Nicholson

The London Guide

**The most comprehensive
guide to London**

ROBERT NICHOLSON PUBLICATIONS

Symbols and abbreviations

L	lunch
D	dinner
B	bar food

Average prices for a meal without wine
(these prices are for guidance only):

£	Under £10 per person
££	£10-£20.00 per person
£££	£20.00-£30.00 per person
£££+	Over £30.00 per person
Reserve	It is advisable to reserve
(M)	Membership necessary
A	Access (incorporating Mastercard, Eurocard)
Ax	American Express
Dc	Diners Club
V	Visa (incorporating Barclaycard)
Opening times	Many places are closed at Xmas, New Year and on Good Friday, and general opening times are subject to change so it is always advisable to check first.

A Nicholson Guide

First published 1967
Eleventh revised edition 1989

© Robert Nicholson Publications 1989

London Map
© Robert Nicholson Publications
based upon the Ordnance Survey with the
sanction of the Controller of Her Majesty's
Stationery Office. Crown Copyright reserved.

London Underground Map by kind
permission of London Regional Transport

All other maps
© Robert Nicholson Publications

Robert Nicholson Publications
16 Golden Square
London W1R 4BN

Great care has been taken throughout
this book to be accurate, but the
publishers cannot accept responsibility
for any errors or their consequences.

Computer typeset by CRB Typesetting Services,
Ely, Cambs

Printed in Great Britain by Scotprint Ltd,
Musselburgh

ISBN 0 948576 26 X

67/11/2250

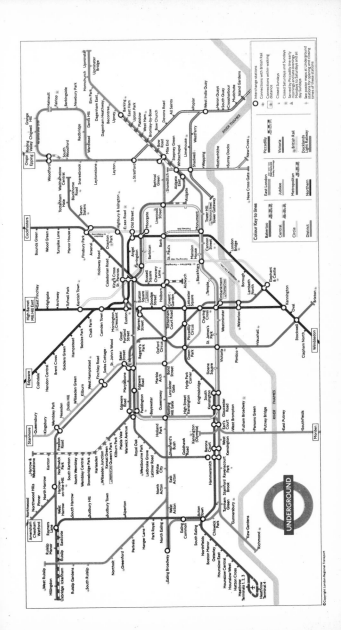

Continued on map 4

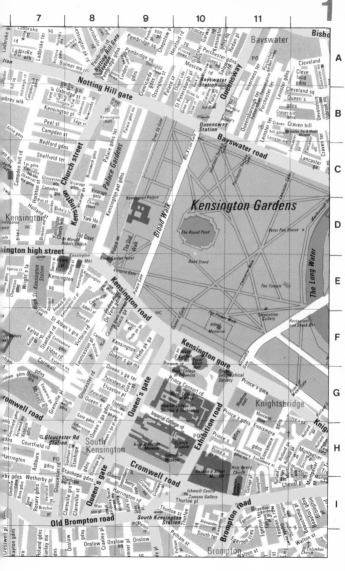

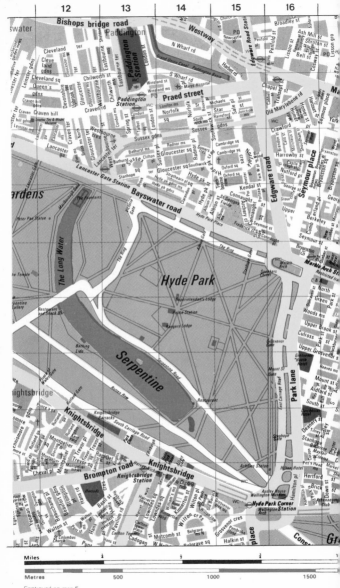

Continued on map 5

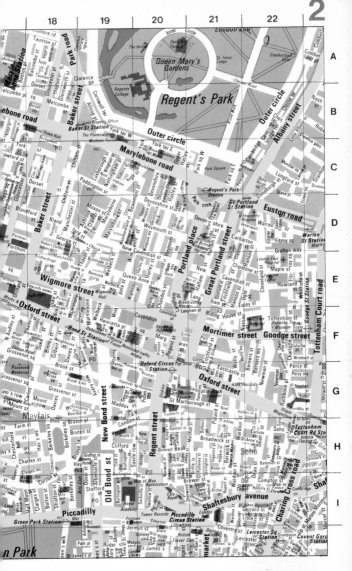

18 19 20 21 22

A

B

C

D

E

F

G

H

I

London Zoo

Inner Circle

Open Air Theatre

Queen Mary's Gardens

St Johns Lodge

Cumberland gate

Cumberland pl

Taunton rd

Park road

Balcombe

Ivor

Clarence ga

Clarence gdns

Gloucester pl

Dorset

Glentworth st

Cornwall ter

Allsop pl

Regents College

Chester Road

Nash st

Melcombe pl

Melcombe

Dorset cotte

Albany street

Outer circle

Outer circle

Regent's Park

ebone road

Baker street

Lost Property Office

The Planetarium

York ter W

York ter E

Outer circle

Madame Tussaud's

WC

Marylebone road

Park sq W

Park Square

Park sq E

Regent's Park Station

Gt Portland St Station

Euston road

Warren St Station

Baker street

Portland place

Great Portland street

Cleveland street

Tottenham Court road

Wigmore street

Oxford street

Bond St Station

Henrietta pl

Cavendish sq

Mortimer street

Goodge street

New Bond street

Oxford Circus Station

Oxford street

Regent street

Soho

Shaftesbury avenue

Charing Cross road

Mayfair

Piccadilly

Green Park Station

Royal Academy

Piccadilly Circus Station

Leicester Sq Station

Covent Gard

n Park

© Robert Nicholson Publications
Crown Copyright Reserved

Continued on map 6

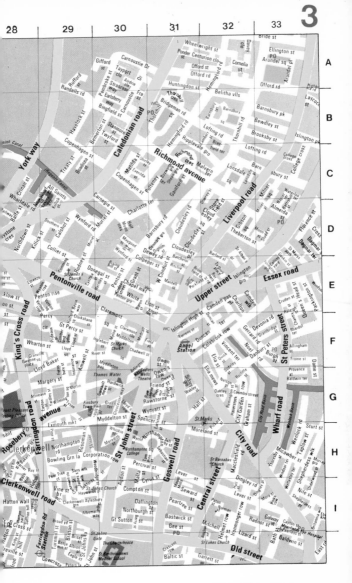

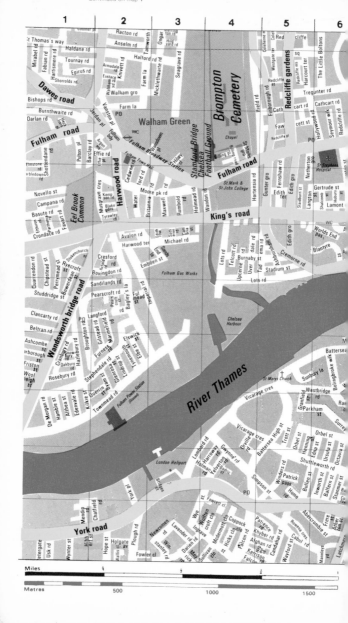

	1	2	3	4	5	6

St Thomas's way

Haldane rd

Mirabel rd
Fabian rd
Flamstmere rd
Tournay rd
Epirus rd
Shorrolds rd.

Bishops rd

Dawes road

Burnthwaite rd
Darlan rd

Fulham road

Elmstone rd
Shottendane rd
Marbledown rd

Novello st
Campana rd
Basuto rd
Fawcett rd
Crondace rd

Quarrendon rd
Chipstead st
Rivercourt st
Perrymead st
Bowerdean st
Studdridge st

Clancarty rd
Beltran rd

Ashcombe
Harborough st
Friston st
Woolneigh st

De Morgan rd
Hamble st
Althea st
Edenvale rd

York road

Racton rd
Anselm rd
Tamworth
Ongar
Held
ford rd

Halford rd
Armadale rd
Knivett rd
Eustace rd
Waldemar
rd
Walham gro

Micklethwaite rd

Seagrave rd

Farm la

Farm la
PO

Walham Green

WC

Brompton Cemetery

Redcliffe gardens

Red cliffe

Colehurne rd
Cole
Westgate ter
Collerne ms

The Little Boltons

Tregunter rd

Cathcart rd
Cathcart rd
Hollywood rd
Seymour wlk
Redcliffe sq

Harcourt ter

Finborough rd
Redcliffe ms
Redcliffe rd

Cath
cart rd
cett st
Redcliffe pl
Faw

Fulham road

St Mark's &
St John College

Hortensia rd

Gunter gro
Edith ter
Edith gro
Fernshaw rd
Slaidburn st
Langton
Blantyre

Netherton gro
Shalcome
Gertrude st
Lamont

St Stephens Hospital

WC
Worlds End
Pas.

Harwood road

Mustgrave cres
Effie rd
Water
ford rd
Cedarne rd
Moore pk rd

Walham gro
Vanston pl
Jerdan pl
Barclay rd
Pulton pl
Effie rd
Fulham
rd

Maxwell rd
Rumbold
Holmead rd
Wandon rd

King's road

Stamford Bridge Chelsea Football Ground

Fulham Broadway Station
Billing rd

Chapel

Held rd

Eel Brook Common

Kemp
son rd
Blake
gdns
Tyrawley rd

Avalon rd
Harwood ter
Michael rd

Cresford
rd
Bovingdon rd
Embden rd

Sandilands rd
Pearscroft rd

Fulham Gas Works

Lots rd
Felcott rd
Uverdale rd
Uverdale rd
Uverdale rd
Stadium st
Lots rd

Cremorne rd

Edith gro

Ashburnham rd

Burnaby st
Lots rd

Michael rd

Stokenchurch
st

Wandsworth bridge road

Broughton rd
Gilstead rd
Marinefield
Elswick
st

Langford
Pearscroft
rd
Bagley's la
Ful
mead
rd
Imperial rd

Chelsea Harbour

Clonmore st
Hazlebury rd
Stephendale rd
Furness rd
Quarrin rd
Bronsart rd
Linstead
Ebury
Oakbury
Roseberry rd

Townmead rd

Fulham Power Station
(Disused)

River Thames

St Marys Church

Vicarage cres

Battersea

Boyinebroke wlk

Granfield
st
Parkham
st

Westbridge
rd

Ras

Mendip
Chatfield

Wolfe
Wolsey
Newcomen
Lavender rd
Plough rd
Wandsworth
IngRave
Stanley
Warrick
Sullivan
Wye st
Fawcett rd
Lombard rd
Halman rd
Harrow rd
Gwynne rd
Orville rd

Vicarage cres

Battersea High st
Trott st
Orbel st
Orbel st
Henning
Edna st
Ursula st
Octavia st

Shuttleworth rd

Winders rd
Patrick
Home
Inworth st
Bollen st
Baltern st
Stanmer st

PO

Simpson st

York road

Hope st
Holgate av
Fowler cl
Hibbt
Walls rd

Newcomen
Quarterly
Winstanley
rd
Falcon
rd

Medmenth clo
Ingrave
Eckstein
Hicks
Sheepcote
Falcon la

Coppock
Patience
Khyber rd
Afghan rd
Candahar rd
Kerrison
Falcon st

Wayford st
Cabul rd
Rowena cres
Frere
Alfer
Latchmere

Abercrombie st

Usk rd
Wynter st
Mendip
Chatfield

Miles

Metres 500 1000 1500

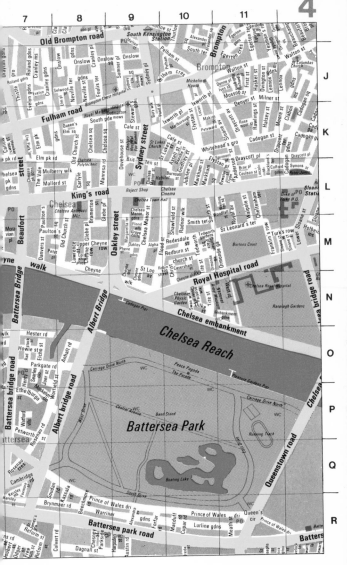

12	13	14	15	16

Hyde Park Corner
Wellington Station
Arch

Constitution

Palace Gardens

Sloane street

Belgrave sq

Grosvenor place

King's road

Belgravia

Buckingham Palace road

Victoria Station

Chelsea bridge road

Pimlico

Ranelagh Gardens

Chelsea Bridge

Queenstown road

Vauxhall bridge road

Belgrave road

Lupus street

River Thames

Battersea park road

Grosvenor road

Nine Elms lane

New Covent Garden Market

Miles		¼		½		¾
Metres	500		1000		1500	

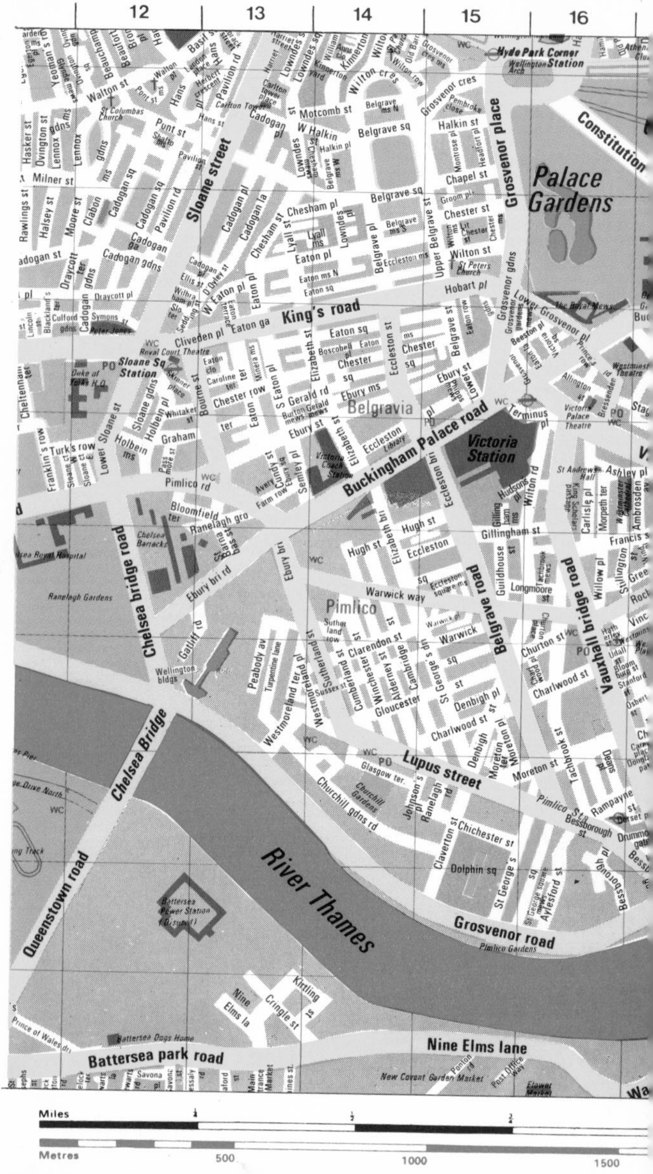

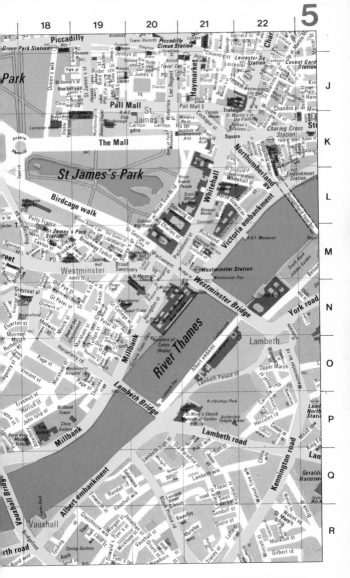

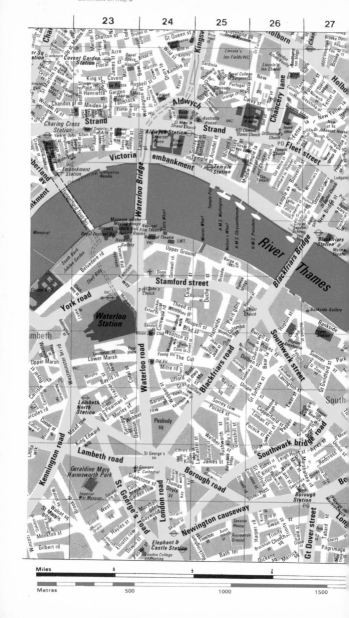

| | 23 | 24 | 25 | 26 | 27 |

Miles

Metres   500   1000   1500

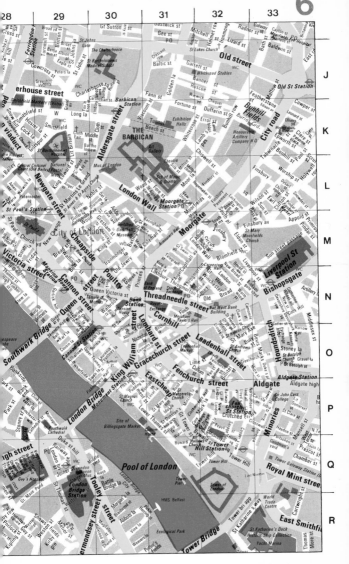

Key to street maps

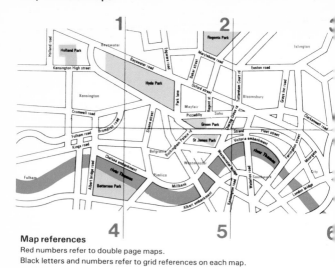

Map references

Red numbers refer to double page maps.

Black letters and numbers refer to grid references on each map.

Street			
Glasgow ter SW1	5	P	14
Glasshill st SE1	6	P	25
Glasshouse st W1	2	I	20
Glasshouse wlk SE11	5	R	19
Glazbury rd W14	1	I	1
Glebe pl SW3	4	L	8
Gledhow gdns SW5	1	I	7
Gledstanes rd W14	1	G	1
Glendower pl SW7	1	I	9
Glenrosa st SW6	4	O	2
Glentworth st NW1	2	A	18
Gliddon rd W14	1	E	1
Globe pl SW3	4	K	8
Globe st SE1	6	R	27
Gloucester Mews west W2	2	A	12
Gloucester ms W2	2	B	12
Gloucester Pl ms W1	2	D	17
Gloucester pl W1	2	A	18
Gloucester rd SW7	1	I	7
Gloucester rd SW7	2	C	14
Gloucester sq W2	5	O	14
Gloucester st SW1	5	O	12
Gloucester ter W2	2	C	12
Gloucester wlk W8	1	C	7
Glyn st SE11	5	R	18
Glynde ms SW3	1	I	11
Godfrey st SW3	4	K	10
Goding st SE11	5	R	18
Godson st N1	3	E	28
Golden la EC1	3	J	31
Golden sq W1	2	H	20
Goldington st NW1	3	B	26
Golford pl NW1	3	A	17
Goodge pl W1	2	F	22
Goodge st W1	2	F	22
Goodman's yd E1	6	Q	33
Goods way NW1	3	B	27
Goodwins ct WC2	5	J	22
Goose yd EC1	3	F	31
Gordon pl W8	1	D	7
Gordon sq WC1	3	E	24
Gordon st WC1	3	E	24
Gore st SW7	1	G	9
Gorleston st W14	1	E	2
Gosfield st W1	2	E	21
Goswell rd EC1	3	H	31
Gough sq EC4	3	G	27
Gough st WC1	3	G	27
Gower ct WC1	3	E	24
Gower ms WC1	3	G	23
Gower pl WC1	3	D	24
Gower st WC1	3	E	23
Gracechurch st EC3	6	O	31
Grafton ms W1	2	D	22
Grafton pl NW1	3	D	25
Grafton st W1	2	H	19
Grafton way W1	2	E	22
Graham st N1	3	G	32
Graham ter SW1	5	M	12
Granby bldgs SE11	5	Q	20
Granby ter NW1	3	B	24
Grand av EC1	3	I	30
Granfield st SW11	4	P	5
Grange ct WC2	6	J	25
Grant st N1	3	E	30
Grantbridge st N1	3	F	33
Granville pl W1	2	D	18
Granville sq WC1	3	F	28
Grape st WC2	3	H	23
Gratton rd W1	1	C	2
Gravel la E1	6	O	33
Gray st SE1	6	O	24
Grays Inn rd WC1	3	G	27
Grays Inn rd WC1	3	I	27
Gt. Castle st W1	2	F	20
Gt. Central st NW1	2	B	18
Gt. Chapel st W1	2	H	22
Gt. College st SW1	5	N	19
Gt. Cumberland pl W1	2	D	16
Gt. Dover st SE1	6	R	27
Gt. George st SW1	5	M	20
Gt. Guildford st SE1	6	P	27
Gt. James st WC1	3	H	26
Gt. Marlborough st W1	2	G	20
Gt. Newport st WC2	2	J	22
Gt. Ormond st WC1	3	G	26
Gt. Percy st WC1	3	F	28
Gt. Peter st W1	5	N	19
Gt. Portland st W1	2	E	21
Gt. Pulteney st W1	2	H	21
Gt. Queen st WC2	3	I	24
Gt. Russell st WC1	3	G	23
Gt. Scotland pl SW1	5	L	21
Gt. Smith st SW1	5	N	19
Gt. St. Helens EC3	6	O	32
Gt. St. Thomas Apostle EC4	6	N	29
Gt. Smith st SW1	5	N	19
Gt. Suffolk st SE1	6	P	26
Gt. Sutton st EC1	3	I	30
Gt. Swan all EC2	6	M	31
Gt. Titchfield st W1	2	F	21
Gt. Tower st EC3	6	P	31
Gt. Turnstile WC2	3	I	26
Gt. Winchester st EC2	6	N	32
Gt. Windmill st W1	2	I	21
Greek st W1	2	H	22
Green st W1	2	F	17
Green ter EC1	3	G	30
Greencoat pl SW1	5	N	17
Greencoat row SW1	5	N	17
Greenhill rents EC1	3	I	29
Greenwell st W1	2	D	22
Greet st SE1	6	O	24
Gregory pl W8	1	D	7
Grenville pl SW7	1	G	7
Grenville st WC1	3	G	26
Gresham st EC2	6	M	30
Gresse st W1	2	G	22
Greville st EC1	3	I	28
Greycoat pl SW1	5	N	18
Greycoat st SW1	5	N	17
Greyhound rd W14	1	G	1
Greystoke pl EC4	3	I	27
Groom pl SW1	5	K	15
Grosvenor Cres ms SW1	2	I	15
Grosvenor cres ms SW1	5	J	15
Grosvenor Gdns ms SW1	5	L	15
Grosvenor gdns SW1	5	L	15
Grosvenor hill W1	2	G	18
Grosvenor pl SW1	5	J	15
Grosvenor rd SW1	5	Q	15
Grosvenor sq W1	2	F	17
Grosvenor st W1	2	G	18
Grove cotts SW3	4	M	9
Guildhouse st SW1	5	N	15
Guilford pl WC1	3	G	26
Guilford st WC1	3	G	26
Gunter gro SW10	4	L	5
Gunterstone rd W14	1	E	1
Gutter la EC2	6	M	29
Guy st SE1	6	R	28
Gwendwr rd W14	1	F	1
Gwynne pl WC1	3	F	28
Gwynne st SW11	4	Q	4
Gye st SE11	5	R	18
Haines st SW8	5	R	13
Haldane rd SW6	1	I	1
Half Moon cres N1	3	D	30
Half Moon st W1	2	I	18
Halford rd SW6	1	J	2
Halkin pl SW1	5	J	14
Halkin st SW1	5	J	15
Hall st EC1	3	G	31
Hallam ms W1	2	E	21
Hallam st W1	2	E	21
Halsey st SW3	4	K	11
Ham yd W1	1	I	21
Hamble st SW6	4	P	1
Hamilton pl W1	2	I	16
Hamilton sq SE1	6	R	28
Hamish pl SE11	5	Q	20
Hammersmith rd W14 & W6	1	D	2
Hampstead rd NW1	3	C	23
Hand ct WC1	3	I	26
Handel st WC1	3	E	25
Hankey pl SE1	6	R	28
Hanover sq W1	2	G	19
Hanover st W1	2	G	20
Hans cres SW1	2	I	13
Hans pl SW1	5	J	12
Hans rd SW3	2	I	13
Hans st SW1	5	J	13
Hansard ms W14	1	I	3
Hanway pl W1	2	G	22
Hanway st W1	2	G	22
Harbet rd W2	2	A	15
Harbledown rd SW6	4	L	1
Harcourt st W1	2	B	17
Harcourt ter SW10	4	I	6
Hardwick st EC1	3	G	30
Harewood av NW1	2	A	17
Harewood row NW1	2	A	17
Harley gdns SW10	4	J	6
Harley pl W1	2	E	20
Harley st W1	2	E	20
Harp all EC4	3	J	27
Harp la EC3	6	P	31
Harper st SE1	6	R	26
Harpsden st SW11	4	R	5
Harpur st WC1	3	H	26
Harriet st SW1	2	I	13
Harriet wlk SW1	2	I	13
Harrington gdns SW7	1	H	7
Harrington rd SW7	1	I	9
Harrington sq NW1	3	A	24
Harrington st NW1	3	B	23
Harrison st WC1	3	E	27
Harrow pl E1	6	O	33
Harrowby st W1	2	C	16
Harrowgate rd SW11	4	R	4
Hartismere rd SW6	4	J	1
Harwood rd SW6	4	L	2
Harwood ter SW6	4	M	2
Hasker st SW3	4	J	11
Hastings st WC1	3	E	26
Hatfields SE1	6	N	25
Hatherley st SW1	5	N	16
Hatton gdn EC1	3	I	28
Hatton wall EC1	3	I	28
Hatton yd EC1	3	I	28
Havelock st N1	3	B	29
Havelock ter SW8	5	R	12
Haverstock st N1	3	G	32
Hay hill W1	2	H	18
Hayes pl NW1	2	A	17
Hayles st SE11	6	R	23
Haymarket SW1	2	I	21
Hayne st EC1	3	I	29
Hays la SE1	6	Q	30
Hazlebury rd SW6	4	O	1
Hazlitt ms W14	1	C	2
Hazlitt rd W14	1	C	2
Headfort pl SW1	5	J	15
Heathcote st WC1	3	F	27
Heaver rd SW11	4	R	4
Heckfield pl SW6	4	K	1
Heddon st W1	2	H	20
Helmet row EC1	3	I	32
Hemingford rd N1	3	B	31
Hemus pl SW3	4	L	9
Henniker ms SW3	4	K	9
Henning st SW11	4	P	5
Henrietta pl W1	2	F	19
Henrietta st WC2	6	J	23
Henty clo SW11	3	O	7
Herbal hill EC1	3	H	28
Herbert cres SW3	5	I	13
Herbrand st WC1	3	E	25
Hercules rd SE1	5	P	22
Hereford rd W2	2	A	10
Hereford sq SW7	1	I	7
Hermes st N1	3	E	30
Hermit st EC1	3	G	31
Herrick st SW1	5	P	18
Hertford pl W1	2	E	22
Hertford st W1	2	I	16
Hesper ms SW5	1	H	6
Hester rd SW11	4	O	7
Hibbert st SW11	4	R	4
Hicks clo SW11	4	R	4
Hide pl SW1	5	O	17
High Holborn WC1	3	I	23
High Timber st EC4	6	N	29
Highbury Sta rd N1	3	B	33
Hilary clo SW6	4	K	3
Hildyard rd SW6	1	I	1
Hill st W1	2	H	17
Hilgate pl W8	1	B	8
Hillgate st W8	1	B	8
Hillsleigh rd W8	1	A	6
Hinde st W1	2	E	18
Hobart pl SW1	5	K	15
Hobury st SW10	4	L	6
Hofland rd W14	1	B	2
Hogarth rd SW5	1	H	6
Holbein ms SW1	5	M	12
Holbein pl SW1	5	M	12
Holborn EC1	3	I	27
Holborn cir EC1	3	I	27
Holborn EC1	6	J	27
Holborn bldgs EC4	6	K	28
Holborn viaduct EC1	3	I	27
Holford pl WC1	3	E	29
Holford st WC1	3	F	29
Holgate av SW11	4	R	3
Holland gdns W14	1	C	3
Holland la SE1	1	D	4
Holland ms W14	1	A	4
Holland Pk av W11	1	A	5
Holland Pk gdns W14	1	A	5
Holland Pk ms W11	1	A	5
Holland Pk rd W14	1	C	4
Holland pk wlk W11	1	B	5
Holland rd W14	1	B	3
Holland st SE1	6	N	27
Holland st W8	1	D	7
Holland Villas rd W14	1	B	3
Holland wlk W8	1	C	6
Hollen st W1	2	G	22
Holles st W1	2	F	20
Hollywood rd SW10	4	K	6
Holman rd SW11	4	Q	4

Street	Map	Col	Row
Pembroke wlk W8	1	F	5
Pembroke wlk W8	1	H	6
Penfold pl NW1	2	A	15
Penfold st NW1 & NW8	2	A	16
Pennant ms W1	1	G	6
Penryn st NW1	3	B	26
Penton gro N1	3	E	29
Penton ri WC1	3	E	29
Penton st N1	3	E	29
Pentonville rd N1	3	E	29
Penywern rd SW5	1	H	5
Pepper st SE1	6	P	26
Pepys st EC3	6	P	32
Percival st EC1	3	H	30
Percy cir WC1	3	F	29
Percy ms W1	2	G	22
Percy st W1	2	G	22
Percy yd WC1	3	F	28
Perham rd W14	1	J	4
Perrymead st SW6	4	M	1
Peter st W1	2	H	21
Petergate SW11	4	R	1
Peters la EC1	6	J	29
Petersham ms SW7	1	G	8
Petersham pl SW7	1	G	8
Peto pl NW1	2	E	19
Petty France SW1	5	L	18
Petworth st SW11	4	P	4
Petyt pl SW3	4	M	8
Petyward st SW3	4	K	10
Phene st SW3	4	M	9
Philbeach gdns SW5	1	G	4
Phillimore gdns W8	1	D	6
Phillimore pl W8	1	D	6
Phillimore wlk W8	1	D	6
Philpot la EC3	6	O	31
Phipps ms SW1	5	L	15
Phoenix pl WC1	3	G	28
Phoenix rd NW1	3	C	25
Piccadilly cir W1	2	I	20
Piccadilly W1	2	I	18
Pickard st EC1	3	G	32
Pickle Herring st SE1	6	R	31
Pickwick st SE1	6	O	26
Picton pl W1	2	E	18
Pilgrim st EC4	6	L	27
Pilgrimage st SE1	6	P	26
Pimlico rd SW1	5	M	12
Pindar st EC2	3	H	33
Pine st EC1	3	D	7
Pitt st W8	1	D	7
Pitt's Head ms W1	2	I	16
Platt st NW1	3	B	26
Playhouse yd EC4	6	M	27
Pleydel ct EC4	6	K	26
Plough pl EC4	6	K	26
Plumtree ct EC4	6	K	28
Pocock st SE1	6	P	25
Poland st W1	2	H	21
Polygon rd NW1	3	C	25
Pond pl SW3	4	K	9
Pond yd SE1	6	O	27
Ponder st N7	4	A	31
Ponsonby pl SW1	5	P	17
Ponsonby ter SW1	5	P	17
Pont St ms SW1	5	J	12
Pont st SW1	5	J	12
Ponton rd SW8	5	R	18
Pooles la SW10	4	M	4
Poplar gro W6	1	A	1
Poplar pl W2	1	B	10
Poppins ct EC4	6	L	27
Porchester Gdns ms W2	1	A	11
Porchester gdns W2	1	A	10
Porchester pl W2	2	C	15
Porchester sq W2	1	B	11
Porchester ter W2	1	B	11
Porlock st SE1	6	R	28
Porten rd W14	1	C	2
Porter st W1	2	E	18
Portland pl W1	2	E	20
Portland rd W11	1	A	5
Portman clo W1	2	D	17
Portman Mews south W1	2	E	17
Portman sq W1	2	D	17
Portman st W1	2	E	17
Portobello rd W11	1	A	8
Portpool la EC1	3	I	27
Portsea pl W2	2	D	15
Portsmouth st WC2	6	J	25
Portsoken st E1	6	Q	33
Portugal st WC2	6	J	25
Post Office way SW8	5	R	15
Potter's fields SE1	6	R	30
Poultry EC2	6	N	30
Powis pl WC1	3	G	26
Praed st W2	2	B	14
Pratt wlk SE11	5	P	21
Prebend st N1	3	F	33
Prescot st E1	6	Q	33
Prices st SE1	6	O	26
Prices yd N1	3	C	30
Prideaux pl WC1	3	F	29
Primrose st EC2	3	F	33
Prince Consort rd SW7	1	G	10
Prince of Wales dri SW11	4	R	8
Prince of Wales ter W8	1	E	8
Prince's ga SW7	1	G	11
Prince's Gate ms SW7	1	H	10
Prince's gdns SW7	1	G	11
Prince's row SW1	5	L	16
Princedale rd W11	1	A	10
Princes ms W2	1	A	10
Princes pl EC4	5	J	19
Princes sq W2	1	A	10
Princes st EC2	6	N	30
Princeton st WC1	3	H	26
Priory wlk SW10	4	J	6
Provence st N1	3	G	33
Providence ct W1	2	F	17
Providence pl N1	3	D	32
Providence row N1	3	D	28
Pudding la EC3	6	P	30
Pulteney ter N1	3	C	31
Pulton pl SW6	4	K	1
Purchese st NW1	3	B	26
Purley pl N1	3	C	33
Quarrendon rd SW6	4	M	1
Queen Anne ms W1	2	E	20
Queen Anne's ga SW1	5	L	19
Queen sq WC1	3	H	26
Queen St pl EC4	6	N	29
Queen st W1	2	H	17
Queen Victoria st EC4	6	M	28
Queen's Club gdns W14	1	G	1
Queen's Elm sq SW3	4	K	8
Queen's Ga gdns SW7	1	G	8
Queen's Ga ms SW7	1	F	9
Queen's Ga Pl ms SW7	1	G	8
Queen's Ga pl SW7	1	G	8
Queen's ga SW7	1	G	8
Queen's Ga ter SW7	1	G	8
Queen's gdns W2	1	B	12
Queen's Head st N1	3	E	33
Queen's Head yd SE1	6	Q	28
Queen's ms W2	1	A	10
Queen's wlk SW1	5	J	18
Queens cir SW11	4	R	11
Queensberry ms SW7	1	I	9
Queensberry pl SW7	1	I	9
Queensberry way SW7	1	I	9
Queensborough ter W2	1	A	11
Queenstown rd SW8	4	Q	11
Queensway W2	1	A	11
Querrin st SW6	4	P	2
Quick st N1	3	F	32
Quilp st SE1	6	O	27
Rabbit row W8	1	B	8
Racton rd SW6	4	I	2
Radley ms W8	1	F	6
Radnor ms W2	2	C	14
Radnor pl W2	2	C	14
Radnor st EC1	3	I	32
Radnor wlk SW3	4	M	10
Radstock st SW11	4	O	7
Railway appr SE1	6	Q	29
Railway pl EC3	6	P	32
Railway st N1	3	D	28
Rainsford st W2	2	B	15
Raleigh st N1	3	E	33
Ramillies pl W1	2	G	21
Ramillies st W1	2	G	21
Rampayne st SW1	5	P	16
Randall clo SW11	4	P	5
Randall rd SE11	5	Q	19
Randell's rd N1	3	A	29
Ranelagh gro SW1	5	M	13
Ranelagh rd SW1	5	P	15
Ranston st NW1	2	A	16
Raphael st SW7	1	H	13
Rathbone pl W1	2	G	22
Rathbone st W1	2	G	22
Ravent rd SE11	5	Q	21
Rawlings st SW3	4	K	11
Rawstorne pl EC1	3	G	31
Rawstorne st EC1	3	G	31
Ray st EC1	3	H	28
Raymond bldgs WC1	3	I	26
Red Lion ct EC4	6	K	26
Red Lion sq WC1	3	H	25
Red Lion st WC1	3	H	25
Redan pl W2	1	A	11
Redan st W14	1	B	1
Redburn st SW3	4	M	10
Redcliffe gdns SW10	1	J	5
Redcliffe ms SW10	4	J	5
Redcliffe pl SW10	4	K	5
Redcliffe rd SW10	4	K	5
Redcliffe sq SW10	1	J	5
Redcliffe st SW10	4	J	5
Redesdale st SW3	4	M	10
Redfield la SW5	1	G	5
Redhill st NW1	3	A	23
Reece ms SW7	1	I	9
Reedworth st SE11	5	R	22
Reeves ms W1	2	F	17
Reform st SW11	4	R	7
Regency st SW1	5	O	17
Regent sq WC1	3	E	26
Regent st SW1 & W1	2	H	20
Regnart bldgs NW1	3	D	24
Relton ms SW7	1	I	12
Remington st N1	3	G	32
Remnant st WC2	6	I	25
Rennie st SE1	6	N	26
Reston pl SW7	1	F	9
Rewell st SW6	4	M	4
Rex pl W1	2	G	16
Rheidol ms N1	3	F	33
Rheidol ter N1	3	F	33
Richmond av N1	3	C	31
Richmond cres N1	3	C	30
Richmond Ter ms SW1	5	M	21
Richmond ter SW1	5	M	21
Richmond way W14	1	A	2
Rickett st SW6	4	I	3
Ridgmount gdns WC1	3	F	23
Ridgmount st WC1	3	F	23
Riding House st W1	2	F	21
Ring the W1	2	E	13
Ripplevale gro N1	3	B	29
Riseborough st SE1	6	P	26
Rising Sun ct EC1 & EC4	6	J	30
Risinghill st N1	3	E	30
Ritchie st N1	3	E	31
River st EC1	3	F	29
Riverside wlk SE1	5	M	22
Robert Adam st W1	2	D	18
Robert st NW1	3	B	23
Robert st WC2	2	K	23
Robinson st SW3	4	M	10
Rochester row SW1	5	N	17
Rochester st SW1	5	N	17
Rockingham st SE1	6	R	25
Rockley rd W14	1	A	2
Rocliffe st N1	3	G	32
Rodmarton ms W1	2	C	18
Rodney st N1	3	E	29
Roger st WC1	3	H	27
Roland gdns SW7	4	J	7
Romilly st W1	2	I	22
Romney st SW1	5	O	19
Rood la EC3	6	P	31
Ropemaker st EC2	6	L	32
Rosary gdns SW7	1	I	7
Roscoe st EC1	3	J	31
Rose & Crown yd SW1	5	J	19
Rose all SE1	6	O	28
Rosebery av EC1	3	I	28
Rosebury rd SW6	4	O	1
Rosemoor st SW3	4	K	11
Rosenau cres SW11	4	P	7
Rosenau rd SW11	4	O	7
Rosoman st EC1	3	H	29
Rossmore rd NW1	2	A	18
Rotary st SE1	6	Q	24
Rotten row SW11	4	Q	11
Rotten row SW7 & SW1	1	G	13
Roupell st SE1	6	N	24
Rowan rd W6	1	C	1
Rowena cres SW11	4	R	5
Roxby pl SW6	4	I	1
Royal av SW3	4	L	11
Royal College st NW1	3	A	24
Royal Hospital rd SW3	4	N	10
Royal Mint st E1	6	Q	33
Royal st SE1	5	O	22
Rufford st N1	3	A	29
Rugby st WC1	3	H	26
Rumbold rd SW6	4	L	3
Running Horse yd SE1	6	P	29
Rupert st W1	2	I	21
Rushworth st SE1	6	P	25
Russell ct SW1	5	J	19

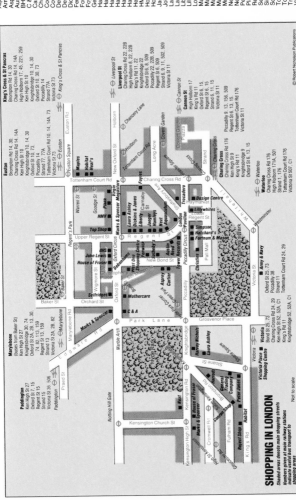

SHOPS

Aquascutum 734 6090
Army & Navy 834 1234
Asprey 493 6767
Austin Reed 734 6789
BHS (Oxford St) 629 2011
C & A 629 7272
Carrier 493 6960
Christie's 839 9060
Conran Shop 589 7401
Covent Garden Market 836 9137
Debenhams 580 3000
Design Centre 839 8000
Dickins & Jones 734 7070
Fenwick 629 9161
Fortnum & Mason 734 8040
Foyles 437 5660
General Trading Company 730 0411
Habitat (King's Rd) 351 1211
Habitat (Tott Ct Rd) 631 3880
Hamleys 734 3161
Harrods 730 1234
Harvey Nichols 235 5000
Hatchard's 437 3924
Heal's 636 1666
HMV 631 3423
House of Fraser (Ken High St) 937 5432
House of Fraser (Oxford St) 629 8800
Jaeger 734 8211
John Lewis 629 7711
Laura Ashley (Regent St) 437 9760
Laura Ashley (Sloane St) 235 9728
Liberty 734 1234
Lillywhites 930 3181
London Pavilion 437 1838
Maples 387 7000
Marks & Spencer (Marble Arch) 935 7954
Marks & Spencer (Oxford St) 437 7722
Marks & Spencer (Ken High St) 938 3711
Mothercare 629 6621
Next (Ken High St) 937 0498
Next (Regent St) 434 2515
Peter Jones 730 3434
Plaza on Oxford St 436 4425
Reject Shop 352 2750
Selfridges 629 1234
Simpson 734 2002
Sotheby's 493 8080
Top Shop 636 7700
Tower Records 439 2500
Trocadero 439 1791
Victoria Place Shopping Centre 931 8811
Virgin Megastore 631 1234

© Robert Nicholson Publications

SHOPPING IN LONDON

Shaded areas denote main shopping streets

Numbers given at main railway stations
indicate useful bus transport to
shopping areas

Not to scale

Paddington
Ken High St 27
Oxford St 7, 15
Regent St 15
Strand 15
Victoria St 36, 506
→ Paddington

Marylebone
(buses from Baker St)
Ken High St 27
Knightsbridge 30, 74
Oxford St 2A, 28, 13, 30,
74, 82, 113, 159
Regent St 13, 159
Strand 13
Victoria St 2A, 2B, 82
→ Marylebone

Euston
Brompton Rd 14, 30
Charing Cross Rd 14, 14A
High Holborn 17, 45, 221, 259
Knightsbridge 10, 14, 30
Oxford St 10, 73
Piccadilly 14
Strand 77, 77A
Tottenham Court Rd 10, 14, 14A, 73
→ Euston

King's Cross & St Pancras
Brompton Rd 14, 30
Charing Cross Rd 14, 14A
High Holborn 17, 45, 221, 259
King's Rd 14
Knightsbridge 10, 14, 30
Oxford St 10, 73
Piccadilly 14
Strand 77
Victoria 73
→ King's Cross & St Pancras

Victoria
Bond St 25, 73
Charing Cross Rd 24, 29
King's Rd 11, 19, 22
Knightsbridge 52, 52A, C1

Waterloo
Charing Cross Rd 176
High Holborn 171A, 501
King's Rd 11
Knightsbridge 9
Tottenham Court Rd 176
Victoria St 507, C1

Charing Cross
Charing Cross Rd 176
Ken High St 9
King's Rd 11
Knightsbridge 9
Oxford St 6, 13, 15

Cannon St
High Holborn 17
King's Rd 11
Regent St 6, 15
Strand 6, 11, 15
Victoria St 11

Liverpool St
Charing Cross Rd 22, 22B
High Holborn 6, 22, 22B
King's Rd 11
Knightsbridge 22
Oxford St 6, 22B, 509
Regent St 6, 509
Strand 6, 9, 11, 502, 509
Victoria St 11

Oxford Circus
Charing Cross Rd 14, 14A
High Holborn 17, 45, 221, 259
King's Rd 11
Knightsbridge 10, 14, 30
Oxford St 10, 73
Piccadilly 14
→ King's Cross & St Pancras

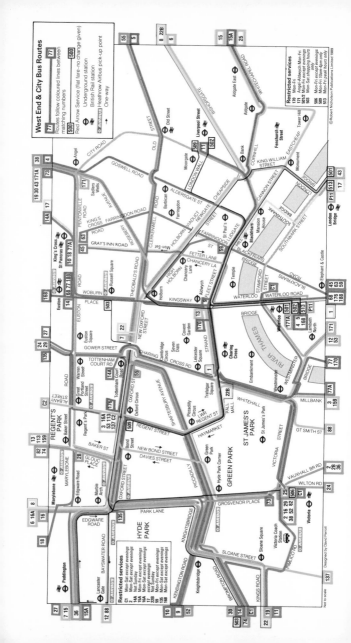

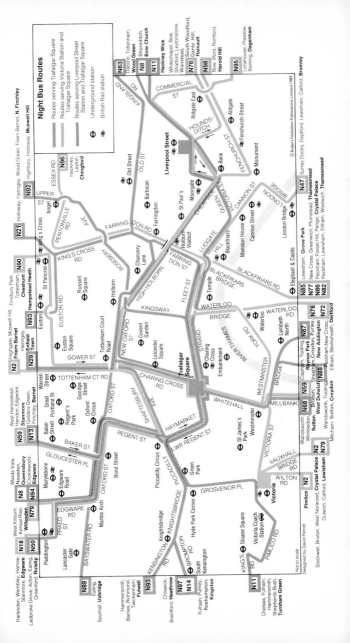

THEATRES

Adelphi 836 7611
Albery 867 1115
Aldwych 836 6404
Ambassadors 836 1171
Apollo 437 2663
Apollo Victoria 828 8665
Arts 836 3334
Astoria 434 0403
Bloomsbury 387 9629
Coliseum 836 3161
Comedy 930 2578
Criterion 867 1117
Dominion 580 9562
Donmar Warehouse 867 1111
Drury Lane, Theatre Royal 836 8108
Duchess (Players) 836 8243
Duke of York's 836 5122
Fortune 836 2238
Garrick 379 6107
Globe 437 3667
Haymarket 930 9832
Her Majesty's 839 2244
Jeannetta Cochrane 242 7040
Lyric 437 3686

Mayfair 629 3036
Mermaid 236 5568
National 928 2252
New London 405 0072
Old Vic 928 7616
Palace 434 0909
Phoenix 836 2294
Piccadilly 437 4506
Playhouse 839 4401
Prince Edward 734 8951
Prince of Wales 839 5987
Queen's 734 1166
Royal Court 730 1745
Royal Festival Hall 928 8800
Royal Opera House 240 1066
St Martin's 836 1443
Shaftesbury 379 5399
Strand 836 2660
Vaudeville 836 9987
Victoria Palace 834 1317
Westminster 834 0283
Whitehall 867 1119
Wyndham's 867 1116
Young Vic 928 6363
Phoenix 836 2294
Piccadilly 437 4506
Prince of Wales 839 5987
Wyndham's 867 1116
Wigmore Hall 935 2141

CINEMAS

Cannon Haymarket 839 1527
Cannon Oxford St 636 0310
Cannon Panton St 930 0631
Cannon Piccadilly 437 3561
Cannon Premiere 439 4470
Cannon Shaftesbury Ave 836 6861
Cannon Tott Ct Rd 636 6148
Curzon Mayfair 499 3737
Curzon Phoenix 240 9661
Curzon West End 439 4805
Empire 1, 2, 3 & 4 437 1234
ICA 930 3647
Lumiere 836 0691

Metro 437 0757
Minema 235 4225
Moulin 437 1653
National Film Theatre 928 3232
Odeon Haymarket 839 7697
Odeon Leicester Sq 930 6111
Odeon Marble Arch 723 2011
Odeon West End 930 5252
Plaza 1, 2, 3 & 4 437 1234
Prince Charles 437 8181
Renoir 837 8402
Warner West End 439 0791

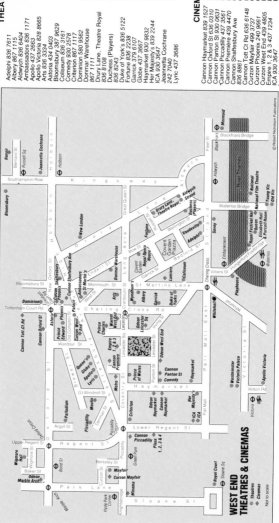

WEST END
THEATRES & CINEMAS

♦ Theatres
♦ Cinemas
Not to scale

© Robert Nicholson Publications

Sightseeing

Tourist information

British Travel Centre 6 J 20
Rex House, 4-12 Lower Regent St SW1. 01-730 3400. New home of the British Tourist Authority Information Centre, incorporating the American Express Travel Service Office, British Rail ticket office and a bureau de change. Details on where to go throughout the UK. Book a room, coach trip or theatre ticket; buy plane tickets, hire a car; all under one roof. Also regular exhibitions, videos, travel bookshop and gift shop. *OPEN 09.00-18.30 Mon-Sat, 10.00-16.00 Sun.*

City of London Information 6 M 28
Centre
St Paul's Churchyard EC4. 01-606 3030. Information and advice with specific reference to the 'Square Mile'. Free literature. Essential to get monthly *Diary of Events* which lists a big choice of free entertainment in the City. *OPEN May-Sep 09.30-17.00 Mon-Sun; Oct-Apr 09.30-17.00 Mon-Fri, 09.30-12.30 Sat.*

Daily Telegraph Information Bureau
Telephone only. Dial 100 and ask for custom call Daily Telegraph Information Bureau. General information service available *09.30-17.30 Mon-Fri. Fixed charge.*

Guildhall Library 6 M 30
Aldermanbury EC2. 01-606 3030. Will tell you anything historical about London. *OPEN 09.30-17.00 Mon-Sat.*

London Transport Travel Information
Centres
London Transport information 01-222 1234. London Transport offices for enquiries on travel (underground, buses and Green Line coaches) and general tourist information. Free maps of underground and buses and information leaflets in French, German and English. *OPENING times vary. Phone for details.*
Euston Underground Station 3 C 24
Heathrow Central Underground Station
King's Cross Underground 3 D 27
Station
Oxford Circus Underground 2 G 20
Station
Piccadilly Circus Underground 2 I 20
Station
Victoria British Rail Station 6 M 15
West Croydon Bus Station

London Tourist Board 5 M 15
Information Centre
Victoria Station Forecourt SW1. 01-730 3488. Travel and tourist information for London and England. Most languages spoken. Also instant hotel reservations, theatre and tour bookings, sales of tourist tickets, guide books and maps. *OPEN Apr-Nov 09.00-20.30 Mon-Sun; Dec-Mar 09.00-19.00 Mon-Sat, 09.00-17.00 Sun. Telephone service available 09.00-18.00 Mon-Fri all year.*
Other tourist information centres at:
Harrods, Knightsbridge SW1 2 I 12
Heathrow Central Underground Station
Selfridges, 400 Oxford St W1 2 E 18
Tower of London, West Gate 6 R 31
E1

Scottish Tourist Board 5 K 21
19 Cockspur St SW1. 01-930 8661. Tourist leaflets and information on mainland Scotland and the islands.

Wales Tourist Board 2 I 20
34 Piccadilly W1. 01-409 0969. Leaflets and information for the visitor to Wales. *OPEN May-Sep 09.00-17.30 Mon-Fri, 09.00-17.00 Sat; Oct-Apr 09.00-17.00 Mon-Fri.*

Telephone services

All London telephone numbers begin with 01- followed by seven figures. If already in London do not dial the 01, only the seven following figures. If dialling from London to an exchange elsewhere, you must find the code of the exchange. The codes are listed in a booklet called The Code Book or the operator (dial 100) will tell you. If you are using a public telephone in London it will almost certainly be a push-button one. You will need 10p, 20p, 50p or £1 coins. The coins must be inserted before you can dial but if you do not get through the money will be refunded when you replace the receiver. More and more public telephones take phonecards as a form of payment. These cards can be bought in post offices or local newsagent's shops to the value of £1-£20, and operate on the basis of 10p per unit. Full instructions on how to use them are displayed in the cardphone booths. Details of all telephone services are in the booklet – this is a summary.

Emergency calls Dial 999 and ask for police, fire or ambulance service.

Directory enquiries 142 for London postal addresses, 192 for other British addresses.

Transfer charge (collect) calls or difficulty in getting through to a number – 100 for the operator.

Telemessages 190 for inland, 193 for international.

International calls You can dial direct to many countries. Codes are listed in *The Code Book* or ask the operator.

Viewpoints

Get a fresh perspective of London by looking down on it from a tall building or a natural high point. You can then appreciate the sheer enormity of London, and there are many places which command a view of almost the entire metropolis.

Alexandra Palace
On Muswell Hill N22. About 250ft (76.3m). View from the terrace over Kent, Surrey, Essex and Hertfordshire.

Eltham Park SE9
View of central London. Best view from the ornamental pond.

Hampstead Heath NW3
Constable's famous view of London. A more comfortable view from Jack Straw's Castle 450ft (137.3m).

Highgate Archway N6
From the top you see the whole of London laid out before you.

Jack Straw's Castle
North End Way NW3. 01-435 8885. Lunch and dinner in the restaurant with long views across London to the distant Kentish hills. *LD. Last orders 22.15 Mon-Sat, 21.45 Sun. CLOSED Sat L.*

Heathrow Airport
Roof of Queen's Building, Heathrow, Middx. 01-759 4321. A favourite for children. Aircraft continuously landing and taking off. *OPEN summer 10.00-18.00, winter 10.00-16.30. Charge.*

Kenwood House
Hampstead La NW3. 01-348 1286. Panorama of almost the whole of London. View from the gazebo by the coach house.

London Hilton   2 I 16
22 Park La W1. 01-493 8000. Roof bar at 320ft (97.6m). Lift. Fine views over Hyde Park, Buckingham Palace and Mayfair.

Monument   6 O 30
Monument St EC3. 01-626 2717. Magnificent view from the top, but it is 202ft (61.6m) high and you have to climb the

stairs. *OPEN Apr-Sep 09.00-17.40 Mon-Fri, 14.00-17.40 Sat & Sun; Oct-Mar 09.00-15.40 Mon-Sat. Charge.*

Point Hill
Blackheath SE10. Commanding view of a wide arc from the docks in the east to Alexandra Palace in the north and the City and Westminster in the west.

Pole Hill
Chingford E4. The high point of Epping Forest. View towards the river and of Shooters Hill south of the river.

Queen's Tower   1 G 10
Imperial College, off Exhibition Rd SW7. 01-589 5111. 287ft (87.5m) high tower in the middle of Imperial College campus offers a unique and uninterrupted view of London. *OPEN Jul-Sep 10.00-17.30 Mon-Sun. Charge.*

St Paul's Cathedral   6 M 28
Ludgate Hill EC4. 01-248 2705. Magnificent view of the City, the Wren churches, the Tower and London Pool. 335ft (102.2m), 727 steps. *OPEN 10.00-16.15 Mon-Fri, 11.00-16.15 Sat. Charge to see the galleries.*

Shrewsbury Park SE18
View of the river, the docks to the north and east along the river towards Tilbury.

Tower Bridge SE1   6 R 31
01-407 0922. Breathtaking views of London and the Thames from high walkways. *OPEN Apr-Oct 10.00-18.30 Mon-Sun; Nov-Mar 10.00-16.45 Mon-Sun. Last admission 45 mins before closing time. CLOSED B. hols. Charge.*

Westminster Cathedral   5 M 16
Ashley Pl, off Victoria St SW1. 01-834 7452. View over Westminster and the Thames from the top of 273ft (83.3m) campanile. Lift usually *OPEN Apr-Sep 09.00-17.00 Mon-Sun. Charge.*

Daily ceremonies and events

Pageantry

These are the main ceremonies which occur throughout the year. Phone the London Tourist Board Information Centre (01-730 3488) for details of events on the day you want to go.

Ceremony of the Keys   6 Q 32
Tower of London, Tower Hill EC3. 01-709 0765. The Chief Warder of the Yeoman Warders, with an escort of the Brigade of Guards, locks the West Gates, the Middle

Tower and Byward Tower. One of the oldest military ceremonies in the world. *21.40 Mon-Sun, by written application to the Governor well in advance, enclosing sae.*

Changing of the Guard   5 K 17
Buckingham Palace SW1. Takes place inside the palace railings and in summer the crowd makes it impossible to see much. An alternative is to see the Guards on their way from Chelsea or Wellington Barracks; phone the Tourist Information Centre to find out which they are leaving from on the day you are going. *Mon-Sun in summer, alternate days in winter.* Leave Chelsea Barracks at *10.45* or Wellington Barracks at *11.00.* Palace ceremony *11.30.*

St James's Palace SW1   5 K 19
A detachment of the Buckingham Palace Guard comes here. Guards change *11.15 (days as above).*

Whitehall SW1   5 L 21
Horse Guards Pde SW1. Changing of the Queen's Life Guard mounted on splendid horses. Guards leave Hyde Park Barracks *10.38 Mon-Sat, 09.39 Sun.* Ceremony *11.00 Mon-Sat, 10.00 Sun.*

Windsor Castle
Windsor, Berks. Windsor 868286. The Queen's out of town and favoured residence. Changing of the Guard at *11.00-11.30 Mon-Sun summer, alternate days winter.* A military band enlivens the pageant.

Commuters: Every working day millions of people come into central London from the suburbs. This is most noticeable in the City where almost nobody lives, so it is left as a ghost town when the commuters leave in the early evening. It is fascinating to watch this daily flow of City workers, many of whom still adhere to the old-fashioned clothing rules of pinstripe suit, bowler and brolly. See it at London Bridge and Waterloo Bridge where the commuters leave the station on the south side of the river in the morning and march across the bridge to their City offices. They charge along the full width of the pavement on the bridge so don't try to walk in the opposite direction! *08.30-09.30 Mon-Fri.*

Speakers' Corner: A remaining vestige of the British tradition of free speech is this institution of impromptu discourses by unknown orators, usually on religion or politics. At Speakers' Corner (Marble Arch corner of Hyde Park, usually on *Sun*). Also

Lincoln's Inn Fields and Tower Hill (*Mon-Fri lunchtime*).

Feeding the pigeons: In Trafalgar Square (5 K 22) – a famous tradition. You will soon be accosted by touts who want to sell you bird-seed and photographs of yourself covered in pigeons.

The following list presents not only the most important annual events but also some of the more obscure London customs in order to cover as wide a field as possible. For exact days, times and places, where not given, and whether or not there is a charge, contact one of the centres given under 'Tourist information'.

Chinese New Year   2 I 22
Gerrard St W1. Papier-mâché dragon and lit-up festivities animate the centre of London's Chinese community. *Jan or Feb.*

International Boat Show   1 H 4
Earls Court Exhibition Centre, Warwick Rd SW5. 01-385 1200. The latest pleasure craft, yachts and equipment. The largest boat show in Europe. *Early Jan.*

International Racing Car Show
Alexandra Pavilion, Alexandra Palace & Park N22. 01-883 6477. *Mid Jan.*

January sales
Most of the London stores have stock-clearing sales after the Xmas shopping spree. Some fantastic bargains but these go quickly – the real fanatics camp outside the store the night before the sale starts to be first in the queue – and there are always big crowds. Start *early Jan.*

Model Engineer Exhibition
Wembley Conference Centre, Wembley Complex, Empire Way, Wembley, Middx. 01-902 1234. Including model cars, trains, planes, boats. *Early Jan.*

Royal Epiphany Gifts   5 J 19
Chapel Royal, St James's Pl, Marlborough Rd SW1. Picturesque ceremony, when two 'Gentlemen Ushers' offer gold, frankincense and myrrh on behalf of the Queen. *6 Jan 11.30.* Admission by ticket only.

Cruft's Dog Show   1 H 4
Earls Court Exhibition Centre, Warwick Rd SW5. 01-385 1200. *Early Feb.*

International Canoe Exhibition
Crystal Palace National Sports Centre SE19. 01-778 0131. *3rd weekend in Feb.*

Psychics and Mystics Fayre
Hammersmith Town Hall, King St W6. 01-748 3020. Meeting point for practitioners of the intuitive sciences such as palmistry, tarot card reading, clairvoyance. *Late Feb.*

March

Chelsea Spring Antiques Fair   4 **L** 9
Chelsea Old Town Hall, King's Rd SW3. 01-352 3619. *Mid Mar.*

Daily Mail Ideal Home Exhibition   1 **H** 4
Earls Court Exhibition Centre, Warwick Rd SW5. 01-385 1200. Very popular and always crowded. *Mid Mar.*

John Stow Memorial Service   6 **O** 32
St Andrew Undershaft, St Mary Axe EC3. The Lord Mayor attends this commemoration of London's first historian and places a new quill pen in the hand of Stow's statue. *Sun in Mar or Apr, 11.30.*

Oranges & Lemons Service   6 **K** 25
St Clement Danes, Strand WC2. 01-242 8282. *No fixed date.*

Oxford v Cambridge Boat Race
River Thames, Putney to Mortlake. University boat race over four miles. View from the banks of the river or one of the bridges. Get there early for a good view. *Sat afternoon in Mar or Apr.*

Royal Film Performance
A selected film gets royal patronage in aid of charity. Celebrities and glitter at one of the big cinemas. *No fixed date.*

Sailboat
Crystal Palace National Sports Centre SE19. 01-778 0131. Britain's largest exhibition of dinghies and small sailing craft. *No fixed date.*

St David's Day
Windsor, Berks. Leeks given to the Welsh Guards. Generally attended by the Duke of Edinburgh. *1 Mar.*

St Patrick's Day
Pirbright, Surrey. Shamrocks given to the Irish Guards by the Queen Mother. *17 Mar.*

Sub-Aqua Exhibition
Crystal Palace National Sports Centre SE19. 01-778 0131. Organised by the British Sub-Aqua Club. *Late Mar.*

Super Stampex   5 **N** 17
Horticultural Halls, Vincent Sq SW1. National stamp exhibition. Contact the Philatelic Traders Society 01-930 6465 for details. *Early Mar.* Also hold Autumn *Stampex late Sep-early Oct.*

Wind & Surf
Alexandra Pavilion, Alexandra Palace & Park N22. 01-883 6477. Everything for the windsurfing enthusiast. *Mid Mar.*

April

Annual Spital Sermon   6 **M** 30
St Lawrence Jewry, Gresham St EC2. 01-600 9478. Governors of the two great hospitals, Christ's Hospital and Bridewell, attend with the Lord Mayor, sheriffs and aldermen. *Coincides with the first meeting of the Aldermen and Court of Common Council.*

Butterworth Charity   6 **K** 29
St Bartholomew-the-Great, Smithfield EC1. 01-606 5171. Presentation of cold-cross buns, traditionally to 'poor widows', now to children. *Good Fri following 11.00 service.*

Easter Procession & Carols   5 **N** 20
Westminster Abbey SW1. 01-222 5152. *Easter Mon.*

Easter Sunday Parade   4 **P** 9
Battersea Park SW11. Colourful carnival procession preceded by a parade of old vehicles. *15.00 Easter Sun.*

London Harness Horse Parade   2 **A** 21
Regent's Park NW1. Fine horses and carts; brewer's vans and drays on parade. Judging *starts at 09.45* followed by a procession twice round the Inner Circle *at about 12.00. Easter Mon.*

The London Marathon   5 **N** 21
The famous 26-mile race starting *09.30* at Greenwich Park SE10 and finishing at Westminster Bridge SW1. For information ring 01-948 7935. *Late Apr.*

Tower of London Church Parade   6 **Q** 32
Tower of London, Tower Hill EC3. 01-709 0765. The Yeoman Warders in state dress are inspected, and parade before and after morning service on *Easter Sun, 11.00.* Also *Whit Sun & Sun before Xmas.*

May

Chelsea Flower Show   4 **N** 11
Royal Hospital Grounds, Chelsea SW3. 01-834 4333. Superb flower displays. *For 3 days late May.*

FA Cup Final
Wembley Stadium, Wembley, Middx.

01-902 1234. The climax of the English football season. *Late Apr/early May.*

Festival of Mind, Body & Spirit   5 N 17

The New Hall, Royal Horticultural Halls, Greycoat St SW1. Human awareness and planetary consciousness. Includes astrology, alternative medicine, crafts, natural foods, religions, ecology, intuitive sciences. Demonstrations and lectures given. Contact 01-938 3788 for information. *Late May.*

Glyndebourne Festival Opera Season
Glyndebourne, nr Lewes, E. Sussex. Brighton 541111. Well-heeled Londoners don evening dress and flock from town to hear superlative singing, and sup on the lawn if the summer air is clement. *Late May-mid Aug.*

Open Air Art Exhibitions   5 L 22
Victoria Embankment Gardens WC2 (next to Embankment Underground station). Artists and their work on exhibition. *2-14 May; Aug, Mon-Sat.* The Terrace, Richmond Hill, Richmond, Surrey. Run by Richmond Art Group. Fine views from terrace. *May or Jun 10.00-20.00 Sat & Sun.* Royal Av, King's Rd SW3. *May-Oct 11.00-18.00 Sat.* The Green Park side of Piccadilly, where a multitude of street artists set up their pictures against the railings. *Every Sun morning.* And along Bayswater Rd, outside Kensington Gardens and Hyde Park.

Putney & Hammersmith Amateur Regattas
Rowing regattas make exciting watching from the banks of the Thames. Contact the Amateur Rowing Assn (ARA) for information 01-748 3632. *Late Apr/early May.*

Rugby League Challenge Cup Final
Wembley Stadium, Wembley, Middx. Contact Rugby Football League. Leeds 624637. *Late Apr/early May.*

Samuel Pepys   6 P 32
Commemoration Service
St Olave's, Hart St EC3. 01-488 4318. The Lord Mayor lays a wreath on Pepys's monument. *Late May or early Jun.*

Summer Art Exhibition   2 I 18
Royal Academy, Burlington House, Piccadilly W1. 01-734 9052. *May-mid Aug.*

June

All England Lawn Tennis Championships
All England Lawn Tennis & Croquet Club, Church Rd, Wimbledon SW19. 01-946 2244. 'Wimbledon Fortnight', the world's most famous championship. Matches from

14.00 Mon-Sat. Last week Jun & 1st week Jul.

Antiquarian Book Fair   2 I 17
Park Lane Hotel, Piccadilly W1. 01-499 6321. International fair with books, documents, musical scores. *Late Jun.*

The Derby
Epsom Racecourse, Surrey. Epsom 26311. One of the most famous horseraces in the world. *Early Jun.*

Election of Sheriffs of the   6 M 30
City of London
Guildhall EC2. 01-606 3030. Lord Mayor and Aldermen in a colourful ceremony. Posies are carried traditionally to ward off 'the plague'. *Midsummer's Day (unless it falls on a Sat or Sun).*

Founder's Day   4 N 11
Royal Hospital, Chelsea SW3. 01-730 0161. Chelsea pensioners parade for inspection, sometimes by royalty. *Early Jun.*

The Garter Ceremony
Service attended by the Queen at St George's Chapel, Windsor, preceded by a colourful procession with the Household Cavalry and Yeomen of the Guard. Ceremony dates from 14thC. *Mon afternoon of Ascot week (usually 3rd week in Jun).*

Lord's Test Match
Lord's Cricket Ground, St John's Wood Rd NW8. Ring 01-289 1615 for tickets. *Jun or Jul.*

Royal Ascot Races
Ascot 22211. A fashionable society event where the hats attract more attention than the horses. *Jun.*

Trooping the Colour   5 L 21
The route is from Buckingham Palace SW1 along the Mall to Horse Guards Parade, Whitehall and back again. Pageantry at its best for the Queen's official birthday. *11.00, Sat nearest 11 Jun.*

July

City of London Festival
01-377 0540. Held in the Barbican, the Tower of London, Mansion House, the City's livery halls, St Paul's Cathedral and many fine churches, and the City's open spaces. Concerts, opera, exhibitions, poetry, drama, dance, jazz, street events and full supporting fringe. *Three weeks in Jul.*

Doggetts Coat & Badge   6 Q 31
Race
The Thames, Tower Pier to Chelsea. 01-626 3531. Rowing race for Thames

Watermen, originated in 1715. Sometimes called the 'Watermen's Derby'. *Late Jul.*

Henley Royal Regatta

Henley-on-Thames, Oxon. Rowing and socialising side by side. *Early Jul.*

Proms (Henry Wood   I   F   10
Promenade Concerts)

Royal Albert Hall, Kensington Gore SW7. 01-589 8212. Concerts of classical music. Ticket qualification system for famous 'Last Night' celebrations. *Late Jul until Sep. No fixed date.*

Richmond Festival

Amateur and professional performing and visual arts. Venues include Richmond Theatre, Richmond Green, the Thames. 01-892 5816. *Mid Jul.*

Royal Tournament   I   H   4

Earls Court Exhibition Centre, Warwick Rd SW5. 01-371 8141. Impressive military spectacle with marching displays and massed brass bands. *Two weeks mid Jul.*

Royal Tournament March   5   L   21
Past

Horse Guards, Whitehall SW1. Colourful parade by all troops taking part in the Royal Tournament. *Sun before Tournament.*

Swan Upping   6   P   29

Starts: London Bridge (Temple Stairs) 09.00-09.30. Ownership of the swans on the Thames is divided between the Dyers Company, the Vintners Company and the Sovereign. Each *Jul* a census of the swans on the reaches up to Henley is taken, and the cygnets are branded by nicking their beaks. *No fixed date.*

August

Greater London Horse Show

Clapham Common SW4. *B.hol Sat-Mon.*

Notting Hill Carnival   I   A   6

Ladbroke Grove and Notting Hill W11. West Indian carnival with colourful floats, steel bands and dancing in the streets. *B.hol Sun & Mon.*

September

Autumn Antiques Fair   4   L   9

Chelsea Old Town Hall, King's Rd SW3. 01-352 3619. *For 10 days mid Sep.*

Battle of Britain Week   5   N   20

Thanksgiving service at Westminster Abbey SW1. 01-222 7110. Biggin Hill Flying Display. *Early Sep.*

Christ's Hospital March

'Bluecoats' march through the City. *St Matthew's Day; on or near 21 Sep.*

Election of Lord Mayor of   6   M   29
London

Procession from the church of St Lawrence Jewry, Gresham St EC2, to the Guildhall EC2. 01-606 3030. *Michaelmas Day, 29 Sep.*

Last Night of the Proms   I   F   10

Royal Albert Hall, Kensington Gore SW7. 01-589 8212. Now a tradition. Audiences sing with the orchestra and wave banners. Tickets by qualification system only. *15 Sep or nearest Sat.*

London to Brighton Walk   5   N   21

Starts Westminster Bridge SW1. Originated in 1903. *Early Sep, 07.00.*

October

Harvest of the Sea   6   P   31
Thanksgiving

St Mary-at-Hill, Lovat La EC3. 01-626 4184. Also a fine display of fish at the church. *11.00, 2nd Sun in Oct.*

Her Majesty's Judges &   5   N   20
Queen's Counsels Annual Breakfast

After special service at Westminster Abbey there is a procession to the House of Lords for the opening of the Law term. *I Oct.*

Quit-Rent Ceremony   6   K   26

The Queen's Remembrancer receives the Quit-rent of a bill-hook, a hatchet, six horseshoes and 61 nails for two holdings from the Comptroller and the City Solicitor: an annual ceremony since 1234. *Tickets from the Chief Clerk to the Queen's Remembrancer, Room 118, Royal Courts of Justice, Strand WC2.*

Trafalgar Day Service &   5   K   21
Parade

Trafalgar Sq WC2. 01-540 8222. Organised by the Navy League. *Sun nearest Trafalgar Day 21 Oct.*

Horse of the Year Show

Wembley Stadium, Wembley, Middx. 01-902 1234. Fine show jumping. *Early Oct.*

November

Admission of the Lord   6   M   30
Mayor Elect

Guildhall EC2. 01-606 3030. The Lord Mayor takes office. Colourful ceremony including handing over of insignia by former Lord Mayor. *Fri before Lord Mayor's show.*

Caravan Camping Holiday   I   H   4
Show

Earls Court Exhibition Centre, Warwick Rd SW5. 01-385 1200. *For 10 days, mid Nov.*

Christmas Lights 2 G 20
Regent St and Oxford St W1. Festive
illuminations to attract Christmas shoppers.
Best seen from 16.00 onwards. Late Nov-6
Jan (12th Night).

Daily Mail International Ski 1 H 4
Show
Earls Court Exhibition Centre, Warwick Rd
SW5. 01-385 1200. Mid Nov.

Guy Fawkes Day
Anniversary of the Gunpowder Plot of 1605.
Private and public firework displays
throughout London. Evening, 5 Nov.

London to Brighton Veteran 2 I 16
Car Run
Hyde Park Corner W1. Cars leave here for
Brighton. Colourful event with contestants
in period costume. Commemorates the
anniversary of Emancipation Day. 08.00,
1st Sun in Nov.

Lord Mayor's Procession & 6 M 30
Show
The newly elected Lord Mayor is driven in
his state coach from the Guildhall to the
Law Courts to be received by the Lord Chief
Justice. The biggest ceremonial event in
the City. 2nd Sat in Nov.

Remembrance Sunday 5 L 21
Poppies sold in the streets to raise money
for ex-servicemen. Service at the
Cenotaph, Whitehall SW1 with a salute of
guns. 11.00, 2nd Sun in Nov.

Royal Command 3 E 27
Performance
Usually at London Palladium, Argyll St W1.
01-437 7373. Variety show in aid of charity
occasionally attended by the Queen. No
fixed date.

State Opening of Parliament 5 N 20
The Queen, in the Irish state coach, is
driven from Buckingham Palace to the
House of Lords. A royal salute is fired from
St James's Park. Early Nov.

December

Annual Ice Show
Wembley Arena, Wembley, Middx. 01-902
1234. Pantomime on ice. Dec-Mar.

Carol Services 5 N 20
Westminster Abbey, Broad Sanctuary
SW1. 01-222 7110. Carol services on 26, 27
& 28 Dec.

Carol Singing 5 K 21
Trafalgar Sq WC2. Recorded on tape.
Early evening from about 14 Dec.

Christmas Tree 5 K 21
Trafalgar Sq WC2. Norwegian spruce
donated each year by the citizens of Oslo.

Brightly lit from 16.00. Carol singing round
the tree. Mid Dec-6 Jan (12th Night).

New Year's Eve 5 K 21
Trafalgar Sq WC2. Singing of 'Auld Lang
Syne' by massed crowds also· dancing
around (sometimes in) the fountains.

Royal Smithfield Show 1 H 4
Earls Court Exhibition Centre, Warwick Rd
SW5. 01-385 1200. Exhibition of agricultural
machinery, supplies and services. Also
livestock. Early Dec.

Tower of London Church 6 Q 32
Parades
Tower Hill EC3. 01-709 0765. The Yeoman
Warders in state dress are inspected and
parade before and after morning service on
the Sun before Xmas. Also Easter
Sun & Whit Sun.

Watchnight Service 6 M 28
St Paul's Cathedral, Ludgate Hill EC4.
01-248 4619/2705. 22.00-24.00, 31 Dec.

London tours

London tours: by coach

Sightseeing tours, usually on double-
decker buses or coaches. Some take several hours and the passengers stay on the
bus listening to a commentary which is
often translated into a number of different
languages. Others take the whole day, and
include guided tours of various sights, plus
lunch. The London Tourist Board Information Centre, Victoria Station Forecourt SW1
(5 M 15), 01-730 3488, sells tickets for a
selection of sightseeing tours; alternatively
you can telephone the organisations direct
to reserve seats.

Cityrama
Silverthorne Rd SW8. 01-720 6663. 20-mile
sightseeing tour of London. Leaves every
30 mins from Trafalgar Sq WC2, Westminster Abbey SW1, Piccadilly W1,
Grosvenor Gdns SW1. Also tours to
Oxford, Cambridge, Stratford and Windsor.

Docklands Tours
Details and booking on 01-252 0742/515
0960. Local tour guides insert news and
views into 2½hr tour of Docklands. Depart
from Tower Hill Underground Station.

Evan Evans 5 K 21
27 Cockspur St SW1. 01-930 2377. Operates a variety of tours; full day, morning,
afternoon, plus a 2½hr general drive
around the capital and 30-min cruise on the
Thames. Also extended tours out of
London.

Frames Rickards   3 F 25
11 Herbrand St WC1. 01-837 3111. Morning
and afternoon tours of the City and the
West End, evening cruises on the Thames,
also (in summer) coach tour to Greenwich
returning by boat. Various tours out of
London.

Harrods   2 I 12
Sightseeing Tours Dept, 4th Fl, Harrods,
Knightsbridge SW1. 01-730 1234. The Neo-
plan Mercedes Benz B10 undoubtedly provides the most luxurious coach tour of
London. The tour takes 2hrs. Taped commentary in eight languages, plus refreshments   served   by   multi-lingual
stewardesses. Harrods also operate tours
to Windsor Castle, Oxford, Stratford,
Blenheim Palace, Bath and Stonehenge.
Ticket reservations and information: 01-581
3603.

**Original London Transport Sightseeing
Tours**
London Coaches, Jew's Row SW18.
01-222 0033. Round London tours in traditional double-decker buses, some of which
are open-topped. London Transport
Information Centres in main tube stations
will give further details and take bookings.

Rock Tour of London   4 R 8
1 Garden Hse, The Cloisters, 8 Battersea
Park Rd SW8. Morning and afternoon tours
of the sights and sounds of the capital.
Double-decker bus complete with video,
music and live commentary. Book through
Keith Prowse 01-730 8191.

**London tours: by private
guide**

The Guild of Guide   5 M 21
Lecturers
2 Bridge St SW1. 01-839 7438. This is the
professional association for Tourist Board
Registered Guides, with over 1000 trained
members, all specialists in their subjects
and speaking more than thirty languages
between them. The Guild compiles an
annual list of Registered Guides and operates a booking bureau for registered tourist
guides throughout the UK.

The London Tourist Board   5 L 15
(Guides Dept)
26 Grosvenor Gdns SW1. 01-730 3450.
Can provide assistance in finding registered guides.

*The following companies all use registered
guides:*
British Tours   2 F 19
6 South Molton St W1. 01-629 5267. Wide

variety of individual tours throughout
London and surrounding areas with
qualified driver/guides.

Go-By-Guides Ltd
67 Clapham Common Northside SW4.
01-350 2408. Sightseeing tours by private
car accompanied by trained driver/guides.
Half, full and multi-day tours covering the
entire UK. 24hr booking service.

London Taxi Guides
18 Monterey Clo, Bexley, Kent. 01-584
3118. Personal sightseeing service by
licensed London taxi drivers who are also
Tourist Board registered guides. 24hr service.

Marketing Support Partnership
Details and booking on 01-538 0022/515
3000x3515. Limousine tour of London
Docklands with local driver and flexible
route. Depart from Tower Hill Underground
Station. Also do coach tours.

Tour Guides Ltd   5 M 21
2 Bridge St SW1. 01-839 2498. A booking
bureau for registered tourist guides
throughout the UK. Uses exclusively Tourist Board registered guides. 24hr service.

London tours: walking

Canal Walks
Inland Waterways Association, 114
Regent's Park Rd NW1. 01-586 2556. Two
walks along the Regent's Canal starting
from Camden Town tube station, then
either west to Little Venice or east to the
City Road Basin.

Citisights of London
145 Goldsmith's Row E2. 01-739 2372.
Archaeologists and historians working in
association with the Museum of London
provide a series of walks and tours concerning the history and archaeology of
London.

Discovering London
11 Pennyfield, Worley, Brentwood, Essex.
Brentwood 213704. Many walks including
Jack the Ripper, Evil London, Night Prowl,
Inns of Court, Great Fire. Leaflet giving
details and times from City Information
Centre.

The Londoners
3 Springfield Av N10. 01-883 2656. Pub
tours, various routes. Bankside, Covent
Garden, Rotherhithe. Visit four or five pubs.
From Temple tube station 19.30 Fri.

London Walks
10 Greenbrook Av, Hadley Wood, Herts.
01-441 8906. Meet at various tube stations
for stimulating walks through London lasting 1½ to 2hrs. Titles include Dickens'

London, Ghosts of the West End. *May-Oct 11.00, 14.00 & 19.30 Mon-Sun; Nov-Apr 11.00, 14.00 & 19.30 Sat & Sun & some weekdays.* Phone to check.

Streets of London
32 Grovelands Rd N13. 01-882 3414. Guided walking tours with regular programme of scheduled tours, regardless of weather. Also private tours for clubs, societies, schools etc.

River trips

The Thames is a fascinatingly beautiful river, never more so than as it passes through London. One of the best ways of appreciating the city is to take a boat trip. The buildings which line the banks range from decrepit warehouses to palaces, conjuring up a whole host of historic, artistic and literary associations. During the summer daily services run from the piers listed below, but travellers may board at any of the other piers en route. It is important to note that times vary according to the tides and the weather and it's always advisable to telephone for details first. The London Tourist Board provides an excellent recorded River Boat Information Service on 01-730 4812. They also sell river trip tickets. NB: always check times of return boats at the pier on arrival.

Downriver services

Charing Cross Pier   6 L 23
Victoria Embankment WC2. 01-930 0971. Trips to the Tower *(20-min journey)* and Greenwich *(45-min journey)* every 30 mins between *10.30-16.00 Apr-Oct;* every 45 mins between *10.30-15.00 Nov-Mar.*

Charing Cross Pier   6 L 23
Catamaran Cruisers, Victoria Embankment WC2. 01-839 2349. Trips to the Tower *(25-min journey)* and Greenwich *(45-60 min journey)* every 30 mins *Apr-Oct from 10.30-16.00 Mon-Sun;* every 45 mins *Nov-Mar from 10.30-15.45 Mon-Sun.*

Greenwich Pier
Return services to Charing Cross Pier *(45-min journey),* Tower Pier *(30-min journey)* and Westminster Pier *(45-min journey).* Telephone the individual piers for details.

Tower Pier   6 Q 31
01-488 0344. Trips to Greenwich *(30-min journey)* every 30 mins *11.00-17.00 (16.00 winter);* to Westminster *(20-min journey)*

every 20 mins *11.00-18.00 (17.00 winter).* Ferry to HMS Belfast *(5-min journey)* every 20 mins when Belfast is open *(11.00-18.00 Mon-Sun, Sat & Sun only in winter).* Ferry service enquiries 01-407 6434.

Westminster Pier   5 M 21
Victoria Embankment SW1. 01-930 4097. Trips to the Tower *(25-min journey)* and Greenwich *(45-60 min journey)* every 20 mins between *10.20-16.00.* Special trips to the Thames Flood Barrier *(1¼hrs each way) 10.00, 11.15, 13.30, 14.45.* Also luncheon cruises *12.15-14.45 (Wed & Sat, May-Oct; Sun all year);* floodlit supper cruises *May-Oct 20.30-22.30 Sun-Fri;* disco cruises *20.00-24.00 Fri & Sat all year.*

Upriver services

Run from Westminster Pier only, all services call at Putney Embankment.

Westminster Pier   5 M 21
Victoria Embankment SW1. Westminster Passenger Services 01-930 4721/01-930 2062. Putney *(30-min journey),* Kew *(1½hr journey),* Richmond *(2hr journey),* Hampton Court *(3-4hr journey).*

Kew Boats leave for Kew at *10.30, 11.15, 12.00,* then at *14.00, 14.45, 15.30, Apr-Oct.*
Richmond Boats leave at *10.00, 10.30, 11.15, 12.00, Apr-Oct.*
Hampton Court Boats leave at *10.00, 10.30, 11.15, 12.00, Apr-Oct.* There are also local services to Hampton Court *(Easter-mid Sep)* from Richmond and Kingston, ring 01-546 2434 for details.

Upper Thames

Salter Bros
Folly bridge, Oxford. Oxford 243421. Salter's steamers run *May-Sep, Mon-Sun.* Trips available from Oxford-Abingdon, Reading-Henley,   Marlow-Windsor, Windsor-Staines. Private hire available.

Canal trips

Canal Water Bus
London Waterbus Co, Camden Lock NW1. 01-482 2550. Boat leaves from Little Venice stopping at the zoo and continuing to Camden Lock. *Apr-Sep 10.00-17.00 Mon-Sun.* Last return boat leaves Camden Lock at *17.00* and the zoo at *17.15.*

Jason's Trip
Opposite 60 Blomfield Rd W9. 01-286

London's river

Twickenham
Little survives of the 18thC elegance of Twickenham, but Walpole's 'little plaything house', Strawberry Hill, which he Gothicised in a whimsical manner, has been restored to his original plans. It is still as charming and convincing a case for the revival as when it was built. It now houses St Mary's Training College and can be viewed by appointment only. Alexander Pope, poet and satirist, lived in a house on the site of the convent in Cross Deep between the road and the river. He laid out large gardens on the other side of the road which were reached by a tunnel – his famous 'Grotto'. This survives but without the original lavish decorations of sea shells and fossils of which Pope was so proud.

Eel Pie Island
The hotel which used to stand on the island had a lively and varied history. In Edwardian days it held tea dances well attended by the equivalent of today's jet-set. In the 1960s it housed a noisy night-club from which many of the most famous groups (including the Rolling Stones) emerged. More recently it was taken over by a commune; after their eviction the hotel was razed to the ground.

Now a luxury housing development. Access by boat or footbridge.

Isleworth
Some lovely 17th-18thC houses and a 15thC church. Syon House, refaced and with a redesigned interior by Robert Adam, still retains much of its original 16thC structure. The most notable sight on this stretch of the river is a splendid, elegant boat-house complete with Ionic columns, attributed to Capability Brown.

Chiswick
The Georgian houses along the waterfront stretch from Kew Bridge to Hammersmith. Originally there were three 18thC mansions with grounds down to the river – Grove House, Sutton Court and Chiswick House. Only the latter remains. Lord Burlington and William Kent, who were largely responsible for the elegance of Chiswick, are buried in St Nicholas' Church. Chiswick Mall is still reminiscent of the wealthy riverside village it was in the 18thC.

Fulham
Long ago a haunt of wildfowl, then a fertile 'garden' area, Fulham today is a mass of untidy buildings. The old Sandford Manor House (possibly the home of Nell Gwynn) is dominated by gasworks, and many other old buildings have been destroyed completely. North End House, 18thC, was the home for

The River Thames

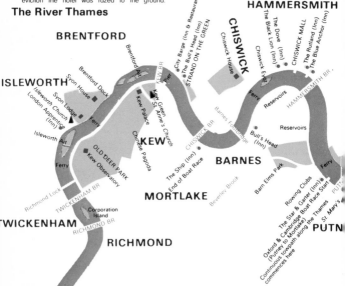

Richmond
A pleasant, almost rural, town which has had long associations with royalty. Richmond Palace, called the Palace of Shene before it was rebuilt by Henry VII in 1497, was a favourite of Elizabeth I. Other famous residents include Joshua Reynolds, first president of the Royal Academy, who had a week-end house here and entertained many of the celebrated literary figures of his time. In this century, Leonard and Virginia Woolf lived at Suffield House and set up the Hogarth Press (publishing among other things the early works of T. S. Eliot).

The park of 2000 acres (810ha) has good herds of deer. Private shooting was stopped in 1904.

Kew
In the Old Deer Park is the Observatory built by Sir William Chambers to enable George III to watch the transit of Venus and Mercury. Kew is most famous for its Botanic Gardens which abound in exotic plants, trees and 'follies' built by order of Queen Charlotte in the late 18thC. Gainsborough and Zoffany are buried in the churchyard on the Green. In 1892 Camille Pissarro, the Impressionist painter, made several studies of Kew and the nearby river.

a time of novelist Samuel Richardson and later of the pre-Raphaelite painter Burne-Jones. John Dwight, potter, was granted a licence to make stone and earthenware in 1671 and the pottery is still on the original site. Fulham Palace is the oldest building in Fulham and has had an uninterrupted ecclesiastical history for over 1200 years. Used to be the main residence of the Bishop of London. Hurlingham House, the only large 18thC house which remains, has grounds to the river and is now an exclusive sports club.

Chelsea

The street with most notable literary and artistic connections in Chelsea is Cheyne Walk. George Eliot lived at No. 10; Rossetti and Swinburne at No. 16; Whistler at No. 21 (also 96 and 101); Carlyle at No. 24; Mrs Gaskell was born at No. 93, Wilson Steer lived at No. 109 and J. M. W. Turner at 119. Tite Street was very popular in the 19thC – Whistler, Sargent, Augustus John and Oscar Wilde all lived here at some time. Both streets are near the river. The Chelsea China Works (which produced some excellent ceramics in the 18thC) was in Lawrence Street where Fielding and Smollett also lived at some time in that century. The nearby Apothecaries' Garden was established in 1673 and it was from here that cotton seeds were first sent to America in 1732. The waterfront is characterised by Georgian houses and, to the west, by houseboats.

Westminster

From the river the stretch from Vauxhall Bridge to Blackfriars affords beautiful views of the north bank

and its many impressive buildings. The Houses of Parliament and Westminster Abbey complement distant views of St Paul's. This part of the river particularly attracted the Impressionist painter, Monet, who came to London in 1899 on a second visit with the express intention of painting the river at that point. Many of the pictures were views from his bedroom window in the Savoy Hotel. Well known is that of the *Houses of Parliament* 1904.

Associations with the area are mainly political, though the Abbey abounds in memorials of scientists, poets and many other notable figures. During World War II Parliament escaped serious damage, but the stained glass of the Henry VII chapel in the Abbey and the Deanery were both badly hit.

The Strand

The road runs parallel with the river from Whitehall to the edge of the City. In the Tudor period it was lined with aristocratic mansions whose gardens spread down to the river. Before that it had been a bridle path 'full of pits and sloughs'. During the 17th and 18thC it was known for its preponderance of coffee houses.

sunsets across the river. In this same church, on 18th August 1782, William Blake, poet, painter and mystic, was married. The power station – a remarkable, if ugly, landmark – was built in 1932-34.

Lambeth

The manor is first mentioned as having been owned by King Hardingcut before 1042. The palace, which was often used as a prison for ecclesiastic or political prisoners, was attacked by Wat Tyler and his followers in 1381. They burnt books and charters and drank the cellar dry. The palace had an even hotter night on 10 May 1940 when it was badly damaged during the biggest air raid on London of World War II.

South Bank Arts Centre

A starkly modern complex built on the south bank of the Thames with a superb view of old London across the river. Started in 1951 with the Festival Hall, the complex now has three concert halls, three theatres, two cinemas, an art gallery and a museum.

Putney

In 1647 Putney was the HQ of Cromwell's Parliamentarian army. In the 19thC Leigh Hunt, Swinburne, Gibbon and George Eliot lived here. There are always eights and sculls rowing here: famous as the start of the Oxford and Cambridge Boat Race.

Wandsworth

Settled as far back as the palaeolithic age. Had a local silk industry until the 19thC. With mechanisation the river Wandle became industrialised and lost what was left of its rural qualities.

Battersea

Away from the pleasure gardens the waterfront is very industrial; it is therefore surprising that in the vestry of the riverside church of St Mary is preserved the chair in which J. M. W. Turner sat and watched

The City

The waterfront from the Temple to the Tower is mainly taken up by warehouses. World War II and many fires destroyed countless valuable buildings and fine churches, but old spires and tall office buildings still dominate the skyline. The most intensive bombing during World War II took place on the night of 10 May 1940 when it was estimated that more than 100,000 bombs were dropped on London. On 29 December the previous year about 60 fires were burning at once, reminding Londoners of the night in 1666 when the Great Fire broke out in Pudding Lane near Eastcheap and spread rapidly throughout the City.

City waterfront

This used to be the most important docking area of London. The 'legal quays and wharfs' were here before the modern docks were built to the east. Queenhithe was the largest wharf and has a very long history. It was here that in the 12thC Queen Maud built the first public lavatory for the 'common use of citizens'. Billingsgate and Custom House form a large complex of trade buildings and the street names between the waterfront and the City often indicate the type of trade which was originally carried out there.

Bankside (Southwark)

A narrow strip of thoroughfare forming the waterfront of Southwark. It was once an Elizabethan pleasure park, between the 'liberty of the Clink and the Paris garden'. Bear-baiting and the theatre formed the central attractions. The 'Rose', 'Swan', 'Globe' and 'Hope' playhouses were here and there were large areas for baiting, wrestling and cock-fighting. The area rapidly became rowdy and dangerous and was eventually known as the 'Stews'. In the 17thC Samuel Pepys was a frequent visitor. Taverns were many – including the 'Anchor' (still there), the 'Cardinal's Cap', 'Falcon', 'Oliphant' and 'Crane'. Small cottages and wharves lined the waterfront; Sir Christopher Wren is said to have watched the rebuilding of St Paul's after the Great Fire of 1666 from one of the houses. The area is now dominated by Bankside power station.

Southwark

A warehouse area. Badly hit during the blitz and very largely rebuilt. In 1898, apparently, Southwark had a street lamp which supplied hot water, tea and cocoa if you 'put a penny in the slot'. The cathedral is built on an old site, probably of a Roman temple and certainly of two previous churches, the first of which was St Mary Overie, a nunnery. In 1905 the church (then St Saviour's) became St George's Cathedral. A famous series of 19thC stained glass windows commemorating dramatists like Shakespeare, Beaumont, Fletcher and Massinger (all associated with Bankside) was totally destroyed during World War II. John Gower, the poet, is buried here.

Bermondsey

The name means 'island of Beormund' and describes the marshy beginnings of the area.

London Bridge marks the western boundary of the Bermondsey waterfront and Cherry Garden Pier, where boats traditionally sounded their horns for Tower Bridge to open, the eastern limit. The latter was a popular place for recreation in the 18thC. The Church of St Mary Magdalen is on the site of one of the earliest Cluniac monasteries established in this country after the Norman conquest. The present church is built in 1680.

Rotherhithe

There are conflicting interpretations of this name but the most realistic translation is from the Anglo-Saxon 'rethra' for mariner and 'hythe' for haven. Once the home of the Surrey Docks, the only docks on the south bank of the river, but now redeveloped as a commercial, residential and entertainment centre.

Deptford

According to a memorial in the church of St Nicholas on Deptford Green, Christopher Marlowe who was killed in a fight at a tavern in Deptford is buried here. Drake's ship the *Golden Hind* was kept in dry-dock for years until it finally collapsed. Henry VIII founded his naval dockyard here, but very little remains.

Greenwich

The church, which had a vast number of medieval relics, was completely burnt out during World War II,

(map labels)

Blackfriars Station
Mermaid Theatre
Puddle Dock
BLACKFRIARS BR
River Fleet emerges under bridge
St Paul's Cathedral
St Andrew-by-the-Wardrobe
St Benet
St Nicholas
St Mary Somerset
St James Garlickhythe
BANKSIDE
St Michael
Fishmongers' Hall
Cannon Street Station
CITY
St Clement
St Magnus the Martyr
The Monument
St Margaret Patterns
Custom House
St Mary
St Dunstan in the East
All Hallows Barking-by-the-Tower
STEPNEY
The Prospect of Whitby (Inn & Restaurant)
The Mint (Restaurant)
Dickens Inn
St Katharine's Dock
Hermitage Entrance
The Town of Ramsgate Inn
Wapping Entrance
The Tower of London
Tower Pier
SOUTHWARK BR
LONDON BR
The Anchor (Inn & Restaurant)
Founders Arms (Inn & Restaurant)
Bankside Power Station
Brewery (site of The Globe Theatre)
Southwark Cathedral
The George Inn
London Bridge Station
TOWER BR
BERMONDSEY
SOUTHWARK
Southwark Park
Cherry Garden Pier
The Angel (Inn & Restaurant)
ROTHERHITHE
St Mary's Church
The Mayflower (Inn)
Brunel's original tunnel now LT
ROTHERHITHE TUNNEL
Globe Pier
Pier
Limehouse
DEPTFORD
Royal Victoria Victualling Yard (remains of)
THE POOL
St Nic...
Deptf...

Tower Bridge
The Gothic towers of the bridge are not purely ornamental – they contain the steam-powered machinery which lifts the drawbridge. Since its installation in 1894 the machinery has only broken down twice – once at the official opening ceremony and once during the heat wave of 1968. A rather spectacular event happened in 1954 when the warning signal failed to sound and a bus had to 'leap' the gap as the bridge was raised. Regrettably with the closing of most of the London docks the bridge is opened so rarely that the steam system is no longer economic and an electrical one has been substituted. On the east side of the bridge is **St Katharine's Dock** which contains the World Trade Centre, a luxury hotel, apartments, restaurants, shops and a yacht basin.

Poplar
The main area of the original parish lies in the Isle of Dogs which was for years an uninhabited and very swampy peninsula. Millwall, on the west, was called Marshwall until the 18thC when seven windmills were built there. In the 19thC the East and West India Docks were built (the East India Company had founded their headquarters at Blackwall in 1612 and had built their ships here) and later the Millwall Dock. In 1982 Billingsgate fish market exchanged its age-old site in the City for a 13.5 acre (5.5ha) expanse on the West India Dock Rd.

The docks
During World War II 3000 convoys sailed from London and munitions from the States and Canada were docked here in millions of tons. Bombing was extremely heavy from August 1940 to 1945, beginning with air raids, then in 1944 with flying bombs and finally late in 1944 with V2 rockets. The docks were a major objective (the bombers following the Thames to London naturally approached over the docks). The huge conglomeration of docks which spread the whole length of the London waterfront is no longer used for shipping and much of the land has been redeveloped providing business accommodation and prestigious housing. The Royal Docks in the east are the least developed but great changes, such as the London City Airport, are already apparent. The Thames Flood Barrier, which crosses the river between Charlton and Silvertown, was completed in 1982.

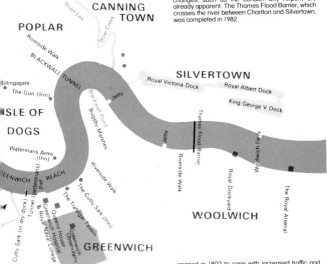

and most treasures were lost including the famous 'Tallis Organ' (Thomas Tallis, musician, 1510-85, is buried here).

In the park the Queen's House, a perfect example of neo-classical architecture by Inigo Jones, houses the Maritime Museum. Marked on the path in front of the Observatory (also in the park but not used) is the zero meridian from which was calculated the Greenwich Mean Time. In 1831 Charles Darwin set off aboard the *Beagle* to South America – and returned to write his famous evolution theory. The *Cutty Sark*, one of the original tea clippers, and Chichester's boat *Gipsy Moth* are in dock near the pier.

Up to the 19thC the only dock system in existence was on the South Bank where the Great Howland Dock had been built in 1696 to take the Greenland whalers. Most ships had to dock at the 'legal quays' where all cargo had to be disembarked between dawn and dusk. The India group of docks were opened in 1802 to cope with increased traffic and combat the smuggling at the overcrowded legal quays. The Royal Docks followed from 1855. In 1909 the three companies which owned these dock areas privately merged into the Port of London Authority, which then had complete control.

After World War II the Old Granary at Shooters Hill became the PLA's private radio station. Since then international VHF and UHF have been installed centred on Greenwich and known as the Thames Navigation Service. Radar was introduced into the port system in 1955 and covers the whole river right down to the estuary mouth.

Woolwich Royal Arsenal
Built as a look-out post to protect Greenwich Palace and to serve as an armoury. Originally called the 'Royal Warren', it was renamed the Arsenal in 1805. During World War II over 40,000 people were employed there making armaments. The site originally covered 1200 acres (486 ha) but has now partly been redeveloped as the Thamesmead Estate.

3428. The traditional narrow boat *Jason* leaves Little Venice for *1½hr* return trip, with commentary, through Regent's Park and zoo to Camden Lock. Disembark to look round the craft shops if you like, or the market at weekends. Refreshments and lunch available. *Depart Apr, May & Sep 12.30 & 14.30; Jun-Aug 10.30, 12.30, 14.30 & 16.30.* Evening trips for groups only, *depart 19.30* and include bar, music and supper if wanted. Private parties of all kinds can be booked.

Jenny Wren Cruises
250 Camden High St NW1. 01-485 4433. *1½hr* round trips along Regent's Canal passing the zoo and Little Venice. Up to 4 tours a day *Easter-Sep Mon-Sun*. Also longer and evening trips. Also runs *My Fair Lady*, a cruising restaurant, for dinner cruise evenings *19.30-23.00 Tue-Sat, & Sun lunch 12.30-15.00*.

Charter boats

Boat Enquiries
43 Botley Rd, Oxford. Oxford 727288. Will arrange cruiser and narrow-boat hire in England.

Catamaran Cruisers
West India Docks Pier, Cuba St, Isle of Dogs E14. 01-987 1185. Motor catamaran can be hired for private parties or business functions. Also a floating restaurant – enquiries on 01-623 1805.

George Wheeler Launches   5 M 21
Westminster Pier SW1. 01-930 4097. Fully licensed. The *Royalty* (120-150 passengers) and the *Rosewood* (220-250 passengers) available for private hire, weddings, dances, etc. Departs from Westminster Pier.

Thames Launches   5 M 21
Westminster Pier SW1. 01-930 7545. Daytime and evening cruises. Fully licensed launches, suitable for private or business entertainment. Embark from Charing Cross or Westminster Piers.

Thames Pleasure Craft
PO Box 15, Blackheath SE3. 01-709 9697/01-488 1939. Daytime and evening cruises. Fully licensed launches with dancing space. Embark from Tower Pier.

Inland Waterways Association
114 Regent's Park Rd NW1. 01-586 2556. Will supply a list of boat-hire firms for canals and rivers.

Woods River Services
PO Box 177 SE3. 01-480 6851. Modern all-weather passenger launches. *Silver Bar-* *racuda* – 280-passenger. *Silver Dolphin* – 160-passenger. *Silver Marlin* – 120-passenger. Fully fitted dance floor, film projector and licensed bar. Guided tours arranged. Private charter only. Luncheon club – *2nd Fri of the month*.

Day trips from London

Every era from prehistoric times has altered, and left its mark on, the English landscape. Ancient heath and moorland contrast with stately gardens and manor houses. Centuries mingle in the architecture along village streets. The ruins of a Norman or Tudor castle are not far from a Victorian cathedral or 14thC parish church. The 19thC pleasure-dome in Brighton is a short drive away from thatched cottages in Sussex and hop fields in Kent. The English countryside is a constantly changing, often magical landscape – well worth exploring. All the places listed below are easily accessible on a day trip from London.
For information about train, coach and bus services out of London see 'Tourist information' at the beginning of this chapter. EC = early closing day.

Ashdown Forest, E. Sussex
Excellent walking. High sandy country of heather and bracken with wind-blown pine trees, silver birch and beech in the valleys – each with its stream. 'Winnie-the-Pooh' country. Start from Crowborough, Hartfield, Forest Row or Three Bridges. London 30 miles (A22).

Battle, E. Sussex
Site of the famous battle of 1066. An abbey, which William the Conqueror had vowed to build should he win the battle, is now in ruins but the Gateway still stands on Battle Hill. Opposite this is the 12thC church of St Mary. London 56 miles (A21).

Brighton, E. Sussex
Known as 'Little London by the Sea', this once poor fishing village has been a lively, bustling seaside resort ever since the Prince Regent set up his court in the fabulous Oriental-domed Pavilion. Fashionable shops, splendid Regency terraces, good pubs and restaurants, cockle stalls, fairs and sport of all kinds. Five miles of beach and a magical Victorian pier. Train *1hr*. EC Wed or Thur. London 48 miles (A23).

Cambridge, Cambs
A great university city of spires, mellow colleges and riverside meadows, bordering

the Cam. The famous 'Backs' and the lovely bridges are best seen by hiring a punt. The 20 or so colleges date from the 13thC onwards including Trinity by Wren, King's by Gibbs and the modern Queens' by Basil Spence. The city contains the superb Fitzwilliam Museum, the notable Botanic Garden and some fine churches. Train 1½hrs. EC Thur. London 55 miles (M11).

Canterbury, Kent
Pleasant, old, walled city on the river Stour, dominated by the magnificent Gothic cathedral, containing the shrine of Thomas à Becket (murdered 1170) and the tomb of the Black Prince. Good local museum in West Gate. Train 1½hrs. EC Thur. London 56 miles (M2).

Chichester, W. Sussex
An old Roman city walled by the Saxons and graced by its beautiful 12thC cathedral. Now mostly Georgian in character. Fine 16thC Butter Cross, a medieval Guildhall and modern Festival Theatre, built 1962. Excellent harbour for sailing. Train 1½hrs. EC Thur. London 63 miles (A3, A286).

The Chilterns
A 40-mile-long ridge of chalk hills with fine views. Open downs, wheat fields, magnificent beech woods and charming villages. Start from Henley, Great Missenden, Stokenchurch, Wendover or Whipsnade. London 20-30 miles.

Colchester, Essex
England's first Roman city, with many visible remains: the city wall, a Mithraic temple, and arches, windows and doorways built from Roman bricks. Norman relics include Colchester castle (now housing a museum) and the ruins of the church of St Botolph. There is a small harbour and an oyster fishery. The famous 'Colchester Oyster Feast' takes place every year, about 20 Oct. Train 1hr. EC Thur. London 52 miles (A12).

Devil's Punchbowl, Surrey
A vast and impressive bowl scooped out of the high open hills. Good views. Start from Haslemere or Hindhead. Train 1hr. London 30 miles (A3).

Henley-on-Thames, Oxon
Situated on a very pretty part of the Thames and most famous for the Regatta, held in early Jul. The arched bridge was built in 1786. In St Mary's churchyard are 16thC almshouses and a rare unspoilt 15thC timber-framed building – the Chantry House. The Regatta is held on the straight mile of the river downstream from the bridge. Train 1hr. EC Wed. London 36 miles (A4).

The North Downs
An outcrop of high chalk hills with magnificent views over the Weald of Kent. The Pilgrim's Way runs along the south face of the hills. Farming country with open beech and oak woods, pleasant villages and pubs. Start from Dorking, Box Hill, Woldingham or Otford. London 15-20 miles.

Oxford, Oxon
A university city of spires and fine college buildings on the Thames and the Cherwell and dating from the 13thC. The Sheldonian Theatre by Wren, the Radcliffe Camera by Gibbs and the 15thC Bodleian Library are particularly notable. Visit also the famous old Botanic Garden and the Ashmolean Museum. Train 1½hrs. EC Thur. London 65 miles (A40).

Southend-on-Sea, Essex
Traditionally the Cockney's weekend seaside resort. Fun-fairs and every sort of entertainment and attraction. Visit Westcliff-on-Sea nearby and Shoeburyness for cockle-beds, boats and paddling. Train 1hr. EC Wed. London 40 miles (A127).

Stratford-on-Avon, Warks
The birthplace of William Shakespeare (1564-1616). The town is still Elizabethan in atmosphere with overhanging gables and timbered inns. Visit the poet's birthplace in Henley St, his house at New Place, Anne Hathaway's cottage and the museum and picture gallery. The Shakespeare Memorial Theatre in Waterside is thriving and progressive. Train 2½hrs. EC Thur. London 90 miles (A40, A34).

Thames Estuary
Unusual and sometimes tough walking along the tidal sea wall. Not everyone's cup of tea; it can be cold, windy or foggy. Take binoculars and wrap up well. Thousands of sea birds, a constant traffic of ships and the lonely marshes. Romantic and isolated but you have to be able to absorb the odd oil refinery or factory and accept that commerce is part of it all. Start from Cliffe, Higham or Gravesend in Kent, Tilbury or Mucking in Essex. London 20-25 miles.

Thaxted, Finchingfield, Great Bardfield, Essex
Perhaps the nicest of all Essex's villages. Thaxted's timbered houses and fine Guildhall are dominated by a magnificent church begun in 1340 and finished in the Reformation period. Finchingfield is a charming village on the edge of the river Pant; nearby Great Bardfield has some splendid 17thC buildings, a fine church and a windmill. It is now an artists' community. EC Wed. London 45 miles (A12, A130).

Winchester, Hants

The ancient Saxon capital of England set among lovely rolling chalk downland. The massive, square-towered Norman cathedral, with its superb vaulted Gothic nave, contains the graves of King Canute, Izaac Walton and Jane Austen. The 'round table of King Arthur' is in the remains of the Norman castle. Train 1½hrs. EC Thur. London 65 miles (A30).

Great houses and gardens near London

England's country houses and their gardens have been loved and written about for nearly 400 years; even the socialist reformer H. G. Wells said of them: 'It is the country house that has opened the way to human equality.' The country house represents a blending of many strands in English history; rural life, great architecture, landscaping, collecting, pride and patronage.

Not that they, any more than other buildings, are unaffected by social and economic change; less than half of the 5000 stately homes reckoned to have been standing in 1920 have survived to the present day. Fortunately, however, not only have many of the most splendid examples been preserved but, thanks to organisations such as the National Trust and English Heritage, a number of these are open to the public. These are some of the great country houses within a 70-mile radius of London, dating from the 11th to the 19thC. Each property has been selected as being characteristic of its period; many were designed by such famous architects as Inigo Jones, Christopher Wren and Robert Adam. The gardens and parks were laid out by various inspired landscape gardeners including Sir John Vanbrugh, William Kent, Capability Brown and Humphry Repton. Almost without exception they contain great richness of interior decoration and ornament, and often famous collections or works of art.

Blenheim Palace

Arundel Castle

Arundel, W. Sussex. Arundel 883136. An imposing feudal stronghold set among the beech woods of the South Downs, overlooking the tidal river Arun. Built at the time of Edward the Confessor, it has been the home of the Dukes of Norfolk for the last 700 years. Completely restored in 1890 by the 15th Duke. Paintings by Van Dyck, Holbein and Gainsborough; important collection of portraits of the Howard family. London 58 miles (A29). *OPEN Apr-May 13.00-17.00 Sun-Fri; Jun-Aug 12.00-17.00 Sun-Fri; Sep & Oct 13.00-17.00 Mon-Fri; B.hols 12.00-17.00. Last admission 1hr before closing. Charge.*

Audley End

Saffron Walden, Essex. Saffron Walden 22399. A great Jacobean mansion standing mellow and serene in its park near the road to Cambridge. Imposing as it now is, Audley End was once three times its present size. Built 1605-14, it served for a while as a royal country palace. In 1721 Vanbrugh demolished two thirds of the building. Fine state rooms – some decorated by Robert Adam, others 19thC neo-Jacobean. London 40 miles (A11). *House OPEN Easter-Sep 13.00-17.00 Tue-Sun & B. hol Mon in Aug 12.00-17.00. Grounds OPEN Easter-Oct 12.00-18.30 Tue-Sun & B. hol Mon in Aug 11.00-18.30. Charge.*

Blenheim Palace

Woodstock, Oxon. Woodstock 811325. A great classical-style ducal palace 1705-22 by Sir John Vanbrugh. The estate was given by Queen Anne to John Churchill, Duke of Marlborough for his victory over Louis XIV at Blenheim in 1704. Winston Churchill was born here. Fine paintings, tapestries and furniture. The park was landscaped first by Wise and later by Capability Brown in 1760, who dammed the small stream to create two great lakes, keeping Vanbrugh's original bridge. London 60 miles (A34). *OPEN Mar-Oct 10.30-17.00 Mon-Sun. Charge.*

Bodiam Castle

Robertsbridge, E. Sussex. Staplecross 436. A romantic and lovely medieval castle completely surrounded by a wide moat. A

Blenheim Palace

mighty fortress built 1385 as a defence against the French. London 45 miles (A21). *OPEN Apr-Oct 10.00-17.30 Mon-Sun; Nov-Mar 10.00-1/2hr before sunset Mon-Sat. CLOSED Xmas. Charge.*

Boston Manor House
Boston Manor Rd, Brentford, Middx. 01-570 7728x4176. Jacobean mansion with park and gardens. *House OPEN May-Sep 14.00-16.30 Sat only. Free. Gardens OPEN dawn-dusk Mon-Sun. Free.*

Buscot Park
Faringdon, Oxon. Faringdon 20786. A charming late 18thC house in the Adam style. Notable for its splendid painted panels by the pre-Raphaelite painter Burne-Jones in the 'Sleeping Beauty' room. Also paintings by Reynolds, Murillo and Rembrandt. Pleasant park and lake. London 70 miles (A417). *OPEN Apr-Sep 14.00-18.00 Wed-Fri, 2nd & 4th weekends. Charge.*

Clandon Park
West Clandon, Surrey. Guildford 222482. Superb Palladian house built c1733 by the Venetian architect Leoni. Magnificent marble halls. Original wallpapers uncovered in restoration. Furniture, porcelain and needlework collections. London 25 miles (A247. Close to M25). *OPEN Apr-mid Oct 13.30-17.30 Sat-Wed. CLOSED Thur & Fri. Charge.*

Claydon
Nr Wimslow, Bucks. Steeple Claydon 349. Built in 1752-68 as an ambitious effort by the 2nd Earl Verney to outdo the slendours of the Grevilles' rival seat at Stowe. Never completed, this remaining wing contains marvellous rococo state rooms decorated by the inspired carvings of a relatively unknown craftsman called Lightfoot. The Chinese Room is notable. Family museum which includes Florence Nightingale memorabilia. Tea rooms. London 45 miles (off A413 & A41). *OPEN Apr-Oct 14.00-18.00 Sat-Wed, 13.00-18.00 B.hols. CLOSED Thur & Fri. Charge.*

Cliveden
Nr Maidenhead, Bucks. Burnham 5069. Superbly sited in wooded grounds overlooking the Thames. An imposing and

famous country house built for the Duke of Sutherland in 1850 by Sir Charles Barry, in Italian palazzo style, replacing the two previous buildings destroyed by fire. Formal gardens with fine sculpture from the Villa Borghese and temples by Giacomo Leoni. *The house is now a hotel. London 25 miles (M4). House (3 rooms) OPEN Apr-Oct 15.00-18.00 Thur & Sun. Gardens OPEN Mar-Dec 11.00-18.00 (or sunset) Mon-Sun. Charge.*

Goodwood
Nr Chichester, W. Sussex. Chichester 774107. An 18thC house planned by James Wyatt to have eight sides, of which only three were completed. Stables by Sir William Chambers. A fine example of building in Sussex flint. Excellent paintings; some of Canaletto's London views and portraits by Van Dyck, Romney, Kneller and Reynolds. Also a particularly interesting collection of early Stubbs. Magnificent Sèvres porcelain, considered to be as fine as any in France; Gobelin tapestries; Louis XV and XVI furniture. Afternoon teas. London 60 miles (off A285 & A286). *OPEN May-Oct 14.00-17.00 Sun & Mon (& Easter Sun & Mon). Also Tue-Thur in Aug. CLOSED on Event days. Charge.*

Hall Place
Bexley, Kent. Crayford 526574. Tudor mansion, 1540, in a park with rose garden, conservatories and fine water garden. *Mansion OPEN Apr-Oct 10.00-17.00 Mon-Sat, 14.00-18.00 Sun; Nov-Mar 10.00-16.00 Mon-Sat only. Free. Park OPEN every day during daylight. Free.*

Ham House
Petersham, Surrey. 01-940 1950. Superb 17thC country house built on an 'H' plan. Lavish Restoration interior. Important collection of Stuart furniture. *OPEN Tue-Sun 11.00-17.00 throughout the year. Charge.*

Hatfield
Hatfield, Herts. Hatfield 62823. A mellow and completely preserved Jacobean mansion with magnificent interior built in 1607-11 by Robert Cecil, 1st Earl of Salisbury and still the home of the Cecil family. The Tudor Old Royal Palace nearby was the home of Queen Elizabeth I. Collection of 16th,

Hatfield House

17th and 18thC portraits, manuscripts and relics. London 20 miles (A1). For Elizabethan banquets phone Hatfield 62055, all year. *House OPEN end Mar-mid Oct 12.00-17.00 Tue-Sat, 14.00-17.30 Sun, 11.00-17.00 B.hols. Charge.*

Hever Castle
Nr Edenbridge, Kent. Edenbridge 865224. 13th and 15thC moated castle once the home of Anne Boleyn who was courted here by Henry VIII. Excellent furnished rooms of the period and many fine portraits. A delightful garden and lake, landscaped by the first Viscount Astor in 1905 and containing a walled Italianate garden with statues, topiary and fountains. London 25 miles (A21). *OPEN end Mar-end Oct 12.00-18.00 Mon-Sun (grounds and gardens from 11.00). CLOSED 16 Jun. Charge.*

Hughenden Manor
High Wycombe, Bucks. High Wycombe 28051. Benjamin Disraeli's country seat from 1847 until his death in 1881, altered from its original Georgian to typical mid-Victorian. Museum of Disraeli relics. Terraced garden. London 30 miles (A40). *OPEN Apr-Oct 14.00-18.00 Wed-Sun & B.hols. Mar 14.00-18.00 Sat & Sun. Charge.*

Knebworth
Knebworth, Herts. Stevenage 812661. A successful and imaginative re-creation from the original Tudor built by the 1st Lord Lytton, the Victorian novelist, in 1844. Pleasant garden with adventure playground for children. Barns restaurant, Stevenage 813825. London 30 miles (A1). *OPEN May-Sep, Tue-Sun; park 11.00-17.30, house and garden 12.00-17.00. Easter school hols & Apr Sat & Sun; B.hols. Guided tours. Parties by arrangement. Charge.*

Knole
Sevenoaks, Kent. Sevenoaks 450608. A great Jacobean country house with a splendid park. The family home of the Sackvilles since 1566. The house and its interior survive intact. It is a treasure house of robust gilded decoration and ornament, fine furniture, tapestries and paintings of 16th-18thC. Many ancient trees in the large park with a fine herd of deer (not to be fed). London 25 miles (A21). *OPEN Easter-end Oct 11.00-17.00 Wed-Sat & B.hols, 14.00-17.00 Sun. Pre-booked guided tours of 25 or more Tue (& Wed-Fri in Oct). Charge. Gardens OPEN 1st Wed of month May-Sep. Charge.*

Leonardslee
Lower Beeding, Horsham, W. Sussex.

Lower Beeding 212. Overlooking the South Downs and containing ancient 'hammer ponds' from the time when the Weald was a great iron producing area. Famous for conifers, azaleas, rhododendrons and camellias. Lovely views and woodland walks. Wallabies and deer. No dogs allowed. Plants for sale. Cafeteria. London 30 miles (M23). *OPEN mid Apr-mid Jun 10.00-18.00 Mon-Fri; Jul-Sep 10.00-18.00 Sat & Sun; Oct 10.00-17.00 Sat & Sun. Charge.*

Luton Hoo
Luton, Beds. Luton 22955. Imposing front of original house designed by Robert Adam 1767. Altered in 1903 and interior decorated in French 18thC style. Park designed by Capability Brown. Particularly notable for the Wernher Collection, several fine gardens, and important private collection of paintings, tapestries, English porcelain, Fabergé jewels and an unusual collection of mementoes and portraits of the Russian imperial family. London 30 miles (M1, Exit 10). *OPEN Easter-mid Oct 14.00-18.00 Tue-Sun & B.hols. Charge.*

Luton Hoo

Marble Hill House
Richmond Rd, Twickenham, Middx. 01-892 5115. Perfect Palladian villa by the Thames. Built 1724-9 for Henrietta Howard, mistress of George II, with interior and furnishings in period. *OPEN Nov-Jan 10.00-16.00 Sat-Thur; Feb-Oct 10.00-17.00 Sat-Thur. Free.*

Nymans Garden
Handcross, W. Sussex. Handcross 400321. One of the great gardens of the Sussex Weald, originally designed by Colonel Messel. Consists of a heather garden, a sunken garden, a walled garden with herbaceous borders and a rose garden. The rhododendrons are features of great beauty and around the lawns are plants from foreign countries, many of which are rarely seen in England. London 40 miles (M23). *OPEN Apr-Oct 11.00-19.00 (or sunset) Tue-Thur, Sat, Sun & B.hols. Charge.*

Osterley Park House
Thornbury Rd, Osterley, Middx. 01-560 3918. Remodelled by Robert Adam 1761-78 on an already fine Elizabethan building built round a courtyard. The magnificent interiors with furniture, mirrors, carpets and tapestry all show the elegance and richness of Adam's genius. *OPEN all*

Penshurst Place

year 11.00-17.00 (last admission 16.30), Tue-Sun; CLOSED Mon (except B.hols). Small charge. Park OPEN all year 10.00-dusk. Free.

Parham

Pulborough, W. Sussex. Storrington 2021. Fine Elizabethan house in a great deer park facing the South Downs, with a superb Great Hall and Long Gallery, and a good collection of portraits. Parham Chuch is in the grounds. London 50 miles (A24). *OPEN Easter Sun-1st Sun in Oct 14.00-17.30 Sun, Wed, Thur & B.hols. Charge. Gardens OPEN 13.00-18.00. Free.*

Penshurst Place

Penshurst, Tonbridge, Kent. Penshurst 870307. A serene medieval house set amidst flat lawns. Built 1340 and enlarged during Elizabeth I's reign. Magnificent Great Hall with carved timber roof, fine portraits of the Sidney family, early Georgian and Chippendale furniture, and a delig:htful formal walled garden with ponds and ancient apple trees. London 30 miles (off A21). *OPEN Apr-Oct 13.00-17.30 (last admission 17.00) Tue-Sun (grounds 12.30-18.00). CLOSED Mon except B.hols. Guided tours by arrangement. Charge.*

Petworth House

Petworth, W. Sussex. Petworth 42207. An impressive 320ft-long (97.6m) house, rebuilt late 17thC and containing a range of magnificent state rooms. Famous for its splendid 'Carved Room' by the greatest carver in wood, Grinling Gibbons, and a most important collection of paintings including Van Dycks, Reynolds, many Dutch pictures and some particularly superb Turners. Fine deer park. London 50 miles (A283). *OPEN Apr-Oct 13.00-17.00 Tue-Thur, Sat, Sun & B.hols. CLOSED Mon, Fri & Tue after B.hols. Extra rooms shown Tue (except Tue following B.hols). Charge.*

Rousham

Steeple Aston, Oxon. Steeple Aston 47110. One of the best remaining examples of the work of William Kent, carried out 1738-40. Original interior decoration, painted ceilings and furniture within the Jacobean house. Kent's delightful classic garden beside the Cherwell, with statues (by Van Nost), glades and cascades, remains unaltered. London 65 miles (A423). *OPEN Apr-Sep 14.00-16.30 Wed, Sun & B.hols. Guided tours. Garden OPEN all year 10.00-16.30 (last admission). Charge.*

Royal Pavilion, Brighton

Old Steine, Brighton, E. Sussex. Brighton 603005. A fantastic Oriental seaside 'villa', complete with onion domes, and minarets, built for the Prince Regent (later George IV), by John Nash in 1815-22. The lavish Chinese style staterooms are breathtaking, the original furniture has been returned from Buckingham Palace and the exemplary restorations, after years of neglect, are due to be completed in 1990. London 45 miles (A23). *OPEN all year 10.00-17.00 Mon-Sun. Charge.*

Sheffield Park Garden

Nr Uckfield, E. Sussex. Danehill 790655. Magnificent garden by Capability Brown 1775. London 43 miles (A22). *OPEN end Mar-beg Nov 11.00-18.00 (or sunset) Tue-Sat, 14.00 (13.00 Oct & Nov)-18.00 (or sunset) Sun & B.hol Mons. CLOSED Mon & Tue following B.hol Mon. Last admission one hour before closing. Charge.*

Royal Pavilion

Sissinghurst Castle
Sissinghurst, Kent. Cranbrook 712850. The soft red-brick remains of the walls and buildings of a once extensive Tudor manor, enchantingly transformed by the late Victoria Sackville-West and Sir Harold Nicolson into numerous enclosed walled gardens. Each is different in character and outstandingly beautiful in its richness of flowers and shrubs. No dogs. London 40 miles (A21). *OPEN Apr-Oct 13.30-18.30 Tue-Fri, 10.00-18.30 Sat, Sun & Good Friday. CLOSED Mon (inc B.hols). Charge.*

Stowe
Stowe School, nr Buckingham, Bucks. Buckingham 813164. Chiefly famous for its succession of notable landscape gardeners and garden architects. Bridgeman, Vanbrugh, James Gibbs, William Kent and Capability Brown. They produced the fine gardens, park, lake and Palladian bridges, temples and garden pavilions. London 55 miles. *OPEN (garden and part of house) Easter & mid Jul-early Sep 13.00-18.00 Mon-Sun. Charge.*

Strawberry Hill
Waldegrave Rd, Twickenham, Middx. 01-892 0051. One of the earliest examples of the Gothic Revival, this romantic, rococo building was converted from 'a little plaything house' (1750-76) by Horace Walpole. It now stands in the grounds of a college. *Appt only.*

Syon House
Park Rd, Brentford, Middx. 01-560 0884. The exterior is the original convent building of the 15thC, but the interior 1762-9 is by Robert Adam. The imaginative elegance and variety in each room is unsurpassed. Garden by Capability Brown. Additional attractions include the London Butterfly House, the Heritage Collection of historic British cars and an excellent garden centre. *House OPEN Apr-Oct 12.00-17.00 Sun-Thur & Good Friday. CLOSED Fri & Sat. Charge. Butterfly House OPEN daily Mar-Nov 10.30-17.00. Charge. Motor Museum OPEN all year 10.30-17.30 (10.30-16.00 Nov-Feb). Charge. Garden centre OPEN daily 09.00-17.00 or dusk.*

Uppark
Petersfield, Hants. Harting 317. Beautifully simple 17thC house on the ridge of the South Downs, by William Talman 1690. Home of Emma Hamilton and H. G. Wells' mother. Faultless 18thC interiors with fine plasterwork and ceilings. London 50 miles (A3). No dogs. *OPEN Apr-late Sep 14.00-18.00 Wed, Thur, Sun & B.hols. Charge.*

Uppark House

The Vyne
Sherborne St John, Basingstoke, Hants. Basingstoke 881337. Early 16thC mansion with private chapel containing original glass. A classic-style portico was added in 1654. Fine Long Gallery with 'linenfold' carving on the panels throughout its length. 18thC staircase by John Chute. London 45 miles (M3). Tea-room and shop. *OPEN Apr-Oct 13.30 (grounds from 12.30)-17.30 Tue-Thur, Sat & Sun, 11.00-17.30 B.hols (CLOSED following Tue). Charge.*

Waddesdon Manor
Nr Aylesbury, Bucks. Aylesbury 651211. An extraordinary house built 1874-89 for baron Ferdinand de Rothschild by the French architect Gabriel-Hippolyte Destailleur, in the style of a great chateau in Touraine. The garden, fountains and large aviary of rare birds are enchanting. The house contains a superb collection of works of art, mostly of the 17th and 18thC. Fine French furniture, Savonnerie carpets, 18thC terracotta figures, and remarkable collections of Sèvres and Meissen porcelain. The paintings include Rubens' *Garden of Love*, eight views of Venice by Guardi, many portraits by Gainsborough and Reynolds, including the latter's *Pink Boy*, and paintings by Watteau and Boucher. London 45 miles (A41). *House OPEN late Mar-late Oct 13.00-17.00 (to*

Waddesdon Manor

Woburn Abbey

18.00 Sat & Sun May-Sep) Wed-Sun, 11.00-18.00 B.hols. CLOSED Wed following B.hol Mon. Grounds and aviary OPEN 13.00-17.00 (to 18.00 Sat & Sun May-Sep) Wed-Sat, 11.30-17.00 Sun. Charge.

West Wycombe Park
High Wycombe, Bucks. High Wycombe 24411. Georgian house rebuilt 1745-71, by Sir Francis Dashwood. Still the home of the Dashwood family, it has good furniture, painted ceilings and frescoed walls. The landscaped grounds are dotted with garden buildings, including Roman and Greek temples, a flint mausoleum and, on the opposite hill, the cave where the notorious 18thC drinking club, the Hell Fire Club, are reputed to have met. London 30 miles (A40). *House and grounds OPEN Jun-Aug 14.00-18.00 Sun-Thur. Charge. Caves OPEN Apr-Sep 11.00-18.00 Mon-Sun; Oct-Mar 13.00-17.00 Mon-Sun. Charge.*

Windsor Castle
Windsor, Berks. Windsor 868286. An imposing 800-year-old medieval fortress. 12thC Round Tower built by Henry II. St George's chapel is fine 16thC perpendicular. Magnificent state apartments. *Castle precinct OPEN Mon-Sun 10.00-17.15 Mar & Apr, Sep & Oct; 10.00-19.15 May-Aug; 10.00-16.15 Nov-Mar. CLOSED Garter Day (2nd or 3rd Mon in Jun) and any State Visit arrival day. State Apartments OPEN May-Oct 10.30-17.00 Mon-Sat, 13.30-17.00 Sun; Nov-Apr 10.30-15.00 Mon-Sat. CLOSED when Queen is in residence – usually 6 weeks at Easter, 3 weeks in Jun and 3 weeks at Xmas. Charge.*

Woburn Abbey
Woburn, Beds. Woburn 290666. The Duke of Bedford's 18thC mansion, set in a fine 3000-acre (1215ha) park landscaped by Humphry Repton (part of which has been converted into a Safari Park). The house retains the quadrangular plan of the medieval monastery from which it also derived its site and name. Remodelling has occurred at different periods; the west front and the magnificent state apartments were done in 1747-60 by Henry Flitcroft; the south side, the lovely Chinese dairy and the orangery in 1802 by Henry Holland. Incomparable collection of pictures by Rembrandt, Van Dyck, Reynolds, Gainsborough, Holbein, and a famous group of fine Canalettos. English and French furniture, porcelain and silver. London 40 miles (M1). *Abbey OPEN Mar-Oct 11.00-17.00 Mon-Sat, 11.00-17.30 Sun & B. hols; Nov-Feb 11.00-17.30 Sat & Sun. Charge. Safari Park OPEN Mar-Nov 10.00-18.00 Mon-Sun. Charge.*

Historic London

London's history begins in AD43 when invading Romans bridged the Thames. Around AD200 they built the London Wall (traces of which are still visible today, see entry below). This was to determine the shape of what we still call the City of London for some 1300 years. The Normans incorporated the Wall into their defences, and despite the extensive devastation and damage caused by the Great Fire of 1666

no radical replanning took place within the 'Square Mile'.
However, post-Fire London was to expand well beyond the historic City and its neighbour Westminster – originally a Saxon religious settlement and a seat of government in Norman times – absorbing in the process numerous surrounding villages which have now given their names to districts of the capital.

London's growth resulted from rising commercial importance (the City is still one of the world's major financial centres), the industrial revolution and, more recently, developing public transport which pushed new suburbs well out into the countryside. Cities change; London has changed more than many. But despite the Blitz and decades of redevelopment, every stage of London's history, including the present, can be traced in her buildings, monuments, churches and famous houses.

Looking at history

The following entries are of important places, buildings, characteristic areas and also some of those elements that make London unique in its people and its history.

Abbey Mills Pumping Station
Abbey La E15. 01-534 6717. An unusual building of cupolas and domes built in 1865 to pump the 83 miles of sewers draining the 100 sq miles of London. This remarkable piece of drainage engineering was the work of the engineer Joseph Bazalgette and still survives intact and perfect after well over 100 years of use. *Visits by arrangement, at 10 days' notice.*

Admiralty Arch   5 K 21
Entrance to the Mall SW1. Massive Edwardian triple arch by Sir Aston Webb 1911. A memorial to Queen Victoria.

Admiralty Arch

Albany   2 I 19
Piccadilly W1. Patrician Georgian mansion 1770-4 by Sir William Chambers. Now privately-owned residences with quiet public forecourt.

Albert Memorial   I F 10
Kensington Gore SW7. Gothic memorial to

Albert Memorial

Prince Albert, consort of Queen Victoria, by Sir George Gilbert Scott 1872.

Annesley Lodge
Platts La NW3. A fine example of an Art Nouveau house by C. F. A. Voysey, built 1895.

Apsley House   2 I 16
149 Piccadilly W1. 01-499 5676. Robert Adam 1771-8 but altered in 1828 by Wyatt. Once the home of the Duke of Wellington, it now houses the Wellington Museum containing paintings, silver plate, porcelain and personal and military relics. Near-naked statue of Napoleon stands a startling 11ft (3.4m) high in the staircase well. *OPEN 11.00-17.00 Tue-Sun. Charge.*

Apsley House

Atlas House   6 M 30
3 King St EC2. One of London's earliest surviving purpose-designed office buildings completed in 1836 by Thomas Hopper for the Atlas Insurance Company.

Ball Court   6 N 31
Next to 39 Cornhill EC3. Straight out of Dickens. Simpson's chop house built in 1757.

Bank of England   6 N 31
Threadneedle St EC2. 01-601 4444. The vaults hold the nation's gold reserves. Outer walls are still the original design by Sir John Soane, architect to the Bank 1788-1833. Rebuilt by Sir Herbert Baker 1925-39. *Visits by appt only. Book well in advance. Free.*

Bank of England

Bankside   6 N 27
Southwark SE1. Thames-side walk with the finest views of St Paul's and the City across the river. Here were Shakespeare's

theatres; his Globe is marked by a plaque in Park St. Number 49 is reputed to be the house in which Wren lodged while St Paul's was being built.

Bedford Park W4

Just north of Turnham Green station, the earliest planned suburb, laid out in 1875 by Norman Shaw, who designed a number of the houses.

Belgravia SW1   5 J 14

Thomas Cubitt converted a swamp almost level with the Thames and intersected by mud banks into the posh village of Belgravia. Draining the site, he turned its clay into bricks, built up its substrata of gravel and, in 1827, started on streets, mansions and houses from designs by George Basevi, Disraeli's uncle. Cubitt died in 1856, but his firm then completed Cubitt Town in Poplar, one of the great industrial parishes on the Thames.

Blackheath SE3

High, open and grassy. Bordered by 18thC houses including 'The Paragon', and the pleasant village of Blackheath.

The Blitz

Although the Docks and the City were prime targets during World War II, bombs rained all over London. The Blitz (prolonged intensive attacks by German bombers) lasted for nine months beginning Aug 1940. In Jun 1944 a renewed assault with V1s ('Doodlebugs') began and lasted nearly a year. Later, V2 rockets arrived with such speed (5000 mph) that they were virtually invisible; the first fell at Chiswick but was heard at Westminster; another hit a New Cross Woolworth's and killed 174 people. Many Londoners spent their nights in air-raid shelters or bedded down in the tube stations. Ten thousand people could fit into Southwark (a disused branch station of the original tube). Over 1.5 million homes were damaged by bombing and 100,000 houses were destroyed. In the City alone, 164 out of 460 acres (66.4 out of 186.3ha) were wiped out. Historic buildings, including churches, were destroyed and damaged.

Bloomsbury Squares WC1   3 H 24

Elegant Regency style houses and squares; Bedford Sq, Russell Sq, Tavistock Sq. etc. Many by Thomas Cubitt, mid 19thC.

Bond Street W1   2 H 19

Fashionable High St. Originally laid out in the 1680s, it no longer has any architectural distinction but is noted for its art dealers' galleries, fashion and quality shops.

Bridges

The tidal Thames has 17 bridges. Noteworthy ones in central London are:

Albert Bridge   4 N 8

Unusual rigid chain suspension. Built by Ordish 1875.

Chelsea Bridge   5 P 12

Original 1858. Rebuilt as suspension bridge by G. Topham Forrest & E. P. Wheeler in 1934.

London Bridge   6 P 29

The site of many replacements. Wooden construction until 13thC; the famous stone bridge that followed carried houses and shops. Granite bridge built in 1832 by Rennie was shipped off to Lake Havasu City, Arizona in 1971. Latest construction completed 1973.

Tower Bridge   6 R 31

Victorian-Gothic towers with hydraulic twin drawbridge. 01-407 0922. Jones and Wolfe-Barry 1894. Enter by the tower closest to the Tower of London and take lift to high walkways for breathtaking views of London and the Thames. The museum on the other side houses the Victorian steam engines that formerly provided the power to operate the bridge. The history, design and operation of the bridge are described and illustrated in exhibition areas within the towers. *OPEN Apr-Oct 10.00-18.30 Mon-Sun; Nov-Mar 10.00-16.45 Mon-Sun. Last admission 45 mins before closing time. Charge.*

Waterloo Bridge   6 L 24

Concrete. Fine design by Sir Giles Gilbert Scott 1940-5.

Westminster Bridge   5 N 21

Graceful cast iron. Thomas Page 1862.

Albert Bridge

Buckingham Palace

Brixton Windmill
Blenheim Gdns SW2. Elegant windmill of the tower type, built 1816. Now restored.

Buckingham Palace 5 K 17
St James's Pk SW1. The official London residence of the Sovereign. Originally built 1705, remodelled by Nash 1825; refaced 1913 by Sir Aston Webb.

Burlington Arcade 2 I 19
Piccadilly W1. 1819 Regency shopping promenade with original shop windows. Still employs a beadle to preserve the gracious atmosphere.

Burlington House 2 I 19
Piccadilly W1. Victorian-Renaissance façade on one of the great 18thC palaces. Houses the Royal Academy and various Royal Societies.

Cadogan Square SW1 5 J 12
A typical 19thC Chelsea square of red-brick houses.

Canals
Many years before railways were built canals carried goods in and out of London. The Grand Union Canal (opened in 1800) provided a link from Brentford to the Midlands; in 1820 a direct link to the Thames dockland was completed. The Regent's Canal, once London's main artery, is still in good condition although its working days are over. At Camden, where the lock starts a 90ft (27.5m) drop to the Thames, you can see houseboats bobbing stem to stern and, occasionally, a cruising pleasure boat. Towpaths there, at Little Venice in Paddington, and a tree-lined cutting that goes through the zoo in Regent's Park afford close-up views of the canal.

Canonbury Tower
Canonbury Pl N1. 01-226 5111. 1530. Tudor brick tower containing fine oak-panelled rooms and staircase. HQ of the successful Tavistock amateur theatre company, whose members will show you round *after the Sat night show. Appts may be made for parties at other times.*

Cemeteries
London cemeteries present a field-day for celebrity-lovers whose idols, if dead, at least can't escape! Cemeteries didn't exist until the 19thC. Before that churchyards sufficed but the pressing burial needs of a rapidly expanding population caused problems of overcrowding (and sometimes cholera). Thus large non-denominational cemeteries were started. They were privately owned and planted out with trees, avenues and vistas – mostly now overgrown – fascinating islands amongst the busy metropolis. The following are notable:

Brompton 4 J 4
Old Brompton Rd SW10. Several extraordinary acres of ornamental Victorian marble tombs and memorials.

City of London
Aldersbrook Rd E12. 200 acres (81ha) of avenues, rhododendrons and Gothic chapels and catacombs.

Highgate
Swains La N6. 01-340 1834. Designed by Stephen Geary. The Friends of Highgate Cemetery guide visitors round the beautiful older western section *on the hour from 10.00-15.00 daily (16.00 in summer). (Also visitors' days five Sun in the year, 13.00-17.00, details from 01-348 0808.)* Thanks to their efforts much of the aggressive sycamore has been removed to allow native woodland to flourish, and wild flowers and birds abound. The eclectic assembly of 19thC society buried here includes bare-fisted prizefighter Tom Sayers, whose grave is guarded by a mastiff who attended his master's funeral in a carriage of his own; and menagerist George Wombwell, lying beneath a colossal, slumbering lion. Other funerary sculpture highlighting the Victorian way of death includes hovering angels, ivy-clad mourners making ephemeral appearances beside winding paths, and the celebrated female figure of *Religion* by Joseph Edwards, lost beneath wreathing ivy for many years. The grand Egyptian gateway leads to the Cedar of Lebanon Circle. Look out for the towering classical mausoleum for financier Julius Beer and for the occasional Gothic shrine. The eastern cemetery, resting place of George Eliot, George Holyoake (pioneer organiser of workers' co-operatives), Herbert Spencer (sociologist and philosopher), Sir Ralph Richardson and, of course, Karl Marx is *OPEN Apr-Sep 10.00-17.00 Mon-Sun;*

Oct-Mar 10.00-16.00 Mon-Sun. CLOSED during funerals. *Donations requested. Charge* for photography by negotiation.

Kensal Green
Harrow Rd W10. In its splendid 56 acres (22.7ha) of stone and marble tombs there can be traced the decline of the 'classic' and the use of the Gothic. Wilkie Collins, the two Brunels, Princess Sophia, the Duke of Sussex, Thackeray and Trollope lie here.

Tower Hamlets
Southern Gro E3. Privately built in 1841 and allowed to deteriorate, it has been transformed from 28 acres (11.3ha) of tangled sycamore interspersed with perilous pits where graves have subsided to woodland walks finely landscaped among the gravestones. An interesting study of nature run wild and cultivation juxtaposed.

The Cenotaph   5   L   21
Whitehall SW1. Designed 1920 by Sir Edward Lutyens to honour the dead of World War I. The annual service of remembrance takes place here.

Chandos House   2   E   20
Chandos St W1. Fine Robert Adam house built 1771.

Charing Cross WC2   5   K   22
The Charing Cross was the last of the stone crosses set up by Edward I to mark the funeral resting places of Queen Eleanor's body on its way to Westminster Abbey. Originally placed where Trafalgar Sq now is, it was demolished in 1647 and the statue of Charles I now stands in its place. The stone cross in the station courtyard is a replica.

Charlton House
See under Greenwich.

Chelsea Physic Garden   4   N   10
Royal Hospital Rd SW3. 01-352 5646. There has been a garden at this site since 1673. Seeds and plants exchanged on a world-wide scale. *OPEN mid Apr-mid Oct 14.00-17.00 Wed & Sun; at other times by appt. Charge.*

Chelsea Royal Hospital   4   N   11
Chelsea Embankment SW3. 01-730 0161. A home for old soldiers. Fine, austere building. 1682 by Wren. Stables 1814-17 by Sir John Soane. Museum (also by Soane, 1819). *OPEN 10.00-12.00 & 14.15-16.00 Mon-Sat, 14.00-16.00 Sun. Free.*

Chiswick House
Burlington La W4. 01-995 0508. Lovely Palladian villa built in the grand manner by 3rd Earl of Burlington 1725-30. Fine interiors and gardens by William Kent. *OPEN mid Mar-mid Oct 09.30-18.30 Mon-Sun;*

Chiswick House

mid Oct-mid Mar 09.30-16.00 Mon-Sat; 14.00-16.00 Sun. Charge.

Chiswick Mall W4
17th-18thC riverside houses.

The Citadel   5   K   19
The Mall SW1. Creeper-covered concrete. Built as a bomb proof unit by the Admiralty 1940.

Clarence House   5   K   18
Stable Yard Gate SW1. Mansion by Nash 1825. Now the home of the Queen Mother.

Cleopatra's Needle   6   L   23
Victoria Embankment SW1. From Heliopolis. 1500BC. Presented by Egypt and set up next to the Thames 1878.

Cock Lane   6   K   28
Look up at the golden boy, marking Pye Cnr, where, poetic licence allows, the Great Fire of London stopped.

41-42 Cloth Fair EC1   6   K   29
A rare domestic survivor of the Great Fire, with its two-storey bay windows of timber (forbidden in post-Fire reconstruction). Peep round the corner in Cloth Ct at the dummy window painted with a somewhat faded Victorian parlour scene.

Cockney or rhyming slang
A particular accent and form of language still exists today which was once the common language of the people of the slums of London, particularly of the East End. To an acute ear a mere sentence at one time would reveal where in London you were born, which school your parents could afford and what your father did for a living. In addition to this very characteristic accent, the petty criminals of the City and the East End developed their own way of communicating by obscuring a dangerous word in a form of 'rhyming slang'. This in turn developed into a general misuse of most words – to the utter mystification of strangers. Instances are: 'apples and pears' for stairs, 'Lady Godiva' for fiver (£5 note); 'Cain and Abel' for table; 'Dickie dirt' for shirt – and countless others.

College of Arms   6   M   28
Queen Victoria St EC4. 01-248 2762. Handsome late 17thC building which houses the official records of English,

Welsh and Irish heraldry and genealogy. *OPEN 10.00-16.00 Mon-Fri.*

Covent Garden Market WC2 6 J 23
Originally designed by Inigo Jones (with his St Paul's church) as a residential square in the 1630s. Market buildings are of 1830 by Fowler, Floral Hall added in 1860 by E. M. Barry, architect of the Royal Opera House (1858). In 1974 the market moved to Nine Elms, but the area survived to become a flourishing new community, with eclectic though expensive shopping centre, restaurants and the London Transport Museum.

Crewe House 2 H 17
15 Curzon St W1. Georgian town house, 1735 by Edward Shepherd, who gave his name to Shepherd Market nearby. It was for many years the home of the Marquess of Crewe.

Crosby Hall 4 M 7
Cheyne Wlk SW3. 01-352 9663. Incorporates 15thC dining hall of city mansion – transplanted here in 1910. Fine timbered roof. Open to the public unless on hire. The Hall serves as a residence for post-graduate women students. *Ring for appt. Free.*

Croydon Palace
Old Palace Rd, Croydon, Surrey. 01-680 5877. A 'standing house' of the Archbishops of Canterbury for over 1000 years, Croydon Palace is now a girls' school. Magnificent 15thC banqueting hall and Tudor chapel. *Tours 14.30 Mon-Sat during certain school hols, Apr, May & Jul. Charge.*

Custom House 6 P 31
Lower Thames St EC3. Rebuilt many times. Admired for its classical river front by Robert Smirke.

Downing Street SW1 5 L 20
17thC street; houses built by Sir George Downing. No. 10 is the official residence of the Prime Minister; No. 11 that of the Chancellor of the Exchequer.

Drapers Company Hall 6 N 31
Throgmorton Av EC2. City Livery Hall dating from 1667 but largely rebuilt in 1870. Fine staircase and collection of plate. For information on tours of all Livery Company Halls contact the City Information Centre, St Paul's Churchyard EC4 (6 **M 28**). 01-606 3030x1456.

Eltham Palace
Off Court Yd, Eltham SE9. 01-859 2112. 15thC Royal Palace until Henry VIII. Also remains of earlier Royal residences. Great Hall with hammer beam roof and a very fine 14thC bridge over the moat. *OPEN Apr-Oct 10.00-19.00 Thur & Sun; Nov-Mar to 16.00. Free.*

Fitzroy Square W1 2 D 22
The south and east sides 1790-4 by Robert Adam. Now pedestrianised with a landscaped garden.

Flamsteed House
See Greenwich: Old Royal Observatory.

Fleet Street EC4 6 K 26
London's 'Street of Ink' associated with printing since Caxton. Most newspapers have moved to new hi-tech offices and only a few remain but the association continues.

Fulham Gasometer 4 M 3
Fulham Gasworks SW6. The oldest gasholder in the world; built in 1830 by Winsor & Mindock. Diameter 100ft (30.5m), capacity 250,000 ft^3 (7075m^3). An extraordinary piece of early industrial engineering.

Fulham Palace
Fulham Palace Rd SW6. 01-736 5821. Ex-residence of the Bishop of London. 16thC building with riverside park. *Tours of palace summer twice a month on Sun at 14.30; three times a month in winter. Charge.*

George Inn 6 Q 28
77 Borough High St SE1. 01-407 2056. Built 1677. London's only surviving galleried inn of the kind which inspired early English theatre design.

Goldsmiths' Hall 6 L 29
Foster La EC2. 01-606 7010. Pre-Victorian classical-style palazzo built in 1835 by Hardwick. Occasional exhibitions. For information on tours of all Livery Company Halls contact the City Information Centre, St Paul's Churchyard EC4 (6 **M 28**). 01-606 3030x1456.

Goodwin's Court 5 J 22
St Martin's La WC2. A completely intact row of bow-windowed 17thC houses.

Gray's Inn 3 I 27
High Holborn WC1. 01-405 8164. Entrance from passage next to City of York pub, 22 High Holborn. An Inn of Court since 14thC. The Hall (16thC) and 'Buildings' restored after bomb damage. Gardens were laid out by Francis Bacon. *Hall OPEN by written application to the Under Treasurer. Gardens OPEN May-13 Sep 12.00-14.30. Free.*

Greenwich
Six miles downriver and associated with England's former sea power. The following are notable:

Charlton House
Charlton Rd SE7. 01-856 3951. Perfect small red-brick Jacobean manor house on an 'H' plan, built 1607-12. Fine ceilings, staircase and some bizarre chimney-pieces. A very active community centre. Staff happy to show visitors round when

circumstances permit. *Lunchtime is easiest. Ring manager for appt. Free.*

The Cutty Sark
King William Wlk SE10. 01-858 3445. Stands in dry-dock. One of the great sailing tea-clippers, built 1869. *Gipsy Moth IV*, the boat in which Sir Francis Chichester sailed round the world in 1966 stands in dry-dock next to the *Cutty Sark*. Both ships *OPEN Apr-Oct 10.30-18.00 Mon-Sat, 12.00-18.00 Sun. Cutty Sark also OPEN Nov-Mar to 17.00. Charge.*

The Queen's House
Romney Rd SE10. 01-858 4422. Now part of the National Maritime Museum. Built by Inigo Jones, 1619, for the Queen of Denmark. *Due to reopen after renovation. Ring to check.*

The Queen's House

Old Royal Observatory
Greenwich Park SE10. 01-858 1167. Formerly the Greenwich Observatory. Part of the National Maritime Museum and includes Flamsteed House. Designed by Wren and founded by Charles II in 1675. Time and astronomical instruments. *OPEN summer 10.00-18.00 Mon-Sat, 14.00-18.00 Sun; winter 10.00-17.00 Mon-Sat, 14.00-17.00 Sun. Charge.* Also a Planetarium: phone for times of showing.

Royal Naval College
Greenwich SE10. 01-858 2154. The site of the former royal palace of the Tudor sovereigns. A fine and interesting group of classical buildings by Webb 1664, Wren 1694 and Vanbrugh 1728. Chapel by James 'Athenian' Stuart 1789 and Painted Hall by Thornhill. *OPEN 14.30-17.00. CLOSED Thur. Free.*

Rotunda Museum
Woolwich Common SE18. 01-854 2242 x 3127. Pavilion by Nash 1814. Renowned museum displaying a highly impressive array of artillery starting with the 1346

Royal Naval College

Crécy bombard. *OPEN Apr-Oct 12.00-17.00 Mon-Fri, 13.00-17.00 Sat & Sun; Nov-Mar 12.00-16.00 Mon-Fri, 13.00-16.00 Sat & Sun. Free.*

Vanbrugh Castle
3 Westcombe Park Rd, Maze Hill SE3. Sir John Vanbrugh's own house 1717-26. Outside of the house can be seen – best view from east side of the park.

Guildhall   6 M 30
Off Gresham St EC2. 01-606 3030. 15thC with alterations to the façade by George Dance, 1789, and later restorations by Sir Giles Gilbert Scott. The Great Hall is used for ceremonial occasions. Medieval groined vaulting in crypts. Library, Art Gallery. Great Hall *OPEN 09.00-17.30 Mon-Sat. Free. Art Gallery opening times vary (new Art Gallery under construction). Usually free. Library OPEN 09.30-17.00 Mon-Sat.*

Guildhall

Gunnersbury Park W3
01-992 1612. Regency house of the Rothschilds. Museum of local history, including transport. Park. *OPEN Mar-Oct 13.00-17.00 Mon-Fri, 14.00-18.00 Sat & Sun; Nov-Feb 13.00-16.00 Mon-Fri, 14.00-16.00 Sat & Sun. Free.*

Hammersmith Mall
Upper & Lower Mall W6. Boathouses, riverside pubs and terraces of Georgian houses, including Kelmscott House, 1780, where William Morris lived and founded his printing press.

Hampstead Garden Suburb
Good pioneering suburban planning. Laid out by Sir Raymond Unwin and Barry Parker, 1907.

Hampstead Village NW3
Still very much a village of Georgian houses and alleyways. Church Row, Holly Mount and Regency houses on Downshire Hill, including Keats' House, are notable.

Hampton Court Palace

Hampton Court Palace
Hampton Court, Middx. 01-977 8441. Royal riverside palace built 1514 for Cardinal Wolsey with later additions by Henry VIII and Wren. Sumptuous state rooms painted by Vanbrugh, Verrio and Thornhill. Famous picture gallery of Italian masterpieces. Orangery, mellow courtyards, the 'great vine' and the maze. The formal gardens are probably among the greatest in the world. A Tudor character is preserved in some of the plants. *OPEN Apr-Sep 09.30-18.00 Mon-Sat, 11.00-18.00 Sun; Oct-Mar 09.30-17.00 Mon-Sat, 14.00-17.00 Sun. Charge.*

Henry VIII's Wine Cellar   5 L 21
MOD, Horseguards Av SW1. Genuine Tudor wine cellar built for Cardinal Wolsey. All that remains of Tudor Whitehall Palace. *OPEN Sat afternoons Apr-Sep by written application for pass from the Dept of the Environment, Property Services Agency, Room 10/39, St Christopher House, Southwark St SE1. 01-921 4849.*

Highgate N6
Here you stand level with the cross of St Paul's. A village full of 18thC surprises.

Highgate Archway N6
Carries Hornsey La across Archway Rd. London's first 'flyover'. Originally built in 1813 and replaced by present structure in 1897. From the top you see the whole of London laid out before you.

Holborn Viaduct EC1   6 K 28
William Haywood, 1869. Fine example of Victorian cast iron, and a pioneer traffic improvement scheme.

Holland House   1 C 6
Off Kensington High St W8. Jacobean house restored after extensive war damage.

Honourable Artillery Company   6 K 32
Armoury House, City Rd EC1. 01-606 4644. Victorian castellated fortress (1857) hides the Georgian (1735) headquarters of the oldest regiment in the British Army. Supplies Guard of Honour for Lord Mayor's Shows and for Royalty visiting the City. *OPEN 12.00-18.00 Mon-Fri. Free.*

House of St Barnabas   2 H 22
1 Greek St W1. 01-437 1894. Early Georgian town house in Soho Sq with mock-Gothic chapel, fine carvings and rococo plasterwork. Connections with Dickens and Gladstone. Now a temporary refuge for distressed women. *OPEN 14.30-16.15 Wed, 11.00-12.30 Thur. Free, with guide.*

Houses of Parliament   5 N 20
St Margaret St SW1. 01-219 3000. Victorian-Gothic building 1840-68 by Sir Charles Barry and A. W. N. Pugin. Westminster Hall was built in 1099 as the Great Hall of William Rufus' new palace; the roof dates from the late 14thC. *Admission to the House of Commons during debates by application to your MP (or embassy for foreigners) or by queuing. Tours of Westminster Hall and the Palace of Westminster by application to your MP. Free.*

Hyde Park Corner SW1   2 I 16
Consists of Constitution Arch at the top of Constitution Hill, and the Ionic screen of three classical-style triumphal arches at the

Houses of Parliament

Wellington Arch

entry to Hyde Park, by Decimus Burton, 1825. Admire too the Duke of Wellington's house, once known as 'Number One, London'.

Inns of Chancery 6 J 27

Before the 18thC, a student of law had first to go through one of the nine Inns of Chancery then existing. They have now mostly disappeared. Staple Inn, High Holborn remains a fine Elizabethan building. Others survive only as names: Clifford Inn, Thavies Inn and Furnival Inn.

Jewel Tower 5 N 20

Old Palace Yd SW1. 01-222 2219. 14thC fragment of the old palace of Westminster. *OPEN Mar-Sep 09.30-19.00 Mon-Sat; Oct-Mar 09.30-16.00 Mon-Sat. CLOSED Sun. Free.*

Jewel Tower

Kensington Palace 1 D 9

Kensington Gdns W8. 01-937 9561. Unostentatious house bought in 1689 by William III and altered by Wren and William Kent; attribution of the Orangery, of exceptionally fine brick, is uncertain. Queen Victoria and Queen Mary born here. State apartments and Costume Museum. *OPEN 09.00-*

17.00 Mon-Sat, 13.00-17.00 Sun (last admission 16.15). CLOSED some B.hols, Xmas Eve and Xmas. Charge.

Kensington Palace Gardens 1 D 8
W8

A street of prosperous town mansions in the grand Italianate style, laid out by Pennethorne in 1843, but continued by other famous architects. No. 8a is by Owen Jones and Decimus Burton; No. 12a James Murray; Nos. 18 & 20 by Banks and Barry; No. 13 by C. J. Richardson.

Kenwood House (Iveagh Bequest)

Hampstead La NW3. 01-348 1286. Robert Adam house and interior 1767-9. English 18thC paintings and furniture. Also fine paintings by Rembrandt, Hals and Vermeer. Gardens and wooded estate of 200 acres (81ha). *OPEN Mon-Sun, Apr-Sep 10.00-19.00; Oct 10.00-17.00; Nov-Jan 10.00-16.00; Feb-Mar 10.00-17.00. Free.* Refreshments in the coach house.

Kew Palace

Kew, Surrey. 01-940 3321. Small red-brick house in Dutch style. 1631. Souvenirs of George III and Queen Charlotte. *OPEN Apr-Sep 11.00-17.30 Mon-Sun.* Kew Gardens *OPEN 09.30 to dusk Mon-Sun. Small charge.*

Lambeth Palace 5 P 21

Lambeth Palace Rd SE1. 01-928 8282. The London residence of the Archbishop of Canterbury since 1197. Remarkable Tudor gatehouse, fine medieval crypt. 14thC Hall with a splendid roof and portraits of archbishops on its walls. The Great Hall, which houses the library, was rebuilt in medieval style in 1633; prominent pendants and blackamoors' heads decorate its elaborate timber roof; the gloves worn by Charles I when he went to the scaffold are on display. Look out for the famous spreading fig tree, planted during Mary Tudor's reign by the last Catholic archbishop, Cardinal Pole; for the brass plate commemorating the negligence of a gardener who put his fork through Archbishop Laud's tortoise, and for the picture of the original Nosy Parker –

Lambeth Palace

archbishop under Elizabeth I and the first to have no allegiance to Rome – so called because he had a big nose. *Tours (very restricted) on a Wed or Thur by written application to the Bursar.*

Lancaster Gate W2　　　　　2　C　12
Area of fine stucco houses 1865, in and around Lancaster Gate. (Queen's Gdns, Cleveland Sq and Cleveland Gdns.)

Lancaster House　　　　　5　K　18
Stable Yd, St James's SW1. Early Victorian London town house. Lavish state apartments and painted ceilings. Used for official functions.

Lancaster House

Law Courts　　　　　　6　K　25
Strand WC2. 01-936 6000. Massive Victorian-Gothic building housing the Royal Courts of Justice. *OPEN to public 09.00-16.30 Mon-Fri.* Over 16s only. Courts not in session *Aug and Sep* but open to public. *Free.*

Leadenhall Market　　　　6　O　31
Gracechurch St EC3. Impressive Victorian glass and iron hall 1881 by Horace Jones preserving the old street pattern; on the site of the Roman basilica.

Lincoln's Inn　　　　　　3　I　25
Lincoln's Inn WC2. 01-405 1393. An Inn of Court 17thC. New Sq, gardens, barristers' chambers and solicitors' offices. A chapel by Inigo Jones (1623) and the 15thC Old Hall. Great Hall was built in 1845. The 'Stone Buildings' are by Sir Robert Taylor and were begun in 1774. Still has Dickensian atmosphere. Gardens and Chapel *OPEN 10.00-16.00 Mon-Fri.* Admission to the Chapel outside these hours, and to the Hall and Library by application to the Treasury Office. *Free.*

Lincoln's Inn Fields WC2　　3　I　25
Seven acres (2.8ha) of gardens laid out by Inigo Jones 1618. Once a famous duelling ground. Criminals were occasionally hanged from its plane trees. Nos. 13 & 14 built 1792 by Sir John Soane. Nos. 57 & 58 built 1730 by Henry Joynes. Nos. 59 & 60 built 1640 by Inigo Jones.

Little Venice　　　　　　2　A　14
Harrow Rd W2. Artists, writers, converted barges and the Grand Union Canal.

Lloyds of London　　　　6　O　32
Lime St EC3. 01-623 7100. World-famous international insurance market. Nearly 33,500 members are represented by underwriters conducting over £12,000m of business a year in 'The Room' which houses the Lutine Bell.

The London Bobby
In the 18thC, highway robbery on new bridges across the Thames and on roads leading from the Angel and Islington across the fields into the city, necessitated armed patrols for convoys of pedestrians. Nevertheless the idea of a permanent police force was considered an infringement of freedom by many Londoners. The Metropolitan Police Act was pressed into being by Home Secretary Robert Peel; thus the first policemen were known as 'Peelers' and 'Bobbies'. They carried rattles in their coat-tail pockets and police batons. In 1860 a whistle replaced the rattle. In the 20thC women were recruited. The London Bobby, relatively the most benign cop in the world, still doesn't carry a gun on his normal duties. Riot shields have, however, been used in recent disturbances.

London Stone　　　　　6　O　30
Cannon St EC4. Set into the wall of the Bank of China opposite Cannon St station. The Roman Millarium from which all road distances were measured.

London's Wall
Surviving parts of the Roman and medieval wall around the old city of London can still be seen at St Alphage on the north side of London Wall EC2; St Giles Churchyard, Cripplegate EC1; Jewry St EC3; off Trinity Sq EC3; and in the Tower of London.

Mansion House　　　　　6　N　30
Walbrook EC4. 01-626 2500. Opposite the Bank of England. Official residence of the Lord Mayor. Palladian building by George Dance 1739. Completed 1752. Sumptuous Egyptian Hall. *OPEN (to parties of 15-40 people only) Tue-Thur by written application. Free.*

Mansion House

Marlborough House　　　　5　K　19
Marlborough Gate, Pall Mall SW1. 01-930 9249. Designed by Wren 1710. Contains a painted ceiling by Gentileschi which was originally designed for the Queen's House at Greenwich. The simple classical-style

Queen's Chapel in the grounds is by Inigo Jones, 1626. Reconstruction work currently underway and will take until at least 1990. *Tours at 11.00 & 15.00 Mon-Fri by telephone application to the Accommodation Manager. Charge.* (A Commonwealth Centre, Marlborough House is closed when conferences are in progress.)

Melbury Road W14   1 D 4
Near Holland Park. Contains several notable houses; No. 9 William Burges' own house 1875-80; Nos. 8 & 11 are by Norman Shaw 1876 & 1877, and No. 1 Holland Park Rd nearby is by Philip Webb.

Monument   6 O 30
Monument St EC3. 01-626 2717. A 17thC hollow fluted column by Wren to commemorate the Great Fire of London. Magnificent view. *OPEN Apr-Sep 09.00-17.40 Mon-Fri, 14.00-17.40 Sat & Sun; Oct-Mar 09.00-15.40 Mon-Sat. Charge.*

Morden College
19 St Germain's Pl, Morden Rd SE3. 01-858 3365. Characteristic Wren domestic architecture in 18thC landscaped grounds. Specialist groups only, by written application. *Free.*

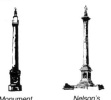

Monument   Nelson's
                  Column

Nelson's Column   5 K 21
Trafalgar Sq SW1. 145ft (44m) high column by William Railton 1840. Weighs 16 tons. At the top a statue of Nelson by Baily 1843.

Old Bailey   6 L 28
Old Bailey EC4. 01-248 3277. The Central Criminal Court. On the site of old Newgate Prison. *Trials open to the public. Gallery OPEN 10.30-13.00 & 14.00-16.00 Mon-Fri. Minimum age 14 (must be accompanied by an adult until 16). Free.*

Old Curiosity Shop   6 J 25
13-14 Portsmouth St WC2. 01-405 9891. London's oldest shop. Tudor style house now an antique and souvenir shop, believed to be the original of Dickens' *Old Curiosity Shop*. If it is not too crowded, the proprietor will fill you in on local history. *OPEN Apr-Oct 09.00-17.00 Mon-Fri, 09.30-16.30 Sat & Sun; Nov-Mar 09.30-16.30 Mon-Sun. CLOSED Good Friday & Xmas.*

Old Operating Theatre   6 Q 29
St Thomas's Hospital
St Thomas St, London Bridge SE1. 01-407 7600x2739. A well-preserved early 19thC operating theatre, located in the ex-parish church and old chapel of St Thomas's Hospital (now the Chapter House of Southwark Cathedral). Owned by the Diocese of Southwark. *OPEN 12.30-16.00 Mon, Wed & Fri. Charge.*

Old Swan House   4 N 10
17 Chelsea Embankment SW3. Late 19thC house by R. Norman Shaw.

Pall Mall SW1   5 J 20
Early 19thC opulence. This fine street and its surroundings express the confidence and wealth of the London of this period. Pall Mall itself contains two fine buildings by Sir Charles Barry, the Travellers' Club, 1829-32 (Italian-Renaissance revival), and his more mature Reform Club, 1837-41.

Piccadilly Circus W1   2 I 20
The confluence of five major thoroughfares. Fountains and statue of Eros by Gilbert 1893, commemorating Victorian philanthropist Lord Shaftesbury. Its fame is largely sentimental.

Pimlico SW1   5 N 15
Laid out by Cubitt in the 1840s as a less grand neighbour to Belgravia.

Postman's Park   6 K 30
Churchyard of St Botolph, Aldersgate EC1. Under an alcove are some remarkable Art Nouveau tiles recording Victorian deeds of bravery (1880).

Prince Henry's Room   6 K 26
17 Fleet St EC4. 01-353 7323. From 1610; oldest domestic building in London. Named after the elder son of James I. Fine plaster ceiling and carved oak panelling. *OPEN 13.45-17.00 Mon-Fri, 13.45-16.00 Sat. CLOSED Xmas, New Year, B.hols. Free.*

Prisons
Prisons were not used for punishment until the 19thC. Before that time they were used only for debtors and for those awaiting trial. In those days the principal punishment was death or transportation to Australia and America. The industrial revolution introduced the 'hulks', prison ships moored in the Thames. In the early 19thC the government built prisons in which the most abominable conditions existed. Things gradually changed after many middle-class suffragettes and conscientious objectors were imprisoned around the time of the First World War. Prison improvement has been badly neglected in recent years so that

most are now seriously overcrowded. Many of London's prisons (from the outside) are formidable and important buildings architecturally – including Brixton, Holloway, Pentonville, Wandsworth and Wormwood Scrubs – a chilling list.

Queen Anne's Gate SW1   5 L 19
Quiet, completely preserved 18thC street in its original state. Close to St James's Park. Statue of Queen Anne near No. 13.

Regent's Canal   2 A 13
Paddington Bridge W2 to Regent's Canal Dock E14. The canal was built by James Morgan in 1820 to connect Paddington with the Thames, thus allowing goods to be shipped direct from Birmingham to the Thames by the canal network. The best way to see the canal is to take a boat trip (see 'Canal trips').

Regent's Park environs   2 B 21
The park and the surrounding Regency architecture were planned almost entirely by John Nash, 1812-26. Particularly notable are Park Cres, Park Sq, Cambridge Ter, York Ter and Chester Ter. Decimus Burton designed the façades of Cornwall Ter and Clarence Ter.

Regent Street   2 H 20
John Nash, asked by George IV (then Prince of Wales) to construct an artery from Carlton House to the royal country home near Regent's Park, not only designed the route for Regent St but also most of the houses. This took many years since it was pieced together to conform with the various architectural styles along the way. Initially acclaimed, its imminent destruction was celebrated in 1927 when King George V and his Queen drove down its flower-decked length; it was then rebuilt from end to end.

Roman Bath   6 K 24
5 Strand La WC2. Disputed origin, restored in the 17thC. Not open but visible from the pathway.

Royal Exchange   6 N 31
Corner of Threadneedle St and Cornhill EC3. Built in 1844 by Tite. The third building on this site. Originally founded as a market for merchants and craftsmen in 1564, and

Royal Exchange

destroyed in the Great Fire. The second building was also burnt down, in 1838. Now houses the London International Financial Futures Exchange (LIFFE).

Royal Mews   5 K 16
Buckingham Palace Rd SW1. 01-930 4832x634. The Queen's horses and carriages including the Coronation coach. OPEN 14.00-16.00 Wed & Thur. CLOSED Royal Ascot week. Charge.

Royal Opera Arcade   5 J 21
Between Pall Mall and Charles II St SW1. John Nash 1816. London's earliest arcade. Pure Regency; bow-fronted shops, glass-domed vaults and elegant lamps.

Royal Society of Arts   6 K 23
6-8 John Adam St WC2. Built 1774. Fine surviving example of Adam architecture, from the original Adelphi area (now almost entirely demolished).

St James's Palace   5 K 19
Pall Mall SW1. Built by Henry VIII with many later additions. Still officially a royal residence. Ceiling of Chapel Royal by Holbein. No admission to palace. Entry to courtyards only. Free.

St James's Street SW1   5 J 19
Contains some of its original 18thC houses and shop fronts. Boodles (No. 28) 1775 by J. Crunden; Brooks (No. 60) 1776 by Henry Holland.

St John's Gate   6 J 29
St John's La EC1. Once a gateway to the Priory of the Knights Hospitallers of St John of Jerusalem. Built in 1504, it is the only monastic gateway left in London.

Skinners Hall   6 O 29
8 Dowgate Hill EC4. 01-236 5629. 17th-18thC buildings and quiet arcaded courtyard. Occasional visits by arrangement with City Information Centre, St Paul's Churchyard EC4 (6 M 28). 01-606 3030x1456.

Smithfield EC1   6 K 29
Once 'Smooth Field'. Historical site of tournaments, public executions, cattle market and the famous Bartholomew Fair. In north-east corner original Tudor gatehouse built over 13thC archway leading to Church of St Bartholomew-the-Great (see 'Churches'). South-east side occupied by St Bartholomew's Hospital, London's oldest hospital, founded in 1123. Gateway (1702) bears London's only statue of Henry VIII. Smithfield Market is the largest meat market in the world (10 acres – 4ha). The Italianate-style market buildings with some ornamental ironwork were designed by Horace Jones and erected between 1868 and 1899.

Soho 2 H 22

An area bounded by Regent St, Oxford St, Shaftesbury Av and Charing Cross Rd. Lively and notorious but perfectly safe, except from touts for peep show, nude encounter and strip joint customers. Narrow 18thC streets full of fascinating foreign food shops, restaurants, street markets, flashing neon and nightlife of all sorts. Visit London's 'Chinatown' around Gerrard St.

Somerset House 6 K 24

Strand WC2. 01-438 6622. On the site of an unfinished 16thC palace. By Sir W. Chambers, 1776. Used to house the register of births, marriages and deaths in England and Wales, now holds the registry of divorce, wills and probate and the Inland Revenue.

Somerset House

Spitalfields E1

This centre of silk-weaving in England was established by the influx of Flemish and French weavers in the 16th and 17thC. The industry reached its height at the end of the 18th and early 19thC when about 17,000 looms were in use and a large area of East London was dependent on these family concerns. Fournier St is a good example of typical Dutch-style houses of the time. The industry collapsed some 100 years ago.

Stations

Some good examples of 19thC 'railway architecture'.

King's Cross 3 D 27

Euston Rd NW1. Functional. 1851, by Lewis Cubitt.

St Pancras 3 D 26

Euston Rd NW1. Victorian Gothic. 1868, by Sir George Gilbert Scott.

Paddington 2 A 13

Praed St W2. 1850-2. 'Railway cathedral' engineering at its best by Brunel; the Gothic ornament by Wyatt and Owen Jones; the Renaissance-style hotel by Hardwick.

Stock Exchange 6 N 31

Old Broad St EC2. 01-588 2355. Entrance to public gallery at corner of Threadneedle St and Old Broad St. Films shown in adjoining cinema. *Gallery OPEN 09.45-16.30 Mon-Fri. Last tour begins 15.45. Free. All visits by arrangement with*

the Public Information Dept. Parties of up to 30 accepted.

Strand WC2 6 K 23

Once a 'Strand' – a walk along the river – bordered in Stuart times with mansions and gardens down to the Thames. Their names still survive in the streets: Bedford, Buckingham, Villiers. A major commercial thoroughfare.

The Temple 6 L 26

Inner Temple, Crown Office Row EC4. 01-353 8462. Middle Temple, Middle Temple La EC4. 01-353 4355. Both are Inns of Court. Enter by the gatehouse, 1685, in Middle Temple La. An extensive area of courtyards, alleys, gardens and warm brick buildings. Step back into the 19thC on misty winter afternoons when the lamplighter lights the gas lamps. Middle Temple Hall 1570. The restored Temple Church is one of only four remaining early Gothic round churches built by the Templars. 12th-13thC. *Inner Temple OPEN 10.30-11.45 & 15.00-16.00 Mon-Fri by arrangement. CLOSED Sat & Sun, B.hols & legal vacations. Middle Temple Hall OPEN 10.00-11.30 & 15.00-16.00 Mon-Fri by arrangement. CLOSED Sat & Sun, B.hols. Aug & during examinations. Free.*

Temple of Mithras, 6 N 30
Bucklersbury House

3 Queen Victoria St EC4. Originally found 18ft (5.5m) underground in Walbrook and moved here with other Roman relics.

Thames Tunnels
Rotherhithe to Wapping

The first tunnel under the Thames built by Sir Marc Isambard Brunel (the elder), and completed in 1843 after many deaths by accident and illness. Now used by underground trains and still a perfect feat of engineering – withstanding over 100 years of train vibration. Original tunnel can be seen at Wapping station – also stairs and handrails.

Blackwall

1897 by Binnie. Now incorporated in a two-way system with the new tunnel, completed in 1967. For vehicles and pedestrians.

Rotherhithe

1908. For vehicles and pedestrians.

Greenwich and *Woolwich*

1902 and 1912. Pedestrians only.

Tower of London 6 Q 32

Tower Hill EC3. 01-709 0765. A keep, a prison and still a fortress. Famous for the Bloody Tower, Traitors' Gate, the ravens, Crown Jewels, the Armouries and the Yeoman Warders. Norman Chapel of St John. *OPEN Mar-Oct 09.30-17.45 Mon-Sat,*

Tower of London

14.00-17.45 Sun; Nov-Feb 09.30-16.00 Mon-Sat. Charge.

Trafalgar Square WC2   5 K 21

Laid out by Sir Charles Barry 1829. Nelson's column (granite) by William Railton 1840. Statue by Baily. Bronze lions by Landseer 1868. Fountains by Lutyens. Famous for political rallies, pigeons and the excesses of New Year's Eve revellers making whoopee.

The Underground

Although overground railways existed in the mid-19thC, a need for more transport to a rapidly expanding London resulted in the 'underground'. The world's first was the Metropolitan Line with 30,000 passengers taking an opening day ride (in March 1863) from Bishops Rd, Paddington to Farringdon St. The original carriages were open trucks drawn by steam trains. The line was cut out by the 'trench' system, usually under a road, lined with brick and the street relaid on top. The Tower subway, opened in 1870, was the world's first iron-lined tube railway. A small cable-hauled car carried 12 passengers at a time from the Tower to Bermondsey. (Today, the 'tube' houses water mains.) Twenty-one years after the Metropolitan opened, the Circle Line was completed. Early underground passengers endured dimly lit carriages and windows closed against smoke. To this day two dummy housefronts in Leinster Gardens W2 puzzle passers-by. They conceal part of the street which had to be demolished for the underground and were built at the insistence of the irate local residents. The underground system has steadily expanded since then – the most recent additions being the Victoria Line and the Jubilee Line.

Watermen's Hall   6 P 31

18 St Mary at Hill EC3. Adam-style front surviving from 1780. Unexpectedly beautiful amid drab surroundings. Visits are arranged in summer through City Information Centre, St Paul's Churchyard EC4 (6 **M 28**). 01-606 3030x1456.

Whitehall

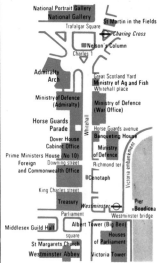

Whitefriars Crypt   6 L 26

30 Bouverie St EC4. 01-353 3030. 15thC crypt belonging to a House of Carmelites. Discovered in 1895 and restored by the proprietors of the *News of the World* and *Sun* when they occupied the offices above.

Whitehall SW1   5 L 21

Wide thoroughfare used for ceremonial and State processions; contains the Cenotaph and several notable statues. Lined with Government offices.

Old Admiralty

1725-8 by T. Ripley. Fine Robert Adam columnar screen 1760. The New Admiralty 1887 lies behind.

Old Scotland Yard

1888. An asymmetrical building by Shaw.

War Office

1898-1907 by William Young. Victorian-baroque.

Horse Guards Parade

1750-60 by William Kent. Changing of the

Horse Guards

Guard in the forecourt daily – see 'Daily ceremonies'.

Banqueting House
01-930 4179. 17thC Palladian-style by Inigo Jones. 1619-25. Rubens ceilings 1630. *OPEN 10.00-17.00 Tue-Sat, 14.00-17.00 Sun. CLOSED Mon except B.hols. Charge.*

Banqueting House

Dover House
1755-8 by Paine. Entrance screen and rotunda 1787 by Henry Holland.

Treasury
1846 by Sir C. Barry. Victorian columned façade on Whitehall. Earlier façade overlooking Horse Guards Parade 1733-6 by William Kent.

Foreign Office
Mid-Victorian palazzo-style by Gilbert Scott. Completed by Ministry of Housing 1920.

White House   4 M 10
35 Tite St SW3. The Chelsea house of Whistler the artist designed by William Godwin in 1879.

Whittington Stone
Highgate Hill N6, near junction with Dartmouth Park Hill. Milestone marking the spot where tradition says young Dick Whittington rested on his way home from London and heard Bow Bells ring out 'Turn again Whittington, thrice Lord Mayor of London', and returned to become London's most famous Mayor.

Woolwich Arsenal
Woolwich SE18. Fine example of early 18thC ordnance architecture. Sir John Vanbrugh, 1716-19. *OPEN by appt only. Free.*

York Watergate   5 K 22
Watergate Wlk, off Villiers St WC2. Built in 1626 by Nicholas Stone as the watergate to York House, it marks the position of the north bank of the Thames before the con-

York Watergate

struction of the Victoria Embankment in 1862. The arms and motto are those of the Villiers family.

Houses of famous people

Visiting the homes of the famous has had its attractions since long before the days of tourism and mass travel. As early as the 17thC, for example, the birthplace of John Milton was one of London's most important sights; while in the next century Boswell anticipated the tourist guides and gazetteers of today by conscientiously listing all the London houses where Dr Johnson had ever lived. Only in rare cases, of course, is the house of someone famous retained as a shrine and opened to the public. Most such houses are simply houses, and they have carried on being lived in as private homes, marked perhaps with a commemorative plaque (see next section). Below, however, is a selection of the most interesting and worthwhile of those houses that are open to the public.

Carlyle's house   4 M 8
24 Cheyne Row SW3. 01-352 7087. A modest early 18thC terraced house where Carlyle lived for 42 years until his death in 1881. *OPEN 11.00-17.00 (last admission 16.30) Wed-Sun and B.hols except Good Friday. CLOSED Nov-Mar. Charge.*

Churchill's house
Chartwell, nr Westerham, Kent. Edenbridge 866368. A famous house full of recent political history. The water gardens, grounds and views of the Weald of Kent are memorable. *OPEN Apr-Oct 12.00-17.00 Tue-Thur, 11.00-17.00 Sat & Sun, 10.00-17.00 B.hols (CLOSED Tue following B.hol). House only OPEN Mar & Nov 11.00-16.00 Wed, Sat & Sun. Charge.*

Darwin's house
Down House, Downe, Kent. Farnborough 59119. Charles Darwin lived and worked here. Two rooms are as they were in his day and others contain exhibitions illuminating his work. Investigate the Sand Walk where Darwin pondered his theory of evolution. *OPEN 13.00-17.30. CLOSED Mon (except B.hols), Fri & Feb. Charge.*

Dickens' house   3 G 27
48 Doughty St WC1. 01-405 2127. Regency terrace house. Relics of Dickens' life and writings. He lived here from 1837 to 1839. Be sure to see the reconstructed drawing room. *OPEN 10.00-17.00 (last*

admission 16.30). *CLOSED Sun and B.hols. Charge.*

Disraeli's house
Hughenden Manor, High Wycombe, Bucks. High Wycombe 32580. Disraeli lived here from 1847 until his death in 1881. Contains much of his furniture, pictures, books and other relics. *OPEN Apr-Oct 14.00-18.00 Wed-Sat, 12.00-18.00 Sun & B.hols; Mar 14.00-18.00 (or sunset) Sat & Sun. Charge.*

Freud Museum
20 Maresfield Gdns NW3. 01-435 2002. This was Freud's last home from 1938-9. The museum contains a major collection of Freud's personal effects: library, correspondence, antiquities, carpets and furniture including the famous couch on which psychoanalysis was pioneered. *OPEN 12.00-17.00 Wed-Sat, 13.00-17.00 Sun. Charge.*

Hogarth's house
Hogarth La, Great West Rd W4. 01-994 6757. The 17thC country villa of William Hogarth; relics and late impressions of his engravings. *OPEN Apr-Sep 11.00-18.00 Mon & Wed-Sat; 14.00-18.00 Sun. Oct-Mar 11.00-16.00 Mon & Wed-Sat; 14.00-16.00 Sun. CLOSED Tue, first 2 weeks of Sep & last 3 weeks of Dec. Free.*

Henry James' house
Lamb House, West St, Rye, E. Sussex. Rye 223763. Georgian house with beautiful garden. Home of Henry James from 1898 to his death in 1916. Three rooms open to the public; study, dining room and parlour all containing pictures and memorabilia. Also the home of the writer E. F. Benson from 1918 to 1940. *OPEN Apr-Oct 14.00-18.00 Wed & Sat. Small charge.*

Dr Johnson's house   6 K 27
17 Gough Sq, Fleet St EC4. 01-353 3745. 17thC house. Relics and contemporary portraits. He lived here from 1748 to 1759. *OPEN May-Sep 11.00-17.30 Mon-Sat; Oct-Apr 11.00-17.00 Mon-Sat. CLOSED Sun & B.hols. Small charge.*

Keats' house
Wentworth Pl, Keats Gro NW3. 01-435 2062. The poet John Keats lived here during his prolific period 1818-20. *OPEN 10.00-13.00 & 14.00-18.00 Mon-Sat, 14.00-17.00 Sun & B.hols except Good Friday & Xmas. Free.*

Kipling's house
Bateman's, Burwash, E. Sussex. Burwash 882302. The house, built in 1634, contains Kipling's furniture and a Kipling exhibition. The surroundings are described in *Puck of Pooks Hill* and *Rewards and Fairies. OPEN*

Apr-Oct 11.00-18.00 Sat-Wed. *CLOSED Thur & Fri. Charge.*

Leighton House   I D 4
12 Holland Park Rd W14. 01-602 3316. Centre for Victorian studies and special exhibitions. Arab hall with decorations of 14th-16thC Oriental tiles. Paintings by Leighton and Burne-Jones. Watts and De Morgan pottery. *OPEN 11.00-17.00 Mon-Sat. CLOSED Sun & B.hols. Free.*

William Morris Gallery
Water House, Lloyd Park, Forest Rd E17. 01-527 5544. 18thC house. Textiles, wallpapers, carpets, woodwork and designs by Morris, pre-Raphaelites and contemporaries, housed in Morris's boyhood home. *OPEN all year 10.00-13.00 & 14.00-17.00 Tue-Sat, 10.00-12.00 & 14.00-17.00 1st Sun in month. CLOSED Mon & B.hols. Free.*

Linley Sambourne House   I D 6
18 Stafford Ter W8. Home of Linley Sambourne, leading *Punch* cartoonist of the late Victorian and Edwardian eras. Unique interior reflecting artistic taste of the period. Contact the Victorian Society, 01-994 1019. *OPEN Wed 10.00-16.00 & Sun 14.00-17.00 Mar-Oct. Parties at other times by appt. Charge.*

Shaw's Corner
Ayot St Lawrence, Welwyn, Herts. Stevenage 820307. George Bernard Shaw lived here from 1906 until his death in 1950. *OPEN Apr-Oct 11.00-18.00 Wed & Sat, 12.00-18.00 Sun & B.hols. CLOSED Nov-Mar except by appt. Charge.*

Wellington Museum   2 I 16
Apsley House, 149 Piccadilly W1. 01-499 5676. Originally known as 'Number One London'. Duke of Wellington's house. Built 1771-8 from designs by Robert Adam and altered 1828 by B. D. Wyatt. Contains Wellington relics, fine Spanish (Velasquez) and Dutch paintings, silver plate and porcelain. *OPEN 11.00-17.00 Tue-Sun. Charge.*

Wesley's house & chapel   6 K 33
47 City Rd EC1. 01-253 2262. John Wesley's possessions and personal relics. His tomb is in the chapel grounds. The chapel crypt houses a new museum which tells the story of Methodism and displays Wesleyan memorabilia. *OPEN 10.00-16.00 Mon-Sat, 12.00-15.00 Sun. (There is also a service at 11.00 on Sun, followed by lunch and a guided tour.) Small charge.*

Wolfe's house
Quebec House, Westerham, Kent. Westerham 62206. Mainly 17thC house where General Wolfe spent his early years. Contains a collection of 'Wolfiana'. *OPEN Apr-*

*Oct 14.00-18.00 Sun-Wed & Fri. CLOSED
Thur & Sat. Charge.*

Commemorative plaques

*Marking houses and other buildings
associated with famous people or events
with the now familiar blue plaques has been
a feature of London's street scene since
1866. Originally on the private initiative of
the Royal Society of Arts, in 1901 they came
under the aegis of the London County
Council, later the Greater London Council.
Since 1 April 1986 the plaques have been
the responsibility of English Heritage.
There are now nearly 400 of them, commemorating important events in the lives of
architects, artists, composers, politicians,
scientists, soldiers and writers. The following are some of the best known.*

Adam, Robert
Lived at 1-3 Robert St, Adelphi   6 K 23
WC2.

Arnold, Matthew
Lived at 2 Chester Sq SW1.   5 L 14

Asquith, Herbert Henry
Lived at 20 Cavendish Sq W1.   2 F 20

Baden-Powell, Robert
Lived at 9 Hyde Park Gate   1 F 9
SW7.

Baird, John Logie
First demonstrated television   2 H 22
at 22 Frith St W1.

Baldwin, Stanley
Lived at 93 Eaton Sq SW1.   5 K 14

Barrie, Sir James M.
Lived at 100 Bayswater Rd   1 B 10
W2
and at 1-3 Robert St, Adelphi   6 K 23
WC2.

Beardsley, Aubrey
Lived at 114 Cambridge St   5 O 14
SW1.

Bennett, Arnold
Lived at 75 Cadogan Sq SW1.   5 J 12

Berlioz, Hector
Stayed at 58 Queen Anne St   2 E 19
W1.

Bligh, William
Commander of the *Bounty*   5 P 21
lived at 100 Lambeth Rd SE1.

Boswell, James
Lived and died on the site of   2 E 21
122 Great Portland St W1.

Browning, Elizabeth Barrett
Lived on site of 50 Wimpole St   2 E 19
W1

and at 99 Gloucester Pl W1.   2 A 18

Brunel, Isambard Kingdom
Lived at 98 Cheyne Walk   4 M 8
SW3.

Burne-Jones, Sir Edward
Lived at 17 Red Lion Sq WC1.   3 H 25

Canaletto, Antonio
Lived at 41 Beak St W1.   2 H 20

Carlyle, Thomas
Lived at 24 Cheyne Row SW3.   4 M 8

Chamberlain, Neville
Lived at 37 Eaton Sq SW1.   5 K 14

Chaplin, Charlie
Lived at 287 Kennington Rd   5 Q 22
SE11.

Chesterton, Gilbert Keith
Lived at 11 Warwick Gdns   1 E 4
W14.

Chippendale, Thomas
and his son had their   5 J 22
workshop near 61 St Martin's La WC2.

Churchill, Sir Winston
Lived at 34 Eccleston Sq SW1.   5 N 15

Clive of India, Lord
Lived at 45 Berkeley Sq W1.   2 H 18

Coleridge, Samuel Taylor
Lived at 7 Addison Bridge Pl   1 E 3
W14
and at 71 Berners St W1.   2 G 22

Conan Doyle, Sir Arthur
Lived not as you might imagine at 221b
Baker St, but at 12 Tennison Rd SE25.

Constable, John
Lived at 40 Well Wlk NW3.

Cook, Captain James
Lived on the site of 88 Mile End Rd E1.

Darwin, Charles
Lived on the site of 110 Gower   3 E 23
St WC1.

Defoe, Daniel
Lived on the site of 95 Stoke Newington
Church St N16.

Dickens, Charles
Lived at 48 Doughty St WC1.   3 G 27

Disraeli, Benjamin
Born at 22 Theobalds Rd WC1   3 H 26
and died at 19 Curzon St W1.   2 H 17

Elgar, Sir Edward
Lived at 51 Avonmore Rd   1 E 3
W14.

Eliot, George (Mary Ann Evans)
Lived at Holly Lodge, 31 Wimbledon Park
Rd SW18 and
died at 4 Cheyne Wlk SW3.   4 M 8

Faraday, Michael
Apprenticed at 48 Blandford St   2 D 18
W1.

Fielding, Henry
Lived at 19-20 Bow St WC2   6 J 24
and at Milbourne House, Station Rd SW13.

Ford, Ford Madox
Lived at 80 Campden Hill Rd 1 C 7
W8.

Franklin, Benjamin
Lived at 36 Craven St WC2. 5 K 22

Freud, Sigmund
Lived at 20 Maresfield Gdns NW3.

Fry, Elizabeth
Lived at St Mildred's Ct, 6 N 30
Poultry EC2.

Gainsborough, Thomas
Lived at 82 Pall Mall SWI. 5 J 20

Galsworthy, John
Lived at Grove Lodge, Hampstead Gro
NW3 and at
1-3 Robert St, Adelphi WC2. 6 K 23

Garrett Anderson, Elizabeth
Lived at 20 Upper Berkeley St 2 D 16
WI.

Gibbon, Edward
Lived on the site of 7 Bentinck 2 E 19
St WI.

Gibbons, Grinling
Lived at 19-20 Bow St WC2. 6 J 24

Gladstone, William Ewart
Lived at 11 Carlton House Ter 5 K 21
SWI
at 10 St James's Sq SWI 5 J 20
and at 73 Harley St WI. 2 E 20

Handel, George Frideric
Lived and died at 25 Brook St 2 G 18
WI.

Hardy, Thomas
Lived at 172 Trinity Rd SW17
and at Adelphi Ter WC2 6 K 23

Hazlitt, William
Lived on the site of 6 Bouverie 6 L 26
St EC4
and died at 6 Frith St WI. 2 I 22

Holman-Hunt, William
Lived and died at 18 Melbury 1 D 5
Rd W14.

Housman, A. E.
Lived at 17 North Rd N6.

Irving, Sir Henry
Lived at 15a Grafton St WI. 2 H 19

James, Henry
Lived at 34 De Vere Gdns W8. 1 F 8

Johnson, Dr Samuel
Lived at 17 Gough Sq EC4 6 K 27
and at Johnson's Ct, Fleet St 6 K 27
EC4.

Keats, John
Lived at Wentworth Pl, Keats Gro NW3 and
was born on the site of
the Swan & Hoop public 6 M 31
house, 86 Moorgate EC2.

Keynes, John Maynard
Lived at 46 Gordon Sq WCI. 3 E 24

Kingsley, Charles
Lived at 56 Old Church St 4 M 8
SW3.

Kipling, Rudyard
Lived at 43 Villiers St WC2. 5 K 22

Kitchener of Khartoum
Lived at 2 Carlton Gdns SWI. 5 K 20

Lamb, Charles
Lived at Colebrook Cottage, 3 F 32
64 Duncan Ter NI.

Lawrence, David Herbert
Lived at I Byron Villas, Vale of Health NW3.

Lawrence, T. E. ('Lawrence of Arabia')
Lived at 14 Barton St SWI. 5 N 19

Lear, Edward
Lived at 30 Seymour St WI. 2 D 16

Lind, Jenny
Lived at 189 Old Brompton Rd 1 I 6
SW5.

Lloyd George, David
Lived at 3 Routh Rd SW18.

Lutyens, Sir Edwin Landseer
Lived at 13 Mansfield St WI. 2 E 20

MacDonald, Ramsay
Lived at 9 Howitt Rd NW3.

Mansfield, Katherine
Lived at 17 East Heath Rd NW3.

Marconi, Guglielmo
Lived at 71 Hereford Rd W2. 1 A 10

Marx, Karl
Lived at 28 Dean St WI. 2 H 22

Maugham, W. Somerset
Lived at 6 Chesterfield St WI. 2 H 17

Millais, Sir John Everett
Lived and died at 2 Palace 1 F 9
Gate W8.

Morris, William
Lived at 17 Red Lion Sq WCI 3 H 25
and at Kelmscott House, 26 Upper Mall
W6.

Mozart, Wolfgang Amadeus
Composed his first symphony 5 M 13
at 180 Ebury St SWI.

Napoleon III
Lived at Ic King St SWI. 5 J 19

Nelson, Lord (Horatio)
Lived on the site of 147 New 2 G 19
Bond St WI
and at 103 New Bond St WI. 2 G 19

Newton, Sir Isaac
Lived on the site of 87 Jermyn 2 I 19
St SWI.

Nightingale, Florence
Lived and died on the site of 10 2 H 17
South St WI.

Palmerston, Lord (Henry John Temple)
Born at 20 Queen Anne's Gate 5 L 19
SWI
Lived at 4 Carlton Gdns SWI 5 K 20

and at Naval and Military Club, 2 I 17
94 Piccadilly W1.

Pepys, Samuel
Lived on the site of 12 & 14   5 K 22
Buckingham St WC2.

Pitt, William
Lived at 10 St James's Sq   5 J 20
SW1.

Pitt, William (The Younger)
Lived at 120 Baker St W1.   2 D 18

Reynolds, Sir Joshua
Lived and died on the site of   5 J 21
Fanum House, 47 Leicester Sq WC2.

Rossetti, Dante Gabriel
Born on the site of 110 Hallam   2 E 21
St W1

Lived at 17 Red Lion Sq WC1   3 H 25
and at 16 Cheyne Wlk SW3.   4 M 8

Ruskin, John
Lived on the site of 26 Herne Hill SE24.

Scott, Captain Robert Falcon
Lived at 56 Oakley St SW3.   4 M 9

Shackleton, Sir Ernest
Lived at 12 Westwood Hill SE26.

Shaw, George Bernard
Lived at 29 Fitzroy Sq W1.   2 D 22

Shelley, Percy Bysshe
Lived at 15 Poland St W1.   2 G 21

Sheraton, Thomas
Lived at 163 Wardour St W1.   2 I 21

Sheridan, Richard Brinsley
Lived at 14 Savile Row W1   2 H 20
and at 10 Hertford St W1.   2 I 16

Stephenson, Robert
Died on the site of 35   2 C 14
Gloucester Sq W2.

Swinburne, Algernon Charles
Lived at 16 Cheyne Wlk SW3   4 M 8
and died at 11 Putney Hill SW15.

Thackeray, William Makepeace
Lived at 16 Young St W8   1 E 8
at 2 Palace Grn W8   1 D 8
and at 36 Onslow Sq SW7.   4 J 9

Trollope, Anthony
Lived at 39 Montagu Sq W1.   2 D 17

Turner, Joseph Mallord William
Lived at 23 Queen Anne St   2 E 19
W1
and at 119 Cheyne Wlk SW3.   4 M 8

Twain, Mark (Samuel L. Clemens)
Lived at 23 Tedworth Sq SW3.   4 M 10

Vaughan Williams, Ralph
Lived at 10 Hanover Ter NW1.

Wallace, Edgar
Lived at 6 Tressillian Cres SE4.

Walpole, Sir Robert
Lived at 5 Arlington St SW1.   2 I 19

Wells, H. G.
Lived and died at 13 Hanover Ter NW1.

Wesley, John
Lived at 47 City Rd EC1.   6 K 33

Whistler, James Abbott McNeil
Lived at 96 Cheyne Wlk   4 M 7
SW10.

Whittington, Richard ('Dick')
House of Whittington stood at   6 N 29
20 College Hill EC4.
'Dick' died in 1423 and was buried in
the church of St Michael   6 N 29
Royal, College Hill EC4.

Wilberforce, William
Lived at 111 Broomwood Rd SW11
and at 44 Cadogan Pl SW1.   5 K 13

Wilde, Oscar
Lived at 34 Tite St SW3.   4 M 10

Wolfe, General James
Lived at Macartney House, Greenwich
Park SE10.

Wood, Sir Henry
Lived at 4 Elsworthy Rd NW3.

Woolf, Virginia
Lived at 29 Fitzroy Sq W1.   2 D 22

Wyndham, Sir Charles
Lived at 43 York Ter NW1.   2 B 19

Yeats, William Butler
Lived at 23 Fitzroy Rd NW1.

Statues

London has some 1700 outdoor statues,
memorials and pieces of historic sculpture.
Their subjects range from classical mytho-
logy to modern statesmen. From such a
number it is only possible to suggest a
selection of some of the best and most
interesting, which are listed below.

Achilles   2 I 16
Hyde Park W1. Westmacott. 1822. Erected
to honour Wellington. London's first nude
statue.

Alfred the Great   6 R 26
Trinity Church Sq SE1. Origin unknown but
it possibly came from Westminster Hall, in
which case it dates from 1395 and is by far
the oldest statue in London.

Queen Anne   6 M 28
In front of St Paul's Cathedral EC4. After
Bird. 1712. This is a copy (1886) of the
original. Surrounding the Queen are figures
representing England, France, Ireland and
North America.

Queen Anne   5 L 19
Queen Anne's Gate SW1. Origin uncertain
but probably by Francis Bond early 18thC:
believed to have stood originally over the
portico of the church of St Mary-le-Strand.

Queen Anne   Boadicea

Boadicea   5 N 21
Westminster Bridge SW1. Thornycroft, 1902. Famous group showing the ancient British Queen with her daughters in her war chariot.

George Canning   5 M 20
Parliament Sq SW1. Westmacott, 1832. Fell over while in the sculptor's studio and killed a man.

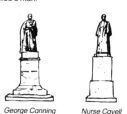

George Canning   Nurse Cavell

Nurse Cavell   5 J 22
St Martin's Pl WC2. Frampton, 1920. Simple and impressive memorial to the nurse who was shot for assisting prisoners to escape during World War I.

Charles I   5 K 21
Trafalgar Sq SW1. Le Sueur, 1633. The oldest equestrian statue in London, and one of the finest. Ordered to be destroyed during the Civil War and hidden until the Restoration. It was erected on its present site between 1675 and 1677.

Charles I   Florence Nightingale

Sir Charles Chaplin   5 J 22
Leicester Sq WC2. John Doubleday, 1981. Bronze. Appropriately surrounded by the cinemas of Leicester Sq. Charlie Chaplin with his characteristic cane and bowler hat is probably still the cinema's greatest comedian.

Sir Winston Churchill   5 M 20
Parliament Sq SW1. Ivor Roberts-Jones, 1973. Large bronze statue of one of Britain's greatest statesmen, half-facing the House of Commons.

Crimea Memorial   5 J 20
Waterloo Pl SW1. Bell, 1859. Figures of Guards cast from melted down cannon taken in battle. A pile of actual cannons decorates the back. Memorial includes a statue of:

Florence Nightingale   5 J 20
Waterloo Pl SW1. Waller, 1915. She is shown holding an oil lamp, whereas the famous lamp which gave her the name 'The lady with the lamp' was actually a candle lantern.

Oliver Cromwell   5 N 20
Old Palace Yd SW1. Thornycroft, 1899. Significantly with his back turned on Parliament.

Oliver Cromwell   Edward VII

Edward VII   5 J 20
Waterloo Pl SW1. Sir Bertram Mackennal, 1921. Memorial statue showing the King in military uniform. Bronze and Portland stone.

Queen Elizabeth I   6 K 26
St Dunstan-in-the-West, Fleet St EC4. Originally stood over Lud Gate. Made during the Queen's lifetime in 1586, it is one of London's oldest statues.

Eros   2 I 20
Piccadilly Circus W1. Gilbert, 1893. Officially the Angel of Christian Charity. It is part of the memorial to the Victorian philanthropist Lord Shaftesbury. Made in aluminium. Fully restored in 1984 and returned in 1986 to a site just south of its original position.

George III   5 K 21
Cockspur St SW1. Wyatt, 1836. The best

Eros   *George III*

statue of this king, on a fine spirited horse.

George IV   5 K 21
Trafalgar Sq WC2. Chantrey, 1843. Rides
without boots on a horse without saddle or
stirrups. Originally intended for the top of
Marble Arch.

George IV   *George V*

George V   5 N 20
Old Palace Yd SW1. Reid Dick, 1947.

Sir Henry Irving   5 J 21
By the side of the National Portrait Gallery,
St Martin's Pl WC2. Brock, 1910.

Sir Henry Irving   *James II*

James II   5 J 22
Outside National Gallery, Trafalgar Sq
WC2. Grinling Gibbons, 1686. One of
London's finest statues.

Dr Samuel Johnson   6 K 25
St Clement Danes churchyard, Strand
WC2. Fitzgerald, 1910.

Abraham Lincoln   5 M 20
Parliament Sq SW1. Saint-Gaudens, 1920.
Replica of the one in Chicago.

Sir Thomas More   4 M 8
Cheyne Wlk SW3. Outside parish church.
Bronze of the Tudor statesman and martyr
by L. Cubitt Bevis unveiled in 1969.

Lord Nelson   5 K 21
On column in Trafalgar Sq WC2. Baily,
1843. The statue is 16ft (4.9m) high; weighs
16 tons. Made of stone, it was hoisted into
position in three pieces.

Peter Pan   2 D 12
Kensington Gardens W2. Frampton, 1912.
Charming fairy figure. Erected overnight as
a surprise for the children.

Richard I   5 N 20
Old Palace Yd SW1. Marochetti, 1860.

Abraham Lincoln   *Richard I*

Franklin D. Roosevelt   2 F 17
Grosvenor Sq W1. Reid Dick, 1948.

Sir Joshua Reynolds   2 I 19
Forecourt of Burlington House, Piccadilly
W1. Drury, 1931.

Royal Artillery Memorial   2 I 16
Hyde Park Corner SW1. Jagger, 1925.
London's best war memorial, with its great
stone howitzer aimed at the Somme where
the men it commemorates lost their lives.
The bronze figures of soldiers are possibly
the finest sculptures to be seen in London.

*Sir Joshua   Royal Artillery
Reynolds   Memorial*

Captain Scott   5 K 20
Waterloo Pl SW1. Lady Scott, 1915. 'Scott
of the Antarctic' modelled by his widow.

William Shakespeare   5 J 22
Leicester Sq WC2. After Scheemakers,
1740. Copy (1874) of the memorial in West-

Captain Scott

William Shakespeare

minster Abbey for which David Garrick is said to have posed.

Victoria Memorial   5 **K** 17
In front of Buckingham Palace SW1. Brock, 1911. Impressive memorial to Queen Victoria which includes a fine dignified figure of the Queen, the best of the many statues of her.

George Washington   5 **J** 21
Outside National Gallery, Trafalgar Sq WC2. Replica of the statue by Houdon in the Capitol at Richmond, Virginia, and presented by that state in 1921.

Duke of Wellington   6 **N** 31
Outside Royal Exchange EC3. Chantrey, 1844. Like the same sculptor's statue of George IV, his horse has no saddle or stirrups and he wears no boots.

Duke of Wellington   2 **I** 16
Hyde Park Corner SW1. Boehm, 1888. Equestrian statue of the Duke. The memorial is distinguished by four well-modelled figures of soldiers in full kit. The Duke rides his favourite horse, Copenhagen, and he looks towards Apsley House, in which he lived.

Duke of Wellington

Victoria Memorial

William III   5 **J** 20
St James's Sq SW1. Bacon, 1807. First proposed in 1697 but not erected until 1808. Beneath one of the horse's hooves is the molehill over which the horse stumbled, killing the King.

Duke of York   5 **K** 20
On column, Waterloo Pl SW1. Westmacott, 1834. Cost £30,000 and was paid for by deducting a day's pay from every officer and man in the British Army.

Modern outdoor sculpture

*Good modern sculpture on open view is still rather rare in London – a reflection of a lack of both private and public commissions – although the Royal parks are regularly used for major displays and there is a permanent exhibition (with changing exhibits) in Regent's Park (south-east corner near Chester Gate NW1, 2 **B** 22). Among the best permanently sited pieces are:*

Michael Ayrton (1921-1974)
Postman's Park, Aldersgate   6 **L** 29
EC2. 'Minotaur' expressing massive energy.

Geoffrey Clark (b. 1924)
Thorn Bldg, Upper St Martin's   2 **I** 22
La WC2. Bronze relief.

Sir Jacob Epstein (1880-1959)
Heythrop College, 11   2 **F** 20
Cavendish Sq W1. Bronze 'Madonna and Child', 1952.
St James's Park Underground   5 **L** 18
Station. Fine sculpture of 'Day and Night'.
South of Nursery Enclosure,   2 **G** 14
Hyde Park. 'Rima'.
Edinburgh Gate, Hyde Park.   2 **H** 13
'Return of Spring'.

Elizabeth Frink (b. 1930)
Carlton Tower Hotel, Cadogan   5 **J** 13
Sq SW1. Beaten copper relief on façade.

Dame Barbara Hepworth (1903-1975)
John Lewis Store, Oxford St   2 **F** 19
W1. Bronze relief.
State House, High Holborn   3 **I** 23
WC1. Fine abstract 'Meridian'.
Hyde Park. 'Family of Man' (on   2 **G** 15
indefinite loan).

Karin Jonzen (b. 1914)
Bassishaw Highwalk, south of   6 **L** 30
London Wall EC2. 'Beyond Tomorrow', male and female figures.

David Kemp
Hay's Galleria, Tooley St SE1.   6 **Q** 30
'The Navigators', a kinetic sculpture in bronze with moving parts.

Bernard Meadows (b. 1915)
TUC Building, Great Russell   3 **H** 23
St WC1. Bronze group.

Henry Moore (1898-1986)
Abingdon St Gdns SW1. 'Knife   5 **N** 20
Edge Two-Piece' bronze, 1967.
Kensington Gardens SW7.   2 **E** 12
'The Arch' overlooking the Long Water. Marble, 1980.
Riverside House, Millbank   5 **Q** 17
SW1. 'Locking Pieces' bronze in garden close to Vauxhall Bridge.

Time & Life Bldg, New Bond St   2 **G** **19**
W1. Fine stone relief.

Walenty Pytel (b. 1941)
Parliament Sq SW1. 'Silver   5 **M** **20**
Jubilee Fountain', a highly elaborate and
impressive steel sculpture.

Places of worship

In their buildings, ruins, sites and associations, London's churches and cathedrals represent nearly 1400 years of Christianity in Britain (the first St Paul's Cathedral is ascribed to the beginning of the 7thC). Norman work survives in St Helen's Bishopsgate and Westminster Abbey and at the time of the Great Fire of 1666 there were over 100 churches in the present area of the City of London, a density peculiar to English cities.

The Fire set the scene for Wren's great rebuilding programme, including St Paul's Cathedral and 50 churches, most of which have survived later demolitions and war damage. Hawksmoor and Inigo Jones were other 17th and early 18thC church designers whose work we can still admire. The Victorians too were great church builders and the 19thC produced a wealth of new churches, many of them in the triumphant Gothic style, for Anglican and other denominations. The neo-Byzantine Westminster RC Cathedral of 1903 is outstanding.

Non-Christian religions also have their part in London's history, with synagogues as at Bevis Marks and, most recently, the Regent's Park Mosque for London's growing Islamic community. London's most important religious buildings are listed below.

Abbeys & cathedrals

St George's RC Cathedral,   6 **P** **29**
Southwark
Lambeth Rd (opp Imperial War Museum) SE1. 01-928 5256. By A. W. Pugin, 1848. Spire never completed. Burnt out in last war and interior restored in 1958.

St Paul's Cathedral   6 **M** **28**
Ludgate Hill EC4. 01-248 4619/2705. Wren's greatest work; built 1675-1710 replacing the previous church destroyed by the Great Fire. Superb dome, porches and funerary monuments. Contains magnificent stalls by Grinling Gibbons. Ironwork

St Paul's Cathedral

by Tijou, paintings by Thornhill and mosaics by Salviati and Sir William Richmond. *OPEN 08.00-18.00 Mon-Sun except during special services. Free. Crypt, ambulatory & galleries OPEN 10.00-16.15 Mon-Fri, 11.00-16.15 Sat. Charge.*

Southwark Cathedral   6 **Q** **27**
Borough High St SE1. 01-407 2939. Much restored. Built by Augustinian Canons 1206. Beautiful early English choir and retrochoir. Tower built c1520, nave by Blomfield 1894-7. Work by Comper includes the altar screen.

Southwark Cathedral

Westminster Abbey   5 **M** **20**
(The Collegiate Church of St Peter in Westminster) Broad Sanctuary SW1. 01-222 5152. Original church by Edward the Confessor 1065. Rebuilding commenced in 1245 by Henry III who was largely influenced by the new French cathedrals. Completed by Henry Yevele and others 1376-1506 (towers incomplete and finished by Hawksmoor 1734). Henry VII Chapel added 1503; fine perpendicular with wonderful fan vaulting. The Abbey contains the Coronation Chair, and many tombs and memorials of the Kings and Queens of England and their subjects. Starting place for pilgrimage to Canterbury Cathedral. *Abbey OPEN 08.00-18.00 Mon-Sun. Free. Royal Chapels OPEN 09.00-16.00 (last tickets) Mon-Fri, 09.00-14.45 & 16.00-16.45 Sat. Charge. 18.00-19.45 Wed*

Westminster Abbey

(photography permitted) free. Sun, services only. Museum OPEN 10.30-16.00 Mon-Sat. Small charge.

Westminster RC Cathedral   5 **M** 16
Ashley Pl SW1. 01-834 7452. Early Christian Byzantine-style church by J. F. Bentley, 1903. The most important Roman Catholic church in England. Fine marbled interior.

Churches & other places of worship

All Hallows-by-the-Tower   6 **Q** 32
Byward St EC3. 01-481 2928. Foundations date from AD675. Audaciously restored by Lord Mottistone after bombing. Fine copper steeple. Crypt museum with Roman pavement. Brass rubbing. *Church OPEN 10.00-17.00 Mon-Sat, 12.30-17.00 Sun. Free. Refectory OPEN 12.00-14.00 Mon-Fri. Crypt OPEN by appt only. Charge.*

All Hallows London Wall   6 **L** 30
83 London Wall EC2. 01-588 3388. Rebuilt 1765-7 by Dance junior. Restored 1962 by David Nye as centre for church art. Charming interior.

All Saints Margaret St   2 **F** 20
Margaret St W1. 01-636 9961. Gothic Revival masterpiece. William Butterfield, 1859. Paintings by Ninian Comper. Fine musical tradition. *OPEN 07.00-19.00 Mon-Sun. Free.*

All Souls Langham Place   2 **F** 20
Langham Pl W1. 01-580 4357. John Nash, 1822-4; Nash's only church. Corinthian columns with needle spire. Restored after bomb damage. Interior refitted 1976. Exterior restored 1987-8.

Bevis Marks Synagogue   6 **O** 33
Heneage La (off Bevis Marks) EC3. 01-283 1167. Avis, 1700. Fine windows. Brass chandeliers from Amsterdam.

Brompton Oratory   1 **I** 11
Brompton Rd SW7. 01-589 4811. Large Italian Renaissance-style church designed by H. Gribble, 1884. Fine marbled interior and original statues from the Cathedral of Siena.

Capel Bedyddwyr Cymreig   2 **G** 21
30 Eastcastle St W1. Highly imaginative Welsh Baptist chapel.

Central Hall   5 **M** 19
Storey's Gate SW1. 01-222 8010. 'Cathedral of Methodism' 1912 by Lanchester & Rickards, the greatest exponents of the baroque style in Edwardian London. Listed building.

Chapel Royal of St John   6 **Q** 32
White Tower, Tower of London EC3. 01-709 0765. The oldest church in London, c1085, original Norman.

Chelsea Old Church, All Saints   4 **M** 8
Chelsea Embankment SW3. 01-352 5627. Rebuilt after severe bombing. 13thC chapels, one restored by Sir Thomas More, 1528. Jacobean altar table, many historic monuments.

Christ Church Newgate St   6 **L** 29
Newgate St EC1. Wren, 1691. Only the tower (1704) and four walls remain.

Christ Church Spitalfields
Commercial St E1. 01-247 7202. Fine church by Hawksmoor, 1714-29, recently partly restored. Notable tower and spire, and lofty interior. Crypt a rehabilitation centre for alcoholics. Annual international music festival.

Christ the King   3 **E** 24
Gordon Sq WC1. 01-387 0670. The University church and the Catholic Apostolic church. Cruciform, cathedral-like building by Raphael Brandon, 1853. West front and tower unfinished.

City Temple   6 **K** 28
Holborn Viaduct EC1. 01-583 5532. City's Free Church, 1874, by Lockwood, restored after bombing.

Cole Abbey Presbyterian Church   6 **M** 28
Queen Victoria St EC4. 01-248 5213. Affiliated to the Free Church of Scotland. Originally by Wren, 1671-81, and restored with similar spire after bombing. Rich stained glass by Keith New.

Crown Court Church of Scotland, Covent Garden   6 **J** 24
Russell St WC2. 01-836 5643. Longest-established Presbyterian church south of the border, dating from 1719. It was rebuilt in 1909 and is situated in the heart of London's theatreland.

Dutch Church   6 **N** 31
7 Austin Friars EC2. 01-588 1684. 14thC origin, given to Dutch Protestants after the

Reformation. Rebuilt 1950-3 after 1940 destruction. Part of the present structure dates from 1550.

French Protestant Church   2 H 22
9 Soho Sq W1. 01-437 5311. By Aston Webb in 1893, externally surprisingly like an office building.

Grosvenor Chapel   2 G 17
South Audley St W1. 01-499 1684. 'Colonial'-looking chapel built 1730. Decorations by Comper added in 1912.

The Guards Chapel   5 L 18
Wellington Barracks, Birdcage Wlk SW1. 01-930 4466. Original chapel (1838) destroyed in 1944 with the loss of 121 lives. New chapel, finished 1963, is austere but complements the original surviving apse.

Holy Trinity   5 L 18
Sloane St SW1. 01-730 7270. By Sedding in 1890. London's most elaborate church of the 'Arts and Crafts' movement.

Immaculate Conception   2 G 17
114 Mount St W1. 01-493 7811. 1849 by J. J. Scoles. Headquarters of the Jesuit Order in Britain.

London Mosque
Hanover Gate NW1. A graceful building on the edge of Regent's Park, it was completed in 1978 and is the religious centre for London's Muslims.

Notre Dame de France   2 I 22
5 Leicester Pl WC2. 01-437 9363. First church 1855, rebuilt 1955 after bombing. Circular. Large Aubusson tapestry, mural by Jean Cocteau and statue of Our Lady by Georges Sanpique.

**Queen's Chapel of the   6 K 23
Savoy**
Savoy Hill, Strand WC2. 01-836 7221. Late perpendicular style, built 1508. Some 13th and 15thC glass.

**The Queen's Chapel, St   5 K 19
James's Palace**
Marlborough Rd SW1. Built by Inigo Jones, 1623. Fine restored woodwork and coffered ceiling. *OPEN (for services only) Easter-end Jul 08.30 & 11.15 Sun.*

St Alban Holborn   3 I 27
Brooke St EC1. 01-405 1831. Originally by Butterfield, 1859. Rebuilt by Adrian Scott after bomb damage. Soaring arches. Sculpture and huge mural by Hans Feibusch.

St Alban Wood St   6 L 30
Wood St EC2. Wren. Only the tower remains 1697-8 (modern pinnacles).

St Andrew Holborn   6 J 27
Holborn Circus EC4. 01-353 3544. Largest of Wren's parish churches. 1686. Restored 1961 after bombing. Pulpit, font,

organ and tomb of Thomas Coram, from the chapel of the 18thC Foundling Hospital.

St Andrew-by-the-Wardrobe   6 M 28
Queen Victoria St EC4. 01-248 7546. Fine City church by Wren, 1685-95. Restored 1959-61, after bomb damage.

St Andrew Undershaft   6 O 32
St Mary Axe EC3. 01-283 7382. Rebuilt 1532. Altar rails by Tijou, font by Nicholas Stone. Monument to John Stow, London's first historian.

St Anne Limehouse
Commercial Rd E14. Hawksmoor, built 1712-24. Highest public clock (added 1839) in Britain after Big Ben. Organ, built for 1851 Great Exhibition, is one of finest unaltered Victorian examples in the country.

St Anne Soho   2 H 22
57 Dean St W1. 01-437 6727. Steeple only, by Cockerell, 1802-6. The church, by Wren, was destroyed by bombing.

St Anne & St Agnes   6 M 30
Gresham St EC2. 01-606 4986. Wren, 1676-87. Attractive church restored after bomb damage.

St Augustine Watling St   6 M 29
Watling St EC4. Wren, 1687. Only tower remains after bombing, with new spire after the original design. Now part of cathedral choir school.

St Bartholomew-the-Great   6 K 29
West Smithfield EC1. 01-606 1575. Norman choir of Augustinian Priory 1123 with later Lady Chapel; the only pre-Reformation font in City. Tomb of founder, who also founded St Bartholomew's Hospital, and other fine monuments.

St Bartholomew-the-Less   6 K 29
West Smithfield EC1. 01-601 8888. Inside 'Barts' hospital (serves as its parish church). Tower and west end medieval, rest rebuilt 1789 and 1823. Octagonal interior.

St Benet Church   6 M 28
Queen Victoria St EC4. 01-723 3104. Attractive church by Wren, 1683, on foundations dating back from 1111. Brick with stone dressings. A Guild Church. Also known as the Metropolitan Welsh Church. The Chapel of the College of Arms. Burial place of Inigo Jones.

St Botolph Aldersgate   6 K 30
Aldersgate EC1. 01-623 6970. Nathaniel Wright, 1788, with additions in 1831. Charming interior.

St Botolph Aldgate   6 O 33
Aldgate High St EC3. 01-283 1670. Rebuilt 1741-4 by Dance senior. Restored by Bentley, 1890s, and again 1966. Fine

monuments. Lies north and south. Renatus Harris organ (1674). Peal of eight bells (18thC). Recent large addition to the crypt, which is a centre for homeless single people.

St Botolph Bishopsgate 6 N 33
Bishopsgate EC2. 01-588 1053. Rebuilt 1725-9 by James Gould. Baroque steeple at east end. Large churchyard.

St Bride's Church 6 L 27
Fleet St EC4. 01-353 1301. Wren, 1670-84. Famous spire 1701-4. Restored after bomb damage. Fine City church.

St Clement Danes 6 K 25
Strand WC2. 01-242 8282. First built by the Danes, 9thC. Spire by Gibbs. Rebuilt by Wren, 1681. Destroyed in air raids 1941 and rebuilt and rededicated in 1958 as the central church of the RAF. Bells ring 'Oranges and Lemons' every 4 hrs. Fine moulded plaster ceiling.

St Clement nr Eastcheap 6 Q 30
Clements La, King William St EC4. 01-226 6992. Wren, 1687. Restored by Butterfield, 1872, and by Comper, 1933. Notable 17thC woodwork and fine organ (1695).

St Columba 5 J 12
Pont St SW1. 01-584 2321. Church of Scotland, new building by Maufe replacing destroyed Victorian one.

St Cyprian 2 A 19
Glentworth St, Clarence Gate NW1. 01-402 6979. Outstanding example of a complete church by Comper, in his early style. 1903. Renowned interior.

St Dunstan-in-the-East 6 P 31
St Dunstan's Hill EC3. Only the delicately poised spire by Wren remains. 1696-1701.

St Dunstan-in-the-West 6 K 26
Fleet St EC4. 01-242 6027. Octagonal church by John Shaw, 1831-3. Restored in 1950. Fine lantern-steeple clock with 'striking jacks' from old church. Orthodox chapel with icon screen brought from Antim Monastery in Bucharest. Monuments to an honest solicitor, and to a swordsman. Also Lord Mayor's sword from Battle of Culloden 1745.

St Dunstan All Saints, Stepney
White Horse Rd E1. 01-790 4194. Mother church of East London, late 15thC. Mostly rebuilt. Fine interior. Notable Saxon crucifix.

St Edmund the King 6 N 30
Lombard St EC3. 01-623 6970. Rebuilt by Wren, 1690, and lies north and south, like the pre-Fire church. Restored after slight damage in both world wars. Fine woodwork, distinctive 90ft (27.5m) steeple.

St Ethelburga 6 N 33
70 Bishopsgate EC2. 01-588 3596. Tiny church, 15thC, later furnished by Comper. Fine mural by Hans Feibusch (1963) on east wall. One of the City Guild Churches.

St Etheldreda 6 J 28
Ely Pl EC1. 01-405 1061. Former bishop's chapel built c1300, restored in the 19thC to Catholic use. Some fine post-war glass.

St George Bloomsbury 3 H 24
Bloomsbury Way WC1. 01-405 3044. Hawksmoor, 1730. Statue of George I on top of steeple, posing as St George. Internal reorientation in 1870. Six-column Corinthian portico. Classical interior.

St George Hanover Sq 2 G 19
St George St W1. 01-629 0874. Classical church by John James, 1721-4. Restored by Blomfield in 1894. Altarpiece of 'Last Supper' by Kent.

St George-in-the-East
Cannon Street Rd E1. 01-709 9074. Remarkable church by Hawksmoor, 1715-23. Modern rebuilding (1964) within the bomb-ruined walls.

St George the Martyr Southwark 6 Q 27
Borough High St SE1. 01-407 2796. A Georgian building with fine ornamental plaster ceiling. 'Little Dorrit's' church. Rebuilt 1734-6 by J. Price.

St Giles Cripplegate 6 L 31
Fore St EC2. 01-606 3630. 14thC church restored 1952 after bombing. Contains Milton's grave. Remains of London Wall in churchyard.

St Giles in the Fields 3 H 23
St Giles High St WC2. 01-240 2532. Flitcroft, 1731-3. Well restored 1952. Wesley's pulpit from West St Chapel is here.

St Helen Bishopsgate 6 N 32
Great St Helen's EC3. 01-283 2231. Built 1150. Has two naves, northern originally a nunnery, southern parochial. Contains fine monuments of many City worthies, some excellent brasses and a notable organ case (Victorian). Original nun's squint.

St James 2 C 13
Sussex Gdns W2. 01-723 8119. Contains an unusual stained glass memorial to Alexander Fleming showing him at work in his laboratory. The discovery of penicillin was made nearby at St Mary's Hospital.

St James Bermondsey
Jamaica Rd SE1. 01-232 2329. A Waterloo church built by James Savage in 1825-9 in the style of a Greek temple with four columned porticos. Has a purpose-built Bishop organ with rare manual keyboard for pedal organ. Original peal of ten bells. Golden dragon weathervane.

St James Clerkenwell 3 I 29
Clerkenwell Grn EC1. 01-253 1568. Rebuilt 1788-92 by James Carr. Fine Wren-like steeple. Good interior. Some monuments from old church.

St James Garlickhythe 6 N 29
Garlick Hill EC4. 01-236 1719. Fine City church by Wren, 1687, well-restored steeple 1713. Good ironwork and woodwork.

St James Piccadilly 2 I 20
Piccadilly W1. 01-734 4511. Wren 1684. Restored by Sir Albert Richardson in 1954 after serious bomb damage. Reredos, organ casing and font by Grinling Gibbons. Famous 'Father Smith' organ presented by Queen Mary in 1691 and brought from Whitehall Palace. Healing ministry. Major programme of concerts and lectures.

St James the Less 5 O 16
Westminster
Thorndike St, Vauxhall Bridge Rd SW1. G. E. Street, 1860; largely unaltered, its furnishings are complete. Remark the patterned brick walls.

St John Clerkenwell 3 I 29
St John's Sq EC1. 01-253 6644. Originally a round church. Became a parish church in 1723. 15thC nave, 16thC gate, well-preserved crypt dating from 1140. Museum of the Order of St John. OPEN Tue, Fri & Sat 10.00-17.00; tours at 11.00 & 14.30. Donation welcome.

St John Smith Sq 5 O 19
Smith Sq SW1. 01-222 2168. Nicknamed 'Queen Anne's Footstool'. Built by Archer, 1721-8. Gutted by fire 1742; interior redesigned. Blitzed 1941; restored to Archer's original design by charitable trust. Opened as a concert hall in 1969. Footstool Gallery has monthly exhibitions. Restaurant & gallery OPEN 11.30-14.45 Mon-Fri. Also OPEN eves if there is a concert.

St John's Wood Church
St John's Wood High St NW8. 01-722 4378. Thomas Hardwick, 1813. White and gold interior with carved ceilings supported by impressive Doric and Etruscan columns.

St John Waterloo Rd 6 O 24
Waterloo Rd SE1. 01-633 0852. Bedford, 1824. Four walls, steeple and portico remained after bombing. Restored by Ford in 1951 as part of the Festival of Britain. There was a fine reredos which has now been replaced by Hans Feibusch murals.

St Katherine Cree 6 O 32
Leadenhall St EC3. 01-283 5733. Rebuilt under Bishop Laud 1631 in hybrid Gothic and classical style.

St Lawrence Jewry 6 M 30
Gresham St EC2. 01-600 9478. Wren,

1670-86. Tower and four walls remained after bombing. Restored in 1957. Replicas of steeple and original Wren ceiling. Official church of City Corporation.

St Leonard Shoreditch
119 High St E1. 01-739 2063. Rebuilt 1736-40 by Dance senior. Fine steeple and woodwork, including the beautiful clock surround. OPEN Mon-Fri 12.00-14.00. Free.

St Luke Chelsea 4 K 9
Sydney St SW3. 01-351 7365/6. Savage, 1824. First church to be built in sumptuous style of early Gothic revival. Dickens married here.

St Magnus the Martyr 6 P 30
Lower Thames St EC3. 01-626 4481. Wren, 1671-87. One of Wren's finest steeples, 185ft (55.9m) high, added 1705-6. Anglo-Catholic baroque interior. Fine pulpit and furnishings.

St Margaret Lothbury 6 N 31
Lothbury EC2. 01-606 8330. Wren, 1686-93. Steeple 1698-1700. Fine fittings, including a 17thC open-work screen. Bust of Ann Simpson by Nollekens. Grinling Gibbons font.

St Margaret Pattens 6 P 31
Rood La, Eastcheap EC3. 01-623 6630. Church by Wren, 1684-9. Fine spire 1698-1702. Unusual canopied pews.

St Margaret Westminster 5 M 20
Parliament Sq SW1. 01-222 6382. Rebuilt 1504-18 and again after repeated war damage. Splendid early 16thC east window and an excellent series of stained glass windows by John Piper. The parish church of the House of Commons.

St Margaret Westminster

St Martin-in-the-Fields 5 K 22
Trafalgar Sq WC2. 01-930 1862. James Gibbs, 1726. Famous spire and portico. Fine Venetian east window and white and gold moulded plaster ceiling. Handsome pulpit. The open space of Trafalgar Square creates a pleasing prominence for the church. Lunchtime music 13.00-14.00 Mon & Tue. Free. Bookshop, brass rubbing

centre, craft market, restaurant & visitor's centre *OPEN 10.00-24.00 Mon-Sat, 12.00-20.00 Sun. Charge for brass rubbing.*

St Martin-in-the-Fields

St Martin Ludgate 6 L 28
Ludgate Hill EC4. 01-248 6054. Wren, 1677-84, now restored. Elegant spire, fine interior, notable woodwork.

St Mary Abbots Kensington I C 8
Kensington Church St W8. 01-937 5136. Scott, 1872. Transitional between early-English and decorated style.

St Mary Abchurch 6 O 30
Abchurch Yd EC4. 01-626 0306. Wren, 1681-7. Fine ceiling by William Snow. Reredos by Grinling Gibbons.

St Mary Aldermary 6 M 29
Watling St EC4. 01-248 4906. Late Gothic rebuilt by Wren. Fine fan vaulting with saucer domes.

St Mary-at-Hill 6 P 31
Lovat La EC3. 01-626 4184. Wren, 1676, tower, 1788. Box pews and magnificent fittings.

St Mary-at-Lambeth 5 P 21
Beside Lambeth Palace, Lambeth Rd SE1. Rebuilt (except tower) by T. Hardwick, 1850. The tomb of Captain Bligh (*Mutiny on the Bounty*) has been restored.

St Mary Islington 3 E 32
Upper St N1. 01-226 3400. Launcelot Dowbiggin, 1750. Restored 1956, after bomb damage. Fine baroque steeple.

St Marylebone Parish Church 2 B 17
Marylebone Rd NW1. 01-935 7315. Thomas Hardwick, 1813-17. Thomas Harris added the chancel in 1884. Imposing white and gold interior.

St Mary-le-Bow 6 M 29
Cheapside EC2. 01-248 5139. The church of 'Bow Bells' fame by Wren, 1680. Crypt dates from 1087. Restored by Laurence King after bomb damage. Superb steeple.

St Mary-le-Strand 6 K 24
Strand WC2. 01-836 3126. James Gibbs, 1714-17. A perfect small baroque church in the middle of the Strand, sadly encircled by heavy traffic.

St Mary-le-Strand

St Mary Magdalen Bermondsey 6 R 29
Bermondsey St SE1. 01-232 2329. Rebuilt 1680. Charming classical interior. Gothic west end, 1830.

St Mary Somerset 6 M 28
Upper Thames St EC4. Wren, 1694. Only the imposing 8-pinnacled tower remains.

St Mary Woolnoth 6 N 30
Lombard St EC3. 01-626 9701. Remarkable 1716-27 baroque Guild Church by Hawksmoor. Church of England services on weekdays. Lunchtime relaxation sessions.

St Michael Chester Square 5 L 14
Chester Sq SW1. 01-730 8889. Cundy, 1846. War memorial chapel added in 1920. Fine coloured alabaster.

St Michael Paternoster Royal 6 N 29
College Hill EC4. 01-248 5202. Wren, 1694, steeple 1713. Recently restored. Dick Whittington buried here (commemorative stained glass window). Tower used as office by The Missions to Seamen.

St Michael-upon-Cornhill 6 N 31
Cornhill EC3. 01-626 8841. Wren, 1677, much restored by Scott. Handsome Gothic tower added 1722. Twelve magnificent bells which are always rung on Sundays. First rate choir and organ.

St Olave Hart St 6 P 32
8 Hart St EC3. 01-488 4318. Originally early 13thC, on the site of a wooden church of 1080, it was enlarged in 1450. Samuel

Pepys' church. Restored by Glanfield after bomb damage. Fine vestry and crypt.

St Pancras New Church   3 D 25
Euston Rd NW1. 01-387 8250. W. and H. Inwood, 1822. One of the finest neo-classical churches in Britain. The largest unsupported ceiling in England. Noted for its choir and organ recitals.

St Pancras Old Church   3 B 26
Pancras Rd NW1. 01-387 7301. Church with country atmosphere. Added to and transformed 1848. 4thC foundations. Saxon altar stone (AD600). Third oldest Christian site in Europe.

St Paul Covent Garden   6 J 23
Covent Garden WC2. 01-836 5221. Fine 'ecclesiastical barn' by Inigo Jones. Rebuilt by Thomas Hardwick after fire of 1795. Pleasant gardens at Bedford St entrance.

St Paul Knightsbridge   2 I 14
32a Wilton Pl SW1. 01-235 3460. Victorian church by Cundy, 1843. Chancel by Bodley. Rich, colourful interior.

St Peter-ad-Vincula   6 Q 32
Tower of London, Tower Hill EC3. 01-709 0765. Much restored church built about 1512. Many historic monuments. *Admission by guided tour only. Frequent tours (except in bad weather) from 09.45 Mon-Sat & Sun afternoons. Charge (included in entrance charge to Tower of London). Sun services at 09.15 & 11.00.*

St Peter-upon-Cornhill   6 N 31
Cornhill EC3. 01-626 9483. Very fine church by Wren, 1677-87. Oldest church site in City, reputedly AD179. Organ built by Schmidt. Fine carved screen. 14th and 15thC plays performed at Xmas.

St Sepulchre Without   6 K 28
Newgate
Holborn Viaduct EC1. 01-248 1660. Rebuilt in 15thC, altered in 1667, possibly by Wren, and again in the 18th and 19thC. Tombs of Sir Henry Wood and Captain John Smith.

St Stephen Walbrook   6 N 30
Walbrook EC4. 01-283 4444. Masterpiece by Wren, 1672-9; steeple 1714-17. Dome, with eight columns, supported by Corinthian pillars, all beautifully restored. Directly under the dome is an intricately carved cylindrical altar in Roman travertine marble sculpted by Henry Moore. Fine fittings. Lord Mayor of London's church and the home since 1953 of 'The Samaritans' who help the suicidal and desperate.

The Temple Church   6 K 26
Inner Temple La EC4. 01-353 1736. Completely restored. 12thC round nave and 13thC choir. Fine effigies. Reredos by Wren.

'Modern' architecture came relatively late to England as compared with the USA or Continental Europe. The 1920s and 1930s provide isolated examples, but the 1950s really set the scene, following the 1951 Festival of Britain, with post-war reconstruction needs (both from the intensive bombing and the growth of London itself) creating the impetus for massive house-building and town centre redevelopment programmes. Town planning became a major new profession, intended originally to guide development in the public interest but, with the property boom of the 1960s, often acting as the willing ally of the new commercial developers with their massive schemes. Too much in too short a time was the result. The Barbican, London Wall, Victoria Street South West and Commercial Union/P & O, all described below, show what could be done, as do some of the schools, hospitals, new towns and universities for which British designers have become internationally renowned. But much of London, as of other cities and towns, suffered from the uncontrolled impact of scale, height, form, materials and building technology. With the collapse of the property boom, however, and the growth of conservationist pressure, both phenomena of the 1970s, more balanced policies prevailed and there was growing interest in the saving and re-use of worthwhile buildings. The recession of the 1980s has adversely affected both new housing and conservation. In the same period a series of proposals for major new office blocks have raised controversy, and the proponents of hi-tech and post-modern architecture have begun to make their contributions to the city, particularly in the City itself and further east, in Docklands. Some of London's most interesting and innovative buildings are listed below.

Alexandra Road Housing
Abbey Rd NW8. LB Camden Architects Dept, Neave Brown 1977. Massive new housing development in which dwellings are stacked in stepped terraces, like the curving contours of artificial hills, enclosing the pedestrian access road in the valley. Dazzling white concrete finish, the detailing of which is of a very high standard.

Alton West Estate (Roehampton)
Roehampton La SW15. London County Council Architects Dept, 1956-61. One of the earliest and most dramatic of

post-war housing schemes, mixing high-and low-rise blocks in a parkland setting in what should have been a blueprint for future developments.

Apollo Victoria   5 M 16
17 Wilton Rd SW1. E. Walmsley-Lewis, 1928-9. London's first cinema built for the 'talkies', its modernistic exterior, in the contemporary Continental horizontal style, concealing a 'fairy palace' of an interior. Now a theatre.

Barbican   6 K 30
London Wall EC2. Chamberlin, Powell & Bon, 1955. A competition-winning city within a city, with over 2,000 flats, some in 40-storey towers, a water garden, the restored St Giles' Church, a girls' school, pubs, shops and an arts centre (see below) all linked by pedestrian decks to the office towers of London Wall (see below).

Barbican Centre   6 K 30
Heralded by jokes about the difficulty of finding the way into it, the country's largest arts centre opened in March 1982. A concert hall, two theatres, three cinemas, a public library, an art gallery and sculpture court and two restaurants are among its wealth of facilities. One among many fascinating statistics is that 130,000 cubic metres of concrete – enough to build over 19 miles of six-lane motorway – were used in its construction.

British Telecom Tower   2 E 22
Howland St W1. Ministry of Public Building & Works, 1966. A dramatic landmark: 580ft (176.9m) tower housing telecommunications equipment, offices. Formerly the Post Office Tower. The revolving restaurant used to provide a spectacular panorama of London but is now closed.

Brunswick Centre   3 F 26
Brunswick Sq WC1. Patrick Hodgkinson, 1973. A scaled-down version of the megastructure concept. Housing, stepped upwards in the form of a ziggurat, overlooks a pleasant raised shopping plaza. Car parking out of sight below.

Bush Lane House   6 N 29
80 Cannon St EC4. Arup Associates, 1976. An inside-out building in which the structural skeleton of stainless steel tubes is exposed, and the transparent skin suspended within a metal cage. This was a solution to the structural constraints imposed by the need to have open floorplans, unimpeded by columns, and restrictions on foundation depth due to the presence of Cannon St station.

Clore Gallery   5 P 18
Millbank SW1. James Stirling, Michael Wilford & Associates, 1986. Housing the Turner Museum, the new gallery forms a striking visual link between its two neighbours, the Tate Gallery and the Edwardian military hospital. It adopts characteristics from each (classical stonework on one side, brickwork on the other).

Commercial Union and   6 O 32
P & O Buildings
Leadenhall St EC3. These buildings represent a unique occurrence in City redevelopment. The two companies, finding that they both needed rehousing, merged to jointly hire the Gollins, Melvin, Ward Ptnrship to design two separate but complementary buildings. Deliberately contrasted, the tall, sheer CU building stands in an open piazza next to the smaller horizontally emphasised P & O building and creates a striking effect.

Economist Building   5 J 19
25 St James's St SW1. Alison & Peter Smithson, 1964-6. A very beautiful and harmonious group of buildings with its own raised piazza. The design was intended to demonstrate a general principle for the redevelopment of dense commercial areas and is a rare example of new building in an area with a traditional street pattern.

Hoover Factory
Perivale on the A40 just outside Central London. Wallis, Gilbert & Ptnrs, 1932. Colourfully decorated blend of Art Deco and Modern Movement.

Lillington Gardens   5 N 16
Vauxhall Bridge Rd SW1. Darbourne & Darke, 1968-72. Award-winning example of the low-rise, high-density public sector housing which followed the over-exploitation of the tower block. Some tenants have their own gardens.

Lloyds Building   6 O 32
Lime St EC3. Richard Rogers Ptnrship, 1986. A new hi-tech monument in the City from the architect jointly responsible for the Pompidou Centre in Paris. This multi-faceted, 12-storey, 6-towered structure is the new headquarters for the international insurance market. The huge dealing room is housed in a 246ft (75m)-high atrium.

London Bridge City   6 Q 30
Tooley St SE1. St Martin's Property Corporation, 1987. Phase I was completed in 1987 and includes Hay's Galleria. This is an elegant and lofty arcade with a barrel-vaulted glass roof, reminiscent of Victorian railway architecture or perhaps the Crystal Palace. Also includes No 1 London Bridge, an office building of pink granite, comprised of two towers – one of 12 storeys, in the

form of an arch, and the other of 9 storeys. Phase 2 of the development is due for completion at the end of 1989.

London Mosque

Regent's Park, entrance by Hanover Gate NW1. Sir Frederick Gibberd & Ptnrs, 1978. Islam's aesthetic and functional needs blend with the constraints of a small and sensitive site adjacent to Nash terraces in a dramatic focus for London's Muslim community.

London Pavilion   2   I   21

Piccadilly Circus W1. Chapman Taylor Ptnrs, 1988. Listed building redeveloped as a shopping and leisure complex. The elegant neo-classical exterior remains as it was originally but two extra storeys have been added and the whole topped with sculptures of classical maidens.

London Wall office   6   L   30
development

London Wall EC2. Early post-1945 comprehensive planning in a badly blitzed area. Six 18-storey office blocks (interspersed with smaller blocks) laid out on the City planners' grid and among the first in Britain with all-glass curtain walling. At the north-west end of London Wall, the most western tower stands on top of the Museum of London.

Museum of London   6   L   30

London Wall EC2. Powell & Moya, 1978. Highly ingenious planning. The Museum (combining the Guildhall and London Museum collections) serves as the podium for an office block (see immediately above) and bridges London Wall to descend into a garden restaurant inside a traffic roundabout.

National Westminster Tower   6   N   32

25 Old Broad St EC2. Extraordinarily slender, shining structure, the closeness of its vertical lines giving a pin-striped effect. Higher than Telecom Tower at 600ft (183m), it gracefully dominates London's skyline. It is Britain's tallest building, and believed to be the tallest cantilevered building in the world. In it is housed the National Westminster Bank's International Division.

New Zealand House   5   J   21

Haymarket SW1. Robert Matthew, Johnson-Marshall & Ptnrs, 1963. A finely modelled 15-storey glass tower on a 4-storey podium. Good material and detailing and an exciting entrance hall. A particularly interesting foil to its flamboyant Victorian neighbour – 'Her Majesty's Theatre'.

Peter Jones Store   5   L   12

Sloane Sq SW1. Slater, Crabtree &

Moberley, 1936. Anticipates much post-1945 architecture in its adventurous curtain walling (see London Wall).

Regent's Park Zoo   2   A   21

North side of Regent's Park NW1. Contains a number of interesting and uninhabited buildings: Gorilla House by Lubetkin & Tecton 1935; Penguin Pool by Tecton 1935; Aviary by Viscount Snowdon, Cedric Price & Frank Newby 1965-6; Elephant House by Casson, Conder & Ptnrs 1965-6; Small Mammal House by Design Research Unit 1967; Sobell Apes & Monkeys Pavilion 1972; and the New Lion Terraces 1976.

St Paul's Cathedral Choir   6   M   29
School

New Change EC4. Architects' Co-Ptnrship, 1967. Incorporates the surviving tower of Wren's war-destroyed St Augustine's, a good example of old blended with new and a better neighbour to the Cathedral than the office plaza to its west.

St Katharine's Dock   6   R   33
development

St Katharine-by-the-Tower E1. The first major bid to regenerate London's former dockland, an £80 million scheme by Taylor Woodrow following a competition in 1969. The World Trade Centre and the Tower Hotel are modern buildings by Renton Howard Wood Levin; the restored Ivory House, a 19thC warehouse, is now apartments, shops, offices, a yacht club and a restaurant.

South Bank Arts Centre   6   M   23

Waterloo SE1. First came the Royal Festival Hall (Robert Matthew and Leslie Martin, LCC Architects Dept), musical focus of the 1951 Festival of Britain which spurred the redevelopment of this run-down area. Most recent is the Museum of the Moving Image (Avery Associates) opened in 1988. In between came the National Theatre (Denys Lasdun) completed in 1977 with its three auditoria; the Hayward Art Gallery and the Queen Elizabeth Hall and Purcell Room, by the Greater London Council Architects Dept in succession to the LCC. Concrete dominates.

Sudbury Town Underground Station

Bridgewater Rd, Wembley, Middx. Charles Holden, 1932. First in a series of modern underground stations.

Thames Flood Barrier

Unity Way, Eastmoor St SE18. This visually and technologically exciting structure, completed in 1982, is designed to swing its gates up through 90 degrees from the river bed and create a stainless steel barrage to stem dangerously high tides which periodically threaten London. The Thames Barrier Visitor Centre houses an exhibition and presentation, illuminating the engineering feats involved in the barrier's construction. *Charge.*

Trocadero 2 I 21
New Coventry St W1. Originally a dance hall and now gutted and rebuilt by Robinson and Arun (1985), the old Victorian façade hides a modern shopping, restaurant and exhibition complex.

TV-AM Breakfast Television Centre
Hawley Cres NW1. Terry Farrell Ptnrship, 1983. A disused garage converted into the colourful London flagship of post-modern architecture 'moored' alongside Regent's Canal. The blank studio walls which front onto the street are enlivened by a huge extruded TV-AM logo.

Vickers' Tower 5 P 18
Millbank SW1. Ronald Ward & Ptnrs, 1960-3. One of London's earliest glass-walled office skyscrapers, and still one of the most elegant.

Victoria Street South West 5 M 16
redevelopment
Victoria St SW1. Elsom Pack & Roberts, 1975. Broken by a piazza giving for the first time a front view of Westminster Cathedral, this is modern commercial development of the highest quality – a notable improvement on the rest of Victoria St.

Museums and galleries

London's national museums and galleries contain some of the richest treasures in the world. Access to special items or collections not on show is willingly and trustfully given. In addition they offer a service of advice and scholarly reference unequalled anywhere in the world. Note that their reference libraries and print collections are further described under 'Reference libraries'. The British Museum, the V & A and other national galleries give expert opinions on the age or identity of objects or paintings – they will not however give you a valuation. Apart from the museums owned by the nation, London is further enriched by other collections open to the public. Most were started as specialist collections by wealthy men or associations but are now available to all, by right or courtesy. It has long been a tradition that national museums and galleries are free and open to all. However some have found it necessary to introduce either voluntary contributions or a fixed admission fee since the mid 80s. Special exhibitions usually charge an entrance fee.

Artillery Museum
The Rotunda, Repository Rd, Woolwich Common SE18. 01-854 2242x5628. The Rotunda was an architectural 'tent' once erected in St James's Park (1814). Notable collection of guns and muskets. Museum refurbished end of 1988. *Usually OPEN 12.00-17.00 Mon-Fri, 13.00-17.00 (16.00 Nov-Mar) Sat & Sun. Please ring to check. Free.*

Battle of Britain Museum
Grahame Park Way NW9. 01-205 2266. A permanent memorial to the men, women and machines involved in the great air battle of 1940. British, German and Italian aircraft, Spitfire, Hurricane, Gladiator, Defiant, Blenheim, Messerschmitt, Heinkel, Junkers, Fiat. Also a replica of the No. 11 Group Operations Room at RAF Uxbridge. Equipment, medals, documents, relics and works of art. *OPEN 10.00-18.00 Mon-Sat, 14.00-18.00 Sun. CLOSED Xmas & Good Friday. Charge.*

HMS Belfast 6 R 31
Symons Wharf, Vine La SE1. 01-407 6434. The largest cruiser ever built for the Royal Navy; now a permanent museum showing the role of this gun ship in wartime. *OPEN 11.00-17.30 Mon-Sun (to 16.30 Nov-Mar). Charge.*

Bomber Command Museum
Grahame Park Way NW9. 01-205 2266. Prize exhibit is the complete – though battered – Lancaster heavy bomber; also the Vickers Wellington. *OPEN 10.00-18.00 Mon-Sat, 14.00-18.00 Sun. Charge.*

British Museum 3 G 24
Great Russell St WC1. 01-636 1555. One of the largest and greatest museums in the world. The Egyptian sculpture gallery on the ground floor was redesigned in 1981 and dramatically highlights colossi of pharaohs, sphinxes, sarcophagi, priests, chantresses, architectural elements and the Rosetta stone. Upstairs mummies pre-

side, striking a chill and thrill to the heart. Other rooms contain tomb paintings and papyri, including editions of the Book of the Dead, and domestic utensils which were used by the living.

Cycladic, Bronze Age and Archaic remains are part of an extensive Greek and Roman collection. The Elgin marbles, sculptures from the Parthenon in Athens, are characterised by fluidity of line and generate a sense of occasion and excitement. Personified breezes in the Nereid room convey a similar sense of movement and life. The Portland Vase and the bronze head of Augustus with staring eyes are remarkable among the Roman exhibits. The Wolfson galleries in the basement also house an immense collection of classical sculpture.

Be sure to see the colossal winged lion and bull with human heads in the Assyrian Transept, the sculptures from the throne-room of the palace at Nimrud, the sculpture of the transport of a colossal winged bull in the Nineveh Gallery, harps and lyres in the Babylonian Room. Coins and Medals, Medieval and Later Antiquities, Oriental Antiquities, Prehistoric and Romano-British Antiquities, Prints and Drawings, are the other collections on view. All are outstanding. Building 1823-47 by Sir Robert Smirke; the domed reading room 1857 is by Sidney Smirke. *Museum OPEN 10.00-17.00 Mon-Sat, 14.30-18.00 Sun. Films Tue-Fri, lectures Tue-Sat, gallery talks. Free. Reading room OPEN to members only.*

Bruce Castle Museum
Lordship La N17. 01-808 8772. Local history explored through changing exhibitions and a fine collection of photographs and watercolours. Also history of the Middlesex Regiment, uniforms, curios back to its foundation in the 18thC. British postal history up to and beyond the introduction of the penny post in 1840. *OPEN 13.00-17.00 Mon-Sun. Regiment museum OPEN 13.00-17.00 Tue-Sat. CLOSED B.hols. Free.*

Cabinet War Rooms   5 L 21
Clive Steps, King Charles St SW1. 01-930 6961. Fascinating reconstruction of the underground emergency accommodation, comprising a suite of 19 rooms, used by Winston Churchill, his War Cabinet and the Chiefs of Staff of Britain's armed forces during World War II. *OPEN 10.00-17.15 Mon-Sun. CLOSED B.hols. Charge.*

Chartered Insurance   6 M 30
Institute's Museum
20 Aldermanbury EC2. 01-606 3835. Collection of Insurance Companies' fire marks.

Fire-fighting equipment, helmets, etc. *OPEN 09.00-17.15 Mon-Fri. CLOSED B.hols. Free.*

Chelsea Royal Hospital   4 N 10
Royal Hospital Rd SW3. 01-730 0161. Small museum housed in a part of the hospital built in 1819 by Sir John Soane. Prints, drawings, manuscripts, uniforms, medals and other items related to the history of the hospital. *OPEN 10.00-12.00 & 14.15-16.00 Mon-Fri, 14.00-16.00 Sun. CLOSED B.hols. Free.*

Church Farm House Museum
Greyhound Hill NW4. 01-203 0130. A 17thC gabled farmhouse, whose stone-floored kitchen with its huge fireplace is equipped with Victorian cooking utensils. Parlour and bedrooms are used for small, changing exhibitions. *OPEN 10.00-13.00 & 14.00-17.30 Mon & Wed-Sat, 10.00-13.00 Tue, 14.00-17.30 Sun. Free.*

Commonwealth Institute   1 D 5
Kensington High St W8. 01-603 4535. 24hr recorded information 01-602 3257. Scenery, natural resources, way of life and industrial development of Commonwealth countries. Reference library of current Commonwealth literature. Cinema, theatre, art exhibitions, bookshop. *OPEN 10.00-17.30 Mon-Sat, 14.00-17.00 Sun. CLOSED B.hols. Free.*

Courtauld Institute Galleries 6 K 24
Somerset House, Strand WC2. 01-580 1015. The Courtauld Collection (moved in July 1989 from Woburn Sq WC1) of French Impressionists (including fine paintings by Cézanne, Van Gogh, Gauguin) and the Lee, Gambier-Parry and Fry Collections. The Princes Gate collection of Flemish and Italian Old Masters on permanent exhibition. *OPEN 10.00-17.00 Mon-Sat, 14.00-17.00 Sun. Charge.*

Crafts Council   5 J 20
12 Waterloo Pl SW1. 01-930 4811. Changing exhibitions of contemporary craft; also an information service on where to learn about or buy crafts; colour-slide library which surveys the best of crafts in Britain. *OPEN 10.00-17.00 Tue-Sat, 14.00-17.00 Sun. CLOSED Mon & B.hols. Charge for special exhibitions.*

Cricket Memorial Gallery
Lord's Cricket Ground NW8. 01-289 1611. The history of cricket. *OPEN (for spectators only) 10.30-17.00 Mon-Sat on matchdays. Donation. At other times by prior appt only.*

Cuming Museum
Newington District Library, Walworth Rd SE17. 01-703 3324. The archaeology and

history of Southwark from earliest times to the present. Also houses the Lovett collection of London superstitions. *OPEN 10.00-17.30 Mon-Fri (19.00 Thur, 17.00 Sat). CLOSED Sun & B.hols. Free.*

Design Museum

Butler's Wharf, 45 Curlew St SE1. 01-403 6933. Opened in July 1989 and sponsored by the Conran Foundation this new museum's range of exhibits includes furniture, cars, gadgets and graphics and aims to make the public more aware of design. Looks at designs past, present and future through permanent and temporary exhibitions. Also has a bookshop, café, restaurant, library and lecture theatre. *OPEN 11.00-18.30 six days a week. CLOSED one day (day unknown at time of going to press. Phone for details).*

Dulwich Picture Gallery

College Rd SE21. 01-693 5254. English, Italian, Spanish, Dutch and French paintings exhibited in one of the oldest and most beautiful art galleries in England. Notable works by Rembrandt, Rubens, Murillo and Gainsborough. Building 1811-14 by Sir John Soane. *OPEN 10.00-13.00 & 14.00-17.00 Tue-Sat, 14.00-17.00 Sun. CLOSED Mon & B.hols. Small charge.*

Fenton House

Hampstead Gro NW3. 01-435 3471. Built in 1693. The Benton Fletcher collection of early keyboard instruments and the Binning collection of porcelain and furniture. *OPEN Apr-Oct 11.00-17.00 Sat-Wed; Mar 14.00-17.00 Sat & Sun only. CLOSED Nov-Feb. Charge.*

Foundling Hospital   3   F   26
(Thomas Coram Foundation for Children)

40 Brunswick Sq WC1. 01-278 2424. Small gallery of 18thC English painters, including Hogarth, Gainsborough and Reynolds. Collection founded by Hogarth. *OPEN 10.00-16.00 Mon-Fri. CLOSED Sat, Sun & B.hols, but visitors are advised to ring and check beforehand. Charge.*

Geffrye Museum

Kingsland Rd E2. 01-739 9893. 18thC almshouses. Period rooms and furniture from 1600 to the 1930s. *OPEN 10.00-17.00 Tue-Sat, 14.00-17.00 Sun. CLOSED Mon except B.hols. Free.*

Geological Museum   I   H   10

Exhibition Rd SW7. 01-938 8765. Physical and economic geology and mineralogy of the world; regional geology of Britain. Moonrock sample, models, dioramas and a large collection of gems, stones and fossils. The *Story of the Earth* exhibition describes the origin of the universe, explores the evolution of the earth and the history of life. The *Treasures of the Earth* exhibition explains the presence of minerals in the earth and man's everyday use of them. Also a new exhibition on plate tectonics. Don't miss the simulated earthquake platform. Regular events – films, lectures, exhibitions (free mailing list). *OPEN 10.00-18.00 Mon-Sat, 13.00-18.00 Sun. Charge (free after 16.30 Mon-Fri).*

Goldsmiths' Hall   6   L   29

Foster La EC2. 01-606 7010. Fine collection of antique plate. The largest collection of modern silver and jewellery in the country. Special public open days: ring for details.

Guildhall Gallery   6   M   30

Aldermanbury EC2. 01-606 3030. Selections from the Guildhall's permanent collection, loan exhibitions and shows of art societies. New gallery currently under construction. *OPENING times vary. CLOSED B.hols. Free.*

Gunnersbury Park Museum

Gunnersbury Park W3. 01-992 1612. Items illustrating the local history of Ealing and Hounslow, including archaeology, costume, transport, domestic life, trades, crafts and industries. Housed in former Rothschild country mansion in large park. *OPEN Mar-Oct 13.00-17.00 Mon-Fri, 14.00-18.00 Sat & Sun; Nov-Feb 13.00-16.00 Mon-Fri, 14.00-16.00 Sat & Sun. Free.*

Hampton Court Palace

Hampton Court, Middx. 01-977 8441. Individual collection of Italian masterpieces. Giorgione, Titian, Tintoretto and early primitives. Also wall and ceiling paintings by Thornhill, Vanbrugh and Verrio. *OPEN Apr-Sep 09.30-18.00 Mon-Sat, 11.00-18.00 Sun; Oct-Mar 09.30-17.00 Mon-Sat, 14.00-17.00 Sun. Charge.*

Hayward Gallery   6   M   23

Belvedere Rd SE1. 01-928 3144. Changing exhibitions of major works of art arranged by the Arts Council. Fine modern building and river setting. *OPEN 10.00-20.00 Mon-Wed, 10.00-18.00 Thur-Sat, 12.00-18.00 Sun. Charge.*

Heinz Gallery   2   D   17

RIBA Drawings Collection, 21 Portman Sq W1. 01-580 5533. Regular exhibitions of architectural drawings. *OPEN 10.00-13.00 Mon-Fri. At other times by appt only. Free.*

Horniman Museum

100 London Rd SE23. 01-699 2339. Natural history, ethnography, musical instruments. The building of 1901 is in C.

Harrison Townsend's distinctive style. Aquarium, education centre and reference library. *OPEN 10.30-18.00 Mon-Sat, 14.00-18.00 Sun. CLOSED B.hols. Free.*

Imperial War Museum 6 Q 23
Lambeth Rd SE1. 01-735 8922. This very popular national museum has undergone a major redevelopment programme.

Imperial War Museum

Collection of models, weapons, paintings, relics on four floors with displays which bring the story of war in this century alive. The building was once a lunatic asylum. *Film shows 15.00 some Sats & Suns. OPEN 10.00-17.50 Mon-Sat, 14.00-17.50 Sun. Free.*

Institute of Contemporary 5 K 20
Arts (ICA)
Nash House, The Mall SW1. 01-930 3647. Three galleries in which changing exhibitions explore new themes and media in contemporary art. Also two cinemas, theatre, video library, lunchtime and evening talks; bar, restaurant and bookshop. *OPEN 12.00-23.00 (Galleries to 20.00) Mon-Sun. Small charge.*

Iveagh Bequest, Kenwood
Kenwood House, Hampstead La NW3. 01-348 1286. Fine house by Robert Adam. Paintings by Rembrandt, Vermeer, Reynolds and Gainsborough. Also sculpture and 18thC English furniture. Music and poetry recitals. *OPEN Apr-Sep 10.00-19.00 Mon-Sun; Oct, Feb & Mar 10.00-17.00 Mon-Sun; Nov-Jan 10.00-16.00 Mon-Sun. Free.*

Jewish Museum 3 E 25
Woburn House, Upper Woburn Pl WC1. 01-388 4525. Jewish festivals and history illustrated by attractive ceremonial objects. Two audio-visual programmes. Parties by appt. *OPEN 10.00-16.00 Tue-Fri (to 12.45 only Fri, Oct-Mar); 10.00-12.45 Sun. CLOSED Sat, Mon, B. & Jewish hols. Free.*

London Transport Museum 6 J 23
The Piazza, Covent Garden WC2. 01-379 6344. Story of London's transport. Historic road and rail vehicles, working exhibits and audio-visual displays. *OPEN 10.00-18.00 (last admission 17.15) Mon-Sun. Charge.*

Madame Tussaud's 2 B 19
Marylebone Rd NW1. 01-935 6861. Among waxwork effigies of the famous and notorious, meet Prince Andrew, Bob Geldof, Benny Hill and Mrs Thatcher. Murderers lurk in the Chamber of Horrors. 'Battle of Trafalgar' reconstruction of gun-deck of *Victory* at height of battle. *OPEN 10.00-17.30 Mon-Sun. CLOSED Xmas Day. Charge.*

Martinware Pottery Collection
Public Library, 9-11 Osterley Park Rd, Southall, Middx. 01-574 3412. Collection of Martinware, including birds, face mugs and grotesques. *OPEN 09.00-19.45 Tue, Thur & Fri, 09.00-17.00 Wed & Sat. CLOSED B.hols. Free.*

Museum of Garden History 5 P 21
St Mary-at-Lambeth, Lambeth Rd SE1. 01-261 1891. The church beside Lambeth Palace was rescued by the Tradescant Trust from demolition in the 1970s, and exhibits the discoveries and travels of the two John Tradescants, father and son, buried in the churchyard beside Captain Bligh of the *Bounty*. Successively gardeners to Charles I and Henrietta Maria, they introduced plants from abroad, some of which feature in the churchyard garden. *OPEN 11.00-15.00 Mon-Fri, 10.30-17.00 Sun. CLOSED Sat. Free.*

Museum of Instruments 1 G 10
Royal College of Music, Prince Consort Rd SW7. 01-589 3643. Almost 500 exhibits, mostly European keyboard, stringed and wind instruments from the 16th-19thC: small ethnological section includes instruments from China, Japan, India, the Middle East and Africa. *OPEN 11.00-16.30 Mon & Wed (termtime) or by appt. Charge.*

Museum of London 6 L 30
London Wall EC2. 01-600 3699. Combined collections of the former London Museum and Guildhall Museum with extra material. A 3-dimensional history of the City and London area, with models, reconstructions and even the Lord Mayor's Coach. *OPEN 10.00-18.00 Tue-Sat, 14.00-18.00 Sun. CLOSED Mon & B.hols. Free.*

Museum of Mankind 2 I 19
6 Burlington Gdns W1. 01-437 2224. Exciting collection of primitives. Changing exhibitions illustrate a variety of non-Western societies and cultures. *Film shows 13.30, 15.00 Tue-Fri. OPEN 10.00-17.00 Mon-Sat, 14.30-18.00 Sun. Free.*

Museum of the Moving 6 M 24
Image
Under Waterloo Bridge, South Bank SE1. 01-928 3535. Part of the South Bank com-

plex, this bright new museum charts the history of moving images from ancient cave paintings to film, television, video and hologram technology. Forty main exhibit areas plus changing exhibitions. Continuous programme of events in the Moving Image workshop – lectures, films, magic lantern shows. *OPEN 10.00-20.00 Tue-Sat, 10.00-18.00 Sun. CLOSED Mon. Charge.*

Musical Museum
368 High St, Brentford, Middx. 01-560 8108. The only musical museum in Europe that has 10 reproducing pianos and 3 reproducing pipe organs all under one roof (which still leaks). In all around 200 instruments, some of which will be played during the 1½ hr tours. *OPEN Apr-Oct 14.00-17.00 Sat & Sun; (also mid Jun-mid Sep 14.00-17.00 Wed-Fri). Donation. No small children. Parties by arrangement. Send sae for list of concerts.*

National Army Museum   4 N 10
Royal Hospital Rd SW3. 01-730 0717. The story of the Army from 1480 to 1982, its triumphs and disasters, its professional and social life all over the world. Uniforms, pictures, weapons and personal relics. *OPEN 10.00-17.30 Mon-Sat, 14.00-17.30 Sun. Free.*

National Gallery   5 J 21
Trafalgar Sq WC2. 01-839 3321. Very fine representative collection of various schools of painting. Includes many world famous pictures. Rich in early Italian (Leonardo da Vinci, Raphael, Botticelli and Titian), Dutch and Flemish (Rembrandt, Rubens, Frans Hals, Van Dyck), Spanish 15-18thC (Velasquez and El Greco), British 18th and 19thC (Constable, Turner, Gainsborough and Reynolds), Impressionists (Monet, Cézanne and Van Gogh). Information palettes in each room assess the pictures and sometimes describe contemporary methods of painting, instead of leaving visitors to wander clueless into yet another room of medieval triptychs, or to wonder at yet another St Sebastian shot through with arrows, and give up. An information sheet, *A Quick Visit to the National Gallery*, leads the time-pressed to 16 masterpieces. Daily guided tours highlight selected pictures. Building 1838 by W. Wilkins. *OPEN 10.00-18.00 Mon-Sat (to 20.00 Wed, Jul-Sep), 14.00-18.00 Sun. Free.*

National Maritime Museum
Romney Rd SE10. 01-858 4422. The finest maritime collection in Britain. Extensive collection of ship models, paintings, navigational instruments, costumes and weapons. The museum incorporates the Queen's House by Inigo Jones, 1616 (closed for renovation 1986-9) and the Old Royal Observatory. *OPEN summer 10.00-18.00 Mon-Sat, 14.00-18.00 Sun; winter 10.00-17.00 Mon-Sat, 14.00-17.00 Sun. CLOSED B.hols. Charge.*

National Portrait Gallery   5 J 22
2 St Martin's Pl WC2. 01-930 1552. Historic collection of contemporary portraits of famous British men and women, forming a fascinating study of human personality. Start with the Tudors on the top floor, portrayed with varying degrees of vivacity and truthfulness. Note the contrast between the Sittow portrait of Henry VII as shrewd statesman and his representation by Holbein as saintly sage. Shakespeare looks strangely modern with an earring in his left ear. Facial expressions are intense and compel attention, as do those of the nearby Stuarts whose costume and hair look less stiff. The 18thC literati include Dr Johnson and his biographer James Boswell, with floridly unromantic visage.
The Victorians dominate the first floor, arranged according to whether their designs were philanthropical, political, colonial, or artistic. The haggard faces of Thomas Carlyle, John Stuart Mill and Matthew Arnold seem better to reflect the struggle with doubt engendered by Charles Darwin's theory of evolution and the ascendancy of the machine, than the smooth young faces of Dickens and Tennyson among the early Victorians.
There are even more striking contrasts among the Edwardians such as the ruthless resolve of Kitchener, softness and sensitivity of Lawrence of Arabia, brilliance and effeteness visible in Aubrey Beardsley's portraits and the rotund avuncular presences of Gilbert and Sullivan.
Revolving displays with zippy titles – *From Vorticism to Video* is one – contribute to the

National Gallery

compelling 20thC gallery on the ground floor. Prince Charles and Princess Diana both feature here, but in separate portraits. Excellent reference section of engravings and photographs. Special exhibitions feature regularly throughout the year. *OPEN 10.00-17.00 Mon-Fri, 10.00-18.00 Sat, 14.00-18.00 Sun. CLOSED some B.hols. Free.*

National Postal Museum   6 L 29
King Edward Bldg, King Edward St EC1. 01-432 3851. Superb displays of stamps including the Phillips collection and the 'Berne' collection. Reference library. *OPEN 09.30-16.30 Mon-Thur, 09.30-16.00 Fri. CLOSED B.hols. Free.*

Natural History Museum   1 H 9
Cromwell Rd SW7. 01-938 9123. The national collections of zoology, entomology, palaeontology, mineralogy and botany. Built in Romanesque style by A. Waterhouse, 1879, and decorated with terracotta mouldings of animals and plants.

Natural History Museum

Dinosaurs are among the favourite exhibits. They tower in the central hall and the apses to the left are devoted to their evolution, lifestyle and extinction. Computer games can be played to see which animals share which characteristics, such as four bony limbs or a backbone. Visit the Hall of Human Biology and find out how your nervous system, brain and muscles function. Upstairs man meets his animal relatives and his closeness to chimpanzees and gorillas is examined. Darwin's theory of the origin of species is explored with many audio-visual aids and computers to help you get things straight. The 90ft (27.5m) model blue whale is a staggering sight among the Mammal Diversity exhibition. *OPEN 10.00-18.00 Mon-Sat, 13.00-18.00 Sun. Charge. (Free 16.30-18.00 Mon-Fri except B.hols and for educational groups booking in advance.)*

North Woolwich Station Museum
Pier Rd E16. 01-474 7244. Housed in what was North Woolwich station are three exhibition galleries telling the story of the Great Eastern Railway in photographs, plans, models, documents and relics. A GER steam locomotive built in 1876 and the restored station booking office bring the museum to life. *OPEN 10.00-17.00 Mon-Sat, 14.00-17.00 Sun & B.hols. Free.*

Old Royal Observatory
See under Greenwich in 'Historic London'.

Passmore Edwards Museum
Romford Rd E15. 01-519 4296. Collections of Essex archaeology, local history, geology and biology. Good collection of Bow porcelain. *OPEN 10.00-18.00 Mon-Fri, 10.00-17.00 Sat, 14.00-17.00 Sun & B.hols. Free.*

Percival David Foundation   3 E 24
of Chinese Art
53 Gordon Sq WC1. 01-387 3909. Chinese ceramics from Sung to Ch'ing dynasty. Reference library. *OPEN 10.30-17.00 Mon-Fri. CLOSED Sat, Sun & B.hols. Free.*

Photographers' Gallery   5 J 22
5 & 8 Great Newport St WC2. 01-240 5511. An exciting contribution to the establishment of photography in the art world. Print room, coffee bar, bookshop. *OPEN 11.00-19.00 Tue-Sat. CLOSED Sun & Mon. Free.*

Planetarium   2 B 19
Marylebone Rd NW1. 01-486 1121. Representation of the universe, with commentary. *OPEN 12.20-17.00 Mon-Fri, 10.20-17.00 Sat & Sun. Regular presentations. Charge.* Also Laserium, 01-486 2242. Laser light concerts *every night. Charge.*

Prince Henry's Room   6 K 26
17 Fleet St EC4. 01-353 7323. One of the few survivors of the Great Fire of 1666. The fine Jacobean ceiling is decorated with the three feathers of the Prince of Wales and with the initials PH (Prince Henry, elder brother of Charles I). The room also contains a small exhibition of 'Pepysiana'. *OPEN 13.45-17.00 Mon-Fri, 13.45-16.30 Sat. CLOSED Sun. Free.*

Public Record Office   6 K 26
Chancery La WC2. 01-876 3444. Permanent display of records on major events in the history of England. Also a display illustrating the story of record making and keeping. *OPEN 09.00-17.30 Mon-Sat. CLOSED Sun & B.hols.*

Queen's Gallery   5 K 17
Buckingham Palace, Buckingham Palace Rd SW1. 01-930 4832. Pictures and works of art from all parts of the Royal collection. Exhibitions changed at intervals. *OPEN 11.00-17.00 Tue-Sat, 14.00-17.00 Sun. CLOSED Mon except B.hols. Charge.*

Royal Academy of Arts 2 I 19
Burlington House, Piccadilly W1. 01-734 9052. Holds a series of major special-loan exhibitions throughout the year. Probably most famous for its annual Summer Exhibition *May-Aug*, in which the work of living artists is displayed, and in most cases on sale. *OPEN 10.00-18.00 Mon-Sun. Charge.*

Royal Air Force Museum
Grahame Park Way NW9. 01-205 2266. (*10-min walk from Colindale station on the Northern Line.*) The first national museum covering all aspects of the RAF and its predecessor the RFC. Opened November 1972 on a former wartime airfield. Aeroplanes, bits of aeroplanes, equipment, paintings, documents, etc. *OPEN 10.00-18.00 Mon-Sat, 14.00-18.00 Sun. CLOSED B.hols. Charge.*

Royal College of Surgeons 6 J 25
The Hunterian Museum, Lincoln's Inn Fields WC2. 01-405 3474. Physiology, comparative anatomy and pathology. Includes most of John Hunter's famous experiments. *OPEN (by written application only) 10.00-17.00 Mon-Fri. CLOSED Aug. Free.*

St Bride's Crypt Museum 6 L 27
St Bride's Church, Fleet St EC4. 01-353 1301. Interesting relics found during excavations. A unique continuity of remains from Roman London to the present day. *OPEN 08.30-16.30 Mon-Fri, occasionally Sat & Sun. Free.*

St Bride Printing Library 6 L 27
St Bride Institute, Bride La EC4. 01-353 4660. Early printing equipment, machinery and books in the exhibition and lecture hall of the library. *OPEN 09.00-17.30 Mon-Fri, appt only. CLOSED B.hols. Free.*

Science Museum 1 H 10
Exhibition Rd SW7. 01-589 3456. The history of science and its application to industry. A large collection of very fine engineering models, steam engines, early motor cars, aeroplanes and all aspects of applied physics and chemistry. Explore the history of printing, textiles, and many other industries through working models. Special features include space exploration, with the actual Apollo 10 space capsule and life-size reconstruction of the Apollo 11 lunar landing module. Exhibited nearby are complicated 'nappies', on board in case the astronauts needed to spend a penny while walking on the moon. The Wellcome galleries examine the history of medicine with thoroughness. A new addition to the museum is 'Launch Pad', an interactive hands-on gallery of large working models which demonstrate scientific principles. *OPEN 10.00-18.00 Mon-Sat, 14.30-18.00 Sun. CLOSED B.hols. Charge. Free lectures & films, or write for brochure.*

Serpentine Gallery 1 F 11
Kensington Gardens W2. 01-402 6075. Changing monthly exhibitions of contemporary art, sculpture, paintings, drawings and prints. *OPEN during exhibitions Apr-Sep 10.00-18.00 Mon-Fri, 10.00-19.00 Sat & Sun; Oct-Mar 10.00-dusk. Free.*

Shakespeare Globe Museum 6 O 28
1 Bear Gdns, Bankside SE1. 01-261 1353. Converted 18thC warehouse on site of 16thC bear-baiting ring and the Hope Playhouse. Formerly the Bear Gardens Museum. Permanent exhibition of Shakespearian theatre and plans for future Globe Theatre reconstruction. The theatre is scheduled for completion in Spring 1992. *OPEN 10.30-16.30 Sat, 13.30-18.00 Sun; weekday times under review, phone for details. Charge.*

St John Soane's Museum 3 I 25
13 Lincoln's Inn Fields WC2. 01-405 2107. Soane's personal collection of antiquities, paintings and drawings, including Hogarth's *Election* and the *Rake's Progress*, original Piranesi drawings and most of the architectural drawings of the Adam brothers. Building designed by Soane, 1812. *OPEN 10.00-17.00 Tue-Sat. Free lecture tour 14.30 Sat (limited to 25 people, no parties. Parties welcome at other times by arrangement). CLOSED B.hols. Free. Library, appt only.*

South London Art Gallery
Peckham Rd SE5. 01-703 6120. Holds 9 or 10 varied exhibitions per year, each lasting three weeks. Founded in 1891, it was the first gallery to open on a Sun. *OPEN during exhibitions 10.00-18.00 Tue-Sat, 15.00-18.00 Sun. CLOSED Mon, B.hols & Aug. Free.*

Tate Gallery 5 P 18
Millbank SW1. 01-821 1313. Information line: 01-821 7128. Representative collections of British painting from the 16thC to the present day; fine examples of Blake, Turner, Hogarth, the pre-Raphaelites, Ben Nicolson, Spencer and Francis Bacon; sculpture by Moore and Hepworth. Also a particularly rich collection of foreign paintings and sculpture from 1880 to the present day, including paintings by Picasso, Chagall, Mondrian, Pollock, Lichtenstein, Rothko, Degas, Marini and Giacometti. Designed 1897 by Sidney H. J. Smith. The

Tate Gallery

Clore Gallery, opened in spring 1987, was built to house the Turner bequest. *OPEN 10.00-17.50 Mon-Sat, 14.00-17.50 Sun. Lectures at various times. Free.*

Theatre Museum   6   J   23
le Tavistock St WC2. 01-831 1227. Outpost of the V & A. Devoted to the theatre: costumes, playbills, scenery, props. *OPEN 11.00-19.00 Tue-Sun. Charge.*

Tower of London, the   6   Q   32
Armouries
Tower Hill EC3. 01-709 0765. The Crown Jewels (heavily guarded). Largest collection of armour and arms in Britain: 10-20thC. *OPEN 09.30-17.45 Mon-Sat (to 16.00 winter), 14.00-17.45 Sun. CLOSED Sun in winter & B.hols. Charge.*

University College: Petrie   3   E   23
Museum of Egyptian Archaeology
Gower St WC1. 01-387 7050. Includes the collections of Amelia Edwards, Sir Flinders Petrie and part of Sir Henry Wellcome's collection. *OPEN 10.00-12.00 & 13.15-17.00 Mon-Fri. CLOSED Sat, Sun & B.hols. Free.*

Victoria and Albert Museum   1   H   10
Cromwell Rd SW7. 01-938 8500. The V & A is Britain's National Museum of Art and Design and has some of the world's finest collections of furniture, ceramics and glass, metalwork and jewellery, textiles and dress from the Middle Ages to the 20thC, as well as paintings, prints and drawings, posters and photographs, and sculpture. It also has superb collections from China, Japan, India and the Middle East. There is a full programme of courses, events and introductory tours. *OPEN 10.00-17.50 Mon-Sat, 14.30-17.50 Sun. Admission by voluntary donation.*

Wallace Collection   2   D   18
Hertford House, Manchester Sq W1. 01-935 0687. A private collection of outstanding works of art which was bequeathed to the nation by Lady Wallace in 1897. Splendid representation of the French 17th and 18thC artists, including many paintings by Boucher, Watteau and Fragonard. There are also several Rembrandts, a Titian, some Rubens, and paintings by Canaletto and Guardi. Important collections of French furniture, Sèvres porcelain, Majolica, Limoges enamel and armour. Also a fine collection of Bonnington oils and watercolours. *OPEN 10.00-17.00 Mon-Sat, 14.00-17.00 Sun. CLOSED some B.hols. Free.*

Westminster Abbey   5   N   20
Treasures
The Cloisters, Westminster Abbey SW1. 01-222 5152. Reopened in spring 1987 after major redecoration, the Cloisters contain the famous wax effigies of British monarchs including Elizabeth I and Charles II, and Admiral Lord Nelson. Also plans, paintings, prints and documents. Forms part of a new complex with the Chapter House and the Chapter of Pyx. *OPEN 09.30-18.00 Mon-Sun (to 16.30 mid Oct-mid Mar). Charge.*

Whitechapel Art Gallery
80 Whitechapel High St E1. 01-377 0107. Frequent public exhibitions of great interest. The Whitechapel has successfully introduced new ideas in modern art into London. *OPEN 11.00-17.00 Tue & Thur-Sun, 11.00-20.00 Wed. CLOSED Mon & B. hols. Free.*

Wimbledon Lawn Tennis Museum
Church Rd SW19. 01-946 6131. Display of tennis through the ages including equipment, dresses, photographs. Also a library of tennis literature. *OPEN 11.00-17.00 Tue-Sat, 14.00-17.00 Sun. CLOSED Mon & B.hols. Charge.*

Zamana Gallery   1   I   10
1 Cromwell Gdns SW7. 01-584 6612. Opposite the V & A, this gallery is part of the beautifully designed Ismaili Centre. Holds three to four exhibitions a year concentrating on art and architecture in the Islamic and developing world. Bookshop. *OPEN 10.00-17.30 Tue-Sat, 12.00-17.30 Sun. CLOSED Mon. Charge.*

Outdoor London

Parks and gardens

London is particularly rich in parks, gardens, commons, forests and heathland with over 80 parks within 7 miles of Piccadilly. They are all that remain of early London's natural surrounding countryside. Many follow river courses and contain lakes and ponds. Left by accident, gift, or long-sighted social intention, they are a welcome breathing space for the Londoner. The 10 royal parks are still the property of the Crown and were originally the grounds of royal homes or palaces. See under 'Children's London' for Playparks and One o'clock clubs.

Alexandra Park & Palace N22
01-365 2121. The Victorian Palace reopened in Jan 1988 following major redevelopment. Set in 196 acres (79.4ha) of parkland overlooking London skyline, the Palace is an exhibition, entertainments and leisure venue. Attractions include a boating lake, pitch & putt, animal enclosure, children's playground, conservation area and arboretum. *OPEN 24 hrs.*

Avery Hill SE9
Bexley Rd SE9. 01-850 2666. The Winter Garden is a second, smaller Kew. Tropical and sub-tropical Asian and Australasian plants in greenhouses. Tennis courts. *OPEN summer 13.00-16.00 Mon-Fri. 11.00-18.00 Sat & Sun; winter 11.00-16.00 Sat & Sun. Park OPEN 07.00-1/2hr before dusk (or 21.00).*

Battersea Park SW11   4 P 8
01-871 7530. An interesting riverside park of 200 acres (81ha). Boating lake, deer park and children's zoo. The London Peace Pagoda which stands close to the river was built by monks and nuns of the Japanese Buddhist order Nipponzan Myohoji and completed in 1985. Based on ancient Indian and Japanese designs, it stands at 110 ft (33.5m) and has a double roof. The park also contains a botanical wild-flower garden, Alpine showhouse, herb garden and greenhouse. Famous Easter parade. *OPEN Easter-Sep dawn-dusk. Greenhouse OPEN 09.30-dusk. Playing fields, athletics track, tennis courts OPEN 06.00-dusk. Floodlit football pitch.*

Blackheath SE3
01-305 1807 (for the area north of the A2,

Shooters Hill). 01-852 1762 (for the area to the south). 275 acres (111.4ha) of open grassland jointly administered by the boroughs of Lewisham and Greenwich and used for general recreation. Ideal for kite-flying and watching the sunset. Good views in all directions especially from Point Hill in the north-west. Play soccer and cricket, sail model boats on Prince of Wales pond. Migratory birds in winter particularly sea-gulls. Occasional circus, festivals. Funfairs at Easter, spring and late summer B.hols. The London Marathon held *every* spring starts from here. The *summer* horse show, aimed at the younger rider, may become an annual event. *OPEN 24 hrs.*

Bostall Heath SE2
01-311 1674. Woods and heath. Fine views of London and the river's dockland. *Bowling green OPEN Apr-Sep 13.30-20.30 Mon-Sat. 10.30-20.30 Sun. Heath OPEN 24 hrs.*

Brockwell Park SE24
Dulwich Rd SE24. 01-674 6141. Fine old English garden with yew hedges. *OPEN 09.00-dusk.*

Clissold Park N16
01-800 1021. Originally a private estate, it was bought by the LCC at the turn of the century and the mansion surrounded by gardens still survives. 54 acres (21.9ha) including a fishing lake, bowling green, playpark for children, croquet lawn, flower garden, rose garden and many chestnut trees which are splendid in spring. Also an aviary of tropical birds; fallow deer graze here. *OPEN 07.00-dusk.*

Crystal Palace SE20
01-778 7148. Named after Paxton's 1851 Great Exhibition building removed here from Hyde Park and unfortunately burnt to the ground in 1936. Now a National Youth & Sports Centre with an Olympic swimming pool and fine modern sports stadium in an open park of 70 acres (28.4ha) on a hill with good views. Has boating and fishing lake. Four islands in the lake are 'colonised' by 20 life-sized replicas of primeval animals, iguanodon, megalosaurus, pterodactyls and primitive reptiles – designed by Richard Owen, 1854. Children's zoo, adventure playground and under-5 play area. Artificial ski slope. *OPEN 08.00-1/2hr before dusk.*

Danson Park
Bexleyheath, Kent. 01-303 7777. Pleasant

200-acre (81ha) park with large lake. 'Old English' garden, rock garden, aviary. Landscaped about 1760 by Capability Brown, Palladian mansion by Sir Robert Taylor, 1756. Wide variety of recreational facilities, including boating and windsurfing. *OPEN 07.30-sunset Mon-Fri. 09.00-sunset Sat & Sun.*

Dulwich Park SE21
01-693 5737. Famous for its rhododendrons and azaleas. A favourite garden of the Queen Mary, wife of George V. Boating lake and tennis courts. Tree trail. The only park in London to produce maps in braille in addition to the more conventional ones. *OPEN 07.30-21.00 summer, 07.30-16.30 winter.*

Eltham Park SE9
01-850 2031. Split by a railway line into two sections, the south is recreational open space but the north is woodland: oaks, chestnuts, birches, bluebells, anemones. The ornamental pond complete with ducks commands a view right across to central London. *OPEN 24 hrs.*

Epping Forest, Essex
6000 acres (2430ha) of natural woodland, six miles long and two miles wide stretching from Chingford to Epping. Opened to the public in 1878, it was 'dedicated to the delectation of the public forever.' Many hornbeam, oak, ash, maple, beech and birch trees; it also offers a superb variety of all kinds of natural life – so many grey squirrels that they have become a problem. High Beech is a popular spot and there are large areas to ramble through where you can get thoroughly lost, or even stumble upon the remains of two ancient British camps at least 2000 years old – Loughton Camp and Ambersbury Banks.

Finsbury Park N4
01-263 5001. 115 acres (46.6ha) opened in 1869. Many sports played – soccer, cricket, fishing, bowling, tennis, boating. Also two children's playgrounds, nursery, tea-room, car park and an athletics track. London plane trees predominate. The oldest aqueduct in London runs through the park and there is a reservoir underground. *OPEN 06.30-1/2hr after sunset.*

Greenwich Park SE10
01-858 2608. A royal park of 200 acres (81ha) with pleasant avenues lined with chestnut trees, sloping down to the Thames. Impressive views of the river, the shipping and the two classical buildings: the Queen's House by Inigo Jones and the Royal Naval College (once a Tudor royal palace). Contains also the Old Royal Observatory and its pleasant garden. 13 acres (5.3ha) of wooded deer park, a bird sanctuary and Bronze age tumuli. *OPEN 07.00 (for traffic, 05.00 for pedestrians)-22.00 summer, 07.00-18.00 (or dusk) winter.*

Hainault Forest, Essex
01-500 3106. Formerly part of the great forest of Essex, or Waltham Forest. Now a Country Park of 1100 acres (445.5ha) of extensive woodland, with a lake, two 18-hole golf courses, a playing field and facilities for angling, riding, picnicking, cross-country running and orienteering. *OPEN 24 hrs.*

Hampstead Heath NW3
01-485 4491/01-455 5183. Open, hilly 800 acres (324ha) of park and woods. Fine views of London. Foxes can sometimes be seen. Crowded on Bank holidays with visitors to the famous fair and the equally famous pubs – the Bull & Bush, the Spaniards and Jack Straw's Castle. Includes Parliament Hill, Golders Hill (containing a fine English town garden) and Kenwood. Ponds, open-air concerts in summer, 10 tennis courts. Olympic track, orienteering, grass skiing, cricket, football, rugby, rounders, putting green, horse riding (for permit holders). Also swimming in Hampstead Ponds (01-485 3873), a children's zoo at Golders Hill, and much of interest to the ornithologist (over 100 species). *OPEN 24 hrs. Kenwood and Golders Hill CLOSED at night.*

Hampton Court & Bushy Park, Middx
01-977 1328. 2000 acres (810ha) of royal park bounded on two sides by the Thames. Hampton is the formal park of the great Tudor palace with ancient courts, superb flower gardens, the famous maze and the 'great vine' planted in 1768 during the reign of George III. Bushy Park is natural parkland with an artificial plantation, aquatic plants and ponds. Two herds of deer, one of red deer, the other fallow deer, run in the park. Both parks have many fine avenues including the mile-long Chestnut Avenue with 'Diana' fountain in Bushy Park. Hampton Court itself is described under 'Historic buildings'. *OPEN 07.45-dusk.*

Holland Park W8   1   B   5
01-602 2226. Behind Kensington High St. 55 acres (22.3ha) of calm and secluded lawns and gardens with peacocks. Once the private park of Holland House (partially restored after bombing during the war). Dutch garden dating from 1812 with fine tulip displays. Also iris and rose gardens, yucca lawn and the Orangery in which

during *May-Sep* craft fairs, art exhibitions and other events are held. On the north side is a remarkable woodland of 28 acres (11.3ha) containing 3000 species of rare British trees and plants, full of birds – woodpeckers, owls, peafowl and British birds generally. Exotic species include Muscovy ducks and Polish bantams, distinguished by feathers on their feet. Open-air theatre in summer. Squash and tennis courts. *OPEN 08.00-sunset summer. 08.00-dusk winter. Flower garden OPEN to 24.00 and illuminated at night.*

Hyde Park W1 2 E 16

01-262 5484. A royal park since 1536, it was once part of the forest reserved by Henry VIII for hunting wild boar and bulls. Queen Elizabeth I held military reviews here (still held on special occasions). It was the haunt of highwaymen until 1750 and even today is patrolled at night by police. The Great Exhibition of 1851 designed by Paxton was held opposite Prince of Wales Gate. Hyde Park now has 340 acres (137.7ha) of parkland, walks, Rotten Row for horse-riders, and the Serpentine – a fine lake for boating and swimming. The Serpentine Bridge is by George Rennie, 1826. The famous Speakers' Corner is near Marble Arch – public executions were held at Tyburn gallows nearby until 1783. Good open-air bar and restaurant overlooking the lake (near the bridge). *OPEN 06.00-24.00. The Lido OPEN May-Sep & B.hols 10.00-18.00. Charge for swimming.*

Kensington Gardens W8 1 D 10

01-937 4848. A formal and elegant addition to Hyde Park. 275 acres (111.4ha) of royal park containing William III's lovely Kensington Palace, Queen Anne's Orangery, the peaceful 'Sunken Garden' nearby, the Round Pond with its busy model sailing-boats, and, on the south, the magnificently Victorian Albert Memorial. The famous Broad Walk, originally flanked by ancient elms, is now replanted with fragrant limes and maples and the nearby 'Flower Walk' is the home of wild birds, woodpeckers, flycatchers and tree-creepers. 'Jubilee Walk', running down the west side of the park, was completely blown down in Oct 1987. Queen Caroline produced both the Long Water (Peter Pan's statue is here) and the Serpentine by ordering the damming of the Westbourne river. A stone balustrade separates the Long Water from formal ponds and fountains. Good children's playground. *OPEN 07.00-1/2hr before dusk.*

Lesnes Abbey Woods SE2

01-310 2777. Commemorates the former 800-year-old abbey, now excavated. Woods and open ground with good views. 20 acres (8.1ha) of wild daffodils in the spring. Café. *OPEN 08.00-16.30 winter. 08.00-20.00 (or dusk) summer.*

Osterley Park

Isleworth, Middx. 01-560 3918. Used to be the private estate of the Earl of Jersey, part of it is still farmland. Also incorporates a bird sanctuary. An open park but some cedars and cork trees. Osterley House is a classic building designed by Robert Adam. *OPEN 11.00-17.00 (last admission 16.30) Tue-Sun. CLOSED Mon. Charge. Park OPEN 10.00-sunset. Free.*

Peckham Rye Park SE15

01-693 3791. Open park with good English, Japanese and water gardens. Sporting facilities include bowling, tennis and football. *OPEN 06.00-1/2hr after sunset.*

Primrose Hill NW8

01-486 7905. A minor royal park of simple grassy hill 200ft (61m) high giving a fine view over London. Children's play areas and a boating lake. Puppet shows in summer. *OPEN 24 hrs.*

Regent's Park NW1 2 B 21

01-486 7905. A royal park of 470 acres (190.4ha), it was originally part of Henry VIII's great hunting forest in the 16thC. The Prince Regent in 1811 planned to connect the park (and a new palace) via the newly built Regent Street to Carlton House. Although never fully completed, the design (1812-26) by John Nash is of great distinction, the park being surrounded by handsome Regency terraces and imposing gateways. Contains London Zoo, the Regent's Canal, a fine boating lake with 30 species of birds, a bandstand, fragrant flower gardens in the Outer Circle and the very fine Queen Mary's rose garden within Nash's Inner Circle. Open-air theatre. Restaurant and cafeterias. Sports facilities include football, baseball and rugby. There are also tennis courts and a running track. *OPEN 05.00 (or dawn)-dusk.*

Richmond Park, Surrey

01-948 3209. A royal park of 2500 acres (1012.5ha) first enclosed as a hunting ground by Charles I in 1637. Retains all the qualities of a great English feudal estate – a natural open park of spinneys and plantations, bracken and ancient oaks (survivors of the great oak forests of the Middle Ages) and over 600 red and fallow deer. Badgers, weasels and the occasional fox can be seen. The Pen Ponds are well stocked with fish. Fine views of the Thames valley from White Lodge (early 18thC and once a royal residence) and the restaurant of Pembroke Lodge. Golf, riding, polo, football. *OPEN 07.00-1/2hr before dusk (from 07.30 in winter).*

Royal Botanic Gardens, Kew
Kew Road, Richmond, Surrey. 01-940 1171. Superb botanical gardens of 300 acres (121.5ha). Founded in 1759 by Princess Augusta. Delightful natural gardens and woods bounded by the river on one side, and stocked with thousands of flowers and trees. Many fascinating hot-houses for orchids, palms, ferns, cacti and alpine plants. *Hothouses OPEN at 10.00.* Also a lake, aquatic garden and pagoda were designed by Sir William Chambers in 1760 and the magnificent curved glass palm house and temperate house, 1844-8, are by Decimus Burton. Its scientific aspect was developed by its two directors Sir William and Sir Joseph Hooker and the many famous botanists who worked here. 17thC Queen's Garden with formal rose-bed. Cafeteria and gift shop in the Orangery. *OPEN 09.30-dusk (or 20.00) summer. Small charge.*

St James' Park & Green   5 K 18
Park SW1
01-930 1793. The oldest royal park, acquired in 1532 by Henry VIII, laid out in imitation 'Versailles' style by Charles II, finally redesigned in the grand manner for George IV by John Nash in the 1820s. A most attractive park, with fine promenades and walks, and a romantic Chinese-style lake, bridge, and weeping willows. The bird sanctuary on Duck Island has some magnificent pelicans and over 20 species of duck and goose. Good views of Buckingham Palace, the grand sweep of Carlton House Terrace, the domes and spires of Whitehall and, to the south, Westminster Abbey. The Mall and Constitution Hill are frequently part of ceremonial and royal occasions. *OPEN dawn-24.00.*

Shooters Hill SE18
01-856 1015. Hundreds of acres of woods and open parkland containing Oxleas Woods, Jackwood and Eltham Parks. Castlewood has a folly erected 1784 to Sir William James for his exploits in India. *OPEN 24 hrs.*

Streatham Common SW16
01-764 5478. The Rookery was formerly the garden of an 18thC mansion; rock garden, wild garden, a 'white' garden and

splendid old cedars. *Common OPEN 24 hrs. Rookery 09.00-dusk.*

Trent Park, Enfield
01-449 8706. Formerly part of the royal hunting forest Enfield Chase. Now a country park of 413 acres (167.3ha) of woodland and grassland, with a water garden, two lakes, animal enclosure, a nature trail, horse rides and several new self-guided trails. Guided walks throughout the year. Picnic facilities and a trail for the blind. *OPEN 24 hrs.*

Victoria Embankment   5 M 21
Gardens WC2
The joy of the lunchtime office worker on a fine summer day. Banked flowers, a band, shady trees, deckchairs and a crowded open-air café.

Victoria Park E9
01-985 1957. With 217 acres (87.9ha) and a 4-mile perimeter, this park was known as 'the lung of the East End'; it is also the oldest, established in 1845 by Sir James Pennythorne. Several historical buildings survive; of note are two alcoves from the original London Bridge which were placed at the east end of the park in 1861, a splendid drinking fountain erected for Burdett Coutts, and two gate pillars at Bonner Bridge. The four gate lodges also date back to 1850. Of natural interest are planes, oaks, birches, hawthorns, cherries, honey locusts, gladitsia, a Kentucky coffee tree and a bitter orange. A wide variety of sports. Also fallow deer, guinea pigs, rabbits and various fowl. Old time dancing *Aug 09.30-21.00 Wed & Sat;* children's shows *11.00 or 15.00 summer hols;* funfairs *Apr, May, Aug (not B.hols). OPEN 06.00-1/2hr after sunset.*

Waterlow Park N6
01-272 2825. Presented by Sir Sidney Waterlow to the people of London in 1889. Contains Lauderdale House (Nell Gwynn lived here) and the site of Andrew Marvell's house. 26 acres (10.5ha). Park, ponds and an aviary. *OPEN 07.30-dusk.*

Wimbledon Common SW19
01-788 7655. 1100 acres (445.5ha), including Putney Heath, comprising wild woodland, open heath and several ponds. Golf course, 16 miles of horse rides. Playing fields. Bronze age remains. Rare and British flora. Protected by act of 1871 as a 'wild area' for perpetuity. Famous old 19thC windmill, composite smock and post type, with a museum inside, *OPEN Apr-Oct 14.00-17.00 Sat, Sun & B.hols.* Park *OPEN 24 hrs. Cars not admitted after dusk.*

Botanic gardens and arboreta

Remember that many of the London parks have living botanical collections; Holland Park has a good arboretum, and others have bog gardens, rock gardens, and extensive rose gardens. Queen Mary's Rose Garden in Regent's Park is particularly fine. Most of the 'great houses' have fine collections of plants, often specialising in one botanical aspect. Also some of the specialist commercial nurseries are almost miniature botanical gardens; for instance Syon Park in Surrey.

Avery Hill

Bexley Rd SE9. 01-850 2666. A second, smaller Kew. Good collection of tropical and temperate Asian and Australasian plants in glasshouses, including a selection of economic crops. *OPEN 13.00-16.00 Mon-Fri, 11.00-18.00 (16.00 in winter) Sat & Sun. Park OPEN 07.00-dusk (or 21.00). Free.*

Bedgebury National Pinetum

Goudhurst, Kent. Goudhurst 212060. First planted in 1924. The forest consists of over 200 species of temperate zone cone-bearing trees laid out in genera. Of great use to foresters and botanists, it is sited in the lovely undulating countryside of the Weald of Kent. *OPEN 10.00-dusk. Charge.*

Borde Hill Arboretum

Haywards Heath, W. Sussex. Haywards Heath 450326. Created by Col Stephenson R. Clarke at the end of the 19thC. The garden and park now extend to nearly 400 acres (162ha). Comprehensive collections of native and exotic trees and shrubs from Eastern Asia. *OPEN Apr-Oct 10.00-18.00 Tue-Thur, Sat, Sun & B.hols. Small charge.*

Cambridge University Botanic Garden

Bateman St, Cambridge. Cambridge 350101. The first garden was established in 1761, moved to its present 40-acre (16.2ha) site 3/4 mile south of the city in 1846. Extensive collection of living plants; fine specimens of trees and shrubs; glasshouses, pinetum, ecological area, chronological bed, scented garden and geographically arranged alpine garden. *OPEN May-Sep 08.00-18.00 Mon-Sat, 14.30-18.30 Sun; Oct-Apr 08.00-16.00 (or dusk) Mon-Sat. Glasshouse 11.00-12.30 & 14.00-16.00 Mon-Sat, 14.00-16.00 Sun. Free.*

Chelsea Physic Garden   4 **N 10**

Royal Hospital Rd, Chelsea SW3. 01-352 5646. Founded in 1673 by the Society of Apothecaries; second oldest botanical garden in UK. Contains fine old trees. Plants grown mainly for teaching purposes. *OPEN Apr-Oct 14.00-17.00 Wed, Sun & other times by appt. Charge.*

Oxford Botanic Garden

Rose La, by Magdalen Bridge, Oxford. Oxford 242737. Oldest botanical garden in Britain founded in 1621 by Henry, Lord Danvers. About 3 acres (1.2ha) within high stone walls, another 3 acres (1.2ha) outside pleasantly situated by the river. Glasshouses, rock garden, some notable trees. Entrance arch by Inigo Jones. *OPEN summer 08.30-17.00 Mon-Sat, 10.00-12.00 & 14.00-18.00 Sun; winter 09.00-16.30 Mon-Sat, 10.00-12.00 & 14.00-16.30 Sun. Greenhouses OPEN 14.00-16.00 Mon-Sun. Free.*

Royal Botanic Gardens, Kew

Kew Rd, Richmond, Surrey. 01-940 1171. One of the world's great botanical gardens. Famous for its natural collections, identification of rare plants, economic botany and scientific research. Nearly 300 acres (121.5ha) of pure aesthetic pleasure. Arboretum, alpine, water and rhododendron gardens. Magnificent tropical orchid, palm, temperate and Australasian houses. Herbarium contains Sir Joseph Hooker's famous *HMS Erebus* and Indian plant collections. Library of rare books on botany and exploration. Kew has been associated with many famous botanists: the Aitons, Sir Joseph Banks, the Hookers and others. *OPEN 10.00-dusk or 20.00 summer. Small charge.*

Savill Garden, Windsor Great Park

Windsor 860222. Approach by Englefield Green. Created by Sir Eric Savill in 1930s. Outstanding woodland garden together with large collections of roses, herbaceous plants and alpines, in 35 acres (14.2ha) and with a lake. *OPEN 10.00-dusk daily throughout the year. Charge.*

Sheffield Park Garden

Nr Uckfield, E. Sussex. Danehill 790655. Gardens with five lakes and house by James Wyatt. Magnificent rhododendrons and azaleas in May and June. Brilliant autumn colours with maples and other shrubs. *OPEN Apr-Nov 11.00-dusk (or 18.00) Tue-Sat, 14.00-dusk (or 18.00) Sun & B.hols. CLOSED Tue following B.hol Mon. Charge.*

Syon Park

Brentford, Middx. 01-560 0881. 55 acres (22.3ha) of gardens surrounding a 16thC mansion house designed by Robert Adam.

The Great Conservatory has orchids. Beautiful lakeside walk and garden sculpture. Garden centre. Vintage motor museum and Butterfly House. *OPEN 10.00-17.00 Mon-Fri, 10.00-17.30 Sat & Sun.*

Wakehurst Place
Ardingly, W. Sussex. Ardingly 892701. A very lovely 500-acre (202.5ha) 'satellite' garden to the Royal Botanic Gardens at Kew; chosen because of its humid climate, clear air, lakes and running streams, and its variety of soils. The open woodland and high forest contain large numbers of rare trees, shrubs and plants from all over the world, particularly from Chile, SE Asia and New Zealand. *OPEN Apr-Sep 10.00-19.00 Mon-Sun; Oct-Mar 10.00-16.00 Mon-Sun. Charge.*

Wisley Gardens
Wisley, Surrey. Guildford 224163. A fine 240-acre (97.2ha) horticultural garden originally created by C. F. Wilson as a wild and woodland garden, acquired by the Royal Horticultural Society in 1904. Famous for its trials and improvements of new varieties. Greenhouses and pinetum. Notable collections of old-fashioned and new roses, rhododendrons, camellias, heathers, rock garden plants and bulbs from the Near East. *OPEN summer 10.00-19.00 Mon-Sun. Last admission 18.15. (Members of RHS only 10.00-14.00 Sun.) Winter 10.00-dusk. Charge.*

Zoos and aquaria

All zoos ask visitors not to bring dogs.

Aquaria

Brighton Aquarium
Marine Pde & Madeira Dri (opp Palace Pier), Brighton, E. Sussex. Brighton 604233. Oldest public aquarium in Britain containing 48 tanks of marine and freshwater fish. Main feature is the Dolphinarium: at feeding times the dolphins perform, including 'walking' on the waters of the pool. *OPEN 10.00-17.00 Mon-Sun. Charge.*

The London Zoo Aquarium 2 A 21
Regent's Park NW1. 01-722 3333. Marine and Tropical Halls. Excellently lit and displayed. A well-stocked aquarium of both sea and freshwater fish and amphibians from European and tropical waters. Particularly notable are the fine sea fish, the octopus and stingrays. *OPEN Apr-Sep*
09.00-18.00 Mon-Sun (09.00-19.00 B.hols and Sun preceding); Oct-Mar 10.00-16.00 Mon-Sun. CLOSED Xmas Day. Charge.*

Zoos: London

The London Zoo 2 A 21
Regent's Park NW1. 01-722 3333. This famous zoo has one of the largest collections of animals in the world. Excellent aviary designed by Lord Snowdon and a 'Moonlight Hall' where day and night are reversed and rarely seen nocturnal animals are kept awake during the day. The zoo was originally laid out by Decimus Burton in 1827; since then many famous architects have designed special animal houses. First-class children's zoo. *OPEN Apr-Sep 09.00-18.00 Mon-Sun (09.00-19.00 B.hols and Sun preceding); Oct-Mar 10.00-16.00 Mon-Sun. CLOSED Xmas Day. Charge.*

Zoos: out of London

Chessington World of Adventures
Leatherhead Rd, Chessington, Surrey. Epsom 27227. A zoo of 65 acres (26.3ha) on outskirts of London. Spectacular family rides set in specially designed areas – The Mystic East, Calamity Canyon, The Fifth Dimension. A monorail travels above the zoo which includes a bird garden, children's zoo and polar bear plunge. *OPEN Apr-Oct (all attractions) 10.00-17.00 Mon-Sun; Nov-Mar (zoo only) 10.00-16.00 Mon-Sun. CLOSED Xmas Day. Charge.*

Colchester Zoo
Standway Hall, Colchester, Essex. Colchester 330253. A good general collection, including an aquarium and reptile house. 40 acres (16.2ha). London 50 miles (A12). *OPEN 09.30-dusk Mon-Sun. Charge.*

Cotswold Wild Life Park
Bradwell Gro, nr Burford, Oxon. Burford 3006. Set in 120 acres (48.6ha) of garden and woodland. Tropical birds, rhinos, zebras and otters. Reptile house. Tropical marine aquarium. *OPEN 10.00-dusk(or 18.00) Mon-Sun. CLOSED Xmas Day. Charge.*

Howletts Zoo Park
Bekesbourne, nr Canterbury, Kent. Hythe 60618. 55 acres (22.3ha) of zoo park including the largest collection of gorillas and tigers in the world. Selection of cats including leopards; African elephants, deer, monkeys. London 60 miles (A2). *OPEN Apr-Oct 10.00-17.00 Mon-Sun; Nov-Mar 10.00-dusk (or 16.00) Mon-Sun. Charge.*

Linton Zoo

Hadstock Rd, Linton, Cambs. Cambridge 891308. A wonderful combination of beautiful gardens and wildlife from all over the world set in over 10 acres (4.1ha) of grassland. Animals include lions, leopards, panthers, reptiles, tarantulas. *OPEN 10.00-dusk Mon-Sun. Charge.*

Longleat Lion Reserve

Warminster, Wilts. Maiden Bradley 328. Visitors to the magnificent Renaissance house can choose to drive through the game park where lions roam at will. You can stop your car and watch in safety but it is extremely foolhardy to get out, however friendly the lions seem. Also has a chimpanzee island. No soft-topped cars allowed. *OPEN mid Mar-Oct 10.00-17.30 Mon-Sun. Charge.*

Longleat House

Marwell Zoological Park

Colden Common, Nr Winchester, Hants. Owslebury 406. 100 acres (40.5 ha) of park with a two-mile road system. Specialises in breeding endangered wildlife species – big cats, wild horses and asses, scimitar-horned oryx. Also a semi-aquatic mammal house. London 70 miles (M3). *OPEN 10.00-18.00 (or 1hr before dusk) Mon-Sun. CLOSED Xmas Day. Charge.*

Mole Hall Wildlife Park

Mole Hall, Widdington, nr Newport, Essex. Saffron Walden 40400. In grounds of moated manor. 25 acres (10.1 ha) of grass. Animals include chimps, otters, llamas, wallabies and flamingos. Butterfly House, pets corner, picnic and play areas, café and shop. London 35 miles (A11). *OPEN 10.30-18.00 (or dusk) Mon-Sun. Charge.*

Port Lympne Zoo Park

Port Lympne, Lympne, nr Hythe, Kent. Hythe 60618. 270 acres (109.4 ha) of spaciously laid out animal park, including 15 acres (6.1 ha) of splendid terraced gardens and Sir Philip Sassoon's historic house. Siberian and Indian tigers, black rhinos, Indian elephants, black panthers, antelope, deer, capucin monkeys, timber wolves. London 60 miles (M20). *OPEN Apr-Oct 10.00-17.00 Mon-Sun; Nov-Mar 10.00-dusk Mon-Sun. Charge.*

Whipsnade Park Zoo

Dunstable, Beds. Whipsnade 872171. A 500-acre (202.5 ha) 'natural' zoo of woods and downland in the Chilterns. Over 2000 animals in large open-air enclosures. Some species roam freely throughout the park. You can picnic in the grounds – take binoculars or use the telescopes provided. Travel within the park in your own car or by miniature motor-coach train. London 35 miles (M1). *OPEN 10.00-dusk (or 18.00) Mon-Fri, 10.00-dusk (or 19.00) Sat & Sun. Charge.*

Windsor Safari Park

Winkfield Rd, Windsor, Berks. Windsor 869841. Drive round the park in the car (long queues in summer) with windows closed, to see the many wild animals. Walks through the tropical plant and butterfly house, chimpanzee enclosure. Noah's Ark adventure centre. Killer-whale, dolphin, sea-lion and parrot shows. *OPEN 10.00-dusk Mon-Sun. Charge.*

Woburn Wild Animal Kingdom & Leisure Park

Woburn, Beds. Woburn 290407. Britain's largest drive-through safari park. Rare European bison, wallabies, llamas, rheas and other animals roam freely. Sea lions, parrot shows and elephant displays. Leisure area with rides, boating lakes, cable car. The 3000-acre (1215ha) park surrounding the Abbey, which is separate from the Animal Kingdom, contains the original herd of Père David deer, saved from extinction by the 11th Duke of Bedford. London 40 miles (M1). *OPEN mid Mar-end Oct 10.00-17.00 Mon-Sun. Charge.*

Animal enclosures in parks

See under 'Children's London'.

Aviaries and wildfowl collections

There are good aviaries at London Zoo and Chessington. Several London parks have small aviaries, notably Brockwell, Clissold, Dulwich, Victoria and Waterlow parks.

Arundel Wildfowl Refuge

Arundel, W. Sussex. Arundel 883355. Extensive Wildfowl Trust collection of outstanding merit with sea-duck a speciality. Wildfowl are attracted here in winter by special feeding programmes. Restaurant and gift shop. *OPEN summer 09.30-18.30 (last admission 17.30) Mon-Sun; winter*

09.30-dusk *Mon-Sun. CLOSED Xmas Day. Charge.*

Bentley Wildfowl Collection
Halland, Lewes, E. Sussex. Halland 573. Private wildfowl collection of 23 acres (10.1ha) with accent on conservation. London 50 miles (A22). *OPEN Mar-Oct 10.00-17.00 (to 17.30 Jul & Aug) Mon-Sun; Nov-Feb 10.30-16.30 Sat & Sun. Last admission ½hr before closing. CLOSED Jan. Charge.*

Birdworld The Bird Park
Holt Pound, on a A325 nr Farnham, Surrey. Bentley 22140. Birds from all over the world living almost naturally in landscaped gardens. Flamingoes, loris, Indian peafowl and penguins among many species. 'Seashore' with waves for seabirds. *OPEN summer 09.30-19.00 (last admission 18.00) Mon-Sun; winter 09.30-dusk Mon-Sun. Charge.*

Child-Beale Wildlife Trust
Church Farm, Lower Basildon, nr Reading, Berks. Upper Basildon 671325. Ornamental pheasants, peacocks, flamingoes, cranes, ducks, geese and other wildfowl. Children's playground. *OPEN Apr-Sep 10.00-18.00 Mon-Sun. Charge.*

Hawk Conservancy
Weyhill, nr Andover, Hants. Weyhill 2252. Specialist collection of birds of prey including hawks, falcons, eagles, owls and kites. Flying demonstrations daily (weather permitting). Refreshments, gift shop. *OPEN Mar-Oct 10.30-16.00 (17.00 in summer) Mon-Sun. Charge.*

Stagsden Bird Garden
Stagsden, Beds. Oakley 2745. Cranes, waterfowl, birds of prey, old English poultry breeds, flamingoes and rare pheasants. London 45 miles (A422). *OPEN 11.00-dusk (or 18.00) Mon-Sun. Charge.*

Children's London

Looking at London

London is full of fascinating things for children (and parents) to see and do – historic sights and ceremonies, ships and museums, festivals and fairs, shows and films, clubs, classes, junior sports and plenty of open spaces. It can also be tiring and expensive, so it's best to plan expeditions round a few places at a time; start with one of the famous sights – Changing of the Guard, St Paul's Dome, the Tower, or a well-known museum – and combine it with a river trip, picnic in a park, swimming pool, or children's show. To find out about special events, local play schemes, holiday sports and entertainment, phone Children's Line: 01-246 8007; 04.00-18.00 Mon-Sat, 09.00-23.00 Sun.

For more information on what London has to offer children see Nicholson's book, Children's London.

Sights

HMS Belfast   6 **R** 31
Symon's Wharf, Vine La SE1. 01-407 6434. Last surviving cruiser from World War II, moored near Tower Bridge. Explore bridge, decks, gun turrets, sick bay, galleys and engine rooms. Educational activities for children: film shows, lectures and quiz sheets. Contact the schools' officer for further information. Cross gangplank from Symon's Wharf, or by ferry from Tower Pier. *OPEN 11.00-17.50 Mon-Sun (to 16.30 Nov-Mar). Charge.*

Cutty Sark & Gipsy Moth IV
King William Wlk SE10. 01-858 3445. Old, romantic sailing ship *Cutty Sark*, fastest of the tea-clippers. Below deck there is a fascinating collection of photographs, ship's logs and figure-heads. *Gipsy Moth IV* nearby, is the small boat Sir Francis Chichester sailed single-handed around the world. *OPEN 10.30-18.00 Mon-Sat, 12.00-18.00 Sun (17.00 winter). Charge.*

Houses of Parliament   5 **N** 20
St Margaret St SW1. 01-219 3000. Site of the old Palace of Westminster. Tours of medieval, beamed Westminster Hall available by contacting local member of parliament to obtain a permit. The appealing, small 14thC Jewel Tower with moat, opposite is a further surviving fragment. Children's guide available on the door. Education sheets on application to the education office. *OPEN 10.00-18.00 Mon-Thur, 09.00-16.30 Fri. CLOSED Sat & Sun. Free.*

London Dungeon　　　6 **Q** 29
34 Tooley St SE1. 01-403 0606. Gruesome and realistic exhibition displaying the darker side of British history – murders, executions and tortures – in an eerie, vaulted cellar. Children under 10 must be accompanied by an adult. *OPEN 10.00-17.30 Mon-Sun (to 16.30 Oct-Apr). Charge.*

London Planetarium　　　2 **B** 19
Marylebone Rd NW1. 01-486 1121. Look at outer space and our neighbours in the solar system. Programmes through the day *11.00-16.30* (special arrangements for school parties *during termtime 12.15-14.00).* Charge. Also Laserium with laser light-shows. For times phone 01-486 2242. *OPEN 11.00-16.30 Mon-Sun. Charge.*

Madame Tussaud's　　　2 **B** 19
Marylebone Rd NW1. 01-935 6861. (Adjoins Planetarium.) Life-size wax figures of historic and contemporary, famous or notorious people. Royalty, pop stars, film stars, statesmen and astronauts all under the same roof, looking incredibly life-like. 'Battle of Trafalgar': reconstruction of gun-deck of *Victory* at height of battle. Chamber of Horrors genuinely gruesome, unsuitable for young children. *OPEN 10.00-17.30 Mon-Sun. Special combined ticket includes admission to Planetarium next door.*

Monument　　　6 **O** 30
Monument St EC3. 01-626 2717. A City landmark – stone column topped by a viewing platform and shining golden urn. Commemorates the Great Fire of 1666 (there's a working diorama of the Great Fire in the Museum of London). Steep spiral staircase (311 steps) inside column leads to a great view. *OPEN Apr-Sep 09.00-17.40 Mon-Sat; May-Sep 14.00-17.40 Sun; Oct-Mar 09.00-15.40 Mon-Sat. Charge.*

Old Royal Observatory
Greenwich Park SE10. 01-858 1167. Information from the National Maritime Museum, 01-858 4422. Houses a collection of old clocks and telescopes, and a marvellous Planetarium. Outside in the courtyard, a brass strip marks the 0° Greenwich Meridian – you can stand astride it with one foot in the Western Hemisphere and one in the Eastern. *OPEN summer 10.00-18.00 Mon-Sat, 14.00-18.00 Sun; winter 10.00-17.00 Mon-Sat, 14.00-17.00 Sun. Free.* Planetarium *OPEN 10.00-15.00 Mon-Fri during school hols. Charge.*

Royal Mews　　　5 **L** 16
Buckingham Palace Rd SW1. 01-930 4832. The Queen's horses and coaches, ready for use on state occasions, including the huge gold Coronation coach and the glass State coach. *OPEN 14.00-16.00 Wed & Thur. CLOSED Royal Ascot Week. Charge.*

St Katharine Docks　　　6 **R** 32
St Katharine's Way, Tower Bridge E1. 01-488 2400. Home to the steam tug *Challenge*, the Nore lightship and magnificent Thames barges. Also a yacht haven, with trendy shops and restaurants.

St Paul's Cathedral　　　6 **M** 28
Ludgate Hill EC4. 01-248 2705. Exciting climb to the Dome, for a terrific view over the roof-tops and river. 259 steps take you to the Whispering Gallery, inside the Dome; 120 more up a narrow stone staircase lead to the broad Stone Gallery, at the base of the Dome; then the final, and most hair-raising climb, is to the Golden Gallery, at the top of the Dome. *OPEN 10.00-16.15 Mon-Fri, 11.00-16.15 Sat (to 15.15 in winter). Charge.*

Thames Flood Barrier
Unity Way, Eastmoor St SE18. 01-854 1373. A shining, technological marvel, built as a bulwark against dangerously high tides. The Thames Barrier Visitor Centre houses an exhibition and an audio-visual presentation every 20 mins, illuminating the engineering feats involved in the barrier's construction, as well as a souvenir shop and cafeteria. *OPEN 10.30-17.00 Mon-Sun. Charge.*

Tower of London　　　6 **Q** 32
Tower Hill EC3. 01-709 0765. The best time to visit the Tower is definitely in winter (between *Nov-Feb*), when it's not only cheaper to get in, but much less crowded. An amazing fortress – you need plenty of time to explore all the different towers, the vast collection of armour and weapons, and the Crown Jewels in their steel-lined underground strongroom. No unaccompanied children under 10. *OPEN Mar-Oct 09.30-17.00 Mon-Sat, 14.00-17.00 Sun; Nov-Feb 09.30-16.30 Mon-Sat. Charge.*

Trafalgar Square WC2　　　5 **K** 21
Always popular with children who like to chase and feed the pigeons, climb the lions and watch the fountains. Parents will enjoy the bustling, colourful crowd which always congregates here. On the north wall, look for the Imperial Standards of Length in yards, feet and inches. Carol singing round a giant Christmas tree every evening for 10 days before Christmas. Revelry New Year's Eve.

Trocadero　　　2 **I** 21
Piccadilly Circus W1. Houses the Guinness

World of Records exhibition (01-439 7331), where you can compare yourself with the tallest man and smallest woman and check your weight against the heaviest man. Tour guides available. *OPEN 10.00-20.00 Mon-Sun. Charge.* Also houses The London Experience (01-439 4938) a filmshow history of London. *OPEN 10.20-22.00 Mon-Sun. Charge.*

Wembley Stadium
Empire Way, Wembley, Middx. 01-903 4864. See behind the scenes and view the famous turf on a guided tour (special tours can be booked for children). Visit the dressing rooms, climb to the Royal box and imagine yourself holding the cup. *Guided tours on the hour, 10.00-16.00 Fri-Wed (except the day of and the days before and after a big match). Charge.*

Westminster Abbey   5 N 20
Broad Sanctuary SW1. 01-222 7110. The Abbey is easiest to explore if you think of it in three sections: the Nave and Transept (with Poets' Corner and the tomb of the Unknown Soldier); Chapel and Shrine of Edward the Confessor (with the Coronation Chair); and Henry VII's Chapel, with a wonderful fan-vaulted roof and the tombs of many kings and queens. The Abbey Museum, in the East Cloister, has a collection of death masks and funeral effigies, including Nelson in his uniform and King Charles II in his garter robes. Royal chapels *OPEN 09.20-16.00 (last tickets) Mon-Fri, 09.20-14.00 & 16.00-17.00 Sat. Charge. 18.00-20.00 Wed (photography permitted). Free.* Museum *OPEN 10.30-16.30 Mon-Sun. Charge.*

Westminster Cathedral   5 M 16
Ashley Pl, off Victoria St SW1. 01-834 7452. Striking Byzantine-style building in red and white brick. See view from the top of Campanile (273ft – 83.7m) over Westminster and the Thames. Lift usually *OPEN 07.00-20.00 Mon-Sun. Charge.*

Trips & tours

See also 'London tours' in 'Sightseeing'.
London from the top of a bus
London Regional Transport do tours which give a bird's eye view or, armed with a (*free*) LRT Bus Map, you can devise your own 'tour' by taking one of the cross-town routes through the centre. For example, the no. 6 bus goes from Marble Arch to St Paul's Cathedral via Oxford St, Regent St, Piccadilly Circus, Trafalgar Sq, Strand, Fleet St and Ludgate Hill.

London Wall Walk
Follow a sequence of tile panels tracing 1¾ miles of the City's Roman and medieval defensive wall – parts of which survive – between the Museum of London and Tower Hill. A map of Roman London on sale in the Museum of London incorporates the route.

Monopoly tours
For Monopoly fans only! Try visiting all the places on the Monopoly board, and take a photo of each one. It'll take several visits to cover them all, but you will have an unusual record of London life.

River trips
See 'Sightseeing'.
On the Thames you can take a trip downriver to Greenwich, or to the docks at Tilbury to see the 'big ships', or upriver to Battersea, or further up towards Hampton Court. Or take a canal trip from Little Venice to Regent's Park Zoo in one of the original painted narrow-boats.

Silver Jubilee Walkway
Map available (*small charge*) from Tourist Information Centres. A well-planned trail (opened in 1977 to celebrate the Queen's Silver Jubilee) covering many interesting sights in central London. The route is indicated by special markers (with the Jubilee symbol) set into the pavement. It's essential to have the map because you can lose the trail, and the map itself is packed with useful information.
Begins at Leicester Sq (NE corner) and makes a round trip covering 10 miles in all, divided into seven easy sections.

Ceremonies

Take advantage of the splendid pageantry which still survives by watching the Changing of the Queen's Guards (daily in summer) or pick one of the seasonal celebrations: Trooping the Colour – one of the most spectacular ceremonies in England which marks the Queen's official birthday in Jun – the Lord Mayor's Procession (Nov), or the Chinese New Year celebrations (Jan/Feb). See 'Sightseeing': 'Daily ceremonies and events' and 'Annual events'.

London at work

See what goes on behind the scenes – some places offer organised tours or group visits, and a chance to see how things work.

Airports

London Gatwick
Horley, Surrey. Crawley 28822. Busy airport with all types of aircraft, including light planes. 800 ft (244 m) viewing gallery gives close view of aircraft movements. *OPEN 09.00-dusk Mon-Sun. Charge.*

London Heathrow
01-759 4321. Underground straight to Heathrow Central. From the viewing terrace above Queen's Building (between Terminals 1 and 2) watch the planes landing and taking off. There's a roof garden, a small children's playground and refreshments. *OPEN Apr-Sep 10.00-18.00 Mon-Sun, Oct-Mar 10.00-16.30 Mon-Sun. Charge.*

Animals

Whitbread Shires Stables 6 J 23
Garrett St EC1. 01-606 4455. A visit to these working stables includes a chance to meet the magnificent shire horses which pull the Lord Mayor's coach on special occasions, and the brewery's drays around the City throughout the year. *OPEN 11.00-12.30, 13.30-15.00 Mon-Fri. Free (charge for over 16s).*

Business & finance

Stock Exchange 6 N 32
Old Broad St EC2. 01-588 2355. Public entrance at corner of Threadneedle St and Old Broad St. Where fortunes are made and lost, trading in stocks and shares. Running commentary and questions answered. Films shown in adjoining cinema . Viewing gallery. *OPEN 09.45-15.30 Mon-Fri. CLOSED B.hols. Parties up to 30, ring or write to PR Dept. Free.*

Diamonds

London Diamond Centre 2 G 20
10 Hanover St W1. 01-629 5511. See the evolution of a diamond from rough stone to glittering gem, as well as the largest collection of diamonds in London. Two days' notice required for groups. *OPEN 09.30-17.30 Mon-Fri, 09.30-13.30 Sat. CLOSED B.hols. Charge.*

Fire stations

Be right on the spot when the siren goes. For permission to visit your local fire station (only for children of 12 years and above) *write to the PR Dept, London Fire Brigade HQ, Albert Embankment SE1.*

Industry

Express Dairies
Milk Bottling Plant, 181 London Rd, South Morden, Surrey. 01-648 4544. Visits arranged by appt in groups only. Audiovisual presentation included. Watch the processes from a viewing platform. Tour round the pasteurising plant. Minimum age 11. Contact Booking Administrator. *Free.*

Ford Motor Co
Dagenham, Essex. 01-592 3000. Fascinating conducted tours of the factory, from engine plant through to final assembly building with completed cars. *Tours at 09.45 and 13.30 Mon-Fri except public and plant holidays. Duration 1¾ hrs. Family tours minimum age 10, group tours minimum age 15. Free.*

The Glasshouse 6 J 23
65 Long Acre WC2. 01-836 9785. Watch glass being blown in the workshop from observation area. *Telephone for details. OPEN 10.00-17.30 Mon-Fri, 11.00-16.00 Sat. CLOSED 13.00-14.00 Mon-Sat & all day Sun. Parties up to 10. Free.*

Law

Old Bailey 6 L 28
Old Bailey EC4. 01-248 3277. Trials in the Central Criminal Court can be watched from the public galleries. Worth going to see the wigs and robes worn by the judges. Minimum age 14. *OPEN 10.30-13.00, 14.00-16.00 Mon-Fri. CLOSED B.hols. Free.*

Music

London Symphony Orchestra 6 K 30
Barbican Centre, Barbican EC2. 01-588 1116. Annual subscription to the LSO club (open to children) gives *free* attendance at final rehearsals.

Royal Festival Hall 6 M 23
SE1. 01-928 3191. Book for guided tours of approx 1¼ hrs, which usually include a visit to the auditorium, backstage, foyers and boiler house. *12.45 and 17.30 daily. Charge.· (Organised school and student groups, max 25 persons, free.)*

Royal Philharmonic	3 I 29	
Orchestra		

16 Clerkenwell Green EC1. 01-608 2381. Promotes concerts at Royal Festival Hall, Barbican and Fairfield Halls. Free attendance at rehearsals for concert ticket-holders only.

Newspapers

Daily Mail 6 L 26
Northcliffe House, Carmelite St EC4. 01-353 6000. Six months waiting list. Groups of 12. Minimum age 14. *Tours 21.00-23.15 Tue & Wed. Contact General Production Manager.*

Postal services

Several of the large central offices offer conducted tours. At each place you can see sorting, postal machinery and the Post Office underground railway. Minimum age 14. In each case, write in advance to the Postmaster Controller. Mark envelope 'Visits'.

King Edward Building 6 L 29
King Edward St EC1. 01-239 5024. Concerned with London and overseas letter post; underground railway. Roman wall. Groups of 20. *Visits Jan-Nov 10.30-16.30 Mon-Thur. Free.*

Mount Pleasant 3 G 28
Rosebery Av EC1. 01-239 2191. Biggest parcel sorting office in the country; underground railway. Groups of 30 (children should be over 10). *Visits Jan-Nov 10.30, 14.30 & 19.30 Mon-Thur. Free.*

West Central District Office 3 H 23
21-31 New Oxford St WC1. 01-239 5726. New fully-mechanised sorting office, also linked to underground railway. *Enquire for visiting details. Free.*

Tea

Tea Brokers Association 6 M 28
John Lyon House, Upper Thames St EC4. 01-236 3368. You may watch tea grown all over the world being auctioned here, each Mon 10.30. Advance booking necessary, groups only. Write to Mrs Mayne (above address). *Charge.*

Telephone services

Telecom Technology 6 N 30
Showcase
135 Queen Victoria St EC4. 01-248 7444.

Displays history of telecommunications, highlighting the best of present-day design and offering a glimpse of the future. *OPEN 10.00-17.00 Mon-Fri. CLOSED B.hols. Free.*

Museums for children

For a full list see 'Museums and galleries'. Most museums will arrange special tours for groups as long as arrangements are made well in advance.

Baden-Powell House I H 8
Queen's Gate SW7. 01-584 7030. Exhibition of the life of Baden-Powell, founder of the scout movement. *OPEN 09.00-18.00 Mon-Sun. Free.*

Bethnal Green Museum
Cambridge Heath Rd E2. 01-980 2415. Fine display of historic toys, dolls and dolls' houses and model theatres, including an 18thC Venetian marionette theatre. Special collection of children's costume. Regular *Sat* workshop *(11.00-13.00, 14.00-16.00)* provides facilities for drawing, puppetry and modelling. Holiday activities include painting competitions, storytelling and Punch and Judy shows with traditional figures. *OPEN 10.00-17.50 Mon-Thur & Sat, 14.30-17.50 Sun. Free.*

Commonwealth Institute I D 5
Kensington High St W8. 01-603 4535. Modern building like a great glass tent. Colourful displays and costumes from the 47 Commonwealth states. Sit in a Wild West saddle (Canadian gallery), try the tropical climate simulator (Malaysian gallery), and see the transparent cow making milk (New Zealand gallery). Special events at weekends and during school hols. *OPEN 10.00-17.30 Mon-Sat, 14.00-17.00 Sun. CLOSED B.hols. Free.*

Geffrye Museum
Kingsland Rd E2. 01-739 8368. 18thC almshouses with period rooms and furniture from 1600 to present day. Activities for children over seven include drawing, painting, puzzles, plays, model-making and outings. Children's room *OPEN Sat mornings in termtime*, special projects in school. *OPEN 10.00-17.00 Tue-Sat, 14.00-17.00 Sun. Free.*

Geological Museum I H 10
Exhibition Rd SW7. 01-589 3444. Real gold, diamonds, minerals, rocks, fossils, impressive collection of gemstones and a piece of

moon rock. Demonstrations, dioramas and films throughout the year. Special feature exhibition *Treasures of the Earth* is a guide to the many minerals dug out of the ground which are important in everyday life. Lectures and demonstrations can be organised for school parties. *OPEN 10.00-18.00 Mon-Sat, 14.30-18.00 Sun. Charge.*

Gunnersbury Park Museum
Gunnersbury Park W3. 01-992 1612. Rothschild family mansion, now a museum with collection of coaches, including a travelling chariot, town chariot and hansom cab. Also dolls, dolls' houses, ancient washing machines, and finds from local excavations. Introductory talks and activities for school parties can be booked. *OPEN Mar-Oct 13.00-17.00 Mon-Fri, 14.00-18.00 Sat & Sun; Nov-Feb 13.00-16.00 Mon-Fri, 14.00-16.00 Sat & Sun. Free.*

Horniman Museum
100 London Rd SE23. 01-699 2339. Collection includes arts, crafts and musical instruments from all over the world. African masks, American Indian and Eskimo art, stuffed animals, live aquaria and an observation beehive. Also a new exhibition of tents from around the world including a North American Indian tent and Chris Bonnington's mountaineering tent. Refreshments. *OPEN 10.30-18.00 Mon-Sat, 14.00-18.00 Sun. Free.* Children's Centre provides crafts, drawing materials etc for children over eight. Art and craft work are based on observation and drawing of the museum exhibits. *OPEN 10.30-16.30 Sat during termtime, Mon-Sat during school hols. CLOSED B.hols.*

Kew Bridge Steam Museum
Green Dragon La, Brentford, Middx. 01-568 4757. Huge Victorian building houses five gigantic beam engines, restored to working order by volunteers. Under steam at weekends. Also a collection of old traction engines and working forge. Tea-room. *OPEN 11.00-17.00 Mon-Sun inc B.hols. Charge (reduced charge Mon-Fri).*

Light Fantastic Gallery of   6 J 23
Holography
48 South Row, Covent Garden WC2. 01-836 6423. A fascinating and constantly changing display of holograms. A hologram is a three-dimensional image produced by a laser on a specially treated plate. The objects on the plate move in relation to one another as you move the plate or walk past it. *OPEN 10.00-18.00 Mon-Sat, 11.00-18.00 Sun. Charge.*

London Toy and Model   2 B 12
Museum
23 Craven Hill W2. 01-262 7905. Toys, dolls and trains including collection of pre-1914 toys, in a Victorian house. Model railway in the garden. *OPEN 10.00-17.30 Tue-Sat, 11.00-17.30 Sun. CLOSED Mon & winter B. hols. Charge.*

Museum of London   6 L 30
London Wall EC2. 01-600 3699. Outstanding museum telling the story of London from earliest times. Walk through different periods of history, from Roman to present day. Well-designed displays, reconstructions of rooms and shops, costumes, etc. Working diorama of the Fire of London. Also the Lord Mayor's Golden Coach. School hol projects. Refreshments. *OPEN 10.00-18.00 Tue-Sat, 14.00-18.00 Sun. CLOSED Mon & B.hols. Free.*

National Army Museum   4 N 10
Royal Hospital Rd SW3. 01-730 0717. Spacious museum tells the story of the British Army from 1485 to the present day. Uniforms, armour, weapon gallery, music and soldiers' songs on push-button machines. Junior Club during summer hols. *OPEN 10.00-17.30 Mon-Sat, 14.00-17.30 Sun. Free.*

National Gallery   5 J 22
Trafalgar Sq WC2. 01-839 3321. Holiday quizzes and slide-tape shows introduce you to the huge collection of paintings. *OPEN 10.00-18.00 Mon-Sat, 14.00-18.00 Sun. Free.*

National Maritime Museum
Romney Rd SE10. 01-858 4422. Vast collections of ship models, navigational instruments, costumes and weapons. Half-deck Club for 7 to 15-year-olds (long waiting list). Meets *Sat* in termtime, *Tue-Thur* in school hols. 'Mess Deck' for picnics. School hol programme. *OPEN Oct-Easter 10.00-17.00 Mon-Sat, 14.00-17.00 Sun. Easter-Oct 10.00-18.00 Mon-Sat, 14.00-18.00 Sun. CLOSED Jan & B.hols.*

National Portrait Gallery   5 J 22
St Martin's Pl WC2. 01-930 1552. Portraits of famous (and infamous) people in history. Children's hol events (*usually Easter and summer*). *OPEN 10.00-17.00 Mon-Fri, 10.00-18.00 Sat, 14.00-18.00 Sun. Free.*

Natural History Museum   1 H 9
Cromwell Rd SW7. 01-589 6323. Fossilised remains and reconstructions of prehistoric animals. Displays of birds, beasts and reptiles from all over the world and a full-size 90ft (27.5m) cast of a blue whale. Lots of push-button machines. Family Centre where adults and children can par-

ticipate in a variety of natural history activities. Also Nature Trails to follow around the museum. *OPEN 10.00-18.00 Mon-Sat, 13.00-18.00 Sun. Charge (free 16.30-18.00 Mon-Fri).*

Pollocks Toy Museum　　　2　F　22
I Scala St W1. 01-636 3452. Old toys, theatres and dolls crammed into two houses. Also toys for sale, including the colourful Victorian cut-out theatres for which Pollocks is famous. *OPEN 10.00-17.00 Mon-Sat. CLOSED Sun & B.hols. Charge.*

Queen Elizabeth's Hunting Lodge
Rangers Rd E4. 01-529 6681. Beautiful old Tudor building, now the Epping Forest Museum. Exhibition of the history of the royal forest. Interesting displays on wildlife, conservation, local archaeology and history, with animal tracks, butterflies, insects, birds, mammals, trees and flowers. *OPEN 14.00-18.00 (or dusk in winter) Wed-Sun. Charge.*

Royal Airforce Museum
Grahame Park Way NW9. 01-205 2266. Plane-spotters will particularly enjoy this impressive collection of aircraft, including a man-lifting kite, airship, historic planes from World Wars I and II, and modern bombers and missiles. *OPEN 10.00-18.00 Mon-Sat, 14.00-18.00 Sun. Free.* Also comprises the Battle of Britain Museum and Bomber Command Museum. *OPEN same hours. Charge.*

Science Museum　　　　　I　H　10
Exhibition Rd SW7. 01-589 3456. Children's Gallery has press-button models and dioramas showing the development of scientific interest. Exploration Gallery has a life-size reconstruction of the moon landing and a real Apollo space capsule. Saturday and half-term lectures have a theme of scientific interest for family groups. *OPEN 10.00-18.00 Mon-Sat, 14.30-18.00 Sun. Charge.*

Tate Gallery　　　　　　　5　P　18
Millbank SW1. 01-821 1313. Trails and special children's tours and other holiday events for children and adults. Pushchairs available. *OPEN 10.00-17.50 Mon-Sat, 14.00-17.50 Sun. Free.*

London's countryside

London's parks and surrounding countryside are surprisingly rich in outdoor pursuits, and there is a great variety of wildlife to be found even in the heart of the metropolis. Some of the opportunities are listed here.

Aeroplanes

The airshow season runs from Apr-Oct, and gives children a chance to see planes at close quarters.

Shuttleworth Collection
Old Warden Aerodrome, nr Biggleswade, Beds. Northill 288. Famous collection of vintage aircraft. Film and introductory talk for pre-booked groups. *OPEN 10.30-17.30 Mon-Sun. Special flying displays Apr-Oct last Sun of every month. Charge.*

Animal & bird enclosures in parks

These are local parks with small animal and bird enclosures. They are open from dawn till dusk Mon-Sun, unless otherwise stated, and all are free. Also see 'Zoos and aquaria'.

Battersea Park SW11　　　　4　O　10
01-871 7540. Small zoo where sheep and pigmy goats are kept. Other animals include monkeys, wallabies, deer and parrots. Pony rides. *OPEN Easter-Sep 13.30-17.30 Mon-Fri, 11.30-18.00 Sat, Sun & school hols. CLOSED Nov-Easter.*

Brockwell Park SE24
01-674 6141. Small collection of birds including quails, doves, canaries and finches.

Clissold Park N16
01-800 1021. Fallow deer, rabbits, guinea pigs, tropical birds including a mynah bird as well as a peacock and a collection of waterfowl.

Crystal Palace SE20
01-778 7148. Small zoo, with some tame animals to pat. Also caged birds. Pony rides. *OPEN Apr-Oct 13.30-17.30 Mon-Fri, 11.00-18.00 Sat, Sun, school hols & B.hols.*

Dulwich Park SE21
01-693 5737. Aviary with quails, doves, touracos, pheasants and other birds. Good collection of waterfowl.

Golders Hill Park NW11
01-455 5183. Fallow deer, pigmy goats, wallaby and guanacos. Birds include pheasants, cranes and flamingoes.

Hainault Forest, Essex
01-500 3106. Ponies, donkeys, cows, a goat and a small herd of llamas. Also small collection of domestic and wildfowl, including peacocks and guinea fowl.

Holland Park W8 | **B** **5**
01-602 2226. Collection of birds, including peacocks, emus, bantams. Muscovy ducks and peafowl. Rabbits too.

Maryon Wilson Park SE7
01-854 0446. Ponies, goats, a donkey, fallow deer and Jacob sheep, as well as rabbits and chickens.

Sydenham Wells Park SE26
Wells Rd. 01-699 8914. Aviary where they breed budgies; also flamingoes, ducks, colourful pheasants and geese. Rabbits in their warrens.

Victoria Park E2
01-985 1957. Deer, rabbits, guinea pigs.

Waterlow Park N6
01-272 2825. Colourful aviary of various birds including mynah birds and toucans as well as waterfowl on the lake including Canada geese. Also lots of wild squirrels, which cadge food.

Architecture

Avoncroft Museum of Buildings
Stoke Heath, Bromsgrove, Worcs. Bromsgrove 31886. All kinds of buildings, spanning seven centuries. Granary, barn, stable, windmill, forge, counting house, and others. Windmill and forge can often be seen working. Summer holiday activities for children. For large groups please book in advance. OPEN Jun-Aug 11.00-17.30 Mon-Sun; Apr-May & Sep-Oct 11.00-17.30 Tue-Sun (& B.hol Mon); Mar & Nov 11.00-16.30 Tue-Thur, Sat & Sun (& B.hol Mon). Charge.

Birdwatching

See 'Natural history' under 'Clubs and classes'.

Cemeteries

Quite a few children find cemeteries fascinating rather than morbid or frightening, and many of London's older cemeteries are wonderful places to explore, not only for their monumental stonework and strange epitaphs but also as the peaceful haunt of many small animals and birds. See 'Looking at history' in 'Historic London'.

Fairs

There are over 200 fairs a week held in England during the summer; the following is a selection of some in London.

Holiday Fairs
Alexandra Park, Blackheath, Hampstead Heath and Wormwood Scrubs (Easter, spring & summer B.hols).

Other Occasional Fairs
Clapham Common (mid Apr), Crystal Palace (early May & Aug), Tooting Bec Common (early May), Victoria Park (early May).

Farms

There are several farms which are open to visit in and around London. In London itself, there are small city farms which welcome visits from families and school groups. Outside London you can visit large working farms which organise open days and farm trails.

Freightliners Farm
Entrance: Sheringham Rd N7. 01-609 0467. Small city farm with cows and calves, ponies, sheep, goats and kids, ducks, chickens, rabbits and guinea pigs. OPEN 11.00-13.00 & 14.00-17.00 Tue-Sun. Free.

Kentish Town City Farm
Grafton Rd NW5. 01-482 2861. Horses, pigs, chickens, sheep, goats and rabbits. OPEN 09.30-17.30 Mon-Sun. CLOSED Xmas. Free.

Manor Farm Museum
Cogges, nr Witney, Oxon. Witney 772602. Working museum. Seeks to show rural England at work in early 1900s. Cotswold stone buildings, display of farm implements, livestock, demonstrations. OPEN 10.30-17.30 Tue-Sun & B.hols. Charge.

Mudchute Farm
Pier St E14. 01-515 5901. Large (32 acre -13ha-) city farm run by staff and volunteers who look after the beef cattle, ponies, sheep, goats, pigs, poultry, rabbits and bees. There is also a riding school and pony club, a classroom and teashop. The Mudchute is the venue for the annual Isle of Dogs Agricultural Show. OPEN 09.00-17.00 Mon-Sun. Free.

Stepping Stones Farm
Stepney Way E1. 01-790 8204. Local volunteers are invited to help out on all sorts of jobs, but everyone is welcome to visit this 4-acre (1.6ha) urban farm in the East End. Activities vary with the seasons, but the livestock population usually includes pigs, goats, cows, sheep, ducks, geese, rabbits and a donkey who gives rides to those under 9 stone! OPEN 09.30-13.00, 14.00-18.00 Tue-Sun. Free (donations welcome).

Surrey Docks Farm
Rotherhithe St SE16. 01-231 1010. 2-acre (0.8ha) site with goats, pigs, donkeys, ducks, quail, geese and hens plus small orchard, vegetable garden and duckpond. Farm shop sells fresh produce. *OPEN 10.00-13.00 & 14.00-17.00 Tue-Sun. CLOSED Mon & Fri in school hols. Free.*

Fish & fishing

The river Thames is now cleaner than it has been for centuries, and supports a growing number of fish including salmon and trout. Many fish are to be found in London's ponds, lakes and canals. See 'Fishing' and 'Fishing: lakes and ponds' under 'Sport'.
London Anglers' Association
Forest Road Hall, Hervey Park Rd E17. 01-520 7477. Junior membership gives information about places to fish and a London Anglers' Licence for coarse fishing on the Grand Union/Regent's Canal and River Lea. *Annual charge.*

Kite flying

Flying your own kite is a great pleasure but you can meet other kite flyers, or see the experts in action, at the following places in London: Blackheath, Clapham Common, Hampstead Heath on the top of Parliament Hill Fields, Primrose Hill, Richmond Park and near the Round Pond in Kensington Gardens.

Model villages

Bekonscot
Warwick Rd, Beaconsfield, Bucks. Beaconsfield 2919. Covers over an acre (0.4ha) with realistic houses, cottages, church, pubs, castle, lighthouse, airport and a model railway. *OPEN Mar-Oct 10.00-17.00 Mon-Sun. Charge.*

Nature reserves & nature trails

Nature Conservancy Council
Northminster House, Peterborough. Peterborough 40345. Will give regional office number and regional offices can supply a list of reserves, and leaflets about individual reserves in Great Britain; also a children's reading list.

Camley Street Natural Park 3 B 27
12 Camley St NW1. 01-833 2311. A park which has been created in a former coal drop on the Grand Union Canal to provide a wildlife refuge and a place to enjoy nature in the city. Phone beforehand to confirm times, but *usually OPEN 10.00-17.00 Mon-Sun. CLOSED B.hols. Free.*

Steam & traction engines

Once common, these early engines have now become collectors' pieces. Rallies are held periodically by clubs in various parts of the country. They are colourful and unusual, and the engines themselves are superb. A useful book is Traction Engines by Harold Bonnett (Shire Publications – Princes Risborough 4301). Apart from the Science Museum, the following collections are worth seeing:
Kew Bridge Steam Museum
See 'Museums for children' section.
National Motor Museum
Beaulieu, Hants. Beaulieu 612345. Every sort of vehicle with various sorts of engines, including 'Lord Nelson' the traction engine. *OPEN 10.00-17.00 Mon-Sun. Charge.*
National Traction Engine Club
Write to: David Pugh, 12 Hillway, Woburn Sands, Milton Keynes, Bucks. Milton Keynes 584737, for a list of steam rallies and clubs.
Thursford Museum
Laurels Farm, Thursford, Norfolk. Fakenham 77477. A superb collection of various engines and machines including fairground and other organs, fairground rides and steam and traction engines – all working. *OPEN Easter-Oct 14.00 (11.00 Jul & Aug)-17.30 Mon-Sun. Charge.*

Windmills

Once a prominent feature of south-east England, though most are now derelict. Discovering Windmills by J. Vince (Shire Publications – Princes Risborough 4301) is an inexpensive introduction and guide. Two remaining in London:
Brixton Windmill
Blenheim Gdns, Brixton Hill SW9. 01-673 5398. A reminder of Lambeth's rural past. The early 19thC tower mill was in use until 1934. *OPEN 08.00-17.00 (to dusk in summer) Mon-Sun. Max 12 people. School parties free, charge for individuals.*
Wimbledon Windmill
Wimbledon Common SW19. Contact:

Ranger's Office, 01-788 7655, for information. A hollow post mill, built in 1817, now housing a museum with models and photographs explaining how windmills work. *OPEN Apr-Oct 14.00-17.00 Sat, Sun & B.hols. Charge.*

Zoos

See under 'Zoos and aquaria' in 'Outdoor London'.

Clubs and classes

In London you can find clubs and classes for just about every hobby and interest you can imagine, from arts, crafts and theatre to natural history, science and sport (see 'Sport'). Scouts, guides and youth clubs are also listed here under 'Youth organisations'.

Archaeology

The best way to get experience, and maybe join in a dig, is to join the junior section of an archaeological society – for local clubs, enquire at your nearest library or museum.
**London and Middlesex   6 L 30
Archaeological Society (LAMAS)**
Contact: Young LAMAS, c/o The Library, Museum of London, London Wall EC2. 01-600 3699. The junior section organises lectures and activities.
Young Archaeologists Club
Write to: United House, Piccadilly, Yorks. York 646411, for details. The Young Archaeologists Club, linked with British Archaeology, organises visits to sites, fieldwork and lectures (usually outside London). Quarterly magazine with news from around the world.

Arts & crafts

Also see 'Community arts centres', 'Family workshops' and 'Museums for children' (several have painting and crafts workshops).
Camden Arts Centre
Arkwright Rd NW3. 01-435 2643. *Sat morning* sessions for children 7-11 in crafts and 12-16 in pottery. Pottery for children 7-11 *Sat & Sun* mornings. Occasional four-week arts and crafts courses for children 5-7 during school hols. *Charge.*

Chelsea Pottery   4 M 10
13 Radnor Walk SW3. 01-352 1366. Good, well-established studio. Classes *Sat*, family or children's, minimum age 4. *Annual membership. Charge.*
Susan Meyer-Michael
99 North End Rd NW11. 01-455 0817. Pottery, and clay modelling. Small groups, family groups, or individual lessons. Sessions by arrangement. *Appt only. Charge.*

Astronomy

Greenwich Planetarium (Old Royal Observatory) and the London Planetarium show projections of the sky and stars (see 'Looking at London'). Morley College has an astronomy class for children and adults on Sat mornings – see 'Family workshops'.
Hampstead Scientific Society
The Secretary, 22 Flask Wlk NW3. 01-794 9341. Organises talks and outings, and also has its own observatory at Lower Ter NW3 (nr Whitestone Pond). President Heinz Wolff. *OPEN Sep-Apr 20.00-22.00 Fri & Sat, 11.00-13.00 Sun, weather permitting. Annual junior subscription.*
Junior Astronomical Society
The Secretary, 36 Fairway, Keyworth, Notts. For interested beginners of any age. Meets four times a year at Holborn Library, Theobalds Rd, London WC1. Quarterly magazine and bi-monthly newsletter sent to members. *Annual subscription.*

Boat clubs

Opportunities to learn canoeing, rowing and sailing. (You can also hire rowing boats by the hour in some parks. See 'Parks and gardens' in 'Outdoor London'.)
The Sports Council   3 D 25
16 Upper Woburn Pl WC1. 01-388 1277. Publishes leaflets listing all the canoeing centres and sailing centres in and around London. Published annually, these include details of special courses and events. Many centres have courses for beginners and/or children. Or ring Sportsline on 01-222 8000.

Book clubs

Bookworm Club
W. Heffer & Sons Ltd, 20 Trinity St, Cambridge. Cambridge 358357. Bookworm is for 5-12-year-olds. Early Worm for

0-7-year-olds. Both clubs are run through schools or groups.

Puffin School Book Clubs   I E 7
c/o Penguin Books Ltd, 27 Wright's La W8. 01-938 2200. Well-established book club for 1-13-year-olds. Encourages an interest in reading and books. *Annual subscription* brings a badge, membership card, book stickers, pupil leaflets and magazine. There are three clubs: Fledgling (0-6 years), Flight (7-9 years) and Post (9-13).

Scholastic Publications
Marlborough House, Holly Walk, Leamington Spa, Warks. Leamington Spa 813910. Promotes a variety of book clubs for ages ranging from 3-12-year-olds and upwards. Monthly *Club News*. Children join through their schools.

Brass rubbing

You can learn how to make your own rubbings at brass rubbing centres, which provide replicas of many historic monumental brasses plus everything you need. The cost of rubbings is graded according to the sizes of the brasses. Once experienced, search out brasses in old churches all over the country.

All Hallows-by-the-Tower   6 Q 32
Byward St EC3. 01-481 2928. At the west end of the church, an appealing assembly of about 30 brasses, although space allows for no more than 10 people to make rubbings at one time. Free instruction available but please check. *OPEN 10.30-17.00 Mon-Sat, 12.30-17.00 Sun. Book for groups of children.*

London Brass Rubbing   5 K 22
Centre
St-Martin-in-the-Fields WC2. 01-437 6023. Replicas on display of 70 British and European brasses ranging from animal figures, children and wool merchants to a crusader knight which stands 7ft (2.1m) tall. Instruction available. *Charge. OPEN 10.00-18.00 Mon-Sat, 12.00-18.00 Sun.*

Community arts centres

These are centres which organise a great variety of activities for both children and adults. Usually a small charge.

Battersea Arts Centre
Lavender Hill SW11. 01-223 6557. Children's day on *Sat*, with workshops on dance, photography, puppetry as well as shows and films. Workshops during school hols.

Inter-Action Social   6 L 26
Enterprise Trust
HMS President (1918), Nr Blackfriars Bridge, Victoria Embankment EC4. 01-583 2652. Facilities for photography, video and computing. Children's workshops and outdoor activities.

Jackson's Lane Community Centre
Archway Rd N6. 01-340 5226. After-school and holiday workshops for children including arts and crafts, dance and shadow puppets, plus an excellent programme of visiting theatre and dance groups.

Moonshine Community Arts Workshop
Victor Rd NW10. 01-969 7959. Dance, drama, West Indian and other arts and crafts, and music. A speciality is an animation workshop, where children's models are filmed and animated. *Workshops after school, on Sat and during school hols. Print shop and adult classes.*

Riverside Studios
Crisp Rd W6. 01-741 2551. Spacious arts centre which organises some children's educational visits and holiday activities. Children's entertainment at *weekends*.

Cricket

Gover Cricket School
172 East Hill SW18. 01-874 1796. All-year-round coaching scheme.

MCC Indoor Cricket School
Lord's Cricket Ground, St John's Wood Rd NW8. 01-286 3649. Coaching from eight years upwards, beginners and advanced.

Cycling

Learn to be a safe and proficient cyclist before venturing on to London's roads.

Cycling Proficiency Tests
Most boroughs organise their own cycling proficiency lessons and tests for 9-13-year-olds. Certificates are issued to those who pass tests in the theory and practice of safe bicycling. Enquire at your local town hall for details or contact the Royal Society for the Prevention of Accidents (ROSPA), 1 Grosvenor Cres SW1 (5 **J 15**), 01-235 6889, for details of their schemes.

Eastway Cycle Circuit
Temple Mills La E15. 01-534 6085. Coaching to improve cycling ability, training ground for more experienced racing cyclists. Book through schools. Bikes for hire. BMX track. Minimum age 7. *OPEN Nov-Feb 08.00-17.00 Mon-Sun, Mar-Oct 08.00-20.00 Mon-Sun. Charge.*

Dancing

English Folk Dance and Song Society
Cecil Sharp House, 2 Regent's Park Rd
NW1. 01-485 2206. Hobby Horse Club.

Imperial Society of   **2 C 17**
Teachers of Dancing
Euston Hall, Birkenhead St WC1. 01-837
9967. Teachers of ballet by the Cecchetti
method and other types of dance. Send sae
for a list of teachers and local dance
schools.

The Place   **3 E 25**
17 Duke's Rd WC1. 01-387 0152. Modern
dance classes for children aged 6-8, 8-10,
10-12 and 13-17 on *Sat* mornings. *Charge.*
Also the home of the London Contemporary Dance Theatre.

Rambert School of Ballet
West London Institute of Higher Education,
Gordon House, 300 St Margaret's Rd,
Twickenham. 01-891 0121 (for application,
auditions and interviews). Classes for children 3½-11, *after school and on Sat mornings. Charge.* This is the junior school of
the famous Ballet Rambert.

Royal Academy of Dancing   **4 P 4**
48 Vicarage Cres SW11. 01-223 0091.
Classes in classical ballet for children aged
5-17, leading to RAD graded examinations.
Charge. Send sae for lists of teachers,
addressed to the Education and Training
Dept.

Royal Ballet School
White Lodge, Richmond Park, Surrey.
01-876 5547. This is the Lower School for
children aged 11-16. Auditions are held to
determine potential for classical ballet training. Accepted children receive a full-time
general education in addition to being
taught classical ballet.

Drama workshops

Anna Scher Children's   **3 D 31**
Theatre in Islington
72 Barnsbury Rd N1. 01-278 2101. Afterschool classes for children from age 6 in
mime, improvisation, poetry, dance, production, stage technique and theory of theatre. 2½-year waiting list for places.
Charge.

Chats Palace
42-44 Brooksby's Wlk E9. 01-533 0227.
Performance workshop *17.00-18.00 Tue,*
when children help prepare the annual
Christmas show – making props, masks,
singing and acting. *Charge.*

Cockpit Theatre
Gateforth St NW8. 01-262 7907 (Box Office

01-402 5081). ILEA theatre and youth arts
workshop. During termtime offers workshops on photography, drama and dance
for girls aged 9-14. *Mon eves. Free.*

Curtain Theatre
26 Commercial St E1. 01-247 6788. ILEA
drama centre catering for the 14+ age
group. No need to have acting ability, there
are courses in do-it-yourself backstage
work. *Free.*

Greenwich Young People's Theatre
Burrage Rd SE18. 01-854 1316. Lively *eve
workshops Mon-Fri* during school terms for
7-21-year-olds, ranging from drama to
music and visual arts. Occasional performances by outside groups. *Charge.*

Mountview Theatre School
104 Crouch Hill N8. 01-340 5885. Runs a
summer school for children. Phone 01-889
8110 for information.

National Youth Theatre
Holloway Rd N7. 01-281 3863. Ages 14-21.
Auditions are held in *Feb & Mar* (closing
date to apply for audition *end Dec*) to select
the casts of plays to be rehearsed and
performed during the summer hols. Only
cost is your own food and accommodation
during the summer and sometimes a few
weekends in between.

Questors Theatre
Mattock La W5. 01-567 0011. Excellent
amateur theatre club with drama playgroups, 'Stage 2' and 'Junior drama' workshop. *Classes 17.00 & 17.30 Mon-Fri.*
Improvisation for under 5's *Sat morning.
Small charge.*

St George's Theatre
Tufnell Park Rd N7. 01-607 7978. Shakespearian productions for education. Workshops in the morning are followed by
performances in the afternoon. Also have a
resources centre and do special workshops
for primary-school children, the Theatre
Experience for 12-14-year-olds and 'A' level
workshops. Shakespearian programme
runs *Oct-Dec & Feb-Apr.* A variety of workshops are held *May-Jul. Charge.*

Theatre Royal E15
Gerry Raffles Sq E15. 01-534 0310. Theatre
workshop for children. *Sat & school hols;
under 14s 12.00-13.30; over 14s
13.30-16.00,* including drama games and
music. Ages 7-17. *Free.*

Family workshops

*These are places which offer special
classes for parents and children together.
Usually a small charge.*

Camden Institute
87 Holmes Rd NW5. 01-267 1414. Family Arts Centre providing many activities, including painting, batik, sculpture, pottery, woodwork, badminton, judo, dance and music. Lunch and refreshments available. *OPEN Sep-Apr 10.00-15.00 Sat.*

Morley College Family   5 O 22
Classes
61 Westminster Bridge Rd SE1. 01-928 8501. *Sat classes* in drama, art and other subjects meet *once a month* Sep-Jun. Send for enrolment details Jul/Aug.

Gymnastics

Most sports centres provide classes and coaching for all ages, including under-5s.
Amateur Gymnastics Association
The Sec, Mrs J. Thatch, 4 Victoria Rd, Chingford, E4. 01-529 9142. Organising body for the sport, which should provide advice and a list of clubs.

Life-saving

Your local swimming baths should provide information about coaching and tests.
North London Rescue Commando
Cordova Rd E3. 01-980 0289. Club for boys only, on the Regent's Canal near Victoria Park. Learn canoeing, life-saving, climbing, sailing, first aid and rescue drill. They also provide a rescue service for local regattas. *Most activities take place Apr-Oct. Charge.*

Music

There is a professional register of music teachers which should be available in the reference section of your library. Ask the librarian.
London College of Music   2 G 20
47 Great Marlborough St W1. 01-437 6120. *Sat morning* junior music school for children over 10. Also individual lessons for any instrument. *Charge.*
London Orchestral   2 I 21
Association
13 Archer St W1. 01-437 1588. Can recommend teachers for any kind of instrument.
National Youth Jazz Orchestra
Meets at the Cockpit Theatre. Details from 11 Victor Rd, Harrow, Middx. 01-863 2717.

National Youth Orchestra of Great Britain
Causeway House, Lodge Causeway, Fishponds, Bristol. Write for detailed information and application forms. Children aged 11-17 can apply for audition to be trained, and once a member of the orchestra remain so until they are 21.
Youth Music Centre
Bigwood House School, Bigwood Rd NW11. 01-907 8018. Lively centre with music school, orchestras and classes on *Sat mornings* during termtime. All types of classical music. High standard. *Charge.*

Natural history & conservation

Young Friends of the Zoo   2 A 21
London Zoo, Regent's Park NW1. 01-722 3333. For 10-15-year-olds. Membership (*charge*) gives free entry to London Zoo or Whipsnade *throughout the year (except B.hols)*, the zoo magazine three times a year, hol lectures, films and outings.
London Natural History Society
Contact: Mike Earp, Secretary, 63 Ivinghoe Rd, Bushey, Watford. Welcomes junior members to the regular outings and meetings in London (Holborn Central Library) and elsewhere. Birdwatching excursions most weekends. Covers the area within a 20-mile radius of St Paul's Cathedral. Newsletter and bulletin every two months. *Charge.*
Young Ornithologists Club
c/o The Royal Society for the Protection of Birds (RSPB), The Lodge, Sandy, Beds. Sandy 80551. Junior membership gives a badge, a bi-monthly magazine (*Bird Life*) and a chance to take part in outings to RSPB reserves and join in special projects. They also organise holiday courses. Family, school and group membership also available. *Charge.*

Poetry

Poetry Society   1 H 5
21 Earl's Court Sq SW5. 01-373 2551. Occasional children's workshops and events including children's poetry competitions. Generous prizes. Also runs the Poets and Schools scheme whereby well-known poets visit schools. Enquiries to Education Officer.

Puppetry

The Puppet Centre Trust
Battersea Arts Centre, Lavender Hill SW11. 01-228 5335. National reference centre for everything to do with puppetry. Offers information and consultancy service, exhibition and shop, training courses and therapy unit. Also supply information about puppet shows. Membership necessary.

Youth organisations

Girl Guides Association   5 **M** 14
17-19 Buckingham Palace Rd SW1. 01-834 6242. For girls aged 7-11 there are Brownie packs and at the age of 10 girls can become Guides. From 14-18 they can join the Rangers.

London Union of Youth Clubs
64 Camberwell Rd SE5. 01-701 6366. To put you in touch with your local clubs. If you live in Greater London you should contact youth and community departments in local boroughs. The Union is for 7-25-year-olds but mainly deals with 12-21-year-olds.

National Association of Boys Clubs
369 Kennington Lane SE11. 01-793 0787. For information about clubs, adventure courses and activity hols.

The Scout Association   I **G** 9
Baden-Powell House, 65 Queen's Gate SW7. 01-584 7030. Headquarters of the movement. They will give you the address of your nearest company. Boys aged 6-8 become Beavers, those aged 8-11 become Cubs and above that age Scouts. 16-21-year-olds can become Venture Scouts.

Playgrounds and playcentres

Most parks offer facilities for children's play – look out for those which provide special attractions such as animal enclosures and children's zoos (see 'London's countryside').

Adventure playgrounds
Community based playgrounds, run by playworkers, who organise activities indoors and out. Children are usually free to build dens, using old timber and junk. For more information contact London Adventure Playground Association, 28 Under-wood Rd E1. 01-377 0314. *OPEN after school, at weekends and during school hols.*

Conventional playgrounds
Provided by borough councils in most local parks. They usually have tarmac surfaces with old equipment (swings, roundabouts, slides, seesaws, climbing frames, and iron rocking-horses). Some of this equipment is potentially dangerous for small children and newer, safer playgrounds have swings made of rubber tyres and built-up slides made of durable plastic. *OPEN 08.00-19.00 (or dusk) Mon-Sun.*

Handicapped Adventure Playground Association
Fulham Palace, Bishops Av SW6. 01-736 4443. The Association runs five playgrounds for the handicapped in London and provides information about its services as well as play ideas for handicapped children. All the playgrounds are carefully planned and landscaped with children with special needs in mind. Also advisory service which gives help to those wishing to set up their own playground.

One o'clock Clubs
Enclosed area in some parks, specially for children under 5. Each club has a building for indoor play (painting, drawing, modelling etc) and an enclosure with climbing frames, swings and sandpit for outdoor play. There are playworkers to supervise activities but a parent or guardian is expected to stay on the premises. Informal and friendly. To find your nearest club, contact the local Borough Council. *OPEN 13.00-16.30 Mon-Fri. Free.*

Playcentres & junior clubs
Playcentres are mainly in schools which are kept open after school hours and during school hols to provide activities for children aged 5-13. Junior clubs are open to children of secondary school age only. They usually offer games, painting and other activities. Teas, snacks and lunch available. *OPEN 09.00-17.30 Mon-Fri.* For a list of playcentres and junior clubs in Inner London, contact your local Education Authority.

Playparks
Intended for children of 5-15 – the aim is towards free play with structures for climbing, swinging etc and playworkers to supervise. You'll find them in Alexandra Park, Battersea Park, Crystal Palace Park, Holland Park and on Hampstead Heath (Parliament Hill Fields). Contact the local Borough Council for information. *OPEN summer 11.30-20.00 Mon-Sun.*

Children's holidays

There are innumerable organisations which arrange holidays for unaccompanied children, and others arrange family holidays. The best way to find out about them is from one of the following:

Central Bureau for   2 E 18
Educational Visits & Exchanges
Seymour Mews House, Seymour Mews W1. 01-486 5101. They publish several excellent guides including *Volunteer Work*, and *Working Holidays*, covering opportunities both at home and abroad.

English Tourist Board   5 L 15
4 Grosvenor Gdns SW1. 01-730 3488. Their annual publication *Activity and Hobby Holidays* is packed with information covering a huge range of holidays in England, from walking, riding, sailing, birdwatching and painting to underwater swimming, archery or fossil hunting. Also multi-activity holidays. There is a special section on holidays for unaccompanied children, and places welcoming families are indicated.

John Ridgeway School of Adventure
Ardmore, Rhiconich, by Lairg, Sutherland. Kinlochbervie 229. International summer school for 12+. Off-shore and dinghy sailing, hill walking, rock climbing, canoeing and survival in remote Highland coastal areas. Dormitories in wooden buildings on the shores of a remote sea loch.

PGL Young Adventure
Station St, Ross-on-Wye, Hereford. Ross-on-Wye 764211. Holidays for ages 7-18. Up to 40 activities including canoeing, pony trekking, sailing, camping, computer and hobby holidays under expert guidance at 30 locations in Britain and abroad. Also family holidays. Brochures available.

YHA Adventure Holidays
Youth Hostel Association, Trevelyan House, St Stephen's Hill, St Albans, Herts. St Albans 55215. Adventure holidays for 11-15-year-olds (in groups of 10-12) with experienced instructors. Large range of special interest holidays as well as multi-activity holidays. YHA members can also arrange their own cycling or walking hols and make use of the YHA hostels.

Exchanges

Amitié Internationale des Jeunes
Beaver House, 10a Woodborough Rd SW15. 01-788 6857. Exchanges between French and British schoolchildren, 11-18-

year-olds. Escorts are provided on the journey between London and Paris.

Robertson's Educational Travel Service
44 Willoughby Rd NW3. 01-435 4907. Long-established. Careful matching up of families for exchanges between France and England. Also arrange paying guest visits for children to France. 12-19-year-olds. Escorted travel from London.

Entertainment

Venues which provide children's shows, films and concerts. See children's section in Time Out.

Children's theatre

The following theatres put on children's shows regularly through the year. Phone for programme details, or see the weekly magazines Time Out, City Limits or What's On. For drama workshops, see 'Clubs and classes'.

Little Angel Marionette   3 D 33
Theatre
14 Dagmar Passage, off Cross St N1. 01-226 1787. London's only permanent puppet theatre, which presents an excellent variety of shows by the resident company and visiting puppeteers. Essential to book (by phone) in advance. Regular performance at *15.00 Sat & Sun* for older children and adults. Special show for the very young (3-6-year-olds) *11.00 Sat*. Extra shows during half-term and school hols.

Mermaid Molecule Theatre   3 E 24
Bloomsbury Theatre, 15 Gordon St WC1. 01-388 5739. Theatre of Science for Young People. Exciting plays that aim to bridge the gap between science and drama. 4-18-year-olds. *Performances Jan, Easter & autumn.*

Polka Children's Theatre
240 The Broadway, Wimbledon SW19. 01-543 4888. Extremely attractive theatre complex. 300-seat theatre with plays, puppet-shows and concerts; exhibitions of toys and puppets; children's workshop, adventure room, garden playground and café catering with children in mind. Age 3 upwards. Full facilities for handicapped children. *OPEN Tue-Sat.*

Puppet Theatre Barge
Bookings and details from 78 Middleton Rd E8. 01-249 6876. A marionette theatre in a

converted Thames barge, which has regular moorings at Little Venice *Sep-May.* Tours up the Thames to Oxford from *May-Sep* and is moored at different places on the waterways. Its position is listed in the London entertainment guides. *Performances Sat & Sun and daily during school holidays.*

St George's Theatre
Tufnell Park Rd N7. 01-607 7978. Children's shows in the autumn and spring *14.30 Sat.* Theatre also offers workshops.

Unicorn Theatre for   2 I 22
Children
Arts Theatre, Great Newport St WC2. 01-836 3334. Well-established children's theatre which presents plays (often specially commissioned) and other entertainment for the 4-12s. Public performances *14.30 Sat & Sun* (extra performances during school hols). Performances for schools *at 14.00 Tue-Fri during termtime.* Also a children's club, which organises workshop sessions.

Young Vic Theatre   6 O 24
66 The Cut SE1. 01-928 6363. Young repertory company putting on a good choice of revivals and new experimental theatre, specially written children's plays and adaptations of Shakespeare. A comprehensive education service, and out-of-school workshops, touring group staging children's plays. Age approx 13 upwards.

Children's films

Institute of Contemporary   5 K 20
Arts (ICA)
Nash House, The Mall SW1. 01-930 6393. Family films, usually *Sat & Sun afternoons.* For children up to 14.

National Film Theatre   6 M 23
South Bank SE1. 01-928 3232. Junior matinees, usually *Sat & Sun afternoons.*

Children's concerts

Several organisations arrange children's concerts (mainly classical music) through the autumn and winter. Also look out for steel bands, brass bands and jazz bands at summer festivals and fairs in the parks.

Arthur Davison Orchestral Concerts
Fairfield Hall, Croydon, Surrey. 01-688 9291. Orchestral concerts for children – selection of short pieces, introducing a wide variety of instruments. *Season tickets available for seven concerts Sep-May 11.00 Sat. Charge.*

Ernest Read Concerts for   6 M 23
Children
Royal Festival Hall, South Bank SE1. 01-928 3191. Orchestral concerts for children over 7, arranged by the Ernest Read Music Association. *Season tickets available for six concerts, Oct-May. Tickets issued from late Apr. Apply Abbey Box Office, 01-870 1655. Or write to: Jennifer Sedgwick, 26 Bartholomew Cl SW18. Charge.*

Morley College Family   5 P 22
Concerts
61 Westminster Bridge Rd SE1. 01-928 8501. Series of informal concerts designed to introduce children and parents to a wide variety of music, from classical to pop, ethnic to electronic. *Season tickets available for eight monthly concerts, Sep-May 10.30-12.30 Sat. Tickets issued in Sep. Also at door. Charge.*

Robert Mayer Concerts for   6 M 23
Children
Royal Festival Hall, South Bank SE1. 01-928 3191. Founded 1923, now sponsored by BBC. Orchestral concerts with a mixture of classical and modern music. *Season tickets available for six Sat morning concerts, Oct-Mar. Tickets issued from late May. Apply to: BBC Yalding House, 156 Great Portland St W1. 01-927 4523. Charge.*

Radio & TV shows

See 'Radio and TV shows' in 'Theatres, cinemas, music and poetry'.

Help for parents

Education & schools

Advisory Centre for Education (ACE)
18 Victoria Park Sq E2. 01-980 4596. The best source of information and advice on schools and teachers, from pre-school to sixth form. Ask for their list of publications. They also publish information sheets and an excellent magazine *ACE Bulletin,* available by annual subscription.

Gabbitas, Truman & Thring   2 I 20
Educational Trust
6 Sackville St W1. 01-734 0161. Expert and free advice on all aspects of private education from nursery to university level. Includes tutorial colleges, secretarial colleges and language tuition.

Independent Schools   5 L 17
Information Service
50 Buckingham Gate SW1. 01-630 8793
(head office). Information about independent and private schools.

National Association for   2 G 17
Gifted Children
1 South Audley St W1. 01-499 1188. Free
advice and help for parents of unusually
gifted children. Publications by subscription; send sae.

Pre-school playgroups

Greater London Pre-school   5 N 16
Playgroups Association
314 Vauxhall Bridge Rd SW1. 01-828 2417.
For information about playgroups in the 22
outer London boroughs.

Inner London Pre-school   5 N 16
Playgroups Association
314 Vauxhall Bridge Rd SW1. 01-828 1401.
For information about playgroups in the 12
inner London boroughs.

Pre-school Playgroups   3 F 28
Association
Head Office, 61 King's Cross Rd WC1.
01-833 0991. For publications and other
information.

Children in hospital

National Association for the 6 N 24
Welfare of Children in Hospital
Argyle House 29-31 Euston Rd NW1.
01-833 2041. Help and advice for parents in
preparing children for hospital stays.

Babysitters & childminders

*The following have a minimum stay of 4
hours; and fares are extra.*
Babysitters Unlimited
London House, King St W6. 01-741 5566.
Covers central London. *Annual membership and fee at each booking. Hourly rate
varies according to time of day.*
Childminders   2 C 19
9 Paddington St W1. 01-935 9763/2049.
Covers 20-mile radius. *Initial fee plus hourly
rate.*

Children's shopping

Books

*Foyles, Dillons, and Hatchards have good
children's book departments. See 'Shopping'.*

Book-Boat
Cutty Sark Gardens SE10. 01-853 4383.
Children's bookshop on a brightly painted
barge, moored near the *Cutty Sark. OPEN
10.00-17.00 Mon-Sun. CLOSED Thur.*

Puffin Bookshop   6 J 23
1 Covent Garden Market WC2. 01-379
6465. Large stock of children's books,
including the full Puffin range. Adult titles
downstairs. *OPEN 10.00-18.00 Mon-Sat.*

Young World   1 D 6
229 Kensington High St W8. 01-937 6314.
The largest selection of children's books in
London with 30,000 titles. Also toys, gifts
and stationery. *OPEN 09.30-18.00 Mon-
Sat, 12.00-18.00 Sun.*

Carnival & party novelties

Barnum's   1 D 2
67 Hammersmith Rd W14. 01-602 1211.
Masks, fairground novelties, balloons,
flags. For hire and sale. *OPEN 09.00-17.30
Mon-Fri, 10.00-16.00 Sat.*

Escapade
150 Camden High St NW1. 01-485 7384.
Get all your party kit here. Stuffed full of
costumes, jokes, tricks, masks, wigs and
novelties. *OPEN 10.00-19.00 Mon-Fri,
10.00-18.00 Sat.*

Theatre Zoo   3 I 23
21 Earlham St WC2. 01-836 3150. Animal
costumes for hire, grotesque and unusual
face masks, false feet, hats, hands and
moustaches, and stage make-up. *OPEN
09.30-17.30 Mon-Fri, 10.00-13.00 Sat.*

Magic, jokes & tricks

Davenports Magic Shop   3 H 23
Charing Cross Underground Stn WC2.
01-836 0408. Jokes, tricks, puzzles, practi-
cal jokes – some at pocket money prices.
Plus elaborate tricks for the professionals.
*OPEN 09.30-17.30 Mon-Fri, 09.30-16.00
Sat.*

Models

See 'Models' under 'Shops and services.'

Party entertainers

Arnold Stoker's Entertainment Agency
32 King's Rd SW19. 01-540 1191. Every
type of entertainment: puppets, clowns,
films, cartoons, conjurors and ventrilo-
quists, for children aged 4-14.

Professor Alexander's Punch & Judy Show
72 Eleanor Rd E8. 01-254 0416. Traditional show lasting 1/2hr or longer.

Len Belmont
48 Morland Estate E8. 01-254 8300. Children's entertainer with ventriloquist, magic and balloon modelling.

Kensington Carnival Co   4 J 4
123 Ifield Rd SW10. 01-370 4358. Provides presents, toys and paper tableware. Hires out low tables and chairs and has a list of recommended entertainers.

Puppet Centre Trust
Battersea Arts Centre, Lavender Hill SW11. 01-228 5335. They can recommend puppeteers and Punch & Judy shows for parties.

Toys & games

Many department stores have very good toy departments, especially Harrods, Selfridges and Heal's. Most of the following specialist shops will send catalogues on request. Remember you can also borrow toys. Contact Play Matters, The National Toy Libraries Association, 68 Church Way NW1 (01-387 9592) for details of your local toy library.

The Dolls House   6 J 23
29 Covent Garden Mkt WC2. 01-379 7243. Wide range of hand-made dolls' houses and miniature furniture in attractive antique styles for children and collectors. *OPEN 10.00-20.00 Mon-Sat.*

Dolls' Hospital   4 J 1
16 Dawes Rd SW6. 01-385 2081. Casualty department for broken limbs, spare part surgery, antique restoration, etc. Also a few toys and dolls for sale. *Phone for opening times.*

Early Learning Centre   1 D 6
225 Kensington High St W8. 01-937 0419. Bright, durable, educational toys for babies upwards. Play area for under-8's. *OPEN 09.00-18.00 Mon-Sat.*

Hamleys   2 H 20
188-196 Regent St W1. 01-734 3161. Largest toyshop in London. Play areas. Has nearly everything. All ages. *OPEN 09.30-18.00 Mon-Sat.*

Kristin Baybars
3 Mansfield Rd NW5. 01-267 0934. Tiny treasure chest which specialises in craftsman-made dolls' houses, miniatures and unusual small toys. *OPEN 11.00-18.00 Tue-Sat. CLOSED Mon.*

Pollocks Toy Shop   2 F 22
1 Scala St W1. 01-636 3452. Fascinating small shop which sells toys, old-fashioned and modern, and the famous Victorian cut-out model theatres. *OPEN 10.00-17.00 Mon-Sat.*

Pollocks Toy Theatres Ltd   6 J 23
44 Covent Garden Mkt WC2. 01-379 7866. In addition to toys and Victorian cut-out model theatres, sells antique dolls for children and collectors. Also specialises in christening presents. *OPEN 10.00-17.00 Mon-Sat.*

The Singing Tree   4 M 1
69 New King's Rd SW6. 01-736 4527. Not just for children, this amazing shop stocks new and antique dolls' houses and everything imaginable to go in them. Collectors' items in miniature. Mail-order service. *OPEN 10.00-17.30 Mon-Sat.*

Tiger, Tiger   4 L 4
219 King's Rd SW3. 01-352 8080. Marvellous window displays. Inside baskets of pocket money toys, dolls and soft and wooden toys. *OPEN 10.00-18.00 Mon-Sat.*

Tree House   1 D 6
237 Kensington High St W8. 01-937 7497. Gift shop for children aged 0-8. Christening gifts and presents for all the family. *OPEN 09.30-18.00 Mon-Sat.*

Virgin Games Centre   2 G 22
100 Oxford St W1. 01-637 7911. Renowned for its incredible fantasy games. Whole department devoted to war games. Also full Trivial Pursuit range and computer games. *OPEN 09.00-19.00 (to 20.00 Thur) Mon-Sat.*

Children's clothes

C & A Modes   2 E 17
501-519 Oxford St W1. 01-629 7272. (Main branch.) Good selection of inexpensive clothes for children up to 16 especially sports kit. *OPEN 09.30-19.00 (to 20.00 Thur) Mon-Sat.*

Laura Ashley   2 G 20
256 Regent St W1. 01-437 9760. Pastoral prints on cotton lawn, corduroys and drills, smocks, shirts and Victorian party dresses. Sailor suits. Straw boaters with lots of flowers. *OPEN 09.30-18.00 (to 20.00 Thur) Mon-Sat.*

Marks and Spencer   2 E 17
458 Oxford St W1. 01-935 7954. (Largest branch, first to get the new ranges.) Foreign mums flock to buy the reasonably priced kilts, footwear, jumpers, macs and underwear; English ones tend to take M&S for

granted as being best value for children's clothes. *OPEN 09.00-20.00 Mon-Fri. 09.00-18.00 Sat.*

Mothercare 2 F 18
461 Oxford St W1. 01-629 6621. (Main branch.) Good quality everyday clothes at reasonable prices. Co-ordinated tops and bottoms as well as accessories for babies and children up to 11. *OPEN 10.00-18.00 (to 20.00 Thur) Mon-Sat.*

Next 1 D 8
54-60 Kensington High St W8. 01-938 3709. Next department store with a special section called B & G full of trendy children's wear: thick cotton tracksuits, tartan duffle coats and a small range of interesting shoes. *OPEN 09.15-18.00 (to 20.00 Thur) Mon-Sat.*

012 2 F 19
22 South Molton St W1. 01-409 1599. Junior version of Benetton. Colourful Italian clothes. Other branches. *OPEN 10.00-18.00 (to 19.00 Thur) Mon-Sat.*

Please Mum 2 G 19
69 New Bond St W1. 01-493 5880. Expen-
sive, dressy, mainly Italian clothes for new-born babies to 14-year-olds. *OPEN 09.30-18.00 (to 19.00 Thur) Mon-Sat.*

Pollyanna 4 L 4
811 Fulham Rd SW6. 01-731 0673. Beautifully designed, practical but unusual clothes for boys and girls up to 12. *OPEN 09.00-17.30 Mon-Sat.*

Small Change
25 Carnegie House NW3. 01-794 3043. Only the best second-hand clothes and toys for toddlers upwards. Clothes are sold on sale or return basis. *OPEN 10.00-16.30 Tue-Fri, 10.00-13.00 Sat. CLOSED Mon.*

The White House 2 G 19
51-52 New Bond St W1. 01-629 3521. Grand store with prices to match. Children's tailored clothes. Mostly French and Italian imports in traditional styles. *OPEN 09.00-17.30 Mon-Fri.*

Zero Four Plus 2 F 19
53 South Molton St W1. 01-493 4920. Mainly Italian and French clothes for 0-14 years, including hand-knits. *OPEN 10.00-18.00 Mon-Sat.*

Student London

Reference libraries

There are over 400 specialist libraries in London. The following selection are the most important and have been classified in sections to both the enquiring visitor and the serious research worker. The British Museum Library can usually solve problems of research because of its vast collections. It is, however, busy and under-staffed, so try other libraries first. Public libraries, maintained by each borough, offer access to magazines, newspapers and reference books. Some have large reference departments specialising in certain subjects.

General

The British Library 3 G 24
Great Russell St WC1. 01-636 1544. This is the national copyright library which holds one copy of every printed book published in the UK. It is also a wide-ranging reference
library with an incomparable collection of books, periodicals and manuscripts in English and foreign languages, but should only be used as a library of last resort. Admission to the Bloomsbury Reading Rooms is restricted to academics and professional researchers, who have to obtain a pass from the Reader Admissions office. Adults over 21 only. *Reading Rooms OPEN 09.00-16.45 Mon, Fri & Sat, 09.00-20.45 Tue-Thur. CLOSED Sun & B.hols.*

British Library Newspaper Library
200 Colindale Av NW9. 01-323 7355. National collection of newspapers from the UK and overseas countries. London newspapers prior to 1801 held at British Museum main building. Adults over 21 only. *OPEN 10.00-16.45 Mon-Sat. Free.*

Government Departments
Extensive collections. Available by appointment only. Official publications, history and information associated with the department. The following few (of many) have particularly large libraries: Treasury; Home Office; Foreign and Commonwealth Office;

Army Dept; Navy Dept; Dept of Environment.

London Library   5 J 20
14 St James's Sq SW1. 01-930 7705. A writers' and scholars' library with many distinguished authors among its members. Permanent collection of standard and authoritative works dating from the 16thC including a unique stock of foreign language books. One million volumes, most of which are on open shelves. Substantial annual membership fee enables readers to take out 10 books at a time. *OPEN 09.30-17.30 Mon-Sat (to 19.30 Thur). Members only.*

Art & architecture

British Architectural Library 2 D 21
66 Portland Pl W1. 01-580 5533. 120,000 volumes; 60,000 photographs. Architecture and related arts, from 15thC to the present day. *OPEN 10.00-17.00 Mon, 10.00-20.00 Tue-Thur, 10.00-19.00 Fri, 10.00-13.00 Sat. CLOSED Aug. Free.*

British Architectural   2 D 17
Drawings Library
Heinz Gallery, 21 Portman Sq W1. 01-580 5533. The most extensive collection of architectural drawings in the world, including practically all the surviving drawings of Palladio. May be consulted on specific research projects *by appt only. OPEN 10.00-13.00 Mon-Fri. CLOSED Aug.*

British Museum   3 G 24
Great Russell St WC1. 01-636 1555. Very extensive collection of original drawings, etchings and engravings in Dept of Prints and Drawings. *OPEN 10.00-13.00 & 14.15-16.00 Mon-Fri, 10.00-12.30 Sat. Pass required – apply to Prints Dept.*

Courtauld Institute of Art   2 D 17
20 Portman Sq W1. 01-935 9292. (Interesting Robert Adam interiors.) 66,000 volumes on the history of art. *OPEN 10.00-18.00 Mon-Fri to students only.* Also the Wick Library, which is open to the public, a collection of over a million photographs, reproductions of paintings and drawings. *OPEN 10.00-18.00 Mon-Fri. Free.*

National Art Library Victoria I H 10
& Albert Museum
Cromwell Rd SW7. 01-589 6371. A million volumes on fine and applied arts of all countries and periods. Sculpture, ceramics, silver, furniture, musical instruments, English costume. Prints and drawings department has extensive collections dealing with art, architecture, pure and applied design

and graphics. *OPEN 10.00-17.00 Tue-Fri, 10.00-13.00 & 14.00-17.00 Sat. CLOSED Mon, Sun & B.hols. Free. Lectures.*

National Monuments   2 H 20
Record
23 Savile Row W1. 01-734 6010. The historic architecture of England. Library of over a million photographs, measured drawings and prints. Sign in at reception. *OPEN 10.00-17.30 Mon-Fri. CLOSED B.hols. Free.*

Royal Academy of Arts   2 D 21
Burlington House, Piccadilly W1. 01-439 7438. Fine Arts. 15,000 volumes, original drawings, mainly 18th-19thC. *OPEN to Friends of the Academy 14.00-17.00 Mon-Fri and to researchers by appt only.*

Royal Society of Arts   6 K 23
8 John Adam St WC2. 01-930 5115. 15,000 books on industrial art and design. May be used for reference by accredited researchers, *by prior appt. OPEN 09.30-17.30 Mon-Fri. CLOSED 12.30-13.30 Tue, Thur & Fri.*

St Bride Printing Library   6 L 27
St Bride Institute, Bride La EC4. 01-353 4660. A public reference library of paper, typography, bookbinding and printing. *OPEN 09.30-17.30 Mon-Fri. CLOSED B.hols. Free.*

Sir John Soane's Museum   3 I 25
Library
13 Lincoln's Inn Fields WC2. 01-405 2107. Art and architecture, 15th-19thC architectural drawings, including many of the drawings from the office of Robert and James Adam and those from Soane's own office. *OPEN 10.00-13.00 & 14.00-17.00 Tue-Fri; 10.00-13.00 Sat. CLOSED Mon. By appt, for specific research enquiries only. Free.*

Westminster Fine Arts   5 J 21
Library
Central Reference Library, St Martin's St WC2. 01-798 2038. English and European books. Painting, drawing, architecture, design, furniture, pottery, costume and sculpture. Periodicals. Also the Preston Blake Library, which contains approx 400 volumes on William Blake. *OPEN 10.00-19.00 Mon-Fri, 10.00-17.00 Sat. Free.*

Ecclesiastic

Dr Williams' Library   3 E 24
14 Gordon Sq WC1. 01-387 3727. Modern and 17th-18thC books on theology, Byzan-

tine history, Dissenting history. 112,000 volumes. *OPEN 10.00-17.00 Mon-Fri (to 18.30 Tue & Thur). CLOSED B.hols. Free.*

Jews' College
Albert Rd NW4. 01-203 6427. Hebraica and Judaica. 80,000 books and manuscripts. *OPEN 09.00-18.00 (to 17.00 in vacations) Mon-Thur, 09.00-13.00 Fri, 09.30-12.30 Sun. CLOSED B.hols & Jewish hols. Free.*

Lambeth Palace   5 P 21
Lambeth Palace Rd SE1. 01-928 6222. The archives of Archbishops of Canterbury from medieval times. 150,000 books, 3500 manuscripts, records, much larger number of archives. *OPEN 10.00-16.50 Mon-Fri to public on production of a letter of introduction. Free.*

Sion College   6 L 26
Victoria Embankment EC4 (entrance in John Carpenter St). 01-353 7983. Theological books from 17thC to present day. 90,000 volumes. *OPEN 10.00-17.00 Mon-Fri. Check times. Appt preferred. Free.*

Westminster Abbey Chapter   5 M 20
Library & Muniment Room
The Cloisters, Westminster Abbey SW1. 01-222 5152. 16th-18thC theology and history of Westminster Abbey. Archives from before the Norman Conquest. 14,000 volumes. *Appt preferred. OPEN 10.00-13.00 & 14.00-16.45 Mon-Fri. Free.*

Film, sound, photo

British Film Institute   2 G 22
21 Stephen St W1. 01-255 1444. The national archive, an extensive collection of over 20,000 films, 750,000 original stills. 19,000 books and scripts. *OPEN 10.00-17.00 Mon-Fri. Members only.*

Hulton Picture Library   2 D 19
Unique House, 21-31 Woodfield Rd W9. 01-266 2662. Ten million photographs and prints on every conceivable subject. Available for reproduction. *OPEN 09.00-18.00 Mon-Fri. Appt only. Charge to reproduce photograph or print.*

National Sound Archive   1 H 10
29 Exhibition Rd SW7. 01-589 6603. National archive of sound recordings. 180,000 discs, tapes and cylinders. Also a library, with documentation on all aspects of sound recording. 150 current periodicals. Record catalogues and release sheets. *Reference only. Listening service (appt only) and library. OPEN 09.30-16.30 (to 21.00 Thur) Mon-Fri. Free.*

Geography

British Library Map Library   3 G 24
Great Russell St WC1. 01-636 1544. Holds over a million printed maps and 20,000 manuscripts. *OPEN 10.00-16.30 Mon-Sat. Identification necessary. Free.*

Royal Geographical Society   1 G 11
1 Kensington Gore SW7. 01-589 5466. Geography in all aspects. 135,000 books, 750,000 maps together with several thousand atlases. Public Map Room. *OPEN 10.00-17.00 Mon-Fri. CLOSED B.hols & part Jun & Jul. Free.*

History

Guildhall Library   6 M 30
Aldermanbury EC2. 01-606 3030. A reference library which also provides the official repository for deposited archives relating to the City of London. 230,000 volumes and printed items of London topography and history. *OPEN 09.30-17.00 Mon-Sat (Prints and Map dept closed Sat). CLOSED B.hols. Free.*

Institute of Archaeology   3 E 24
University of London. 31-34 Gordon Sq WC1. 01-387 6052. Archaeology. particularly Europe. Western Asia. Latin America. world prehistory. conservation and human environment. 800 current periodicals. 48,000 monographs and 27,000 journals. *OPEN termtime only 10.00-20.00 Mon-Fri. 10.00-18.00 Sat. Free.*

Institute of Classical   3 E 24
Studies
University of London. 31-34 Gordon Sq WC1. 01-387 7697. Includes the Hellenic and Roman Societies Library. 60,000 volumes. Classical Antiquity. Open to members of Roman or Hellenic societies. *OPEN 09.30-18.00 Mon-Fri. 10.00-17.00 Sat. CLOSED every Sat & last two weeks in Aug. Free.*

Institute of Historical   3 F 24
Research
University of London. Senate House. Malet St WC1. 01-636 0272. 120,000 volumes. Concentrates on principal sources for British and foreign medieval and modern history. Holds regular research seminars. *OPEN 09.00-21.00 Mon-Fri. 09.00-17.00 Sat. Members only.*

Library of the Museum in Docklands
Project
10 Prestons Rd E14. 01-515 1162. Houses Port of London Authority archive and has a large and unique collection of material on

the London Docks including 10,000 photographs, prints and engravings. *OPEN 10.00-17.00 Mon-Fri by appt. CLOSED Sat & B.hols.*

Museum of London Library 6 L 30
London Wall EC2. 01-600 3699. London history and topography. *Appt only Mon-Fri. CLOSED Sat & B.hols.*

National Maritime Museum Library
Romney Rd SE10. 01-858 4422. Large collection of prints and drawings. 50,000 books, maps, charts. Portraits. *Open to anyone for genuine research. Identification necessary. For longer projects ticket issued. OPEN 10.00-17.00 Mon-Fri, 14.00-17.00 Sat. Free. Appt required on Sat.*

Society of Antiquaries 2 I 19
Burlington House, Piccadilly W1. 01-734 0193. Archaeological and antiquarian research. 130,000 volumes. *OPEN 10.00-17.00 Mon-Fri by appt only.*

Law & public records

British Library Official 3 G 24
Publications and Social Sciences Service
Great Russell St WC1. 01-636 1544. Official British publications and political and educational journals. *Reader's pass required. OPEN 09.30-16.45 Mon, Fri & Sat, 09.30-20.45 Tue-Thur. CLOSED B.hols.*

Inns of Court
The principal law libraries (Inner Temple, Middle Temple, Lincoln's Inn and Gray's Inn) *only available by special permission.*

Institute of Advanced Legal 3 F 24
Studies
University of London, 17 Russell Sq WC1. 01-637 1731. Centre for legal studies. 105,000 volumes. *OPEN 10.00-20.00 Mon-Thur, 10.00-17.30 Fri, 10.00-12.30 Sat. Free to academic researchers. Charge to commercial organisations.*

Public Record Office 6 K 26
Chancery La WC2. 01-876 3444. Government archives and records of the Courts from 11thC to 1800. Records from 1800 to present day stored in Ruskin Av, Kew. For access to either need reader's pass. *OPEN 09.30-17.00 Mon-Fri. CLOSED B.hols and first two weeks of Oct for stock-taking.*

Literature

The British Library 3 G 24
Great Russell St WC1. 01-636 1544. The most comprehensive literary collection in London of printed books and manuscripts. Adults over 21 only. *Reader's pass required. OPEN 09.00-16.45 Mon, Fri & Sat, 09.00-20.45 Tue-Thur. Free.*

Poetry Library 6 M 23
Royal Festival Hall, South Bank Centre SE1. 01-921 0664. Collection of poetry for loan and reference plus information on poetry events.

Medicine

British Library Science 6 J 24
Reference & Information Service
Aldwych Reading Room, 9 Kean St WC2. 01-636 1544x7288. Historical medical books. All current British clinical publications and foreign periodicals. *OPEN 09.30-17.30 Mon-Fri. Free.*

British Medical Association 3 E 24
Library
Tavistock Sq WC1. 01-387 4499. Over 80,000 books and 2000 modern medical periodicals. British and foreign. *OPEN 09.00-19.00 Mon-Thur, 09.00-17.00 Fri. BMA members free. Charge to non-BMA members.*

Medical Research Council
The Ridgeway NW7. 01-959 3666. All branches of medical science (except clinical science). 14,000 volumes and 600 periodicals. *OPEN 09.00-17.15 Mon-Fri to members only, or by application to director or librarian.*

Pharmaceutical Society 5 Q 20
1 Lambeth High St SE1. 01-735 9141. Pharmaceutical subjects. Historical collections of pharmacopoeias, herbals and botanical works. 60,000 volumes. *OPEN 09.00-17.00 Mon-Fri for bona fide students of pharmacy and allied subjects.*

Royal College of Physicians 2 C 22
11 St Andrews Pl NW1. 01-935 1174. History and biography of medicine. Medical portraits. 50,000 volumes and pamphlets. *OPEN 09.30-17.30 Mon-Fri for serious researchers.*

Royal College of Surgeons 6 J 25
Lincoln's Inn Fields WC2. 01-405 3474. Medical and surgical books and journals including large historical collections on anatomy and surgery. 160,000 volumes. Portraits. *OPEN 10.00-18.00 Mon-Fri. Letter of introduction from a Fellow or another library necessary.*

Wellcome Institute for the 3 D 24
History of Medicine
183 Euston Rd NW1. 01-387 4477. History

of medicine and allied sciences. Original texts. 400,000 volumes. *OPEN 09.45-17.15 (to 19.30 Thur) Mon-Fri. Identification required.*

Westminster Public Library   2 B 17 (Medical)
Marylebone Rd NW1. 01-798 1039. Includes nursing, dentistry, psychiatry, speech and music therapy. Textbooks and periodicals. *Ticket. OPEN 09.30-19.00 Mon-Fri, 09.30-17.00 Sat.*

Music & drama

BBC Music Library   2 E 21
156 Great Portland St W1. 01-580 4468. All forms of printed music. *OPEN 09.30-17.30 Mon-Fri to non-BBC employees by appt with the Librarian only. Charge.*

British Library Music   3 G 24 Library
Great Russell St WC1. 01-636 1544. Printed music and books about music. *Reader's pass required. OPEN 09.30-16.30 Mon, Fri & Sat, 09.30-20.30 Tue-Thur. CLOSED B.hols.*

British Theatre Association   2 A 20
Inner Circle, Regent's Park NW1. 01-935 2571. Comprehensive collection of plays and critical works on the theatre. 250,000 volumes, 65,000 sets of plays. *Play library OPEN 10.00-17.00 Mon-Fri (to 19.30 Wed). Only members may take books out.*

Central Music Library   5 M 14
160 Buckingham Palace Rd SW1. 01-798 2192. (Westminster City Libraries.) Books on music, music scores and parts, music periodicals. *OPEN 09.30-19.00 Mon-Fri, 09.30-17.00 Sat. Free.*

Natural science

British Library Science   6 J 24 Reference & Information Service
Aldwych Reading Room, 9 Kean St WC2. 01-636 1544x7288. Periodicals, books and pamphlets on the life sciences and technologies, medicine, earth sciences, astronomy and pure mathematics. *OPEN 09.30-17.30 Mon-Fri. Free.*

Geological Society   2 I 19
Burlington House, Piccadilly W1. 01-734 2356. 300,000 volumes and papers. 39,000 maps. *OPEN 10.00-17.30 Mon-Fri to Fellows only (or to bona fide researchers introduced by a Fellow).*

Linnean Society   2 I 19
Burlington House, Piccadilly W1. 01-434 4479. Reference library. Botany, biology

and zoology. Historical, biological manuscripts. 100,000 books. *OPEN 10.00-17.00 Mon-Fri by appt only. Letter of Introduction required.*

Natural History Museum   1 H 9
Cromwell Rd SW7. 01-589 6323. Research library. Botany, zoology, entomology, palaeontology, mineralogy and anthropology. Large collection of manuscripts, drawings and prints. 760,000 volumes. *Academics or professional researchers only. Identification necessary. OPEN 10.00-16.30 Mon-Fri.*

Royal Botanic Gardens, Kew
Kew Rd, Richmond, Surrey. 01-940 1171. Botany and travel. Prints and drawings. Extensive and historical record of millions of dried specimens of plants from all over the world. 100,000 volumes. *OPEN Mon-Fri to bona fide researchers only. Appt and opening times by written application to the Director.*

Royal Horticultural Society   5 N 17
Lindley Library, Vincent Sq SW1. 01-834 4333. Over 40,000 volumes of horticultural and botanical books. Collection of original 18th and 19thC plant drawings. Large number of periodicals. *OPEN 09.30-17.30 Mon-Fri. Appt preferred.*

Zoological Society
Regent's Park NW1. 01-722 3333. 150,000 volumes on zoology and related subjects, original zoological drawings and prints. Photographic library. *OPEN 09.30-17.30 Mon-Fri to members, associate members and non-members once they have purchased a ticket.*

Politics, economics & social sciences

British Library Humanities &   3 G 24 Social Sciences
Great Russell St WC1. 01-636 1544. Extensive collection of historical and current works. *Reader's pass required. OPEN 09.00-16.45 Mon, Fri & Sat, 09.00-20.45 Tue-Thur. CLOSED B.hols.*

British Library of Political &   6 J 25 Economic Science
London School of Economics, 10 Portugal St WC2. 01-405 7686. Social science. 790,000 bound volumes, including pamphlets, periodicals and manuscripts in addition to special collections and rarities. *OPEN to research scholars by special permit: Oct-Jun 09.30-21.20 Mon-Fri, 10.00-17.00 Sat; Jul-Sep 09.30-17.00 Mon-Fri only. CLOSED B.hols.*

City Business Library   6 **M** 30
Gillett House, 55 Basinghall St EC2. 01-638 8215. Public reference library. One of the major sources of British and overseas directory material, company reports and financial information. Also newspapers, periodicals, timetables, statistical handbooks and series on commodities and overseas markets. *OPEN 09.30-17.00 Mon-Fri. Free.*

House of Lords Record   5 **N** 20
Office
Palace of Westminster SW1. 01-219 3074. Law and parliamentary history. 100,000 volumes, and manuscripts. *OPEN 09.30-17.00 Mon-Fri, to persons undertaking research of volumes not available elsewhere. Appt necessary. Free.*

Institute of Bankers' Library   6 **N** 30
10 Lombard St EC3. 01-623 3531. Comprehensive professional library on banking and allied subjects. 30,000 volumes. *OPEN 09.00-17.00 Mon-Fri. Appt only to non-members.*

Institute for the Study of   3 **I** 28
Drug Dependence (ISDD)
1-4 Hatton Pl, Hatton Gdn EC1. 01-430 1993. Reference library and information service covering all aspects of the non-medical use of drugs. Over 35,000 journals, articles and books; extensive press cuttings. *OPEN 09.30-17.30 Mon-Fri. Free.*

Science

British Library Science   6 **J** 26
Reference & Information Service
Holborn Division, 25 Southampton Bldgs, Chancery La WC2. 01-323 7496. Formerly known as the Patent Office, it contains periodicals, books, patents, trade marks, literature and reports on inventive sciences, engineering, industrial technologies and commerce. Main library *OPEN 09.30-21.00 Mon-Fri, 10.00-13.00 Sat (for opening times of annexes check with main library). CLOSED B.hols. Free.*

Aldwych Branch   6 **J** 24
9 Kean St WC2. 01-636 1544 x 7288. Has all the rest of the scientific literature with emphasis on life sciences and technologies, medicine, biotechnology, earth sciences, astronomy and pure mathematics. *OPEN 09.30-17.30 Mon-Fri. CLOSED B.hols. Free.*

Institution of Civil Engineers   5 **M** 20
Great George St SW1. 01-222 7722. All branches of engineering; 19thC engineering history. Film library. 100,000 books and

pamphlets. *OPEN 09.15-17.30 Mon-Fri to members and members of the Institution of Mechanical Engineering. Non-members on application to the librarian.*

Royal Aeronautical Society   2 **I** 16
4 Hamilton Pl W1. 01-499 3515. One of the finest collections in the world of historical and modern aeronautical books, prints and photographs. *OPEN 10.00-17.00 Mon-Fri. Charge for non-members.*

Royal Astronomical Society   2 **I** 19
Burlington House, Piccadilly W1. 01-734 4582. 27,000 volumes. Astronomy and geophysics. *OPEN 09.30-17.30 Mon-Fri to Fellows. Non-Fellows should contact the librarian in writing. Identification necessary.*

Royal Institution of Great   2 **I** 19
Britain
21 Albemarle St W1. 01-409 2992. General science and history of science since 1799. Many complete scientific periodicals. Biography. Portraits. 50,000 volumes. *OPEN to non-members by appt 10.00-17.30 Mon-Fri.*

Royal Society of Chemistry   2 **I** 19
Burlington House, Piccadilly W1. 01-437 8656. Early works, periodicals. 100,000 volumes. *OPEN 09.30-17.30 Mon-Fri by appt only to non-members. Letter of introduction necessary.*

Science Museum   1 **H** 10
Imperial College Rd SW7. 01-589 3456. A national reference library of pure and applied science, specialising in the history of science, technology and medicine. More than 450,000 volumes. *OPEN 10.00-17.30 Mon-Sat. Free.*

Cultural institutes

Will provide comprehensive information on their country. Most organise language tuition, exhibitions and filmshows. Some also run summer courses and exchanges.

Austrian Institute   2 **H** 12
28 Rutland Gate SW7. 01-584 8653.

Commonwealth Institute   1 **D** 5
Kensington High St W8. 01-603 4535.

Goethe Institut   1 **G** 11
50 Prince's Gate SW7. 01-581 3344.

Greek Institute
34 Bush Hill Rd N21. 01-360 7968.

Hispanic & Luso Brazilian   5 **J** 14
Council
2 Belgrave Sq SW1. 01-235 2303.

Institut Français du   1 **I** 9
Royaume-Uni
17 Queensberry Pl SW7. 01-589 6211.

Italian Cultural Institute   5   J   14
39 Belgrave Sq SW1. 01-235 1461.
Polish Institute   2   E   21
73 New Cavendish St W1. 01-636 6032.
Society for Cultural Relations with the USSR
320 Brixton Rd SW9. 01-274 2282.
Spanish Institute   5   K   14
102 Eaton Sq SW1. 01-235 1484 5.
Swedish Cultural Dept   2   C   17
11 Montagu Pl W1. 01-724 2101.

Language tuition

A cosmopolitan city such as London offers a wide variety of facilities for learning almost any language. in colleges. cultural centres and private schools. where you can choose between group or individual tuition. Prices and standards vary enormously. There is no centrally maintained register of private language schools. although most can be found in the Yellow Pages. The ILEA organises a large number of language courses which are listed in Floodlight (available from libraries and newsagents). Private tutors may be found by contacting embassies or cultural institutes. by looking in the local newspaper or putting an advert in the paper yourself. You can also enquire at local colleges if staff or foreign students could assist. For information about facilities. methods and tuition contact:

Centre for Information on   2   A   20
Language Teaching and Research (CILT)
Regent's College. Inner Circle, Regent's Park NW1. 01-486 8221.

English as a foreign language

Association of Recognised   6   P   24
English Language Schools
2 Pontypool Pl, Valentine Pl SE1. 01-242 3136. Gives information and advice on the many English language schools within the association in the Greater London area. They are recognised by the British Council as being of a high standard.
Cambridge School of   3   F   25
English
8 Herbrand St WC1. 01-734 4203. Classes at all levels for students of 16+. Literature and film-study courses. Preparation for London Chamber of Commerce exam.
Canning School   1   E   6
4 Abingdon Rd W8. 01-937 9060. Intensive

business-orientated training courses for managers from international European and Far Eastern companies. Small groups and one-to-one. Specialised courses in negotiation and presentation.
International House   2   I   18
106 Piccadilly W1. 01-491 2598. General and executive courses for all levels. Also teacher training courses. Language laboratory and social club.
Sels College   3   J   23
64-65 Long Acre WC2. 01-240 2581. Intensive courses throughout the year. All levels from beginners to Cambridge Proficiency. Accommodation and excursions arranged.

Other languages

The schools and colleges listed below offer tuition in practically any language.
All Languages Ltd
Nelson House, 362 Old St EC1. 01-739 6641.
Conrad Languages   2   G   22
77 Oxford St W1. 01-434 0113.
Inlingua School of   5   M   17
Languages
170 Victoria St SW1. 01-834 0606.
Language Studies Ltd   6   J   23
Woodstock House, 10-12 St James St W1. 01-499 9621.

Secretarial training

Pitman Central College   3   G   25
154 Southampton Row WC1. 01-837 4481. Courses of varying length and intensity including typing, shorthand, secretarial administration, business communication, audio-typing, word processing. Special courses for overseas students.
Sight & Sound   2   I   22
118-120 Charing Cross Rd WC2. 01-379 5742. Full- or part-time, day or evening courses in copy-typing, audio, shorthand, word processing, book-keeping, computing, data processing, PAYE.
Speedwriting/Speedtyping   2   F   19
59-61 South Molton St W1. 01-493 3401. Day and evening courses in secretarial skills, office practice and word processing. Also refresher courses.

Student information

Nowhere is it more exciting to be a student than in London. Cheap theatre and enter-

tainment abound (see 'Theatres, cinemas, music and poetry') and there are many restaurants offering unusual and inexpensive food (see 'Eating and drinking'). London has some of the best stocked reference libraries in the world (see the section 'Reference libraries').

Grants, charitable trusts & sponsorships

Advisory Centre of Education
18 Victoria Park Sq E2. 01-980 4596. Publishes *ACE Bulletin* which reports on all aspects of the state sector of education.

Association of   3   E   24
Commonwealth Universities
36 Gordon Sq WC1. 01-387 8572. Publishes *Scholarships Guide for Commonwealth Postgraduate Students* which gives details of awards to all Commonwealth and UK postgraduates studying in UK and Commonwealth countries. Provides an information service to personal callers (phone first for an appointment) on general aspects of UK and Commonwealth universities.

British Council   5   K   21
10 Spring Gdns SW1. 01-930 8466 (for all London offices). And 65 Davies St W1 (2 G 18). Publishes *Scholarships Abroad* listing scholarships to British students by overseas governments and universities. Also offers grants to foreign postgraduate students wishing to study in the UK and administers overseas students under the government technical education agreement.

Charities Aid Foundation   3   G   27
18 Doughty St WC1. 01-831 7798. Information service. Publishes *Directory of Grant-making Trusts.*

Charity Commission   5   J   21
St Alban's House, 6th Floor, 59 Haymarket SW1. 01-210 4405. Keeps a fully comprehensive register of educational trusts for England and Wales.

Inner London Education   5   N   22
Authority (ILEA)
Education Officer (Ref EO/FHE6/TF), County Hall SE1. 01-633 8865. The ILEA has at its disposal a number of trust funds from which small supplementary grants are made in cases of hardship.

National Council for   3   G   23
Voluntary Organisations
26 Bedford Sq WC1. 01-636 4066. Their *Voluntary Organisations – and NCVO Directory* lists 1400 national voluntary organisations, and includes details of membership, staffing, recruitment of volunteers and funding for research.

National Union of Students   3   E   24
461 Holloway Rd N7. 01-272 8900. Maintains an educational grants advisory service to student unions. Non-union members must write in for information. Also publishes *Grants Information Sheet* – a breakdown of what constitutes eligibility for LEA grants.

Macmillan Press
Brunel Rd, Houndmill Estate, Basingstoke. Basingstoke 29242. Publishes the *Grants Register*, which covers grants world-wide.

Useful organisations

British Council   5   K   21
10 Spring Gdns SW1. 01-930 8466 (for all London offices). And 65 Davies St W1. Promotes Britain abroad – a thorough cultural, educational and technical co-operation between Britain and other countries.

British Youth Council   3   D   25
57 Chalton St NW1. 01-387 7559. Made up of representatives from national youth organisations and local youth councils. Aims to represent the views of young people and to look at ways of giving them a voice in society at local, national and international levels.

National Union of Students   3   E   24
461 Holloway Rd N7. 01-272 8900. At least 2 million students are members. Represents students' rights. Organises and advises on social, cultural and educational events. Research staff deal with welfare problems. Trains student union officers. Produces publications including *The Welfare Manual.*

Social clubs & societies

British Federation of   4   M   8
University Women
Crosby Hall, Cheyne Wlk SW3. 01-352 5354. Membership open to women graduates of all nations. Club facilities and hostel.

International Students'   2   E   21
House
229 Great Portland St W1. 01-631 3223. Open to all full-time students, professional trainees, foreign language assistants, au pairs (over 17) and student nurses. Excellent social and recreational facilities – most sports catered for. Coach visits to places of interest. Also a hostel.

London Union of Youth Clubs
64 Camberwell Rd SE5. 01-701 6320.
Will provide details of local youth clubs with
social, recreational and community facilities.

Student Christian Movement
St Benets House, 327A Mile End Rd E1.
01-981 2010. Inter-denominational fellow-
ship open to all students. Local and international branches. Meetings. Magazine
Movement five times a year.

Victoria League   **5 K 22**
18 Northumberland Av WC2. 01-930 1671.
Hospitality in British homes arranged for
Commonwealth students and nurses.
Comfortable club and programme of social
activities. London hostel.

Student accommodation

*Reasonably priced accommodation is
notoriously difficult to find in London. College accommodation services only deal
with their own students – but don't rely on
them. Initially it may well be necessary to
settle for a temporary solution like one of
the hostels listed below. Foreign students
can try the welfare office of their London
embassy. Flat shares are advertised in the
Evening Standard and Time Out.*

**King's Campus Vacation   4 L 4
Bureau**
552 King's Rd SW10. 01-351 2488. Can
arrange accommodation for visitors and
foreign students during the vacation period
in various halls of residence. Single and
twin rooms.

**London Council for the   3 H 23
Welfare of Women & Girls**
57 Great Russell St WC1. 01-430 1524.
Accommodation advisory service. Also
publish a useful booklet *Hostels in London.*

London Tourist Board   5 M 15
Information Centre, Victoria Station Forecourt SW1. 01-730 3488. Bookings in hostels, guest houses and hotels. Information
on youth accommodation, self-catering and
camping. *OPEN 09.00-20.30 Mon-Sun.*
Also at Heathrow Airport.

**University of London   3 F 24
Accommodation Office**
Union Building, Malet St WC1. 01-636 2918.
They find accommodation for London University students only, but will supply any-
body with a list of halls of residence, many
of which are open to all students during
vacations particularly *Jul-Sep.*

*There is a large selection of hostel accom-
modation in London. Rooms are spartan
but very clean, usually shared. Accommodation is mainly bed and breakfast and
is mixed unless otherwise shown. Mostly
for young people. Prices vary depending on
how long you stay. Weekly rates tend to be
better value than daily rates. It is cheaper to
share a room or a dormitory than to have a
single room. For bed and breakfast for a
day you should expect to pay £7.00-
£15.00.*

*b = bed only, bb = bed and breakfast
fb = full board, sc = self-catering*

Carr-Saunders Hall   2 E 22
18-24 Fitzroy St W1. 01-580 6338. Accom-
modaton only available during summer
vacation *(Jul-Aug).* TV lounge. Mostly
single rooms, some twin. 130 beds. *bb.* Also
have 150 beds in flats. *sc.*

Central Club   3 H 23
16-22 Great Russell St WC1. 01-636 7512.
Short-term accommodation provided (up to
1 week) in 178-bed hostel. Other facilities
include a concert hall, function room and
coffee shop. *b.*

**Central University of Iowa   3 G 24
Hostel**
7 Bedford Pl WC1. 01-580 1121. TV lounge.
Twin and dormitory accommodation. 33
beds. 2 weeks maximum stay. *bb.*

Centre Français   1 A 9
61-69 Chepstow Pl W2. 01-221 8134.
Single, double and multi-bedded rooms for
young people. 166 beds. Maximum stay 3
months (1 week in dormitories). Restaurant, TV room, library and conference
room. *bb.*

Globetrotters Travel Centre   1 G 4
60 Warwick Rd SW5. 01-748 4834. TV
lounge and kitchen. Double, twin and dormitory rooms. 21 beds. No maximum stay.
sc.

International Friendship League
3 Creswick Rd W3. 01-992 0221. Dormitory
accommodation. 50 beds. Games room,
library, TV lounge, garden. Advance booking necessary. Short-stay hostel. *bb.*

**International Students'   2 E 21
House**
229 Great Portland St W1. 01-631 3223.
Mostly single, double or twin rooms and
dormitory accommodation in summer. TV
lounge, games room, squash court. 294
beds. *bb & sc.*

O'Callaghans   1 G 5
205a Earl's Court Rd SW5. 01-370 3000.

TV lounge. Accommodation in shared and twin rooms. No breakfast, but kettles in every room. *b.*

Passfield Hall   3 E 24
1 Endsleigh Pl WCl. 01-387 3584. Accommodation only available during vacations (*Mar-Apr & Jul-Sep*). TV lounge, games room. Single, twin and triple accommodation. 198 beds. *bb.*

Rosebery Avenue Hall   3 H 28
90 Rosebery Av ECl. 01-278 3251. Accommodation only available during vacations (*Mar-Apr & Jul-Sep*). TV lounge and bar. Single rooms; some double and twin. 195 beds. *bb.*

Saney Guruji Hostel   1 B 3
18a Holland Villas Rd W14. 01-603 3704. TV lounge. Dormitory accommodation. 40 beds. *sc.*

Sass House   2 C 12
11 Craven Ter W2. 01-262 2325. TV lounge. Mostly dormitory rooms but also single, double and twin. 36 beds. *bb.*

YMCA London Central Hotel 3 H 23
& Hostel
George Williams House, 112 Great Russell St WCl. 01-637 1333. Mixed hostel for long stays. Single, twin and double rooms each with shower and toilet. 596 beds. There is also a short-stay hotel with single, twin and triple rooms. 168 beds. Excellent sports centre, including swimming pool, attached for members and their families. *There are many other YMCA hostels in London, mainly for men only. Applications must be made to individual hostels, numbers in telephone directory.*

YMCA: London   2 C 12
Metropolitan Region
31 Craven Ter W2. 01-723 0071. Will give addresses and telephone nos of hostels.

YWCA Holborn   3 H 23
Helen Graham House, 57 Great Russell WCl. 01-430 0834. 300 beds. Single and double rooms. Long-term accommodation only (6 months +). *sc.*

YWCA: London Regional   3 H 23
Office
16-22 Great Russell St. 01-580 4827. Provides current information on all 18 London hostels. *Applications must be made to individual hostels, numbers in telephone book.*

Youth Hostel Association   6 J 23
(YHA)
Members only. Join at YHA 14 Southampton St WC2. 01-836 8541. Also large shop with wide range of maps, guides, clothing and equipment. Travel service open to non-members. Dormitory accommodation. Maximum stay 3 nights. Cost per night varies with age. *CLOSE at 23.30.*
London hostels are at:
All Saints Hall of Residence, White Hart La N17. 01-458 9054 *(Jul-Sep only).*
38 Bolton Gdns SW5.   1 H 5
01-373 7083.
36 Carter La EC4.   6 M 28
01-236 4965.
84 Highgate West Hill N6. 01-340 1831.
Holland House, Holland Wlk   1 C 6
W8. 01-937 0748.
4 Wellgarth Rd NW11. 01-458 7196.
Wood Green Halls of Residence, Brabant Rd N22. 01-458 9054. *(Jul-Sep only.)*

Money and business services

Money

Currency

The unit of currency is the pound sterling (£) divided into 100 pence (p). There are coins for 1p, 2p, 5p, 10p, 20p, 50p and £1, with notes for £5, £10, £20 and £50. Some old one shilling and two shilling pieces are still in circulation, and are the same size and value as 5p and 10p pieces respectively.

Exchange facilities

There is no exchange control in Britain, so you can carry any amount of money through customs, in or out of the country. The best rate of exchange is always to be found in a bank. Bureaux de change will exchange most currencies and cash cheques, but charge more to do so. They can be found at airports, main-line stations, central tube stations and in the larger department stores. Bureaux de change stay open outside banking hours. The larger hotels sometimes have facilities for changing major currencies, and will accept travellers' cheques in payment of bills. Most restaurants will also accept travellers' cheques as long as they are accompanied by a valid form of identification.

Chequepoint Bureau de Change

13 Davies St W1. 01-409 1122.	2	G	18
220 Earl's Court Rd SW5. 01-373 9515.	1	G	5
Marble Arch, 548 Oxford St W1. 01-723 2646.	2	E	16

Eurochange Bureaux Ltd

95 Buckingham Palace Rd SW1. 01-328 4953.	5	L	16
Leicester Sq Tube Stn, 45 Charing Cross Rd WC2. 01-439 2827.	5	J	22
Paddington Tube Stn, 179 Praed St W2. 01-258 0442.	2	B	13
Tottenham Court Rd Tube Stn W1. 01-734 0279.	3	H	22

Thomas Cook Ltd

39 Tottenham Court Rd W1. 01-637 1313 x367.	3	F	23
123 High Holborn WC1. 01-405 8316.	3	I	25
104 Kensington High St W8. 01-937 3673.	1	D	7
100 Victoria St SW1. 01-828 0437.	5	M	16
Selfridges, 400 Oxford St W1. 01-629 1234.	2	E	18

Banks

Banks are open 09.30-15.30 Mon-Fri. They are closed B.hols and often close early on the day before a B.hol. Some selected branches open on Sat. Longer banking hours at Heathrow and Gatwick Airports: 24hr opening all year; at Luton Airport: OPEN 06.00-23.00 in summer.

England's main high-street banks are Barclays, Lloyds, Midland, National Westminster and the TSB (Trustee Savings Bank). Their head offices are listed below together with several other British banks and international departments.

Barclays Bank plc	6	N	30
54 Lombard St EC3. 01-626 1567.			
Barclays Bank International	6	O	31
168 Fenchurch St EC3. 01-283 8989.			
Bank of Ireland	6	N	29
36 Queen St EC4. 01-329 4500.			
Bank of Scotland	6	N	31
38 Threadneedle St EC2. 01-628 8060.			
Coutts & Co	6	O	30
International Dept, 27 Bush La, Cannon St EC4. 01-623 3434.			
Lloyds Bank plc	6	N	30
71 Lombard St EC3. 01-626 1500.			
Lloyd's Bank International Ltd	6	P	30
11-15 Monument St EC3. 01-407 1000.			
Midland Bank plc	6	N	30
Poultry EC2. 01-260 8000.			
Midland Bank International Division	6	N	29
110 Cannon St EC4. 01-260 6000.			
National Westminster Bank plc	6	N	31
41 Lothbury EC2. 01-726 1000.			
National Westminster Bank International Division	6	N	32
25 Old Broad St EC2. 01-920 5555.			
TSB	6	N	30
60 Lombard St EC3. 01-623 6000.			

Credit cards

The major credit cards – Access, American Express, Diners Club, Visa – are accepted in most places as a form of payment. Carte Blanche is less popular.

Access card
Joint Credit Card Company, Access House, 200 Priory Cres, Southend-on-Sea, Essex. Southend-on-Sea 352211. To report lost or stolen cards contact your own bank immediately or phone the above number outside office hours.

American Express	5 J 21	

6 Haymarket SW1. 01-930 4411. *OPEN 09.00-17.00 Mon-Fri, 09.00-12.00 Sat.* Customer service handles any enquiry or billing problem. Acts as travel agent, sells and cashes personal cheques on an emergency basis if customer has an American Express card. If card is lost the company can issue an emergency replacement card. To report lost or stolen cards call 01-222 9633 for a *24hr* emergency service.

Barclaycard
Barclaycard Centre Dept G, Northampton, Northants. Northampton 234234. To report lost or stolen cards during office hours contact any Barclays bank or ring the above number (*24hr service*) and write a confirming letter within seven days.

Diners Club card
Diners Club House, Kingsmead, Farnborough, Hants. Farnborough 516261. *24hr service* for reporting lost cards and the telephone call should, within seven days, be followed by a confirming letter.

Eurocard
See under 'Access' above.

Eurocheque card
In case of loss contact issuing branch or telephone this emergency number: 01-588 3600. Confirm the loss in writing within seven days.

Mastercard
See under 'Access' above.

Visa
See under 'Barclaycard' above.

Taxes

Most goods and services purchased in the UK are subject to VAT (value added tax) at the standard rate of 15%. Luxury items – tobacco, perfume, alcoholic beverages and motor vehicles – are subject to higher rates. Overseas visitors can reclaim the VAT paid on high value items by obtaining a VAT 407 form from the retailer. On returning home the goods must be certified by the customs officer. Evidence of this plus the form must then be returned to the retailer, who will send the refund to the visitor's country of origin. However, this procedure can be lengthy. A good alternative is to shop in stores showing the London Tax Free Shopping sign. This system entails filling in a voucher, presenting it to customs with the goods and returning it to the London Tax Free Shopping organisation who will then immediately refund your money in the currency of your country of residence.

Tipping

Should be an expression of pleasure for service rendered and never a duty; it is still possible not to tip at all if the circumstances justify this. These guidelines give some idea of the average tip:

Restaurants Many now add on a service charge, usually 10%, but do not always say so – if in any doubt ask them. They usually say if it is *not* included. 10% is the minimum; give up to 15% for above average service.
Taxis 10-15%.
Women's hairdressers 15% to the hairdresser, 5% to the shampooer.
Men's hairdressers 15%.
Cloakroom attendants 10p per article when collected.
Washroom services 10p if individual attention is given.
Commissionaires For getting a taxi. Up to 50p depending on the effort expended.
Pubs & bars Never at the bar, but buy the barman a drink if you wish. For waiter service in the lounge, from 10p per drink.
Hotels Almost all add it to your bill, usually 10%. Give extra to individuals for special service, from 50p.
Porters 50p-£1 per case depending on how far it is carried.

Business services

London offers a number of back-up services to make life easier for the travelling business man or woman. There are organisations which hire out offices or conference rooms by the hour, day or month along with complete secretarial and communication services. They will provide you with a London address while you are overseas and a message service whereby someone will handle telephone calls and forward your telexes. Other agencies deal with secretarial and staffing services only. It is worth enquiring about the amenities available at your hotel, as most of the major ones help their business guests by providing communication facilities.

Angela Pike Associates 2 I 18
9 Curzon St W1. 01-491 1616. *24hr emergency secretarial and staffing services. 7 days a week.*

Business Space 2 I 20
35 Piccadilly W1. 01-439 8985. Luxury offices and conference rooms for hire with all the necessary services.

Heathrow Business Centre
Heathrow Airport Terminal 2. 01-759 2434. For high-flyers. Private office accommodation, work cubicles and services including the use of a personal computer between flights.

Inter-Continental Hotel 2 I 16
Hyde Park Corner W1. 01-409 3131. Print shop, stenographer, couriers. *24hr telex and electronic mail systems. For residents only.*

Nightingale London 2 H 18
Secretariat
3 Berkeley Sq W1. 01-629 6116. Office hire and all business requirements. *Membership.*

Conference services

Conference Services Ltd
9-15 Aldine St W12. 01-740 8121. Professional conference organisers who arrange everything from the budgeting to

the hosting of any size meeting or conference.

Video/Audio Conferencing

British Telecom organises national and international video conferencing. Phone the Conference Booking Centre 01-606 0541 for details.

Conference centres

Alexandra Palace & Park
Wood Green N22. 01-883 6477.

Barbican Arts and   6   **L**   **31**
Conference Centre
Barbican EC2. 01-638 4141.

Earl's Court Exhibition   I   **G**   **4**
Centre
Warwick Rd SW5. 01-385 1200.

Olympia Exhibitions   I   **C**   **2**
Olympia W14. 01-603 3344.

Queen Elizabeth II   5   **M**   **19**
Conference Centre
Broad Sanctuary SW1. 01-222 5000.

Wembley Conference Centre
Wembley Complex, Empire Way, Wembley, Middx. 01-902 8833.

Courier services: international

The following all offer door-to-door collection and delivery services around the world.

Datapost
Dial 100 and ask the operator for Freephone Datapost for a speedy door-to-door collection and delivery service.

DHL
01-890 9000.

IML Air Couriers
01-890 8888.

Intelpost   6   **N**   **31**
Stock Exchange Bldg, 24 Throgmorton St EC2. 01-638 1901. Public facsimile system enabling copies of documents to be transmitted to twenty-nine countries on four continents.

TNT Skypack
01-561 2345.

Courier services: nationwide

See Yellow Pages *for extensive listings of motorcycle and van messengers.*

Employment agencies

There are many different agencies all over London (see Yellow Pages for listing). The ones given below are the main offices of some of the largest firms, which have branches in most commercial districts.

Alfred Marks Group
84 Regent St W1. 01-437   2   **H**   **20**
7855.

Atlas
194 Bishopsgate EC2. 01-283   6   **N**   **33**
6644.

71 Oxford St W1. 01-636 4000.   2   **G**   **21**

Brook Street Bureau
63 Oxford St W1. 01-437 8622.   2   **G**   **22**
131 Cannon St EC4. 01-623   6   **N**   **29**
3966.

Reed Employment
116 Moorgate EC2. 01-638   6   **M**   **31**
1021.
5 High Holborn WC1. 01-405   3   **H**   **24**
6525.

Financial information

Citycall
Dial 0898 121212 for information from the London and international stock exchanges. For sterling and US dollar conversion rates ring 0898 121230.

Storage

Berkley Safe Deposit Co   2   **G**   **18**
13-15 Davies St W1. 01-409 1122. Rental of strong boxes.
Metro Store
81-89 Carnwath Rd SW6. 01-736 5433. Rents out warehouse space by the week.

Translation

Conference Interpreters Group
10 Barley Mow Pass W4. 01-995 0801. Internationally recognised interpreters in most widely spoken languages.
Interlingua/TTI   6   **J**   **24**
Imperial House, 15-19 Kingsway WC2. 01-240 5361. Rapid translations done in over 70 languages. Also interpreters for meetings and conferences. Typesetting, printing and executive language tuition done in-house.

Transport

For taxis and car-hire see 'Travel and holiday information' section.

Air London
Crawley 549555. Can organise any plane from executive jets to air ambulances, from air taxis to 747s.

Business information

These are the major organisations available to help the business man or woman with trade enquiries and export and import information. Do not overlook the assistance you can get from your bank, your own trade association, or the trade sections of embassies and chambers of commerce who do much to promote trade between countries.

Association of British   2 I 21
Chambers of Commerce
Sovereign House, 212a Shaftesbury Av WC2. 01-240 5831.
British Exporters   5 M 19
Association
16 Dartmouth St SW1. 01-222 5419.
Central Office of   5 P 22
Information
Hercules Rd SE1. 01-928 2345.
Chamber of Commerce   6 N 29
69 Cannon St EC4. 01-248 4444.
Companies House   6 K 33
55-71 City Rd EC1. 01-253 9393. Searches undertaken for information on any company registered under the Companies Act for £1 fee.
Confederation of British   3 H 23
Industry (CBI)
Centrepoint, 103 New Oxford St WC1. 01-379 7400.
Department of Trade   6 L 28
1 Victoria St SW1. 01-215 7877. The Enquiry Service will put you through to the appropriate officer of the DTI's Export Services for information and advice on exporting. Market assessments; Export Intelligence Service (subscribers are informed of export opportunities in their area of business as they arise); appointment of overseas agents; reports on standing of overseas traders; foreign tariff and import regulations; assistance for companies at overseas trade fairs and exhibitions; service for foreign business visitors wishing to buy British goods.
Design Council   5 J 21
28 Haymarket SW1. 01-839 8000.
Institute of Export   6 L 33
Clifton House, 64 Clifton St EC2. 01-247 9812.
Institute of Practitioners in   5 J 14
Advertising
44 Belgrave Sq SW1. 01-235 7020.
National Economic   5 O 19
Development Office
Millbank Tower, Millbank SW1. 01-211 3000.

Travel and holiday information

Passports

Applications for, and renewals of, full 10-year passports can be handled by your bank or travel agency for a small charge. Personal applications to the Passport Office only and a birth certificate must be produced. British Visitors passports, valid for one year, can be obtained from main post offices. These are for holiday-makers only and are valid in Canada and many European countries, usually those that don't require visas. They are issued on production of a medical card, birth certificate or expired but uncancelled passport.

Passport Office   5 L 18
Clive House, Petty France SW1. 01-279 3434. *OPEN 09.00-16.30 Mon-Fri. Emergencies 16.30-18.00 Mon-Fri, 10.00-12.00 Sat.*
Home Office   5 L 19
50 Queen Anne's Gate SW1. 01-273 3000.
Immigration Office
Lunar House, Wellesley Rd, Croydon, Surrey. 01-686 0688. Deals with questions concerning the granting of British visas to foreigners and entry under the Commonwealth Immigration Act. Subject to approval, visas are then supplied by the Foreign Office.

Passport photographs

These can be done by any photographer, who will know the size and other require-

ments. Basically you should submit two identical black and white (certain colour photos are also acceptable), full face photographs of yourself without a hat. The size should be no more than 50mm by 38mm (2in by 1½in). The paper should be ordinary photographic paper, unglazed and unmounted. It is possible to have the photos taken in one of the street or station photograph machines. The Passport Office will accept photos taken in machines which have marked on them somewhere the words 'Passport' or 'Passport approved'.

Inoculations and vaccinations

These can be carried out by your own doctor under the National Health Scheme free – though the doctor may make a charge for signing the certificate. The certificate should then be taken for stamping to the Health department of the local authority in which the vaccinator practises. International certificates are required for cholera and yellow fever. The Department of Health and Social Security, Alexander Fleming House, Elephant & Castle SE1, 01-407 5522, will send out details of international requirements.

British Airways   2 H 20
Immunisation Clinic
75 Regent St W1. 01-439 9584. All inoculations including yellow fever. OPEN 08.30-16.30 Mon-Fri. Also at Heathrow Airport 01-562 5453. OPEN 09.00-12.30, 14.00-16.30 Mon-Fri (appt only). Also at 101-102 Cheapside EC2. 01-606 2977. OPEN 09.00-12.45, 14.00-16.15 (appt only).

Hospital for Tropical   3 A 26
Diseases
St Pancras Hospital, 4 St Pancras Way NW1. 01-387 4411. New patients need a doctor's letter. Yellow fever inoculations. OPEN 11.15 Mon-Fri. All others appt only 11.45 Mon-Fri. Charge.

Unilever House   6 M 27
Blackfriars EC4. 01-822 6017. Appt only. OPEN 14.10 & 16.00 Mon-Fri for all main inoculations required for travelling.

Vaccinating Centre   2 D 16
53 Great Cumberland Pl W1. 01-262 6456. A centre for vaccinations and inoculations. OPEN Mon-Fri 09.00-16.45. No appt necessary.

Money: currency exchange

For full details on currency and exchange facilities see 'Money' section of 'Money and business services'.

Lost property

British Rail

If you lose something on a train, contact the station where the train terminates. They will be able to inform you whether your belongings have been recovered and where they have been taken to.

London Transport

Lost Property Office   2 B 19
200 Baker St W1 (next to Baker St Station). For enquiries about lost property please call in person (or send another person with written authority) or apply by letter. No telephone enquiries. OPEN 09.30-14.00 Mon-Fri. CLOSED B.hols.

Air travel

Lost property is held by each individual airline. For property lost in the main airport buildings enquire: British Airport Authorities Lost Property Office MSCP2, London Airport, Heathrow, Middx. 01-745 7727/8. OPEN 09.00-16.00 Mon-Sun.

Taxis

Apply 15 Penton St N1 (3 E 30) or nearest police station.

Lost anywhere

Apply to the nearest police station. Lost property found in the street is usually taken there.

Lost children

Will be cared for by the railway police if lost on British Rail, or ask at the nearest police station if lost elsewhere.

Lost dogs

May have been taken to Battersea Dogs Home, 4 Battersea Park Rd SW8 (5 **R** 12). 01-622 3626. Unwanted dogs should be taken to the same address by the owner or by a representative with a letter. Dogs can also be purchased here. *OPEN 10.30-16.15 Mon-Sat.*

Embassies

All have Consulates in the same building unless a separate address is given. They all deal with emigration. A full list of embassies is in the London Diplomatic List, *available from the HMSO Bookshop, 49 High Holborn WCl (β* **I** 26).

Austria   5   **J**   14
18 Belgrave Mews West SWl. 01-235 3731.

Belgium   5   **K**   14
103 Eaton Sq SWl. 01-235 5422.

Brazil
32 Green St Wl. 01-499 0877.   2   **F**   17
Consulate: 6 St Alban's St   5   **J**   21
SWl. 01-930 9055.

Bulgaria   I   **G**   9
186-188 Queen's Gate SW7. 01-584 9400.

Chile   2   **D**   20
12 Devonshire St Wl. 01-580 6392. Consulate: 01-580 1023.

China   2   **E**   20
31 Portland Pl Wl. 01-636 5726.

Cuba   3   **I**   26
167 High Holborn WCl. 01-240 2488.

Czechoslovakia   I   **D**   8
25 Kensington Palace Gdns W8. 01-229 1255. Consulate: 30 Kensington Palace Gdns W8. 01-727 9431.

Denmark   5   **K**   12
55 Sloane St SWl. 01-235 1255.

Egypt   2   **G**   17
75 South Audley St Wl. 01-499 2401.

Finland   5   **J**   19
38 Chesham Pl SWl. 01-235 9531.

France
58 Knightsbridge SWl. 01-235   2   **I**   14
8080.
Consulate: 24 Rutland Gate   2   **H**   12
SW7. 01-581 5292.

Germany   5   **J**   14
23 Belgrave Sq SWl. 01-235 5033.

Greece   I   **A**   5
1a Holland Park W11. 01-727 8040.

Hong Kong   2   **H**   19
6 Grafton St Wl. 01-499 9821.

Hungary   5   **K**   14
35 Eaton Pl SWl. 01-235 4048. Consulate: 35b Eaton Pl SWl. 01-235 2664.

Iceland   5   **L**   13
I Eaton Ter SWl. 01-730 5131.

Iran   I   **G**   11
27 Prince's Gate SW7. 01-584 8101.

Iraq   I   **G**   9
21-22 Queen's Gate SW7. 01-584 7141.

Ireland   5   **J**   15
17 Grosvenor Pl SWl. 01-235 2171. Passport office: 01-245 9033.

Israel   I   **D**   8
2 Palace Grn, Kensington Palace Gdns W8. 01-937 8050.

Italy
14 Three Kings Yd Wl. 01-629   2   **G**   18
8200.
Passport office: 38 Eaton Pl   5   **K**   14
SWl. 01-235 9371.

Japan   2   **G**   18
46 Grosvenor St Wl. 01-493 6030.

Jordan   I   **C**   8
6 Upper Phillimore Gdns W8. 01-937 3685.

Kuwait   I   **G**   9
45 Queen's Gate SW7. 01-589 4533.

Lebanon   I   **D**   8
21 Kensington Palace Gdns, 01-229 7265.
Consulate: 15 Palace Gdns   I   **B**   9
Mews W8. 01-727 6696.

Luxembourg   5   **J**   14
27 Wilton Cres SWl. 01-235 6961.

Mexico   5   **J**   15
8 Halkin St Wl.01-235 6393.

Morocco   I   **H**   8
49 Queen's Gate Gdns SW7. 01-584 8827.

Nepal   I   **D**   8
12a Kensington Palace Gdns W8. 01-229 1594.

Netherlands   I   **F**   9
38 Hyde Park Gate SW7. 01-584 5040.

Norway   5   **J**   14
25 Belgrave Sq SWl. 01-235 7151.

Pakistan   2   **I**   13
35 Lowndes Sq SWl. 01-235 2044.

Peru   5   **K**   12
52 Sloane St SWl. 01-235 1917. Consulate: 01-235 6867.

The Philippines   I   **E**   8
I Cumberland House, Kensington High St W8. 01-937 3646.

Poland
47 Portland Pl Wl. 01-580   2   **E**   30
4324.
Consulate: 73 New Cavendish   2   **E**   21
St Wl. 01-636 4533.

Portugal   5   **J**   14
11 Belgrave Sq SWl. 01-235 5331.

Consulate: 62 Brompton Rd   I   **L**   II
SW3. 01-581 8722.
Romania   I   **D**   8
4 Palace Grn, Kensington Palace Grn W8.
01-937 9666.
Saudi Arabia   5   **K**   14
30 Belgrave Sq SW1. 01-235 0831. Consu-
late: 01-235 0303.
South Africa
South Africa House, Trafalgar   5   **K**   21
Sq WC2. 01-930 4488.
Consulate: 8 Duncannon St   5   **K**   22
WC2. 01-839 2211.
Spain   4   **K**   II
20 Draycott Pl SW3. 01-581 5921.
Sweden   2   **C**   17
II Montagu Pl W1. 01-724 2101.
Switzerland   2   **C**   17
16 Montagu Pl W1. 01-723 0701.
Thailand   I   **G**   9
30 Queen's Gate SW7. 01-589 0173.
Tunisia   I   **G**   II
29 Prince's Gate SW7. 01-584 8117.
Turkey   5   **J**   14
43 Belgrave Sq SW1. 01-235
5252.
Consulate: Rutland Gdns   2   **H**   12
SW7. 01-589 0360.
USA   2   **F**   17
24 Grosvenor Sq W1. 01-499 9000.
USSR   I   **D**   8
13 Kensington Palace Gdns W8. 01-229
3628. Consulate: 5 Kensington Palace
Gdns W8. 01-229 3215.
Venezuela   I   **G**   7
I Cromwell Rd SW7. 01-584
4206.
Consulate: 56 Grafton Way   2   **H**   19
W1. 01-387 6727 (Visas Dept).
Yugoslavia   I   **F**   6
5 Lexham Gdns W8. 01-370 6105. Consu-
late: 7 Lexham Gdns W8.

High Commissions

*All these offices deal with emigration. A full
list of high commissions is in the* London
Diplomatic List *available from the HMSO
Bookshop, 49 High Holborn WC1.*
Australia   6   **K**   24
Australia House, Strand WC2. 01-379
4334.
Bahamas   2   **H**   17
10 Chesterfield St W1.01-408 4488.
Bangladesh   I   **G**   9
28 Queen's Gate SW7. 01-584 0081.
Barbados   3   **H**   23
I Great Russell St WC1. 01-631 4975.

Canada   2   **F**   17
MacDonald House, I Grosvenor Sq W1.
01-629 9492.
Cyprus   2   **F**   17
93 Park St W1. 01-499 8272.
Ghana   5   **J**   14
13 Belgrave Sq SW1. 01-235 4142.
Guyana   I   **B**   10
3 Palace Ct, Bayswater Rd W2. 01-229
7684.
India   6   **J**   24
India House, Aldwych, WC2. 01-836 8484.
Jamaica   5   **J**   19
63 St James's St SW1. 01-499 8600.
Kenya   2   **G**   19
24-25 New Bond St W1. 01-636 2371.
Malaysia   5   **J**   14
45 Belgrave Sq SW1. 01-235 8033.
Malta   I   **E**   7
16 Kensington Sq W8. 01-938 1712.
New Zealand   5   **J**   21
New Zealand House, 80 Haymarket SW1.
01-930 8422.
Nigeria   5   **K**   22
Nigeria House, 9 Northumberland Av WC2.
01-839 1244.
Sierra Leone   2   **E**   20
33 Portland Pl W1. 01-636 6483.
Singapore   5   **K**   13
5 Chesham St SW1. 01-235 9067/8.
Sri Lanka   2   **D**   14
13 Hyde Park Gdns W2. 01-262 1841.
Tanzania   2   **I**   16
43 Hertford St W1. 01-499 8951.
Trinidad & Tobago   5   **J**   14
42 Belgrave Sq SW1. 01-245 9351.
Zambia   I   **F**   9
2 Palace Gate W8. 01-589 6655.
Zimbabwe   6   **K**   23
429 Strand WC2. 01-836 7755.

Tourist offices

*National Tourist Offices provide advice,
specialised knowledge and literature.*
Australia   2   **H**   20
Australian Tourist Commission, Heathcote
House, 20 Savile Row W1. 01-434 4371.
Austria   2   **G**   19
Austrian National Tourist Office, 30 St
George's St W1. 01-629 0461.
Bahamas   2   **H**   17
Bahama Island Tourist Office, 10 Chester-
field St W1. 01-629 5238.
Barbados   3   **F**   23
Barbados Tourist Board, 263 Tottenham
Court Rd W1. 01-636 0090.

Belgium 2 I 19
Belgian National Tourist Office, 38 Dover St WI. 01-499 5379.

Bermuda 4 L 10
Bermuda Dept of Tourism, 6 Burnsall St SW3. 01-734 8813.

Britain 5 L 15
National Tourist Information Centre, 26 Grosvenor Gdns SWI. 01-730 3488.

Bulgaria 2 G 20
Bulgarian National Tourist Office, 18 Princes St WI. 01-499 6988.

Canada 5 K 21
Canadian Government Travel Bureau, Canada House, Cockspur St SWI. 01-629 9492.

Czechoslovakia 2 I 19
Czechoslovak Travel Bureau Cedok (London), 17-18 Old Bond St WI. 01-629 6058.

Denmark 2 H 20
The Danish Tourist Board, Sceptre House, 169-173 Regent St WI. 01-734 2637.

Egypt 2 I 18
Egyptian Tourist Centre, 168 Piccadilly WI. 01-493 5282.

Finland 5 J 21
Finnish Tourist Board, 66 Haymarket SWI. 01-839 4048.

France 2 I 18
French Government Tourist Office, 178 Piccadilly WI. 01-499 6911.

Germany 2 H 19
German National Tourist Office, 61 Conduit St WI. 01-734 2600.

Gibraltar 5 K 22
Gibraltar National Tourist Office, 179 The Strand WC2. 01-836 0777.

Greece 2 I 20
The National Tourist Organisation of Greece, 195-197 Regent St WI. 01-734 5997.

Holland 5 L 17
Netherlands National Tourist Office, 25-28 Buckingham Gate SWI. 01-630 0451.

Hong Kong 5 J 21
Hong Kong Tourist Association, 125 Pall Mall SWI. 01-930 4775.

Hungary 2 H 19
Hungarian Travel Centre, 6 Conduit St WI. 01-493 0263.

Iceland 3 E 23
Iceland Tourist Information Bureau, 172 Tottenham Court Rd. 01-388 5599.

Ireland 2 G 18
Irish Tourist Office, Ireland House, 150 New Bond St WI. 01-493 3201.

Israel 2 G 20
Israel Government Tourist Office, 18 Great Marlborough St WI. 01-434 3651.

Italy 2 G 20
Italian State Tourist Dept (ENIT), I Princes St WI. 01-408 1254.

Jamaica 5 J 19
Jamaica Tourist Board, 50 St James's St SWI. 01-493 3647.

Japan 2 I 20
Japan National Tourist Organisation, 167 Regent St WI. 01-734 9638.

Jersey 2 I 19
Jersey Tourist Information Office, 35 Albemarle St WI. 01-493 5278.

Kenya 2 H 20
Kenya Tourist Office, 13 New Burlington St WI. 01-839 4477.

Lebanon 2 I 18
Lebanese Tourist Office, 90 Piccadilly WI. 01-409 2031.

Luxembourg 2 I 18
Luxembourg National Tourist Office, 36/37 Piccadilly WI. 01-434 2800.

Malta I E 7
Malta Government Tourist Office, Suite 207, College House, Wright's La W8. 01-938 2668.

Mexico 2 H 19
Mexico Tourist Board, 7 Cork St WI. 01-734 1058.

Morocco 2 H 20
Moroccan National Tourist Office, 174 Regent St WI. 01-437 0073.

New Zealand 5 J 21
New Zealand Government Tourist Bureau, New Zealand House, 80 Haymarket SWI. 01-930 8422.

Northern Ireland 2 I 18
Northern Ireland Tourist Board, 11 Berkeley St WI. 01-493 0601.

Norway 5 J 20
Norwegian Tourist Board, 20 Pall Mall SWI. 01-839 6255.

Poland 2 F 21
Polish Travel Office, 82 Mortimer St WI. 01-580 8028.

Portugal 2 G 19
Portuguese Tourist Office, 1-5 New Bond St WI. 01-493 3873.

Scotland 5 K 21
Scottish Tourist Board, 19 Cockspur St SWI. 01-930 8661.

South Africa 2 H 20
South African Tourist Corporation, Regency House, 1-4 Warwick St WI. 01-439 9661.

Spain 5 J 19
Spanish National Tourist Office, 57 St James's St SWI. 01-499 0901.

Sweden 2 H 19
Swedish National Tourist Office, 3 Cork St WI. 01-437 5816.

Switzerland   2 I 22
Swiss National Tourist Office, Swiss Centre, I New Coventry St WI. 01-734 1921.

Thailand   2 I 19
Thailand Tourist Office, 9 Stafford St WI. 01-499 7679.

Tunisia   2 I 19
Tunisian National Tourist Office, 7a Stafford St WI. 01-499 2234.

Turkey   2 I 18
Turkish Tourism and Information Office, 170-173 Piccadilly WI. 01-734 8681.

USA   2 I 20
United States Travel and Tourism Administration, 22 Sackville St WI. 01-439 7433.

USSR   2 H 20
Intourist Moscow, 292 Regent St WI. 01-580 4974.

Wales   2 I 20
Wales Tourist Board, 34 Piccadilly WI. 01-409 0969.

Yugoslavia   2 H 20
Yugoslavia National Tourist Office, 143 Regent St WI. 01-734 5243.

Zimbabwe   2 I 19
Zimbabwe Tourist Office, 52 Piccadilly WI. 01-629 3955.

Travel agents and tour operators

Travel agents, who retail package holidays and travel tickets, can be found all over London. Most belong to the Association of British Travel Agents (ABTA); if they do they can only sell the holidays of tour operators who also belong to ABTA. Buying from ABTA agents is a good idea since any complaints can be addressed to the Association if the agent and operator do not give satisfaction. Any ABTA travel agent can sell the full range of ABTA holidays, which include standard package holidays to all parts of the world and specialist holidays from archaeology to wine-tasting. All-inclusive tours sold by ABTA tour operators are covered by a bond to safeguard holiday-makers' money. Agents and operators advertise in newspapers and magazines, and operators' brochures are available at travel agents. You can often book directly with the operator. Agents also sell train and air tickets, insurance and travellers' cheques.

Association of British   2 G 22
Travel Agents
55 Newman St WI. 01-637 2444.

London Tourist Board   5 K I5
Information Centre
26 Grosvenor Gdns SWI. 01-730 3488. Information on travel and holidays in Britain.

Thomas Cook   2 I 18
45 Berkeley St WI. 01-499 4000. The biggest travel agency and also a tour operator. Sell their own travellers' cheques.

Passenger shipping lines

Since flying has become so fast, cheap and popular very few shipping lines have survived, but if you have the time or inclination for a less hectic way of getting to your destination try these lines which sail from the UK.

Baltic Shipping   2 H 20
CTC Lines (agents), I Regent St SWI. 01-930 5833. Sailings between Helsinki & Talli, Stockholm & Leningrad, Leningrad & Helsinki, Helsinki & Riga.

Cunard Line   5 J 9
30-35 Pall Mall SWI. 01-930 4321. Sailings to New York on the QE2.

Polferries   6 J 33
Gdynia America Shipping Lines (agents), 238 City Rd ECI. 01-251 3389. London to Gdynia, Poland. Some cars taken. Gdynia Shipping Lines have destinations all over the world.

P & O Cruises   3 H 23
77 New Oxford St WCI. 01-831 1234. Regular cruises from Southampton to the Mediterranean and destinations further afield – Egypt, the Caribbean, Africa. Also a three-month world cruise every *Jan*. Also operate Swan Hellenic cruises.

Car ferries

All routes carry passengers as well as cars. It is advisable to book as early as possible, especially for Jul & Aug. Your travel agent, or the operators listed below, will make bookings and supply information including details of special reduced fares, which are normally lower in winter, mid-week and for short-stay trips.

B & I Line   2 H 19
150 New Bond St WI. 01-734 4681.

Brittany Ferries
The Brittany Centre, Wharf Rd, Portsmouth, Hants. Portsmouth 827701.

DFDS Seaways
Scandinavia House, Parkestone Quay, Harwich, Essex. Harwich 241234.

Fred Olsen Lines
Crown House, Crown St, Ipswich, Suffolk. Ipswich 233022.

Olau-Line
Old Paymaster's House, 104 Anchors La, Sheerness Docks, Kent. Sheerness 666666.

Sally Line	2 I	18

81 Piccadilly W1. 01-409 2240.

Sealink	5 M	15

Sealink Travel Centre, Platform 2, Victoria Station SW1. 01-828 1940. Reservations also on Wye 47047.

P & O European Ferries	2 H	20

127 Regent St W1. 01-437 5644.

Ferry routes

There are more sailings in summer than in winter. Most ferries do not operate on Xmas Day or Boxing Day.

Belgium
Dover-Ostend. P & O. *3¾hrs.* 10 departures daily.
Dover-Zeebrugge. P & O. *4½hrs.* 6 departures daily.
Felixstowe-Zeebrugge. P & O. *5hrs.* 2 departures daily.

Denmark
Harwich-Esberg. DFDS Seaways. *19hrs.* Approx. 5 departures per week.

Eire
Holyhead-Dun Laoghaire. Sealink. *3½hrs.* 2 departures daily.
Fishguard-Rosslare. Sealink. *3½hrs.* 1-2 departures Mon-Sat, also Sun mid Jun-mid Sep.
Holyhead-Dublin. B & I Line. *3½hrs.* 2 departures daily.
Liverpool-Dunleavy. B & I Line. *8hrs.* 1 departure daily.
Pembroke-Rosslare. B & I Line. *3½hrs.* 1 departure daily, 2 in summer.
Stranraer-Larne. B & I Line. *2½hrs.* 9 departures daily.

France
Dover-Boulogne. P & O. *1¾hrs.* 10 departures daily.
Dover-Calais. Sealink. *1½hrs.* Up to 20 departures daily.
Dover-Calais. P & O. *1¼hrs.* 10-19 departures daily.
Ramsgate-Dunkerque. Sally Line. *2½hrs.* 5 departures daily.
Folkestone-Boulogne. Sealink. *1¾hrs.* Up to 8 departures daily.

Newhaven-Dieppe. Sealink. *4½hrs.* 4-6 departures daily.
Plymouth-Roscoff. Brittany Ferries. *6hrs.* Up to 3 departures daily in peak season.
Portsmouth-Caen. Brittany Ferries. *5¾ hrs.* Up to 3 departures daily.
Portsmouth-Cherbourg. Sealink. *4¾hrs.* 3-4 departures daily.
Portsmouth-Cherbourg. P & O. *4¾hrs.* Up to 5 departures daily.
Portsmouth-Le Havre. P & O. *5¾hrs.* 2-5 departures daily.
Portsmouth-St Malo. Brittany Ferries. *8½ hrs.* 1 departure daily, 2 in summer.
Weymouth-Cherbourg. Sealink. *4hrs.* 2 departures daily.

Netherlands
Harwich-Hook of Holland. Sealink. *6½hrs.* 2 departures daily.

Norway
Harwich-Kristiansand. Fred Olsen Lines. *24hrs.* 1 departure per week. Jun-Aug. (DFDS can provide a service to Norway via Denmark, see above.)

Spain
Plymouth-Santander. Brittany Ferries. *24 hrs.* 2 departures per week.

Sweden
Harwich-Goteborg. DFDS Seaways. *23 hrs.* Departures every even date.

West Germany
Harwich-Hamburg. DFDS Seaways. *20 hrs.* 3-4 departures per week.
Sheerness-Vlissingen. Olau Line. *7hrs.* 2 departures daily.

Hovercraft

Take cars as well as passengers.

Hoverspeed (UK) Ltd
International Hoverport, Ramsgate, Kent. Reservations can be made on 01-554 7061, or through any travel agent.

Hovercraft routes

France
Dover-Boulogne. *40mins.* Up to 6 departures daily.
Dover-Calais. *35mins.* Up to 23 departures daily.

Jetfoil

P & O European Ferries, 127 Regent St W1 (2 **H 20**). 01-437 5644.
Dover-Ostend. Passengers only. *100mins.*

5 (4 in winter) daily departures. Connecting express boat trains and coaches to and from port. Jetfoil tickets and combined Jetfoil and coach tickets available from P & O. Combined Jetfoil and rail tickets available from European Rail Centre, Victoria Station SW1. 01-834 2345.

Taxis and mini-cabs

Taxis

The famous London black taxi cabs can be hailed in the street (some are now painted different colours and carry limited advertising, but are still bound by the same strict regulations); they are available for hire if the yellow light above the windscreen is lit. All these taxis have meters which the driver must use on all journeys within the Metropolitan Police District (most of Greater London and out to Heathrow Airport); for longer journeys the price should be negotiated with the driver beforehand. There is also a minimum payable charge which is shown on the meter when you hire the cab. Expect to pay extra for large luggage, journeys between 20.00-06.00, at weekends and B.hols. There are over 500 ranks throughout London, including all major hotels and British Rail stations. For your nearest rank, look in the telephone book under 'Taxi', or try:

Computer-cab: 01-286 0286.
Owner Drivers Radio Taxi Service: 01-286 4848.
Radio Taxicabs: 01-272 0272. *24hrs.*

Mini-cabs

These cannot be hailed in the street, and in any case they are indistinguishable from private cars. Unlike the black cabs they are not licensed and neither do their drivers take the same stringent tests, but they are cheaper on longer runs. Negotiate the price with the company, for any journey, when you phone. Your nearest mini-cab office is listed in Yellow Pages.

Car-hire

Self-drive car hire

Prices differ greatly from company to company and depending on make of car and the season. There is a basic daily, weekly or monthly charge, sometimes inclusive of mileage, and you will also have to leave a deposit. Normally you will have to be over 21 and have held a licence, valid for use in the UK, for at least a year.

Avis Rent-a-Car   5   **J**   **15**
35 Headfort Pl SW1. 01-245 9862. For bookings anywhere in London. *OPEN 07.00-20.00 Mon-Sun.*
World-wide reservations at Trident House, Station Rd, Hayes, Middx. 01-848 8733.
Budget
01-935 3518 for your nearest branch in London. *OPEN 07.30-19.30 Mon-Fri, 07.30-15.30 Sat & Sun.*
Car Hire Centre
230 Burlington Rd, New Malden, Surrey. 01-949 8122. Free reservation centre for most British car-hire groups. Arrange hire in GB and world-wide.
J. Davy
606 High Rd, Wembley, Middx. 01-902 7771. *OPEN 08.00-18.00 Mon-Fri, 08.00-15.00 Sat, 08.00-12.00 Sun. CLOSED B.hols.*
Eaton Self-Drive Car Hire   5   **N**   **13**
48-56 Ebury Bridge Rd SW1. 01-730 3554. *OPEN 08.00-18.00 Mon-Fri, 08.00-13.00 Sat. CLOSED Sun.*
Godfrey Davis (Eurocar)   5   **M**   **16**
Davis House, Wilton Rd SW1. 01-834 8484. For London bookings. *OPEN 08.00-20.00 Mon-Sun.* Central reservations at Bushey House, High St, Bushey, Watford, Herts. 01-950 5050. *OPEN 08.00-19.00 Mon-Fri, 08.00-13.00 Sat.*
Hertz, Rent a Car
Radnor House, 1272 London Rd SW16. 01-679 1799. Self or chauffeur driven. Branches throughout GB and Continent. *OPEN 08.00-18.00 Mon-Fri, 08.00-17.30 Sat. CLOSED Sun.*
Kenning   3   **C**   **28**
1 York Way N1. 01-833 3211. Self-drive cars. Branches throughout GB at airports and abroad. (International reservations on 0246 208888. *OPEN 08.30-17.30 Mon-Fri.*) *OPEN 07.30-18.30 Mon-Fri, 08.00-14.00 Sat & Sun.*
Sportshire   1   **I**   **8**
6 Kendrick Pl, Reece Mews SW7. 01-589 8309. MGB, Morgan, Golf GTI, Audi Quattro and Porsche 944 for hire. *OPEN 09.30-19.00 Mon-Fri, 10.00-13.00 Sat.*
Swan National
1 National House, 3 Warwick St, Uxbridge, Middx. Uxbridge 33300. Phone here for your nearest branch. *OPEN 08.30-18.00 Mon-Fri, 09.00-13.00 Sat.*

Travelwise Car Hire   5   **K** 12
77 Pavilion Rd SW1. 01-235 0751. *OPEN 08.00-19.00 Mon-Fri, 08.00-14.00 Sat, 09.00-12.00 Sun.*

Chauffeur drive

Patrick Barthropp   5   **J** 15
Headfort Pl SW1. 01-245 9171. Bentleys, Silver Spirits and Silver Spurs with liveried chauffeurs. Also saloons. *OPEN 07.00 (08.00 Sun)-24.00 Mon-Sun.*

Arthur Monk
Monk House, 823 Western Rd NW10. 01-965 5333. Chauffeur driven Granada saloons and a wide range of vehicles from 6-to 35-seater. *OPEN 07.00-18.00 Mon-Fri. 24hr telephone service.*

Cycle hire

The bike offers an alternative form of transport worth considering when it costs 50p to travel one stop on the tube in central London. Danger to health through breathing noxious fumes is not nearly as great as the benefit gained from the exercise of cycling. Test the experience for yourself by hiring before buying a bike, or contact the London Cycling Campaign (01-928 7220) for information.

Chelsea Cycles   4   **L** 6
13-15 Park Wlk SW10. 01-352 3999.

On Your Bike   6   **Q** 29
52-54 Tooley St, London Bridge SE1. 01-407 1309 & Duke Street Hill SE1. 01-378 6669. Over 100 cycles available.

Saviles Cycle Stores
97-99 Battersea Rise SW11. 01-228 4279. No advance bookings. 40 bicycles for hire.

Coach hire

Greens
2 Priory Av E17. 01-520 1138.

Grey-Green Coaches
53-55 Stamford Hill N16. 01-800 4549.

Heathrow Coach Centre
Sipson Rd, West Drayton, Middx. 01-897 6131.

London Transport   5   **M** 18
Tours & Charter Office, 55 Broadway SW1. 01-222 5600.

R & I Coaches   1   **G** 7
118 Cromwell Rd SW7. 01-370 0322.

Sheenway Coaches
66 Stanley Rd SW14. 01-876 4243.

Public transport

London has a fairly good system of public transport with an improved night service. There are three different services – red buses, the underground (tube) and British Rail overground trains. The system is supposed to be integrated so that all three connect with each other wherever practicable, but bus and train timetables don't always coincide. To find your way around, use the underground and bus maps in this book.

London Transport   5   **M** 18
Travel Information Centre, 55 Broadway SW1. 01-222 1234. LT operates buses and the underground. Other travel information centres at these underground stations: Euston, Heathrow, King's Cross, Oxford Circus, Piccadilly Circus and Victoria (British Rail station).

The underground

For the stranger to London, this is the simplest way of getting around. Very efficient in central London and very quick. Few lines run south of the river where BR offers a better service. For journeys starting from the centre, tubes run *approx 05.30-00.15 Mon-Sat, 07.30-23.30 Sun.* Start 30 minutes earlier if coming from the suburbs or if you have to change; all tube stations have a notice showing the times of first and last trains. Fares are graduated according to zones and, for the regular traveller, weekly, monthly, quarterly or annual Travelcards provide considerable savings. Travelcards can be used on both the underground and buses. Capitalcards are also available on a weekly, monthly, quarterly or annual basis and are valid for use on buses, tubes and BR trains in the Greater London area. To save queuing at ticket offices, keep some 10p, 20p, 50p and £1 coins handy to use in ticket machines. Cheap day returns are available if you start your journey *after 10.00 Mon-Fri or any time Sat & Sun.*

Buses

Slower, especially in the rush hours, but more pleasant and you see so much more. They cover the whole of Greater London. They run *approx 06.00-24.00 Mon-Sat, 07.30-23.30 Sun.* First and last times of bus routes are indicated on bus stops but buses are not always reliable so don't depend on these. Again fares are graduated, apart from a few flat-fare routes, notably the Red Arrow buses in the centre. Return tickets are not available. On some buses you pay the driver as you get on but others (including all those with the entrance at the back of the bus) have a conductor who collects the fares as the bus goes along. Both give change but do not like being handed notes, especially large ones. If you are waiting at a request stop you must raise or wave your arm to make the bus stop for you. Once on the bus, if you wish to alight at a red request stop, you must ring the bell once, in good time. At other bus stops, called compulsory stops (white), this is not necessary. There are now all-night buses serving London every night, with a greatly extended service to the suburbs as well. Consult *Buses for Night Owls* for night buses, available from LT and BR travel information centres.

British Rail trains

See rail terminals below. BR run inter-city trains all over Britain but also run many suburban lines, especially in south London. These trains generally run *06.00-24.00 Mon-Sat, 07.00-22.30 Sun.* There are some one-off trains during the early hours; check with your station to see if there is a suitable one. Fares on BR trains are graduated and cheap day returns are available but not *Mon-Fri* on busy trains during rush hours (*approx 08.00-09.30 and 16.30-18.00*). Many BR stations connect with the underground.

Green Line coaches

Enquiries 01-668 7261. These are express buses run by London Country bus company. Most run from central London to outlying areas such as Windsor. The main starting point for these is Eccleston Bridge, Victoria SW1 (5 **M** 15); others from Regent St just north of Oxford Circus (2 **F** 20). Three unique services: route 700 from Victoria to Windsor Castle, special express via M4 motorway; route 727 from Crawley via Gatwick & Heathrow; route 747 from Gatwick via Heathrow to Luton airport. Services generally run *every hour*. Green Line can be used for travel within central London but the bus stops are quite far apart and the fares are high for short journeys.

Coaches

Victoria Coach Station   5 **M** 14
164 Buckingham Palace Rd SW1. 01-730 0202. The main provincial coach companies operate from here, travelling to destinations throughout Britain and the Continent. Booking necessary.

Riverbus

Thames Line Riverbus
West India Dock Pier, Cuba St E14. 01-987 0311. New service making use of London's great river. *Runs, at 15 minute intervals, between Chelsea Pier and Docklands 07.00-22.00 Mon-Fri & 10.00-18.00 Sat & Sun.*

Rail terminals

British Travel Centre   5 **J** 20
4-12 Lower Regent St SW1. 01-730 3400. And British Rail Travel Centres are also at 14 Kingsgate Pde, Victoria St SW1 (5 **M** 17), 87 King William St EC4 (6 **O** 30), 407 Oxford St W1 (2 **F** 18), Heathrow Airport. Booking centre for rail travel in Britain, rail and sea journeys to the Continent and Ireland, motorail and rail package holidays and tours. Several languages spoken.
Blackfriars   6 **M** 27
Queen Victoria St EC4. Information 01-928 5100. South and south-east London suburbs. Built in 1864, rebuilt 1977. *CLOSED Sat & Sun.*
Cannon Street   6 **O** 29
Cannon St EC4. Information 01-928 5100. South-east London suburbs, Kent, E. Sussex. Built 1866; rebuilt with office block above in 1965. *CLOSED Sat & Sun.*
Charing Cross   5 **K** 22
Strand WC2. Information 01-928 5100. South-east London suburbs, Kent. Built 1864. Trains from here go over Hungerford Bridge.
Euston   3 **C** 24
Euston Rd NW1. Information 01-387 7070. Fast trains to Birmingham, Liverpool, Manchester, Glasgow, Inverness. Suburban line to Watford, Northampton. The original station was built in 1837, designed by Robert Stephenson. It had a famous Doric portico which was 72ft (22m) high. The station was completely rebuilt in 1968 and is now a modern functional terminal.

Fenchurch Street   6 P 32
Railway Pl, Fenchurch St EC3. Information 01-283 7171. Trains to Tilbury and Southend. Built 1841 and currently being redeveloped with office block above.

Holborn Viaduct   6 K 28
Holborn Viaduct EC1. Information 01-928 5100. South and south-east London suburbs. Built 1874, rebuilt 1963. *CLOSED Sat & Sun.*

King's Cross   3 D 27
Euston Rd N1. Information 01-278 2477. Fast trains to Leeds, York, Newcastle, Edinburgh, Aberdeen. Built by Lewis Cubitt in 1851, a more modern concourse was added some years ago. The clock on the tower was taken from the original Crystal Palace in Hyde Park.

Liverpool Street   6 M 33
Liverpool St EC2. Information 01-283 7171. East and north-east London suburbs, fast trains to Cambridge, Colchester, Norwich and Harwich harbour. Built 1874-5 and currently being renovated.

London Bridge   6 Q 29
Borough High St SE1. Information 01-928 5100. South and south-east London suburbs, Kent, Sussex, East Surrey. First opened in 1836, expanded in 1839 and 1864.

Marylebone   2 A 17
Boston Pl NW1. Information 01-262 6767. Suburban lines to Amersham, High Wycombe, Banbury, Aylesbury. Last of the main-line terminals to be built, 1899.

Moorgate   6 M 32
Moorgate EC2. Information 01-278 2477. Recently opened for suburban services to Welwyn Garden City and Hertford. Constructed in 1904 as an underground station with tunnels to Drayton Park and thence overground. The tube tunnels are 16ft (4.9m) diameter, the largest in London.

Paddington   2 A 13
Praed St W2. Information 01-262 6767. Fast trains to Bath, Bristol, Cardiff, Hereford, Swansea, Devon and Cornwall. Some 125 mph services. Built in 1854 by Brunel, it was the London terminus of his Great Western Railway and one of his dreams was to run a service from Paddington to New York — by rail to Bristol and high-speed steamship across the Atlantic. The railway hotel, built by Hardwick, is a superb edifice in French renaissance style.

St Pancras   3 D 26
Euston Rd NW1. Information 01-387 7070. Fast trains to Nottingham, Leicester, Sheffield, Derby; suburban to Luton, St Alban's, Bedford. An imposing Victorian Gothic glass and ironwork structure, it is more like a cathedral than a railway station with its 100ft (30.5m) high roof. Designed by Sir George Gilbert Scott and opened in 1868. The frontage was once a grand hotel but has now been refurbished and is used for offices.

Victoria   5 M 15
Terminus Pl, Victoria St SW1. Information 01-928 5100. South and south-east London suburbs, Kent, Sussex, east Surrey. Fast trains to Brighton. Built in two parts; Brighton side in 1860, Dover side in 1862. Fast service to Gatwick Airport (30-min journey). *Every 15mins, 05.00-01.00; less frequent at night.*

Waterloo   6 N 23
SE1. Information 01-928 5100. South-west London suburbs, west Surrey, Hampshire, Dorset. Fast trains to Portsmouth, Southampton, Bournemouth. Built 1848, partly modernised 1922. There is also a separate Waterloo (East) station where all trains from Charing Cross stop.

Airports

London City Airport
King George V Dock, Connaught Rd E16. 01-474 5555.
London Gatwick Airport
Horley, Surrey. Crawley 28822.
London Heathrow Airport
Bath Rd, Heathrow, Middx. 01-759 4321.
London Stansted Airport
Stansted, Essex. Bishop's Stortford 502380.
Luton Airport
Luton, Beds. Luton 405100.
Southend Airport
Southend-on-Sea, Essex. Southend 340201.
Westland Heliport   4 Q 3
Lombard Rd SW11. 01-228 0181.

Air services

Check-in facilities for most major airlines are now based at the airports. For information contact airline booking offices. See telephone directories for details.

British Airways   5 M 15
Central London Air Terminal, Victoria Station SW1. 01-834 9411. *OPEN 06.00-22.00 Mon-Sun.*

Airport bus services

London Transport
A1 Heathrow, Cromwell Rd, Victoria.
A2 Heathrow, Bayswater, Oxford Circus, Euston.
Flightline
747 Gatwick, Heathrow
757 Luton, Victoria
767 Heathrow, Victoria
777 Gatwick, Victoria

Cheap air tickets

Considerable savings can be made on full price air tickets – any travel agent can give details of arrangements which vary according to destination. ABC (Advance Booking Charter) and APEX (Advance Purchase Excursion) return tickets are available to many worldwide destinations including N. America and Australia; tickets for these must be bought 21 or 30 days in advance and neither outward nor return dates can be altered. The classified ads in Time Out *are a source of other less official cheap flights. If you are a student, special rates are available – check with the student travel office.*

Airlines

Most of the world's airlines operate services to London and many have booking offices here (listed in the telephone directory). Travel agents will also make bookings.
British Airways Sales Shops
01-897 4000. British Airways sell tickets and make bookings for any airline that belongs to IATA (International Air Transport Association). If you book by phone, you can have your ticket sent by mail or collect and pay for it at one of the Sales Shops. *OPEN 07.00-22.45 Mon-Sun.*

101-102 Cheapside EC2.	6	K	29

OPEN 09.00-17.30 Mon-Fri.
52 Grosvenor Gdns SW1.   5 **K** 15
OPEN 09.00-17.30 Mon-Fri, 09.00-13.00 Sat.
Hilton Hotel, Park La W1.   2 **I** 16
OPEN 09.00-17.00 Mon-Fri, 09.00-13.00 Sat.
421 Oxford St W1.   2 **F** 18
OPEN 09.00-18.00 Mon-Fri, 09.00-17.00 Sat.
Portman Hotel, 22 Portman Sq   2 **D** 17
W1. *OPEN 09.00-17.00 Mon-Fri.*

65-75 Regent St W1. *OPEN*   2 **I** 20
09.00-18.00 Mon-Fri, 09.00-17.00 Sat.
110-111 Strand WC2.   6 **K** 23
OPEN 09.00-17.30 Mon-Fri.
Nr Platform 13, Victoria BR   5 **M** 15
Station SW1. *OPEN 07.00-22.00 Mon-Sat, 08.00-22.00 Sun.*
Cromwell Rd SW7.   1 **G** 7
OPEN 08.00-17.00 Mon-Fri, 08.00-16.00 Sat.
Subject to alteration.

Specialist air and helicopter charter

All the big airlines also operate charter flights for all purposes, subject to availability.
Air Amiga Ltd
Stapleford Aerodrome, Stapleford Tawney, Essex. Stapleford 361. Five Bell Jet Rangers, three Robinson R22s (for training pilots). Can supply many sizes of aircraft.
Alan Mann Helicopters
Fairoaks Airport, Chobham, Surrey. Chobham 7471/7037. Operates a fleet of six 4-seater Jet Ranger helicopters, two 109s and one Bell 47 for training. Contact Jenny McKenna for bookings.
Autair International   2 **E** 18
75 Wigmore St W1. 01-935 1151. Fleet of helicopters for hire or sale. Phone Bedford 751243 for bookings.
Cabair
Elstree Aerodrome, Elstree, Herts. 01-953 4411. Piper, Drummond-Kougar, Jet Ranger and Navajo air-taxi operators and helicopter charter.
Clark Air International   6 **Q** 30
Clark Air House, 85 Tooley St SE1. 01-407 8831. Plane and helicopter brokers and consultants.
Dollar Air Services
Hangar 6, Coventry Airport, Coventry. Coventry 304231. Fleet of helicopters for all types of charter.
Instone Air Transport   6 **Q** 28
Bridge House, 4 Borough High St SE1. 01-407 4411. Freight specialists, air brokers and aviation consultants.
London Airtaxi Centre   6 **Q** 29
New City Court, 20 St Thomas St SE1. 01-378 6935. Helicopter and aircraft charter. Will supply almost any size of aircraft.
Thurston Aviation
London Stansted Airport, Stansted, Essex. Bishop's Stortford 815027. *24-hour* air-taxi, helicopter charter and handling.

Accommodation

Hotel booking agents

Accommodation Service of   5   M   15
the London Tourist Board
London Tourist Board Information Centre, Victoria Station Forecourt SW1. 01-730 3488. They give information and make bookings. *OPEN 09.00-20.30 Mon-Sun. Also at Heathrow Airport. Charge.*

Concordia Worldwide Hotel   5   L   15
Reservations
52 Grosvenor Gdns SW1. 01-730 3467. All kinds of hotels in London, Britain and worldwide. *OPEN 07.00-19.00 Mon-Sat.* Also sales desk at Victoria Station, Platform 9. 01-828 4646. *OPEN 07.00-23.00 Mon-Sun. Charge.*

Expotel Hotel Reservations
Dial 01-568 8765 to make hotel reservations. Covers the whole of Great Britain. *OPEN 08.30-18.00 Mon-Fri. Free.*

Global Grange Ltd   6   N   33
Platform 9, Liverpool Street Station EC2. No telephone. Hotel reservations in London only. *OPEN 08.00-09.00 Mon-Sun. Charge.*

Hotel Booking Service   2   H   20
Cashmere House, 13-14 Golden Sq W1. 01-437 5052. Excellent and knowledgeable service to business firms and general public. All types of hotel reservations in London, UK and worldwide. *OPEN 09.30-17.30 Mon-Fri. Free.*

Hotel Finders
20 Bell La NW4. 01-202 7000. All kinds of hotels. *OPEN 09.00-17.30 Mon-Fri, 09.00-16.00 Sat. Free.*

Hotel Guide   2   I   22
Faraday House, 8-10 Charing Cross Rd WC2. 01-836 7677. Hotel accommodation service. *OPEN 09.00-17.00 Mon-Fri. Free.*

Hotelpacc Group Services   5   J   15
Ltd
40-46 Headfort Pl SW1. 01-235 9696. Hotel accommodation for groups (10 people or more) in London, UK and worldwide. Facilities for coach and tour operators and conference organisers. *OPEN 09.00-18.00 Mon-Fri. Free.*

Hotel Reservations Centre   5   M   14
10 Buckingham Palace Rd SW1. 01-828 2425. *OPEN 09.00-17.00 for bookings all over Britain. Free.*

Room Centre
Kingsgate House, Kingsgate Pl NW6. 01-328 1790. Worldwide hotel and conference booking service. *OPEN 09.00-17.30 Mon-Fri. Free.*

It is compulsory for hotels to display their prices. Visitors should make sure exactly what is included in the price, ie breakfast, VAT, service, etc. Many hotels have facilities for conferences, banquets, receptions, etc, but in each entry we refer to this as conference facilities. Capacity, where given in numbers, is approximate at the upper end of the scale – check first. Small conference facilities means capacity for 20 people or less. Large conference facilities means the capacity is flexible according to the requirements, air cond = air conditioning, conf cap = conference capacity, P = parking, s pool = swimming pool. Credit cards: A = Access (incorporating Mastercard/Eurocard). Ax = American Express, Dc = Diners Club, V = Visa (incorporating Barclaycard).
For inexpensive accommodation see 'Student London'.

Hotels: top prices

Over £100 per night, single room with bath or shower. Prices should be checked because they may vary considerably within the category and breakfast, VAT and service may not be included in the charge.

Athenaeum   2   I   18
116 Piccadilly W1. 01-499 3464. Comfortable modern hotel in good taste. 112 rooms all with bath and TV. Small conf room. Air cond. A. Ax. Dc. V.

Belgravia Sheraton   5   K   13
20 Chesham Pl SW1. 01-235 6040. Small luxury hotel, personal service. 90 rooms. Air cond. Conf cap 20. A. Ax. Dc. V.

Berkeley   2   I   14
Wilton Pl SW1. 01-235 6000. Modern building. Interior stylish and elegant. Two good restaurants. 160 rooms. TV. S pool. Air cond. P. Conf cap 200. A. Ax. Dc. V.

Britannia 2 F 17
Grosvenor Sq W1. 01-629 9400. Modern international hotel. Three restaurants. 356 rooms. Conf cap 50. Air cond. A. Ax. Dc. V.

Browns 2 I 19
Albemarle St W1. 01-493 6020. Traditional, restful, oak-panelled. Courteous service. 127 rooms. 8 conf rooms. A. Ax. Dc. V.

Cadogan 5 K 12
75 Sloane St SW1. 01-235 7141. Comfortable and friendly. Restaurant. 69 rooms. Small conf facilities. A. Ax. Dc. V.

Cavendish 2 I 19
Jermyn St SW1. 01-930 2111. Modern and sophisticated. 253 rooms all with bath and TV. P. Large conf facilities. A. Ax. Dc. V.

Churchill 2 D 17
30 Portman Sq W1. 01-486 5800. Modern international hotel. 485 rooms. Air cond. P. Conf cap 250. A. Ax. Dc. V.

Claridges 2 G 18
Brook St W1. 01-629 8860. Quiet luxury and lavish traditional atmosphere. Haute cuisine in the restaurant and good smörgåsbord in the Causerie. 200 rooms. Secretarial service. A. Ax. Dc. V.

Connaught 2 G 18
Carlos Pl W1. 01-499 7070. Dignified and distinguished. Excellent service. Restaurant with unrivalled reputation. 90 rooms all with bath and TV. A.

Dorchester 2 H 16
Park La W1. 01-629 8888. Luxury with courteous, efficient service. Dinner dances in the Terrace Restaurant. Good food. 279 rooms. P (limited). Conf cap 500. A. Ax. Dc. V.

Dukes 5 J 18
35 St James's Pl SW1. 01-491 4840. Unique situation on secluded gas-lit courtyard. Good restaurant. 58 rooms including 22 suites. Banqueting and small conf facilities. A. Ax. Dc. V.

Grosvenor House 2 G 16
Park La W1. 01-499 6363. Unobtrusive luxury and service. 390 rooms, 70 suites, 160 apartments. Air cond. S pools, saunas, banqueting and conf cap 1800. Bookshop, boutique, garage and restaurants. A. Ax. Dc. V.

Hilton 2 I 16
22 Park La W1. 01-493 8000. Modern luxurious hotel overlooking Hyde Park. Good roof restaurant with views and dancing. 501 rooms. Air cond. P. Sauna. Conf cap 1000. A. Ax. Dc. V.

Hilton International Regent's Park
18 Lodge Rd, St John's Wood NW8. 01-722 7722. Modern hotel overlooking Lord's Cricket Ground. Minski's Restau-

rant. 377 rooms. P. Air cond. Conf facilities. A. Ax. Dc. V.

Holiday Inn Chelsea 5 K 12
17-25 Sloane St SW1. 01-235 4377. Modern hotel with Mediterranean-style restaurant. King-size beds. 220 rooms. Conf cap 100. Air cond. A. Ax. Dc. V.

Holiday Inn Marble Arch 2 D 17
134 George St W1. 01-723 1277. Modern hotel with s pool, sauna. Air cond. P. 241 rooms. Conf cap 150. A. Ax. Dc. V.

Holiday Inn Mayfair 2 I 18
3 Berkeley St W1. 01-493 8282. Modern hotel with elegant interior. 186 rooms. Conf cap 50. A. Ax. Dc. V.

Howard 6 K 25
Temple Pl WC2. 01-836 3555. Modern, elegant hotel. 135 rooms. Air cond. P. Conf cap 200. A. Ax. Dc. V.

Hyatt-Carlton Tower 5 K 13
Cadogan Pl SW1. 01-235 5411. International standards of luxury and service in this sophisticated hotel. Good food in the Chelsea Room, roast beef in the Rib Room. 224 rooms. Air cond. P. Conf facilities. A. Ax. Dc. V.

Hyde Park 2 H 14
66 Knightsbridge SW1. 01-235 2000. Traditional standards of luxury and comfort. Restaurant and Grill. 186 rooms. Air cond. A. Ax. Dc. V.

Inn on the Park 2 I 16
Hamilton Pl, Park La W1. 01-499 0888. Luxurious modern hotel, with every comfort. Two haute cuisine restaurants. Views over Hyde Park. 228 rooms. P. Air cond. Conf facilities. A. Ax. Dc. V.

Inter-Continental 2 I 16
Hyde Park Corner W1. 01-409 3131. Good modern hotel. Excellent central location. 490 rooms. Air cond. Sauna, health club and hairdressing. P. Conf facilities. A. Ax. Dc. V.

Le Meridien 2 I 20
Piccadilly W1. 01-734 8000. Deluxe hotel with own health club attached. Three restaurants. 365 rooms. Air cond. Conf facilities. A. Ax. Dc. V.

May Fair 2 I 18
Stratton St W1. 01-629 7777. Traditional hotel refurbished to modern standards. Air cond. Theatre. 310 rooms. Conf cap 300. A. Ax. Dc. V.

Portman Inter-Continental 2 D 17
22 Portman Sq W1. 01-486 5844. Modern with traditional atmosphere designed to make the business person feel at home: secretarial, teletext and telefax facilities. Nouvelle cuisine. 275 rooms. Air cond. P. Conf cap 750. A. Ax. Dc. V.

Ritz 2 I 18
Piccadilly W1. 01-493 8181. Grandeur and elegance. Period rooms. Unobtrusive efficient service. Beautiful restaurant. 128 rooms. Air cond. A. Ax. Dc. V.

Royal Garden 1 E 8
Kensington High St W8. 01-937 8000. Comfortably modern, pleasantly run. Two restaurants. Good food. 395 rooms. Valet and secretarial services. Conf cap 500. A. Ax. Dc. V.

Royal Lancaster 2 C 12
Lancaster Ter W2. 01-262 6737. A tall modern block geared to business people and conferences. Magnificent views over Kensington Gardens and Hyde Park. La Rosette restaurant specialises in seasonal French and English dishes. 418 rooms. Air cond. P. Valet, secretarial and interpreting services. Conf cap 1000. A. Ax. Dc. V.

Savoy 6 K 23
Strand WC2. 01-836 4343. World-famous in reputation and clientele. Edwardian in atmosphere and service, yet still faultlessly up-to-date. Impeccable standards. Outstanding cuisine. Air cond. 202 rooms. Secretarial service. A. Ax. Dc. V.

Selfridge 2 E 17
Orchard St W1. 01-408 2080. Traditional comfort plus modern facilities. All bedrooms are soundproofed with controllable air cond and bath, TV, radio. Two restaurants. 298 rooms. Conf facilities. A. Ax. Dc. V.

Sheraton Park Tower 2 I 14
101 Knightsbridge SW1. 01-235 8050. Modern hotel with beautiful glass-encased restaurant. P. 293 rooms including 25 suites. Air cond. Secretarial service. Conf cap 250. A. Ax. Dc. V.

Stafford 5 J 19
16-18 St James's Pl SW1. 01-493 0111. Elegant and comfortable. Good restaurant. Private dining rooms. 62 rooms. Small conf facilities. A. Ax. Dc. V.

Westbury 2 H 23
Conduit St W1. 01-629 7755. Modern with American standards of luxury and efficiency. Restaurant. 256 rooms. Conf cap 120. A. Ax. Dc. V.

Hotels: medium prices

£50-£100 per night, single room with bath or shower. Continental breakfast and inclusive of VAT and service charge. Prices should be checked as they may vary considerably within the category.

Academy 3 F 23
17-21 Gower St WC1. 01-631 4115. Small, elegant Georgian hotel refurbished in 1987/8 to a high standard. Good service. 35 rooms. TV. Bar. A. Ax. Dc. V.

Basil Street Hotel 2 I 13
Knightsbridge SW3. 01-581 3311. Victorian decor, country house atmosphere. Two restaurants and wine bar. The Parrot Club for ladies is here. 103 rooms. Small conf facilities. A. Ax. Dc. V.

Blakes 4 J 7
33 Roland Gdns SW7. 01-370 6701. Informal with Chelsea atmosphere. Showbiz clientele. Each room individually and luxuriously decorated. 50 rooms including 16 suites. Air cond. A. Ax. Dc. V.

Bloomsbury Crest 3 F 25
Coram St WC1. 01-837 1200. Modern tourist hotel. Coffee shop and restaurant. Conf facilities. 175 rooms. A. Ax. Dc. V.

Bonnington 3 G 25
92 Southampton Row WC1. 01-242 2828. Modernised well-established hotel. Restaurant. 240 rooms. Conf facilities. A. Ax. Dc. V.

Charing Cross 5 K 22
Strand WC2. 01-839 7282. Victorian, spacious but modernised and comfortable. Cocktail bar and carvery. Men's sauna. Hairdresser. 218 rooms. Conf facilities. A. Ax. Dc. V.

Cora 3 E 25
Upper Woburn Pl WC1. 01-387 5111. Close to Euston Station. Regency hotel. Restaurant. 162 rooms. Conf facilities. A. Ax. Dc. V.

Cumberland 2 E 16
Marble Arch W1. 01-262 1234. Large, busy, modernised hotel. Valeting service. Coffee shop and restaurant. 935 rooms. Air cond. Conf cap 300. A. Ax. Dc. V.

De Vere Park 1 F 9
1 De Vere Gdns, 60 Hyde Park Gate W8. 01-584 0051. Victorian, spacious and modernised. Restaurant. 96 rooms. A. Ax. Dc. V.

Drury Lane 3 I 24
Drury La WC2. 01-836 6666. Ultra-modern hotel in the heart of theatreland. Maudie's Restaurant is good. 128 rooms. Air cond. Conf cap 100. A. Ax. Dc. V.

Durrants 2 D 17
George St W1. 01-935 8131. Elegant family-owned hotel. 96 rooms including 3 suites. Restaurant. Conf facilities. A. Ax. V.

Forum Hotel London 1 G 7
97 Cromwell Rd SW7. 01-370 5757. Mod-

ern hotel with restaurant, shops, theatre desk. 907 rooms with bath. P. Conf facilities. A. Ax. Dc. V.

Gloucester I H 7
Harrington Gdns SW7. 01-373 6030. Very modern large hotel. Air cond and shopping arcade. Renaissance floor with butler service. 530 rooms. Conf cap 500. A. Ax. Dc. V.

Great Eastern 6 N 32
Liverpool St EC2. 01-283 4363. Spacious, modernised old-style hotel. Three restaurants. 164 rooms. Conf and beautiful banqueting facilities. A. Ax. Dc. V.

Great Northern 3 D 27
King's Cross N1. 01-837 5454. Spacious, comfortable old-style hotel. New decor. Restaurant. 80 rooms. Conf facilities. A. Ax. Dc. V.

Great Western Royal 2 B 13
Paddington Station W2. 01-723 8064. Traditional, spacious and modernised. Efficient service and comforts. Two restaurants. 170 rooms. Conf facilities. A. Ax. Dc. V.

Grosvenor 5 M 14
101 Buckingham Palace Rd SW1. 01-834 9494. The building is reputed to be the finest example of French Renaissance-style architecture in Britain. 350 rooms with bath. Conf cap 200. A. Ax. Dc. V.

Holiday Inn Swiss Cottage
128 King Henry's Rd NW3. 01-722 7711. Modern building outside the centre but within easy access. S pool, sauna, gym, air cond, inhouse movies. P. 304 rooms. Executive floor with own check-in facilities. Conf cap 200. A. Ax. Dc. V.

Hospitality Inn I B 10
104 Bayswater Rd W2. 01-262 4461. Competently run modern hotel overlooking Hyde Park. 175 rooms. Air cond. P. Small conf facilities. A. Ax. Dc. V.

Hotel Russell 3 F 24
Russell Sq WC1. 01-837 6470. Victorian splendour. Shop. 318 rooms all with bath and TV. Two restaurants. Conf facilities. Special weekend rates throughout the year. A. Ax. Dc. V.

Kensington Close I E 7
Wright's La W8. 01-937 8170. Good-value hotel with plenty of facilities. S pool, saunas, sun-beds, gym and squash. Garden. 530 rooms. Conf facilities. A. Ax. Dc. V.

Kensington Hilton I A 5
179-199 Holland Park Av W11. 01-603 3355. Modern, well-furnished building with sandstone finish and smoked glass windows. Shops. Entertainment. 606 rooms

with bath. Air cond. P. Conf cap 300. A. Ax. Dc. V.

Kensington Palace I E 9
De Vere Gdns W8. 01-937 8121. Restful and modernised traditional hotel. Kensington Restaurant. 298 rooms. Large conf facilities. A. Ax. Dc. V.

Kingsley 3 H 24
Bloomsbury Way WC1. 01-242 5881. Modernised hotel for the business person and tourist. Restaurant. 146 rooms. Small conf facilities. A. Ax. Dc. V.

London Embassy Hotel I B 10
150 Bayswater Rd W2. 01-229 1212. Modern hotel overlooking Kensington Gardens. Restaurant and cocktail bar. 193 rooms all with TV. Conf facilities. A. Ax. Dc. V.

The Londoner 2 E 19
Welbeck St W1. 01-935 4442. Well-appointed, friendly and modern. Valeting service. 143 rooms. A. Ax. Dc. V.

London International I G 7
147 Cromwell Rd SW5. 01-370 4200. Modern hotel with restaurant and the Fountain Brasserie. 420 rooms. P. Conf facilities. A. Ax. Dc. V.

London Tara I E 7
Scarsdale Pl, Wright's La W8. 01-937 7211. Modern hotel with restaurant and brasserie. 840 rooms with bath. P. Conf facilities. A. Ax. Dc. V.

Mountbatten 3 I 23
Monmouth St WC2. 01-836 4300. Theatreland hotel with luxurious marble interior. Valet service. Restaurant, cocktail bar. 127 rooms including 7 suites. Air cond. Conf facilities. A. Ax. Dc. V.

Norfolk I I 9
Harrington Rd SW7. 01-589 8191. Elegantly modernised Victorian hotel close to the Natural History Museum and the V & A. 97 rooms all with spa baths. Air cond. Gym. Brasserie, winery, tavern. Conf cap 60. A. Ax. Dc. V.

Novotel
Shortlands W6. 01-741 1555. Concrete edifice near Hammersmith flyover. Traditionally furnished. 640 rooms. Air cond. P. Conf facilities. A. Ax. Dc. V.

Park Court I C 11
75 Lancaster Gate W2. 01-402 4272. Full range of services for guests with children. 442 rooms with bath. Conf facilities. A. Ax. Dc. V.

Regent Crest 2 D 22
Carburton St W1. 01-388 2300. Modern hotel which is very popular with tourists. Coffee shop. Boulevard restaurant. 322 rooms all with bath. Air cond. P. Conf facilities. A. Ax. Dc. V.

Regent Palace Hotel 2 I 20
Piccadilly Circus W1. 01-734 7000. At the heart of the West End. Carvery, coffee shop, bars. 1034 rooms. A. Ax. Dc. V.

Rembrandt 1 I 10
Thurloe Pl SW7. 01-589 8100. Modernised, well run. Restaurant with carvery. Conservatory. Romanesque health club. 200 rooms. Conf cap 200. A. Ax. Dc. V.

Royal Angus 5 J 21
39 Coventry St W1. 01-930 4033. Traditionally furnished and central. Pavilion Restaurant. 92 rooms. A. Ax. Dc. V.

Royal Court 5 L 12
Sloane Sq SW1. 01-730 9191. Attractive, luxurious, country-house-style hotel. 102 rooms including 6 suites, all with bath or shower. 'Twelve Sloane Square' international restaurant. A. Ax. Dc. V.

Royal Horseguards 5 L 22
2 Whitehall Ct SW1. 01-839 3400. Victorian building facing across the Thames to the Festival Hall. Traditionally furnished and comfortable. 285 rooms all with bath and TV. Restaurant. Conf facilities. A. Ax. Dc. V.

Royal Kensington 1 D 4
380 Kensington High St W14. 01-603 3333. Large, modern hotel, next to Olympia and near the motorail terminal. Brasserie/restaurant. 400 rooms with bath. P. Conf facilities. A. Ax. Dc. V.

Royal Trafalgar 5 J 21
Whitcomb St WC2. 01-930 4477. Hotel behind the National Gallery. Restaurant. Has its own pub 'The Battle of Trafalgar'. 108 rooms. Special weekend rates. A. Ax. Dc. V.

Sherlock Holmes 2 D 18
108 Baker St W1. 01-486 6161. Spacious modern hotel with its name as a theme. 126 rooms with bath. Restaurant. Conf facilities. A. Ax. Dc. V.

Strand Palace 6 K 23
372 Strand WC2. 01-836 8080. Large, practical and accommodating hotel. Three restaurants. Shops. 771 rooms. Conf facilities. A. Ax. Dc. V.

Tower Thistle 6 R 33
St Katharine's Way E1. 01-481 2575. Large modern hotel next to Tower Bridge and the Tower of London. 3 restaurants, 1 overlooking the river. 826 rooms. Air cond. P. Conf facilities. A. Ax. Dc. V.

Waldorf 6 J 24
Aldwych WC2. 01-836 2400. Edwardian-style elegance. Suitable for the business executive. Modernised and central. Brasserie, restaurant, wine bar, tea dances in the 'Palm Court' *Fri-Sun*. 310 rooms. Conf facilities. A. Ax. Dc. V.

Washington 2 I 17
Curzon St W1. 01-499 7030. Up-to-date fashionable hotel. Efficient service. 159 rooms. Conf cap 150-400. A. Ax. Dc. V.

White House 2 C 22
Albany St NW1. 01-387 1200. Former apartment hotel now offering full service. Overlooks Regent's Park. First class public rooms. Restaurant with good reputation. Wine bar. Coffee shop. 577 rooms. Conf facilities. A. Ax. Dc. V.

White's 1 C 11
90-92 Lancaster Gate W2. 01-262 2711. Charming, balustraded exterior, unobtrusive and modernised. Overlooks Hyde Park. Restaurant. 55 rooms. Air cond. P. Conf facilities. A. Ax. Dc. V.

Bed and breakfast

Mostly found in streets around main line stations, but also scan notice boards outside newsagents and look in local papers. There are hundreds of small guest-houses so look around areas like Victoria, Earl's Court, Bayswater and Bloomsbury. It is much easier to find a room in winter than in summer. Beware of hotel touts who operate at the main stations, particularly Victoria; the accommodation they offer is usually inadequate and expensive.

Camping sites

Certainly the cheapest accommodation in London, camping can provide a pleasant alternative for the visitor. Own tent essential. Book in advance in summer.

Caravan Harbour
Crystal Palace Pde SE19. 01-778 7155. *OPEN all year.*

Co-operative Woods Camping and Caravanning Site
Federation Rd, Abbey Wood SE2. 01-310 2233. Electric hook-ups available for caravans. *OPEN all year.*

Debden House Campsite
Debden Green, Loughton, Essex. 01-508 3008. *OPEN all year.*

Hackney Camping
Millfields Rd E5. 01-985 7656. *OPEN Jun-Aug.*

Lee Valley Park
Picketts Lock Centre, Picketts Lock La N9. 01-803 4756. *OPEN all year.*

Lee Valley Regional Park
Eastway Cycle Circuit, Temple Mills La E15. 01-534 6085. *OPEN Apr-Oct.*

Tent City
Wormwood Scrubs, Old Oak Common La W3. 01-749 9074. *OPEN Apr-Oct.*

Hotels near Heathrow Airport

All these are air conditioned and provide free transport to and from the airport. Prices vary considerably. £40-£90 per night, single room with bath or shower. Breakfast is often extra. Inclusive of VAT and service charge.

The Ariel
Bath Rd, Hayes, Middx. 01-759 2552. Circular in design. Restaurant open all day. 177 rooms with bath and TV. Conf facilities. A. Ax. Dc. V.

Arlington
Shepiston La, Hayes, Middx. 01-573 6162. Transit hotel for the airport. Restaurant. 75 rooms. Special weekend rates. A. Ax. Dc. V.

Excelsior
Bath Rd, West Drayton, Middx. 01-759 6611. Fully soundproofed. Indoor pool. Restaurant. 24hr service. 665 rooms. Health and fitness centre. Conf facilities. A. Ax. Dc. V.

Heathrow Park Hotel
Bath Rd, Longford, Middx. 01-759 2400. New hotel built as near as possible to the airport and geared to cater for transit visitors. Restaurant. 303 rooms. Conf cap 500. A. Ax. Dc. V.

Heathrow Penta Hotel
Bath Rd, Hounslow, Middx. 01-897 6363. Pleasant modern exterior. S pool. Two restaurants. Two bars. 670 rooms with bath, TV, mini bar, air cond. Conf facilities. A. Ax. Dc. V.

Holiday Inn Heathrow
Stockley Rd, West Drayton, Middx. West Drayton 445555. Modern hotel with 9-hole golf course, pool, sauna, gym. Two restaurants. All rooms have bath, TV, telephone, radio, in-house movies. 400 rooms. Conf facilities. A. Ax. Dc. V.

Master Robert
366 Great West Rd, Hounslow, Middx. 01-570 6261. 3 miles from Heathrow, 10 miles from central London. 100 soundproofed rooms with bath and TV. Conf facilities. Restaurant and carvery. A. Ax. Dc. V.

Post House
Sipson Rd, West Drayton, Middx. 01-759 2323. All rooms have bath, TV, telephone; mini bars, babysitting service. 594 rooms. Four conference rooms. A. Ax. Dc. V.

Sheraton Heathrow
Colnbrook By-pass, West Drayton, Middx. 01-759 2424. Built in 1973, with a well-designed interior. Shops, s pool, sauna, coffee shop. Free transport links with central London four times a day. 440 rooms, all with TV and soundproofing. Conf facilities. A. Ax. Dc. V.

Sheraton Skyline
Bath Rd, Hayes, Middx. 01-759 2535. Luxurious hotel. Quadrangular in design. Gourmet restaurant. Night club, sauna, s pool, babysitting service. 353 soundproofed rooms including 5 suites. A. Ax. Dc. V.

Skyway
Bath Rd, Hayes, Middx. 01-759 6311. Built in 1971. Well designed. Outdoor s pool. Restaurant, coffee shop, bar. 445 soundproofed rooms with TV and bath. Conf facilities. A. Ax. Dc. V.

Hotels near Gatwick Airport

All these provide free transport to and from the airport. £50-£70 per night, single room with bath or shower. Breakfast is often extra. Inclusive of VAT and service charge.

Chequers Thistle Hotel
Brighton Rd, Horley, Surrey. Horley 786992. Fully modernised country-house-style hotel. Restaurant, snack bar. Outdoor s pool. 78 rooms. Conf facilities. A. Ax. Dc. V.

Crest Hotel
Langley Dri, Tushmore Roundabout, Crawley, W. Sussex. Crawley 29991. Modern, efficient airport hotel recently refurbished. Restaurant. 231 rooms. Conf cap 350. A. Ax. Dc. V.

George Hotel
High St, Crawley, W. Sussex. Crawley 24215. 15thC building retaining original features yet providing modern, well-equipped bedrooms in the rear extension. Restaurant. 75 rooms. Conf facilities. A. Ax. Dc. V.

Post House
Povey Cross Rd, Horley, Surrey. Horley

771621. New, spacious hotel. Heated outdoor s pool. Two restaurants. Facilities for the disabled. 218 rooms. Conf facilities. A. Ax. Dc. V.

Estate agents

Mainly deal in the sale of property but sometimes in rented property as well. Normally operate very much on a local basis and they advertise in the local papers which is a good source for assessing the market in any particular area. Estate agents may belong to one of the following associations, who can give you the names of member agents in any particular area and to whom complaints against member agents should be addressed.

Incorporated Society of   5 **K** 12
Valuers and Auctioneers
3 Cadogan Gate SWI. 01-235 2282. Also for auctioneers, valuers and surveyors.
National Association of Estate Agents
Arbon House, 21 Jury St, Warwick, Warks. Warwick 496800.
Royal Institution of   5 **M** 20
Chartered Surveyors
12 Great George St SWI. 01-222 7000. Also for surveyors.

Flat-sharing

Publications like the Evening Standard and Time Out are good sources for flat-sharing advertisements, as are local newsagents' windows.
Agencies will help you find a place in a ready established flat, or else find you a kindred spirit to search with. They do try to match up carefully according to age, interests, background, etc and may charge a fee for their services.
Apex Flats   2 **I** 21
39 Wardour St WI. 01-734 1619.
Flatmates   I **I** 11
313 Brompton Rd SW3. 01-589 5491.

Furnished & unfurnished flats

The address will generally indicate the district in which the agent specialises.
Around Town Flats   I **A** 5
120 Holland Park Av W11. 01-229 9966. Good quality luxury furnished property to let for 6 months to 1 year.
Benham & Reeves Residential Letting Office
14 Upper Kingswell, Heath St NW3. 01-435 9681. Furnished and unfurnished flats and houses.
Britton, Poole & Burns
5 Wellington Pl NW8. 01-722 1166. And in Knightsbridge and South Kensington.
Claridges
West Heath House, 32 North End Rd NW11. 01-455 0007. Furnished and unfurnished lets only. Min 6 months. Visitors and company
Cluttons   2 **H** 18
45 Berkeley Sq WI. 01-408 1010. Mostly unfurnished properties.
Keith Cardale Groves   2 **F** 17
22 Grosvenor Sq WI. 01-629 6604.
Marsh & Parsons   I **D** 8
5 Kensington Church St W8. 01-937 6091 (head office). Several other branches in West London.
Residential Property   I **D** 8
Services
116 Kensington High St W8. 01-937 7244. And in Mayfair, Hyde Park, Notting Hill Gate, Chelsea, Pimlico.

Accommodation agencies

For cheaper houses, flats and bedsits.
Derek Collins   5 **J** 21
25 Haymarket, Panton House, Panton St SWI. 01-930 7986.
Downtown Flats   2 **B** 14
189 Praed St W2. 01-723 2741.
Jenny Jones   2 **F** 19
40 South Molton St WI. 01-493 4801.
London Accommodation   I **A** 11
Bureau
102 Queensway W2. 01-727 5062.

Eating and drinking

Restaurants

These have been chosen primarily for authentic food and good cooking. No restaurant is included just because it is expensive or pretentious – alternatively some of the cheaper ones here give excellent value and the cooking can be first class. For more detailed information on where and what to eat see Nicholson's London Restaurant Guide.

The Restaurant Switchboard, 01-888 8080 offers free up-to-the-minute information and advice on London's restaurants from 09.00-20.00 Mon-Sat. Average prices for a full meal for one including VAT but without wine:

£	Under £10	£££	£20-£30
££	£10-£20	£££+	Over £30

Reserve	It is advisable to reserve
OPEN	Last orders
to . . .	
A	Access (incorporating Mastercard, Eurocard)
Ax	American Express
Dc	Diners Club
V	Visa (incorporating Barclaycard)
B	Breakfast
L	Lunch
D	Dinner

Service charge: many restaurants now add service on to the bill, usually at 10%, but do not always say so – if in doubt ask. However they do usually say if service is not included. 10% is normally the minimum; give up to 15% for above average service. Cover charge: not to be confused with the service charge. This is for napkins, bread and water and is normally added to the bill. However, many restaurants have now dispensed with this charge.

African & Caribbean

Caribbean (or Creole) cooking is based on African, with French and Spanish influences. Maize flour, vegetables, rice and coconut are widely used, with meat or fish stews. Food tends to be spicy and filling.

Afric-Carib
1 Stroud Green Rd N4. 01-263 7440. Restaurant and takeaway specialising in spicy Nigerian dishes. Chicken, beef or fish with plantains and yams. Palm wine and African music. Relaxed, informal atmosphere. *LD OPEN to 23.00. A.V.* **£**

The Calabash 6 J 23
38 King St WC2. 01-836 1976. African cooking in the basement of the Africa Centre in Covent Garden. Masks, head-dresses and African textiles adorn the walls and a tasty selection of regional dishes is available. Beef with green bananas and coconut cream, couscous, chicken and groundnut stew. Friendly service. *LD OPEN to 22.30. CLOSED L Sat & LD Sun. Ax. Dc. V.* **££**

Caribbean Sunkissed
49 Chippenham Rd W9. 01-286 3741. Authentic West Indian cooking. Try Calaloo soup, pork calypso or curried goat followed by banana suprise. *LD OPEN to 23.30. CLOSED Sun. A. Ax. V.* **££**

American

Chicago Pizza Pie Factory 5 J 19
17 Hanover Sq W1. 01-629 2669. Eat American deep-pan pizzas surrounded by Chicago paraphernalia including tapes of the local radio station and US football videos flown in weekly. *LD OPEN to 23.30 (Sun to 22.30).* No credit cards. **£**

Chicago Rib Shack 2 H 13
1 Raphael St SW7. 01-581 5595. Wood-smoked barbecued meats with salads and trimmings. Cheesecake, pecan pie and ice-cream to follow. *LD OPEN to 23.30 (Sun to 23.00).* No credit cards. **££**

Drones 5 J 12
1 Pont St SW1. 01-235 9638. Stylishly spread over two floors. Elaborate menu includes one hamburger. *LD Reserve. OPEN to 23.30. A. Ax. Dc. V.* **£££**

Hard Rock Café 2 I 16
150 Old Park La W1. 01-629 0382. Ever popular hamburger joint, just off Hyde Park Corner. Vast room on two levels with a shorts bar. Good quality food and non-stop rock. Expect long queues outside. *LD OPEN to 24.15 (Fri & Sat to 24.45).* No credit cards. **££**

Joe Allen 6 K 23
13 Exeter St WC2. 01-836 0651. In a converted Covent Garden warehouse, the London 'Joe Allen' follows the pattern of the New York and Paris restaurants. First-rate

cocktail bar for diners, blackboard menu of steaks, hamburgers, delicious spinach salad, spare ribs and chilli, followed by cheesecake or brownies. A fashionable place. *LD Reserve. OPEN to 24.45 (Sun to 24.00).* No credit cards. ££

Parsons   4 **K   8**
311 Fulham Rd SW10. 01-352 0651. American-style restaurant with trendy clientele. Large portions of pasta (second helping free), puff pastry pies, salads and burgers. Some Mexican dishes too. *LD OPEN to 24.30.* A. Ax. Dc. V. ££

Anglo-French

These restaurants generally offer French-style dishes, without forfeiting favourite English staples such as Stilton, steak and kidney and, of course, traditional Sunday lunch. Attractive and fairly expensive, they are pleasant and relaxing places in which to eat.

Bunny's
7 Pond St NW3. 01-435 1541. Ground-floor brasserie and larger à la carte restaurant. Fixed price set menu in brasserie. Imaginative food in relaxed atmosphere in restaurant – carré d'agneau en croûte, filet de boeuf Parisienne. *D (L Sun) OPEN to 22.30 Mon-Fri, to 23.00 Sat. CLOSED Sun D.* A. Ax. V. Brasserie ££, restaurant £££

Chanterelle   I **I   6**
119 Old Brompton Rd SW7. 01-373 7390. Attractive fresh decor in this crowded restaurant. Generous portions of distinctive Anglo-French dishes. Set lunch and dinner; dinner menu changes fortnightly and includes a mousse of Stilton and Armagnac, trout marinated in white wine. Lunch menu (set lunch only) changes every other day. Good value. *LD Reserve. OPEN to 23.30.* A. Ax. Dc. V. ££

Corney & Barrow   6 **M 31**
118 Moorgate EC2. 01-628 2898. Stylish modern restaurant, handy for the Barbican. French and English menu – sole, caviar, lemon sole, fillet steak. Menu changed weekly. Champagne bar on the ground floor. *LD OPEN to 19.30 Mon-Fri.* A. Ax. Dc. V. £££

Dolphin Brasserie   5 **P 15**
Dolphin Sq, Chichester St SW1. 01-828 4257. Anglo-French food is served in this sparkling and unusual restaurant reminiscent of a 1930s ocean liner. Try the apple and celery soup followed by fillet of beef with wild mushrooms. A pianist plays every night and there is live jazz *Fri & Sat. D*

OPEN to 22.45 Mon-Fri, to 23.15 Sat. CLOSED Sun. A. Ax. Dc. V. £££+

Julie's   I **A   5**
135 Portland Rd SW10. 01-352 8692. Champagne bar, open fire, forge and bellows, conservatory – something for everyone at this smart, popular restaurant. The pretty courtyard garden (now covered) is heated on cool evenings. Interesting menu – aubergine and sour cream mousse with toasted pumpkin seeds, roast pheasant with chestnut stuffing and rowan jelly. Vegetarian dishes. *LD Reserve. OPEN to 23.15. CLOSED Sun.* A. Ax. Dc. V. £££

Langan's Bistro   2 **D 20**
26 Devonshire St W1. 01-935 4531. Original Hockneys and Proctors decorate the walls, while Japanese parasols open above your head. Gratin of Arbroath smokies, avocado and tomato salad with hazelnut sauce, poached salmon trout with dill sauce, breast of chicken with tarragon sauce. Reports of Mrs Langan's chocolate mousse have spread far and wide and they vary – you'll just have to try it. *LD Reserve. OPEN to 23.30. CLOSED L Sat & LD Sun.* A. Ax. Dc. V. £££

Odin's   2 **D 20**
27 Devonshire St W1. 01-935 7296. Stylish, luxurious restaurant decorated with interesting photographs, prints and paintings. Frequently changing à la carte dishes. Red mullet pâté, stuffed roast duck, rack of lamb, plus seasonal specialities such as game, lobster and mussels. Home-made ice-cream or lemon curd tart to follow. *LD Reserve. OPEN to 23.15. CLOSED L Sat & LD Sun.* Ax. V. £££

Savoy Hotel Grill Room   6 **K 23**
Strand Embankment WC2. 01-352 0206. World-famous, well-deserved reputation for classic English and French cooking and near-perfect service. Delightful panelled room, soft lighting and a very fine wine list. Harpist plays every *weekday evening. LD Reserve. OPEN to 23.15. CLOSED Sun.* A. Ax. Dc. V. £££+

Chinese

Contrary to popular belief, Chinese cuisine offers a huge variety of styles and ingredients. Nearly all the Chinese restaurants in this country are Cantonese, and unfortunately many have made concessions to English taste. However, authentic Cantonese cooking is very good indeed; highly savoury and cooked simply and quickly in order to bring out the natural flavour of the food. Blends of meat and seafood, stir-fried vegetables and steamed dim sum are traditional. Pekingese food from the north is considered the highest form of Chinese cuisine. Drier and more highly seasoned than Cantonese, it shows Muslim and Mongolian influences. Great dishes are Peking duck and Mongolian hot-pot. Szechuan cooking from western China is chewy, aromatic and highly spiced. Double-cooked pork and tea-smoked duck are specialities. Gerrard Street in Soho is the heart of London's Chinatown.

Chuen Cheng Ku   2   I   21
17 Wardour St W1. 01-437 1398. Authentic Cantonese restaurant, popular with Chinese customers. Delicious fish, dim sum and excellent value lunches. *LD Reserve D. OPEN to 23.45.* A. Ax. Dc. V. **££**

City Friends   6   L   28
34 Old Bailey EC4. 01-248 5189. Popular lunchtime venue in the city. Wide choice of Chinese food. *LD Reserve L. OPEN to 23.15.* **££**

Dragon Gate   2   I   22
7 Gerrard St W1. 01-734 5154. The first and probably the best Szechuan restaurant in London. Sliced pork with garlic and chilli, tea-smoked duck. Pancakes or almond curd to follow. *LD OPEN to 23.15.* Ax. Dc. V. **££**

Dumpling Inn   2   I   22
15a Gerrard St W1. 01-437 2567. Small, lively restaurant with genuine Pekingese cooking. Very crowded. Prawns in chilli sauce, beef and dumplings in oyster sauce. *LD OPEN to 23.00, to 23.30 Fri & Sat.* A. Ax. V. **££**

Gallery Rendezvous   2   H   20
53-55 Beak St W1. 01-734 0445. Delicious Pekingese food, many specialities. Snow prawn balls, shark fin soup, Peking duck. Banqueting suite where you can dine in splendour. *LD Reserve. OPEN to 23.00, to 23.30 Fri & Sat.* Ax. Dc. V. **££**

Good Friends
139-141 Salmon La E14. 01-987 5498. Cantonese restaurant in the original Chinatown of Limehouse, where the docks used to be. Excellent reputation. *LD Reserve. OPEN to 23.00.* A. Ax. Dc. V. **££**

Ho-Ho   2   G   19
29 Maddox St W1. 01-493 1228. New-style restaurant offering Pekingese, Szechuan and Singaporean cuisine. Cheerful atmosphere. Try crispy seaweed or Chinese fondue. *LD OPEN to 22.30. CLOSED Sun.* A. Ax. Dc. V. **£££**

I Ching   I   G   5
40 Earl's Court Rd W8. 01-937 0409. Fine

Szechuan and Cantonese cooking in an exquisite setting. Small garden for aperitifs in summer. Witty menu. Spring rolls wrapped in lettuce are a speciality. *LD Reserve. OPEN to 24.00.* A. Ax. Dc. V. **£££**

Ken Lo's Memories of China 5 M 13
67-69 Ebury St SW1. 01-730 7734. The windows are etched with Tang dynasty horses and the menu features regional specialities: Shanghai sea bass, Szechuan crispy beef. Cantonese seafood with black bean sauce. *LD OPEN to 23.00. CLOSED Sun.* A. Ax. Dc. V. **£££+**

Kuo Yuan
217 Willesden High Rd NW10. 01-459 2297. Some of the best Pekingese food in London is served in this modest, 'local' restaurant. Try the Peking duck. *D (Reserve Sat) OPEN to 23.00. L Sat & Sun only.* No credit cards. **££**

Lee Ho Fook   2   I   22
15-16 Gerrard St W1. 01-734 9578. Renowned Cantonese cooking, very popular with local Chinese. Huge portions at reasonable prices. Dim sum at lunchtime. *LD OPEN to 23.30 (to 22.30 Sun).* A. Ax. Dc. V. **££**

Mr Chow   2   H   13
151 Knightsbridge SW1. 01-589 7347. Pekingese food with Italian overtones. Modern decor and paintings. Peking duck, sole in wine, green prawns. *LD Reserve. OPEN to 23.45.* A. Ax. Dc. V. **£££**

Mr Kai of Mayfair   2   H   17
65 South Audley St W1. 01-493 8988. Simple decor, slow but meticulous service. Sizzling lamb, chilli prawns in fresh pineapple, crispy Peking duck. *LD Reserve. OPEN to 23.15.* A. Ax. Dc. V. **£££+**

Poons   2   I   21
4 Leicester St WC2. 01-437 1528. Wind-dried meats are a speciality at this unpretentious, family-run Cantonese restaurant. Also unlicensed branch at 27 Lisle St WC2. 01-437 4549. (£.) *LD Reserve. OPEN to 23.30. CLOSED Sun.* No credit cards. **££**

Poons of Covent Garden   6 J 23
41 King St WC2. 01-240 1743. The decor has been kept simple and the restaurant built around the kitchen of this more up-market Covent Garden branch. The menu lists some 350 Cantonese dishes, including wind-dried meats. Special menus for parties. *LD Reserve D. OPEN to 23.30. CLOSED Sun.* Ax. Dc. V. **££-£££**

Sailing Junk   I   F   6
59 Marloes Rd W8. 01-937 2589. Float through the ten-course Dragon Festival dinner in an old Chinese sailing junk, candles flickering and soft Mandarin music pip-

ing. Food is a mixture of Cantonese and Pekingese. Special steamboat soup is cooked at the table. *LD Reserve (Sat & Sun). OPEN to 23.30.* A. Ax. Dc. V. ££

English

In all English restaurants look out for fresh meat and vegetables – it is the quality of the food and not the sauces that makes good English food. Mentioned here is a selection of carveries where for a set price, which usually includes a starter and sweet, customers can carve or be served generous portions from enormous, succulent joints of beef, lamb or pork. Many pubs also serve good lunches based on traditional English cooking. See 'Pubs' section.

Baker & Oven　　　　　　2 C 19
10 Paddington St W1. 01-935 5072. A restaurant in a converted Victorian bakery. Original bakers' ovens still used to cook enormous portions of English food. Soups, pies, roasts and pheasant in season. All very good. *LD Reserve. OPEN to 22.30. CLOSED L Sat & LD Sun.* A. Ax. Dc. V. ££

Baron of Beef　　　　　　6 M 29
Gutter La (off Gresham St) EC2. 01-606 6961. First-class food eaten in great comfort. Good service. Roast Scotch beef, braised oxtail, steak and oyster pie, steak and kidney pie, fresh fruit. *LD Reserve. OPEN to 20.00. CLOSED Sat & Sun.* A. Ax. Dc. V. £££+

Betjeman Carving Restaurant　　5 K 22
Charing Cross Hotel, Strand WC2. 01-839 7282. *LD OPEN to 22.30 (to 22.00 Sun).* A. Ax. Dc. V. ££

City Gates Restaurant　　　6 N 33
Great Eastern Hotel, Liverpool St EC2. 01-283 4363. Carvery. *LD OPEN to 22.00.* A. Ax. Dc. V. ££

The Cut Above　　　　　　6 L 31
Barbican Centre, Silk St EC2. 01-588 3008. Carvery. *LD. Last orders 30 mins after last performance.* A. Ax. Dc. V. £££

The English House　　　　4 J 11
3 Milner St SW3. 01-584 3002. Intimate restaurant in the style of an English country house. Classic English cooking. *LD Reserve. OPEN to 23.30 (to 22.00 Sun).* A. Ax. Dc. V. £££+

Friths　　　　　　　　　2 H 22
14 Frith St W1. 01-439 3370. 'New British' cuisine. Menu changes monthly and offers an imaginative range of dishes. Broccoli mousse with baked walnuts, turbot baked with tarragon and roast partridge. *LD Reserve. OPEN to 22.30. CLOSED L Sat & LD Sun.* A. Ax. Dc. V. £££

George & Vulture　　　　6 N 31
3 Castle Ct, off Cornhill EC3. 01-626 9710. Built in 1170 and restored after the Great Fire, this hostelry was one of Dickens' haunts. Traditional English fare like Dover sole, roast beef, liver and bacon, sherry trifle. *L OPEN to 14.45. CLOSED Sat & Sun.* A. Ax. Dc. V. ££

Greenhouse　　　　　　2 H 17
27a Hays Mews W1. 01-499 3331. White walls with lush green plants create a summery effect. Start with cod's roe pâté or creamy shrimp bisque, followed by roast rack of lamb with rôti potatoes or calf's liver with sautéed onions. Interesting puds too, including chocolate brandy cream and rice pudding with strawberry jam. *LD Reserve. OPEN to 23.00. CLOSED L Sat & LD Sun.* A. Ax. Dc. V. £££

Hyatt Carlton Rib Room　　5 K 13
Cadogan Pl SW1. 01-235 5411. A sophisticated restaurant notable for its plush decor as well as the excellence of its beef. Fine wine list, welcoming service and an entertaining happy hour when the glass-topped piano is played. *LD OPEN to 22.45 (to 22.00 Sun).* A. Ax. Dc. V. £££+

Lockets　　　　　　　　5 O 18
Marsham Ct, Marsham St SW1. 01-834 9552. Richly panelled and dignified, close to the Houses of Parliament. Attractively presented English dishes. Saddle of hare, spiced beef cooked in strong ale. Fine wine list. *LD Reserve L. OPEN to 23.00. CLOSED Sat & Sun.* A. Ax. Dc. V. £££+

Maggie Jones　　　　　　1 D 8
6 Old Court Pl, Kensington Church St W8. 01-937 6462. Cosy and pleasant with its wooden settles and country atmosphere. Home-made pâtés, baked mackerel with gooseberries, steak and mango casserole, chocolate and banana pots. Cheaper set meals also available, with set lunch only Sun. *LD Reserve. OPEN to 23.30 (to 23.00 Sun).* A. Ax. Dc. V. £££

Master's　　　　　　　　1 G 9
190 Queen's Gate SW7. 01-581 5666. Long, elegant cocktail bar; downstairs restaurant with homely Victorian atmosphere. Venison with honey, poppy, sesame and mustard seed sauce. White chocolate terrine to follow. Live piano music. *D Reserve Fri & Sat. OPEN to 23.30. L Sun only. CLOSED D Sun & LD Mon.* A. Ax. Dc. V. £££

Mrs Beeton's
58 Hill Rise, Richmond, Surrey. 01-940 9561. Each day one of a group of housewives comes in to prepare the English

menu of her choice, so individual inspiration characterises the result. A vegetarian dish always included. Unlicensed. *LD Reserve.* OPEN to 22.30. No credit cards. **£**

Porters   6 **J** 23
17 Henrietta St WC2. 01-836 6466. Large, pillared dining room lined with old carvings and mirrors. Imaginative, good value English fare in the form of pies – Billingsgate, lamb and apricot, turkey and chestnut. Good old bread and butter pudding, rhubarb crumble or Stilton to follow. Traditional Sunday lunch. *LD OPEN to 23.30.* No credit cards. **£**

Printer's Pie   6 **I** 27
60 Fleet St EC4. 01-353 8861. Pretty, old house. Competently prepared simple English dishes; grills, pies and steak and kidney pudding, traditional sweets. *LD Reserve L.* OPEN to 22.00. CLOSED D Sat & LD Sun. A. Ax. Dc. V. **££**

Rules   6 **J** 23
35 Maiden La, Strand WC2. 01-836 5314. Something of a landmark. Genuine Edwardian eating house with very good traditional English food like jugged hare, steak and kidney pie or pudding, venison and grouse. Seasonal menu. On the tourist circuit so booking essential. *LD Reserve.* OPEN to 24.00. CLOSED Sun. A. Ax. Dc. V. **££**

Simpson's-in-the-Strand   6 **K** 23
100 Strand WC2. 01-836 9112. A famous restaurant with an Edwardian club atmosphere. The attentive service and the large carvings from enormous joints of beef and lamb are excellent. Booking and correct dress essential. *LD Reserve.* OPEN to 22.00. CLOSED Sun. A. Ax. Dc. V. **££**

Strand Palace Hotel   6 **K** 23
Strand WC2. 01-836 8080. Carvery. OPEN to 22.00 (to 21.00 Sun). A. Ax. Dc. V. **££**

Tate Gallery Restaurant   5 **P** 18
Millbank SW1. 01-834 6754. Ideally located for art lovers on the lower ground floor of the Tate. Elegant lunchtime restaurant offering historical English fare and a distinguished wine list. Chef's choice, veal kidneys Florentine and Joan Cromwell's grand salad are favourites. *L Reserve.* OPEN to 15.00. CLOSED Sun. No credit cards. **££**

Throgmorton Restaurant   6 **N** 31
27a Throgmorton St EC2. 01-588 5165. A very friendly, club-like atmosphere pervades this City establishment. Generous portions of roast beef, fried fish, and steak and kidney pie served in the oak-panelled dining room. Slightly pricier steaks and chops in the long, mirrored grill. *L Reserve.* OPEN to 14.45. CLOSED Sat & Sun. A. Ax. Dc. V. **££**

Tiddy Dol's   2 **I** 18
55 Shepherd Market W1. 01-499 2357. Comfortable, intimate interior. Fillet of venison Parvarat, beef Wellington and the original gingerbread Tiddy Dol. *D OPEN to 23.30.* A. Ax. Dc. V. **£££**

Tower Thistle Hotel   6 **R** 23
St Katharine's Way E1. 01-481 2575. Carvery. *LD OPEN to 22.00.* A. Ax. Dc. V. **£££**

Wiltons   5 **J** 19
55 Jermyn St SW1. 01-629 9955. Serve the best oysters in town. Excellent plain cooking. Baby lobsters, crabs, salmon, halibut, sole and turbot. Chops, grills, marvellous game. Stilton to follow. Fine wine list, good port. *LD Reserve.* OPEN to 22.30. CLOSED L Sat & LD Sun. A. Ax. Dc. V. **£££+**

Fish

As well as those restaurants, some of which are listed here, that specialise in elaborately cooked fish dishes, London has a large number of fish and chip 'take away' shops, mostly to be found in residential areas. Fish and chips is a national dish which you can take away soused with vinegar, salt and pepper. Eaten hot it can be delicious and good value. (The following restaurants are not fish and chip shops.)

Bentley's   2 **I** 20
11-15 Swallow St W1. 01-734 4756. Famous seafood restaurant and oyster bar. Excellent oysters from Bentley's own beds, prawns, crabs and fish of many sorts. *LD Reserve.* OPEN to 23.00. CLOSED Sun. A. Ax. Dc. V. **£££**

Café Fish   5 **J** 21
39 Panton St SW1. 01-930 3999. Blackboard menus list wide selection of fish cooked in various styles served with vegetables or salad. No starters but cover charge includes fish pâté and French bread. Good cheeseboard and wine list. Pianist every night. Downstairs wine bar. *LD Reserve.* OPEN to 23.30. CLOSED D Sun. Wine bar OPEN to 23.00. A. Ax. Dc. V. **££**

La Croisette   4 **J** 4
168 Ifield Rd SW10. 01-373 3694. Ingeniously lit, crowded, basement restaurant. Single fixed-price menu with good, but limited, choice which may include plateau de fruits de mer or rougets en papillote. Efficient service. *LD OPEN to 01.00.* CLOSED LD Mon & L Tue. A. Ax. Dc. V. **£££**

Manzi's   2 **I** 22
1-2 Leicester St WC2. 01-734 0224. Old-established Italian fish restaurant on two

floors. Wide range of fish and shellfish; opt for the simpler dishes such as poached salmon or grilled turbot. Busy but lots of atmosphere. *LD Reserve. OPEN to 23.30. CLOSED L Sun. (upstairs CLOSED LD Sun).* A. Ax. Dc. V. **££**

Overton's   5 **L** 15
4-6 Victoria Bldgs, Terminus Pl SW1. 01-834 3774. Long-established fish restaurant of character. Also at 5 St James's St SW1 (5 **J** 19). 01-839 3744. 'Old-world' atmosphere in the nicest sense. Oysters, lobsters, Dover sole. *LD Reserve. OPEN to 22.30. CLOSED Sun.* A. Ax. Dc. V. **£££**

Poissonnerie de l'Avenue   4 **K** 11
82 Sloane Av SW3. 01-589 2457. Beautifully cooked fresh fish dishes in an intimate French atmosphere. Coquilles St Jacques au vin blanc, moules, sole, turbot, oysters, Dublin Bay prawns. *LD Reserve. OPEN to 23.30. CLOSED Sun.* A. Ax. Dc. V. **£££**

Scott's   2 **G** 17
20 Mount St W1. 01-629 5248. Long-established, traditional, expensive. Splendid oysters and fresh, skilfully cooked fish. Plats du jour lend variety to the menu, including cutlets and pepper steaks. Lobster bisque, sole Véronique. *LD Reserve. OPEN to 22.45. CLOSED L Sun.* A. Ax. Dc. V. **£££+**

Sheekey's   5 **J** 22
28-32 St Martin's Ct WC2. 01-240 2565. Established since 1896, it is noted for its shellfish and seafood. Fresh salmon, steamed turbot with lobster sauce, stewed eels. Crowded. Theatrical. *LD Reserve. OPEN to 23.00. CLOSED Sun.* A. Ax. Dc. V. **££**

Le Suquet   4 **K** 11
104 Draycott Av SW3. 01-581 1785. French fish restaurant. Relaxed atmosphere with efficient and helpful service. Massive plateau de fruits de mer a speciality. Delicious desserts. *LD Reserve. OPEN to 24.00.* A. Ax. Dc. V. **£££+**

Sweetings   6 **N** 29
39 Queen Victoria St EC4. 01-248 3062. Tiny 150-year-old City eatery. Fish parlour, with excellent service. Sit at the bar and eat herrings with mustard, whitebait, excellent fish pie. Very popular. Queuing often necessary as they don't take bookings. *L OPEN to 15.00. CLOSED Sat & Sun.* No credit cards. **££**

Trattoria dei Pescatori   2 **F** 22
57 Charlotte St W1. 01-580 3289. Bustling and hectic. Excellent Italian fish dishes in nautical atmosphere. Sauces especially tasty. Red mullet, lobster, fish soup, fried octopus. *LD Reserve. OPEN to 23.15 (Mon & Tue to 22.15). CLOSED Sun.* **££**

Wheeler's
A group of 17 restaurants specialising in expertly cooked fish dishes. Welcoming atmosphere with sophistication. Scallops, lobster Normande, sole Egyptian and shellfish. Some are listed below:

Alcove   1 **D** 4
17 Kensington High St W8. 01-937 1443. As in all Wheeler's restaurants, only fresh ingredients of high quality are used in the preparation of fish dishes: whitebait, sole bonne femme, prawn thermidor. *LD Reserve. OPEN to 22.45 (Sun to 22.15).* A. Ax. Dc. V. **£££**

Antoine's   2 **F** 22
40 Charlotte St W1. 01-636 2817. Small restaurant on three floors specialising in seafood. Lobster, smoked salmon, moules marinières and many ways of serving sole and halibut. *LD Reserve. OPEN to 22.45. CLOSED Sat.* A. Ax. Dc. V. **£££**

Carafe   5 **J** 13
15 Lowndes St SW1. 01-235 2525. *LD Reserve. OPEN to 22.45.* A. Ax. Dc. V. **£££**

Wheeler's   2 **I** 22
19 Old Compton St W1. 01-437 2706. *LD Reserve. OPEN to 22.40 (Sun to 22.15).* A. Ax. Dc. V. **£££**

Wheeler's Ivy   2 **I** 22
1 West St WC1. 01-836 4751. *LD Reserve D. OPEN to 23.00. CLOSED L Sat & LD Sun.* A. Ax. Dc. V. **£££**

French

The following all serve French cooking at its best. Some specialise in simple French provincial dishes, others in highly sophisticated haute cuisine. It should also be noted that French cuisine is amongst the most expensive in the world.

Ark   1 **C** 8
122 Palace Gdns Ter W8. 01-229 4024. Basic building but cosy and friendly atmosphere. Good French provincial food. Onion soup, noisette d'agneau, foie de veau. Another branch at 35 Kensington High St W8. 01-937 4294. *LD Reserve. OPEN to 23.15. CLOSED L Sun.* A. V. **££**

Berkeley Hotel Restaurant   2 **I** 14
Wilton Pl SW1. 01-235 6000. French cuisine of consistent excellence in strikingly decorated room. Many of the dishes are the chef's variations on classical themes. Exemplary service. *LD Reserve. OPEN to 22.45. CLOSED Sat.* A. Ax. Dc. V. **£££+**

Le Bistingo   2 **I** 22
57 Old Compton St W1. 01-437 0784.

Excellent Soho bistro serving provincial French and Italian cooking. Blackboard menu including fresh pasta, moules marinières, coquilles St Jacques, scampi provençale, coq au vin. Carafe wines. Other branches. *LD OPEN to 24.00. A. Ax. Dc. V.* **££**

Boulestin 6 **J 23**
25 Southampton St WC2. 01-836 7061. There are many new and interesting specialities on the menu of this famous old restaurant. Crabe à l'artichaut, ballotine de turbot farcie au homard, tulipe de sorbets maison. Fine wines, dignified service. *LD OPEN to 23.15. CLOSED L Sat & LD Sun. A. Ax. Dc. V.* **£££+**

Café du Commerce
Business Efficiency Centre, 3 Limeharbour E14. 01-538 2030. Very busy and smart. Popular for business breakfasts, champagne and smoked salmon, and lunches with set menu and à la carte. *LD Reserve L. OPEN 08.30-20.30 Mon-Fri. A. Ax. Dc. V.* **££-£££**

Café Pelican 5 **J 22**
45 St Martin's La WC2. 01-379 0309. Narrow Parisian-style brasserie serving traditional French day-long dishes; croissant, croque m'sieur, onion soup. Also fixed price and à la carte. Busy all day with the trendy and artistic. Service can be slow. (Another branch at Hay's Galleria, Tooley St SE1. 01-378 0097.) *LD Reserve. OPEN to 02.00. Snack menu only from 23.00. A. Ax. Dc. V.* **£££**

Café Royal Grill Room 2 **I 20**
68 Regent St W1. 01-439 6320. The days of Oscar Wilde and the 'old' Café Royal still linger in the grill room. Good scampi Oscar Wilde, caneton, tournedos flambé au poivre verte, langoustine, crêpe flambé Café Royale. *LD Reserve. OPEN to 22.45. A. Ax. Dc. V.* **£££+**

Camden Brasserie
216 Camden High St NW1. 01-482 2114. A good, honest brasserie near the canal serving quality food, mostly grilled meat or fish with pommes frites. An open fire in winter adds to the relaxed ambience. *LD Reserve D. OPEN to 23.30 Mon-Sat, to 22.30 Sun. No credit cards.* **££**

Chez Solange 5 **J 22**
35 Cranbourn St WC2. 01-836 5886. Busy but roomy. Typical French cuisine. À la carte menu changes weekly, also set lunch and pre-theatre menu. Cervelle au beurre noir, mignons de veau gratinée Lyonnaise, coq au vin, delicious filling desserts. *LD Reserve. OPEN to 24.15. Closed Sun. A. Ax. Dc. V.* **£££**

Chez Victor 2 **I 21**
45 Wardour St W1. 01-437 6523. Old-fashioned restaurant. Consistent standard of cooking and faithful clientele. Classic French dishes; French onion soup, tripes à la mode de Caen, daily specials. *LD OPEN to 24.00. CLOSED L Sat & LD Sun. A. V.* **££**

Claridges Restaurant 2 **G 18**
Brook St W1. 01-629 8860. Distinguished French cooking in luxurious surroundings. The atmosphere is typical of the sedate thirties. Polished service. Large and notable wine list. *LD Reserve. OPEN to 24.00. A. Ax. Dc. V.* **£££+**

Connaught Restaurant 2 **G 17**
Carlos Pl W1. 01-491 0668. Well-earned reputation for outstanding cuisine. Splendid room with panelling, mirrors and chandeliers. Connaught terrine, ouefs de cailles Maintenon, filet de boeuf en croûte, langoustine. Superb wine list. Very formal – jacket and tie must be worn. *LD Reserve. OPEN to 22.30. Grill room CLOSED Sat & Sun. A.* **£££+**

A L'Ecu de France 2 **I 19**
111 Jermyn St SW1. 01-930 2837. Superlative food in traditional, formal setting. Notable wine list. *LD Reserve. OPEN to 23.30. CLOSED L Sat & LD Sun. A. Ax. Dc. V.* **£££+**

L'Escargot 2 **H 22**
48 Greek St W1. 01-437 2679. Brasserie on the ground floor offers reasonably priced starters and mains. Upstairs the restaurant is more formal and pricey. Menu changes every 2 months. Excellent wine list. *LD Reserve. OPEN to 23.15. CLOSED L Sat & LD Sun. A. Ax. Dc. V.* **£££**

Le Français 4 **K 7**
259 Fulham Rd SW3. 01-352 3668. Comfortable, with excellent service. Serious minded approach to its excellent French provincial cooking. A fixed carte of well-chosen dishes, reliably cooked and a selection – changed weekly – of regional specialities. Fine wine list. *LD OPEN to 23.00. CLOSED Sun. Ax. V.* **£££**

Le Gastronome
309 New King's Rd SW6. 01-731 6993. Previously Gastronome One but a move along the road has seen a change of name. Quality of the food remains excellent and the clientele enthusiastic. Nouvelle cuisine style. Set three-course meals. Vegetarian dishes available. *LD Reserve D. OPEN to 22.30. CLOSED L Sat & LD Sun. A. Ax. V.* **£££**

Le Gavroche 2 **F 16**
43 Upper Brook St W1. 01-408 0881. One of the best restaurants in London,

renowned for its luxurious atmosphere and imaginative *haute cuisine*. Cooking and service faultless. *D Reserve. OPEN to 23.00. CLOSED Sat & Sun.* A. Ax. Dc. V. **£££+**

Harvey's

2 Bellevue Rd SW17. 01-672 0114. South London restaurant with excellent reputation. Leek terrine stuffed with scallops and langoustines, roast rabbit with wild mushrooms. Terrine of fresh fruit. Outdoor tables in warm weather. *LD Reserve. OPEN to 23.00. CLOSED L Sat & LD Sun.* A. Ax. Dc. V. **£££**

Inigo Jones　　　　　　　　5 **J** 22

14 Garrick St WC2. 01-836 6456. Extremely popular restaurant in converted Victorian stained-glass workshop. Brick walls, large windows and distinctive lighting create a truly romantic setting. Imaginative nouvelle cuisine style menu changes monthly. Quail in tangerine sauce, grilled breast of duck with carrot and cauliflower purée, carré d'agneau en croûte. *LD Reserve. OPEN to 23.30. CLOSED L Sat & LD Sun.* A. Ax. Dc. V. **£££+**

Au Jardin des Gourmets　　2 **H** 22

5 Greek St W1. 01-437 1816. Ambitious French classical cuisine. Snails, frogs, aiguillettes de canard au poivre rose, quenelles de brochette. Good wines. *LD Reserve. OPEN to 23.15. CLOSED L Sat & LD Sun.* A. Ax. Dc. V. **£££**

Langan's Brasserie　　　　2 **I** 19

Stratton St W1. 01-493 6437. (See Anglo-French section for Langan's Bistro.) Vast L-shaped room seating 200. Popular and very trendy. Small menu, erratic service. Live music every night. *LD Reserve. OPEN to 23.00. CLOSED L Sat & LD Sun.* A. Ax. Dc. V. **£££**

Ma Cuisine　　　　　　　　4 **J** 11

113 Walton St SW3. 01-584 7585. Small and simple restaurant. Galettes de lotte et St Jacques au pistou, aiguillettes de canard Paloise. *LD Reserve. OPEN to 23.00. CLOSED Sat & Sun.* Ax. Dc. **£££**

Mon Marche　　　　　　　　3 **I** 23

63 Endell St WC2. 01-836 2320. Small, cosy and intimate. Specialises in regional cooking. Duck pâté, fish pancakes, grilled goat's cheese. Blackboard menus which change every few months. Set price pre-theatre menu. Serves vegetarian dishes. *LD Reserve. OPEN to 23.00, to 23.15 Sat. CLOSED L Sat & LD Sun.* A. Ax. Dc. V. **££**

Mon Plaisir　　　　　　　　3 **I** 23

21 Monmouth St WC2. 01-836 7243. Small, typically French restaurant. Friendly atmosphere and helpful service. Short,

unpretentious menu: escalope à la crème, coq au vin. *LD Reserve. OPEN to 23.15. CLOSED L Sat & LD Sun.* A. Ax. Dc. V. **££**

Monsieur Frog　　　　　　3 **E** 33

31a Essex Rd N1. 01-226 3495. Charming, small restaurant very popular with Islington residents. Modern style food using good, fresh ingredients. Sautéed scallops. fricassée of monkfish in lobster sauce, chocolate and raisin cake with crème fraîche. *LD Reserve. OPEN to 23.30. CLOSED L Sat & LD Sun.* No credit cards. **£££**

Monsieur Thompson's　　I **A** 8

29 Kensington Park Rd W11. 01-727 9957. Fresh, homely decor. Daily menu may include smoked quail with watercress sauce and Parma ham gratin, warm red mullet mousse with fresh ginger sauce, kidneys in blackcurrant and ginger. *LD Reserve. OPEN to 22.30. CLOSED Sun.* A. Ax. Dc. V. **£££**

Le Petit Montmartre　　　2 **E** 19

15 Marylebone La W1. 01-935 9226. Good French cooking: médaillons de boeuf orientals, salad Moulin Rouge, crêpes suzette. Good fresh vegetables. *LD Reserve. OPEN to 23.00. CLOSED L Sat & LD Sun.* A. Ax. Dc. V. **£££+**

Pollyanna's

2 Battersea Rise SW11. 01-228 0316. On two floors with pleasant decor. Imaginative French à la carte with daily specialities: tournedos of beef poached in red wine, fresh salmon with basil, chocolate ramekins. Attentive service, extensive wine list. *D Reserve. OPEN to 24.00. L (Reserve) Sun only.* A. Ax. Dc. V. **££**

Le Poulbot　　　　　　　　6 **M** 29

45 Cheapside EC2. 01-236 4379. Expense account lunches downstairs, less expensive fare upstairs in this City partner of 'Le Gavroche'. Excellent food – menu changes daily. Polished service and fine wine list. *L Reserve. OPEN to 15.00. CLOSED Sat & Sun.* A. Ax. Dc. V. **£££+**

La Poule au Pot　　　　　5 **L** 14

231 Ebury St SW1. 01-730 7763. Informal and friendly, with reasonable prices. Limited menu at lunchtime, more varied in the evening. Carbonnade de boeuf, lapin aux deux moutardes. *LD Reserve. OPEN to 23.15. CLOSED L Sat & LD Sun.* A. Ax. Dc. V. L**££**, D**£££**

Au Provençal

295 Railton Rd SE24. 01-274 9163. Fine French provincial cooking in a popular local restaurant. Moules marinières, wild duck, chicken with tarragon. Vegetarian dishes on request. Sorbets to follow. *D Reserve. OPEN to 22.30. CLOSED Sun.* A. V. **££**

Simply Nico   5 N 17
48a Rochester Row SW1. 01-630 8061.
The chef, Nico Ladenis, is one of London's
most well-known and most inventive chefs,
formerly of Chez Nico and the Ortolan. This
is one of the rare English restaurants with
two stars in the *Guide Michelin* which
should speak for itself – a dining experience. Short but comprehensive wine list.
*LD Reserve. OPEN to 23.00 Mon-Fri.
CLOSED Sat & Sun.* No credit cards. L£££,
D£££+

Thierry's   4 L 7
342 King's Rd SW3. 01-352 3365. One of
the more rewarding restaurants in the
King's Road. French proprietor and authentic French cooking. Robust dishes like rack of lamb,
canard sauvage and saddle of hare. Spinach tart, moules, soufflé au fromage. Interesting wines and sometimes preoccupied
service. *LD Reserve D. OPEN to 23.30.
CLOSED Sun.* Ax. Dc. V. £

German & Austrian

Kerzernstuberl   2 E 18
9 St Christopher's Pl W1. 01-486 3196.
Authentic Austrian food, accordion music,
dancing and yodelling. Leberknödel soup,
pork chop Serbischesart, venison with red
cabbage and dumplings. Sachertorte to follow. *LD Reserve. OPEN to 23.00. Licensed
to 01.00. CLOSED L Sat & LD Sun.* A. Ax.
Dc. V. ££

Old Vienna   2 G 19
94 New Bond St W1. 01-629 8716. Authentic Austrian atmosphere, music and excellent cooking. Large varied menu with over
20 Viennese specialities. *LD OPEN to
01.00, to 22.30 Sun.* A. Ax. Dc. V. ££

Twin Brothers   1 D 8
51 Kensington Church St W8. 01-937 4152.
Intimate, old-style German restaurant
started up by twin brothers and still run by
one – a very colourful character. Bismarck
herring, Schweizer onion soup, Wiener or
Holsteiner schnitzel and apple cake are just
some of the traditional dishes served. *D
OPEN to 23.00. CLOSED Sun.* No credit
cards. ££

Greek, Turkish & Cypriot

*Many Greek restaurants are run by
Cypriots who have absorbed the best of
both Greek and Turkish dishes into their
style of cooking.*

Beotys   5 J 22
79 St Martin's La WC2. 01-836 8768. Comfortable establishment with authentic Greek
cooking. Stuffed vine leaves, kalamarakia
(squid cooked in its own ink with wine),
moussaka. Usual sweet pastries – baklava
and kadeifi. Very courteous service. *LD
OPEN to 23.30. CLOSED Sun.* A. Ax. Dc.
V. ££

Chaglayan
86 Brent St NW4. 01-202 8575. Well-
prepared food appetisingly presented; charcoaled kebabs, lamb on the bone,
moussaka, salads. *LD Reserve Sat & Sun.
OPEN to 24.00. CLOSED L Sun.* A. Dc. V. £

Cypriana Kebab House   2 G 22
11 Rathbone St W1. 01-636 1057. Greek
Cypriot food. Pleasant and slightly cheaper
than most of the Cypriot restaurants in this
area. Friendly service. Specialities are
kleftiko, afelia, moussaka, dolmades. *LD
OPEN to 23.30. CLOSED L Sat & LD Sun.*
A. Ax. Dc. V. £

Hellenic   2 E 19
30 Thayer St W1. 01-935 1257. Noisy,
crowded bistro atmosphere with friendly
service. Fish kebabs, afelia, stifado,
moussaka, loukomades. Good Greek
farmhouse cooking. *LD Reserve. OPEN to
23.00. CLOSED L Sat & LD Sun.* ££

Mega Kalamaras   1 A 11
76 Inverness Mews W2. 01-727 9122. Also
smaller and less expensive **Mikro
Kalamaras** 66 Inverness Mews W2.
01-727 9122. True taverna atmosphere.
Bouzouki players on some evenings.
Dancing. Superb national dishes ranging
from dolmades to baklava. *D Reserve.
OPEN to 24.00. CLOSED Sun.* A. Ax. Dc.
V. ££

Mykonos   2 H 22
17 Frith St W1. 01-437 3603. Bright and lively
taverna in Soho, popular with media folk.
Renowned for their moussaka, lamb
kebabs with pimentos, tomatoes and
onions, and tasty kleftiko. Ouzo, Greek wine
and brandy. *LD OPEN to 23.00. CLOSED L
Sat & LD Sun.* No credit cards. £

White Tower   2 G 22
1 Percy St W1. 01-636 8141. Elegant; first-
class cuisine. Agreeable and leisurely service. Moussaka, shashlik and duck with
bulghur. *LD Reserve. OPEN to 22.30.
CLOSED Sat & Sun.* A. Ax. Dc. V. £££

Hungarian

*Hungarian food is distinguished by unusual
but extremely tasty dishes. Fish are all of*

the freshwater variety. Carp and pike are presented in an impeccable style.

Gay Hussar　　　　　　　**2　H　22**
2 Greek St W1. 01-437 0973. Intimate, cosy much-loved Soho restaurant. Cold wild cherry soup, pike with beetroot sauce, roast saddle of carp, goulash. To follow, orange curd pancakes or berries with whipped cream. *LD Reserve. OPEN to 22.30. CLOSED Sun. No credit cards.* **££**

Le Mignon　　　　　　　**1　A　11**
2 Queensway W2. 01-229 0093. Typical Hungarian food, cheerful atmosphere and live gipsy orchestra. House sulz, chicken paprika, fantanyeros. *LD OPEN to 24.00. A. Ax. Dc. V.* **££**

Indian

The farther south in India the hotter the spices. Madras, Bindi and Vindaloo mean climbing degrees of heat. For the European however there is no particular virtue in hotness – many Indians also enjoy (and prefer) mild curries. Hindu cooking uses vegetables in rich liquid juices; Muslims use more meat and the food is drier. The best cooking uses the traditional clay oven and adds spices individually to each dish, giving a distinctive and piquant flavour.

Bombay Brasserie　　　　**1　H　7**
140 Gloucester Rd SW7. 01-370 4040. Large, fashionable, colonial-style venue, with plants, fans and wicker chairs. Dishes from several regions including Bombay thali, chicken dhansak, Goan fish curry. Cobra coffee flambé to finish. *LD Reserve D. OPEN to 24.00. A. Ax. Dc. V.* **£££**

Diwan-E-Khas　　　　　　**2　E　22**
110 Whitfield St W1. 01-388 1321. Cave-like setting to enjoy excellent tandoori dishes from northern India. Also Mogul chicken or lamb. *LD OPEN to 23.45. A. Ax. Dc. V.* **££**

Ganges　　　　　　　　　**2　B　14**
101 Praed St W2. 01-723 4096. Small, simple, family-run restaurant offering a superb range of Bengali dishes. Try giant fried prawns, fish masala, Bengal chicken or chicken tikka. *LD Reserve. OPEN to 23.30. A. Ax. Dc. V.* **£**

Gaylord　　　　　　　　　**2　F　21**
79-81 Mortimer St W1. 01-636 0808. Authentic north Indian food. Spices added individually to each dish giving some delectable flavours. Tandoori chicken masala, lentils in cream and interesting Indian sweetmeats. *LD OPEN to 23.30. A. Ax. Dc. V.* **£**

Goan　　　　　　　　　　　**3　C　28**
16 York Way N1. 01-837 7517. Home-cooked, authentic Goan dishes. Specialities include sweetbreads and a prawn curry; nans are delicious. Drink wine, Indian beer or lassi with your meal. *LD OPEN to 01.00. A. Ax. Dc. V.* **£**

Khan's
13-15 Westbourne Gro W2. 01-727 5420. Vast room with oriental arches, palm tree pillars and a bar in one corner. Kofti dilruba – spiced curried meatballs with fresh cream and herb sauce – is one of the specialities. Hot and noisy, but good fun if you enjoy a lively atmosphere. *LD Reserve D. OPEN to 24.00. A. Ax. Dc. V.* **£**

Last Days of the Raj　　　**6　J　24**
22 Drury La WC2. 01-836 1628. Bengali specialities in crowded theatreland restaurant. Meat thali, lamb tandoori, hot and sour chicken. *LD Reserve. OPEN to 23.30. CLOSED L Sun. A. Ax. Dc. V.* **££**

Maharani　　　　　　　　**2　H　21**
77 Berwick St W1. 01-437 8568. Popular Soho curry house with a good reputation for tandoori dishes. Excellent chicken tikka. *LD OPEN to 24.00 (Fri & Sat to 01.00). A. Ax. Dc. V.* **££**

Oval Tandoori
64a Brixton Rd SW9. 01-582 1415. Cosy alcoved seating. Chicken dupiaza, mutton badam pasanda, kashmiri nan are among the delicacies on offer. *LD OPEN to 24.00. A. Ax. V.* **££**

Ravi Shankar　　　　　　**3　C　23**
133-135 Drummond St NW1. 01-388 6458. Inexpensive southern Indian cooking. Authentic vegetarian dishes. Excellent Mysore masala dosai, thali and tasty snacks. *LD OPEN to 23.00. A. Ax. Dc. V.* **£**

The Red Fort　　　　　　**2　H　22**
77 Dean St W1. 01-437 2410. Attractively decorated, luxurious restaurant serving excellent, delicately spiced Mogul dishes: quails in mild spice, chicken korahi, tandooris and nan. Delicious kulfi to follow. Meat or vegetarian thalis and buffet lunch on Sunday. Have a cocktail in the elegant bar while waiting for your table. *LD Reserve. OPEN to 23.30. A. Ax. Dc. V.* **££**

Star of India　　　　　　**1　I　7**
154 Old Brompton Rd SW5. 01-373 2901. Excellent Indian food and good service. Order Mogul dishes a day in advance. Also prawn biryani, whole stuffed tandoori chicken, kebabs. *LD OPEN to 24.00, to 23.30 Sun. A. Ax. Dc. V.* **££**

Tandoori of Chelsea　　　**4　J　10**
153 Fulham Rd SW3. 01-589 7749. Excellent food cooked in traditional clay ovens.

Pleasant decor with soft music. Tandoori chicken, chicken tikka masala, roghan josh. *LD OPEN to 24.00, to 23.30 Sun.* A. Ax. Dc. V. **££**

Tandoori of Mayfair 2 I 18
37a Curzon St W1. 01-629 0600. Charming and elegant, hung with colourful batiks and abundant foliage. Specialities include fish tikka and lamb dishes such as Sali Boli – cooked with dried apricots – and Raan. *LD Reserve. OPEN to 24.00, to 23.30 Sun.* A. Ax. Dc. V. **££**

Veeraswamy's 2 I 20
99-101 Regent St (entrance in Swallow St) W1. 01-734 1401. Authentic food in atmosphere of pre-War Indian club. Moglai, Delhi, Madras, Ceylon and Vindaloo curries. *LD Reserve. OPEN to 23.30, to 22.00 Sun.* A. Ax. Dc. V. **££**

Viceroy of India 2 A 18
3-5 Glentworth St NW1. 01-486 3401. Large and elegant. Appetising cooking with skilful use of spices and herbs. Several varieties of nan. *LD OPEN to 23.30, to 23.00 Sun.* A. Ax. Dc. V. **££**

Inexpensive eating

Places where you can eat a three-course meal for £8 or under. The café serving 'sausage, egg and chips' is not included here, however excellent some may be. Neither are the international 'fast food' chains which can be found on nearly every High Street. This list prizes distinctive or unusual cooking and atmosphere – but particularly good value for money.

Alpino 2 D 19
42 Marylebone High St W1. 01-935 4640. Alpine-style restaurant. Busy at all times. Quick service. Generous portions of pasta, or try some veal, fish or chicken dishes. *LD OPEN to 23.30. CLOSED Sun.* A. Ax. Dc. V.

Barocco Bar 2 I 22
13 Moor St W1. 01-437 2324. Simple Italian restaurant and coffee shop. Good food at very low prices. Pasta, omelettes, veal. *LD OPEN to 22.45. CLOSED Sun.* No credit cards.

Bistro Vino
1 Old Brompton Rd SW7. I I 9
01-589 3888.
303 Brompton Rd SW3. 4 J 10
01-589 7898.
5 Clareville St SW7. I I 8
01-373 3903.
A chain of separately managed but similar style informal restaurants. Good simple

bistro food at very reasonable prices in cheerful if noisy surroundings. *LD OPEN to 23.45. D only at Clareville St.* A. V.

Chelsea Kitchen 4 L 10
98 King's Rd SW3. 01-589 1330. Part of the Stockpot group. The daily menu offers a good choice of hot cheap dishes. Soup, moussaka, spaghetti. Licensed. *LD OPEN to 23.45.* No credit cards.

Costas Grill I B 8
14 Hillgate St W8. 01-229 3794. Good, friendly Greek restaurant where you can eat outside in the summer. Also fish and chip shop next door. *LD OPEN to 22.30. CLOSED Sun.* Fish shop also *CLOSED Mon.* No credit cards.

Daquise I I 9
20 Thurloe St SW7. 01-589 6117. Simple, very cheap Polish food. Pirozhky, shashlik, bortsch. Many Polish customers. *LD OPEN to 22.45.* No credit cards.

Fatso's Pasta Joint 2 I 22
13 Old Compton St W1. 01-437 1503. Lively, bright and cheerful. Renowned for quantity as much as quality. *Mon-Thur* eat as much pasta as you like for one price. *Mon* half-price cocktails. *LD OPEN to 24.00 Mon-Thur, to 01.00 Fri & Sat, to 23.00 Sun.* No credit cards.

Geales I B 8
2-4 Farmer St W8. 01-727 7969. Large selection of excellent fish and chips; cod's roe, clams, sole. Wine list. *LD OPEN to 23.00. CLOSED Sun & Mon.* A.

India Club 6 K 23
143 Strand WC2. 01-836 0650. Excellent South Indian specialities in this down-at-heel canteen. Popular with students for its generous portions. *LD OPEN to 22.00, to 20.00 Sun.* No credit cards.

Jimmy's 2 H 22
23 Frith St W1. 01-437 9521. Greek-Cypriot basement restaurant, especially popular with students. Huge helpings at very reasonable prices. Beef stew, moussaka, lamb tava, plus fresh salads, baklava, kataifi. *LD OPEN to 22.30. CLOSED Sun.* No credit cards.

Justin de Blank 2 E 18
54 Duke St W1. 01-629 3174. Attractive, leafy, self-service restaurant. Food very fresh and well-presented; the bread is all home-baked. Always one vegetarian dish on offer. *LD OPEN to 21.00. CLOSED D Sat & LD Sun.* A. V.

The Lantern
23 Malvern Rd NW6. 01-624 1796. Amazing variety and quality at low prices; predictably busy. French bistro with simple, candlelit ambience, soft music, blackboard

menu and wine list. *LD (Reserve Fri & Sat). OPEN to 24.00, to 23.00 Sun.* A. V.

Maggie Brown's   4 P 5
179 Battersea High St SW11. 01-228 0559. Old-style eel and pie shop. Stewed or jellied eels, sausages, pie and mash, apple pie. A real taste of England! *LD OPEN to 18.30 Mon & Tue, to 15.00 Wed, to 19.00 Thur, Fri & Sat. CLOSED Sun.* No credit cards.

My Old Dutch   3 H 24
132 High Holborn WC1. 01-242 5200. Traditional Dutch farmhouse decor, pine tables and chairs, prints of Dutch masters on the wall. Over 100 Dutch pancakes; some savoury, some dessert. *LD OPEN to 23.30, to 24.30 Fri & Sat.* A. Ax. Dc. V.

The Nautilus
27-29 Fortune Green Rd NW6. 01-435 2532. As its name suggests, seafood is the order of the day – 18 different sorts including scampi and sole. Soups and salads, too, and a wide range of ice-creams. *LD OPEN to 22.30. CLOSED Sun.* No credit cards.

Pizza Express   3 H 24
30 Coptic St WC1. 01-636 2244. Modern pizza parlour with a large red pizza oven in the middle. Many varieties. Good ice-creams. Numerous branches. Jazz as well as pizza at 10 Dean St W1. 01-437 9595. *LD OPEN to 24.00.* A. Ax. V.

Pizza House   2 F 22
54-56 Goodge St W1. 01-636 9590. Excellent pasta, pizza and meat dishes. Italian desserts such as zabaglione or ice-cream. Lively, bustling atmosphere, quick service. *LD OPEN to 23.00. CLOSED Sun.* No credit cards.

Spaghetti House   5 J 22
24 Cranbourn St WC2. 01-836 8168. There are several branches of this restaurant and the Trattoria dei Cacciatories, Vecchia Milano and Villa Carlotta are also in the chain. Genuine Italian spaghetti houses, friendly and busy. Minestrone, pasta, gnocchi. Delicious pastries or ice-cream to follow. *LD OPEN to 23.00. CLOSED Sun.* A. Ax. Dc. V.

Standard
23 Westbourne Gro W2. 01-727 4818. Large, popular Indian restaurant serving over 80 specialities including tandoori and vegetarian dishes. Also fish masala. *LD Reserve. OPEN to 24.00.* A. Ax. Dc. V.

Stockpot   5 J 21
40 Panton St SW1. 01-839 5142. Crowded, noisy and excellent value. Home-made soups, casseroles and puds at popular prices. *LD OPEN to 23.30 (Sun to 22.00).* Also at 6 Basil St SW3. 01-589 8627. *LD*

OPEN to 22.30. CLOSED Sun. No credit cards.

Up All Night   4 L 4
325 Fulham Rd SW10. 01-352 1996. True to its name. Steaks, hamburgers, chilli, spaghetti, kebabs. *LD OPEN to 06.00.* A. Ax. V.

Veritable Crêperie   4 L 7
329 King's Rd SW3. 01-352 3891. Large range of sweet and savoury crêpes. Normandy cider, constant classical music. *LD OPEN to 24.00.* No credit cards.

Wong Kei   2 I 21
41-43 Wardour St W1. 01-437 8408. Cheap and cheerful. Large Cantonese restaurant on four floors, always busy and bustling. *LD OPEN to 23.15.* No credit cards or cheques.

International

We have listed a range of restaurants at all levels that do not specialise in the food of any particular country. These restaurants pick from the best dishes of the world, frequently blending styles and flavours to provide quite distinctive cooking.

Bill Stickers   2 H 22
18 Greek St W1. 01-437 0582. Unusual decor – zebra stripes, gilt and strange props. Dishes include burgers of many varieties, steaks, ribs, chicken dishes, Mexican and Cajun food. *LD Reserve. OPEN to 03.00, to 24.00 Sun.* A. Ax. Dc. V. **££**

Meantime
47 Greenwich Church St SE10. 01-858 8705. Intimate English and Spanish restaurant worth remembering on a trip to Greenwich. Short menu with a weekly speciality. Mussels, paella Valencia, Dover Sole. *LD Reserve. OPEN to 23.00. CLOSED L Sat & LD Sun.* A. Ax. Dc. V. **££**

Ménage à Trois   2 I 12
14-15 Beauchamp Pl SW3. 01-584 9350. Starters (some very elaborate) and desserts only in this smart nouvelle cuisine establishment. Scotch lobster, crudités, caviar, ménage à trois – pastry parcels of cheese or seafood. Summer pudding, ice-cream daquiris, terrine of chocolate and black cherries. *LD Reserve. OPEN to 24.15. Closed L Sat & LD Sun.* A. Ax. Dc. V. **£££**

Le Mercury
140a Upper St N1. 01-354 4088. Popular and excellent for an inexpensive but elegant lunch. Asparagus soup, muffin with smoked salmon, sour cream and caviar are typical starters. Chicken Peter or vegetarian cornmeal crêpes with seaweed and

wild mushrooms may follow. Nutritional data on the menu. *LD Reserve D. OPEN to 01.00, to 23.00 Sun. A. V. £*

Neal Street Restaurant　　3　I　23
26 Neal St WC2. 01-836 8368. Chic and modern restaurant. Cooking matches the elegant decor – king prawns wrapped in bacon, charcoaled on a skewer and served with a spicy mayonnaise, roast duck with apple sauce. *LD Reserve. OPEN to 23.00. CLOSED Sat & Sun. A. Ax. Dc. V. £££+*

Pomegranates　　5　Q　15
94 Grosvenor Rd SW1. 01-828 6560. Highly original and adventurous restaurant with truly international menu. Welsh, Turkish, Malaysian, Greek, French, Italian and Chinese dishes all prepared from first-class ingredients. Multi-national wine list too. *LD Reserve D. OPEN to 23.15. CLOSED L Sat & LD Sun. A. Ax. Dc. V. £££+*

South of the Border　　6　O　25
8 Joan St SE1. Farmhouse atmosphere with a bar on the ground floor overlooked by a balcony – outside terrace for dining in summer. South-Pacific-style and Indonesian food such as rijstafel, Japanese-style tempura prawns and some Australian dishes including Carpet Bag Australasian. Home-made desserts, ice cream and cheese. *LD OPEN to 22.30. CLOSED L Sat & LD Sun. A. Ax. Dc. V. ££*

Italian

The largest group of foreign restaurants in London. One can eat cheaply or expensively and almost always get good food. These are some of the best:

Biagi's　　2　D　16
39 Upper Berkeley St W1. 01-723 0394. Well-run, intimate trattoria decorated with fishing nets. Good varied Italian dishes. Scalloppine alla crema, entrecôte alla pizzaiola, saltimbocca. *LD Reserve. OPEN to 23.00. A. Ax. Dc. V. ££*

La Capannina　　2　I　22
24 Romilly St W1. 01-437 2473. Popular Soho trattoria. Music in the evening. Petto di pollo, vitello alla Gianni, gnocchi. *LD OPEN to 23.30. CLOSED L Sat & LD Sun. A. Ax. Dc. V. ££*

Casa Cominetti
129 Rushey Grn SE6. 01-697 2314. Good Italian food in a gastronomic wasteland. Home-made cannelloni, veal Milanese. *LD OPEN to 22.00. CLOSED Sun & Mon. A. Ax. Dc. V. ££*

Como Lario　　5　M　12
22 Holbein Pl SW1. 01-730 2954. Lively and crowded trattoria. Generous helpings. Gnocchi particularly good, also plenty of reliable veal and chicken dishes. Italian wines. *LD Reserve D. OPEN to 23.30. CLOSED Sun. No credit cards. ££*

Luigi's　　6　J　23
15 Tavistock St WC2. 01-240 1795. Something of an institution now. Luigi's is crowded and popular with after-theatre diners. Photographs of entertainment personalities decorate the walls. Good, authentic food: cannelloni, mussels grilled with garlic and breadcrumbs, veal and chicken dishes. *LD Reserve. OPEN to 23.30. CLOSED Sun. A. V. ££*

Mimmo d'Ischia　　5　L　14
61 Elizabeth St SW1. 01-730 5406. Bright, exciting restaurant on two floors. Original and imaginative dishes. Good spigola. *LD Reserve. OPEN to 23.15. CLOSED Sun. A. Ax. Dc. V. £££*

Monte Bello　　2　E　21
84 Great Titchfield St W1. 01-636 3772. Crowded trattoria on two floors serving simple but good food; spaghetti, lasagne and chicken dishes. *LD Reserve L. OPEN to 23.00. CLOSED Sun. £*

Montpeliano　　2　I　12
13 Montpelier St SW7. 01-589 0032. Crowded Knightsbridge restaurant. Basic Italian menu with regional specialities which change daily. Spaghetti dolcelatte, veal Montpeliano (stuffed with cheese, ham and garlic sauce), game and seafood in season. The chef's cold crêpes, covered with ground biscuits and Tia Maria, are famous. *LD Reserve. OPEN to 24.00. CLOSED Sun. No credit cards. £££*

Pizzeria Condotti　　2　G　19
4 Mill St W1. 01-499 1308. Sophisticated and stylish restaurant serving pizzas plus tasty salads and fish dishes. Good starters: the chocolate truffle cake is also recommended. *LD Reserve. OPEN to 24.00. CLOSED Sun. A. Ax. Dc. V. £££*

Portofino　　3　E　32
39 Camden Pas N1. 01-226 0884. Small, popular. Good friendly service and excellent cooking. Generous portions. Fresh fish in season. Guitarist Thur, Fri & Sat. *LD OPEN to 23.30. CLOSED Sun. A. Ax. Dc. V. ££*

San Frediano　　4　L　4
62 Fulham Rd SW3. 01-584 8375. Bright and lively trattoria with friendly service. Excellent Italian dishes, particularly good fish and a tempting sweet trolley, all at reasonable prices. Clam salad, scalloppino uccellato. *LD Reserve. OPEN to 23.15. CLOSED Sun. A. Ax. Dc. V. £££*

San Lorenzo   2 **I** 12
22 Beauchamp Pl SW3. 01-584 1074. One of London's best known Italian restaurants offering a different menu every day. Fashionable clientele who enjoy excellent pasta and bollito misto. Unusual veal and chicken dishes. *LD Reserve. OPEN to 23.30. CLOSED Sun.* **£££**

Terrazza Est   6 **J** 26
109 Fleet St EC2. 01-353 2680. Lively atmosphere in this basement restaurant where opera singing begins around 20.00 Mon-Fri. The Villa Claudius, 10a The Broadway SW1 (5 **M** 18), 01-222 3338, is part of the same chain. Set à la carte menu, salads and pasta dishes are the mainstay. Good desserts. *LD Reserve. OPEN to 23.30. CLOSED Sat & Sun.* A. Ax. Dc. V. **££**

Topo Gigio   2 **I** 21
46 Brewer St W1. 01-437 8516. Appetising Italian food at reasonable prices. Good minestrone, cannelloni, petto di pollo, veal escalopes. Helpful service, large portions. *LD Reserve. OPEN to 23.30.* A. Ax. Dc. V. **££**

Trattoo   1 **E** 6
2 Abingdon Rd W8. 01-937 4448. Excellent food under a glass roof, surrounded by greenery. Spaghetti with clams, pollo sorpresa, rack of lamb with rosemary and garlic. *LD Reserve. OPEN to 23.50, to 23.00 Sun.* A. Ax. Dc. V. **£££**

Japanese

Ginnan   6 **L** 28
5 Cathedral Pl EC4. 01-236 4120. Crowded; polite and efficient service. Raw fish sashimi, excellent soups, soba and domburi dishes. Food fried in front of you. Traditional tempura (deep fried sea food with subtle sauces). *LD Reserve. OPEN to 22.00. CLOSED Sun.* A. Ax. Dc. V. **££**

Hiroko   1 **A** 5
Hilton International Kensington, 179 Holland Park Av W11. 01-603 5003. Courteous staff. Sashimi (raw fish) may well begin the meal – then watch sankaiyaki, thin slices of beef, chicken, prawns and oysters, being cooked at the table. À la carte or two set menus. *LD Reserve. OPEN to 22.00. CLOSED L Mon.* A. Ax. Dc. V. **£££+**

Hokkai   2 **I** 21
61 Brewer St W1. 01-734 5826. Authentic restaurant with imaginative menu. Set lunches include the familiar choice of sashimi, tempura and teriyaki. Dinner includes king prawns and a rich fish stew. *LD Reserve. OPEN to 22.30. CLOSED Sun.* A. Ax. Dc. V. **££**

Masako   2 **E** 18
6-8 St Christopher's Pl W1. 01-935 1579. Authentic Japanese restaurant with private dining rooms attended by charming waitresses in kimonos. Completely oriental atmosphere. Try the set sukiyaki or tempura meals. *LD OPEN to 22.00. CLOSED Sun.* A. Ax. Dc. V. **£££+**

Jewish

Bloom's
90 Whitechapel High St E1. 01-247 6001. And 130 Golders Green Rd NW11. 01-455 1338. Bustling Kosher restaurants. Large helpings; lockshen and meatballs, salt beef, stuffed kishka. *LD OPEN to 21.30. CLOSED Fri, Sat & Jewish hols.* A. V. **££**

Harry Morgan's
31 St John's Wood High St NW8. 01-722 1869. All-Jewish menu care of Mrs Morgan. Very reasonable prices. Gefilte fisch, latkes (sweet, fried, crisp potato pancakes), blintzes, Hungarian goulash, black cherry cheesecake. *LD OPEN to 22.00. CLOSED LD Mon & D Fri.* No credit cards. **£**

Reuben's   2 **D** 18
20a Baker St W1. 01-935 5945. Simple, kosher deli and take-away with first-floor restaurant, in the oldest building in Baker St. Salt beef, chopped liver, gefilte fisch, lockshen pudding. *LD Reserve Sun. OPEN to 21.30. CLOSED D Fri & LD Sat.* Dc. V. **££**

Widow Appelbaum's   2 **F** 19
46 South Molton St W1. 01-629 4649. American-Jewish deli offering 101 dishes. Mirrors and photos of New York in the jazz age. Wooden bench seating with tables outside in summer too. Matzo balls, hot salt beef and pastrami, apfelstrudel and ice-cream sodas. *LD OPEN to 21.00. CLOSED D Sat & LD Sun.* No credit cards. **£**

Korean

A relatively new arrival here, Korean food has rapidly developed a following. Fresh, often raw ingredients and marinades are widely used. Rice forms the basis of many dishes with lots of vegetables and shredded beef. Desserts are simple, but fruit-cutting is a Korean art.

Arirang   2 **G** 21
31-32 Poland St W1. 01-437 9662. Green

and white decor, lacquered vases and a bamboo ceiling. Waitresses in Korean dress steer you through the large menu which includes kim chee (hot pickled cabbage), yuk kwe (beef strips with sugar, pears and spices), ojingo pokum (hot, sweet squid), and tangsaoyuk (sweet and sour meatballs). *LD Reserve. OPEN to 23.00. CLOSED Sun.* A. Ax. Dc. V. £

Korea House   2 G 19
10 Lancashire Ct W1. 01-493 1340. Attractive, popular restaurant specialising in dishes from Seoul. Extensive menu of seafood, pork, chicken, marinated beef. Order raw fish 24 hours ahead. Try the very strong Korean saké or fojoo. *LD Reserve. OPEN to 22.45. CLOSED Sun L.* A. Ax. Dc. V. £

Malaysian, Indonesian & Singaporean

Coconut, peanut and coriander are some of the characteristic flavours in this cuisine. For hotter tastes try sambals (fiery pickles served as condiments). Malaysian specialities include salad with peanut sauce and satay. Mild and creamy curries from Singapore; Indonesia is famous for rijstafel (a collection of small dishes served with rice).

Equatorial   2 I 22
37 Old Compton St W1. 01-437 6112. A cheerful Singaporean restaurant on three floors. Fruit and vegetables in shrimp dressing, coconut rice with fried fish and prawns. *LD Reserve Fri & Sat. OPEN to 23.15, to 23.00 Sun. CLOSED L Sat & LD Sun.* A. Ax. Dc. V. ££

Malaysian Kitchen   1 I 5
234 Old Brompton Rd SW5. 01-370 2421. Small, friendly eatery. Try satay, crispy duck or chillied king prawns then cool off with exotic desserts. *D OPEN to 23.00, to 23.30 Fri & Sat, to 22.30 Sun.* Ax. Dc. V. ££

Melati   2 H 21
31 Peter St W1. 01-437 2011. And 1 Great Windmill St W1. 01-437 2754. Very popular Indonesian restaurants. Rice and noodle dishes, meat and seafood specialities. Fried rice with shredded chicken and shrimps, fish cutlets in coconut sauce. *LD Reserve. OPEN to 23.30. CLOSED Sun.* A. Ax. Dc. V. ££

Rasa Sayang   2 H 22
10 Frith St W1. 01-734 8720. Unpretentious restaurant serving authentic Singaporean, Indonesian and Malaysian food. Try the beef satay, prawns, orange chicken. *LD Reserve D. OPEN to 22.45. CLOSED L Sat & LD Sun.* Ax. Dc. V. ££

Mexican

The main Mexican dishes are largely variations on the theme of tortillas (thin corn or flour pancakes), minced or shredded meats, frijoles or refried beans (red beans cooked soft and mushy) and chilli. Rice is a common accompaniment.

Café Pacifico   3 I 23
5 Langley St WC2. 01-379 7728. Crowded cantina in a converted warehouse. No booking at night, but have a cocktail while you wait. Young clientele. Guacamole, nachos, tacos, enchiladas, quesadillas, tostados, chilaquiles. Fresh pineapple or helados to follow. *LD Reserve L. OPEN to 23.45, to 22.45 Sun.* A. V. ££

La Cucaracha   2 H 22
12-13 Greek St W1. 01-734 2253. London's first Mexican restaurant, in the cellars of a converted monastery. Hacienda-style decoration with sunny covered terrace at the back. Ceviche, tacos, carnitas, avocado Mexicana (baked and stuffed with crabmeat), enchiladas. Spicy and delicious. *LD OPEN to 23.30.* A. Ax. Dc. V. ££

Los Locos   6 J 24
24 Russell St WC2. 01-379 0220. Mexican bar and restaurant with lots of Tex-Mex specials. Nachos, tacos, carnitas, steaks, alligator, enchiladas, grilled shrimps, fajitas — cooked over mesquite wood. Limited wine list, Mexican beer and cocktails. Disco from 23.30 every night. *D OPEN to 03.00.* A. Ax. Dc. V. ££

Middle Eastern

Charcoal grilling is a popular method throughout the area, and dishes are often spicy. Yoghurt is a common ingredient. Ginger, almonds, nutmeg, coriander and cinnamon are also widely used.

Baalbeck   1 G 5
18 Hogarth Pl SW5. 01-373 7199. Plain, informal and economical Lebanese restaurant offering tabbouleh, couscous and kibbeh sinieh — baked lamb, crushed wheat and eggs stuffed with mince meat and pine nuts. Separate vegetarian and vegan menus and if the wine list doesn't appeal you can bring your favourite with you. Taped music. *LD Reserve D. OPEN to 23.00. CLOSED Sun.* No credit cards. £

Buzkash
4 Chelverton Rd SW15. 01-788 0599. Traditional Afghani restaurant decorated with

local antiques, rugs and guns. Try ashak (pasta stuffed with leeks, mince and yoghurt), kormos (grilled lamb) and firni (Afghani rice pudding). Excellent value set lunch. *LD OPEN to 23.00. CLOSED L Sun.* A. Ax. Dc. V. **££**

Caravan Serai   2   C   19
50 Paddington St W1. 01-935 1208. Younler brother of Buzkash, with the same menu but more Western decor. *LD Reserve. OPEN to 22.30 Mon-Fri, to 23.00 Sat & Sun. CLOSED L Sun.* A. Ax. Dc. V. **££**

Falafel House
95 Haverstock Hill NW3. 01-722 6187. Candlelit tables, casual, relaxed atmosphere and simple homely food in this popular restaurant. Falafel and pitta, chicken liver with onion, egg and spices, many vegetarian dishes, brandy trifle. *D Reserve. OPEN to 23.30.* V. **£**

Lebanese   2   D   16
60 Edgware Rd W2. 01-723 9130. Eat genuine Lebanese dishes in an oriental atmosphere. Mirrors, arches, dim wall lights and carved chairs inlaid with brass. Montabar (baked eggplant with sesame sauce, lemon, olive oil and garlic) or kibbeh (fresh raw lamb pourri served with spices and wheat). Arab music. *LD OPEN to 24.00.* A. Ax. Dc. V. **££**

Open air

The following places have a few tables on the pavement or in the garden, in an enclosed courtyard or conservatory, or on a terrace. Restaurants in some areas whip out tables and chairs at the first glimmer of sun, particularly the Greek ones around Charlotte St and the cafés off Oxford St.

Anemos   2   F   22
34 Charlotte St W1. 01-580 5907. Friendly, crowded and noisy. Eat outside at the pavement tables in summer. Humous, excellent kebabs, moussaka. *LD Reserve D. OPEN to 01.00. CLOSED Sun.* A. Ax. Dc. **££**

L'Artiste Assoiffé
122 Kensington Park Rd W11. 01-727 5111. Authentic French food can be eaten under the trees of a small front garden during fine weather. Filet de Dijon, foie de veau des gourmets. *D OPEN to 23.30. L Sat only. CLOSED Sun.* A. Ax. Dc. V. **£££**

Au Bon Acceuil   4   K   10
19-21 Elystan St SW3. 01-589 3718. Tables set out on the pavement in summer. Comfortable French restaurant with good unpretentious cooking – seafood crêpes, venison casserole, jugged hare, pheasant

in red wine. *LD Reserve. OPEN to 23.30. CLOSED L Sat & LD Sun.* A. Ax. Dc. V. **££**

Barbican, Waterside Café   6   K   30
Level 5, Barbican Centre EC2. 01-638 4141. Modern self-service café by the man-made lake of the arts centre. Snacks or full meals. *LD OPEN to 20.00.* No credit cards. **£**

Dan's   4   K   9
119 Sydney St SW3. 01-352 2718. Bright, airy room with hanging plants and seating for 20 in the garden. Anglo-French cuisine – warm spinach mousse with basil, rack of lamb with honey and mustard, chocolate truffle cake to follow. *LD OPEN to 23.00. CLOSED Sat & Sun.* Ax. Dc. V. **£££**

La Famiglia   4   L   5
7 Langton St SW10. 01-351 0761. Attractive, with pretty rear garden seating 32. Southern Italian cooking. Fourteen types of pasta. Italian wine. *LD OPEN to 24.00.* A. Ax. Dc. V. **££**

Jakes   4   K   6
14 Hollywood Rd SW10. 01-352 8692. Ground floor and basement restaurant leading out onto an attractive patio with seating for 30 at lunchtime. Relaxed atmosphere in which to sample beef Wellington, chicken en croûte, Jakes' own blinis or hamburgers. *LD Reserve. OPEN to 23.45. CLOSED D Sun.* A. Ax. Dc. V. **££**

Old Rangoon
201 Castelnau SW13. 01-741 9656. Spacious, colonial-style restaurant with large terrace and floodlit garden, ideal for summer eating. Varied menu with an emphasis on chargrilled dishes – thalis a speciality. Cocktail bar. *LD OPEN to 23.00.* A. Ax. Dc. V. **£££**

Rose Garden Buffet   2   A   20
Queen Mary's Rose Garden, Regent's Park NW1. 01-935 4010. Open-air eating in a London park. Self-service for unadventurous English food, but the surroundings at the right time of the year make it idyllic. *LD OPEN to 16.00 winter, 20.30 summer.* No credit cards. **£**

San Lorenzo Fuoriporta
Worple Rd Mews SW19. Cheerful, lively trattoria with tables in the garden during summer. Traditional menu – scalloppine di vitello alla San Lorenzo, petti di pollo, good fresh vegetables. *LD Reserve. OPEN to 23.00, to 22.00 Sun.* A. Ax. Dc. V. **££**

Serpentine   2   F   12
Hyde Park W2. 01-723 8784. Overlooks the Serpentine, and it is worth a visit for the excellent view of the park. Charcoal-grilled fish – sole, salmon trout – a speciality, and you can watch it cooking. Good salads.

Tables on the verandah in summer. LD
OPEN to 22.30. A. Ax. Dc. V. £££

Russian & Polish

*If you like fish, try some of the restaurants
listed below. You'll also find bortsch (cold
beetroot soup) and blinis (savoury or sweet
pancakes).*

Borshtch n'Tears   2 I 12
46 Beauchamp Pl SW3. 01-589 5003.
Crowded, informal, lively restaurant. Russian music on the ground floor, pop downstairs. Try the bortsch, beef Stroganoff,
chicken Dragomirof (with white wine,
cream and gherkin sauce), golubtsy
(stuffed cabbage leaves) or blinis. D OPEN
to 01.30. A. Ax. Dc. V. ££

Daquise   I I 9
20 Thurloe St SW7. 01-589 6117. Very
popular with Polish emigrés, this restaurant
serves simple, inexpensive but very well
prepared dishes. Bortsch, stuffed cabbage,
bigor and sausages, shashlik. Also open for
morning coffee and afternoon tea, with
some of the most delicious pastries in
London. LD OPEN to 22.45. No credit
cards. £

Lowiczanka
238-246 King St W6. 01-741 3225. Spacious first-floor restaurant in dusty pink and
brown with fresh flowers and traditional
paper wall-ornaments. Changing menu
always includes some Polish dishes. Try
pike in cream sauce, pirozki or tripe casserole. Home-made cakes. Dancing *from
20.00 Fri & Sat.* LD OPEN to 22.30, to
22.00 Sun. A. Ax. Dc. V. £

Luba's Bistro   I I II
6 Yeoman's Row SW3. 01-589 2950. Individual, down-to-earth, spartan atmosphere.
Seating at long tables. Bring your own wine.
Authentic Russian cooking. Bortsch, beef
Stroganoff, kooliebiaka (salmon pie),
zrazra (chicken with vegetables), golubtsy,
pojarsky. D OPEN to 24.00. CLOSED Sun.
A. Ax. V. ££

Scandinavian

Anna's Place
90 Mildmay Pk N1. 01-249 9379. Small,
intimate restaurant offering personal service and Scandinavian and French dishes
in Anna's own home. For starters, camem-
bert with parsley, then gravad lax, beef or
herring, duck breast with Swedish cabbage. LD Reserve. OPEN to 22.15.
CLOSED Sun & Mon. No credit cards. ££

Garbo's   2 C 17
42 Crawford St W1. 01-262 6582. Pleasant
pink restaurant serving Scandinavian
home cooking. Try the herring salad Baltic,
cabbage stuffed with minced pork, beef and
rice or the smoked eel. Imported Swedish
beer and schnapps as well as wine. LD
Reserve D. OPEN to 23.30. CLOSED L Sat
& LD Sun. A. Ax. Dc. V. ££

Spanish & Portuguese

*Both cuisines are similar and ideal for
lovers of fish and garlic. Portuguese cooking is not as oily as Spanish. Beware of
dishes spiced with piri piri, a type of pepper,
which can be very hot.*

El Bodegon   4 L 6
9 Park Wlk SW10. 01-352 1330. Intimate,
cool and popular. Mainly Spanish dishes,
excellently cooked. Gambas al pil-pil
(prawns in a hot garlic sauce), paella,
zarzuela. Year round patio seating. LD
OPEN to 23.45. A. Ax. Dc. V. ££

Caravela   2 I 12
39 Beauchamp Pl SW3. 01-581 2366.
Small, intimate, mainly seafood restaurant.
King prawns piri piri, fresh grilled sardines,
or regional specialities. Delicious orange
roll dessert. Wine list exclusively Portuguese. Guitars play every eve, with
singers from Tue-Sun. LD Reserve. OPEN
to 01.00, to 24.00 Sun. CLOSED L Sun. A.
Ax. Dc. V. ££

Fogareiro
16-18 Hendon La N3. 01-346 0315. Marine
decor to match emphasis on fish specialities. Try the seafood pancake flamed in
brandy to start. Other dishes include – king
prawn piri piri, lagosta Portuguese, diced
steak fried in herbs and garlic or assiette de
fruits de mer. LD Reserve. OPEN to 23.30.
CLOSED Sun. A. Ax. Dc. V. £££

Hispaniola   6 L 23
The Thames at Victoria Embankment,
Charing Cross WC2. 01-839 3011. A float-
ing restaurant. Romantic setting and good
Spanish food on upper or lower deck. LD
Reserve. Upper Deck OPEN to 24.00. Main
deck OPEN to 21.30. CLOSED LD Mon, L
Sat & LD Sun. A. Dc. V. £££

O Fado   2 I 12
50 Beauchamp Pl SW3. 01-589 3002. A
genuine Portuguese restaurant with music
in the basement. Delicious fish dishes. Sardines and the chicken speciality –
franquintos a Fado – are superb. Good
carafe wine. LD OPEN to 01.00, to 23.30
Sun. A. Ax. V. ££

Ports   2 I 12
11 Beauchamp Pl SW3. 01-581 3837.
Relaxed Portuguese restaurant which concentrates on traditional seafood dishes.
Smoked swordfish, bacalhau (sun-dried
cod) or arroz de marisco (a rice and fish
dish). Wine list exclusively Portuguese. Set
price lunch. *LD OPEN to 23.30. CLOSED
Sun.* A. Ax. Dc. V. ££

Valencia   I I 3
1 Empress App, Lillie Rd SW6. 01-385
0039. Authentic Spanish restaurant with
singing waiters, guitarists and flamenco on
Sun. Good regional dishes and wines. *D
OPEN to 24.15.* A. V. ££

Swiss

St Moritz   2 I 21
161 Wardour St W1. 01-734 3324. Two
floors rigged out like a ski hut in the famous
resort. Cheese and beef fondues are a
house speciality. Also assiette de grison
(mountain-air dried and cured beef), veal in
cream and mushroom sauce. Nightclub
downstairs (membership required). *LD
Reserve. OPEN to 23.30, to 24.30 Fri &
Sat. CLOSED L Sat & LD Sun.* A. Ax. Dc. V.
££

Swiss Centre   2 I 22
2 New Coventry St (Leicester Sq) W1.
01-734 1291. Large shop and restaurant
complex comprising five venues at different
price ranges serving Swiss provincial food.
Fondue, raclette, grisons, gateaux, chocolates, coffee all available. Childrens' and
vegetarian menus also available. *LD
OPEN to 24.00, to 23.00 Sun.* A. Ax. Dc. V.
£-£££

Thai & Vietnamese

*Thai cuisine is rich and highly seasoned
with chilli and spices. Rice and fish predominate, and many recipes include nam
pla, a salty fish sauce. Exotic vegetables
and flowers are often served raw with
sauces to dip into. Salads such as rose
petal or water chestnut are recommended.
Desserts include lotus seeds, cassava
roots and coconut, scented with jasmin.*

Bangkok   I I 9
9 Bute St SW7. 01-584 8529. Simple, neat
restaurant which serves beef satay in peanut sauce. Thai noodles or chicken fried in
garlic or prepared with ginger. *LD Reserve.
OPEN to 22.45. CLOSED Sun.* ££

Busabong   4 L 4
331 Fulham Rd SW10. 01-352 4742. Infor-

mal surroundings with Thai dancers performing. Try fisherman's soup, mint pork
with minced water chestnuts and wonton
sauce, coconut banana. *LD Reserve.
OPEN to 23.15.* A. Ax. Dc. V. ££

Chiang Mai   2 H 22
48 Frith St W1. 01-437 7444. This calm
authentic restaurant serves steamed crab
claws in soy sauce, pepper and herbs, or
kai yad sai (omelette with pork and vegetables). *LD Reserve. OPEN to 23.00.* A. Ax.
V. ££

Mekong   5 N 16
46 Churton St SW1. 01-630 9568. Sample a
blend of Vietnamese and Chinese cuisine
in this simple bistro-like restaurant. Spring
rolls, sugar cane prawns, beef in lemon
grass. Vegetarian dishes and set price
menus. *LD Reserve. OPEN to 23.00.
CLOSED Sun.* A. V. ££

Saigon   2 H 22
45 Frith St W1. 01-437 7109. A very popular
Soho restaurant serving exotic starters –
papaya salad with pork and prawns; followed by seafood specialities such as
spiced crab with garlic, lemon grass and
herbs. *LD Reserve. OPEN to 23.30.
CLOSED Sun.* A. Ax. Dc. V. ££

Van Long   2 H 22
40 Frith St W1. 01-434 3772. Attractive,
modern Vietnamese restaurant with pretty,
pastel decor. Excellent soups. Superior
seafood dishes. Long menu but set meals
help the uninitiated. *LD Reserve. OPEN to 23.15.* A.
Ax. Dc. V. ££

Vegetarian & wholefood

*Vegetarian restaurants are very popular in
London and some of the best are listed
below. See also the 'Indian' and 'Inexpensive' sections. For further information contact the Vegetarian Society 53 Marloes Rd
W8 (01-937 7739). It publishes the International Vegetarian Health Food Handbook. This is a directory of vegetarian
restaurants, shops, guest houses and
hotels throughout the UK and the world.*

Chutneys   3 C 23
124 Drummond St NW1. 01-388 0604.
Bright, white restaurant serving very good
Indian vegetarian food. Lunchtime 'eat as
much as you like' buffet very popular. Dinner à la carte and more relaxed. A speciality is the de luxe thali comprising dhal
soup, papadam, bhajis, four curries, pillau
rice, raita, pickles, pooris and a dessert.
Good selection of dosas (pancakes filled
with vegetables). Wine, beer, lassi or herbal

teas. *LD Reserve. OPEN to 24.00. A. Ax. Dc. V.* £

Cranks 2 H 21

8 Marshall St W1. 01-437 9431. This branch was the first of London's original healthfood restaurants. Hot and cold vegetarian dishes, soups, pies, salads, yoghurt, cakes, biscuits, bread, scones, fruit and vegetable juices. Licensed. Other branches. *LD Reserve D. OPEN to 23.00. CLOSED Sun. A. Ax. Dc. V.* £-££

Diwana Bhel-Poori House 3 C 23

121 Drummond St NW1. 01-387 5556. Indian food at very reasonable prices. Samosas, thalis, bhajis. Also at 50 Westbourne Gro W2, 01-221 0721, and 114 Drummond St NW1, 01-388 4867. *LD OPEN to 23.00. CLOSED Mon. A. V.* £

East West 6 J 32

188 Old St EC1. 01-251 4076. Serious macrobiotics' delight in a pretty, tranquil setting. Miso, tofu, seitan, sushi and vegetable dishes. Home-made, sugar-free sweets. Licensed: organic wines and naturally fermented beers. *LD OPEN to 21.15, to 15.00 Sat & Sun.* No credit cards. £

Food for Thought 3 I 23

31 Neal St WC2. 01-836 0239. Vegetarian wholefood in a cheerful Covent Garden basement. Soups, stews, stir fries, bakes, quiches, salads, yoghurt, fruit salads, hot and cold desserts. Drink tisanes or bring your own wine. *LD OPEN to 20.00. CLOSED Sat & Sun.* No credit cards. £

Gardner's 4 L 4

156 Chiswick High Rd W4. 01-995 1656. Pretty, discreet restaurant serving naturally and humanely produced red meat, free-range fowl, fish and imaginative vegetarian dishes. Set price three-course menu includes cheese and spinach puff, chicken mousse, vegetable moussaka, stuffed crêpes, fish of the day. *D Reserve. OPEN to 23.00. CLOSED Sun. A. Ax. Dc. V.* ££

Mandeer 2 G 22

21 Hanway Pl W1. 01-323 0660. Highly acclaimed Indian vegetarian and wholefood restaurant. Deserves good reputation as the food is cooked to a very high standard. Specialities include aubergine bhajis, thali Mandeer or puffed lotus savoury. Generous set menu available. Also a very reasonable self-service cafeteria. Licensed. *LD OPEN to 22.15. CLOSED Sun. A. Ax. Dc. V.* £

Nuthouse 2 H 20

26 Kingly St W1. 01-437 9471. Buffet service vegetarian health food on two floors. Nut roasts, quiches, carrot cake. The food is all organically grown and cooked. Drink

wine, fresh fruit or herb teas. *L OPEN to 19.00, to 17.00 Sat. CLOSED Sun.* £

Oodles 3 I 25

113 High Holborn WC1. 01-405 3838. Not strictly a vegetarian restaurant but offers a wide variety of vegetarian dishes and salads. Another branch at 42 New Oxford St WC1. 01-580 9521. *LD OPEN to 21.00, to 14.30 Sat. CLOSED Sun. A. Ax. Dc. V.* £

Raw Deal 2 B 17

65 York St W1. 01-262 4841. Hot dishes, salads, quiches. Wholemeal pies, cakes and trifles to follow. Unlicensed, but bring your own wine. Guitarist on *Thur & Sat. LD OPEN to 21.30, to 22.30 Sat. CLOSED Sun.* No credit cards. £

Sharuna Restaurant 3 H 23

107 Great Russell St WC1. 01-636 5922. South Indian vegetarian restaurant. Curries, delicately spiced, yoghurt and fruit. *LD OPEN to 21.00, to 18.00 Sun.* No credit cards. £

Slenders 6 L 28

41 Cathedral Pl EC4. 01-236 5974. In a modern square beside St Paul's Cathedral. Delicious home-made soups, vegetable casseroles and flans. Wide choice of desserts. *L OPEN to 18.15. CLOSED Sat & Sun.* No credit cards. £

Vijay

49 Willesden La NW6. 01-328 1087. Traditional south Indian vegetarian food served here as well as tasty meat curries for any non-vegetarian friends. Try their masala dosai, sambar or vegetables cooked in yoghurt and coconut. To follow genuine Indian sweets – almond cakes and kulfi. *LD Reserve. OPEN to 22.45, to 23.45 Fri & Sat. A. Ax. Dc. V.* £

Windmill Wholefood 4 K 1

486 Fulham Rd SW6. 01-385 1570. Counter service during the day, waitresses in the evening. Large portions of salads, quiches and hot savoury dishes – all home-made. A vegan dish is always available. Crumble, banana cream or cake to follow. Large range of organic wines, also additive-free beers and ciders. Tranquil tapes. *LD OPEN to 23.00. CLOSED Sun L.* No credit cards. £

Breakfast and brunch

A selection to suit all tastes. Times are given for breakfast or brunch only. Price symbols for this section only are: £ *under* £4; ££ £4-£7; £££ *over* £7.

Cafés & brasseries

Bartholomew's 6 K 29
57a West Smithfield EC1. 01-606 3903.
Traditional English. *OPEN 07.30-11.30.
CLOSED Sat & Sun.* A. Ax. Dc. V. £-££

La Brasserie 4 J 10
272 Brompton Rd SW3. 01-584 1668.
Upmarket range served all day. *OPEN
08.00-11.30 Mon-Sat, 10.00-11.30 Sun.* A.
Ax. Dc. V. £££

Gate Diner 1 A 8
184a Kensington Park Rd W11. 01-221
2649. American-style restaurant open in
the morning for coffee and desserts from
the menu. Special *Sun* brunch with bagels,
eggs, salmon etc. *OPEN 11.30 onwards.*
Reserve. A. V. ££

Harry's 2 H 20
19 Kingly St W1. 01-734 3140. Popular,
friendly all-night café serving cooked
breakfasts, toasted sandwiches and
snacks. *OPEN 22.00-10.00 Mon-Sun.
CLOSED Sun night.* £

The Hermitage 3 E 26
19 Leigh St WC1. 01-387 8034. A friendly,
stylish café where baguettes, croissants,
pain au chocolat and brioches are cooked
on the premises. Newspapers provided.
OPEN 10.00 onwards. V. £

Messrs C 5 J 22
10 New Row WC2. 01-836 0563. Bright,
cheerful café serving traditional fry-ups
throughout the day. *OPEN 08.30-19.30.
CLOSED Sun.* £-££

Quality Chop House 3 H 28
94 Farringdon Rd EC1. 01-837 5093.
Authentic English. *OPEN 06.30-11.00.
CLOSED Sat & Sun.* £

Le Tire Bouchon 2 H 20
6 Upper James St W1. 01-437 5348. Continental. *OPEN 08.00. CLOSED Sat & Sun.*
££

Hotels

Basil Street 2 I 13
Basil St SW3. 01-581 3311. English or Continental. *OPEN 07.45-10.00.* A. Ax. Dc. V.
££-£££

Cadogan 5 J 13
75 Sloane St SW1. 01-235 7141. English or
Continental. *OPEN 07.30-10.00.* A. Ax. Dc.
V. ££-£££

Claridge's 2 G 18
Brook St W1. 01-629 8860. English, à la
carte or Continental. *OPEN 07.30-10.00.* A.
V. ££-£££

Hyde Park, Park Room 2 H 14
66 Knightsbridge SW7. 01-235 2000. English, Continental or à la carte. *OPEN
07.00-10.00 (08.00-11.00 Sun & B.hols).* A.
Ax. Dc. V. £££

Portman 2 E 17
22 Portman Sq W1. 01-486 5844. English
buffet, à la carte or Continental. *OPEN
07.00-11.00.* A. Ax. Dc. V. £££

Ritz 2 I 18
Piccadilly W1. 01-493 8181. English, à la
carte or Continental. *OPEN 07.30-10.30.* A.
Ax. Dc. V. £££

Savoy 6 K 23
Strand & Embankment WC2. 01-836 4343.
English or Continental. *OPEN 07.30 (08.00
Sun)-10.30.* A. Ax. Dc. V. £££

Afternoon teas

*Afternoon tea is a British institution: at one
time very fashionable, sociable, leisurely,
gossipy. This list gives some of the remaining strongholds.*

Tea & cakes

Bendicks 5 K 12
195 Sloane St SW1. 01-235 4749. Breakfast, morning coffee, lunch and cream tea
with all the trimmings. *OPEN 08.30-19.00
(19.30 Wed) Mon-Sat, 10.30-18.30 Sun.* A.
Ax. Dc. V.

Maison Sagne 2 D 19
105 Marylebone High St W1. 01-935 6240.
Traditional tea shop with its own bakery and
delicious patisserie. Serves coffee and
croissants from *09.00*, lunch and tea.
*OPEN to 17.00 (Sat to 12.30). CLOSED
Sun.* No credit cards.

The Muffin Man 1 E 7
12 Wright's La W8. 01-937 6652. Breakfast,
morning coffee, light lunches and a range of
set teas: Devon, 'Muffin Man', traditional.
*OPEN 08.15-17.45 (17.00 Sat). CLOSED
Sun.* No credit cards.

Patisserie Valerie 2 I 22
44 Old Compton St W1. 01-437 3466. Soho
patisserie with tea, coffee and hot chocolate. Good cream cakes and sandwiches.
OPEN to 19.00. CLOSED Sun. No credit
cards.

Teas in hotels

*Always good with excellent service and a
comfortable sense of welcome. Often*

some quiet background music and usually a reasonable bill at the end.

Brown's 2 H 19
Albemarle St W1. 01-493 6020. Very English, country house setting. Sandwiches, cakes, tarts. *15.00-18.00.*

Claridge's 2 G 18
Brook St W1. 01-629 8860. A touch of class in the comfortable reading room, where liveried footmen serve sandwiches and assorted pastries. *Reserve. 16.00-17.15.*

Dorchester 2 H 16
Park La W1. 01-629 8888. Dainty sandwiches, cakes and pastries in the main lounge. *15.00-17.45.*

Ritz 2 I 18
Piccadilly W1. 01-493 8181. A good comfortable hotel. Tea in the Palm Court, with dainty sandwiches, pastries and cream cakes. *Reserve.* Tea served at *15.15 & 16.30.*

Teas in stores

Most large department stores provide teas as well as the two that follow.

Fortnum & Mason 2 I 19
181 Piccadilly W1. 01-734 8040. Afternoon tea is available at three locations in the store *Mon-Sat.* St James' Restaurant serves a set tea of sandwiches, scones, cake, tea or coffee to a piano accompaniment *15.00-16.55.* The Patio Bar and Soda Fountain offer an à la carte tea menu *14.30-17.00.* (Soda Fountain to *18.00*).

Harrods Georgian Restaurant 2 I 12
Knightsbridge SW1. 01-730 1234. Enjoy a buffet tea of coffee or fruit juice with bread and butter, scones, cakes and pastries while listening to the pianist. All-inclusive price. Served from *15.45.* Alternatively have tea served on the Terrace from *15.30.* Slightly more expensive.

Thé dansant

Café de Paris 2 J 21
3 Coventry St W1. 01-437 2036. Dancing *Wed, Thur, Sat & Sun 15.00-17.45* & in the evening to *01.00 Mon & Thur-Sun.*

Waldorf Hotel 6 J 24
Aldwych WC2. 01-836 2400. Opulent Pancock tea lounge with comfort and good service. Edwardian elegance. Dancing to the band and full set tea *Fri-Sun 15.30-18.30.*

Ice-cream

Baskin-Robbins
Delicious American ice-cream, 31 flavours. *OPEN 11.00-23.00.*
Empire Cinema, Leicester Sq 5 J 22
WC2. 01-734 8222.
259 Finchley Rd NW3. 01-435 0665.

Dayvilles
More delicious ice-cream. 32 flavours. *OPEN 11.00-24.00.*
264A Earls Court Rd SW5. 1 G 5
01-370 0083.
56 Edgware Rd W2. 01-723 2 D 16
3243.
62 Gloucester Rd SW7. 01-581 1 H 7
5508.
2 The Mall W5. 01-567 3778.

Marine Ices
Haverstock Hill NW3. 01-485 8898. Huge choice of Italian ice-cream and water ices. Also restaurant. *OPEN 10.30-23.00.*

Pubs

A 12thC wit noted two plagues in London: fire and drink. Children drank beer as a preventative to typhoid. The Royal Navy issued a gallon per man per day! Workmen's wives of the 16thC easily blended malt, yeast, water and perhaps sugar at home. Hops were thought of later. (Today's ale is lower in hops, higher in sugar than beer; both are generally processed.) Spirits made of fermented cereals, potatoes or malted barley were sold literally everywhere. Chemists distributed gin as a cure-all but the public, egged on by William of Orange, soon made its own (rye combined with juniper berries). By 1733, almost 100 gin shops in St Giles conveniently adjoined tuppenny brothels. A publican's placard in Southwark promised: 'Drunk for 1d. Dead drunk for 2d. Clean straw for nothing.' The rise of splendidly ornamental gin palaces resulted from the Beerhouse Act of 1830 permitting the unlicensed sale of beer. Throngs of gin palace patrons spurred the brewers into improving their own premises. Out of these taverns, inns (offering drink, food and lodgings) and gin mills the 7,000 pubs of London evolved. Darts, dominoes and skittles survived bawdier times. Innovations like scampi or ham rolls, pool or hired entertainment, Public Bars through one door, more expensive Saloons through the other, and decor to match the clientele

produced a great variety of 'locals'. When the blue-mouthed parrot in Dr Samuel Johnson's favoured 'Cheshire Cheese' (in Fleet St) caught a cold his death was solemnly announced on the BBC; such has ever been the impact on Londoners of these homes from home. The hours vary slightly and should be checked to avoid disappointment, but usually are Mon-Sat 41.00/11.30-15.00 and 17.30-23.00; Sun 12.00-14.00 and 19.00-22.30. These licensing hours were introduced during World War I to get the workers up in time for work the next day and back at work in the afternoon. In 1988 they were relaxed and pubs are officially allowed to open 11.00-23.00 Mon-Sat, 19.00-22.30 Sun. However, many licensees do not choose to remain open all day. NB: many of the pubs in the City are closed on Sat & Sun. Most pubs sell drink to take away (off sales). By law they must have WCs and display a price for drinks. Remember to ask for lager if you want what the rest of the world calls beer.
L lunch; D dinner; B bar food. Most pubs serve snacks.

Nicholson's London Pub Guide gives more detailed information on where to drink in the capital.

Admiral Codrington   4   J   11
17 Mossop St SW3. 01-589 4603. Wood-panelled, gaslit house and 38-seater restaurant with a varied menu. Big garden with overhanging grape vine. Good 'up-market' Chelsea local, complete with cocktail bar. **L D**

Antelope   5   L   13
22 Eaton Ter SW1. 01-730 7781. Hearty early 19thC pub. Wine bar on first floor serving hot and cold food six days a week. Lunchtime food in bar. **B**

Blackfriar   6   M   28
174 Queen Victoria St EC4. 01-236 5650. Triangular building near Blackfriars station. Stunning Art Nouveau temple of marble and bronze; lunchtime hot and cold bar food and cold buffet in the evening. **B**

Buckingham Arms   5   L   18
62 Petty France SW1. 01-222 3386. Attractive mid-Victorian pub. Gathering place for business people. **B**

Bunch of Grapes   1   I   11
207 Brompton Rd SW3. 01-589 4944. Popular Victorian pub with finely engraved 'snob-screens' separating the bars and impressively carved wooden pillars. Traditional ales, home-baked lunches and evening bar snacks. **L B**

Captain's Cabin   5   J   2
4-7 Norris St, Haymarket SW1. 01-930

4767. A cosy nautical pub well situated for a pre-theatre drink. **B**

Cartoonist   6   K   27
76 Shoe La EC4. 01-353 2828. In the heart of the old newspaper world, this Victorian pub is wallpapered with cartoons, some famous and all amusing. Headquarters of the Cartoonist Club of Great Britain. **B**

Chelsea Potter   4   L   10
119 King's Rd SW3. 01-352 9479. Trendy meeting place for the locals with an alternative juke box in the bar. Filling lunches and snacks throughout the day. **B**

Cheshire Cheese, Ye Olde   6   K   26
145 Fleet St EC4. 01-353 6170. Rebuilt after the Great Fire with low ceilinged interiors, oak tables, sawdust on the floor. The pub probably hasn't changed much since Dr Johnson used to drop in. Snacks and good traditional English cooking for those in search of a meal. **L D**

Cheshire Cheese   6   K   25
5 Little Essex St WC2. 01-836 2347. Intimate Jacobean pub with original oak beams and three bars. **B**

Cittie of York   3   I   26
22-23 High Holborn WC1. 01-242 7670. A huge pub in the Victorian grand manner with cosy cubicles for discreet couples. This is where lawyers used to have confidential chats with their clients. Cellar bar. **B**

Cock Tavern, Ye Olde   6   K   26
22 Fleet St EC4. 01-353 8570. Good journalists' tavern with literary and Dickensian associations and mementoes. Carvery restaurant which also serves fish, puddings, pies and vegetarian dishes. **B L**

Cross Keys   4   M   8
2 Lawrence St SW3. 01-352 1893. Popular Chelsea local with very friendly staff and excellent hot and cold food. Walled garden. **B**

Crown and Two Chairmen   2   H   22
31 Dean St W1. 01-437 8192. Earned its name nearly 200 years ago by playing host to royalty who arrived by sedan chair – a crown carried by two chairmen. Real ale, cocktails, hot and cold bar food. Rub shoulders with writers and people from the film world. **B**

Dirty Dick's   6   N   33
202-204 Bishopsgate EC2. 01-283 5888. The original pub named after Nat Bentley, well-known 18thC miser of the ballad. No longer dirty since cobwebs and stuffed cats were removed. Remnants preserved behind glass. Upstairs wine bar serving three-course lunches. **B L**

Dog and Duck   2   H   22
18 Bateman St W1. 01-437 3478. Built in

1773, and not updated, the Dog and Duck has one small bar, gleaming with polished wood and tiles. **B**

Dover Castle　　　　　　　2　D　20
43 Weymouth Mews W1. 01-636 9248. Mews pub patronised by the BBC staff. Home-cooked food. **B**

Duke of Clarence　　　　　　1　A　5
203 Holland Park Av W11. 01-603 5431. Medieval-style interior with typically Victorian bar. Beautiful courtyard with barbecues in summer. **B**

Duke of Cumberland
235 New King's Rd SW6. 01-736 2777. Edwardian elegance prevails. Popular with the young and trendy. Summertime drinking on Parson's Green. Real ale. **B**

Duke of Wellington　　　　　5　L　13
63 Eaton Ter SW1. 01-730 3103. Traditional pub – pictures of the Iron Duke abound as do brass and copperware. Used by shoppers and workers as well as Chelsea locals. Good snacks. **B**

Eagle　　　　　　　　　　3　I　33
2 Shepherdess Wlk N1. 01-253 4715. Victorian music-hall pub immortalised in the song *Pop goes the Weasel*. Hot and cold snacks. Restaurant serving traditional English fare, carvery and summer barbecue. **B L D**

Edgar Wallace　　　　　　6　K　25
40 Essex St WC2. 01-353 3120. On an original Elizabethan site but now with the famous writer as the theme of the pub. Dr Johnson and his circle used to meet here regularly once a week. Small upstairs restaurant. **B L**

Empress of Russia　　　　　6　J　29
362 St John St EC1. 01-837 1910. Cheerful pub near Sadler's Wells with hot and cold food lunchtimes and evening. **B**

Fox and Grapes
Camp Rd, Wimbledon Common SW19. 01-946 5599. Julius Caesar camped near here. Mock Tudor pub rambling right on to the common. Good lunches, though limited menu on *Sun*. **B**

Flask
77 Highgate West Hill N6. 01-340 3969. Old tavern named after the flasks which people used to buy here to fill with water at the Hampstead wells. English restaurant. Crowded forecourt for outdoor drinking. **B L**

Freemasons Arms
32 Downshire Hill NW3. 01-435 4498. Popular Hampstead pub with enormous garden, courtyard and terraces. **B**

The French House　　　　　2　H　22
49 Dean St W1. 01-437 2799. Centre for the Free French during the war. De Gaulle

drank here as did Brendan Behan and Dylan Thomas. Not immediately appealing. Good wines. **B**

George　　　　　　　　　6　K　23
213 Strand WC2. 01-353 9238. Fine old timbered inn opposite the Royal Courts of Justice. Upstairs carvery. **B L**

George Inn　　　　　　　6　Q　28
77 Borough High St SE1. 01-407 2056. Unique galleried coaching inn rebuilt in 1679 and featured in Dickens' *Little Dorrit*. Courtyard entertainment in summer. Wine bar with good selection of wines, pâtés and cheeses. Restaurant. **B L D**

Globe　　　　　　　　　6　J　24
37 Bow St WC2. 01-836 0219. Nearest pub to the Royal Opera House, frequented by members of the orchestra. Used in Hitchcock's *Frenzy*. Good food. **B**

Golden Lion　　　　　　　5　J　19
25 King St SW1. 01-930 7227. Theatrical and literary pub. Oscar Wilde and Lily Langtry associations. **B**

Green Man
Putney Heath SW15. 01-788 8096. 15thC ale house overlooking Putney Common. Associated with duels and highwaymen. Barbecues in summer. **B L D**

Grenadier　　　　　　　　2　I　14
18 Wilton Row SW1. 01-235 3074. Mews pub where the ceiling is covered with wine labels. Duke of Wellington played cards here. Wellingtonia, good restaurant. **B L D**

Greyhound
82 Kew Green, Kew. 01-940 0071. Tiny, family pub, with a mock Tudor exterior and an imitation olde-worlde interior, that attracts a mixed crowd. **B**

Hand and Shears
1 Middle St EC1. 01-600 0257. Sometimes called the Fist and Clippers. Either way, the name comes from the nearby Cloth Fair. The local for St Bartholomew's Hospital. **B**

Holly Bush
22 Holly Mount, Heath St NW3. 01-435 2892. Unspoiled, pleasant and small, in picturesque setting. Olde-worlde, Victorian mirrors, gas lighting, beer advertisements and open fires in winter. **B**

Island Queen　　　　　　　3　F　32
87 Noel Rd N1. 01-226 5507. Looming papier mâché figures dominate the bar in this popular local. Pool room and restaurant. **B D**

King of Bohemia
10 Hampstead High St NW3. 01-435 6513. Bow fronted Georgian pub – a fashionable local. **B**

King's Head　　　　　　　1　A　10
33 Moscow Rd W2. 01-229 4233. A popu-

lar pub. The King's Head Chess Club meets here each evening *from 19.00*. **B**

King's Head and Eight Bells   4   M   8
50 Cheyne Wlk SW3. 01-352 1820. 18thC decor with pots, jugs and prints of old Chelsea. Quite a few famous regulars. **B**

Lamb   3   H   26
94 Lamb's Conduit St WC1. 01-405 0713. A busy Bloomsbury local with some intriguing music-hall photographs and Hogarth prints. Original snob-screens. **B**

Lamb and Flag   6   J   23
33 Rose St WC2. 01-836 4108. Originally called 'The Bucket of Blood' because the pub was the centre for fighting in the area (Dryden apparently got the 'once-over' here). Now a popular, mellow bar. **B**

Marquis of Anglesey   6   J   24
39 Bow St WC2. 01-240 3216. Popular with local workers and journalists. Good beer. Upstairs bar-cum-restaurant. **B L D**

Marquis of Granby   5   J   22
51-52 Chandos Pl WC2. 01-836 7657. Cheerful pub round the back of Trafalgar Square. Very busy at lunchtimes. **B**

Museum Tavern   3   H   23
49 Great Russell St WC1. 01-242 8987. Opposite the British Museum, the tavern attracts students and sightseers. Mirrored Victorian intcrior. **B**

Nag's Head   6   J   23
10 James St WC2. 01-836 4678. Famous and lively Edwardian pub with a strongly theatrical flavour. **B**

Old Bull and Bush
North End Way NW3. 01-455 3685. The famous pub of the Florrie Forde song. Drink on the forecourt and gaze at Hampstead Heath opposite. **B**

Old Coffee House   2   H   20
49 Beak St W1. 01-437 2197. As the name suggests started life as a coffee house. Cosy, jolly establishment with good food. **B L D**

Olde Butler's Head   6   M   31
Mason's Av, Coleman St EC2. 01-606 3504. Pleasant, renovated 17thC inn with English cooking. **B L D**

Olde Mitre Tavern   6   J   28
1 Ely Ct EC1. 01-405 4751. Built in 1546 by the Bishop of Ely for his servants. Associations with Elizabeth I and Dr Johnson. **B**

Printer's Devil   6   K   26
98 Fetter La EC4. 01-242 2239. A printers' and journalists' pub taking its title from the traditional nickname for a printer's apprentice. Notable collection of early printing curios. Wine bar upstairs. **B L**

Punch Tavern   6   L   27
99 Fleet St EC4. 01-353 8338. Popular with

reporters. Fascinating cartoons and framed old newspapers. **B**

Queen's Elm   4   K   4
241 Fulham Rd SW3. 01-352 9157. So-called because Elizabeth I took shelter under a nearby elm in 1567. Lively and popular with writers and publishers. **B**

Red Lion   5   J   20
2 Duke of York St SW1. 01-930 2030. Plenty of Victoriana in this friendly pub. Beautifully preserved mirrors and rich mahogany panelling. **B**

Red Lion   2   H   17
1 Waverton St W1. 01-499 1307. Lovely 17thC Mayfair inn with forecourt. Frequented by models, actors and young businessmen. **B L D**

Roebuck
Richmond Hill, Richmond. 01-940 0607. Large ground floor with wood beams and prints of old Richmond. Upstairs restaurant. Terrific Thames views. **B L D**

Rose and Crown   2   I   16
2 Old Park La W1. 01-499 1980. 200-year-old country pub now surrounded by Park Lane houses. Tyburn associations. Five hot dishes every lunchtime and cold buffet in the evening. **B L D**

Rossetti
23 Queen's Gro NW8. 01-722 7141. Airy pub-trattoria with Rossetti etchings on the walls. English beer, good Italian food. **B L D**

Running Footman   2   H   17
5 Charles St W1. 01-499 2988. Pub which once had the longest name in London, 'I am the Only Running Footman'. Popular with staff from the clubs nearby. **B L D**

St Stephen's Tavern   5   M   21
10 Bridge St SW1. 01-930 3230. Local for Members of Parliament – the Division Bell rings here. Political journalists' gossip might be worth hearing. **B**

Salisbury   5   J   22
90 St Martin's La WC2. 01-836 5863. Glittering Edwardian pub in the heart of theatreland. Cut-glass mirrors and first-class hot and cold buffet. A famous meeting place for theatre people. **B**

Seven Stars   6   J   26
53 Carey St WC2. 01-242 8521. Behind the Law Courts stands this early 17thC pub, one of the smallest in London. **B**

Sherlock Holmes   5   K   22
10 Northumberland St WC2. 01-930 2644. Upstairs is a perfect replica of Holmes's study at 221b Baker St. **B L D**

Spaniards Inn
Spaniards Rd NW3. 01-455 3276. Famous 16thC inn with literary and Dick Turpin associations. Pretty garden. **B**

Spotted Dog
212 Upton La, Forest Gate E7. 01-472 1794. 17thC inn used by City merchants during the great plague. Dick Turpin associations though the decor is mostly Tudor. Oak beams, plaster whitewash, prints. **B L D**

Still and Star   6 **P 33**
1 Little Somerset St, Oldgate E1. 01-488 3761. The only one of its name in England, and set in 'blood alley' where Jack the Ripper committed dire deeds. IPA on four pumps. **B**

Watling, Ye Olde   6 **M 29**
29 Watling St EC4. 01-248 6252. Oak-beamed tavern rebuilt by Wren after the Great Fire of 1666. **B, L** in upstairs bistro.

White Horse   6 **K 26**
90 Fetter La EC4. 01-242 7846. Old City coaching inn haunted by Sebastian – a friendly presence. Very good home-cooked food. **B L**

Williamson's Tavern   6 **M 29**
1-3 Grovelands Courts, Bow La EC4. 01-248 6280. Inviting City tavern built after the Great Fire. Basement wine bar. **B**

World's End   4 **L   4**
459 King's Rd SW10. 01-352 7992. Generous, robust and Victorian. **B**

Wrestlers, Ye Olde
98 North Rd N6. 01-340 4297. L-shaped bar with leaded glass windows, named for the wrestling that was once a regular event here. **B L D**

Riverside pubs

Anchor   6 **O 28**
1 Bankside/34 Park St SE1. 01-407 1577. 18thC replacement of original destroyed by Great Fire of 1666. Exposed beams, large open fireplace and general Olde-English decor. **B L D**

Angel
101 Bermondsey Wall East SE16. 01-237 3608. 15thC Thames-side pub on piles, with extensive views over the river and the pool of London. Low ceilings, wooden beams and English cooking. **B L D**

Black Lion
2 South Black Lion La W6. 01-748 7056. Lovely old riverside pub with a prize-winning garden. **B**

Bull's Head
Strand on the Green W4. 01-994 0647. 350-year-old Chiswick waterfront tavern with Cromwellian links. **B**

City Barge
27 Strand on the Green W4. 01-994 2148.
15thC Elizabethan charter inn on Chiswick waterfront. **B L**

Cutty Sark
Ballast Quay, Lassell St SE10. 01-858 3146. Quiet Georgian pub with wooden interior. Overlooks river and wharves near *Cutty Sark* dry-dock. **B L D**

Dickens Inn   6 **R 32**
St Katharine's Way E1. 01-488 2208. Pub in the Dickensian style. Fine views of diverse craft in St Katharine Docks. Two restaurants. **B L D**

Dove
19 Upper Mall W6. 01-748 5405. 18thC pub with a terrace overlooking the river. James Thomson wrote *Rule Britannia* here. **B L**

Grapes
76 Narrow St E14. 01-987 4396. Traditional atmospheric riverside pub with balcony overlooking river. **B L D** in fish restaurant upstairs.

London Apprentice
62 Church St, Old Isleworth. 01-560 1915. Famous 16thC Thames-side pub with fine Elizabethan and Georgian interiors. Prints of Hogarth's 'Apprentices'. **B L D**

Mayflower
117 Rotherhithe St SE16. 01-237 4088. Tudor inn connected historically with the Pilgrim Fathers. The only pub in England licensed to sell British and American stamps. Drink on the jetty in good weather. Restaurant. **B L D**

Prospect of Whitby
57 Wapping Wall E1. 01-481 1095. Historic dockland tavern with many famous and infamous associations. Decorated with nautical souvenirs and fine pewter. Excellent English menu in upstairs restaurant. Food bar overlooking the river. **B L D**

Samuel Pepys   6 **N 28**
Brooks Wharf, 48 Upper Thames St EC4. 01-248 3048. Converted warehouse in Jacobean style. Two large bars and a two-tier terrace overlooking the river. **B L D**

Ship
Ship La SW14. 01-876 1439. 16thC pub with terrace at the Mortlake end of the Oxford and Cambridge boat race course. **B L**

Three Pigeons
87 Petersham Rd, Richmond. 01-940 0361. Old riverside inn with beer garden and restaurant which projects over the water. **B L D**

Trafalgar Tavern
Park Row SE10. 01-858 2437. Smart Thames-side inn close to Wren's imposing Royal Naval College. Good English cooking in the restaurant. **B L D**

White Swan
Riverside, Twickenham. 01-892 2166. Attractive black-and-white balconied pub overlooking the river. Excellent lunchtime food. **B**

Music pubs

These vary enormously from pubs with a pianist who plays old-time favourites to those with professional facilities and large audience space for rock and jazz bands. The pubs listed below are all established live music venues, but it's always best to check beforehand what is happening each night. Most pubs with a separate music room ask for gate money, though it is rarely more than £4-£5 and often less.

Bull & Gate
389 Kentish Town Rd NW5. 01-485 5358. Jazz, R & B or blues, *seven nights a week.* **B**

Bull's Head
373 Lonsdale Rd SW13. 01-876 5241. Modern jazz by top English and international musicians *every night*, plus *Sat & Sun L.*

Cockney Pride   2 I 19
6 Jermyn St W1. 01-930 5339. Nostalgic reconstruction of a Victorian Cockney pub right down to the bubble and squeak! Live music *every eve* featuring piano, singsongs, contemporary rock and country & western. **B L D**

Empress of Russia   6 J 29
362 St John St EC1. 01-837 1910. The Islington folk club meets here *every Thur eve.*

Greyhound
175 Fulham Palace Rd SW6. 01-385 0526. Rock and pop *Mon-Sat eve* and striptease *Sun-Fri lunchtimes.* **B**

Half Moon
93 Lower Richmond Rd SW15. 01-788 2387. Music *every night* including rock, folk and jazz bands; jazz *Sun L* too.

Hog's Grunt
The Production Village, 110 Cricklewood La NW2. 01-450 9361. Wild-west style decor and good sounds *every night* – anything from jazz to reggae. Also a disco.

King's Head   3 E 32
115 Upper St N1. 01-226 1916. Live music at *22.00 Mon-Sat* after the stage performance. Folk, rock or jazz.

Minogues   3 D 32
80 Liverpool Rd N1. 01-354 4440. Live music *every night*, generally traditional Irish, but occasionally other styles as well.

New Merlin's Cave   3 G 29
34-38 Margery St WC1. 01-837 2097. Barnlike pub offering rock music *nightly*. Jazz session *Sun L.* **B**

New Pegasus
109 Green Lanes N16. 01-226 5930. Live music *every night* – mostly rock, occasionally country. **B**

Pied Bull   3 D 32
1 Liverpool Rd N1. 01-837 3218. Once Sir Walter Raleigh's house, now a pleasant pub. One bar has a stage. Variety of live music *Fri & Sat eve.* **B**

Plough
90 Stockwell Rd SW9. 01-274 3879. Jazz and blues *Wed-Sun eve.* **B**

Prospect of Whitby
57 Wapping Wall E1. 01-481 1317. 400-year-old Tudor tavern overlooking the Thames (see also 'Riverside pubs'). Live music *every night* including guitar, jazz and folk. **B L D**

Ruskin Arms
386 High St North E12. 01-472 0377. Visiting bands play heavy rock *Thur-Sun.* Boxing gym upstairs.

St James's Tavern   2 I 21
45 Great Windmill St W1. 01-437 5009. Pleasant, Victorian pub. Irish folk music *Mon, Tue & Thur.* **L B**

Sir George Robey
240 Seven Sisters Rd N4. 01-263 4581. Live music *every eve.* Blues *Sun L.*

Swan   4 K 2
1 Fulham Bdwy SW6. 01-385 1840. Mixed bands and R & B *six nights a week Mon-Sat & Sun L.* Hot bar food. **B**

Swan Tavern   1 B 10
66 Bayswater Rd W2. 01-262 5204. Illuminated at night, this popular beer garden opposite Hyde Park is a busy rendezvous for tourists. Honky-tonk piano *every eve except Sun.* **B**

Torrington
4 Lodge La N12. 01-445 4710. Visiting bands play wide range of music on *Fri & Sun eve.* **B**

Tufnell Park Tavern
Tufnell Park Rd N7. 01-272 2078. 1930s decor provides a suitable backdrop for live jazz *Thur-Sun eve.*

White Lion   3 I 31
37 Central St EC1. 01-253 4975. Real East End pub where punters can sing along to the piano played *Fri-Mon eve & Sun L.*

Yorkshire Grey   3 H 25
2 Theobald's Rd WC1. 01-405 2519. Dance to the 'golden oldie' hits of the 50s and 60s and 70s on *Tue eve;* jazz *Thur, Sat & Sun eve.*

Gay pubs

Gay and drag pubs have been combined because while not all gay pubs offer drag acts, all pubs with drag acts attract an at least partially gay clientele. For further information contact Gay Switchboard 01-837 7324. See also 'Gay nightlife'.

Black Cap
171 Camden High St NW1. 01-485 1742. Two bars. Second offers drag shows *every night & Sun L.*

The Britannia
12 Chilton St E2. 01-729 6502. Small, intimate and cosy pub. Different features *every eve.* **B**

Elephant and Castle
2 South Lambeth Pl SW8. 01-735 0217. Disco and drag cabaret *every night except Sun.*

Fallen Angel
65 Graham St N1. 01-253 3996. Pub which also functions as a vegetarian café. *Tue & Sat* are very popular women-only nights. Exhibitions held in refurbished bar. **B**

King's Arms   2 H 21
23 Poland St W1. 01-734 5907. Busy, friendly gay men's pub in central position. **B**

Market Tavern   5 R 15
Market Towers, 1 Nine Elms La SW8. 01-622 5655. Atmospheric and friendly pub with separate, quieter bar. Different theme nights. **B**

Royal Oak
62 Glenthorne Rd W6. 01-748 2781. Drag cabaret *Mon, Thur-Sun eve & Sun L.* **B**

Royal Vauxhall Tavern
372 Kennington La SE11. 01-582 0833. Drag shows *every night & Sun L.* **B**

Theatre pubs

*It is sometimes necessary to become a member (**M**) of the theatre club before being able to watch the performance. The fee is usually small.*

Aba Daba Theatre   3 G 27
The Water Rats, 328 Gray's Inn Rd WC1. 01-837 7269. 17thC pub decorated with cinema posters and theatre bills. The rear bar-cum-restaurant has a small stage and is *licensed to 24.00.* Old-time music hall *Thur-Sat.* Also occasional pantomime and live music. Enjoy a traditional English meal beforehand and drinking and singing during the performance. **B L D**

Bush Theatre
Shepherd's Bush Grn W12. 01-740 0501. Box office: 01-743 3388. Theatre above the pub with curtainless stage and raked seating. First productions of new plays from Britain and abroad. *Tue-Sun.* **M**

Gate at the Prince Albert   1 A 8
11 Pembridge Rd W11. 01-727 7362. Bookings: 01-229 0706. New works, adaptations of novels and revivals of lesser known plays by important writers. Proper stage and lighting facilities. *Mon-Sat.*

King's Head   3 E 32
115 Upper St N1. 01-226 8561. Box office: 01-226 1916. Probably the best known and most widely reviewed of theatre pubs. Decorated with theatre bills. You can have a meal before you see the show and stay at your table for the performance. *Lunchtime and evening shows. Mon-Sat.* **M L D**

Latchmere Theatre   4 R 6
503 Battersea Park Rd SW11. 01-228 2620. Good reputation for plays, cabaret and reviews. There is also a theatre bar. Check listings for late-night shows and Sunday performances. Pub recently refurbished. *Theatre Mon-Sat.*

Man in the Moon   5 L 14
392 King's Rd SW3. 01-351 2876. Very comfortable pub theatre in a converted cold store. Enterprising management presents predominantly modern plays – two different productions each night. The pub itself is worth a visit – lovely engraved glass, real ale and lunchtime snacks. *Theatre Tue-Sun.*

Orange Tree
45 Kew Rd, Richmond. 01-940 0944. Bookings: 01-940 3633. Popular performances above this friendly, attractive pub. Small and informal. *Theatre Mon-Sat Sep-Apr.* **L D**

Wine bars

Cheaper and more informal than restaurants and as an alternative to the pub, wine bars provide excellent meeting places for locals and visitors alike. Wine is served by the bottle or the glass and a selection of cheeses, pâtés and salads is usually available. Many bars have their own restaurants. Booking is often advisable. Wine bars have been opening (and closing again) in London at an astonishing rate over recent years. Below we list a selection of the best, well-established ones. Assume the bars

are open normal pub hours except where otherwise indicated.
L *lunch* **D** *dinner* **B** *bar food.*

Andrew Edmunds 2 H 21
46 Lexington St W1. 01-437 5708. Small but charming wine bar/restaurant which serves excellent wines and imaginative food. Daily specials. *OPEN to 23.00. CLOSED Sat & Sun.* **B L D**

Archduke 6 M 23
Concert Hall Approach SE1. 01-928 9370. Underneath the railway arches. Good range of wines, live jazz and blues nightly. Upstairs restaurant specialises in sausages from around the world. *OPEN to 22.30 (restaurant to 23.00). CLOSED L Sat & L Sun.* **L D**

Balls Bros
One of the oldest wine bar chains in London, especially useful for City workers. *OPEN to 19.30 (unless otherwise stated). CLOSED Sat & Sun.* **B L**

Hay's Galleria, Tooley St SE1. 6 Q 30
01-407 4301.

3 Budge Row, Cannon St 6 N 29
EC4. 01-248 7557. *CLOSES 20.00.*

Laurence Pountney Hill EC4. 6 O 23
01-283 2947. *CLOSES 20.00.*

2 Old Change Ct, St Paul's 6 M 28
Churchyard EC4. 01-248 8697.

St Mary-at-Hill EC3. 01-626 6 P 31
0321. *CLOSES 19.00.*

5 Carey La EC2. 01-606 4787. 6 L 29

6 Cheapside EC2. 01-248 6 M 29
2708.

Moor House, London Wall 6 L 31
EC2. 01-628 3944.

42 Threadneedle St EC2. 6 N 31
01-283 6701.

Bill Bentley's Wine Bar 2 I 12
31 Beauchamp Pl SW3. 01-589 5080. Dark, cosy bar in the old-fashioned tradition with an excellent fish restaurant upstairs. The wine, mostly good quality French, is reasonably priced and complemented well by the delicious snacks from the oyster bar. Other branches. *OPEN to 22.30. CLOSED Sun.* **B L D**

Bow Wine Vaults 6 M 29
10 Bow Churchyard EC4. 01-248 1121. Victorian bar very definitely within the sound of Bow Bells! Popular with City gents, the bar offers a good selection of over 100 well chosen French, Spanish, Californian and German wines, imaginative bar food and a lunchtime restaurant. *L OPEN to 15.00. CLOSED Sat & Sun.* **B L**

Brahms & Liszt 6 J 24
19 Russell St WC2. 01-240 3661. Lively, crowded Covent Garden wine bar. Very

popular upstairs and cellar bar. Music is rather loud, food varied, with the emphasis on cheeses and salads. Some hot dishes. Upstairs *OPEN to 23.00, to 22.30 Sun.* **L D** (*CLOSED Sun L*). Downstairs *OPEN to 01.00, CLOSED Sun.* **L D**

Le Beaujolais 2 I 22
25 Litchfield St WC2. 01-836 2277. Lively, mixed clientele in this popular, yet intimate wine bar. Good French wines and authentic French cooking. *OPEN to 23.00. CLOSED L Sat & L D Sun.* **L D**

Café des Amis du Vin 6 J 23
11-14 Hanover Pl WC2. 01-379 3444. Close to the Royal Opera House and always very busy early evening. Good range of French, German, Spanish and Californian wines accompanied by plat du jour or the impressive choice of cheeses. *OPEN to 23.30. CLOSED Sun.* **L D**

Café St Pierre 3 I 29
29 Clerkenwell Grn EC1. 01-251 6606. Brasserie and art deco wine bar on the ground floor, more expensive restaurant above. *OPEN to 23.00. CLOSED D Sun.* **B L D**

Charco's 4 L 11
1 Bray Pl SW3. 01-584 0765. Near Sloane Sq. Interesting salads and game pies. Pavement tables in summer. *OPEN to 23.00. CLOSED Sun.* **B**

Cork and Bottle 5 J 22
44-46 Cranbourn St WC2. 01-734 7807. Spacious basement with unusual variety of top-class bargain wines. Excellent salads and hot food. *OPEN to 23.00. CLOSED L Sun.* **B**

Covent Garden 6 J 23
1 The Piazza WC2. 01-240 6654. Parisian café ambience. Pavement seating in summer. Short menu with daily specials. Good wine list, mostly French. *OPEN to 23.00, to 22.30 Sun.*

Davy's Wine Bars
Dusty barrels, old prints and sawdust-covered floors create the Victorian image of these houses, the names of which date back to the wine trade of 100 years ago. The chain offers a good selection of wines and tasty fish appetisers plus other light dishes. Phone to check opening times. The City bars *close at 20.00 or 20.30. Most branches are closed Sat & Sun.* The following list is a selection:

Boot and Flogger 6 Q 27
10-20 Redcross Way SE1. 01-407 1184.

Bung Hole 3 I 23
57 High Holborn WC1. 01-242 4318.

City Boot 6 L 31
7 Moorfields High Wlk EC2. 01-628 2360.

Davy's Wine Vaults
165 Greenwich High Rd SE10. 01-858 7204.

Mother Bunch's 6 L 28
Arches F & G, Old Seacoal La EC4. 01-236 5861.

Tappit Hen 5 K 22
5 William IV St WC2. 01-836 9811.

Downs 2 I 17
5 Down St W1. 01-491 3810. Excellent food and French wines. Two floors but crowded at lunchtime with Mayfair clientele. Have a late lunch to avoid the rush. *OPEN 12.00-24.00.* **B L D**

Ebury Wine Bar 5 M 13
139 Ebury St SW1. 01-730 5447. Crowded and cramped, but pleasant atmosphere. Comprehensive wine list. Restaurant. *OPEN to 22.15.* **L D**

El Vino 6 K 26
47 Fleet St EC4. 01-353 6786. Something of an institution. Thoroughly masculine atmosphere popular with journalists and lawyers. Women must wear skirts, men a jacket and tie. Downstairs restaurant. *OPEN to 20.00. CLOSED D Sat & LD Sun.* **B L**

Five Lamps 6 P 32
3 Railway Pl EC3. 01-488 1587. Popular and crowded basement wine bar frequented by staff from nearby Lloyd's of London. *OPEN to 20.30. CLOSED Sat & Sun.* **B L**

Lincoln's 3 I 25
49A Lincoln's Inn Fields WC2. 01-405 3349. Cosy wine bar with restaurant downstairs and hot and cold buffet on ground floor. *OPEN to 23.00. CLOSED Sat & Sun.*

Shampers 2 H 20
4 Kingly St W1. 01-437 1692. Always a congenial atmosphere here and a very fine selection of wines. Tasty hot and cold buffet, imaginative salads. Downstairs is a brasserie. Taped jazz. *OPEN to 23.00. CLOSED D Sat & LD Sun.* **B**

Soho Soho 2 H 22
11-13 Frith St W1. 01-494 3491. Spacious, colourful French wine bar, café and brasserie. French food. *OPEN to 23.00. CLOSED Sun.* **B L D**

Tracks 2 H 22
17a Soho Sq W1. 01-439 2318. Agreeable modern decor. Wines mainly French with a sprinkling of Italian. Cold buffet and a few hot dishes. Continental breakfast and afternoon teas also served. *OPEN to 23.00. CLOSED Sat & Sun.* **B**

Nightlife

For a city as big as London, with a reputation to match, the late night scene is a lot less obvious than you might expect. Once the theatres and cinemas, pubs and wine bars have disgorged their patrons at about 23.00, the streets can be virtually deserted by midnight. This is because the late night places are not exclusively situated in the West End but are spread farther out around the city – north west to Camden Town and Hampstead, south west to Knightsbridge and South Kensington, and west to Earl's Court and Kensington. In fact, by and large, London tends to go to bed earlier than many other cities in the world. There are, however, places where you can kick-on into the small hours but you have to know what you want, where to go, and how much you are prepared to pay. You can choose from live music venues, discos with theme nights, dinners accompanied by lavish entertainment, expensive nightclubs, gambling dens or clubs which combine dinner, dancing, gambling and a little of whatever you fancy – if you can afford it! However, you don't need an expense account to enjoy a night on the town and there are enough places to choose from to suit almost any pocket. For more detailed information see Nicholson's London Nightlife Guide.
£ = low priced ££ = medium priced £££ = high priced.

Club membership

The Clubman's Club 2 I 19
5 Albemarle St W1. 01-493 4292. For an annual subscription fee, you can obtain free membership or benefits at several hundred clubs all over Britain and worldwide. Also discounts for car hire and hotels.

Night clubs

These are fairly exclusive clubs. Some have dancing and most have restaurants. Many London night clubs employ hostesses whose job it is to boost the sales of drinks. Most of them have an expensive taste in champagne and you will have to pay for the pleasure of their company.
Membership: *For most of these clubs you have to be a member, although short-term membership is usually available for visitors. You can only enter a gaming house as a member or a guest of a member. By law, when you join a gaming club, you will not be admitted until you have filled in a declaration of your intent to gamble and 48 hours have elapsed from the time you signed this declaration. Membership charges vary considerably. In some clubs visitors from overseas get reduced rates or free membership. A few clubs may insist on a potential member being proposed by an existing member. These clubs generally operate* 14.00-04.00 Mon-Sat (03.00 Sat), 16.00-04.00 Sun. *The number* **48** *after the club's entry means that the 48 hours rule applies. (M) means that membership is usually necessary for entry.*

Alibi   5 L 14
38 King's Rd SW3. 01-584 7346. Attracts a wide-ranging clientele including show-biz personalities. Relaxed ambience. Restaurant with full menu. Dancing in a separate area. (M) *OPEN to 02.00 Mon-Sat.* A. Ax. Dc. V. ££

Bristol Suite   2 H 18
14 Bruton Pl W1. 01-499 1938. Hostesses, music and an international cuisine. *OPEN to 04.00 Mon-Fri.* A. Ax. Dc. V. £££

Casanova   2 G 18
52 Grosvenor St W1. 01-629 1463. Roomy and comfortable. Regency decor. Not cheap but good value. (M) *OPEN to 04.00.* ££ (48)

Charlie Chester Casino   2 I 21
12 Archer St W1. 01-734 0255. Modern night club with a restaurant. (M) *OPEN to 04.00.* £ (48)

Clermont Club   2 H 18
44 Berkeley Sq W1. 01-493 5587. An opulent 18thC town house. À la carte restaurant with Arab cuisine. (M) *OPEN to 04.00.* A. Ax. Dc. V. £££ (48)

Director's Lodge   2 I 19
13 Mason's Yard, Duke St SW1. 01-839 6109. Wine, dine and dance to a resident band and guest singer. Entrance fee. *OPEN to 03.00 Mon-Fri.* A. Ax. Dc. V. ££

Gaslight of St James's   5 J 20
4 Duke of York St SW1. 01-930 1648. Two bars with attractive hostesses. Restaurant. (M) or entrance fee. *OPEN to 02.00 Mon-Sat (to 02.30 Sat).* A. Ax. V. ££

Golden Horseshoe   2 I 21
79-81 Queensway W2. 01-221 8788. À la carte restaurant. (M) *OPEN to 04.00.* £ (48)

New Georgian Club   2 G 19
4 Mill St W1. 01-629 2042. Club with cabaret twice nightly. Lounge bar and hostesses, hot food served. (M) *OPEN to 03.00 Mon-Fri.* A. Ax. Dc. V. £££

Pinstripe   2 H 20
21 Beak St W1. 01-437 5143. Victorian decor and topless waitresses. Restaurant and bar. (M) or entrance fee. *OPEN to 03.00 Mon-Fri.* A. Ax. Dc. V. ££

Stork Club   3 I 20
99 Regent St W1. 01-734 1393. Luxury restaurant serving French cuisine. Dance Band. Singers and dancers from 22.00. Spectacular cabaret twice nightly. *OPEN 20.30-03.30 Mon-Sat.* Dinner, supper and breakfast. A. Ax. Dc. V. £££+

Nightspots

Nightspots are prone to changes in fashion trends and in London they are continually opening and closing, or changing their image, according to the current whims of the clientele. Some nightspots also have different themes depending what night of the week it is and this affects dance, dress and music styles. It is a good idea to check Time Out *or* City Limits *for the theme of the day or ring the club beforehand because what is correct dress in one place may be totally unsuitable in another.*

Annabel's   2 H 18
44 Berkeley Sq W1. 01-629 2350. Legendary retreat for the rich and famous, aristocracy and royalty. Exclusive, expensive and very difficult to join. (M) – long waiting list. Temporary membership (3 weeks) available. *OPEN to 03.00 Mon-Sat.* £££

Café des Artistes   4 K 7
266 Fulham Rd SW10. 01-352 6200. Entrance in Redcliffe Gdns. Lively, casual atmosphere with plenty of dimly-lit alcoves and disco every evening. *OPEN to 02.00.* £

Café de Paris   5 J 21
3 Coventry St W1. 01-437 2036. An attractive period building which hosts tea dances and club nights *on Tue & Wed* (M). Ring for details of what's on or check the music

press. *OPEN to 01.00 Mon & Thur, to 03.00 Fri & Sat, to 24.00 Sun.* ££

Camden Palace 3 A 25
1a Camden High St NW1. 01-387 0428. Spacious and lively disco which attracts the young and trendy. Different theme nights. Restaurant. *OPEN to 02.30 Tue-Sat.* £

Empire Ballroom 5 J 22
Leicester Sq WC2. 01-437 1446. Resident band provides the music. Very crowded. Diner serving burgers, steaks and salads. Bars. *OPEN to 03.00 Mon-Sat, to 01.30 Sun.* (M) for Sun. £

The Fridge
Town Hall Pde, Brixton Hill SW2. 01-326 5100. A large venue with projectors and over 100 video screens, so you can watch while you bop. Various club nights. Wholefood restaurant. *OPEN to 02.00 Mon-Sat.* £

The Hippodrome 2 I 22
Hippodrome Cnr WC2. 01-437 4311. Lavish nightspot. Black and silver decor complemented by an amazing laser system. Six bars and a restaurant. Attracts young trendies. *OPEN to 03.30 Mon-Sat.* £

Jacqueline's 2 G 21
201-205 Wardour St W1. 01-434 4285. New nightclub with disco. Designer decor, aiming for an upmarket clientele. Restaurant. *OPEN to 03.30 Mon-Sat.* ££

Lacey's 5 J 22
80-81 St Martin's La WC2. 01-240 8187. Upstairs disco and light show. *OPEN to 03.00 Mon-Sat.* £

Legends 2 H 19
29 Old Burlington St W1. 01-437 9933. Decor in chrome and contrasting colours. Constant non-commercial funk, attracts big names from the music business. *OPEN to 02.00 Mon-Thur, to 03.00 Fri & Sat.* ££

Limelight 2 I 21
136 Shaftesbury Av W1. 01-433 0572. Situated in a converted church this club is on three levels. A live band plays on the ground floor, below is a jazz lounge and the top floor is the VIP bar and a balcony. *OPEN to 03.00 Mon-Sat.* £

Le Palais 1 A 1
242 Shepherd's Bush Rd W6. 01-748 2812. Revamped in art deco style with the latest in disco technology – laser systems, video wall, fast-food restaurants, bar and theme party nights. Regularly hosts live acts. *OPEN to 03.00 Tue-Sat.* £

Pal Joey 2 H 20
62 Kingly St W1. 01-439 7242. Upmarket, international-style club. À la carte French restaurant. Piano bar, champagne bar, light show and dance floor. (M) or entrance fee. *OPEN to 03.30 Mon-Sat.* ££

The Park 1 D 4
38 Kensington High St W8. Ultra-modern sophisticated disco. Impressive lighting system. Bars and snack foods. *OPEN to 03.30 Mon-Sat except Tue.* ££

Roof Gardens 1 D 7
99 Kensington High St W8. 01-937 7994. Exclusive international private nightclub set in roof garden. Very select membership. Dinner and dancing. (M) or entrance fee (at the discretion of the doormen). *OPEN to 03.00 Thur & Sat.* ££

Samantha's 2 H 20
3 New Burlington St W1. 01-734 6249. Long-established, ever-popular split-level disco with two dance floors, four bars, cocktail bar and games room. A comfortable club with an interesting 'swing bar'. *OPEN 03.30 Mon-Sat.* £

Stringfellows 5 J 22
16-19 Upper St Martin's La WC2. 01-240 5534. Celebrity spot. Art deco motifs in restaurant. Mirrored walls create endless reflections of pulsating coloured lights in disco below. (M) or entrance fee. *OPEN to 03.00 Mon-Sat.* £££

Tokyo Joe's 2 I 18
85 Piccadilly W1. 01-409 1832. Fashionable and exclusive basement nightclub. Two bars and a restaurant serving French food. Attracts a prestigious clientele. (M) *OPEN to 03.00 Mon-Sat.* ££

The Wag 2 I 21
35 Wardour St W1. 01-437 5534. Graffiti-painted walls create a certain atmosphere in this popular Soho haunt. Loud music, theme nights. Wag-goers tend to be cool, alternative and trendy. *OPEN to 03.30 Mon-Sat.* Members only Fri & Sat. ££

Xenon 2 I 20
196 Piccadilly W1. 01-734 9344. Laser light and water shows and cabaret acts. Upmarket club. Live jazz in the cocktail bar. Good range of food available. *OPEN to 03.00 Mon-Sat.* ££

Zanzibar 3 I 24
30 Queen St WC2. 01-405 6153. Decor reminiscent of a 30s liner. Exotic cocktails and a huge selection of alcohol from all over the world. Live jazz on various nights. (M) *OPEN to 02.00 Mon-Sat.* ££

Dinner and entertainment

These are not membership clubs. Booking is advisable. Also see 'Restaurants' because a few have music and dancing.

Barbarella I 4 L 4
428 Fulham Rd SW6. 01-385 9434. Stylish and sophisticated disco. Unusual Italian food. *OPEN to 03.00 Mon-Sat.* A. Ax. Dc. V. ££

Beefeater by the Tower of London 6 R 32
Ivory House, St Katharine's Way E1. 01-408 1001. Five-course medieval banquets are served nightly with jugglers and magicians performing between courses. Henry VIII in full costume proposes the toasts. *OPEN to 23.00 Mon-Sun.* A. Ax. Dc. V. £££+

La Bussola 5 J 22
42-49 St Martin's La WC2. 01-240 1148. Cosy restaurant in the heart of theatreland, which still provides table d'hôte pre-theatre dinners. Dance band, pianist and excellent Italian cuisine of consistently high standard. *OPEN to 01.30 Mon-Fri (Sat to 02.00).* A. Ax. Dc. V. £££

L'Entrecôte 3 G 25
124 Southampton Row WC1. 01-405 1466. Romantic candlelit restaurant with wide-ranging menu. Resident dance band *Mon-Sat 21.00-01.00.* Guitarist *early evening & Sun.* Last orders 23.45 (22.45 Sun). A. Ax. Dc. V. ££

Flanagan's 2 C 18
100 Baker St W1. 01-935 0287. Also at 9 Kensington High St W8 (1 E 7), 01-937 2519, 55 Queensway W2 (1 B 10), 01-229 0615 and 14 Rupert St W1 (2 I 21), 01-434 9201. Completely phoney but enjoyable Victorian dining rooms, with sawdust on the floor, stalls, cockney songs and colourful extravaganza. Elegantly costumed waiters and serving girls. The pianist slams his piano at you and the waitresses sing as do the customers. Tripe, jellied eels, game pie, enormous plates of fish and chips and hearty golden syrup pudding. *LD OPEN to 23.00.* A. Ax. Dc. V. ££

Gallipoli 6 N 32
8 Bishopsgate Churchyard EC2. 01-588 1922. Exotic and unusual. Twice nightly cabaret of enjoyable Eastern belly dancing. Excellent Turkish food. Shish kebab, buryan Gallipoli, red mullet. *OPEN to 02.00. CLOSED Sun. Cabaret 22.00 & 01.00.* Ax. Dc. V. £££

L'Hirondelle 2 I 20
99-101 Regent St W1. Entrance in Swallow St. 01-734 6666. Theatre restaurant with two floor-shows nightly and a cabaret. International à la carte menu. *OPEN to 03.30 Mon-Sat.* Floor shows *23.15 & 01.30.* A. Ax. Dc. V. ££

Kerzenstuberl 2 E 18
9 St Christopher's Pl W1. 01-486 3196. Dinner dancing. Plenty of 'gute stimmung' here to warm the heart; an informal, hearty atmosphere and loads of goodwill backed up by excellent Austrian cooking. Jolly rhythmic accordion music nightly. *OPEN to 01.00 Mon-Sat.* A. Ax. Dc. V. ££

Lord Byron Taverna 2 H 20
41 Beak St W1. 01-437 0708. Delightful Greek restaurant whose speciality is lamb cooked on a spit. A warm and friendly ambience with lively dancing to Greek musicians. *OPEN to 01.30 Mon-Sat. Dancing to 03.00.* A. Ax. Dc. V. ££

My Fair Lady
250 Camden High St NW1. 01-485 4433. Dine aboard an attractive canal wide-boat whilst gliding down Regent's Canal. English cuisine with Continental overtones. Menu changes regularly. *OPEN to 23.00 Mon-Sat. (Sun L 12.30-15.30.)* A. V. ££

Roof Restaurant 2 I 16
Hilton Hotel, Park La W1. 01-493 8000. The view is all you would imagine, the decor light and modern. Two bands. French food. *OPEN to 02.00 Mon-Sat.* A. Ax. Dc. V. £££

Savoy Restaurant 6 K 23
Savoy Hotel, Strand WC2. 01-836 4343. Elegant and formal with resident quartet. Worldwide and well-deserved reputation for classic cooking and service. *OPEN to 24.00 Mon-Thur (to 24.30 Fri, to 01.00 Sat).* A. Ax. Dc. V. £££

Talk of London 3 I 24
Drury La cnr Parker St WC2. 01-408 1001. Modern purpose-built theatre restaurant with tiered seating. 'International' menu. Features some of London's most popular cabaret acts. *OPEN to 01.00 Mon-Sun.* A. Ax. Dc. V. ££

Terrace Restaurant 2 H 16
Dorchester Hotel, Park La W1. 01-629 8888. Stately and gracious. Live music. Dinner à la carte. *OPEN to 01.00 Mon-Sat.* A. Ax. Dc. V. £££

Tudor Rooms 2 I 20
17 Swallow St W1. 01-240 3978. Jesters and troubadours entertain while you eat your five-course meal. Specialities include 'olde Englishe' beef, roast pork and whole baby chicken. Much mead. Disco. *OPEN to 24.30.* A. Ax. V. £££

Villa Dei Cesari 5 Q 15
135 Grosvenor Rd SW1. 01-834 9872. Converted riverside warehouse with a fine view over the Thames. Classical decor. Italian and international food. Dance floor with band. *OPEN to 02.30 Tue-Sun.* Ax. Dc. V. ££

Live music venues

Outside the USA Britain, and especially London, is the main centre for live music. The venues range from massive arenas to club basements and the music from heavy rock to jazz, reggae and folk. We have listed below some of the most popular and established venues, irrespective of size (see also 'Music pubs' in 'Eating and drinking'). Consult Time Out, City Limits and the music press to check who's playing where, and when.

Almeida Theatre   3 D 33
Almeida St N1. 01-359 4404. Mainly contemporary music with a lot of jazz. Concerts on *Sun* night and *sometimes* mid-week. Contemporary music festival in *Jun* and various music weeks throughout the year.

Astoria Theatre   3 H 23
157 Charing Cross Rd WC2. 01-437 1801. Large auditorium for live music – anything from hard rock to classical. Restaurant and bars. *OPEN to 03.00 Mon-Sun.*

Africa Centre   6 J 23
38 King St WC2. 01-836 1973. African bands on *Fri & Sat* from about 21.30.

Bass Clef
35 Coronet St, off Hoxton Sq N1. 01-729 2476. A very popular venue to hear jazz, Latin American and African music. *Tue* – open house (modern jazz). *Free. Wed, Thur & Sun* – jazz; *Fri* – Latin American; *Sat* – African. *Charge.* The atmosphere is relaxed and the restaurant offers tasty meals. *OPEN to 02.00 Tue-Sat, to 24.00 Sun.*

100 Club   2 G 22
100 Oxford St W1. 01-636 0933. Jazz club that is historically the home of trad jazz. Friendly and comfortable it features live jazz groups (trad, modern and African) and the occasional new-wave band. *OPEN to 01.00 Mon-Sun.*

Dingwalls
Camden Lock NW1. 01-267 4967. A good selection of live bands most nights in this club by Regent's Canal. R&B, reggae, soul. *OPEN to 02.00 Mon-Sat, to 23.30 Sun.*

Dominion   3 F 23
Tottenham Court Rd W1. 01-580 9562. Major London venue for well-known performers.

Earl's Court Exhibition Centre   1 H 4
Warwick Rd SW5. 01-385 1200. Massive hall for top pop and rock stars.

Fairfield Hall
Croydon, Surrey. 01-688 9291. A modern concert hall with a number of large bands or soloists.

Hammersmith Odeon
Queen Caroline St W6. 01-748 4081. Regular appearances by many known stars playing different types of music.

Hog's Grunt
The Production Village, 110 Cricklewood La NW2. 01-450 9361. Village consists of two pubs and a restaurant. Hog's Grunt is the music venue. Wild-West style decor and good sounds. Hear anything from jazz to reggae. Also a disco. *OPEN to 24.00 Sun-Wed, to 01.00 Thur, to 02.00 Fri & Sat.*

Marquee   2 I 21
90 Wardour St W1. 01-437 6603. One of the original London rock clubs. Bars. *OPEN to 23.00 Mon-Sun. £*

Palookaville's   6 J 23
13a James St WC2. 01-240 5857. Lively basement restaurant and wine bar serving a wide variety of bistro-style dishes to the accompaniment of modern or traditional live jazz *from 21.00. OPEN to 01.30 Mon-Sat. ££*

Pizza Express   2 H 22
10 Dean St W1. 01-437 9595. Jazz sessions in the basement restaurant. *OPEN to 01.00 Tue-Sun. £*

Pizza on the Park   2 I 14
11 Knightsbridge SW1. 01-235 5550. Two restaurants with modern and traditional jazz played in the basement. Reserve Fri & Sat. *OPEN to 24.30 Mon-Sun (no music Sun). £*

Rock Garden   6 J 23
67 The Piazza, Covent Gdn WC2. 01-240 3961. Restaurant upstairs and on street level. Hamburgers, spare ribs, various house specialities. Cocktail bar. Live concerts downstairs in a converted vegetable warehouse. Five bands a night with focus on new, up-and-coming bands. *OPEN to 03.00 Mon-Sat, to 24.00 Sun.*

Ronnie Scott's   2 H 22
47 Frith St W1. 01-439 0747. Reputedly the best jazz in London. On the stand a succession of big name jazz men and women. Can be typically hot, smoky and sleazy on a busy night. Food and drink available but it's the sounds that people come for. Advisable to book. *Charge.*

Royal Albert Hall   1 F 10
Kensington Gore SW7. 01-589 8212. Has a varied selection of artistes throughout the year.

Town & Country Club
9-17 Highgate Rd NW5. 01-267 3334. An authentic 1930s theatre hall complete with chandeliers and balconies allowing excel-

lent viewing and plentiful dancing space. Live music four or five nights a week, a wide range including African, reggae, jazz, rock and blues bands. *OPEN to 23.30 Mon-Sat.*

Wembley Arena

Empire Way, Wembley, Middx. 01-902 1234. Enormous capacity auditorium for really major concerts.

Gay nightlife

These are just a few of the many gay clubs and pubs in London. For details of other venues contact the **Lesbian & Gay Switchboard** *01-837 7324 (24 hr service) and see also 'Gay pubs' in 'Eating & drinking'. For an alternative to the 'scene', ring* **London Friend** *(01-837 3337) which runs various social/support groups.*

Bang's (at Busby's)   2 I 22

157 Charing Cross Rd WC2. 01-734 6963. Enormous barn-like disco with lasers and video screens. Outrageous gay nights (but everyone welcome) *Mon* & *Thur*, Mudclub *Fri*, disco *Sat*. *OPEN to 03.00*.

The Bell   3 D 28

259 Pentonville Rd N1. 01-837 5617. Large, comfy pub next to the Scala cinema, with different alternative discos every night. Very popular with a young, lively and varied clientele. *OPEN to 24.00 Sun-Wed, to 01.00 Thur, to 02.00 Fri & Sat.*

Brief Encounter   5 J 22

41 St Martin's La WC2. 01-240 2221. Centrally situated gay men's bar, especially popular with theatre-goers. Neo-thirties style, with pianist playing *(Mon, Wed & Sat)* in the lower bar which has a slightly quieter atmosphere. *OPEN pub hrs.*

Club Copa   1 G 5

180 Earl's Court Rd SW5. 01-373 3407. Men only, lively, atmospheric disco and bars venue. One of the most popular in south west London. *OPEN to 02.00 Mon-Sat.*

The Drum (at the Pied Bull) 3 D 32

1 Liverpool Rd N1. 01-837 3218. Very popular women's venue with good dancefloor, lights and quieter space for talking. Women only *20.00-01.00 Thur.*

Heaven   5 K 22

The Arches, Villiers St WC2. 01-839 3852. Stark and imaginative hi-tech decor. Fantastic lighting system in the downstairs

disco. Upstairs a more relaxed atmosphere centred around an octagonal bar. Dancing every night *from 22.00. OPEN to 04.00 Tue-Sat.*

London Apprentice   6 J 32

333 Old St EC1. 01-739 5577. Two large bars, plus dancefloor, pool tables, videos, atmospheric lighting. Predominantly gay male crowd. *OPEN to 02.00 Mon-Thur, to 03.00 Fri & Sat, to 24.00 Sun.*

Madame Jo Jo   2 I 21

8-10 Brewer St W1. 01-734 2473. Camp, comfortable and fun transvestite venue where everyone has a good time. Drag acts and cabaret *24.00 & 01.30. OPEN to 03.00 Mon-Sat.*

Roy's Restaurant   4 K 6

206 Fulham Rd SW10. 01-352 6828. Reputedly London's best gay restaurant. Very lively with frequent live entertainment – and entertaining waiters. Good, mainly English, food. *OPEN to 23.30 Mon-Sat, to 23.00 Sun.*

Sex and sleaze

Owing to new licensing laws, the number of legal strip clubs in Soho, the once notorious red-light area of London, has fallen considerably. The unwary punter should, however, be aware of the sex shops, hostess bars and peep shows where he will see little and lose a lot of money. The hostess bars are not licensed to serve alcohol so you may pay far too much for a fizzy drink, and most of the peep and bed shows have suffered under the new licensing laws and either exist illegally or provide a long and expensive wait for what may finally prove to be a fully-clothed show! The remaining licensed clubs are listed below.

Carnival   2 I 22

12 Old Compton St W1. 01-437 8337. Continuous performances *12.00-23.00 Mon-Sat.*

Raymond Revuebar   2 I 21

Walkers Ct, off Brewer St W1. 01-734 1593. Considered the most 'respectable' of its kind and the source of many a magazine feature. Performances at *20.00 & 22.00 Mon-Sat.*

Sunset Strip   2 H 22

30a Dean St W1. 01-437 7229. Continuous strip shows *12.30-23.00 Mon-Sat.*

Theatres, cinemas, music and poetry

Theatre ticket agencies

Will book tickets for all occasions – but remember they charge a commission. List of current theatre, cinema, dance and music programmes can be found in the daily papers, Time Out, City Limits *and* What's On & Where to Go. *Further theatre ticket agencies in Yellow Pages.*

For further details of all arts events in London see Nicholson's Arts and Cultural Guide.

H. J. Adams   2 **B** 18
1 Melcombe St NW1. 01-935 3883. Credit card line.

Thomas Cook   2 **I** 18
45 Berkeley St W1. 01-499 4000. Main office.

Fenchurch Booking Agency   6 **O** 26
94 Southwark St SE1. 01-928 8585. Head office.

Fringe Box Office   5 **J** 22
Duke of York's Theatre, St Martin's La WC2. 01-379 6002.

Keith Prowse   3 **F** 23
Banda House, Cambridge Gro W6. 01-741 7441. Head office (administrative centre). Bookings 01-741 9999.

Society of West End Theatre 5 **J** 22
Half-Price Ticket Booth
Leicester Sq WC2. Unsold tickets at half-price on the day of performance from this red, white and blue pavilion opposite the Swiss Centre.

Ticketmaster UK Ltd   5 **J** 22
78 St Martin's La WC2. 01-379 4444.

Theatres

The tradition of live theatre in London has flourished for more than four centuries, since the first regular playhouse – aptly named the Theatre – went up in Shoreditch in 1576. A penny bought standing room in the circular roofless building; tuppence included a stool for 'quiet standing'. Mar-lowe's Tamburlaine *electrified audiences with its new style of 'great and thundering speech'. During a performance of Dr Faustus the Theatre actually cracked. In 1597 bankruptcy (due to inflation) set in and the building's timber and materials were transported across the river to become the Globe, made famous by Shakespeare. The Drury Lane, where Pepys caught cold from draughts in 1663, still stands on its original site despite fire, plague and World War II bombs. Covent Garden, built in 1732, and the Haymarket, 1721, are national monuments, while the number and quality of theatre people and stageworks – from Garrick to Frohman, from Nell Gwyn to Bernhardt, from Sheridan to Shaw, from Chaplin to the Ballet Rambert – that made London theatre renowned has never been equalled. Government subsidies during and after World War II sustained this tradition which partly gave way in the 70s to sex, farce and formula: the West End's answer to inflation. Subsidised companies such as the National and the Royal Shakespeare continue to stage quality productions in the 1980s including new plays, revivals, Shakespeare and large-scale musicals. The Theatre of Comedy Company, formed in 1982, has also made a significant contribution to the nature of West End theatre during the 80s with its nucleus of leading actors, actresses, writers and directors presenting limited seasons of high-quality comedies. Fringe theatre adds an alternative – and usually less expensive – source of vitality, providing opportunities for new talent and new ideas.*

See 'Theatres & Cinemas Map'.

Adelphi   6 **K** 23
Strand WC2. 01-836 7611. Musicals including Me and My Girl.

Albery   5 **J** 22
St Martin's La WC2. 01-836 3878. Originally the New Theatre. Renamed 1973. Musicals, comedy and drama.

Aldwych   6 **J** 24
Aldwych WC2. 01-836 6404. Former London home of the RSC. Offers a varied programme of plays, comedies and musicals.

Ambassadors   2 **I** 22
West St WC2. 01-836 6111. Small theatre. Original home of *The Mousetrap*.

Ambassadors

Apollo   2 **I** 21
Shaftesbury Av W1. 01-437 2663. Old tradition of musical comedy. Now presents varied productions, including musicals, comedy and drama.

Apollo Victoria   5 **M** 16
17 Wilton Rd SW1. 01-828 8665. Auditorium completely transformed to accommodate the hit rollerskating railway musical *Starlight Express*.

Barbican   6 **K** 30
Barbican Centre, Barbican EC2. 01-638 8891. Purpose-built for the Royal Shakespeare Company; main auditorium for large-scale productions in repertory and The Pit, a smaller studio theatre, where mainly new work is performed.

Comedy   5 **J** 21
Panton St SW1. 01-930 2578. Good intimate theatre showing unusual comedy and small-cast plays.

Criterion   2 **I** 18
Piccadilly Circus W1. 01-930 3216. A listed building and the only theatre in London with the auditorium completely underground. Descend to the Upper Circle through the Victorian tiled lobby. Small, comfortable theatre. Plays, revues and comedies are among its productions.

Drury Lane (Theatre Royal)   6 **J** 24
Catherine St WC2. 01-836 8108. Operated under Royal charter by Thomas Killigrew in 1663 and has been burnt or pulled down and rebuilt 4 times. Nell Gwyn was an actress here and Orange Moll sold her oranges. Garrick, Mrs Siddons, Kean and others played here. General policy now is vast productions of musical plays.

Duchess   6 **J** 24
Catherine St WC2. 01-836 8243. Opened 1929. Plays, serious drama, light comedy and musicals.

Duke of York's   5 **J** 22
St Martin's La WC2. 01-836 5122. Built by 'Mad (Violet) Melnotte' in 1892. Associated with names like Frohman, G. B. Shaw, Granville Barker, Chaplin and the Ballet Rambert. Refurbished by the present owners, Capital Radio, for major productions.

Duke of York's

Fortune   6 **J** 24
Russell St WC2. 01-836 2238. Small compared with its neighbour, Drury Lane. Intimate revues (Peter Cook and Dudley Moore shot to fame here in *Beyond the Fringe*), musicals and modern drama.

Garrick   2 **I** 22
Charing Cross Rd WC2. 01-379 6107. Built 1897. Notable managers included Bourchier and Jack Buchanan. Varied bills.

Garrick

Globe   2 **I** 21
Shaftesbury Av W1. 01-437 3667. A wide variety of successful plays and comedies. The third theatre of this name in London.

Globe

Greenwich Theatre
Crooms Hill SE10. 01-858 7755. Stages a season of eight plays annually including new works, revivals and classics, often with famous names in the cast. Bar and restaurant.

Haymarket

Haymarket (Theatre Royal)   5 **J** 21
Haymarket SWI. 01-930 9832. Originally built in 1721 as the little Theatre in the Hay it became Royal 50 years later. The present theatre was built by Nash in 1821 and is sometimes enlivened by the ghost of Mr Buckstone, Queen Victoria's favourite actor-manager. He no doubt approves of the policy to present plays of quality.

Her Majesty's

Her Majesty's   5 **J** 21
Haymarket SWI. 01-839 2244. A fine Victorian baroque theatre founded by Beerbohm Tree. Successes include *West Side Story, Fiddler on the Roof* and *Amadeus.*

London Palladium   2 **G** 20
8 Argyll St WI. 01-437 7373. Second in size to the Coliseum; houses top variety shows and the annual Royal Command Performance.

Lyric   2 **I** 21
Shaftesbury Av WI. 01-437 3686. Oldest theatre in Shaftesbury Av (built 1888). Eleonora Duse, Sarah Bernhardt, Owen Nares and Tallulah Bankhead all had long runs here. Plays.

Lyric

Lyric Hammersmith
King St W6. 01-741 2311. Rebuilt and restored to original Victorian splendour inside modern shell. Also studio theatre. Spacious foyers, bar, restaurant and terrace. Wide-ranging productions.

Mayfair   2 **I** 18
Stratton St WI. 01-629 3036. In the May Fair Hotel. A luxurious but very small theatre, which limits the type of plays which can be performed here. *The Business of Murder* ran for eight years.

Mermaid   6 **M** 27
Puddle Dock, Blackfriars EC4. 01-236 5568. Renovated and reopened 1981. Plays and musicals. Restaurant; two bars overlooking the Thames.

National Theatre   6 **M** 24
South Bank SEI. Box office 01-928 2252. Complex of three theatres, Olivier, Lyttelton and Cottesloe. Home of the National Theatre Company. Stages a wide mixture of plays in repertory, including new works, revivals, Shakespeare and musicals. Also foyer entertainment, bookstall, and tours of the building including backstage and workshops. Restaurants, bars, exhibitions. *OPEN 10.00-23.30 Mon-Sat. CLOSED Sun.*

New London Theatre   3 **I** 24
Drury La WC2. 01-405 0072. Can convert from a 900-seat conventional theatre to an intimate theatre-in-the-round within minutes. Opened 1972 on the site of the old Winter Gardens. The hit musical *Cats* is well-established here.

Old Vic   6 **O** 24
Waterloo Rd SEI. 01-928 7616. Built 1818. For a long time the home of the National Theatre Company, then housed the Prospect Theatre Company. It now shows plays and musicals amid recreated Victorian decor.

Palace   2 **I** 22
Shaftesbury Av WI. 01-434 0909. Listed building. Originally intended by D'Oyly Carte to be the Royal English Opera House but eventually became the Palace Theatre of Varieties. Staged performances by Pavlova and Nijinski. Became a musical comedy house in the 20s and still is,

Palace

although occasional plays are staged. Housed longest running musical in British theatre history – *Jesus Christ Superstar*.

Phoenix 2 **I** 22
Charing Cross Rd WC2. 01-836 2294. A large theatre showing comedies, plays and musicals.

Piccadilly 2 **I** 21
Denman St W1. 01-437 4506. A pre-war theatre which showed the first season of 'Talkies' in Britain. A varied post-war history of light comedy, plays and musicals. Many RSC productions staged here. Transformed into a cabaret theatre 1983.

Playhouse 5 **K** 22
Northumberland Av WC2. 01-839 4401. Edwardian theatre used as a BBC studio and then closed in 1975. Restored to former glory and reopened in late 1987. Seats 800. Stages musicals, serious drama and comedies.

Prince Edward 2 **I** 22
Old Compton St W1. 01-734 8951. Started life as a cabaret spot called the London Casino in 1936 and has also been a cinema. Now a large theatre where musicals are staged, including the hit show *Evita* which ran for 2900 performances.

Prince of Wales 2 **I** 21
Coventry St W1. 01-839 5989. Rebuilt 1937, this large, modern theatre has housed many musicals.

Queen's 2 **I** 21
Shaftesbury Av W1. 01-734 1166. Very successful between wars. Still presents good drama and varied productions. Wheelchair accommodation by prior arrangement.

Royal Court 5 **L** 12
Sloane Sq SW1. 01-730 1745. Home of the English Stage Company which produces many major experimental plays.

St Martin's 2 **I** 22
West St WC2. 01-836 1443. Intimate playhouse with unusual polished teak doors. *The Mousetrap* continues its record run here having transferred from the Ambassadors, its original home.

Savoy 6 **K** 23
Strand WC2. 01-836 8888. Entrance is in the forecourt of the Savoy hotel. It was the first London theatre to be fully electrically lit and fireproofed. Produces a variety of plays, comedies and musicals.

Shaftesbury 2 **I** 21
Shaftesbury Av WC2. 01-379 5399. Permanent base of the Theatre of Comedy Company.

Strand 6 **J** 24
Aldwych WC2. 01-836 2660. Large theatre presenting a mixture of straight plays, comedies and musicals.

Vaudeville 6 **K** 23
Strand WC2. 01-836 9987. Listed building which originally ran farce and burlesque (hence the name), then became 'straight' (which for the most part it remains).

Vaudeville

Victoria Palace 5 **L** 16
Victoria St SW1. 01-834 1317. Musicals, variety shows and plays. Once home of the Crazy Gang and the Black and White Minstrel Show.

Westminster 5 **L** 17
Palace St SW1. 01-834 0283. Arts centre opened in 1931, but now a general theatre. Plays and musicals and the occasional schools workshop when there are children's programmes. Snackbar on performance evenings. Some facilities for the disabled.

Whitehall 5 **K** 12
14 Whitehall SW1. 01-930 7765. Closed down in 1983; reopened in 1986 with the interior restored to its full art deco splendour. Now one of the Wyndham Theatres group staging varied productions.

Wyndham's 2 **I** 22
Charing Cross Rd WC2. 01-836 3028. Small, pretty and successful theatre founded by Sir Charles Wyndham, the famous actor-manager. Edgar Wallace was a manager for a while. Plays, comedy and musicals.

Arts centres

Many of these have appeared in London over the last decade. They put on shows – theatre, music, dance – usually have workshop facilities and give classes in a variety of arts skills.

Africa Centre 6 **J** 23
38 King St WC2. 01-836 1973. Courses in African languages, dance and politics. Library, art gallery, exhibition space, bookshop. Hall for film shows, plays, dance or music performances by travelling companies. Restaurant and bar.

Tom Allen Centre

Grove Crescent Rd E15. 01-555 7289. East End community arts centre with cinema, theatre, exhibition space and workshops (including workshops for disabled people and women's workshops) on the current exhibitions, drama, dance and music. Café and bar.

Barbican   6 **K 30**

Barbican Centre, Barbican EC2. 01-638 8891. No workshops or classes, but plenty of entertainment. A concert hall, two theatres, three cinemas, a public library, an art gallery and sculpture court. Two restaurants.

Battersea Arts Centre

Old Town Hall, Lavender Hill SW11. 01-223 6557. A lively, informal community arts centre. A theatre, small cinema, gallery and bookshop. Dance studio, dark rooms and café. Variety of classes and workshops.

Brentford Watermans Arts Centre

40 High St, Brentford, Middx. 01-568 1176. Broad range of arts activities and entertainment. Theatre, cinema and exhibition gallery. Studio where youth drama and dancing classes are held. Bar and self-service restaurant overlooking the river.

Commonwealth Institute   I **D 5**

230 Kensington High St W8. 01-603 4535. Showplace for the cultural and economic life of the Commonwealth with exhibition galleries, art gallery, library, resource centre and separate arts centre where music, dance, drama and films are on offer regularly. Bookshop, giftshop and restaurant. Occasional festivals and carnivals.

Drill Hall Arts Centre   3 **F 23**

16 Chenies St WC1. 01-637 8270. Extensive fringe programme of drama, cabaret, live music and opera. Drama and dance workshops; photography courses and darkrooms available. Popular with feminist companies. *Women-only night Mon, free crèche facilities Mon, Fri & Sat eves.* Bar and restaurant.

**Institute of Contemporary   5 K 21
Arts (ICA)**

Nash House, The Mall SW1. 01-930 3647. A good range of arts entertainment. Three galleries, theatre, two cinemas, seminar-room for lectures and talks, video reference library, arts bookshop, bar and restaurant. Membership available on daily basis.

Oval House

54 Kennington Oval SE11. 01-735 2786. Two theatres for fringe and experimental work. Workshops and classes in theatre, dance, mime, tai-chi and photography. Holi-day projects for children. Coffee bar and restaurant.

Riverside Studios

Crisp Rd W6. 01-748 3354. Mixture of events – theatre, dance, films, visual arts and all kinds of music. Classes in contemporary dance. Workshops, lectures, discussions. Gallery with varied exhibitions. Bar and restaurant serving excellent food. *CLOSED Mon.*

South Bank Arts Complex   6 M 23

South Bank SE1. Consists of National Theatre (01-928 2252), the Royal Festival Hall (01-928 3191), the Queen Elizabeth Hall (01-928 3191), the Purcell Room (01-928 3191), the Hayward Gallery (01-928 3144), the National Film Theatre (01-928 3232) and the Museum of the Moving Image (01-928 3535). See separate entries in relevant sections.

Fringe, pub & experimental theatre

The best weekly listings are in Time Out. *Tickets for many of London's fringe venues are available from the Fringe Box Office, Duke of York's Theatre, St Martin's La WC2* (5 **J 22**). 01-379 6002. *Many fringe theatres are clubs. If membership (M) is necessary it can be bought before the performance.*

Almeida

Almeida St N1. 01-359 4404. Best known for international contemporary dance, theatre and music work.

Arts Theatre   2 **I 22**

6 Great Newport St WC2. 01-836 3334. A 340-seat theatre showing plays for adults, performed by touring companies, in the evening and performances by the Unicorn Theatre for Children which has programmes at *10.30 & 14.00 Tue-Fri* for schools, and for general public at *14.30 Sat & Sun.* Lounge and vegetarian snackbar.

Bloomsbury   3 **E 24**

15 Gordon St WC1. 01-387 9629. Owned by University College, London and used by the students 12 weeks a year. International plays, dance, cabaret and opera.

Bush Theatre

Above a large, busy pub. Shepherds Bush Grn W12. 01-743 3388. Première performances of British and international plays, some of which transfer to the West End. (M)

Canal Café Theatre

Bridge House, Delamere Ter W2. 01-289 6054. Lively, friendly upstairs theatre restaurant. Flexible programme of plays or cabaret and late-night satirical review. Ring for details. Good, simple blackboard menu; changes daily. All-inclusive price for complete evening or separate dinner and either show.

Cockpit Theatre
Gateforth St NW8. 01-402 5081. Fringe theatre venue for professional and amateur companies with a modern theatre-in-the-round which is also adaptable to other forms of staging. Weekly shows of drama, music and experimental theatre. Mainly young companies giving first performances.

Cottesloe   6 M 24
National Theatre, South Bank SE1. 01-928 2252. Based on a Shakespearian theatre with a pit and two galleries, it is the experimental section of the NT and stages new productions.

Donmar Warehouse   3 I 23
41 Earlham St WC2. 01-379 6565. 240-seat theatre which welcomes touring companies and mounts its own productions. Diverse productions from future West End hits to satirical late-night cabaret and concerts.

Half Moon
213 Mile End Rd E1. 01-790 4000. The theatre seats 400, with a bar and a restaurant. Musical, political and popular plays.

Hampstead Theatre
Swiss Cottage Centre, Avenue Rd NW3. 01-722 9301. Dedicated to the presentation of new plays and the encouragement of new writers. Productions change every six to eight weeks. Bar and snacks. (M)

Jeannetta Cochrane   3 H 25
Theatre
Southampton Row WC1. 01-242 7040. Central School of Art and Design uses the facilities during termtime. During vacations productions are staged by such companies as the National Youth Theatre, National Youth Music Theatre, PATH (Practical Arts & Theatre with the Handicapped), Royal College of Music and the Old Vic Youth Theatre.

King's Head Theatre Club   3 D 33
115 Upper St N1. 01-226 1916. Pub with a theatre at the back. You can have a meal before the show starts and stay at your table for the performance. One of London's leading fringe theatres with many West End transfers. Encourages new work but also performs revivals. Lunchtime and evening shows. (M)

Latchmere Theatre   4 R 6
503 Battersea Park Rd SW11. 01-228

2620. Recently refurbished. Varied programme of plays and cabaret. Evening performances *Mon-Sat.* (M)

The Man in the Moon   4 L 8
392 King's Rd SW3. 01-351 2876. Successful fringe theatre that performs lots of new plays or revives old plays that haven't been performed for some time. *CLOSED Mon.*

Offstage Downstairs
37 Chalk Farm Rd NW1. 01-267 9649. Basement theatre below a performing arts bookshop. Accent on good-quality new plays. *CLOSED Mon.* (M)

Orange Tree
45 Kew Rd, Richmond, Surrey. 01-940 3633. Highly successful fringe theatre above an early Victorian pub. Wide range of plays often featuring local writers and performers. *Evenings Sep-Apr.* In the summer there are shows for children and theatre studies for post O and A level students. Some lunchtime shows *Jul & Aug.*

Players'   6 J 24
c/o Duchess Theatre, Catherine St WC2. 01-839 1134. Last stand of the Victorian music-hall tradition in this successful private theatre. Drinks and sandwiches served during the show and there is a restaurant. (M) *only, but temporary membership available in advance of booking date. Apply 48hrs in advance. CLOSED Mon.*

Soho Poly Theatre Club   2 F 21
16 Riding House St W1. Small basement performance space launching new work by new writers (including the work of the winner of the Verity Bargate award for a new and unperformed play). Writers' workshops throughout the year. Light snacks available.

Theatre Royal Stratford East
Gerry Raffles Sq E15. 01-534 0310. Joan Littlewood's brainchild; has its own company which stages new plays and musicals. Bar and snack bar.

Theatre Upstairs   5 L 12
Royal Court Theatre, Sloane Sq SW1. 01-730 2554. New plays and playwrights in a small studio space above the main theatre.

Tramshed Theatre
51 Woolwich New Rd SE18. 01-317 1495. Housed, as the name suggests, in a converted tramshed. Lively venue for rock *Thur & Fri,* cabaret *Sat,* and jazz *Sun.* Bar serves food and drinks.

Tom Allen Centre
Grove Crescent Rd E15. 01-555 7289. Touring companies, workshop produc-

tions, youth theatre and films in this community arts centre.

Tricycle Theatre
269 Kilburn High Rd NW6. 01-328 8626. Well-established fringe theatre (rebuilt after a fire in 1987) where an excellent selection of new plays is performed. *Sat morning children's shows at 11.30.* Occasional *Sun concerts.* Youth theatre workshop, art gallery, restaurant and bar.

Vanbrugh   3 **F** 23
Malet St WC1. 01-580 7982. Theatre club presenting a complete range of classic and contemporary drama by RADA students. Three theatres. Members bar. (M) details from RADA, 62 Gower St WC1.

Young Vic   6 **O** 24
66 The Cut SE1. 01-928 6363. Young people's repertoire theatre mainly showing the classics and established modern plays, but also some new plays and musicals. Also Education and Community theatre and workshops.

Marionette theatre

The Little Angel   3 **D** 33
14 Dagmar Pas, Cross St N1. 01-226 1787. The first real puppet theatre in London for over 100 years. Excellent shows *15.00 daily during school holidays (5s and over).* Otherwise *15.00 Sat & Sun only,* and *11.00 Sat (3 to 5-year-olds).*

Puppet Theatre Barge
Little Venice W9. 01-249 6876. Marionette performances in a converted barge. Moored in London *Sep-Easter,* travels up the Thames as far as Oxford in summer. *Shows at 15.00 Sat, Sun & B.hols; 15.00 Mon-Fri during school holidays.* Book in advance to avoid disappointment.

Open-air theatre

Holland Park Theatre   1 **C** 5
Holland Park W8. 01-602 7856. 600-seat open-air theatre (covered by canopy) which gives performances of dance, opera and theatre *Jun-Aug.* Days and times vary so check with booking office.

Regent's Park Open-Air   2 **A** 21
Theatre
Inner Circle, Regent's Park NW1. 01-486 2431. Lovely in good weather. Plays of Shakespeare and sometimes others. *End May-Sep 19.45 Mon-Sat and 14.30 Wed, Thur & Sat.* Book in advance.

Opera, ballet and dance

English ballet lagged almost two centuries behind the Danes and Russians with the founding of the Royal Academy of Dancing in 1920. By 1930, Marie Rambert's Ballet Club had landed with some éclat on the West End stage. That same year Ninette de Valois was assembling the Sadler's Wells company up in Islington. One night in 1934 an unknown dancer stepped out of the Sadler's corps to do her first solo at the Old Vic; in 1946 that same dancer and company opened at Covent Garden to mass hysteria. Margot Fonteyn in her 40 years as a ballerina became the embodiment of British ballet history. The première of Benjamin Britten's Peter Grimes, also in 1946, marked the birth of British opera. Very shortly thereafter a permanent British opera school and orchestra was established; regular and festival seasons came into being; a string of high achievers suddenly appeared. Such composers as Walton, Tippett, Searle, Bennet and Davies provided an exciting repertory that boosted British opera onto a world-wide scale.

Coliseum   5 **J** 22
St Martin's La WC2. 01-836 3161. Largest London theatre, seating 2400. Houses the resident English National Opera *Aug-Jun,* and visiting companies during summer months.

Covent Garden   6 **J** 23
Royal Opera House, Bow St WC2. 01-240 1066. Recorded information 01-836 6903 (24hr). The world-famous Royal Ballet and Royal Opera companies maintain an international reputation.

The Place   3 **D** 25
17 Duke's Rd WC1. 01-387 0161. This 250-seat theatre is the home of the London Contemporary Dance Theatre and the London School of Contemporary Dance, an exciting and creative modern dance company. Immaculate production with interesting choreographic ideas.

Sadler's Wells   3 **G** 30
Rosebery Av EC1. 01-278 8916. Recorded information 01-278 5450. Once a spa (the original well discovered by Richard Sadler is under a trap-door at the back of the stalls). Birthplace of the English National Opera and the Royal Ballet Company. Now the home of the New Sadler's Wells Opera. Host to leading national and international ballet, dance and opera companies.

Poetry

The societies and venues listed below are well established. There are many other poetry readings and discussions on offer every week but as the venues change, new groups are formed and others fade, it is advisable to check the weekly listings in Time Out and City Limits.

Apples & Snakes
The Broadway Studio, Catford Bdwy SE6. 01-690 9368. Different programme every week performed in various pubs to make poetry more accessible to everyone. Regular meetings on *Sat* but venue changes.

City Lit 3 I 24
City Lit, Stukeley St WC2. 01-242 9872. Day and evening classes on the writing and appreciation of verse, contemporary poetry, verse speaking and poetry workshops. *Sep-May main course, Jun-Jul summer school.*

Institute of Contemporary 5 K 20
Arts (ICA)
Nash House, The Mall SW1. 01-930 3647. Occasional lectures and readings by distinguished poets followed by discussion.

Poetry Library 6 M 23
Royal Festival Hall, South Bank Centre SE1. 01-921 0644. Information on poetry competitions, workshops, day and evening classes and readings. Lists of poetry groups, magazines and bookshops are also available. New audio and video collection and special children's poetry information service.

Poetry Society I H 5
21 Earl's Court Sq SW5. 01-373 7861. Produces a quarterly journal *Poetry Review* in which both new and established poets can appear. Holds readings and discussions. Poetry bookshop.

Poetry South East London
Kidbrooke House Community Centre, 90 Mycenae Rd SE3. Contact: 01-854 4899. Poetry workshop *20.00 alternate Thur.*

Stratford Poets
Durning Hall, Earlham Gro E7. 01-555 1814. Fortnightly workshops to read and discuss the work of members and established poets. *20.00-22.00 Mon.*

Sub-Voicive 7 J 22
White Swan, New Row WC2. Contact: 01-340 6224. Fortnightly meetings in the room above the pub. Avant-garde, experimental work. *20.00 Tue.*

Troubadour Poets I I 7
Downstairs Theatre, Troubadour Coffee House, 265 Old Brompton Rd SW5. 01-874 8218. Live music and live poetry in a relaxed coffee house atmosphere. *21.00-23.00 Mon.*

Concert halls

Barbican Hall 6 K 30
Barbican Centre EC2. 01-638 6891. Base of the London Symphony Orchestra. Three one-month seasons a year. Otherwise used for visiting opera, jazz and light classical music.

Camden Centre 3 D 26
Bidborough St, rear of Camden Town Hall WC1. 01-278 4444x5000. Seats 900. Multi-purpose hall – opera, dramatics, concerts, bazaars, meetings etc.

Central Hall 5 M 19
Storeys Gate SW1. 01-222 8010. A large hall seating 2640. Organ recitals, orchestral concerts. Also used for conferences, exhibitions and meetings. Listed building – housed the first meeting of the General Assembly of the United Nations in 1946.

Conway Hall 3 H 25
Red Lion Sq WC1. 01-242 8032. Seats 550. A large hall, small hall and meeting rooms. Chamber music (*Sun eve Oct-Apr*), concerts, meetings, rehearsals and recordings. Acoustic ceiling especially designed for quartets.

Old Town Hall
Haverstock Hill NW3. 01-278 4444x2441. Seats 300. Multi-purpose hall, housing concerts, meetings and other events.

Purcell Room 6 M 23
South Bank SE1. 01-928 3191. Smallest of the three South Bank concert halls so ideal for chamber music and solo concerts.

Queen Elizabeth Hall 6 M 23
South Bank SE1. 01-928 3191. Shares foyer with Purcell Room. Orchestral and choral works, chamber music and recitals. Also film shows.

Royal Albert Hall I F 10
Kensington Gore SW7. 01-589 8212. Victorian domed hall named after Prince Albert, built 1871. Orchestral, choral, pop concerts, sporting events and public meetings. Famous for the 'Proms'.

Royal Albert Hall

Royal College of Music | G 10
Prince Consort Rd SW7. 01-589 3643. Chamber, orchestral and choral concerts plus operas performed by the students in their own theatre (*termtime only*). High standard. Also museum *OPEN (by appt only to parties) 11.00-16.30 Mon & Wed (termtime only).*

Royal Festival Hall   6 M 23
South Bank· SE1. 01-928 3191. General information on events 01-928 3002. Built in 1951 for the Festival of Britain. Seats 3000. Orchestral and choral concerts. *Foyer music 12.30-14.00 Mon-Sun & 17.15-18.15 Fri.* Stages ballet in summer and at Xmas. Forms the South Bank Arts Centre with the Queen Elizabeth Hall, Purcell Room, National Film Theatre, Hayward Gallery, the National Theatre and the Museum of the Moving Image.

St John's   5 O 19
Smith Sq SW1. 01-222 1061. Unique 18thC church whose appearance has been likened to an upside-down footstool. Regular lunchtime and evening concerts. Solo recitals, chamber, orchestral and choral works. Seats approx 800. Restaurant. Art exhibitions held in the crypt.

Wigmore Hall   2 E 19
36 Wigmore St W1. 01-935 2141. Seats 540. Instrumental, song, chamber music and chamber orchestral recitals. Fine acoustics for chamber music and solo recitals. Popular Coffee Concerts *11.30 Sun.* Intimate atmosphere.

Cinemas

Cinema came to Britain before World War I and became so popular that moralists feared for the future of church attendance and novel reading. Picture palaces sprung up everywhere in the 20s. The ornate, gilded buildings with huge chandeliers, elaborate ceilings and luxurious carpets certainly lived up to their name at first but were gradually reclassified by the audience as 'flea pits' and 'dumps'. With the advent of television after World War II it seemed there would be no need for cinemas and many did close down or become bingo halls. However, in the 70s the cinema was saved from economic collapse by the development of complexes whereby one large cinema became at least two smaller ones, each showing a different new release. These cinemas have even survived videos. There has been increasing interest in foreign, experimental and classical films

and these audiences are catered for by specialist organisations like the National Film Theatre and the Institute of Contemporary Arts, but also by cinemas which present 'alternative', rather than 'blockbuster/commercial' films.
The main central London cinemas are listed below. For current programmes see the Evening Standard, Time Out or City Limits. Alternatively telephone the cinemas, many of which have 24hr answering services giving details of programmes. See local papers for suburban programmes. All cinemas show general new release films unless otherwise indicated. (M) = membership.

Astral   2 I 21
3-7 Brewer St W1. 01-734 6387. Censored sex films.

Barbican   6 K 30
Barbican Centre EC2. 01-638 8891. Cinema 1 shows general current releases, 2 repertory and 3 is usually used for conferences.

Camden Plaza
211 Camden High St NW1. 01-485 2443. Quality films.

Cannon 1 & 2 Baker Street   2 B 19
Station Approach, Marylebone Rd NW1. 01-935 9772. Two modern cinemas adjacent to Baker St tube station. *Late shows 23.00 Fri & Sat.*

Cannon Bayswater 1, 2 & 3   2 A 12
89 Bishop's Bridge Rd W2. 01-229 4149. Long-running films and new releases. *Late shows 23.15 Fri & Sat.*

Cannon Chelsea 1, 2, 3 & 4   4 L 4
279 King's Rd SW3. 01-352 5096.

Cannon Fulham Road 1, 2,   4 K 6
3, 4 & 5
Fulham Rd SW10. 01-370 2636.

Cannon Hampstead 1, 2 & 3
Pond St NW3. 01-794 4000. Three screens showing new releases. *Late shows 23.00 Fri & Sat (when one screen shows double feature revival).*

Cannon Haymarket 1, 2 & 3   5 J 21
Haymarket SW1. 01-839 1527. Three screens showing long-running British and American releases and new releases. *Late shows 23.15 Fri & Sat.*

Cannon Oxford Street 1, 2, 3,   2 G 21
4 & 5
Oxford St W1. 01-636 0310. Five cinemas. *Late shows 23.15 Fri & Sat.*

Cannon Panton Street 1, 2, 3   5 J 21
& 4
Panton St SW1. 01-930 0631. Four small cinemas under one roof showing long-running and very new releases.

Cannon Piccadilly 2 I 20
215-217 Piccadilly W1. 01-437 3561. *Late shows 23.15 Fri & Sat.*

Cannon Premiere 2 I 22
Swiss Centre, Leicester Sq WC2. 01-439 4470. Complex of four cinemas.

Cannon Royal 2 I 22
35-37 Charing Cross Rd WC2. 01-930 6915. *Late shows 23.15 Fri & Sat.*

Cannon Shaftesbury 3 I 23
Avenue 1 & 2
135 Shaftesbury Av W1. 01-836 8861.

Cannon Tottenham Court 3 F 23
Road 1, 2 & 3
Tottenham Court Rd W1. 01-636 6148. *Late shows 23.15 Fri & Sat.*

Chelsea Cinema 4 L 4
King's Rd SW3. 01-351 3742. Good films, spacious seating.

Coronet Cinema I A 8
Notting Hill Gate W11. 01-727 6705. *Late night show 23.00 Sat.*

Curzon Mayfair 2 I 17
Curzon St W1. 01-499 3737. Specially selected new films in very plush surroundings.

Curzon Phoenix 2 I 21
Phoenix Theatre, Charing Cross Rd WC2. 01-240 9661. Under same management as Curzon Mayfair and showing a similar selection of films.

Curzon West End 2 I 22
93 Shaftesbury Av W1. 01-439 4805. Formerly the Columbia; now under the same management as the Curzon Mayfair and showing a similar selection of films.

Empire 1, 2 & 3 5 J 22
Leicester Sq WC2. 01-200 0200. Bookable first releases in cavernous 'movie palace'. Adjustable seats, perfect vision, Dolby stereo. *Late shows 23.30 Fri & Sat.*

Everyman
Holly Bush Vale NW3. 01-435 1525. Weekly classic revivals.

Gate Cinema I A 8
Notting Hill Gate W11. 01-727 4043. Quality art films. Adventurous and interesting selection. *Late shows 23.15 Fri & Sat.*

ICA 5 K 19
Nash House, The Mall SW1. 01-930 3647. Two cinemas with bookable seats. Films by contemporary directors. Also seasons of foreign and unusual theme films. Day, associate or full (M) on-the-spot.

Leicester Square Theatre 5 J 22
Leicester Sq WC2. 01-930 5252. Preserved exterior with completely modernised interior. Built by Jack Buchanan – licensed bar named after him. New releases. *Late shows 23.45 Fri & Sat.*

Lumière 5 J 22
St Martin's La WC2. 01-836 0691. Première-release cinema. Interesting programmes. *Late shows 23.15 Fri & Sat.*

Metro 1 & 2 2 I 21
11 Rupert St W1. 01-437 0757. New independent cinema showing first-run films.

Minema 2 I 14
45 Knightsbridge SW1. 01-235 4225. Intimate cinema showing modern classics. Available for private hire.

Moulin 1, 2, 3, 4 & 5 2 I 21
43 Great Windmill St, Piccadilly Circus W1. 01-437 1653. Sex films.

Museum of London 6 L 30
London Wall EC2. 01-600 3699. Two seasons annually of film archive material called the 'Made in London' series. Seasons run *Apr-Jul & Sep-Dec.*

National Film Theatre 6 M 24
South Bank SE1. 01-928 3232. Shows rare foreign films, revivals of classics and seasons of notable directors' works. Serious museum studies of styles, stars, retrospectives and movie history. London Film Festival *each Nov.* Two cinemas. Weekend junior programmes. (M)

Odeon Haymarket 2 H 21
Haymarket SW1. 01-839 7697. Mainly new releases but also revivals in separate performances. *Late shows 23.30 Fri & Sat.*

Odeon Kensington High I D 4
Street 1, 2, 3 & 4
Kensington High St W8. 01-602 6644. *Late show 23.15 Sat.*

Odeon Leicester Square 5 J 22
Leicester Sq WC2. 01-930 6111. *Late shows 23.45 Fri & Sat.*

Odeon Marble Arch 2 E 16
Marble Arch W2. 01-723 2011. Claimed to be the most advanced cinema in Britain, with closed circuit TV. Premières and 'U' film blockbusters.

Odeon Swiss Cottage 1, 2 & 3
Finchley Rd NW3. 01-722 5905.

Phoenix
High Rd N2. 01-883 2233. Mixed programme of classics and popular films. *Late shows 22.45 Fri & Sat.*

Plaza 1, 2, 3 & 4 5 J 20
Lower Regent St W1. 01-200 0200. Varied programmes – often first releases. *Late shows 23.45 Fri & Sat.*

Prince Charles 5 J 22
Leicester Pl, Leicester Sq WC2. 01-437 8181. Small cinema. Latest releases. *Late shows 23.15 Fri & Sat.*

Renoir 1 & 2 3 F 28
Brunswick Sq WC1. 01-837 8402. Formerly the Gate Bloomsbury, now redesigned

and refurbished. Quality films, some sub-titled.

Rio
Kingsland High St E8. 01-254 6677. Mixed programme. *Late show 23.15 Sat.*

Ritzy Cinema Club
Brixton Rd SW2. 01-737 2121. Repertory of double bills. *Late shows 23.15 Fri & Sat.* (M)

Riverside Studios
Crisp Rd W6. 01-748 3354. Mixed pro-gramme. Often have themes to coincide with Studio theatre productions.

Scala
275-277 Pentonville Rd N1. 01-278 0051. Ever-changing repertory of double bills plus Scala Cinema Club (01-278 8052) *all-night show 23.30 Sat.* (M)

Screen on Baker Street 1 & 2   **2 D 18**
96 Baker St NW1. 01-935 2772. *Late shows 23.15 Fri & Sat.*

Screen on the Green   **3 E 32**
Islington Grn, Upper St N1. 01-226 3520. Usually first-run films. Occasional double-bills. *Late shows 23.15 Fri & Sat.*

Screen on the Hill
203 Haverstock Hill NW3. 01-435 3366. Usually shows quality films not on general release. *Late shows 23.15 Fri & Sat.*

Warner West End 1, 2, 3,   **5 J 22**
4 & 5
Leicester Sq WC2. 01-439 0791. *Late shows 23.10 Fri & Sat.*

Radio and TV shows

Free tickets obtainable. Write enclosing stamped addressed envelope and prefer-ence of programme.

BBC Radio & Television   **2 E 20**
Ticket Unit, Broadcasting House, Portland Pl W1.

London Weekend Television   **6 M 24**
Kent House, Upper Ground SE1. 01-261 3434.

Thames Television   **2 D 22**
Ticket Unit, 306 Euston Rd NW1.

Church music

The following churches generally have above average choirs or organists.
All Hallows-by-the-Tower, Byward St EC3; All Saints, Margaret St W1; All Souls, Langham Pl W1; Bloomsbury Central,

Shaftesbury Av WC2; Brompton Oratory, Brompton Rd SW7; Central Hall, Storey's Gate SW1; St Botolph St, Aldgate High St EC3; St Bride, Fleet St EC4; St Giles Cripplegate, Fore St EC2; St James, Spanish Pl W1; St Lawrence Jewry, Gresham St EC2; St Martin-in-the-Fields, Trafalgar Sq WC2; St Mary the Virgin, Bourne St SW1; St Michael-upon-Cornhill, Cornhill EC3; St Paul's Cathedral, Ludgate Hill EC4; Southwark Cathedral, London Bridge SE1; Westminster Abbey, Broad Sanctuary SW1; Westminster Cathedral, Ashley Pl SW1.

Lunchtime concerts

Mostly held in the City churches at lunchtime Mon-Fri for the office worker. Chamber music, choral music, violin, piano and organ recitals. The interiors of the churches are also rewarding in themselves.
All Hallows-by-the-Tower   **6 Q 31**
Byward St EC3. 01-481 2928. Mainly clas-sical hi-fi recordings *13.00 Mon.* Organ reci-tals by Prof Gordon Phillips *12.15 and 13.15 Thur. Free.*

Bishopsgate Institute   **6 N 33**
230 Bishopsgate EC2. 01-247 6844. Clas-sical and chamber music. *13.05 Tue Jan-end Apr.* One week during City of London July Festival and autumn season. *Free.*

St Bride   **6 L 27**
Fleet St EC4. 01-353 1301. Organ recitals *13.15 Wed.* Song, piano or chamber recitals Tue & Fri *13.15.* During City of London July Festival recitals every lunchtime except Sun. *Free.*

St John's   **5 O 19**
Smith Sq SW1. 01-222 1061. Solo recitals and chamber music in unique 18thC church. *13.00 Mon (for BBC Radio broad-cast) & 13.15 alt Thur* in the crypt. Concerts most eves (phone for details). Restaurant and Footstool Gallery. *OPEN 11.30-14.45 Mon-Fri & during eve concerts. Charge.*

St Lawrence Jewry   **6 M 30**
Gresham St EC2. 01-600 9478. Concert pianist recitals *13.00 Mon except B.hols.* Organ recitals *13.00 Tue. Free.*

St Martin-in-the-Fields   **5 K 22**
Trafalgar Sq WC2. 01-839 1930. Wide vari-ety of classical music. *13.05 Mon & Tue. Free.*

St Mary-le-Bow   **6 M 29**
Cheapside EC2. 01-248 5139. Live clas-sical music concerts. *13.05 Thur. Free.*

St Mary Woolnoth   6 N 30
Lombard St EC3. 01-626 9701. City Singers rehearse *13.05 Mon*, and *13.05* there is a 'singers workshop' to rehearse church music. Visitors welcome. *Free.*

St Michael-upon-Cornhill   6 N 31
Cornhill EC3. 01-626 8841. Organ recitals *13.00 Mon. Free.*

St Olave   6 P 32
Hart St EC3. 01-488 4318. Lunchtime recitals of chamber music *13.05 Wed & Thur. Free.*

St Paul's Cathedral   6 M 28
Ludgate Hill EC4. 01-248 4619. Organ recitals *12.30 Fri. Free.*

St Sepulchre Without   6 K 28
Newgate
Holborn Viaduct EC1. 01-248 1660. Live recital of vocal, instrumental and organ music *13.10 Fri.* Choral service *13.10 Thur. Free.* Occasional Memorial concerts.

Southwark Cathedral   6 Q 27
Borough High St SE1. 01-407 3708. Organ recitals *13.10 Mon.* Live music recitals *13.10 Tue.* Recorded music *13.10 Thur. Free.*

Open-air music

There is a surprising variety of summertime outdoor music in London: lunchtime bands and light orchestral music in the City squares and gardens for office workers (see below for details), more serious evening concerts and old-time concert parties in famous gardens and parks, as well as country dancing demonstrations after which the audience dances too. Many of these entertainments are free, and when there is a charge, it is generally nominal. For current programmes, see Time Out *and* What's On & Where to Go.

Alexandra Park
Wood Green N22. 01-883 7173. Very enthusiastic community music programme. International music and dancing *Jun-Aug 15.00-17.00 Sun.* Mixed performances *school summer hols 14.00-15.00 Thur. Free.*

City Sites
Information from City Information Centre, St Paul's Churchyard EC4. 01-606 3030. There are often lunchtime musical events in the summer but dates and times vary so it is advisable to collect a copy of the Diary of Events, *issued monthly, for exact details.*

Finsbury Circus Gardens   6 M 32
Moorgate EC2. Lunchtime band concerts. *Free.*

Paternoster Square   6 L 28
EC4. Mostly military bands. Eat lunch at an open-air cafe and listen to the music. *Free.*

St Paul's Steps   6 M 28
St Paul's Cathedral, Ludgate Hill EC4. Delightful setting facing St Paul's. Military bands. *Free.*

Greenwich Park
SE10. 01-212 3833. Brass bands. *End May-end Aug 15.00 & 18.00-19.30 Sun & B.hols. Free.*

Holland Park   1 C 5
W11. Varied programme in the Court Theatre in the evening. *Charge.*

Hyde Park   2 H 15
W2. 01-262 5484. Military and brass bands. *End May-end Aug 15.00-16.30 & 18.00-19.30 Sun & B.hols. Free.*

Kenwood
Hampstead La NW3. Contact English Heritage 01-734 6010 for details. Lakeside symphony concerts by leading orchestras, opera, jazz and brass in fine park. *Jun-Jul 20.00 Sat.* Also recitals in the Orangery of the 18thC house. *Apr-May & Aug-Oct 19.30 Sun.* Booking 01-633 1707.

Lincoln's Inn Fields   3 I 25
WC2. Military bands entertain *some summer lunchtimes. Free.*

Marble Hill House
Richmond Rd, Twickenham, Middx. 01-734 6010. Orchestral concerts, brass bands or jazz, sometimes accompanied by fireworks. *Early Jul-early Aug 19.30 Sun. Charge.*

Regent's Park   2 B 21
NW1. 01-486 7905. Military and brass bands. *End May-end Aug 12.30-14.00 & 17.30-19.00 Mon-Sat, 15.00-16.30 & 18.00-19.30 Sun & B.hols. Free.*

St James's Park   5 L 19
SW1. 01-930 1793. Military and concert bands. *End May-end Aug 12.30-14.00 & 17.30-19.00 Mon-Sat, 15.00-16.30 & 18.00-19.30 Sun & B.hols. Free.*

Tower Place   6 Q 31
EC3. Military bands play in a modern pedestrian square with fine views of the Tower and the Thames. *Some summer lunchtimes. Free.*

Victoria Embankment   5 L 22
Gardens
Nr Embankment Tube Station WC2. Riverside setting for military bands, massed bands and light orchestras. *Some summer lunchtimes. Free.*

Sport, health and fitness

Sports centres

Britannia Leisure Centre
40 Hyde Rd N1. 01-729 4485. Large indoor centre. Squash, badminton, weight-training, table tennis, basketball, volleyball, martial arts, swimming pool with wave machine and waterfall, sauna, sunbed, spa bath. Also tennis courts (some grass), and five-a-side courts, all floodlit. Tuition in most activities, over-50s classes, activities for the disabled, clubs for children and adults. *No membership requirement. Charge.*

Brixton Recreation Centre
Brixton Station Rd SW2. 01-274 7774. Indoor sports centre. Squash, badminton, weight-training, swimming pool, bowls, sauna, solarium. Classes plus social and cultural activities. *No membership requirement. Charge (reduced rates 09.00-12.00, 14.00-16.00).*

Chelsea Sports Club   4 M 9
Chelsea Manor St SW3. 01-352 6985. Facilities for swimming, squash, badminton, table tennis, yoga, volley ball, weight-training, aerobics. Gymnasium, sauna, solarium and spa bath. *No membership requirement. Charge.*

Crystal Palace National Sports Centre
Crystal Palace SE19. 01-778 0131. Beautifully situated in Crystal Palace Park. Opened in 1964, this is the largest multi-sports centre in the country. Superb facilities for over 50 different sports include a floodlit stadium (seating 16,000 spectators), Olympic-size swimming and diving pools, a large indoor sports hall and a dry-ski slope. Important national and international events are frequently staged, including swimming, water polo, athletics and basketball events. Courses in many sports including skiing, squash and swimming. *Modest annual membership fee. Charge.*

Finsbury Leisure Centre   3 I 32
Norman St EC1. 01-253 4490. Indoor centre with facilities for football, netball, badminton, squash, weight-training, outdoor tennis, basketball, martial arts, roller-skating. Also swimming pool and Turkish bath. *No membership requirement. Charge.*

Jubilee Sports Centre
Caird St W10. 01-960 5512. Indoor facilities for most sports including tennis, cricket, martial arts, squash, swimming. *No membership requirement. Charge.*

Latchmere Sports Centre   4 R 6
Latchmere Rd SW11. 01-871 7470. Sports hall, projectile room, snooker room, multi-gym, meeting rooms, crèche and bar. Also leisure pool and activity room. *No membership requirement. Charge.*

Michael Sobell Sports Centre
Hornsey Rd N7. 01-609 2166. Large indoor centre adaptable to most sports. Classes in badminton, basketball, cricket, gymnastics, martial arts, netball, squash, table tennis, volleyball, weight-lifting and yoga. There is also an ice rink, a sauna and a baby-bounce. *Modest annual membership fee. Charge.*

Picketts Lock Centre
Picketts Lock La N9. 01-803 4756. Indoor facilities for soccer, gymnastics, badminton, basketball, hockey, netball, volleyball, martial arts, roller skating, shooting, bowls and swimming. Outdoors: soccer, hockey, tennis and golf. Tuition available in most sports. *Membership not essential. Charge.*

Queen Mother Sports   5 N 16
Centre
223 Vauxhall Bridge Rd SW1. 01-798 2125. Large indoor centre with multi-gym and swimming pool. Facilities for badminton, weight-training, squash, table tennis, martial arts, aerobics, yoga, gymnastics and short tennis for children. Tuition available for most activities. *Membership required only for squash. Charge.*

Swiss Cottage Sports Centre
Winchester Rd NW3. 01-586 5989. Indoor facilities for badminton, basketball, netball, volleyball, gymnastics, keep fit, martial arts, squash and swimming. *No membership requirement. Charge.*

Tottenham Sports Centre
703 High Rd N17. 01-801 6401. Facilities for archery, shooting, bowling, gymnastics, children's football, martial arts, table tennis, boxing, badminton, aerobics, yoga. *No membership requirement. Charge.*

YMCA: London Central   3 H 23
112 Great Russell St WC1. 01-637 8131. Indoor only. Badminton, basketball, gymnastics, martial arts, keep fit, aerobics, sub aqua, swimming, table tennis, volleyball and yoga. Also weight-training, short tennis and sunroom. *Membership necessary.*

Ticket agents: sport

Tickets are available for most events but sometimes they must be bought months in advance. Apply to the box office of the venue concerned or try:

Keith Prowse
Banda House, Cambridge Gro W6. 01-741 8955. Head office. They will give you the address of their nearest ticket agency.

Sport

London has facilities for nearly all types of sport and has a formidable number of clubs, sports grounds and associations. This list gives the main authorities, places and events not only for the spectator but also for those who want to take part. There are numerous facilities for inexpensive tuition and training; the Sports Council and ILEA run hundreds of courses all over London. For sports equipment see the 'Specialist shops & services' section.

Greater London & SE Region Sports Council
PO Box 480, Crystal Palace SE19. 01-778 8600. Answers individual enquiries about sport in the London area. Information on grants and loans, facilities and events. Runs 'Sportsline', 01-222 8000, which gives details of clubs and events in the London area.

Sports Council　　　　　　3　**E**　25
Information Centre, 16 Upper Woburn Pl WC1. 01-388 1277. Answers all kinds of enquiries about sport and physical recreation nationally and internationally. Also produces a calendar of events.

Archery

There are about 20 archery clubs in London each of which has some facilities for shooting. The County of London outdoor championships are held in Aug. Indoor championships in Feb. Numerous inter-county matches throughout the year.

County of London Archery Association
Hon Sec, Mr Miller, Flat 9/N, Peabody Av, Sutherland St SW1. 01-821 1735. For information on the sport in London.

Grand National Archery Society
National Agricultural Centre, 7th St, Stoneleigh, Kenilworth, Warks. Coventry 696631. Will supply information about archery.

Southern Counties Archery Society
Hon Gen Sec, Mr A. L. Francis, 5 Fordington Rd, Winchester, Hants. Winchester 54932. For information about archery in all the southern counties and London.

Athletics

The major events are held at Crystal Palace.

Amateur Athletics　　　　　5　**N**　16
Association
Francis House, Francis St SW1. 01-828 9326. For all information on athletics.

Badminton

All England championships at Wembley in Mar; also many other tournaments throughout the country during the year. All England junior championships held at Watford, Herts.

Badminton Association of England
National Badminton Centre, Bradwell Rd, Loughton Lodge, Milton Keynes, Bucks. Milton Keynes 568822. Gives information on local clubs, promotes all national and international events in England, and supplies a diary of events and handbook.

Ballooning

British Balloon & Airship Club
122 Fazeley St, Digbeth, Birmingham. Birmingham 643 3224. Will supply a list of clubs.

Baseball

There are National League and Southern Baseball League clubs at Sutton, Croydon, Hendon, Purfleet and Wokingham.

Basketball

Championship play-offs take place at Wembley, which also hosts the occasional visit by the internationally-renowned Harlem Globetrotters.

English Basketball Association
Calomax House, Lupton Av, Leeds, W. Yorks. Leeds 496044. Will supply a club list.

Billiards & snooker

Over 300 clubs in London and a variety of leagues and competitions.

Billiards and Snooker Control Council
Coronet House, Queen St, Leeds, W.
Yorks. Leeds 440586. For information on
clubs and events.

Bowls

*National championships held at Beach
House Park, Worthing, W. Sussex in Aug.
Public greens in Battersea Park, Finsbury
Park, and many other London parks.*
English Bowling Association
The Secretary, Lyndhurst Rd, Worthing, W.
Sussex. Worthing 820222. For information.

Boxing

*ABA championships held in May. Bouts
take place at Wembley and the Royal
Albert Hall. For detailed listings, consult
Boxing News.*
**British Boxing Board of   5 N 16
Control**
70 Vauxhall Bridge Rd SWI. 01-828 2133.
Controls and administers professional box-
ing.
**London Amateur Boxing   6 O 26
Association**
Suite 68, Hop Exchange, Southwark St
SEI. 01-407 2194. Supplies a list of London
clubs.

Canoeing

*Various suitable rivers such as the
Thames, Kennet, Wey, Medway, Rother
and Stour – all within easy reach of London.*
British Canoe Union
Flexel House, 45-47 High St, Addlestone,
Surrey. Weybridge 841341. For information
and advice.

Clay pigeon shooting

Clay Pigeon Shooting Association
107 Epping New Rd, Buckhurst Hill, Essex.
01-505 6221. For a list of clubs. Organises
home and overseas championships.

Cricket

*Many amateur clubs throughout London
and first-class cricket at Lord's and the Oval
which also stage at least one test match
each, every year. For latest scores of test
matches played in England, phone
Cricketline, 154. The season is Apr-Sep.*

National Cricket Association
Lord's Cricket Ground, St John's Wood Rd
NW8. 01-289 6098. Gives information on
amateur clubs and coaching facilities.
Lord's Cricket Ground
St John's Wood Rd NW8. 01-289 1615. The
most famous cricket ground in the world.
Historic home of the MCC. Stages Mid-
dlesex county matches throughout the sea-
son, cup finals and a test match.
Oval Cricket Ground
Kennington Oval SEII. 01-582 6660.
Stages Surrey county matches and a test
match, usually in *Aug*. For latest scores of
matches played here phone 01-735 4911.

Croquet

Croquet Association
Mr B. C. Macmillan, The Secretary,
Hurlingham Club, Ranelagh Gdns SW6.
01-736 3148. For information and advice.

Cycling

*The spectacularly fast 6-day indoor event is
held at Wembley Arena and the Round-
Britain Milk Race takes place in May-Jun.*
British Cycling Federation   3 E 25
16 Upper Woburn Pl WCI. 01-387 9320.
Information on road, track and circuit racing.
Eastway Cycle Circuit
Temple Mills La E15. 01-534 6085. An
enclosed road circuit with facilities for
recreational riding, racing, training and
coaching. BMX track. Camp site.

Drag racing

*Events take place infrequently at various
airfields around London.*
British Drag Racing Association
29 Westdrive, Caldicott, Cambs. Crafts Hill
210028. Arranges meetings at Santa Pod.
Santa Pod Raceway
c/o PO Box 196, Bromley, Kent. Meetings
are held regularly at England's only permanent drag racing venue, Santa Pod Raceway, Podington, Nr. Wellingborough,
Northants. Wellingborough 313250.

Fencing

**Amateur Fencing   I G I
Association**
83 Perham Rd WI4. 01-385 7442. For
information and lists of events and clubs.

Fishing

To fish anywhere in the Thames area it is necessary to hold a Thames Water Authority Rod Licence. An additional permit is needed to fish in royal parks. The season is between 16 Jun-14 Mar.

Anglian Water Authority Colchester Division

33 Sheepen Rd, Colchester, Essex. Colchester 763344. Division licence covers coarse and game fishing; reductions for children and OAPs. Regional licence covers wider area and is more expensive. Weekly licences available.

London Anglers' Association

Forest Road Hall, Hervey Park Rd E17. 01-520 7477. Gives information on clubs and offers associate membership.

Southern Water Authority

Kent Division, Capstone Rd, Chatham, Kent. Medway 830655. Kent river licences are granted for trout and coarse fish. Reduction for under-16s; OAPs and disabled free (for coarse fishing but licence still required).

Thames Water Authority

Customer Services (Rivers Division), Nugent House, Vastern Rd, Reading, Berks. Reading 593777. Further details and licences for fishing in their reservoirs, rivers, etc.

Fishing: lakes & ponds

To fish here you must hold a permit or day ticket from the local borough councils, unless marked free. Reductions for under-16s and OAPs. To fish anywhere in the Thames area you must hold a Thames Water Authority Rod Licence.

Battersea Park   4 P 9

Roach, bream, flat-fish and very large carp. *Free.*

Chestnut Abbey Cross Pit, Herts

Good pike, perch, roach, tench. Crowded in summer.

Chingford Connaught Waters

All species. Crowded in summer. *Free.*

Clapham Common Eagle Pond

Good carp, some roach, pike, bream. *Free.*

Crystal Palace Boating Lake

Good carp, pike, roach, tench, gudgeon and perch.

Epping, Copped Hall Estate Pond

Carp, tench, perch, gudgeon, some rainbow trout. *Summer only.*

Finsbury Park

Carp, perch, tench and roach.

Hampton Court Ponds

Tench, pike, roach, perch. Beautiful water but often crowded.

Hampstead Heath Ponds

Good tench, roach, bream, pike. *Free.*

Hollow Ponds

Whipps Cross E17. Tench, pike, eels *(but get there very early in the morning). Free.*

Hyde Park Serpentine   2 F 12

Good roach, perch.

Northmet Pit, near Cheshunt, Herts

Good summer tench and winter pike, also perch, roach, rudd.

Osterley Park, Middx

Tench, perch, roach.

Richmond Park Pen Ponds

Good roach and perch.

Rickmansworth Lakes, Herts

Good roach, perch, tench, bream, pike.

Seven Islands, Mitcham Common, Surrey

Pike, perch, bream. *Free.*

South Weald Park, Essex

Good tench, crucian carp, roach, rudd, pike, perch.

Tooting Common Pond

Roach, perch, carp.

Victoria Park Lake E9

Good eels, pike, perch, bream, gudgeon.

Wandsworth Common Pond

Carp, roach, bream.

Windsor Great Park

Obelisk Pond, Johnson's Pond and Virginia Water. Carp, tench, pike, roach, rudd, bream and perch. Permits from Crown Estate Office, Great Park, Windsor, Berks (enclose sae). Windsor 860222.

Fishing: reservoirs

A number of Thames Water reservoirs are well stocked. Season 16 Jun-14 Mar for coarse fishing, 15 Mar or 1 Apr-30 Nov for trout. Thames Water licence needed. Day tickets from gate, but written applications only for seasons (two types – midweek and weekend) to:

North London Division

New River Head, Rosebery Av, London EC1, for **Barn Elms** – trout.

Eastern Division

The Grange, Crossbrook St, Waltham Cross, Herts, for **Walthamstow** – coarse, trout.

Fishing: rivers & canals

Grand Union Canal

Denham, Bucks. From Black Jack's Lock (No. 85) to Denham Lock (No. 87).

Lee Relief Channel Fishery
Waltham Abbey to Fishers Green. All species and the occasional trout. Day permits.

River Lee
Walthamstow to Hertford. Best fishing above Enfield Lock at Waltham Abbey, Cheshunt, Broxbourne, Rye House and St Margarets.

River Thames
Fishing starts above Kew. Probably England's best coarse fishing river. All species. Various stretches.

Aircraft Owners & Pilots   5 O 14
Association
50a Cambridge St SW1. 01-834 5631. For information, help and advice on all aspects of light aviation.

London School of Flying
Elstree Aerodrome, Elstree, Herts. 01-953 4343. Training and use of aircraft. Gulfstream American aircraft available for training. Also training in helicopter flying.

This is far and away the most popular British sport from both the player's and spectator's point of view. The English Football League has 92 clubs divided into 4 divisions; the London clubs are listed here. Then there are the Southern and Isthmian League clubs, many of them in London and well worth watching. Finally there are hundreds of amateur clubs which encourage new players of all standards. Football League matches are played every Sat and most B.hols at 15.00, occasional midweek matches at 19.30. The season lasts from Aug to Apr. Occasional international matches at Wembley Stadium, domestic and European knock-out competitions at club grounds. The FA and League Cup Finals are held at Wembley, but it's impossible to get in unless you already have a ticket.

London Football Association
Aldworth Gro SE13. 01-690 9626. For information on Leagues and clubs.

Arsenal FC
Highbury Stadium, Avenell Rd N5. 01-226 0304. Recorded ticket information 01-359 0131.

Charlton Athletic FC
Selhurst Park SE25. 01-771 6321.

Chelsea FC   4 L 4
Stamford Bridge, Fulham Rd SW6. 01-385 5545.

Crystal Palace FC
Selhurst Park SE25. 01-653 4462.

Fulham FC
Craven Cottage, Stevenage Rd SW6. 01-736 6561.

Millwall FC
The Den, Cold Blow La SE14. 01-639 3143.

Orient FC
Brisbane Rd E10. 01-539 2223.

Queen's Park Rangers FC
South Africa Rd W12. 01-743 0262.

Tottenham Hotspur FC
White Hart Lane Ground, 748 High Rd N17. 01-801 3411.

West Ham United FC
Boleyn Ground, Green St E13. 01-472 2740.

Wimbledon FC
49 Durnsford Rd SW19. 01-946 6311.

British Gliding Association
Kimberley House, Vaughan Way, Leicester, Leics. Leicester 531051. For information and help, club list and details of training courses.

London Gliding Club
Tring Rd, Dunstable, Beds. Dunstable 63419. The home of British gliding. Contact the secretary for a familiarisation flight on a temporary membership basis so that you can see what it's about before committing yourself.

The Daily Telegraph Golf Course Guide published by Collins, gives details and maps of all the courses in the British Isles. A useful book for the travelling golfer. Also the Golfers' Handbook can be obtained from most libraries.
Municipal courses, where it is not necessary to be a member, can be found at:

Addington Court
Featherbed La, Addington, Croydon, Surrey. 01-657 0281. Two 18-hole courses, a 9-hole course and a pitch and putt course of 18 holes.

Beckenham Place Park
Beckenham Hill Rd, Beckenham, Kent. 01-650 2292. 18 holes.

Coulsdon Court
Coulsdon, Coulsdon, Surrey. 01-660 0468. 18 holes.

Hainault Forest
Chigwell Row, Hainault, Essex. 01-500

2470. Two 18-hole courses, a putting green and practice field.

Home Park
Hampton Wick, Kingston-upon-Thames, Surrey. 01-977 6645. 18 holes.

Picketts Lock Centre
Picketts Lock La N9. 01-803 4756. 9-hole course.

Royal Epping Forest
Forest Approach, Station Rd, Chingford, Essex. 18 holes.

Golf clubs in and near London for which membership is necessary, although many will extend guest facilities to members of comparable clubs from overseas:

Hampstead GC
Winnington Rd N2. 01-455 0203. 9 holes. Bar lunches served.

Highgate GC
Denewood Rd N6. 01-340 3745. 18 holes. Lunches served.

North Middlesex GC
Friern Barnet La, Whetstone N20. 01-445 1604. 18 holes. Bar lunches except *Mon*. Full lunch *Sun* only.

RAC Country Club
Wilmerhatch La, Woodcote Park, Epsom, Surrey. Ashstead 76311. Two 18-hole courses. Meals and accommodation by arrangement.

Richmond GC
Sudbrook Park, Petersham, Richmond, Surrey. 01-940 4351. 18 holes. Lunches served.

Royal Mid-Surrey GC
Old Deer Park, Richmond, Surrey. 01-940 1894. 36 holes. Men's 6331 yds (5786m); ladies' 5544 yds (5067m). Lunches served.

Sandown Golf Centre
Sandown Park, More La, Esher, Surrey. Esher 65921. Two 9-hole courses; one 9-hole pitch and putt course.

Sunningdale GC
Ridgemount Rd, Sunningdale, Berks. Ascot 21681. 36 holes. Two courses. Lunches served except *Mon*.

Wentworth GC
Wentworth Dri, Virginia Water, Surrey. Wentworth 2201. Two 18-hole and one 9-hole course. Visitors by arrangement. Lunches served.

Grass skiing

British Grass Ski Congress 5 K 14
118 Eaton Sq SW1. 01-245 1033. Events take place throughout the country *Apr-Oct* with skiing at weekends. Provides list of slopes for members.

Greyhound racing

It is advisable to check times with evening newspaper.

Catford Stadium
Catford Bridge SE6. 01-690 2261. *19.30 Mon, Wed & Sat.*

Hackney Stadium
Waterden Rd E15. 01-986 3511. *14.00 Tue & Thur, 11.00 Sat.*

Walthamstow Stadium
Chingford Rd E4. 01-531 4255. *19.30 Tue, Thur & Sat.*

Wembley Stadium
Empire Way, Wembley, Middx. 01-902 8833. *19.30 Mon, Wed & Fri.*

Wimbledon Stadium
Plough La SW17. 01-946 5361. *19.45 Tue, Thur & Sat, 19.15 Sat.*

Gymnastics

Competitions at the Royal Albert Hall and Crystal Palace. See 'Children's: Clubs and classes'.

Hang gliding

British Hang Gliding Association
Cramfield Airfields, Cramfield, Milton Keynes, Bucks. Write for information.

Hockey

Men's internationals held at Willesden Sports Centre, women's at Wembley.
All England Women's 2 D 28
Hockey Association
Argyle House, 29-31 Euston Rd NW1. 01-278 6340.
The Hockey Association 3 D 28
16 Northdown St N1. 01-837 8878.

Horse racing

Courses in and near London: Ascot, Berks (famous for its Royal meeting in Jun); Epsom, Surrey (stages the world-famous Derby in Jun and also the Oaks); Kempton Park, Sunbury-on-Thames, Middx; Lingfield Park, Surrey; Sandown Park, Esher, Surrey (famous for the Whitbread Gold Cup); and Windsor, Berks. Flat racing season Mar-Nov. Steeplechasing Aug-Jun. Point to point racing (amateur) season Mar-Apr.

Jockey Club (incorporating   2   D   17
the National Hunt Committee)
42 Portman Sq W1. 01-486 4921. Governing body, responsible for rules, meetings, training and promotion of horse racing.
Racecourse Publicity Agency
Winkfield Rd, Ascot, Berks. Ascot 25912. Can supply information on all aspects of racing.

Ice hockey

British Ice Hockey Association
The Secretary, 40 Hambledon Rd, Bournemouth, Dorset. Bournemouth 432583. For information on clubs and events.

Karting

Royal Automobile Club   5   J   14
31 Belgrave Sq SW1. 01-235 8601. Controls karting and sells *Motor Sports Yearbook* for regulations and maintenance.

Lacrosse

The main events are held Feb-Apr, including the Clubs and Colleges Tournament and a home international in London.
All England Women's   5   N   16
Lacrosse Association
Francis House, Francis St SW1. 01-931 8899. For lists of coaching courses, clubs and fixtures.
English Lacrosse Union
The Secretary, Mr R. Balls, Lynton, 70 High Rd, Rayleigh, Essex. Rayleigh 770758. Men only. Gives details of events and coaching courses.

Martial arts

Amateur Karate   3   E   26
Association
120 Cromer St WC1. 01-837 4406.
British Judo Association   3   E   25
16 Upper Woburn Pl WC1. 01-387 9340. Supplies free explanatory leaflet and details of clubs.
Martial Arts Commission
15 Deptford Bdwy SE8. 01-691 3433.
Judokan Club
Latymer Ct, Hammersmith Rd W6. 01-748 6787. Classes in judo and karate.
London Judo Society
89 Lansdowne Way SW8. 01-622 0529. Judo and karate club.

Tunbridge Karate Club   3   E   26
80 Judd St WC1. 01-278 5608.

Motorcycle racing

Road racing at Brands Hatch.
Auto-Cycle Union
Miller House, Corporation St, Rugby, Warks. Rugby 540519. Governs all motorcycle competitions. Also trials and grass track. Publishes a handbook of forthcoming road racing and scrambling events.

Motor racing

Several clubs in the London area.
British Automobile Racing Club
Thruxton Racing Circuit, nr Andover, Hants. Weyhill 2696. For details of club, championships and general information.
British Racing & Sports Car Club
Brand Hatch Circuit, Fawkham, nr Dartford, Kent. Ash Green 874445. Stages meetings at Brands Hatch and seven other car circuits. Also organises major international events in this country.
Royal Automobile Club   5   J   14
Competitions Dept, 31 Belgrave Sq SW1. 01-235 8601. Controls competitions. Supplies list of championship events.

Mountaineering

British Mountaineering Council
Crawford House, Precinct Centre, Booth St East, Manchester. Manchester 273 5835. Supplies a list of clubs and information on where to find mountain huts etc.

Netball

Played lunchtimes in Lincoln's Inn Fields WC2.
All England Netball   5   N   16
Association
Francis House, Francis St SW1. 01-828 2176. For information and advice.

Orienteering

This sport can be enjoyed by people of all ages and involves competitive navigation on foot with map and compass. Events take place most Sundays.
British Orienteering Federation
Riversdale, Dale Rd North, Darley Dale, Matlock, Derbyshire. Matlock 734042.

Parachuting

British Parachute Association
Kimberley House, 47 Vaughan Way, Leicester, Leics. Leicester 519778. For information, a list of clubs and help.

Polo

Played Apr-Sep at Smiths Lawn, Windsor, Berks. Matches most weekends, B.hols & during Ascot week; Sun at Ham House, Richmond; Tue, Thur & Sat at Richmond Park (nr Roehampton Gate); Wed, Fri, Sat, Sun & B.hols at Cowdray Park, Midhurst, W. Sussex, also Wed & Thur during the British Open Championships (beginning Jul) and during Goodwood week; Wed, Sat & Sun at Woolmers Park, Hereford. Play starts middle or late afternoon.

Hurlingham Polo Association
Ambersham Farm, Midhurst, W. Sussex. Lodsworth 277.

Rackets & real tennis

Real tennis is the original form of tennis and Henry VIII's court at Hampton Court still exists. Nowadays it's rather obscure, as is rackets which is a form of squash but with a much larger court.

Tennis & Rackets Association
c/o Queen's Club, Palliser Rd W14. 01-381 4746. Actively promotes both sports.

Queen's Club
Palliser Rd W14. 01-385 3421. Stages matches in both sports. Real tennis events Oct-Apr.

Riding

Association of British Riding Schools
Old Brewery Yard, Penzance, Cornwall. Penzance 69440. Deals with general equestrian matters ranging from insurance and legal matters to helping those interested in a career with horses. Publishes a handbook listing approved riding schools.

British Horse Society
British Equestrian Centre, Stoneleigh, Kenilworth, Warks. Coventry 696697. For information on riding and breeding, career advice, and list of approved riding schools.

Rowing

The most famous event is the Oxford and Cambridge boat race from Putney to Mort-

lake in Mar or Apr. The Head of the River event on the Thames is held in Mar and is one of the largest of its kind in the world. Important regattas are held at Chiswick, Hammersmith, Henley-on-Thames, Kingston, Putney, Richmond, Twickenham and Walton.

Amateur Rowing Association
6 Lower Mall W6. 01-748 3632. Publishes the British Rowing Almanac annually, which gives a list of clubs and coming events. Also a monthly club newspaper.

Rugby union

Twickenham is the home of rugby union and some international matches are staged there. Besides this there are a number of top-class clubs in the London area which provide excellent spectator sport and a plethora of lesser clubs which encourage new members of all standards.

Rugby Football Union
Whitton Rd, Twickenham, Middx. 01-892 8161. Controlling body of the sport and headquarters of rugby. The important matches, including internationals, are played there.

Sailing & yachting

International Yacht Racing   2 H 14
Union
60 Knightsbridge SW1. 01-235 6221. Publishes an annual international fixture list and booklet on racing rules.

Royal Ocean Racing Club   5 J 18
20 St James's Pl SW1. 01-493 2248. To become eligible you must have taken part in two Ocean races or one Fastnet race.

Royal Yachting Association
Romsey Rd, Eastleigh, Hants. Eastleigh 629962. National authority providing information on all forms of yachting, sailing and powered boating.

Shooting

The most important competitions held at Bisley Camp are: The Services Meeting, beginning of Jul; NRA Small-bore Meeting later in Jul; NSRA British Small-bore Meeting later in Jul; NSRA British Small-bore Rifle Championship in Aug.

National Rifle Association
Bisley Camp, Brookwood, Woking, Surrey. Brookwood 2213. Full-bore. Will re-

commend a suitable club (by letter only), but these are rare in London.

National Small-bore Rifle Association
Lord Roberts House, Bisley Camp, Brookwood, Woking, Surrey. Brookwood 6969. Small-bore and air weapons. Will recommend a suitable club on receipt of sae.

Showjumping

The two major events are: the Royal International Horse Show at Wembley in Jul and the Horse of the Year Show at Wembley in Oct. There are also notable events staged at Windsor, Richmond and Clapham Common. See also 'Riding'.

British Show Jumping Association
British Equestrian Centre, Stoneleigh, Kenilworth, Warks. Coventry 696516.

Skateboarding

The craze has died down since its heyday and many skateparks have closed but there are still a few in and around London, both commercial and local authority ones.

English Skateboard Association
Mr D. Thompson, Flat 2, Northcliff Heights, Kidderminster, Worcs. Kidderminster 744293. Can supply information on skateparks both in London and nationally.

Skating

National Skating   6   J   30
Association of Great Britain
15-27 Gee St EC1. 01-253 3824. For information and advice on ice and rollerskating.

Queen's Ice Skating Club   1   B   10
17 Queensway W2. 01-229 0172. Membership fee. Fee for skate hire. Tuition available. *OPEN 10.00-12.00, 14.00-16.30 & 19.30-22.00 Mon-Fri, 10.00-12.00, 14.00-17.00 & 19.30-22.30 (19.00-22.00 Sun) Sat & Sun.*

Richmond Ice Rink
Clevedon Rd, East Twickenham, Middx. 01-892 3646. Admission and skate-hire charge. *OPEN 10.00 (10.30 Sat)-12.30, 14.30-17.00, 19.30-22.00 (22.30 Fri & Sat) Mon-Sun.*

Streatham Ice Rink
386 Streatham High Rd SW16. 01-769 7861. Admission and skate-hire charge. *OPEN 10.00-12.30, 21.00-23.00 (20.00-*

22.30 Sat) Mon-Sun. Also 14.00-16.30 Mon, Tue & Thur, 16.00-17.00 Wed, 15.45-16.45 Fri & 14.30-17.30 Sat & Sun.

Skiing

The National Recreation Centre at Crystal Palace runs classes on its fine outdoor artificial slope.

British Ski Federation   5   K   14
118 Eaton Sq SW1. 01-235 8228.
Ski Club of Great Britain   5   K   14
118 Eaton Sq SW1. 01-245 1033. National club for recreational skiing. Equipment advice for members.

Speedway

The season is Mar-Oct. Events in London at:
Hackney Stadium
Waterden Rd E15. 01-985 9822. *19.30 Fri.*
Wimbledon Stadium
Plough La SW17. 01-946 5361. *19.45 Wed.*

Squash

A number of sports centres have public squash courts – prior booking essential.
Squash Rackets   5   N   16
Association
Francis House, Francis St SW1. 01-828 3064. Publishes the *SRA Annual* which gives a list of clubs and courts. Also *Squash News* bimonthly.

Stock car racing

Noisy, colourful, exciting and only slightly dangerous. Contrary to popular opinion, the drivers do actually try to avoid hitting each other. Events mostly staged Sat eve Mar-Sep.
Spedeworth International
Aldershot Stadium, Tongham, nr Farnham, Surrey. Aldershot 20182. For information on events.
Wimbledon Stadium
Plough La SW17. 01-946 5361.

Sub aqua

British Sub Aqua Club   3   E   25
16 Upper Woburn Pl WC1. 01-387 9302.

For information on local branches where training courses are run. To join you will have to pass a swimming test, produce a certificate of fitness signed by your doctor, and evidence of a satisfactory chest X-ray. BSAC training is recognised worldwide as being of the highest order. Holborn branch and London branch are well-equipped, active groups who train throughout the year and dive regularly. See also 'Sports equipment: sub aqua' under 'Shopping'.

<hr>

Swimming

Magnificent Olympic-standard pool at the Crystal Palace Recreation Centre. High-standard competitions. Excellent tuition and facilities for members.

Public baths (indoor)

Chelsea Manor St SW3. 01-352 6985.	4	**M**	9
Ironmonger Row EC1. 01-253 4011.	3	**I**	32
Marshall St W1. 01-439 4678.	2	**H**	21
Oasis, 32 Endell St WC2. 01-836 9555. Also an outdoor pool May-Oct.	3	**I**	23
Porchester Rd W2. 01-798 3689.	1	**A**	11
Queen Mother Sports Centre, 223 Vauxhall Bridge Rd SW1. 01-798 2125.	5	**N**	16
Seymour Pl W1. 01-723 8019.	2	**D**	16

Swimming in the parks (outdoors)
OPEN May-Sep 07.00-19.00 Mon-Sun; Oct-Apr 07.30-10.00 Mon-Sun. Free before 09.00.

Eltham Park South Baths SE9. 01-850 9890.

Hampstead Pond NW3. 01-435 2366. *Free.*

Highgate Ponds N6. 01-340 4044. Men only. *OPEN Apr-Sep 06.30-20.30 Mon-Sun; Oct-Mar 07.00-15.00 Mon-Sun. Free.*

Kenwood Pond N6. 01-340 1033. Women only. *Free.*

London Fields Baths E8. 01-254 7494.

Parliament Hill Lido NW5. 01-485 3873. *Free before 09.30 (09.00 Sep-Jan).*

Peckham Rye Park Baths SE22. 01-635 8221.

Serpentine Hyde Park W2. 01-724 3104.	2	**F**	12

Southwark Park Baths SE16. 01-237 6572.

Tooting Bec Lido SW17. 01-871 7198.

Victoria Park Lido E9. 01-985 6774.

Amateur Swimming Association
Harold Fern House, Derby Sq, Loughborough, Leics. Loughborough 230431. The authority governing national swimming events.

<hr>

Table tennis

English Table Tennis Association
21 Claremont, Hastings, E. Sussex. Hastings 433121.

<hr>

Tennis

Public courts in most London parks but there is a great variety in the quality of the courts. There are also plenty of clubs to join. The major event, of course, is Wimbledon fortnight which is held at the end of Jun; it is best to apply for tickets by ballot from the All England Lawn Tennis Club or queue for standing room on the day. There are also various other tournaments held in London, those which take place immediately before Wimbledon usually include several top professionals.

All England Lawn Tennis & Croquet Club
Church Rd SW19. 01-946 2244. Stages 'Wimbledon Fortnight' (perhaps the world's top sporting event) *last week Jun & first week Jul.*

Lawn Tennis Association
Palliser Rd W14. 01-385 2366. The governing body of lawn tennis in Britain. Will supply a list of clubs.

Queen's Club
Palliser Rd W14. 01-385 3421. For membership enquiries.

<hr>

Ten pin bowling

The closing times given here are approximate: bowling alleys quite often stay open much later.

British Ten Pin Bowling Association
Postal address: 19 Canterbury Av, Ilford, Essex. 01-478 1745. No bowling centre, but provides list of bowling centres and other information and advice.

Airport Bowl
Bath Rd, Harlington, Middx. 01-759 1396. *OPEN 10.00-01.00 Mon-Sun. CLOSED during occasional matches.*

Bexleyheath Bowling Centre
Broadway, Bexleyheath, Kent. 01-303 3325. *OPEN 10.30-24.00 Mon-Sun.*

Lewisham Bowl
11-29 Belmont Hill SE13. 01-318 9691. 24 lanes, automatic scoring, fast food and bar. *OPEN 10.00-24.00 Mon-Sun.*

Princess Bowl
New Rd, Dagenham, Essex. 01-592 0347.
24 lanes. OPEN 11.00-22.30 Mon-Thur,
11.00-23.00 Fri, 10.00-23.00 Sat, 10.00-
22.30 Sun.

Volleyball

National League season runs Oct-Mar.
English Volleyball Association
21 South Rd, West Bridgford, Nottingham,
Notts. Nottingham 816324. Supplies a list of
clubs and fixtures.

Water polo

Occasional games at Crystal Palace.
Amateur Swimming Association
Harold Fern House, Derby Sq,
Loughborough, Leics. Loughborough
230431 for details.

Water skiing

Several clubs to join and championships to
watch. The season is May-Sep.
British Water Ski Federation
390 City Rd EC1. 01-833 2855. For information and club lists. Residential summer
courses.

Weight-lifting

National championships held at Crystal
Palace.
**British Amateur Weight-Lifters
Association**
3 Iffley Turn, Oxford, Oxon. Oxford 778319.
Comprises 12 regional associations which
organise meetings, clubs, championships
etc. Will supply information on local clubs
and events.
**Greater London Amateur Weight-
Lifters Association**
The Secretary, Mr H. Turner, 4 Buchanans
Clo, Aveley, Essex. South Ockenden
861808.

Windsurfing

Windsurfing Information Centre
RYA, Romsey Rd, Eastleigh, Hants. Eastleigh 629962. Contact for full details of
clubs, classes, equipment hire, events and
venues.

Wrestling

Main professional bouts at the Royal Albert
Hall.
British Amateur Wrestling Association
Administration, 16 Choir St, Salford. Man-
chester 832 9209. Write for information.

Health and fitness

With the increasing awareness of the
importance of health and fitness, clubs and
dance centres have sprung up all over
London, offering the opportunity to take
classes in aerobics, dance or yoga; or simply to relax in the sauna or spa bath. Beauty
treatments are often available in these
centres along with bar and restaurant facilities (serving health foods of course). Some
clubs require membership, some an
entrance fee which varies depending on
which equipment is used. A selection of
clubs and dance centres is listed below.
Local newspapers and newsagents' windows carry announcements of classes in
your area. Local council education authorities also offer tuition. Check your library or
Floodlight for details. Time Out and City
Limits are also useful sources.

Dance & keep fit

Keep Fit Association   3 **E 25**
16 Upper Woburn Pl WC1. 01-387 4349.
Answers all kinds of enquiries about keep fit
and dance.
Big Apple Health Studio   2 **J 22**
10 Great Newport St WC2. 01-240 1701.
Dance and exercise studios for jazz, body
conditioning, aerobics and stretch classes.
Also sauna (women only), spa bath
(women only), solarium and beauty treatments. Membership not essential.
Dancercise Studios
The Barge, Durban Lion Wharf, Old Isleworth, Middx. 01-560 3300. There are several Dancercise Studios in central and
suburban London offering classes combining jazz, Broadway, ballet, contemporary
and disco. Enrolment at beginning of term.
Contact above address for list of studios.
Fitness Centre   6 **J 23**
11-12 Floral St WC2. 01-836 6544. Aerobics, stretch, rock, jazz, ballet, tap, karate,
sauna, steam room. Gymnasium with nautilus and free weights, health bar and swim-

ming pool. *No membership requirement. Charge.*

Lotte Berk   2 D 18
29 Manchester St W1. 01-935 8905. Also at 465 Fulham Rd SW6. 01-385 2477. Exercises to get you into shape prescribed by the lithe Lotte who is a marvellous advert for her work. *No membership requirement. Charge.*

Pineapple Dance Studio   5 J 23
7 Langley St WC2. 01-836 4004. Other Pineapple studios: Pineapple West, 60 Paddington St W1. 01-487 3444. Pineapple Kensington, 38 Harrington Rd SW7. 01-581 0466. Qualified teachers for every type of dance imaginable from belly to break. Also gymnasium for weight training, hydro fitness, body control studios (Pilates technique), café-bar, resident osteopath and masseur.

Health clubs

City Gym (Al Murray)   6 L 31
New Union St EC2. 01-628 0786. Fitness training, sauna, gymnasium and weight training. Specialises in cardiac rehabilitation for people referred by their doctors. Sessions for men and women (women *Tue & Thur from 12.30*). *Membership.*

Cannons Sports Club   6 O 29
Cousin La EC4. 01-283 0101. Large City club for men and women. Nautilus gym, cardiac exercise equipment, aerobics, 11 squash courts including an all-glass 'telecourt', swimming pool, sauna, solarium, snooker, restaurant. Full-time beautician and coaching staff. *Membership.*

Dave Prowse Fitness Centre   6 Q 27
12 Marshalsea Rd SE1. 01-407 5650. Two gymnasiums, sauna, solarium and showers. Dance classes. *Membership.*

Hogarth Club
1a Airedale Av W4. 01-995 4600. American-style club with nautilus gym, spa bath, sauna, swimming pool, squash and tennis courts. Dance and exercise classes. Bar and restaurant. *Daily membership available.*

Morle Slimming & Beauty   1 D 4
Centre
176 Kensington High St W8. 01-937 9501. Gym, sauna and sunbeds; anti-stress, relaxation, dietary control and slimming treatments, massage, hydrotherapy, facials and beauty treatments. Women only. *Membership.*

Ravelle's Health Club   3 F 26
52 Brunswick Centre WC1. 01-278 2754.

Men's health club and ladies' health and beauty centre. Individual schedules devised for a 3-month period. Latest equipment, saunas. Also at Marble Arch, Portsea Pl W2. 01-402 7684. (**2 D** 15). *Members only.*

The Sanctuary   6 J 23
12 Floral St WC2. 01-240 9635. Exotic setting for sauna, solarium, steam room, swimming pool, spa bath. For the real sybarite. Women only. *Daily membership available.*

Town & Country Health &   1 I 11
Beauty Salon
2 Yeoman's Row SW3. 01-584 7702. Membership which allows unlimited visits for exercise and saunas under personal supervision. Women only.

Saunas

Telephone for appointment as times vary considerably. See also under 'Health clubs' and 'Turkish baths'.

The Body Feminine
Clarendon Court Hotel, Maida Vale W9. 01-286 8080. Sauna and massage. Women only. *No membership required.*

Charing Cross Hotel Sauna   5 K 22
Strand WC2. 01-839 7282. Ladies' day on *Mon*, otherwise a male preserve. *No membership required.*

City Saunas   6 L 32
City Wall House, 22 Finsbury St EC2. 01-628 7117. Men only. *No membership required.*

Harrods Beauty Salon   2 I 12
Knightsbridge SW1. 01-584 8881. Excellent salon with sauna facilities. Comprehensive range of treatments. *No membership required.*

Oasis   3 I 23
Endell St WC2. 01-836 9555. Swimming pools, paddling pool, sauna, warm baths and showers. Heated outdoor pool and sunbathing facilities in summer. *No membership required.*

Unisex Sauna
2 New College Parade, Finchley Rd NW3. 01-586 4422. *OPEN 24hrs. No membership required.*

Turkish baths

Ladywell Baths
Lewisham High St SE13. 01-690 2123. Excellent and inexpensive. Also indoor pool and public baths.

Porchester Centre   I A II
Porchester Rd W2. 01-798 3688. Public
and inexpensive. Three dry heat rooms,
steam room, cold plunge, massage,
exercise room. Also two swimming pools.

Rainbow Centre
41 East St, Epsom, Surrey. Epsom 26252.
Turkish bath plus other facilities including
sauna, sun beds, swimming pool, conditioning gym and indoor bowls.

Mind, body and spirit

*Life in a hi-tech society has brought about a
return to ancient and natural forms of
therapy. This, combined with the idea of
prevention rather than cure, has made
alternative medicine a regular practice for
many people. Some treatments are available under the National Health Service, but
most are private. Health food shops and
health magazines (also Time Out and City
Limits) often advertise practitioners and
teachers, some of whom are registered,
some not. The Institute for Complementary
Medicine Year Book is a comprehensive
guide to all aspects of alternative medicine
which is updated each year and available in
most bookshops. Below are listed some of
the bodies which will give advice about the
various therapies and supply a list of registered practitioners. See also under 'Hospitals'.*

General

Community Health   6 J 32
Foundation
188 Old St EC1. 01-251 4076. Oriental medicine based on the theories of the movement of energy between two poles, the yin
and the yang. Shiatsu massage (like acupuncture it concentrates on energy points
of the body), iridology (diagnosis of the
body through the eye) and reflexology
(therapeutic massage of the feet to promote health throughout the body). Also
macrobiotic cookery classes with a dietary
counsellor. *OPEN 09.30-13.00, 14.00-
17.30 Mon-Fri for information. Evenings and weekends for classes and treatment.*

Institute of Complementary   2 E 20
Medicine
21 Portland Pl W1. 01-636 9543. Provides
detailed information on all aspects of alternative medicine.

The Isis Centre for Holistic Health
362 High Rd N17. 01-808 6401. Individual
and group sessions of a medical and counselling nature. Treatments in homoeopathy, osteopathy, touch for health,
psychotherapy and healing. Regular group
sessions in active birth, tai-chi, bioenergetic
exercise, constructive movement, co-
counselling, creative problem solving,
transactional analysis, dream therapy,
body image and pulsing. Workshops are
also organised for some weekends. *OPEN
Mon-Fri by appt.*

Neal's Yard Therapy Rooms   3 I 23
2 Neal's Yard WC2. 01-379 7662. Individual
consultations (by appt only) for acupuncture, Alexander technique, antogenic
training, aromatherapy, bach flower
remedies, biodynamic therapy, biofeed-
back, chiropractic, counselling, cranial
osteopathy, healing, herbalism, homoeopathy, hypnotherapy, iridology, applied
kinesiology, massage, naturopathy, nutrition and diet, osteopathy, polarity therapy,
psychotherapy,   reflexology,   sexual
therapy, shiatsu, touch for health.

Acupuncture

*Chinese method of treating ailments by
pricking the skin or tissue with needles.*
British Acupuncture   5 O 14
Association
34 Alderney St SW1. 01-834 1012. *OPEN
09.00-17.00 Mon-Fri. Appt only.*

Alexander technique

*The re-education of the body in order to
achieve the posture that nature intended
and to carry out bodily activities with maximum ease and a minimum of energy and
tension.*
Society of Teachers of the   4 L 4
Alexander Technique
10 London House, 266 Fulham Rd SW10.
01-351 0828. Will supply a list of qualified
teachers (send sae).

Chiropractic

*The correction of spinal displacements by
manipulation of the spine to ensure the flow
of nervous energy from the spine to all parts
of the body is unimpaired.*
British Chiropractic   5 N 18
Association
Premier House, 10 Greycoat Pl SW1.
01-222 8866. Will provide information and
addresses of recognised practitioners.

Homoeopathy

Natural medicine based on the principle of treating like with like – ie a substance which would produce symptoms of sickness in a healthy person will cure a sick person showing those same symptoms.

British Homoeopathic   2   D   20
Association
27a Devonshire St W1. 01-935 2163. Provides a list of medical doctors trained in homoeopathy (send sae).

Royal London   3   G   26
Homoeopathic Hospital
Great Ormond St WC1. 01-837 8833. NHS treatment by registered homoeopaths (appt only). *OPEN 09.00-17.00 Mon-Fri.*

Society of Homoeopaths
47 Canada Gro, Bognor Regis, W. Sussex. Bognor Regis 860678. Maintains a register of professional homoeopaths who practise according to the Society's registration standards and code of ethics. Send sae for a copy.

Hypnotherapy

The Hypnotherapy Centre   2   D   16
1 Wythburn Pl W1. 01-262 8852. Provides information and a list of registered practitioners of cure by hypnosis.

Osteopathy

Manipulation of the joints to correct structural imbalance as the body cannot function effectively unless structurally sound.

British Osteopathic   2   A   17
Association
8 Boston Pl NW1. 01-262 5250. *Clinic*

10.00-12.30 Mon, 10.00-15.00 Tue-Fri by appt. Also provides a list of registered osteopaths.

British School of   5   J   21
Osteopathy
1-4 Suffolk St SW1. 01-930 4601. *OPEN 09.00-17.00 Mon-Fri by appt. Specialist sports injury clinic 11.00-16.00 Sat.*

Reflexology

Massage treatment which stimulates nerve-centres in the feet.

British School of Reflexology
Holistic Healing Centre, 92 Sheering Rd, Old Harlow, Essex. Harlow 29060. Information and addresses of practitioners.

International Institute of Reflexology
28 Hollyfields Av N11. 01-368 0865. Provides information and addresses of practitioners. Seminars.

Yoga & meditation

Iyengar Yoga Institute
223a Randolph Av W9. 01-624 3080. Classes for all levels from beginners to teacher training.

London Buddhist Centre
51 Roman Rd E2. 01-981 1225. Specialises in meditation, also holds classes in yoga, Alexander technique, tai-chi, massage and Buddhism. *Meditation classes for beginners 19.00 Wed.*

Sivananda Yoga Centre
50 Chepstow Villas W11. 01-229 7970. Courses and beginners classes available in meditation and yoga. Yoga for pregnancy and pre-pregnancy. Courses on vegetarian cookery. Fasting clinic. Indian music. Also arranges retreats.

Shops and services

London has a truly amazing array of shops where one can purchase just about anything; from the many department stores which have a huge selection of all sorts of goods to the small specialist shops.

Consumer protection

Always keep the receipt for goods you buy and, if you're not satisfied, take them back to the shop and ask to speak to the manager. If the fault is entirely theirs you don't have to accept a credit note: ask for cash. The *Trade Descriptions Act* protects the consumer against fraudulent claims made for goods, and the *Sale of Goods Act* against merchandise not up to standard – contact your Trading Standards Officer at the local Town Hall, your local Consumer Advice Centre or the Citizens Advice Bureau.

Opening times

Generally shops *open 09.00/10.00-17.30/18.00 Mon-Sat and are closed on Sun and B.hols*. West End shops stay *open late on Thur to 19.30/20.00, and until the same time on Wed* in Knightsbridge, King's Rd and Sloane Sq. A lot of Bond St shops *do not open on Sat*. In cases where a shop's hours differ from the standard times above, the opening hours appear in italic at the end of the entry.

Shopping areas

The West End
The capital's biggest shopping area consisting of three main streets. Oxford St is over a mile long and has nearly all the major department stores including Selfridges, London's largest Marks & Spencer and an overwhelming assortment of individual fashion shops. It gets very crowded here, especially on *Sat* and at *lunchtime*. Regent St is less hectic and offers luxurious items at Liberty's, plus several china, glass and clothing stores. (Gathering place for the young, and undergoing a face-lift some years after its decline as a 60s hotspot, Carnaby St – just off Regent St – is still worth a visit. The High Street chains are moving in among the novelty shops.) For real luxury try New Bond St, particularly shoes, jewellery, pictures, prints and designer clothes. Two pedestrian-style streets just off Oxford St are well worth exploring – St Christopher's Place (2 E 18) and South Molton St (2 F 19). Both are packed with stylish small shops and attractive eating places.

Brent Cross
This vast shopping complex at the head of the M1 on the North Circular is North London's 'West End'. Ample free parking so ideal way to avoid central London traffic and still visit branches of the main central London stores. Also has smaller, more individual, shops. *OPEN 10.00-20.00 Mon-Fri, 09.00-18.00 Sat.*

Camden
Trendy and popular canalside area lined with shops and huge, sprawling market. Very busy on a *Sat afternoon*. Shops deal in period clothes, alternative books, imported records, pine furniture and artefacts.

Charing Cross Road & Bloomsbury
This is the area for books – new, second-hand, antique, specialist or best-sellers. Also prints and maps.

Covent Garden
Once the site of the famous fruit and vegetable market, this refurbished area is now a trendy pedestrianised piazza. The arcades are lined with small specialist fashion and gift shops, plus lots of places to eat and drink. There are also open-air craft stalls, an antiques market and a craft market on certain days. Leading off the piazza the streets hold an interesting variety of shops and restaurants where you can find the latest in fashion, hi-tech household equipment and foods.

Hampstead
A quaint and pleasant place to browse. As well as the usual chain stores there are a number of exclusive clothes shops and narrow streets with arcades of antique and art dealers. Also plenty of wine bars, cafés and brasseries.

Kensington High Street
Less hectic than Oxford St, though a similar range of shops, plus House of Fraser – its own department store. Delve into the roads leading off for more individual fashion shops.

King's Road/Chelsea
As much a place to be seen as to see; this area comes alive on *Sat* with the parading trendies out-doing one another for outrageousness. This is the centre for up-to-the-minute fashion. The King's Rd is particularly good for shoes and men's clothing.

Knightsbridge
A fashionable area for the rich and famous, Knightsbridge is dominated by Harvey Nichols and Harrods, which can supply almost every demand if you are willing to pay the price. Exclusive furniture, jewellery and clothes can also be found in Beauchamp Pl.

Piccadilly/Trocadero/London Pavilion
Quality and tradition at Fortnum & Mason, Hatchard's, Simpson and Lillywhites; also the historic Burlington Arcade. The Trocadero and the London Pavilion cater for the more up-to-date market, providing one-stop shopping, refreshment and entertainment, while Tower Records now dominates Piccadilly Circus from the old Swan & Edgar building.

Portobello Road
Most famous for its huge market where you can alternate from the expensive antique dealer to the rag-and-bone merchant, finding a variety of household goods and second-hand clothes in between. There are also unusual art deco and craft shops to

discover in the surrounding streets; excellent delis too.

Soho
Sex shops and porno cinemas are now giving way to excellent specialist food shops, oriental supermarkets, designer clothes shops, restaurants and wine bars. Berwick St Market and Chinatown are definitely worth a visit. For more details see Nicholson's *Inside Soho*.

Tottenham Court Road
Stretching north from the end of Oxford St, this area is buzzing with shops selling electronic equipment (stereos, videos, cameras). Furniture and modern design also feature at Heal's and Habitat, with many smaller shops also selling sofas, sofa-beds and futons.

Department stores

There are several large stores in London where you can buy practically anything, others are slightly more specialised, but still offer a wide choice of goods. Most have coffee shops and restaurants serving good, reasonably priced lunches and teas; many also have hairdressing salons.

Army & Navy   5 M 17
101-105 Victoria St SW1. 01-834 1234. Excellent food hall and wine department. Clothes, cosmetics, household goods, toys, books, china and glass. Hairdressing salon, coffee shop, restaurant.

British Home Stores   2 F 20
252 Oxford St W1. 01-629 2011. Inexpensive high-street chain for clothes and household goods. Extensive home lighting department.

Debenhams   2 F 19
344-348 Oxford St W1. 01-580 3000. Fashion clothes at reasonable prices. Good departments for kitchenware, lingerie, hosiery, cosmetics.

Dickins & Jones   2 G 20
224 Regent St W1. 01-734 7070. Fashionable store selling classy ladies' and men's clothes, accessories and haberdashery. Excellent dress fabrics. Shopping adviser. Restaurant and coffee shops.

Fenwicks   2 G 19
63 New Bond St W1. 01-629 9161. Good fashions and accessories. Imaginative gifts and stationery. Books. Also large store at Brent Cross Shopping Centre NW4. 01-202 8200.

Fortnum & Mason   2 I 19
181 Piccadilly W1. 01-734 8040. World-famous. Luxury goods and exotic foods. Superb hampers for all occasions. Designer collection clothes.

Harrods   2 I 12
Knightsbridge SW1. 01-730 1234. The world's most famous department store. Superb men's, ladies' and children's fashions and accessories. Perfumery, gifts, china and glass, pets, toys, books, furniture, fabrics. Edwardian marble food halls – a luxury emporium. Hairdressing/beauty salon, gentlemen's barber. Restaurants, tea and coffee shops. Also a wide range of services.

Harvey Nichols   2 I 14
Knightsbridge SW1. 01-235 5000. Stylish clothes from top British, Continental and American designers. Home furnishing and household goods. *OPEN 10.00-20.00 Mon-Fri, 10.00-18.00 Sat.*

House of Fraser, Kensington   1 E 7
63 Kensington High St W8. 01-937 5432. Good general store selling fashionable clothes, household and electrical goods. Hairdressing/beauty salon.

House of Fraser, Oxford St   2 F 19
318 Oxford St W1. 01-629 8800. Straightforward store with an excellent lingerie department. Unusual sizes well catered for in the dress department. Astral Sports in the basement.

John Lewis   2 F 19
278-306 Oxford St W1. 01-629 7711. One of the largest dress fabric departments in Europe. Furniture, furnishings, china and glass, fashions. Good haberdashery and craft materials. Bureau de change, export bureau and interpreters. Several branches including Brent Cross Shopping Centre NW4. 01-202 6535.

Liberty   2 G 20
210-220 Regent St W1. 01-734 1234. Fashionable and famous, especially for its distinctive fabrics and unusual luxury goods. Good, unusual fashion jewellery, wide range of glass and china, oriental rugs, prints and gifts. Designer collection clothes.

Littlewoods   2 E 17
508-520 Oxford St W1. 01-629 7840. Inexpensive high-street chain for clothing and household goods.

Marks & Spencer   2 E 17
458 Oxford St W1. 01-935 7954. Also at 173 Oxford St W1, 01-437 7722; plus numerous other branches. Excellent quality clothes and accessories for men, women and children. Wide range of foods, home furnishings, cosmetics. Nothing can be tried on, but anything can be exchanged/

refunded. Good value. Bureau de change.
*OPEN 09.00-20.00 Mon-Fri, 09.00-18.00
Sat.*

Next   I D 7
54-60 Kensington High St W8. 01-938
3709. Offers the fashions which made its
name but also cosmetics, lingerie, accessories, flowers, home furnishings and its
newest clothing range, BG, for children.
Restaurant and snack bar. *OPEN
10.00-19.00 Mon-Fri, 10.00-18.00 Sat.*

Peter Jones   5 L 12
Sloane Sq SW1. 01-730 3434. Modern and
antique furniture; glass, china, household
goods. Large furnishing fabric department.
Excellent linens: wide range of plain coloured sheets and towels in all sizes. Fashion   clothes,   hairdressing   salon.
Interpreters.

Selfridges   2 E 18
400 Oxford St W1. 01-629 1234. Limitless
household department. Furniture, men's
and women's fashions, toys, food hall,
sports clothing and equipment. Bank,
information desk, garage with parking facilities for 700 cars.

Clothes stores

*Nearly all London's department stores also
have extensive collections of clothes and
accessories. These are the specialists:*

Aquascutum   2 I 20
100 Regent St W1. 01-734 6090. Fine
quality British raincoats, coats, suits, knitwear and accessories for men and women.

Austin Reed   2 I 20
103 Regent St W1. 01-734 6789. English
and Continental suits and accessories for
men. Accent on quality. Valet service and
barber. Options department for ladies, selling executive and designer wear suits and
classic dresses. Luncheon room.

Burberrys   5 J 21
18 Haymarket SW1. 01-930 3343. Classic
raincoats for men and women cut in English
style. Hats, scarves, suits and accessories.
Other branches.

C & A   2 E 17
501-519 Oxford St W1. 01-629 7272. Vast
selection of reasonably priced fashions and
classics for all the family including skirts,
dresses, coats, knitwear, suits and
leathers. Avanti collection for young men.
Sportsworld department includes large
seasonal collection of ski-wear. Full fashion
range for 14 to 25-year-olds in the Clock
House. Other branches.

Jaeger   2 H 20
204 Regent St W1. 01-734 8211. Four floors
of well-cut fashionable English clothes.
Suits, coats, knitwear and casual wear for
men. Dresses, suits and separates for
women in colour co-ordinated departments. Cashmere, camel and knitted garments. Original accessories, jewellery,
perfumes and Italian footwear.

Lillywhites   5 J 20
Piccadilly Circus SW1. 01-930 3181. All
sporting clothes and equipment plus Sports
Council information desk.

Moss Bros & Attitudes   6 J 23
88 Regent St W1. 01-494 0666. Moved to
Regent Street in 1988 after 150 years in
Covent Garden. Moss Bros is well known
for classic menswear, including service uniforms. Attitudes stocks cosmetics,
women's designer clothes, jewellery and
accessories.

Simpson   2 I 20
203 Piccadilly W1. 01-734 2002. High-
quality clothing for men and women. Suits,
knitwear, dresses, separates. Daks country
clothes, Squadron sportswear, luggage
and accessories. Wine bar, restaurant, barber's shop.

Children's clothes

*See 'Children's shopping' section in 'Child-
ren's London' for details of shops.*

Men's clothes

See also 'Clothes stores'.

Bespoke tailors

*Savile Row for expensive but long-lasting
hand-tailored clothes in the finest cloths.*

Anderson & Sheppard   2 H 19
30 Savile Row W1. 01-734 1420.

Blades   2 H 19
8 Burlington Gdns, Savile Row W1. 01-734
8911.

Douglas Hayward   2 G 17
95 Mount St W1. 01-499 5574.

Gieves & Hawkes   2 H 20
1 Savile Row W1. 01-434 2001. Classic but
fashionable bespoke and ready-made
clothes.

Henry Poole   2 H 19
15 Savile Row W1. 01-734 5985.

Huntsman & Sons 2 H 20
11 Savile Row W1. 01-734 7441. King of
Savile Row from before 1800.

Kilgour, French & Stanbury 2 H 20
8 Savile Row W1. 01-734 6905.

Nutters of Savile Row 2 H 20
35a Savile Row W1. 01-437 6850. Exclusive but adventurous men's tailor.

Tom Gilbey 2 H 20
2 New Burlington St W1. 01-734 4877. An
appointment is necessary at this design
house where any type of suit can be made-
to-measure. Women are also catered for. A
new venture is Tom Gilbey's Waistcoat
Gallery which has a large selection of
bespoke and ready-to-wear waistcoats.

Designer clothes

*Internationally known names, very chic and
rather expensive.*

Browns 2 F 19
23 South Molton St W1. 01-491 7833.
Selection of Europe's foremost ready-to-
wear designs exclusive to the shop.

Crolla 2 I 19
35 Dover St W1. 01-629 5931. Classical
designs in unusual fashion fabrics. Also
made-to-measure and accessories.

Malcolm Levene 2 D 18
13-15 Chiltern St W1. 01-487 4383. Men's
classic fashion and contemporary design.
Hand-made shoes, designer suits, trousers
and jackets. Exclusive UK stockists of
Kiehls – a range of the purest skin and hair
products.

Piero de Monzi 4 L 4
68-70 Fulham Rd SW3. 01-581 4247. Chic
Italian styles.

St Laurent 'Rive Gauche' 2 G 19
113 New Bond St. 01-493 1800. Exclusive
own-label Paris clothes for men and
women.

Vincci 2 I 19
60 Jermyn St SW1. 01-629 0407. Top Italian designs in unusual fabrics exclusive to
the shop.

Fashion shops

Burtons 2 H 20
114 Regent St W1. 01-734 1951. Suits and
accessories at reasonable prices.

Cecil Gee 2 I 21
39-45 Shaftesbury Av W1. 01-734 8651.
Well-made designer suits, ties, coats.

Classic Nouveau 4 L 11
65 King's Rd SW3. 01-730 6575. Part of the
Fiorucci company. Casual, sporty, practical
clothes and accessories.

Coopers 2 H 20
89 Regent St W1. 01-734 3292. Good range
of classic and business suits. Casual wear
and accessories. Also shoes. Larger sizes
catered for.

Dunn & Co 2 I 20
56-58 Regent St W1. 01-734 1904. Classic
suits and tweed jackets with a modern influ-
ence.

French Connection 3 J 23
55-56 Long Acre WC2. 01-379 6560.
Stocks only French Connection clothes for
men. Colourful, fashionable styles. *OPEN
10.30-19.00 (to 20.00 Thur) Mon-Sat,
11.30-17.00 Sun.*

Hackett 4 M 2
65b New King's Rd SW6. 01-731 2790. Well
known for classic English style but stock
ranges from formal to sportswear. Good
accessories.

Herbie Frogg 2 H 19
38 New Bond St W1. 01-499 2029. Stylish,
classic suits by Hugo Boss and Valentino.
High fashion casual wear by Armani and
Cerutti.

Hornes Menswear 2 G 22
4 Oxford St W1. 01-580 9104. Casual wear,
suits and shoes with the emphasis on co-
ordination.

Jones 4 L 10
129 King's Rd SW3. 01-352 5323. Exciting
young designs at average prices. Jeans,
leather jackets, shirts, shoes.

Les 2 Zebras 6 J 23
38 Tavistock St WC2. 01-836 2855. Specialises in very chic, casual clothes for men
by French, Italian and English designers.
Knitwear, accessories, shoes and leather
goods. *OPEN 10.30-18.30 (to 19.00 Thur)
Mon-Sat.*

Next Man 2 F 19
62 South Molton St W1. 01-493 5076. Colour co-ordinated fashion separates. Suits
and casual wear. Shoes and accessories.

Review 2 H 20
69 King's Rd SW3. 01-730 5533. Fashion
for the image-conscious male. Co-
ordinated fashions in both original and classic styles.

Tie Rack 1 D 7
15a Kensington Shopping Mall, Kensington
High St W8. 01-937 5168. Chain of small
shops selling ties in a range of different
fabrics.

Top Man 2 F 20
Oxford Circus W1. 01-636 7700. Large
shop for variety of inexpensive men's fashions in styles to suit most tastes.

Way In   2 I 14
Harrods, Knightsbridge SW1. 01-730 1234.
Fashionable clothes department within the
famous store.
Woodhouse   2 G 21
99-101 Oxford St W1. 01-437 2809. Extensive range of fashionable clothes.

Clothes hire

Kritz   2 B 18
19 Melcombe St NW1. 01-935 0304. Gents'
dress-wear hire service since 1904.
Moss Bros   6 J 23
88 Regent St W1. 01-494 0666. Men's ceremonial and formal wear. Arrange to hire a
week in advance.
Young's Dress Hire   2 G 22
1-2 Berners St W1. 01-437
4422.
Also at: 19-20 Hanover St W1.   2 G 20
01-493 5192.
Formal wear with a difference. A full range
of morning suits, dinner suits, lounge suits,
daywear and white tuxedos.

Clothing fabrics

*Also refer to the fabric shops under
'Women's clothes' for materials suitable for
shirts, ties, etc.*
Allans   2 E 18
56-58 Duke St W1. 01-629 3781. Spe-
cialises in men's light-weight suitings and
ladies' fabrics.
W. Bill   2 F 19
93 New Bond St W1. 01-629 2837. British
tweeds, cashmeres and suitings. Tweed
jackets made to order, knitwear. World-
wide mail-order.
Dormeuil   2 H 20
14 Warwick St W1. 01-437 4433. World-
famous 'Tonik' cloths, mohairs, tropical
worsteds, etc.
Hunt & Winterbotham   2 H 19
19 Savile Row W1. 01-437 1425. Wide
range of quality suiting fabrics, tweeds,
cashmere, etc. 24hr delivery service.

Hats

Bates   2 J 19
21a Jermyn St SW1. 01-734 2722.
Edwardian-fronted men's hat shop, also
favoured by the ladies.
Herbert Johnson   2 H 19
30 New Bond St W1. 01-408 1174. Everything from crash helmets to yachting caps.

James Lock   5 J 19
6 St James's St SW1. 01-930 5849. Hats for
every occasion. Felt hats, tweed hats and
caps. Famous for bowlers. Also top-quality
riding hats.

Knitwear

W. Bill   2 F 19
93 New Bond St W1. 01-629 2837. Wide
range of British knitwear including
lambswool, cashmere, intarsia and Argyle
sweaters. Hand-knitted Icelandic, Fair Isle,
Aran and cricket sweaters. Shetland Eve-
rests exclusive to the shop.
The Scotch House   1 I 11
2 Brompton Rd SW3. 01-581 2151. Also at
84 Regent St W1. 01-734 0203. A wide
selection of Fair Isle, Shetland and Pringle
knitwear. Tartans too.
S. Fisher of Burlington   2 I 19
Arcade
22-23 & 32-33 Burlington Arcade W1.
01-493 4180. Very popular with overseas
visitors for cashmere, lambswool and classic knitwear and kilts.

Leather clothes

*See under 'Women's clothes' and 'Second-
hand clothes'. For a cheaper range of fashion leather coats and jackets try the markets, especially in Kensington, and
boutiques.*

Military & naval dress

Moss Bros   6 J 23
88 Regent St W1. 01-494 0666. War uni-
forms for officers in any of the services. War
medals and ribbons. Ceremonial accoutre-
ments can be hired.

Second-hand clothes

*Don't miss the markets, especially Anti-
quarius, Portobello Rd and Camden Lock
for period clothes.*
Angel   2 I 21
119-123 Shaftesbury Av WC2. 01-836
5678. Military full dress uniform 1800
onwards for professional use. Hire only.
Eat Your Heart Out   4 L 7
360 King's Rd SW3. 01-352 3392. 30s, 40s
and 50s suits, jackets, shirts, and evening
wear. Large selection including jewellery,

bric-à-brac and some new, classical clothes.

Hackett 4 L 2
117 Harwood Rd SW6. 01-731 2790. Second-hand formal wear.

Lawrence Corner 3 C 23
62-64 Hampstead Rd NW1. 01-388 6811. Uniforms and Army/Navy surplus from World War II onwards. To hire or buy.

Shirts

These firms make top-quality shirts to measure:

Coles Ltd 5 K 12
131 Sloane St SW1. 01-730 7564.

Harvie & Hudson 2 I 19
77 & 97 Jermyn St SW1. 01-930 3949.

Hawes & Curtis 2 H 19
2 Burlington Gdns W1. 01-493 3803.

Hilditch & Key 2 I 19
73 Jermyn St SW1. 01-930 5336.

Turnbull & Asser 2 I 19
71 Jermyn St SW1. 01-930 0502. Also at 23 Bury St SW1. Ready-made and bespoke English cottons and silks.

Shoes

Refer to 'Women's shoes' – many also have a good men's department.

Church's 2 I 19
58-59 Burlington Arc W1. 01-493 8307. The famous high quality classic men's shoes. Wide range of fittings.

John Lobb 5 J 19
9 St James's St SW1. 01-930 3664. Top-quality, hand-made, made-to-measure shoes. Also women's shoes.

Maxwell's 2 H 20
11 Savile Row W1. 01-734 9714. Hand-made bespoke boots and shoes of the highest quality.

Pinet 2 G 19
47 New Bond St W1. 01-629 2174. Shoes in all kinds of skins exclusive to the shop. Evening wear and a large range of casual wear.

Trickers 2 I 19
67 Jermyn St SW1. 01-930 6395. Quality hand-made and ready-made shoes at reasonable prices.

Sportswear

Lillywhites and Simpson have very extensive stocks of sports and casual wear. See also 'Sports equipment' under 'Specialist shops and services'.

J. C. Cording 2 I 20
19 Piccadilly W1. 01-734 0830. Weatherproof and country clothing plus typical English fashion. Famous for old-fashioned, classic look cords and trousers. Exclusive luggage.

Swaine, Adeney, Brigg 2 I 19
185 Piccadilly W1. 01-734 4277. Wide selection of English and Continental country and shooting clothes.

Unusual sizes

Cooper's All Size 2 D 16
72 & 74 Edgware Rd W2. 01-402 8635. Also at 89 Piccadilly W1. 01-734 3292. Ready-to-wear clothes for the tall and small. Chest sizes 34-60 in (86-152cm). Alterations service.

High and Mighty 2 I 12
177 Brompton Rd SW3. 01-589 7454. Everything ready-to-wear for the big or tall man. Chest sizes 44-58 in (112-147cm) up to 6ft 9in (2.06m) in height. Shoes to size 15.

Magnus
63 Southend Rd NW2. 01-435 1792. Out-size shoes for men sizes 11-15 and women sizes 8-11.

Women's clothes

See also 'Department stores' and 'Clothes stores'.

Fashion chains

Up-to-date fashion without the expensive price tags of more exclusive designs. Main branches only are listed below.

Benetton 2 G 20
255-259 Regent St W1. 01-493 8600. Large range of colourful Italian knitwear and separates.

Boules 6 J 23
22-23 James St WC2. 01-379 7848. Own label fashions and accessories at affordable prices. *OPEN 11.00-19.30 Mon-Fri, 10.30-19.00 Sat, 13.00-18.00 Sun.*

Chelsea Girl 1 D 4
124 Kensington High St W8. 01-937 0224. Popular young styles at very reasonable prices. Good tops and skirts, shoes, tights and handbags.

Country Casuals 2 I 20
146 Regent St W1. 01-734 1727. Colour co-ordinated separates in classic and high fashion ranges. Matching accessories.

The Gap 2 G 20
208 Regent St W1. 01-434 2091. American-style casual wear for men, women and children. Co-ordinated colours.

Hennes 2 E 17
481 Oxford St W1. 01-493 8557. Also at 261-271 Regent St W1. 01-493 4004. High fashion clothes to suit every mood. Children's and men's clothes too.

Jigsaw 6 J 23
21 Long Acre WC2. 01-240 3855. Casual, sporty styles in natural fibres. Limited number of co-ordinating colours available but stock changes frequently. Accessories, lingerie and shoes. OPEN 10.00-20.00 Mon-Fri, 10.00-19.00 Sat, 13.00-18.00 Sun.

Laura Ashley 2 G 20
256 Regent St W1. 01-437 9760. Distinctive cotton print dresses and separates in romantic styles. Nighties, evening and wedding dresses. Also corduroy and woollens for winter. Accessories include boots, shoes, hats and jewellery.

Miss Selfridge 2 E 18
40 Duke St W1. 01-629 1234. Enormous selection of fashionable clothes. Excellent sweaters and shirts. Tights, jewellery, cosmetics and a good shoe shop.

Monsoon 6 J 23
23 Covent Garden Mkt WC2. 01-836 9140. Up-market Indian cottons, silks and velvets. Good for party clothes. Visit the Monsoon accessories shop 'Accessorize' next door for co-ordinating belts, hats, jewellery and shoes.

Next 2 F 19
160 Regent St W1. 01-434 2515. Colour co-ordinated fashion separates. New styles each season. Shoes and cosmetics.

Richards 2 F 18
374 Oxford St W1. 01-629 0640. Large selection of dresses, separates, coats and sportswear.

Stefanel 2 F 19
15 South Molton St W1. 01-499 9907. Italian knitwear and separates in bright fashion colours.

Top Shop 2 G 20
214-216 Oxford St W1. 01-636 7700. Basement complex of boutiques carrying all major designers of young fashion. Range from inexpensive to nearly up-market.

Wallis 2 E 17
215 Oxford St W1. 01-439 8669. Large range of dresses and well-cut quality fashions. Specialise in colour co-ordinates.

Warehouse 2 G 20
19 Argyll St W1. 01-437 7101. Young fashion from young designers at reasonable prices.

Designer wear

The following shops have been chosen for the quality and individuality of their goods. Prices vary – the South Molton St and Knightsbridge areas tend to be expensive. London is full of interesting individual fashion shops which a day's browsing will reveal.

Arte 4 L 10
55 King's Rd SW3. 01-730 3607. Bold and unusual fashions for the daring dresser.

Browns 2 F 19
23-27 South Molton St W1. 01-491 7833. The very best of British and international designer clothes exclusive to the shop.

Cacharel 2 G 19
103 New Bond St W1. 01-629 1964. Sleek, stylish, quality clothes. Now have a range of clothes for the younger working woman.

Daniel Hechter 2 H 19
105 New Bond St W1. 01-493 1153. Dashing designs using bold and original colour schemes and quality fabrics, with the assured touch of French style.

Feathers 2 I 13
40 Hans Cres SW1. 01-589 0356. Well-chosen collection of continental clothes and accessories. Good knits, shoes, bags and belts.

Fiorucci 2 I 12
48 Brompton Rd SW3. 01-584 3683. High fashion designer labels for men and women. Bright 'fun' clothes and accessories for the young at heart including own label jeans and tops.

Friends 1 D 4
170 Kensington High St W8. 01-937 4665. Bright dresses and separates from the French Connection range. Tailored-look Stephen Marks clothes. Good accessories including hats, belts and jewellery.

Giorgio Armani 2 H 19
123 New Bond St W1. 01-499 7545. Beautiful designs by Armani for men and women. Chic and expensive.

Gorgissima 2 I 14
57 Knightsbridge SW1. 01-235 8414. Expensive French and Italian designer wear by the top names, including Lanvin and Givenchy.

Hyper Hyper 1 D 4
26-40 Kensington High St W8. 01-937 6964. A fashion forum on two floors featuring the work of exciting young designers in individual units. A large variety of avant garde clothing for men and women. Also shoes and accessories for all occasions. Café on each floor.

Issy Miyake 5 K 12
21 Sloane St SW1. 01-245 9891. Everything from tailored skirts to ethnic looking scarves are carefully designed and, unfortunately, expensive. Stocks a classic line as well as Issy Woman for the younger woman. Men's shop at 311 Brompton Rd SW3. 01-589 5924.

Joseph Bis 5 K 12
6 Sloane St SW1. 01-235 2467. Clothes by top French, Italian and English designers with prices to match.

Joseph Tricot 2 F 19
16 South Molton St W1. 01-629 9617. Joseph's fashions converted into wool. Some suede and leather garments.

Katharine Hamnett 1 I 11
264 Brompton Rd SW3. 01-584 1136. Huge hall of mirrors fashion palace. Strong on unfussy casual wear for men and women. All her latest themes are stocked here.

Kenzo 5 K 12
17 Sloane St SW1. 01-235 1991. Unusual clothes in colours that change every season. The whole look.

Koko 5 J 22
4 Garrick St WC1. 01-836 9511. Chic clothes for women of all ages and a few accessories including some interesting hats and bags. OPEN 10.30-19.00 (to 18.30 Sat) Mon-Sat.

Parkers 2 G 18
31 Brook St W1. 01-493 3412. Cross-section of high fashion mixed in with general classics. Good accessories, especially belts.

Piero de Monzi 4 K 7
68-70 Fulham Rd SW3. 01-581 4247. Sporty but expensive clothes from Italy for men and women. Excellent knitwear.

Polo Ralph Lauren 2 G 19
143 New Bond St W1. 01-491 4967. Expensive designer collection, ready-to-wear classic range and casual wear. Accessories. Also men's collection.

Valentino 2 H 19
160 New Bond St W1. 01-493 2698. A shop for the woman who loves to dress well and has the money to indulge her tastes. The grand evening dresses take some beating.

Wardrobe 2 D 18
17 Chiltern St W1. 01-935 4086. Also at 3 Grosvenor St W1. 01-629 7044. Good quality fashion for all ages. Consultancy service for working women with advice on clothes, make-up and hair.

Whistles 6 J 23
20 Covent Garden Mkt WC2. 01-379 7401. Expensive, up-market clothes with envi-able labels. OPEN 10.30-18.30 Mon-Wed, 11.00-19.00 Thur-Sat & 12.00-17.00 Sun.

Classic styles

Belville-Sassoon 5 K 12
73 Pavilion Rd SW1. 01-235 5801. Extravagant and elegant dresses for day, cocktail and evening wear.

Caroline Charles 2 I 12
11 Beauchamp Pl SW3. 01-589 5850. Pretty feminine clothes exclusively designed. All ages.

Galicia 6 J 24
24 Wellington St WC2. 01-836 2961. Classic and fashion clothes. Separates, dresses, suits, coats and rainwear.

James Drew 2 I 19
3 Burlington Arc W1. 01-493 0714. Classic tailored suits for women in the finest materials. Beautiful silk shirts. All ready-to-wear but couture-made in their own workrooms.

Panache 2 I 12
24 Beauchamp Pl SW3. 01-584 9807. A selection of the best designs from top international ready-to-wear collections. Printed silks, jersey, and French and Italian knits. Day and evening wear.

Peal & Co 2 I 19
37 Burlington Arc W1. 01-493 5378. Fashionable and classic knitwear and separates in cashmere and wools. Also cater for men.

Valbridge 2 I 12
60 Beauchamp Pl SW3. 01-589 7939. Huge stock of silk and cotton blouses in a dozen different qualities. Silks in 55 colours. Also a made-to-measure service. Orders despatched anywhere in the world.

The White House 2 G 19
51 New Bond St W1. 01-629 3521. Famous for their beautiful linen but also specialise in lovely clothes for women and children from little-known French, Italian and Swiss designers which keep their collection unique. Also exquisite lingerie.

Couturiers

These are the great internationally famous fashion houses. Appointment necessary.

Christian Dior London 2 G 20
9 Conduit St W1. 01-499 6255.

Hardy Amies 2 H 20
14 Savile Row W1. 01-734 2436.

Lachasse 2 H 17
4 Farm St W1. 01-499 2906.

Norman Hartnell 2 H 18
26 Bruton St W1. 01-629 0992.

Bridalwear

Most large department stores have good bridalwear departments. There are also large specialist shops with extensive collections and fitters on hand to advise. Smaller, even more specialised, shops deal in exclusive styles sometimes using antique fabrics.

Berkertex Brides   2   F   19
81 New Bond St W1. 01-629 9301. Biggest bridal store in the country. Lots of satins, taffetas and lace. Good stock of formal registry office wedding dresses.

Catherine Buckley
302 Westbourne Gro W11. 01-229 9786. Designer of exclusive, elaborate wedding gowns often made in antique textiles to Edwardian styles. New and antique lace used with embroidery and beading.

David Fielden   4   L   10
137 King's Rd SW3. 01-351 1745. Glamorous wedding dresses and evening wear made to order using an exotic array of materials.

Droopy & Browns   2   E   18
16 St Christopher's Pl W1. 01-935 3198. Wedding dresses by Angela Holmes who will design and make up anything from a flowing traditional church number to a quirky registry office suit.

Laura Ashley   2   G   20
256-258 Regent St W1. 01-437 9760. Tradition, nostalgia and femininity are Laura Ashley's trademarks in wedding dresses. Natural fabrics and reasonably priced.

Liberty   2   G   20
210-220 Regent St W1. 01-734 1234. Liberty has 12 designers working on its wedding dresses. Sample stock from which stock sizes made up although made-to-measure service available from some designers.

Pronuptia de Paris   2   G   20
19-20 Hanover St W1. 01-493 9152. Large collection of bridalwear which changes every season. Full fitting service by specialists.

Dress hire

Act One
2a Scampston Mews, Cambridge Gdns W10. 01-960 1456. Specialists in evening and cocktail dresses dating from the 1920s-1950s. Also accessories. *OPEN 10.00-19.00 Mon-Fri. Sat by appt only.*

Blackout   2   I   21
33 Great Windmill St W1. 01-439 1998.

40s, 50s and 60s clothing for hire. Cocktail dresses a speciality. If you really like something, Blackout will make you up a copy of the original. *OPEN 12.00-19.00 (to 20.00 Thur) Mon-Fri, 11.00-18.00 Sat.*

Dress to Kill   2   H   20
13 Newburgh St W1. 01-434 0168. Flamboyant range of ladies designer evening wear – stocked for the showbiz set. *OPEN 11.00-18.00 Mon-Fri.*

Hire Society
310b King St W6. 01-741 5210. Wonderful range of glamorous ball gowns and cocktail dresses as well as day wear, maternity and bridal dresses.

One Night Stand   5   M   13
44 Pimlico Rd SW1. 01-730 8708. Ball gowns, cocktail and dinner wear. Over 400 garments in stock with new styles each season.

Simpsons   6   J   23
Moss Bros, Bedford St WC2. 01-240 4567. The in-store dress-hire department specialises in ball gowns and evening attire generally.

Fabrics

The following are recommended for men's and women's fabrics.

Dickins & Jones   2   G   20
224 Regent St W1. 01-734 7070. Superb women's wool and novelty fabrics in addition to good general stock.

Harrods   2   I   12
Knightsbridge SW1. 01-730 1234. Exclusive and exquisite women's fashion fabrics.

Harvey Nichols   2   I   13
Knightsbridge SW1. 01-235 5000. Dress fabrics and delightful range of furnishing fabrics.

The Irish Shop   2   E   18
11 Duke St W1. 01-935 1366. Hand-woven Donegal tweeds, among large range of tweeds and other fabrics.

Jacob Gordon   2   E   18
75 Duke St W1. 01-629 5947. Couture fabrics from European collections at half-price.

Jason's   2   G   20
53 New Bond St W1. 01-629 2606. Exclusive fine silks.

John Lewis   2   F   19
278-306 Oxford St W1. 01-629 7711. One of the finest general selections of fabrics in the world at very reasonable prices.

Laura Ashley   2   G   20
256 Regent St W1. 01-437 9760. Special dress and furnishing fabric collection in

plain and patterned cotton/cambric. Cords and drills in exclusive patterns.

Liberty   2 H 20
210-220 Regent St W1. 01-734 1234. Superb silk, wool and cotton fabrics. Art nouveau and flower prints. Continental couture fabrics and Chinese silks. Furnishing fabrics.

Liberty Prints   4 L 8
340a King's Rd SW3. 01-352 6581. Beautiful printed fabrics in a medley of colours and a variety of materials.

Peter Jones   5 L 12
Sloane Sq SW1. 01-730 3434. Good general selection of materials at low prices.

The Scotch House   2 H 13
2 Brompton Rd SW1. 01-581 2151. Several branches including 84 and 191 Regent St W1; 7 Marble Arch W1. Excellent tartans.

Selfridges   2 E 18
400 Oxford St W1. 01-629 1234. Excellent general selection.

Knitwear

Bond Street Boutique   2 G 19
99 New Bond St W1. 01-629 5326. Large collection of colourful cashmere sweaters and skirts.

Carolyn Brunn   2 I 12
211 Brompton Rd SW3. 01-584 9065. Fashion knitwear, dresses, jackets, coats. Pretty, slinky dresses and silk shirts.

Crochetta   2 I 12
61 Beauchamp Pl SW3. 01-589 1266. Hand-made exclusive knitwear in silk, wool, cotton. Dresses and separates.

Jaeger   2 H 10
204 Regent St W1. 01-734 8211. Fashion and classic knitwear.

Lewis Henry   2 I 18
43 Berkeley St W1. 01-493 3628. Specialise in hand-crocheted clothes – even bikinis. Very attractive and original styles. Jersey and chiffon dresses with crocheted trimming.

Marks & Spencer   2 E 14
458 Oxford St W1. 01-935 7954. Very reasonably priced woollens of high-tested manufacturing standards.

Patricia Roberts   6 J 23
31 James St WC2. 01-379 6660. Beautiful and imaginative designer knitwear. An extensive collection of mohairs, Shetlands, cashmeres and cotton bouclés in bright primary colours.

The Scotch House   2 H 13
2 Brompton Rd SW1. 01-581 2151. Enormous range of Scottish knitwear – Shetland, cashmere and lambswool.

Scottish Merchant   5 J 22
16 New Row WC2. 01-836 2207. Seasonally changing stock of hand-made British designer sweaters. Also traditional Fair Isles, Guernseys and heavy rib-knits.

Westaway & Westaway   3 H 23
62-65 Great Russell St WC1. 01-405 4479. Specialists in woollens and cashmere.

Leather, suede & sheepskin clothes

Flint
614 Fulham Rd SW6. 01-731 4987. Suede and leather clothes in all colours of the rainbow. Also made-to-measure.

Leather Rat   2 F 19
37 South Molton St W1. 01-629 2208. Stocked with a wide variety of styles.

Loewe   2 I 19
25a Old Bond St W1. 01-493 3914. Quality hand-made Spanish leather and suede coats, dresses and suits for men and women.

Natural Leather   3 I 23
62 Neal St WC2. 01-240 7748. A safe bet if you want to buy a straightforward, good quality designer leather jacket. *OPEN 11.00-19.00 Mon-Sat.*

Skinshades   4 L 10
113 King's Rd SW3. 01-352 2480. Leather, suede and sheepskin fashions. *OPEN 10.00-19.00 Mon-Sat.*

Lingerie, hosiery & nightwear

Marks & Spencer, Littlewoods and Fenwicks carry good, inexpensive lingerie and nightwear while Harvey Nichols, Harrods and Fortnum & Mason are excellent for the more elegant, dreamy styles.

Bradleys   2 I 14
85 Knightsbridge SW1. 01-235 2902/3. Speciality shop for fine lingerie, nightwear and beachwear.

Courtenay   2 G 18
22 Brook St W1. 01-629 0542. Pretty lingerie in silk, cotton, lace; swimwear and accessories.

Fogal   2 I 12
51 Brompton Rd SW3. 01-225 0472. Tights, stockings and socks made from silk, cashmere and other exotic fabrics in all sizes, colours and patterns.

Janet Reger   1 I 12
2 Beauchamp Pl SW3. 01-584 9368. Also at 12 New Bond St W1. Glamorous, expen-

sive nightwear and lingerie. Collector's item catalogue also available.

Knickerbox 2 G 20
189 Regent St W1. 01-439 6430. High-street chain selling various styles of underwear for men and women.

Night Owls 4 J 9
78 Fulham Rd SW3. 01-584 2451. Unique little shop selling exquisite nightwear.

Rigby & Peller 2 F 19
12 South Molton St W1. 01-629 6708. Exclusive corsetières. Made-to-measure underwear and high-class Continental beachwear.

Sock Shop 2 G 22
89 Oxford St W1. 01-437 1030. High-street chain of small shops stocked full with all colours and styles of socks, tights and stockings. *OPEN 08.30-20.00 Mon-Fri, 08.30-19.00 Sat.*

Maternity clothes

It is worth looking in the chain stores because they often stock their own range of maternity clothes.

Balloon 4 J 11
77b Walton St SW3. 01-589 3121. Elegant, expensive maternity wear.

Great Expectations 4 J 9
78 Fulham Rd SW3. 01-584 2451. Stylish, youthful and quite trendy maternity clothes but unfortunately rather expensive.

Mothercare 2 E 17
461 Oxford St W1. 01-629 6621. (Main branch.) Good quality maternity and baby clothes and equipment at practical prices.

Second-hand clothes

Markets are your best bet for period clothes – especially Portobello Rd and Camden Lock.

Annie's 3 E 32
10 Camden Pas N1. 01-359 0796. Original clothes and accessories of the 20s, 30s and 40s, plus large selection of antique lace dresses, blouses, etc.

Antiquarius Antique Market 4 L 9
135-141 King's Rd SW3. 01-351 5353. Victorian nighties, 20s flapper dresses and crêpe dresses, 30s velvet evening dresses and more recent items. Quite expensive.

Cornucopia 5 O 16
12 Upper Tachbrook St SW1. 01-828 5752. Good range of second-hand clothes, shoes, jewellery and accessories, dating from 1910 into the 1960s, at reasonable prices.

Flip 3 J 23
125 Long Acre WC2. 01-836 7044. Large selection of second-hand American clothing.

The Frock Exchange 4 L 4
450 Fulham Rd SW6. 01-381 2937. Nearly new clothes and accessories.

Gallery of Antique Costume & Textiles
2 Church St NW8. 01-723 9981. Selection of period clothes spanning three centuries. Some reproductions. Also large stock of decorative textiles including wall hangings and quilts. Film and theatre suppliers.

Pandora Dress Agency 5 L 12
54 Sloane Sq SW1. 01-730 5722. Very good used model garments bought and sold on commission. Will be moving to new premises at 16-22 Cheval Pl SW7 (2 I 12) at some point as building scheduled for redevelopment.

Shoes

There are many good shoe-shop chains in addition to the more expensive individual shops. This is a selection of both:

Anello & Davide 3 I 24
30-35 Drury La WC2. 01-836 1983. Beautifully made shoes and boots in long-lasting styles and at good prices. Specialise in dance shoes.

Bally 2 I 19
30 Old Bond St W1. 01-493 2250. Good quality shoes for men and women.

Bertie 2 F 18
409 Oxford St W1. 01-493 2250. More imaginative styles than many and usually stock unconventional colours.

Charles Jourdan 2 I 12
39-43 Brompton Rd SW3. 01-581 3333. Beautiful shoes imported from France for men and women.

Deliss 2 I 12
41 Beauchamp Pl SW3. 01-584 3321. Exclusive designs in all kinds of shoes and boots, made-to-measure in a week from fabrics and leather. Bags and accessories.

Derber 1 D 7
80 Kensington High St W8. 01-937 1578. Popular and stylish shoes and boots for women. High fashion range for men.

Dolcis 2 F 19
350 Oxford St W1. 01-629 5877. Popular chain with many branches.

Faith 2 F 18
383 Oxford St W1. 01-499 2176. Reasonably priced classic everyday styles.

Ferragamo 2 I 19
24 Old Bond St W1. 01-629 5007. Italian shoemakers. Smart, comfortable shoes.

Frederick Freed   5 J 22
94 St Martin's La WC2. 01-240 0432. Specialists in theatrical and ballet shoes. Also make excellent boots to order. Contact 01-985 6121.

Gamba Shoes   2 I 12
3 Garrick St WC2. 01-437 0704. Ballet shoes, character shoes, pumps in satin and leather. Dyeing service for satin shoes – can match almost any colour.

Gucci   2 I 19
27 Old Bond St W1. 01-629 2716. Pricey, but well-made and distinctive styles.

Hobbs   2 F 19
47 South Molton St W1. 01-629 0750. Classic and fashion shoes in a good range of colours; lots of flatties.

Kurt Geiger   2 F 19
95 New Bond St W1. 01-499 2707. Exclusive shoes and handbags. Also at Harrods, Dickins & Jones and other big stores.

Lilley & Skinner   2 F 18
360 Oxford St W1. 01-629 6381. One of many branches for fashion shoes at reasonable prices.

Midas   2 H 20
22 Carnaby St W1. 01-730 3527. Eye-catching, colourful fashion shoes of all kinds. Also clothes and accessories.

Natural Shoe Store   3 I 23
21 Neal St WC2. 01-836 5254. Ultra-comfortable, foot-shaped shoes for men, women and children.

Peter Lord   2 G 21
167 Oxford St W1. 01-637 1638. Stock quality shoes in wide fittings as well as fashion shoes and children's footwear. Large stockist of Clark's shoes.

Pied à Terre   2 F 19
19 South Molton St W1. 01-629 1362. Unusual styles for men and women, including exotic suede slippers. Also do a cheaper range called Basics.

Ravel   2 F 20
248 Oxford St W1. 01-499 1949. Fashion-shoe chain with many branches.

Rayne   2 G 19
66 New Bond St W1. 01-629 7022. Smart, well-made shoes, tend to be on the expensive side.

Russell & Bromley   2 H 19
24 New Bond St W1. 01-629 6903. Fine hand-made shoes from Spain, France and Italy.

Sacha   2 E 17
351 Oxford St W1. 01-499 7272. Modern shoes in up-to-date styles for the younger woman.

Saxone   2 E 17
502 Oxford St W1. 01-629 2138. Popular modern shoes at competitive prices.

Unusual sizes

The Base   3 I 23
55 Monmouth St WC2. 01-240 8914. Half the clothes here are designed by Yugoslav Rushka Murganovic and the rest come from Europe or America. Bold designs and fun colours.

Buy & Large   5 L 12
4 Holbein Pl, Sloane Sq SW1. 01-730 6534. Full selection of clothes in fittings from 16-24. Good for evening wear.

Crispins   2 D 18
28-30 Chiltern St W1. 01-935 7984. Court shoes, boots, sandals and espadrilles in large sizes (8-11); plus narrow fittings in sizes 4-11.

Evans   2 E 17
538-540 Oxford St W1. 01-499 5372. General selection of clothes for the larger woman from size 14.

Lilley & Skinner   2 F 18
360 Oxford St W1 01-629 6381. Special department for large and small size fashion shoes at reasonable prices.

Little Women   3 I 23
4 Langley Ct WC2. 01-836 9640. Co-ordinating fashion clothes for the 5ft 2in (1.57m) and under. *OPEN 10.30-18.30 Mon-Sat.*

Long Tall Sally   2 D 18
21 Chiltern St W1. 01-487 3370. Specialises in elegant clothes for tall women, sizes 12-20. Lingerie, separates, specially designed evening wear.

Mary Fair   2 C 17
61 Crawford St W1. 01-262 9763. Individually designed clothes in small sizes.

Sassa   5 N 17
76b Rochester Row SW1. 01-834 2260. The name stands for Sixteen and Several Sizes Above. Dresses, and separates in silk, cotton and wool, made-to-measure and ready-to-wear.

Tall Girls   2 G 19
17 Woodstock St W1. 01-499 8748. Everything for girls from 5ft 9in (1.75m) to 6ft 5in (1.96m). Shoes from 8-11, lingerie, stockings and tights.

Accessories

General

Accessorize   6 J 23
Unit 22, Covent Garden Mkt WC2. 01-240 2107. A large selection of earrings, costume jewellery, bags, belts, shoes and

watches. *OPEN 10.00-20.00 Mon-Sat, 12.00-18.00 Sun.*

American Retro   2 I 22
35 Old Compton St W1. 01-734 3477. Sells original 50s American garb and natty accessories.

Brats   4 L 7
281 King's Rd SW3. 01-341 7674. An upmarket accessory shop but all good designs and value for money.

Cobra
5 Portobello Green, 281 Portobello Rd W10. 01-960 4874. Own label flamboyant designer jewellery, bags, belts and wallets.

Gallery   2 J 19
1 Duke of York St, off Jermyn St SW1. 01-930 5974. Specialise in high quality accessories for men – blazer buttons and crests for various schools, universities and regiments. Also shirts, ties, cuff links, belts and braces.

Gucci   2 I 19
27 Old Bond St W1. 01-629 2716. Classic, matching accessories all emblazoned with the recognisable Gucci 'G's.

Hermes   2 H 19
155 New Bond St W1. 01-499 8856. Expensive, chic quality bags, scarves, jewellery and perfumes.

Mary Quant   2 H 20
21 Carnaby St W1. 01-494 3277. Bursting with novel accessories, including fancy tights, make-up and undies. Stock changes regularly.

Nec;cessory   2 F 19
11 South Molton St W1. 01-629 0550. Small shop full of jewellery, hats, bags and hosiery.

Next Accessories/Essential   1 E 7
Next
123c Kensington High St W8. 01-938 3709. Accessories in sophisticated colours and styles. Essentials are a range of useful, well-designed objects which make great gifts – torches, diaries, luggage etc.

Filofax

Filofax Centre   2 G 20
21 Conduit St W1. 01-499 0457. Filofaxes to fit every pocket and an amazing range of inserts.

Just Facts   2 H 21
43 Broadwick St W1. 01-734 5034. Stocks the entire Filofax range.

Handbags & luggage

Carried by most fashion and shoe shops.

Alba Handbags   2 B 18
189 Baker St NW1. 01-935 3410. Good modern bags at all prices, exciting shapes and colours.

The City Bag Store   2 F 19
3 South Molton St W1. 01-499 2549. Wide range of bags including tapestry, canvas and leather. Stockists for 'le sport sac' of New York and Enny of Italy.

Mulberry   2 E 18
12 Gees Court, St Christopher's Pl W1. 01-493 2546. Full range of Scotch grain and leather luggage, fashion handbags and briefcases.

Salisburys
68a Oxford St W1. High street chain selling wide range of inexpensive bags, handbags and luggage generally.

Hats

David Shilling   2 D 19
44 Chiltern St W1. 01-487 3179. Famous and exclusive hat creations; as immortalised by Mr Shilling's mother at Ascot. Chic and elegant hats for everyday wear.

The Hat Shop   3 I 23
58 Neal St WC2. 01-836 6718. A wide variety of hats for men and women, ranging from classic panamas and boaters to designer specials.

Herbert Johnson   2 H 19
30 New Bond St W1. 01-408 1174. A fine range of hats for men and women to suit all occasions.

Jane Smith Straw Hats
131 St Philip St SW8. Amazing selection of straw hats and pins to keep them on.

Sandra Phillips   1 D 8
Hyper Hyper, 26-40 Kensington High St W8. 01-937 8904. Classic but adventurous styles in quality materials. Made-to-measure service.

Simone Mirman   5 J 14
11 West Halkin St SW1. 01-235 2656. Unusual high-fashion hats and accessories.

Specialist shops and services

London is an international centre of art, fashion, antiques and collectors' items. Many shops have specialised in certain goods and have become world-famous names. The list below represents only a selection of some of the best shops in each category.

Some shops close on Sat afternoon and stay open late on Wed or Thur evenings.

'Which?' Magazine   2 B 17
Consumers' Association, 2 Marylebone Rd NW1. 01-486 5544. The best subscription periodical for unbiased testing of everyday products and services. Available at libraries for reference.

Animals

Animal Fair   1 E 6
17 Abingdon Rd W8. 01-937 0011. Animals and services such as boarding (for small animals) and grooming. Agency for kennels in the country.

Battersea Dogs Home   4 R 12
4 Battersea Park Rd SW8. 01-622 3626. Dogs and cats, some with pedigrees, but all deserving cases.

Friends of Animals League
Foal Farm, Jail La, Biggin Hill, Kent. Biggin Hill 72386. Mainly dogs, cats, and other domestic animals, rescued and available for adoption by carefully vetted homes.

National Canine Defence League
1 Pratt Mews NW1. 01-388 0137. Rehouses abandoned dogs and provides information on canine problems and care.

Town & Country Dogs   2 I 13
35b Sloane St SW1. 01-730 5792. Long-established dog agency. Specialise in Yorkshire Terriers and Shihtzu but will direct you to the breeder of any dog. Also clipping and shampooing and help with exporting.

Antiques

English homes are still rich in antiques, as is reflected in the amount of 18th and 19thC furniture, china and objets d'art available in the hundreds of antique shops in London. Good hunting grounds are the King's Rd, Portobello Rd, Camden Passage in Islington, Kensington Church St, Fulham Rd and Camden Town.

Antique fairs

Antiquarian Book Fair   2 I 17
Park Lane Hotel, Piccadilly W1. 01-499 6321. International fair with books, documents, musical scores. *Late Jun.*

Chelsea Antiques Fair   4 L 4
Chelsea Old Town Hall, King's Rd, SW3. 01-937 5464. *Held annually in Sep,* this well-established fair offers a wide range of antiques and works of art.

Antique hire

Michael Carleton
77-81 Haverstock Hill NW3. 01-722 2277. Furniture, pictures and decorative items available for hire for film, TV or photographic use.

Antique shops

Bluett & Sons   2 G 18
48 Davies St W1. 01-629 4018. Mainly Chinese, and some south-east Asian, ceramics and works of art.

T. Crowther   1 G 2
282 North End Rd SW6. 01-385 1375. Period lead, bronze and stone figures, gates, mantelpieces, wrought-iron work, panelling and beautiful furniture.

Gallery of Antique Costume and Textiles
2 Church St NW8. 01-723 9981. One of Europe's largest suppliers of antique costumes and textiles. Pillows of London at 48 Church St is part of the Gallery.

Jeremy   4 L 8
255 King's Rd SW3. 01-352 0644. English and French furniture and objets d'art.

John Sparks   2 G 17
128 Mount St W1. 01-499 2265. Oriental objets d'art.

Jonathan Harris   1 D 8
54 Kensington Church St W8. 01-937 3133. Fine quality and unusual European and Oriental furniture and works of art.

Mayorcas   2 J 19
38 Jermyn St SW1. 01-629 4195. Well-known dealers in antique textiles – costumes, embroidery, vestments, tapestry.

Myriad   1 A 5
131 Portland Rd W11. 01-229 1709. Painted and decorative furniture and general antiques too.

Pelham Galleries   4 J 10
163-165 Fulham Rd SW3. 01-589 2686. Specialists in English and Continental furniture, works of art, musical instruments and tapestries.

Spink & Son   5 J 19
5-7 King St, St James's SW1. 01-930 7888. English paintings and water-colours. Silver, jewellery, paperweights, Oriental, Asian and Islamic art, textiles, medals and coins.

Antique markets

These covered antique markets can be found in Camden Passage, Portobello Rd, King's Rd and as follows:

Alfie's Antique Market
13-25 Church St NW8. 01-723 6066. Four floors of antique stalls selling just about everything, also some repairs done. Coffee bar.

Antiquarius   4   L   9
135-141 King's Rd SW3. 01-351 5353. All aspects of fine, applied and decorative arts. Also worth visiting for the antique clothing.

Chelsea Antique Market   4   L   8
245-253 King's Rd SW3. 01-352 9695. A large, busy market covering all collectors' items.

Furniture Cave   4   L   4
533 King's Rd SW10. 01-352 4229. Several companies under one roof selling a wide range of non-contemporary furniture. Also have a large architectural and sculpture range.

Grays Market   2   G   18
1-7 Davies Mews W1. 01-629 7034. Two giant covered markets selling huge selection of antiques.

Antiques: restorations

P. Levi
115 Power Rd W4. 01-995 1848. Terracotta and wooden sculptures repaired. Picture framing.

R. Wilkinson & Son
43-45 Wastdale Rd SE23. 01-699 4420. Expert restorations and reproduction of glass. Manufacturers of reproduction chandeliers and restorers of old ones. Art metal work.

Antiquities

The following shops deal in ancient works of art and objects.

Charles Ede   2   G   18
37 Brook St W1. 01-493 4944. Roman, Greek, Egyptian and Near Eastern antiquities. *OPEN Tue-Fri 12.30-16.30 or by appt.*

Ian Auld   3   E   32
1 Gateway Arc, Camden Passage N1. 01-359 1440. Mixed stock of antiquities and ethnographical items, with an emphasis on the latter.

Aquaria

Aquapets
17 Leeland Rd W13. 01-567 2748. Excellent general stock of fish, tanks and equipment.

Queensborough Fisheries
111 Goldhawk Rd W12. 01-743 2730. Excellent selection of various tropical and pond fishes. Also equipment, tanks and water plants.

Tachbrook Tropicals   5   N   16
244 Vauxhall Bridge Rd SW1. 01-834 5179. Importers and growers of over 200 species of tropical water plants for the aquarium. Also import fish. Accessories. Maintenance and servicing of aquaria.

Artists materials

See 'Crafts & art supplies'.

Auctioneers: general

W. & F. C. Bonham & Sons   2   H   12
Montpelier Galleries, Montpelier St SW7. 01-584 9161. Paintings, furniture, carpets, porcelain, jewellery and silver.

Christie's   5   J   19
8 King St, St James's SW1. 01-839 9060. Internationally famous. Comprehensive fine art auctioneers since 1766.

Christie's South Kensington   1   I   9
85 Old Brompton Rd SW7. 01-581 2231. All sorts of antique and antiquarian objects, including pictures, jewellery, silver, glass, ceramics, furniture and books.

Croydon Auction Rooms
144-150 London Rd, West Croydon, Surrey. 01-688 1123. Miscellaneous sales *10.00 Sat.*

Harvey's Auctions   3   I   23
14-18 Neal St WC2. 01-240 1467. Sales of antique and general furniture, ceramics, pictures, drawings, prints, clocks and modern objets *every Wed.*

Lots Road Galleries   4   M   4
71 Lots Rd SW10. 01-351 5784. General assorted sales *every Mon 18.00.* View Mon 09.00-17.00, Fri 09.00-15.00, Sat & Sun* 10.00-13.00.

Phillips   2   G   19
7 Blenheim St, New Bond St W1. 01-629 6602. Fine arts auctioneers and valuers.

Phillips Marylebone Auction   2   A   17
Rooms
Hayes Pl, Lisson Gro NW1. 01-723 2647. Sale of paintings only *11.00 Fri* (specialist sales *14.00 Fri).* Viewing *09.00-19.00 Thur* (specialist viewing *Wed).*

Sotheby's   2   G   19
34-35 New Bond St W1. 01-493 8080. Internationally famous for antiques and works of art. Paintings, ceramics, glass, furniture, silver, jewellery, books, manu-

scripts, photographic material and collectors' items.

Auctions: stamps & coins

Glendining 2 G 19
7 Blenheim St, New Bond St W1. 01-493 2445. Coins, military and naval medals. *About 20 sales a year.*

London Stamp and Coin Exchange 5 K 22
5 Buckingham St, Strand WC2. 01-930 1413. *One-two auctions annually.*

Royale Stamp Co 6 J 23
42 Maiden La WC2. 01-836 6122. *Six-seven postal auctions a year.*

Stanley Gibbons 6 K 23
399 Strand WC2. 01-836 8444. Stamps, postal history, albums and catalogues. *Twelve auctions a year.*

Bath repair

Renubath
248 Lillie Rd SW6. 01-381 8337. Bath resurfacing. Chemical cleaning, specialist repairs to enamel and porcelain. Good range of colours.

Bathrooms

Armitage Shanks 3 I 26
303-306 High Holborn WC1. 01-405 9663. Room settings of bathroom equipment.

Bathroom Discount Centre
297 Munster Rd SW6. 01-381 4222. Suites by Ideal, Twyfords and Armitage Shanks all at a discount.

Bonsack Baths 2 G 17
14 Mount St W1. 01-629 9981. Luxury baths and bathroom fittings, all custom-made.

British Bathroom Centre
602-604 Seven Sisters Rd N15. 01-802 6493. Bathroom products of well-known manufacturers displayed as rooms.

Czech & Speake 2 J 19
39c Jermyn St SW1. 01-439 0216. Brass taps and shower fittings (some thermostatic) moulded from Edwardian originals. Also sell accessories and toiletries.

Sitting Pretty 4 J 1
131 Dawes Rd SW6. 01-381 0049. Lavatory seats in mahogany or obeche (the latter can be stained to any colour). Also unfinished mahogany seats for the DIY enthusiast and reproduction, period suites.

Beauty specialists

Nicholson's Looking Good in London gives information on all aspects of health and beauty treatments available in the capital.

Alternative & Orthodox Medicine Clinic 2 C 20
56 Harley Hse, Marylebone Rd NW1. 01-486 8087. Treatments include aromatherapy, reflexology, facials and stress alleviation. Own range of natural products designed to treat specific skin problems and types.

The Body Shop 6 J 23
13 Covent Garden Mkt WC2. 01-836 5113. Other branches. These shops sell a large range of preparations based on fruit, flowers, spices and woods, formulated by herbalists. Non-animal derived products.

Cosmetics à la Carte 5 J 14
19b Motcomb St SW1. 01-235 0596. 'Beauty workshop' with advice and a chance to experiment.

Delia Collins 2 I 12
19 Beauchamp Pl SW3. 01-584 2423. Well-known and long-established beauty specialists. Sell their own preparations.

Helena Harnik 2 D 16
19 Upper Berkeley St W1. 01-724 1518. Specialise in electrolysis and the treatment of problem skins.

Joan Price's Face Place 4 K 11
33 Cadogan St SW3. 01-589 9062. Also at 31 Connaught St W2. 01-723 6671. Make-up lessons using many different products from various ranges. Also body and facial massages, pedicure and manicure, waxing, lash tinting, electrolysis.

Ray Cochrane Beauty School 2 C 18
118 Baker St W1. 01-486 6291. Deals with skin troubles, figure problems and unwanted hair. Facials, manicures and pedicures by advanced students under supervision. Consultants very capable.

Yves Rocher 4 L 11
9 Gees Ct W1. 01-409 2975. Shop packed with their famous beauty products – everything from shampoo to perfume. The emphasis is on natural beauty.

Bedroom shops

And So To Bed. . . 4 L 3
638-640 King's Rd SW6. 01-731 3593. Specialists in antique and reproduction four-posters, bedsteads and headboards in wood and brass. Complete range of bed-linen.

London Bedding Centre 2 I 13
26 Sloane St SW1. 01-235 7541. Comprehensive selection of beds from the practical to the ostentatious, including a large range of sofa beds. Available in 15 sizes, soft, medium and firm.

Upstairs Shop 4 K 10
33 Elystan St SW3. 01-581 9959. Specialists in pretty and exclusive bedroom furnishings, fabrics and wallpaper.

Books: children's

See under 'Children's shopping' in 'Children's London'.

Books: new

Most major department stores have book departments, the better ones being Harrods, Selfridges and Liberty. The following bookshops are recommended:

Barbican Business Book 6 L 31
Centre
9 Moorfields EC2. 01-628 7479. Wide range of business and finance books.

Books Etc 2 H 22
120 Charing Cross Rd WC2. 01-379 6838. Well-organised general book store.

Cinema Bookshop 2 H 23
13-14 Great Russell St WC1. 01-637 0206. Specialists in books, including out-of-print titles, magazines and all material relating to the cinema.

Claude Gill Books 2 E 18
10-12 James St W1. 01-629 4773. Excellent general bookshop. Other branches.

Collet's International 2 H 22
Bookshop
129-131 Charing Cross Rd WC2. 01-734 0782. Wide selection of books including travel, politics, economics, sociology; plus left-wing and trade union literature.

Collet's Penguin Bookshop 2 I 22
66 Charing Cross Rd WC2. 01-836 6306. Large selection of Penguins and Pelicans. Second-hand section too.

Compendium
234 Camden High St NW1. 01-485 8944. Contemporary bookshop specialising in political and feminist literature. US fiction. Also the occult, mysticism, psychology and fringe subjects. *OPEN Mon-Sat 10.00-18.00, Sun 11.00-17.00*

David & Charles Bookshop 2 C 18
36 Chiltern St W1. 01-935 6739. Specialises in railway and transport books. Also general books.

Denny's 6 J 30
2 & 4 Carthusian St EC1. 01-253 1311. General, scientific, medical and technical books.

Dillon's 3 F 23
82 Gower St WC1. 01-636 1577. Large academic and general stock including science and language. Some antiquarian and second-hand books.

The Economists' Bookshop 6 J 25
Clare Market, Portugal St WC2. 01-405 5531. Specialists in social science and business books. Second-hand dept.

European Bookshop 2 H 20
4 Regent Pl (off Regent St) W1. 01-734 5259. Mainly French books but also Spanish, German and Italian plus European periodicals.

Forbidden Planet 3 H 23
71 New Oxford St WC1. 01-379 6042. Specialists in science fiction, fantasy and horror. Large stock of comics, games and posters.

Foyles 2 H 22
119-125 Charing Cross Rd WC2. 01-437 5660. The biggest – has practically every English book in print.

French's Theatre Bookshop 6 J 23
52 Fitzroy St W1. 01-387 9373. Books on the theatre and play scripts.

Gay's the Word 3 F 25
66 Marchmont St WC1. 01-278 7654. Gay and feminist bookshop. *OPEN 11.00-19.00 Mon-Sat, 14.00-18.00 Sun.*

Grant & Cutler 2 G 21
55-57 Great Marlborough St W1. 01-734 2012. New and second-hand books in German, French, Spanish, Portuguese and Italian.

Hatchards 2 I 20
187 Piccadilly W1. 01-439 9921. Comprehensive selection of general books. Knowledgeable staff.

HMSO Bookshop 3 I 26
49 High Holborn WC1. 01-211 5656. HMSO publications on every subject from cooking to parliament. No fiction.

London Art Bookshop 1 D 7
7 Holland St W8. 01-937 6996. International books and magazines on art, architecture and photography.

Motor Books 5 J 22
33-36 St Martin's Ct WC2. 01-836 5376. Specialists in books on cars and aviation. Also military and railway books. World-wide mail-order service.

Murder One 3 H 23
23 Denmark St W1. 01-497 2200. Specialises in English language mystery and thriller titles plus magazines, videos, pos-

ters and section on rare and out-of-print titles.

Pan Bookshop   4 K 6
158-162 Fulham Rd SW10. 01-373 4997. Wide selection of paperbacks and most new hardbacks. *OPEN long hours: 10.00-22.00 Mon-Sat: 14.00-21.00 Sun.*

The Penguin Bookshop   6 J 23
10 Covent Garden Mkt WC2. 01-379 7650. Almost complete range of Penguin titles and a good range of other paperbacks and hardbacks.

Sherratt & Hughes   2 I 13
205 Sloane St SW1. 01-235 2128. Good general bookshop and court stationers.

Silver Moon   2 I 22
68 Charing Cross Rd WC2. 01-836 7906. Good selection of feminist literature.

W. H. Smith
Branches throughout London and at railway stations.

Travis & Emery   5 J 22
17 Cecil Ct WC2. 01-240 2129. Music and new and second-hand books on music. Theatrical and musical prints. Catalogues issued.

Waterstones   I E 6
193 Kensington High St W8. 01-937 8432. Good general bookshop.

Watkins Books Ltd   5 J 22
19-21 Cecil Ct WC2. 01-836 3778. Mysticism, the occult, religions and astrology.

Wholefood   2 D 18
24 Paddington St W1. 01-935 3924. Books on nutrition and health, diets, natural childbirth, ecology and agriculture.

A. Zwemmer   2 I 22
80 Charing Cross Rd WC2. 01-836 4710. 24 Litchfield St WC2. Comprehensive stock of international books on art, architecture, design, fashion, film and photography.

Book binding & restorations

Sangorski & Sutcliffe Zaehnsdorf
175r (entrance at 159) Bermondsey St SE1. 01-407 1244. Two companies at the same address. Hand binding in all styles and materials, design service. Repair and restore leather bindings.

Books: rare & antiquarian

The book collector is fortunate in having over 250 bookshops in London, many specialising in particular subjects. Charing Cross Rd, Cecil Ct and around the British Museum are good areas for browsing.

Andrew Block   3 H 24
20 Barter St WC1. 01-405 9660. Drama, entertainment and conjuring books, prints and ephemera. *OPEN 11.30-16.30 Mon-Fri (to 20.00 Wed).*

Bell Book & Radmall   6 J 23
4 Cecil Ct WC2. 01-240 2161. Modern first editions of English and American literature. Plus detective, science and fantasy fiction.

Bernard Quaritch   2 H 20
5-8 Lower John St, Golden Sq W1. 01-734 2983. Illuminated manuscripts, early printed books, English literature pre-1900, natural history, science and travel.

Dance Books   5 J 22
9 Cecil Ct WC2. 01-836 2314. All aspects of dancing and human movement. Also posters, photos, records and video cassettes.

David Drummond   5 J 22
11 Cecil Ct WC2. 01-836 1142. 19th and early 20thC juvenilia. Theatrical souvenirs and playbills and a large collection of classified postcards. Plus books and ephemera of the performing arts. *Unusual hours: 11.00-14.30, 15.30-17.45 Mon-Fri, 11.00-14.15 first Sat in month (other Sats by appt only).*

Hatchards   2 I 18
187 Piccadilly W1. 01-439 9921. Fine, illustrated second-hand books above a modern bookshop. Search facility.

G. Heywood Hill   2 I 17
10 Curzon St. W1. 01-629 0647/8. Books with fine colour plates. Also an extensive collection of 19th and early 20thC children's books and general second-hand books. New books stocked as well.

Maggs Bros   2 H 18
50 Berkeley Sq W1. 01-493 7160. Rare and fine books, illuminated manuscripts, autographed letters.

Marlborough Rare Books   2 H 19
144-146 New Bond St W1. 01-493 6993. Illustrated books, bibliography and architecture.

Otto Haas
49 Belsize Park Gdns NW3. 01-722 1488. One of the best stocks of music, musical literature and autographs in the world. *By appt only.*

Pickering & Chatto   5 J 19
17 Pall Mall SW1. 01-930 2515. Rare and antiquarian books. English literature, science, medicine, economics. Literary manuscripts.

Sotherans   2 I 20
2-5 Sackville St W1. 01-439 6151. Established in London 1815. Antiquarian books, maps, prints, periodicals and some modern books. Also binding and restoration. Sepa-

rate Print Gallery at 80 Pimlico Rd SW1
(5 **M 12**). 01-730 8756.

The Building Centre 3 **F 23**
26 Store St WC1. 01-637 1022. Information
on building materials, equipment and techniques. Large permanent exhibition and
special solid fuel advisory service. Also
Build Electric and Infodisc. For product
information dial Winkfield Row 884999.

The London Door Company
165 St John's Hill SW11. 01-223 7243. Offer
a made-to-measure service in different
woods and glass. Showroom with samples
on display.

Metalcraft
6-40 Durnford St, Seven Sisters Rd N15.
01-802 1715. Supply all kinds of metalwork
– railings, spiral staircases, fire escapes,
gates, brackets and structural or ornamental metalwork – in modern or Victorian
designs.

Redland Brick 5 **O 18**
28 Maiden La WC2. 01-379 7142. Showroom with a wide range of handmade and
quality handmade bricks.

Thomas & Wilson 4 **K 3**
454 Fulham Rd SW6. 01-381 1161. Made-
to-order ceiling centres and cornices plus a
range of ready-mades.

J. Williams
2 Buller Rd NW10. 01-969 0022. All kinds of
roofing materials and components including Welsh slate tiles.

*Try the markets – Camden Lock for art
deco styles.*
Button Box 6 **J 23**
44 Bedford St WC2. 01-240 2716. Huge
variety of buttons – all shapes, colours and
sizes – in wood, glass, pearl, horn, plastic.
Mail-order service available. Also a market
stall at Camden Lock.

Button Queen 2 **E 18**
19 Marylebone La W1. 01-935 1505. Specialise in antique, old and modern buttons,
buckles, etc.

Taylors Buttons
1 Silver Pl W1. 01-437 1016. Largest variety
of buttons in London.

See under 'Photographic equipment'.

See under 'Sports equipment'.

Bernardout & Bernardout 1 **I 10**
7 Thurloe Pl SW7. 01-584 7658. Oriental
rugs and carpets, tapestries and needlework. Some French and English stock.
Expert cleaners and repairers.

Bond Street Carpets 2 **G 19**
31 New Bond St W1. 01-629 7825. Big stock
of Oriental and Persian rugs.

David Black Oriental 1 **A 5**
Carpets
96 Portland Rd W11. 01-727 2566. Specialist in antique tribal rugs, carpets, kilims,
embroideries, dhurries and rare textiles.
Valuations, restoration, cleaning. Also new
carpets and kilims. Publishes 6 vols on
antique carpets and sells books by other
publishers on antique carpets. *OPEN
11.00-18.00 or by appt.*

C. John 2 **G 17**
70 South Audley St W1. 01-493 5288. Oriental and Persian carpets.

Kilim Warehouse
28a Pickets St SW12. 01-675 3122. A vast
selection of antique, decorative and new
kilims from all parts of the world. Cleaning
and restoration service.

Mayorcas 5 **J 19**
38 Jermyn St SW1. 01-629 4195. Outstanding stock of European carpets, textiles and
tapestries.

Samad's 2 **I 14**
33 Knightsbridge Rd SW1. 01-235 5712.
Variety of Oriental carpets and rugs.

Consult Yellow Pages.

*The big stores such as Heal's, John Lewis,
Liberty, Maples and Selfridges have large
stocks.*
Afia Carpets 2 **D 18**
60 Baker St W1. 01-935 0414. Well-known
shop with a large selection of modern fitted
carpets and rugs. Two-tone range in a great
choice of colours.

Charles H. Hall 6 **R 30**
136-148 Tooley St SE1. 01-403 0249. Carpets – and just about everything else – sold
at reduced prices.

Resista Carpets
255 New King's Rd SW6. 01-731 2588.
Massive stocks of plain and subtly patterned carpets.

Carpet & textile restorers

Anglo-Persian Carpet Co
6 South Kensington Station Arc SW7.
01-589 5457. Oriental carpets and tapestries.

Bernardout   2 I 14
5 William St SW1. 01-235 3360. Oriental
rugs and carpets.

David Black Oriental   1 A 5
Carpets
96 Portland Rd W11. 01-727 2566. Cleaning and repair service for Oriental and other antique carpets.

Catering service

Fortnum & Mason   2 I 20
181 Piccadilly W1. 01-734 8040. Supply
superb picnic hampers. Any size of order
catered for.

Moveable Feasts
83-85 Holloway Rd N7. 01-607 2202. Vast
selection of 3-course lunch and dinner
menus. Cater for weddings, parties, etc;
supply staff, cutlery and plates.

Party Planners   1 A 6
56 Ladbroke Gro W11. 01-229 9666. Run by
the Queen's cousin. Organise all types of
parties from dinners to balls. Also conferences, overseas groups and weddings.

Searcy Tansley & Co   2 I 12
136 Brompton Rd SW3. 01-584 9207. Highclass catering for cocktail parties, dances,
etc.

Toastmasters Incorporated
6 Gladstone House, High Rd N22. 01-888
7098/2398. After-dinner speakers and professional toastmasters to officiate at any
type of function can be supplied at short
notice.

Ceramic restorations

China Repairers
64 Charles La NW8. 01-722 8407. Specialise in repairing antique and modern
china and glass.

Robin Hood's Workshop   5 L 13
18 Bourne St SW1. 01-730 0425. China
repairs and tuition in ceramic restoration.
By appt only.

Ceramics: antique

*The principal areas for antique ceramic
shops are Kensington Church St and
Knightsbridge – remember to look in the
back streets.*

Alistair Sampson Antiques   2 I 12
156 Brompton Rd SW3. 01-589 5272. Early
English and some medieval pottery. Also
17th and 18thC oak furniture, English brass,
needlework, primitive pictures and treen.

Antique Porcelain Company   2 G 19
149 New Bond St W1. 01-629 1254. Fine
18thC English and Continental china and
porcelain.

Haslem and Whiteway   1 D 8
105 Kensington Church St W8. 01-229 1145.
Late 19thC Arts and Craft Movement pieces.

Vandekar   1 I 11
138 Brompton Rd SW3. 01-589 8481. Said
to have the largest collection of pre-1830
pottery, porcelain and glass in Europe.

Charity shops

*School and church halls often hold beneficiary jumble sales where both donations and
buyers are welcome.*

Oxfam Shops
202b Kensington High St W8.   1 D 4
01-937 6683.
13 Marylebone High St W1.   2 D 19
01-487 3852.
There are about 50 of these shops in
London which offer excellent value in good
second-hand clothes, jewellery, books and
bric-à-brac in good condition.

Salvation Army Warehouse
122-124 Spa Rd SE16. 01-237 1107.
Second-hand chairs, tables, wardrobes.
3-piece suites, gas stoves, etc and clothing.

Chemists

*In addition to the numerous independent
chemists, both Boots and Underwoods are
dispensing chemists with branches
throughout London. Two of their largest
stores are:*

Boots   2 H 20
182 Regent St W1. 01-734 4934. The most
comprehensive chemist in London with
three floors selling everything from toothpaste to computers.

Underwoods   5 K 22
7 Strand WC2. 01-839 5240. Toiletries,
perfume, films and electrical equipment.

China, glass & porcelain

Chinacraft   2 E 17
499 Oxford St W1. 01-499 9881. Fine English china, crystal and figurines. Over 15 branches, most in central London.

Craftsmen Potters Shop   2 H 21
William Blake House, 7 Marshall St W1. 01-437 7605. Only members of the Craftsmen Potters Association can sell work here. This demands a high standard.

General Trading Co   5 K 12
144 Sloane St SW1. 01-730 0411. Some of the best designs in contemporary English and Continental glass and china. Large stock.

Gered   2 I 19
173-174 Piccadilly W1. 01-629 2614. Large showroom displaying and selling Spode, Royal Crown Derby, Royal Doulton and Wedgwood.

The Glasshouse   3 I 24
65 Long Acre WC2. 01-836 9785. Here you can see craftsmen making glass – and everything is for sale. Restoration work undertaken.

Lalique Ltd   2 G 17
24-25 Mount St W1. 01-493 7041/5. Elegant displays of Lalique crystal, Limoges porcelain and Christofle silver.

Lawleys   2 H 20
154 Regent St W1. 01-734 2621. Popular chain selling Wedgwood, Royal Doulton, Waterford crystal and other top names.

Reject China Shop   2 I 12
33-35 Beauchamp Pl SW3. 01-581 0737. Also at 134 Regent St W1. Reject china at low prices – a bargain as the flaws tend to be hardly noticeable.

Rosenthal China Shop   2 I 20
137-141 Regent St W1. 01-734 3076. Specialises in Rosenthal china, glass and porcelain.

Villeroy & Boch   2 H 20
155 Regent St W1. 01-434 0249. Villeroy & Boch were established in 1748. Only English showroom stocking own china, porcelain and cutlery plus Atlantis crystal.

Chocolates & confectionery

Fortnum & Mason, Harrods and Selfridges all have excellent confectionery departments selling hand-made English and Continental chocolates.

Bendicks   2 E 19
53-55 Wigmore St W1. 01-935 7272. Famous for their bittermints, but also stock a wide range of chocolates.

Charbonnel et Walker   2 I 19
28 Old Bond St W1. 01-629 4396. Handmade, mainly soft-centred chocolates. Exotic, extravagant presentation boxes in silk or satin, but they will fill anything with their chocolates!

Prestat   2 I 19
14 Princes Arc, Piccadilly W1. 01-629 4838. Delicious hand-made chocolates and fresh cream truffles. Seasonal novelties.

Rococo   4 L 7
321 King's Rd SW3. 01-352 5857. Traditional chocolatier. Over 50 types of loose hand-made chocolates. Delicious fresh cream truffles. Will design anything in chocolate.

Thornton's   6 J 23
2 Covent Garden Mkt WC2. 01-836 2173. Continental chocolates, toffee and seasonal novelties.

Clocks & watches: antique

Aubrey Brocklehurst   1 G 7
124 Cromwell Rd SW7. 01-373 0319. Specialise in longcase and bracket clocks, also barometers. Clock and furniture restorations.

Camerer Cuss   3 H 23
17 Ryder St W1. 01-930 1941. Antique watches and clocks.

Garrard & Co   2 H 20
112 Regent St W1. 01-734 7020. Pieces by the great English clockmakers of the past and an extensive range of French period carriage clocks. Top quality.

Pearl Cross   5 J 22
35 St Martin's Ct WC2. 01-836 2814. Antique jewellery, silver and presentation gold watches from 1880 onwards.

Peter K. Weiss
18 Silver Vaults, Chancery La WC2. 01-242 8100. Antique clocks and watches.

Philip & Bernard Dombey   1 D 8
174 Kensington Church St W8. 01-229 7100. Manly French 18th and 19thC clocks.

Ronald A. Lee   2 H 18
1-9 Bruton Pl W1. 01-629 5600. 17th and 18thC clocks of very high quality. Some furniture and works of art too.

Clock restoration

See also under 'Clocks: antique'.
Clock Clinic
85 Lower Richmond Rd SW15. 01-788 1407.

Rowley Parkes 3 I 29
17 Briset St EC1. 01-253 3110.

J. Walker 2 F 19
1st Floor, 64 South Molton St W1. 01-629
3487. Modern clock repairs too.

Clocks & watches: modern

*Good selections at Harrods and Selfridges
and at most leading jewellers such as
Bentleys and Kutchinsky.*

AM.PM I E 7
Kensington Arc, Kensington High St W8.
01-937 4914. The UK's first comprehensive
specialist watch shop. All 600 designs are
clearly displayed so you don't have to keep
asking an assistant to unlock endless
showcases. Prices range from £6.00 to
£6,000.

Watches of Switzerland 2 H 8
16 New Bond St W1. 01-493 5916. Vast
selection of watches, anything from the
cheap and cheerful to the most expensive
designs. Stocks all the most renowned
manufacturers.

Coffee & tea

Algerian Coffee Stores 2 I 22
52 Old Compton St W1. 01-437 2480.
Established in 1887, the shop sells 30 different blends of coffee and over 100 leaf,
flavoured and herb teas. Also coffee-
making equipment.

Drury Tea & Coffee Co 3 I 24
37 Drury La WC2. 01-836 2607. Long-
established company offering 28 different
types of coffee and 35-40 types of tea. Also
coffee-making equipment and good quality
biscuits and preserves.

Ferns 2 G 22
27 Rathbone Pl W1. 01-636 2237. Old-
established firm selling 14 blended coffees
and a good selection of leaf, flavoured and
herb teas. All own-label.

H. R. Higgins (Coffee man) 2 E 18
79 Duke St W1. 01-629 3913. Over 40
different types of coffee including original
and blended, light, medium and dark
roasts. Also over 20 teas.

The Tea House 3 I 23
15a Neal St WC2. 01-240 7539. More than
50 own-label leaf teas and tisanes in this
striking red and black shop devoted to tea
and 'teaphernalia'. Vast selection of tea-
pots including unusual and novelty; cad-
dies, preserves, biscuits. *OPEN 10.00-
19.00 Mon-Sat.*

Coins & medals

A. H. Baldwin 6 K 23
11 Adelphi Ter WC2. 01-930 6879. Good
general selection. Ancient, medieval and
modern; commemorative and military.

Dolphin Coins
2c Englands La NW3. 01-722 4116. Ham-
mered coins in gold and silver. Rare colonial coins. Foreign coins, banknotes and
medals.

B. A. Seaby 2 F 20
8 Cavendish Sq W1. 01-631 3707. One of
the largest coin shops in the world and
publishers of standard coin catalogues for
British, Roman and Greek coins.

Spink 5 J 19
5-7 King St SW1. 01-930 7888. They stock
or can acquire any coin wanted by a collector. Also mint commemorative medals.

Copper & brass

The Copper Shop 3 I 23
48 Neal St WC2. 01-836 2984. Copper
cookware, kettles, jugs, tankards, planters,
coal scuttles, lamps, lanterns, jewellery,
etc. Mail-order catalogue.

Jack Casimar I A 8
23 Pembridge Rd W11. 01-727 8643. Large
stock of antique brass, copper and pewter.

Crafts & art supplies

Alec Tiranti 2 D 22
27 Warren St W1. 01-636 8565. Large
range of tools and material for wood and
stone carving. Also plaster, resins,
fibreglass and cold-pouring rubbers.

J. Blundell & Sons 2 I 21
199 Wardour St W1. 01-437 4746. Jewellery 'findings' and supplies. *OPEN
09.30-16.00 Mon, Tue, Thur & Fri.*

Candle Makers Supplies I A I
28 Blythe Rd W14. 01-602 4031. Sell everything for making your own candles as well
as equipment for batik and silk-painting.
Also wax dye-craft and resin casting.
Candle-making, batik and silk-painting
classes *some Sat.* Vast range of candles.

Cass Arts & Crafts 2 I 22
13 Charing Cross Rd WC2. 01-930 9940.
Stock all leading brands of paints, paper,
artists' materials and picture frames.

Cornelissen 3 H 23
105 Great Russell St WC1. 01-636 1045.
Fine art, restoration and print-making
materials.

Daler Rowney Ltd 2 G 22
12 Percy St W1. 01-636 8241. Large and varied stock of general artists' paints and materials.

Felt & Hessian Shop 6 J 28
34 Greville St EC1. 01-405 6215. Colourful materials for soft-toy making, craft and display work. Extensive range of soft toys. OPEN 11.00-15.00 Mon-Fri.

Fulham Pottery
8-10 Ingate Pl SW8. 01-720 0050. All potters' materials from clay to kilns.

The Handweaver's Studio & Gallery
29 Haroldstone Rd E17. 01-521 2281. Fleece, yarns, dyes and other equipment for weaving and spinning. Books. Also tuition.

Langford & Hill 2 H 20
10 & 38-40 Warwick St W1. 01-437 9945. The place in London to find a selection of the latest American and German commercial art materials, films, coloured papers, special inks, drawn curves, etc. Expert advice.

T. N. Lawrence 6 J 28
2 Bleeding Heart Yd, Greville St EC1. 01-242 3534. Everything for the engraver, etcher and printmaker.

Paperchase 3 G 23
213 Tottenham Court Rd W1. 01-580 8496. Exciting collection of papers and card. All types of artists' papers, book papers, Japanese papers, foils and display papers.

Reeves Dryad 1 D 4
178 Kensington High St W8. 01-937 5370. Think of a craft and they'll sell you the materials for it.

Russell & Chapple 3 I 23
23 Monmouth St WC2. 01-836 7800. Supply artists' fabrics.

Thorpe Modelmakers 3 G 27
98 Gray's Inn Rd WC1. 01-405 1016. Balsa wood, trees, cars and people for model making and accessories.

Times Graphic Centre
Unit 11, Westminster Sq, Durham St SE11. 01-735 0524. Supply all sorts of graphic equipment.

Winsor & Newton 2 G 22
51-52 Rathbone Pl W1. 01-636 4231. Good general selection of artists' materials, papers and paints.

Craft shops

Contemporary Applied Arts 3 I 23
43 Earlham St WC2. 01-836 6993. Comprehensive display of work by craftsmen in many materials including many British pieces.

Naturally British 5 J 22
13 New Row WC2. 01-240 0551. High-quality hand-made British goods. Pottery, toys, gifts, clothes, hand-knits and jewellery.

V & A Craft Shop 1 G 7
Victoria & Albert Museum, Cromwell Rd SW7. 01-589 5070. High-quality British contemporary crafts.

Crafts: national

Africa 6 J 23
Kikapu, The Africa Centre, 38 King St WC2. 01-240 6098. Baskets, jewellery, clothes.

Australia 6 K 23
Australian Gift Shop, Western Australia House, 113-116 Strand WC2. 01-836 2292. Aboriginal crafts and Australian-made gifts and souvenirs; books and food products including Vegemite.

Denmark 2 G 19
Royal Copenhagen Porcelain and Georg Jensen Silver, 15 New Bond St W1. 01-499 6541. Also Holmegaard glass.

France 4 J 9
Souleiado, 171 Fulham Rd SW3. 01-589 6180. Provençal fabrics and accessories.

Greece & Turkey 2 F 22
Byzantium, 1 Goodge St W1. 01-636 6465. Clothes and footwear.

Ireland 2 E 18
The Irish Shop, 11 Duke St W1. 01-935 1366. Waterford crystal, Donegal tweed, Irish linen, Belleek china, Aran sweaters, Celtic jewellery.

Japan 5 I 19
Mitsukiku, 15 Old Brompton Rd SW7. 01-589 1725. Other branches. Kimonos, health sandals, fans, rice bowls, china.

New Zealand 5 J 22
Kiwifruits, 25 Bedfordbury WC2. 01-240 1423. Gifts, crafts, books. Kiwifruits New Zealand Book Shop, 6 Royal Opera Arc SW1 (5 **J 21**). 01-930 4587.

Peru 5 M 14
Inca, 45 Elizabeth St SW1. 01-730 7941. Colourful, hand-made Peruvian clothes, sweaters, accessories and gifts.

Russia 3 I 26
The Russian Shop, 278 High Holborn WC1. 01-405 3538. Russian dolls, painted trays, lacquered boxes and other handicrafts.

Scotland 1 I 11
The Scotch House, 2 Brompton Rd SW1. 01-581 2151. Also 84 and 191 Regent St W1 (2 **I 20** and 2 **G 20**). Excellent tartans, kilts, rugs, foods and Fair Isle, Aran and Shetland woollens.

Spain   6 **J** 23
Casa Fina, 9 Covent Garden Mkt WC2. 01-836 0289. Spanish porcelain. Casa Pupo, 56 Pimlico Rd SW1 (5 **M** 12). 01-730 7111. Spanish, Italian and Portuguese furniture.

Switzerland   5 **J** 22
Swiss Centre, Leicester Sq WC2. 01-734 0444. Cuckoo clocks, army knives, cheese raclettes, dolls, chocolates.

Curtains & covers

John Lewis offers an excellent cutting and making up service for loose covers and curtains.

De Winter   1 **D** 8
223 Kensington Church St W8. 01-229 4949. Made-to-measure curtains and loose covers. The shop carries a large selection of all types of fabrics. Upholstery work, tapestries, tapestry kits made up into cushions, blinds, carpets and furniture.

Tulley's of Chelsea   4 **L** 4
289-297 Fulham Rd SW10. 01-352 1078. Classic sofas and chairs to have covered, cover yourself or buy with interchangeable loose covers. Thousands of fabrics to choose from.

Cycles

Selfridges and Harrods are good for standard machines. See Time Out *for advertisements for latest news on the bike scene.*

Beta Bikes
275 West End La NW6. 01-794 4133. Huge range of bicycles and everything to do with cycling. Stock includes tandems, custom-made bikes and touring bikes.

Edwardes
223 Camberwell Rd SE5. 01-703 3676. Wide range of cycles for children and adults. Cycling accessories, second-hand bikes and repair service.

W. F. Holdsworth
132 Lower Richmond Rd SW15. 01-788 1060. Holdsworth custom-built bikes plus a wide range of other makes. Full range of accessories.

Stuart Cycles
1 Ascot Pde, Clapham Park Rd SW4. 01-622 4818. Hand-built and production bikes. Full range of services.

Tandem Centre
281 Old Kent Rd SE1. 01-231 1641. All sorts of bikes as well as tandems. They make all their own tandems. Repairs and spares.

Cycle hire

See under 'Travel and holiday information'.

Design

The Design Centre   5 **J** 21
28 Haymarket SW1. 01-839 8000. An exciting showroom of the best British domestic design – always up to date. Free and helpful advice from experts and a comprehensive Design Centre Selection – a photographic sample record of over 10,000 consumer goods. Also sell what is on display. *OPEN 10.00-18.00 Mon & Tue, 10.00-20.00 Wed-Sat, 13.00-18.00 Sun.* Bookshop and coffee shop.

Discount shopping

Cheap buys and bargains can often be found by looking in the local newspapers, at newsagents' notice-boards or in Time Out, London Weekly Advertiser, Exchange & Mart *and* The Evening Standard. *Charity shops, jumble sales and the markets are also useful for the low-budget shopper.*

Do-it-yourself

The Building Centre   3 **F** 23
26 Store St WC1. 01-637 1022. Supply information on anything connected with building.

Hire Service Shops   3 **E** 33
192 Campden Hill Rd W8. 01-727 0897. Hire out every conceivable piece of DIY tackle/scaffolding, sanders, strippers, etc. Many other branches.

Knobs & Knockers   4 **L** 7
385 King's Rd SW10. 01-352 5693. All kinds of door furnishings.

Magnet
153 Hurlingham Rd SW6. 01-731 7304. Doors, windows, kitchens, bathrooms, bedrooms, stairs, double-glazing, timber, sheet materials. More than 30 branches in Greater London.

Michel & Polgar   2 **D** 18
41 Blandford St W1. 01-935 9629. Have a wide range of perspex materials, sheet plastics and unit furniture.

W. H. Newson   5 **M** 12
61 Pimlico Rd SW1. 01-730 6262. Specialise in doors of which they have a very large selection. Also hardware and other DIY materials.

Tile Mart 2 E 21
151 Great Portland St W1. 01-580 3814.
Also at 107 Pimlico Rd SW1. 01-730 7278.
One of the largest ranges of ceramic tiles in
London. English and Continental designs,
many of which are unique.

Domestic help

Also refer to the classified adverts in The
Lady *magazine, 40 Bedford St WC2.
01-836 8705.*
Belgravia Bureau 2 I 13
35 Brompton Rd SW3. 01-584 4343. Supply cooks, cleaners, housekeepers, secre-
taries, chauffeurs, butlers and gardeners.
Can supply couples who work as a team.
Childminders 2 C 19
9 Paddington St W1. 01-935 4386. Babysitters (mostly trained nurses) supplied to the
home and to hotels in central London and
most suburban areas.
Curzon Cleaning Services
598 Kingston Rd SW20. 01-543 7022. For
all kinds of household, window and specialist cleaning – not decorating. Not daily
cleaning.
London Domestics 1 I 11
271-273 King St W6. 01-741 5868. Can
provide cleaners and babysitters.
Lumley Employment 5 O 15
85 Charlwood St SW1. 01-630 0545. If you
want a Cordon Bleu cook for a special
occasion, this is the place to come. Catering services agency.
The Nanny Service 2 C 19
9 Paddington St W1. 01-935 3515. Temporary, permanent and maternity nannies.
Residential and non-residential available
for positions in London and the Home
Counties.
Thames Cleaning Company
16 Hatherley Rd, Sidcup, Kent. 01-300
5888. Clean carpets, dry-clean curtains,
polish hard floors and clean windows and
venetian blinds. A full cleaning service.
Universal Aunts 4 L 11
250 King's Rd SW3. 01-351 5767. Babysitting, shopping, escorting children at beginning and end of term, temporary
housekeeping, mother's helps, removal
packing. Children's tours of London organised.

Dry-cleaning & laundry

**Association of British Laundry
Cleaning & Rental Services**
7 Churchill Ct, 58 Station Rd, Nth Harrow

Middx. 01-863 7755. A national trade body
with about 350 parent company members
who are themselves responsible for approx
2000 dry cleaners and 500 laundries, all of
whom display an ABLC code of practice
sign. The association also operates a consumer complaints service.
Dry Cleaning Information Bureau (DIB)
c/o 7 Churchill Ct, 58 Station Rd, Nth Harrow, Middx. Operates the 24hr DIB Hotline:
01-863 8658, offering free advice on just
about any cleaning problem or disaster.
*There are many reliable dry-cleaners and
launderers in London. Sketchley Cleaners
is one of the largest chains, with branches
on most high streets. For specialist treatment go to:*
Elegant Cleaners 2 D 15
30-31 Kendal St W1. 01-402 6108. Specialists in silk, evening gowns, suede, leather
and fur.
Jeeves 5 J 12
8-10 Pont St SW1. 01-235 1101. A personal
service. Everything is hand-finished and
the prices are reasonable. They collect and
deliver in central London and have a postal
service. Also carry out repairs and various
other services.
Lewis & Wayne Ltd 4 L 11
13-15 Elystan St SW3. 01-589 5730. For
garment cleaning and hand-finishing of
evening gowns and bridal wear. Taking
down and rehanging curtains, on-site carpet cleaning. All types of hand-finished
laundry.
Liliman & Cox 2 H 18
34 Bruton Pl W1. 01-629 4555. Highest
quality cleaning of special garments such
as beaded and embroidered dresses.
Suede Services
2a Hoop La NW11. 01-455 0052. Specialise
in cleaning, restoring, remodelling and
repairing all skin garments, including
pigskin.

Electrical

Electrical Contractors' 1 B 9
Association
32-34 Palace Ct W2. 01-229 1266. 450
member firms in London area. High standard of work guaranteed.

Electronics shops

*The area around Tottenham Court Rd and
St Giles Circus is packed with shops selling
electronic, video, radio and tape recording*

equipment at competitive prices. Edgware Rd also has a good selection.

Henry's   2 G 15
404 Edgware Rd W2. 01-723 1008. Electronic and radio components, amplifiers. Specialises in test equipment. Prompt mail-order service and personal computing. Also at 301 Edgware Rd W2.

Lasky's   3 G 23
42 Tottenham Court Rd W1. 01-636 0845. Wide range of TVs, videos, stereos and computers.

Lion House   3 G 23
227 Tottenham Court Rd W1. 01-580 0395. Europe's first electronics department store. Three floors of hi-fi, radio, video, TV and computer equipment. Hi-fi department has at least four demonstration studios.

Sonic Foto Centre   3 G 23
256 Tottenham Court Rd W1. 01-580 5826. Extensive selection of hi-fi, audio and video equipment.

Tandy   2 B 16
234 Edgware Rd W2. 01-723 4705. Chain selling a range of audio and video equipment. Many branches.

Fabrics: furnishing

The big stores, particularly Peter Jones, John Lewis, Heal's and Liberty, have a large range of furnishing fabrics.

Afia   2 C 18
96-97 Crawford St W1. 01-724 1341. Huge comprehensive stock. Will replace old curtains or covers and copy original design.

Designers Guild   4 L 8
271 & 277 King's Rd SW3. 01-351 5775. Beautiful fabrics, wall-coverings, carpets, furniture and accessories in plain, floral or abstract designs.

Distinctive Trimmings   1 D 8
17 Kensington Church St W8. 01-937 6174. Full range of furnishing trimmings (tiebacks, staircase ropes, etc) which they will dye to match your decor.

The Fabric Shop   4 K 9
6 Cale St SW3. 01-584 8495. International designers' fabrics, many of them originals. Will custom-make and supply carpets, upholstery etc.

Habitat
196 Tottenham Ct Rd W1. 01-631 3880. Range of reasonably priced fabrics. Can choose your sofa and curtains to match.

Liberty   2 G 20
210-220 Regent St W1. 01-734 1234. Rich fabrics in floral, geometric or abstract designs. Considered very British.

Sanderson   2 G 22
52 Berners St W1. 01-636 7800. Famous for wide selection of floral and co-ordinated designs to match their renowned wall coverings. Great selection of paints, tiles and vinyls.

Fancy dress hire

Bermans & Nathans   5 J 22
18 Irving St WC2. 01-839 1651. Vast range of costumes for men and women.

Charles Fox   6 J 23
22 Tavistock St WC2. 01-240 3111/3. Theatrical make-up for sale.

Theatre Zoo   5 J 22
21 Earlham St WC2. 01-836 3150. All types of animal costumes and masks. Also wigs, jewellery and make-up.

Fireplaces

Acquisitions
269 Camden High St NW1. 01-485 4955. Specialise in reproduction Victorian and Edwardian fireplaces, and all fireplace accessories. Distributors and retailers of gas, coal and log-effect fires.

La Belle Cheminée   2 B 22
81-85 Albany St NW1. 01-486 7486. Over 100 fireplace designs on show for all kinds of fires.

Cast Iron Fireplace Co
99-103 East Hill SW18. 01-870 1630. Original and reproduction cast iron, tiled, wooden and marble fireplaces. Gas coal-and log-effect fires; and all accessories.

National Fireplace Council
PO Box 35, Stoke-on-Trent, Staffs. Stoke-on-Trent 744311. For a small charge will send a brochure on the various types and styles of fireplaces available and their stockists.

Fish

See under 'Aquaria'.

Fishing tackle

See under 'Sports equipment'.

Flowers

See also under 'Gardening'.
Flower House   2 E 19
130 Wigmore St W1. 01-486 1388. Good exotic plants and flowers.

Jane Packer Floral Design 2 E 18
56 James St W1. 01-935 2673. Bouquets,
baskets, fresh and dried flowers. Delivery
service.

Justin de Blank 5 M 13
114 Ebury St SW1. 01-730 2375. Fresh and
dried flowers delivered daily. Also herbs,
herb seeds and honey.

Moyses Stevens Floral Arts 2 H 18
6 Bruton St W1. 01-493 8171. Fresh and
dried flowers. Delivery service.

Selwyn Davidson 2 H 21
31 Berwick St W1. 01-437 0881. Smallish
shop, good selection.

Food: health shops

Ceres Grain Shop 1 A 8
269a Portobello Rd W11. 01-229 5571. Vegetarian, including macrobiotic, food. Complete range of chemical-free herbs,
vegetables and grains. Wholefood take-
away food cooked on the premises.

Cranks 2 H 21
8 Marshall St W1. 01-437 2915. Appetising
health shops, dried fruits and grains. Restaurant next door.

Health Foods 4 L 4
767 Fulham Rd SW6. 01-736 8848. Macrobiotic foods such as organically grown
rice, millet, chick peas and soya. Also
creams, honeys, fruit juices, cereals and
biochemical remedies.

Holland & Barrett 2 F 18
Unit C12/C13 West One Shopping Centre,
Oxford St W1. 01-493 7988. Complete
range of wholefoods and cooking herbs.
Cosmetics made with natural ingredients,
natural vitamin supplements. Wide range of
take-aways.

Wholefood 2 C 18
24 Paddington St W1. 01-935 3924. Organically grown products, free-range eggs, gro-
ceries and even wines.

Food shops

*Soho is an area full of small Continental
shops crammed with exotic foods, wines
and spices. See under 'Markets' for
cheaper buys and fresh foods.*

Bartholdi 2 F 22
4 Charlotte St W1. 01-636 3762. Swiss food
specialists. Fresh meat, cheeses, Continental sausages, chocolates.

Cheong-Leen 2 I 22
4-10 Tower Hill WC2. 01-836 5378. Chinese
supermarket with a large selection of gro-
ceries.

Fortnum & Mason 2 I 19
181 Piccadilly W1. 01-734 8040. Exotic and
unusual tinned and bottled foods from all
over the world. Famous for hampers.

Fratelli Camisa 2 H 21
1a Berwick St W1. 01-437 7120. Good
Continental delicatessen. Wines, fresh
pasta and seasonal delicacies such as
truffles.

German Food Centre 2 H 13
44-46 Knightsbridge SW1. 01-235 5760.
Meat, sausages, cheeses, coffee, chocolates, biscuits.

Harrods 2 I 13
Knightsbridge SW1. 01-730 1234. International selection of top-quality fresh, tinned and bottled foods.

Hobbs & Co 2 G 17
29 South Audley St W1. 01-409 1058.
Gourmet food and drink; cheeses, pâtés,
wines, fruit and vegetables, served in elegant surroundings. Hampers made up to
order.

Justin de Blank 5 L 14
42 Elizabeth St SW1. 01-730 0605. Wide
range of freshly prepared dishes and prime
fruit and vegetables. Fresh home-made
bread daily.

Lina Stores 2 I 21
18 Brewer St W1. 01-437 6482. Amazing
selection of Italian foods. Excellent fresh
pasta, bread and olives.

The London Cheese Co 2 F 22
21 Goodge St W1. 01-631 4191. Over 400
cheeses. Wines and fresh sandwiches.

Maison Sagne 2 D 19
105 Marylebone High St W1. 01-935 6240.
Croissants, superb sausage rolls, pastries.
Excellent gateaux and special occasion
cakes made to order.

Ninjin Food Store 2 E 21
244 Great Portland St W1. 01-388 2511.
Japanese food specialists. Fresh meat and
fish too.

Pak Continental Food Stores
191 Shepherds Bush Mkt W12. 01-743
5389. Specialise in African and West Indian
food.

Paxton & Whitfield 5 J 20
93 Jermyn St SW1. 01-930 0259. Famous
for superb English and Continental
cheeses, traditional hams, teas, home-
made pies and pâtés. Small selection of
wines.

Products from Spain 2 F 22
89 Charlotte St W1. 01-580 2905. Importers
of a vast range of Spanish foods – retail and
wholesale.

Randall & Aubin 2 I 21
16 Brewer St W1. 01-437 3507/8. Pâtés,

cheeses of all sorts, assorted cooked and fresh meats and game.

Richards 2 I 21
11 Brewer St W1. 01-437 1358. Nothing but fish; shellfish, live crabs and lobsters, squid, fresh salmon and sea trout.

Viniron 3 C 23
119 Drummond St NW1. 01-387 8653. Drummond St is full of Indian shops and restaurants. Viniron is one of the best – spices, curries and vegetables from India.

Foreign newspapers & periodicals

Many of the Soho and Queensway news-agents deal in foreign papers. European magazines are usually available at the larger newsagents and at the station and airport branches of W. H. Smith and John Menzies. The following shops stock a good selection of both:

Harrods 2 L 14
Knightsbridge SW1. 01-730 1234.
Librairie Parisienne 2 I 22
48 Old Compton St W1. 01-437 2479.
NSS Newsagents I A 8
6 Pembridge Rd W11. 01-229 8020.
Selfridges 2 G 21
400 Oxford St W1. 01-629 1234.
Solosy 2 I 22
50 Charing Cross Rd WC2. 01-836 6313.

Furniture: antique

See under 'Antique shops'.

Furniture: modern

Adeptus 3 F 23
110 Tottenham Court Rd W1. 01-388 5965. Adaptable, versatile modern designs at reasonable prices.
Ciancimino International 4 L 7
307-311 King's Rd SW3. 01-352 2016. Sculptor turned furniture designer – tables and chairs of aluminium and wood in an interlocking system that allows for adapta-tion in shape and size; office or residential. Made to order.
Futon Company 3 F 23
82-83 Tottenham Court Rd W1. 01-636 9984. Sells the traditional Japanese mat-tresses and a range of furniture with ele-ments of Japanese design.
Habitat 3 F 23
196 Tottenham Court Rd W1. 01-631 3880. Not so much a shop, more a way of life.

Popular international furniture and colourful household goods.

Harrods 2 I 14
Knightsbridge SW1. 01-730 1234. Widest range of every kind of furniture.
Heal's 3 F 23
196 Tottenham Court Rd W1. 01-636 1666. Big selection of the best British and Conti-nental designs.
Liberty 2 G 20
210-220 Regent St W1. 01-734 1234. Good contemporary international furniture.
Maples 3 D 23
145 Tottenham Court Rd, W1. 01-387 7000. 50,000sq ft of furniture, plus car parking space. All types and styles of furniture, including reproduction, futuristic and office furniture. Huge range of soft furnishings. Curtain-making service from Maples own range of fabrics. English and Oriental car-pets and rugs. Contract and design service.
Next Retail I D 8
54-60 Kensington High St W8. 01-938 4211. Stylish and co-ordinated furniture and accessories displayed in a large show-room. The full range can be seen in the *Next Directory.*
Pine Village 3 H 20
1 Pembridge Villas W2. 01-221 7044. Wide range of modern and restored pine furniture from mirrors to dressers.
Sofas & Sofa-Beds 3 F 23
219 Tottenham Court Rd W1. 01-636 6001. Wide range of sofas, in many different fab-rics, which convert into double beds.
Wesley-Barrell 3 F 23
86 Tottenham Court Rd W1. 01-580 6979. Sells own-make settees, sofa-beds, beds and chairs, but also stocks other makes of dining-room furniture.
Zarach 2 G 17
48 South Audley St W1. 01-491 2706. Ultra-modern furniture and fittings in chrome, leather, etc.

Furniture restorers

Clifford Tracy
6/40 Durnford St N15. 01-800 4774. Antique furniture restorers and cabinet makers. Excellent personal service.
W. R. Harvey & Co (Antiques)
67-70 Chalk Farm Rd NW1. 01-485 1504. Specialist restorers of fine antique furniture.
Phoenix Antique Furniture 6 Q 25
Restoration Ltd
96 Webber St SE1. 01-928 3624. Cabinet work, polishing, upholstery, pieces made to commission.

A. J. Theobald   5 **R** 17
120 Wandsworth Rd SW8. 01-720 6509.
Antique furniture restoration. Caning and
rushing of chairs.

Galleries: prints, paintings & sculpture

Most picture galleries are grouped in and around Bond St, South Kensington and St James's. Camden Lock is an interesting area for contemporary pictures and pottery, as are the open-air exhibitions by London's major parks.
This is a selection of specialist galleries often showing exhibitions of individuals' work. See the daily papers, Time Out and the art press for current listings.

Agnew   2 **I** 19
43 Old Bond St W1. 01-629 6176. Outstanding selection of old masters.

Angela Flowers   2 **F** 22
11 Tottenham Mews W1. 01-637 3089. Represent and exhibit the work of younger British artists.

Annely Juda Fine Art   2 **F** 22
11 Tottenham Mews W1. 01-637 5517. Russian constructivism and contemporary paintings, drawings and sculpture.

Browse & Derby   2 **H** 19
19 Cork St W1. 01-734 7984. 19th and 20thC French and English paintings, drawings and sculpture.

Crane Kalman   1 **I** 11
178 Brompton Rd SW3. 01-584 7566. 20thC British and European paintings and sculpture.

Curwen Gallery   2 **F** 22
4 Windmill St, off Charlotte St W1. 01-636 1459. Originals and prints by young British artists; also original prints by Henry Moore and Barbara Hepworth.

Editions Alecto   1 **F** 7
46 Kelso Pl W8. 01-937 6611. Contemporary and historical original prints including the official facsimile of the *Domesday Book*.

Editions Graphiques   2 **H** 19
3 Clifford St W1. 01-734 3944. 19th and 20thC prints, graphics and paintings from 1880. Art nouveau and art deco objects.

Gimpel Fils   2 **G** 18
30 Davies St W1. 01-493 2488. Contemporary British, American and European art.

Malcolm Innes Gallery   4 **J** 11
172 Walton St SW3. 01-584 0575. Paintings, watercolours and prints of the 19th and 20thC, specialising in Scottish and sporting subjects.

Marlborough Fine Art   2 **I** 19
6 Albemarle St W1. 01-629 5161. 19th and 20thC 'master' paintings, contemporary art and sculpture.

Marlborough Graphics   2 **I** 19
6 Albemarle St W1. 01-629 5161. Large selection of graphics: Kokoschka, Moore, Richards, Sutherland, Nolan, Kitaj, Pasmoore. Also contemporary graphics and photography.

Mayor Gallery   2 **H** 19
22a Cork St W1. 01-734 3558. Contemporary paintings, drawings and sculpture.

Redfern Gallery   2 **H** 19
20 Cork St W1. 01-734 1732. 20thC paintings, drawings, sculpture and graphics.

Tyron & Moorland Gallery   2 **H** 19
23 Cork St W1. 01-734 6961. Sporting and rural pictures and paintings.

Waddington   2 **H** 19
2, 4, 5, 11 & 34 Cork St W1. 01-437 8611. 20thC painting, works on paper, sculpture and graphics.

Zella 9   4 **L** 6
2 Park Wlk SW10. 01-351 0588. Limited edition contemporary prints.

Games

Games Workshop
1 Dalling Rd W6. 01-741 3445. Science fiction and military board games. Role-playing games and lead miniatures.

Just Games   2 **I** 21
71 Brewer St W1. 01-437 0761. Up-to-date selection of board and card games and executive toys. More traditional games too.

Gardening

See also under 'Flowers'.
Camden Garden Centre
66 Kentish Town Rd NW1. 01-485 8468. Garden and indoor plants. Terracotta pots and troughs.

The Chelsea Gardener   4 **K** 9
125-147 Sidney St SW3. 01-352 5656. Trees, shrubs, roses, house plants. Garden furniture.

Clifton Nurseries
5a Clifton Villas W9. 01-289 6851. A very comprehensive range of gardening plants; specialists in town gardens and window boxes. Landscaping service.

Dial A Gardener
The Old Factory, Carpenter's Pl, 111 Clapham High St SW4. 01-498 0500. Young and enthusiastic firm tackling garden design. They'll take on any size job down to window boxes or just tidying up a scruffy corner.

New Covent Garden Market 5 R 15
Vauxhall SW8. 01-720 2211. Cheapest way to buy plants in London – but you must buy by the box. Flower market *OPEN Mon-Fri until 11.00.*

Rassells I E 5
80 Earl's Court Rd W8. 01-937 0481. Everything for the greenfingered; terracotta pots and fibreglass tubs, trelliswork, hanging baskets, window boxes, house plants and herbs, perennials, bulbs and bedding plants. Fresh cut flowers.

Suttons Seeds 6 J 24
33 Catherine St WC2. 01-836 0619. The showplace of the famous seed company, offering a very wide selection. Also bulbs and garden supplies. Mail-order and export service.

Syon Park Garden Centre
Syon Park, Brentford, Middx. 01-568 0134. Housed in the old riding school are all the implements needed for gardening plus a large selection of garden plants.

Thompson & Morgan
London Rd, Ipswich, Suffolk. Ipswich 688588. Seeds usually ordered by mail – this is one of the very best for quality. Particularly good for vegetables and unusual varieties.

Garden furniture & ornaments

Crowther of Syon Lodge
Syon Lodge, London Rd, Busch Corner, Isleworth, Middx. 01-560 7978. Vast selection of period and period-style garden ornaments. Furniture and chimneypieces.

T. Crowther
282 North End Rd SW6. 01-385 1375. Antique lead, stone and marble garden ornaments including fountains, statues, entrance gates.

Garden Crafts
158 New King's Rd SW6. 01-736 1615. Ornaments and garden furniture.

Mallet at Bourdon House 2 G 18
2 Davies St W1. 01-629 2444. Garden statuary and furniture. Antique dealers.

Peter Jones 5 L 12
Sloane Sq SW1. 01-730 3434. Hold the more exclusive and expensive lines but John Lewis also has a good department. Both departments stock full furniture range *mid Mar-mid Sep only.*

Gemmology

Gemmological Association 6 J 25
St Dunstan's House, Carey La EC2.

01-726 4374. Supply crystal specimens and ornamental materials for students. Gem testing equipment. Also run courses.

R. Holt & Company 3 I 28
98 Hatton Gdn EC1. 01-405 0197. Semi-precious and precious stones, cut and uncut. Facilities provided for testing stones. Some jewellery. Bead-stringing and stone-cutting on the premises.

Genealogy & heraldry

To help you trace your predecessors and make up the 'family' coat of arms try:

College of Arms 6 M 28
Queen Victoria St EC4. 01-248 2762. Will undertake research and help identify coats of arms. Houses official records of all coats of arms ever granted in England.

Heirloom & Howard 2 H 18
1 Hay Hill W1. 01-493 5868. Specialist in armorial antiques.

The Heraldry Society 3 H 24
28 Museum St WC1. 01-430 2172. Membership open to all. Small library. Sell heraldic books.

Society of Genealogists 6 J 30
14 Charterhouse Bldgs, off Goswell Rd EC1. 01-251 8799. Help to trace your ancestors. Library if you want to do your own research.

Geology

Gregory, Bottley & Lloyd I I 3
8-12 Rickett St SW6. 01-381 5522. Fascinating stock of minerals, fossils, meteorites. Geology equipment.

Gifts

Covent Garden General Store 6 J 23
111 Long Acre WC2. 01-240 0331. Well-established shop on two floors selling a huge range of tasteful gifts including pottery, comestibles, caneware and ornaments.

Crabtree and Evelyn I E 4
55-57 South Edwardes Sq W8. 01-937 3177. Unusual range of comestibles, toiletries and soaps all delightfully packaged. Books and cards. Mail-order service.

Design Centre 5 J 21
28 Haymarket SW1. 01-839 8000. Tasteful and innovative gift ideas.

F. Fwd (Fast Forward) 2 H 20
14a Newburgh St W1. 01-439 0091. Useful range of gadgets and trendy gifts.

The Gift Centre 3 G 25
140 Southampton Row WC1. 01-837 4084.
Wide selection of gift ideas.

Halcyon Days 2 G 18
14 Brook St W1. 01-629 8811. Beautiful
enamelware, little boxes for all occasions,
thimbles, pin-cushions and needlecases.
Some small antique items and antique
enamel boxes. Catalogue.

Neal Street East 3 I 23
5 Neal St WC2. 01-240 0135. Interesting
and enterprising gifts with a definite Chinese flavour: books, prints, clothes,
ceramics, baskets, toys.

Old Curiosity Shop 6 J 25
13 Portsmouth St WC2. 01-405 9891.
Immortalised by Dickens, the shop now
sells gifts, curios and antiques. *OPEN
09.30-17.30 Mon-Sun.*

Tortoiseshell & Ivory House 2 D 18
24 Chiltern St W1. 01-935 8031. Imported
goods including jade.

Unirose
125 Askew Rd W12. 01-749 9735. Gifts
(brochure available) which can be delivered in central London the same day.

*Most antique dealers have good 18th-19thC
glass as part of their stock in trade. See also
under 'Antique shops & supermarkets'.*

W.G.T. Burne 4 K 10
11 Elystan St SW3. 01-589 6074. English
and Irish glass. Wine glasses, candelabra
and chandeliers from the early 18th and
early 19thC.

Howard Phillips 2 F 19
11a Henrietta Pl W1. 01-580 9844. English,
Irish, Dutch, Venetian, Roman, German
and Spanish glass. Outstanding varieties.

Lloyd 2 I 14
5a Motcomb St SW1. 01-235 1010. Good
stock of glass of all periods, including selection of 18th and 19thC decanters. *By appt.*

See under 'China, glass & porcelain'.

Peter Dale 5 J 21
11-12 Royal Opera Arc, Pall Mall SW1.
01-930 3695. Antique weapons, armour
and militaria for the collector.

Boss 2 H 19
13 Dover St W1. 01-493 0711. Manufacturers of top quality sporting shot guns. A
long waiting list for purchasers.

Holland & Holland 2 H 18
33 Bruton St W1. 01-499 4411. The top
London gunsmiths.

James Purdey & Sons 2 G 17
57 South Audley St W1. 01-499 1801. Fine
gunsmiths.

John Rigby & Co 6 P 26
(Gunmakers)
66 Great Suffolk St SE1. 01-734 7611.
Maufacturers and dealers of high-quality
hand-made modern sporting guns and
rifles.

Swaine, Adeney, Brigg 2 I 19
185 Piccadilly W1. 01-734 4277. Piccadilly
Gun Rooms. Agents for Westley Richards
and Atkin, Grant, Lang. Stock modern and
antique guns and accessories.

Fishers 6 L 28
28 Cathedral Pl, St Paul's Churchyard EC4.
01-236 1767. Modern and pleasant –
convenient for City executives. Women's
styling too.

Gavin Hodge at Sweenys 2 I 12
48 Beauchamp Pl SW3. 01-589 3066/7.
Fashionable barber in an elegant club
atmosphere. Women's hairdressing too.

Stanley Alwin 2 I 21
110 Shaftesbury Av W1. 01-437 8933.
Some of the leading London hairdressers
come here to get their own hair cut.

Trumper 2 I 17
9 Curzon St W1. 01-499 1850. A very
famous establishment. Superb shopfront
and interior.

Vidal Sassoon 2 G 18
56 Brook St W1. 01-409 0925. Also at 44
Sloane St SW1 (2 I 13). 01-235 1957.
Adventurous styles.

*Nearly all the big department stores have
hair-dressing salons and men's styling.
Most modern hairdressers cater for men &
women.*

Alan International 4 K 8
281 Fulham Rd SW10. 01-351 1123. Popular modern salon.

André Bernard Hair International 2 I 14
41 Knightsbridge SW1. 01-235 6851. Specialists in styling for both young and older women.

Crimpers 2 D 18
80a Baker St W1. 01-486 4522/3. High-fashion styles for the young of both sexes.

Ginger Group 2 I 13
47-49 Brompton Rd SW3. 01-584 4714. Up-to-date styling. Many branches.

Hebe 5 K 22
38 William IV St WC2. 01-836 1132. Full range of perms, colours and highlighting products.

Jingles 5 M 16
125 Wilton Rd SW1. 01-834 0032. Good quality service including cutting, colouring and perming.

Mane Line 2 F 18
22 Weighhouse St W1. 01-493 4952. Trendy place for men and women, convenient if you work in the West End.

Michaeljohn 2 I 19
23a Albemarle St W1. 01-629 6969. Modern and fashionable.

Molton Brown 2 F 19
58 South Molton St W1. 01-629 1872. For a totally natural look. Hair products, accessories and cosmetics. Men's cutting. 01-493 5236.

Ricci Burns 2 D 17
94 George St W1. 01-935 3657. Eye-catching styles designed to suit the individual. Beauty salon.

Robert Fielding 2 H 20
215 Regent St W1. 01-734 3381. Fashionable styles for all ages; beauty treatments available. Many branches. Also a hairdressing school.

Sissors 4 L 11
46a King's Rd SW3. 01-589 9471. High-fashion styles for men and women. Other branches.

Stage Door 3 I 24
16 Drury La WC2. 01-836 6425. Good modern styles for men and women.

Steiner 1 E 8
Royal Garden Hotel, Kensington High St W8. 01-937 1228. A world-famous salon linked with high-quality hair-care products. Branches in several hotels and at Victoria and Euston railway stations.

Toni & Guy 2 G 18
10-12 Davies St W1. 01-629 8348. Ultramodern and stylish salon. Hairdressing to a high standard.

Trevor Sorbie 6 J 24
10 Russell St WC2. 01-379 6901. All types of hairstyling, colouring and perming.

Vidal Sassoon 5 K 12
44 Sloane St SW1. 01-235 7791. Also at 60 South Molton St W1 (2 **F 19**). 01-491 8848. And 130 Sloane St SW3 (5 **J 13**). 01-730 7288. Famous avant garde styles.

Handbag & luggage repairs

Jeeves 5 J 12
7 Pont St SW1. 01-235 1101. Handbag, luggage and shoe repairs and renovations.

Herbalists

G. Baldwin & Co
171-173 Walworth Rd SE17. 01-703 5550. Locally renowned, long-established shop with huge range and helpful advice. Sells health foods too.

Culpeper 2 H 18
21 Bruton St W1. 01-629 4559. Also at 8 Covent Garden Mkt WC2 (6 **J 23**). 01-379 6698. And 9 Flask Wlk NW3. 01-794 7263. Also specialists in pure cosmetics, pot pourri and pomanders.

Neal's Yard Apothecary & Therapy Rooms 3 I 22
2 Neal's Yd WC2. 01-379 7222. Herbal remedies. Bach flower remedies and natural cosmetics, books and leaflets.

Home accessories

Anthony Redmile 4 M 5
97 Lots Rd SW10. 01-730 0557. Unusual, decorative objects. Specialise in antler furniture.

Casa Fina 6 J 23
9 Covent Garden Mkt WC2. 01-836 0289. Ceramics from Italy and Portugal. Pine furniture from Spain. Vast range of lighting and cachepots.

Casa Pupo 5 M 12
56-60 Pimlico Rd SW1. 01-730 7111. Spanish ceramics, glassware, rugs, ornaments and bedcovers at fairly reasonable prices.

Covent Garden General Store 3 J 23
111 Long Acre WC2. 01-240 0331. Large selection of out of the ordinary home accessories.

Deans Blinds
Haslemere Ind Est, Ravensbury Ter, SW18. 01-947 8931. Make roller blinds to order. Wide range of materials to choose from.

General Trading Company 5 K 12
144 Sloane St SW1. 01-730 0411. A miscellany of antiques, china, glass and soft furnishings – all in elegant 'private house' setting.

Graham & Green
4 & 7 Elgin Cres W11. 01-727 4594. Home accessories, many in individual styles, and furniture with the natural look. Cushions covered in Victorian and Edwardian lace. Basketware specialists.

Liberty 2 G 20
210-220 Regent St W1. 01-734 1234. Very attractive household department with lots of ideas.

The Reject Shop 3 F 23
209 Tottenham Court Rd W1. 01-580 2895. Also at 245 Brompton Rd SW3 (1 I 11). And 234 King's Rd SW3 (4 L 9). Big selection of home accessories and furniture, lighting, cookware, etc. Low prices.

Icons

Maria Andipa's Icon Gallery 4 J 11
162 Walton St SW3. 01-589 2371. Byzantine, Greek, Russian and Ethiopian icons. Also ethnic jewellery.

Temple Gallery 1 I 11
4 Yeoman's Row, Brompton Rd SW3. 01-589 6622. Russian, Greek and Byzantine icons.

Ironwork

G. & S. Allgood 2 D 22
297 Euston Rd NW1. 01-387 9951. Well-designed architectural ironmongery.

J. D. Beardmore 2 G 22
3-4 Percy St W1. 01-637 7041. Very large selection of good reproduction and architectural ironmongery and cabinet fittings.

Comyn Ching 6 J 31
110 Golden La EC1. 01-253 8414. An enormous range of ironmongery designs still produced from old patterns. Architectural and builders' ironmongers.

Jewellery & silver: antique

Many antique shops deal in silver and jewellery, particularly those in the Burlington Arcade, but the markets and antique supermarkets are best for a variety of choice and price.

Ann Bloom 2 H 19
10a New Bond St W1. 01-491 1213. Exclu-

sive collection of fine period jewellery and period silver photograph frames.

Armour-Winston 2 I 19
43 Burlington Arc W1. 01-493 8937. Fine jewels and clocks.

Asprey 2 H 19
165 New Bond St W1. 01-493 6767. Unusual antique and modern jewellery. Also an excellent range of luxury gifts.

Bentley 2 G 19
65 New Bond St W1. 01-629 0651. Long-established. Superb jewels and antique silver. Also Fabergé pieces. Buys as well as sells.

Bond Street Silver Galleries 2 G 19
111-112 New Bond St W1. 01-493 6180. 15 showrooms of antique, modern and second-hand jewellery and silver.

Collingwood 2 H 19
171 New Bond St W1. 01-734 2656. Long-established jewellers to the Queen – antique and modern gold and silverware.

Garrard 2 I 20
112 Regent St W1. 01-734 7020. Jewellers to the Queen. Fine antique and modern silver.

Green's Antique Galleries 1 D 8
117 Kensington Church St W8. 01-229 9618. Victorian jewellery and rings. Also silver.

Langfords Silver Galleries 6 J 26
46-47 Chancery La WC2. 01-405 6402. Antique and modern silver and plate. Also model ships.

The London Silver Vaults 6 J 26
Chancery House, 53-64 Chancery La WC2. 01-242 3844. Underground vaults like an Aladdin's cave crammed with antique and modern silver and plate.

Paul Longmire 5 J 19
12 Bury St SW1. 01-930 8720. Suppliers of jewellery to the Queen and Queen Mother. Vast selection of cuff links; seal engraved rings. Extensive display space as this shop has the largest windows of any privately-owned jewellers in the West End.

Philip Antrobus 2 H 19
11 New Bond St W1. 01-493 4557. Fine gold and gem-set jewellery ranging from antique to modern.

S. J. Phillips 2 G 19
139 New Bond St W1. 01-629 6261. Fine jewels, silver and objets d'art from England and the Continent.

Sac Frères 2 I 19
45 Old Bond St W1. 01-493 2333. Antique amber jewellery and works of art. Established over 120 years.

Shrubsole 3 H 24
43 Museum St WC1. 01-405 2712. Fine

antique English silver and old Sheffield plate for the discerning collector.

Tessiers   2 G 19
26 New Bond St WI. 01-629 0458. Fine old firm of silversmiths. Antique jewels. Valuations and repairs of modern and antique jewellery.

Jewellery & silver: modern & costume

London is rich in fine specialist jewellery shops. Many are world-famous. Good areas to shop are: Bond St, the Burlington Arcade, Knightsbridge.

Acsis   6 J 23
Unit 31, Covent Garden Mkt WC2. 01-836 9356. Designer costume jewellery mostly imported from Italy and France. Also fun watches and some 9ct gold items.

Argenta   4 J 8
82 Fulham Rd SW3. 01-584 1841. Stunning modern silverware from Scandinavia and modern English designs. Their silversmith will make up pieces for individual customers.

Butler & Wilson   4 K 8
189 Fulham Rd SW3. 01-352 3045. Selection from Art Deco and Celtic pieces to modern jewellery.

Cartier   2 H 19
175 New Bond St WI. 01-493 6962. Top-class internationally famous jewellers.

Ciro Pearls   2 I 19
48 Old Bond St WI. 01-493 5529. Specialists in cultured and imitation pearl jewellery of all kinds. Also large selection of superior costume jewellery.

Cobra & Bellamy   2 I 13
149 Sloane St SWI. 01-730 2823. Specialises in Art Deco silver and costume jewellery from the 1920s to 1950s.

Electrum Gallery   2 F 19
21 South Molton St WI. 01-629 6325. Exhibits and sells contemporary designer jewellery to suit all the latest tastes.

Georg Jensen Silver   2 G 19
156 New Bond St WI. 01-499 6541. Modern Danish jewellery and silver.

Ken Lane   2 I 12
50 Beauchamp Pl SW3. 01-584 5299. Wide range of exciting and daring costume jewellery.

Kutchinsky   2 H 19
179 New Bond St WI. 01-629 2876. Fine jewels, and top-quality Swiss watches.

Mappin & Webb   2 H 20
170 Regent St WI. 01-734 3801. High-quality jewellery and silver.

Jewellery: hire

Charles Fox   6 J 23
22 Tavistock St WC2. 01-240 3111. Magnificent artificial jewellery for hire.

Jewellery: repairs & restorations

Hilwoods
148 Station Rd, Edgware, Middx. 01-952 5067. Repairs and restoration to all types of jewellery and antique clocks. Also make jewellery to order.

Key cutting

Selfridges, Harrods, many branches of Woolworths have a while-you-wait service: also many small local ironmongers, shoe repairers and some of the larger tube stations.

Kitchen equipment

Try the small shops in Soho which supply the local restaurants. Heal's, Selfridges and Habitat have excellent kitchen departments. The Design Centre in the Haymarket exhibits the best designs. Also visit the Building Centre in Store St WCl, for a pre-selection of kitchen units and fittings.

Covent Garden Kitchen Supplies   6 J 23
3 Covent Garden Mkt WC2. 01-836 9167. Wide range of kitchen equipment from France. Other ranges as well.

David Mellor   5 L 12
4 Sloane Sq SWI. 01-730 4259. Also at 26 James St WC2 (6 J 23). 01-379 6947. All sorts of kitchen equipment, some pottery, basketware.

Divertimenti   2 E 19
68-72 Marylebone La WI. 01-935 0689. Wide selection of cookware and tableware.

Elizabeth David   5 L 12
46 Bourne St SWI. 01-730 3123. Complete range of kitchen pots, pans, knives and pastrycook's equipment from France and elsewhere.

William Page   2 I 22
121 Shaftesbury Av WC2. 01-379 6334. Excellent functional 'down to earth' pots, pans and cutlery as used by the local restaurant trade.

Kitchen planning

Just Kitchens
206-208 Upper Richmond Rd West SW14. 01-876 6106. Also at 242 Fulham Rd SW10 (4 **K 6**). 01-351 1616. Many makes and types of kitchen equipment. Good displays.

Kitchen Mart
291 Holloway Rd N7. 01-607 3575. Will order virtually any make of fitted kitchen.

Knitting yarns

Most of the big department stores stock a range of knitting yarns and patterns. Harrods and Dickins & Jones are particularly good.

Colourspun
18 Camden Rd NW1. 01-267 6317. Large range of natural fibre yarns. Tweeds, silk, angora, cashmere, alpaca, mohair.

Colourway
112a Westbourne Gro W12. 01-229 1432. Yarns are mainly by Rowan and Christian de Falbe. Also have tapestry kits, designer sweaters and books.

Patricia Roberts   6 **J 23**
31 James St WC2. 01-379 6660. Pure yarns in a vast range of seasonally changing colours. Patricia Roberts original patterns or buy the jumpers ready-knitted downstairs.

Ries Wools of Holborn   6 **J 27**
242 High Holborn WC1. 01-242 7721. Knitting wools and homecrafts.

Left-handed

Anything Left-handed   2 **H 20**
65 Beak St W1. 01-437 3910. Potato peelers, pen nibs, scissors – every gadget is designed for the left-handed. Mail-order service and catalogue.

Lighting

Good lighting departments at Heal's, Harrods, Habitat, John Lewis, Selfridges and British Home Stores.

Christopher Wray's Lighting   4 **L 6**
Emporium
600 King's Rd SW6. 01-736 8434. Over 2000 genuine, restored oil and gas lamps. Also a lamp workshop to service, restore, repair or convert to electricity any oil or gas lamp.

The London Lighting Co   4 **L 4**
135 Fulham Rd SW3. 01-589 3612. Excellent, pricey collection of modern light fittings.

Mr Light   4 **L 4**
275 Fulham Rd SW10. 01-352 7525. Large range of indoor and outdoor lights including desk lamps, corner lamps and spotlights. Designs very modern or traditional.

Thorn EMI   2 **G 19**
4 Tenterden St, Hanover Sq W1. 01-836 2444. Customer advisory service on lighting and things electrical.

Linen

Givans Irish Linen Stores   4 **L 9**
207 King's Rd SW3. 01-352 6352. Top-quality linen from this well-stocked shop with an air of old-fashioned gentility.

Irish Linen   2 **I 19**
35 Burlington Arc W1. 01-493 8949. Tiny shop with expensive, beautifully made table cloths, napkins, pillowcases, etc.

Linen Cupboard   2 **F 20**
21 Great Castle St W1. 01-629 4062. Cut-price .household linen and baby linen. Stocks all the famous makes.

London Bedding Centre   2 **I 13**
26 Sloane St SW1. 01-235 7542. Bed linen of all kinds – duvets, quilts, etc. Lots of beds too!

Vantona International Linen   2 **H 19**
28 Savile Row W1. 01-629 5000. Table linen and initialled handkerchiefs sold in a rather grand, exclusive atmosphere.

The White House   2 **G 19**
51 New Bond St W1. 01-629 3521. Stocks the most luxurious and expensive linen in London. Exquisite hand-embroidery and hand-made lace edges. Also silk and satin lingerie and regal children's wear.

Locksmiths

Barry Bros   2 **B 14**
121-123 Praed St W2. 01-262 9009. Wide range of fire and crime prevention equipment. Operates an emergency service 08.00-24.00 Mon-Sun.

Magazines

The Vintage Magazine Shop   2 **I 21**
39-41 Brewer St W1. 01-439 8525. Vintage magazines from the turn of the century, especially 30s, 40s and 50s, sheet music,

theatre programmes, children's annuals. Also movie shop with film star mags and posters. American comic shop, and vintage pop and rock ephemera shop.

Maps: antique

Cartographia   3 H 24
Pied Bull Yd, Bury Pl WC1. 01-404 4050. Antique maps and engravings from the 15thC onwards. Framing service.
The Map House   2 I 12
54 Beauchamp Pl SW3. 01-589 4325. Antique maps, engravings, prints, atlases and globes.
Robert Douwma (Prints & Maps)   3 H 23
4 Henrietta St WC2. 01-836 0771. Very large selection of decorative prints, atlases and old maps.

Maps: modern

Geographia Map Shop   6 L 28
58 Ludgate Hill EC4. 01-248 3554. Stocks an extensive range of maps of all parts of the world, including Ordnance Survey maps, atlases and globes. Good choice of guide books as well.
The London Map Centre   5 M 18
22-24 Caxton St SW1. 01-222 2466/4945. Stockists of Ordnance Survey and other maps.
Stanfords   6 J 23
12-14 Long Acre WC2. 01-836 1321. Maps of GB and the rest of the world; Ordnance Survey maps, globes. Will obtain any map, to any scale, of any part of the world – but it may take time. Also guide books and foreign geology section.

Matchbox labels

The British Matchbox Label Society
B. Griffin (Secretary), 22 Githa Rd, Hastings, E Sussex. Hastings 431236. Will supply information.

Media

BBC World   6 K 23
Bush House, Strand WC2. 01-257 2575. Information-centred shop – geared mainly to world and external services, but also deals with home radio and TV. London showroom for BBC English courses. Large range of technical manuals and media books. Sells BBC publications, records, cassettes and videos. *CLOSED Sat & Sun.*

Militaria shops

See also under 'Antiques', 'Guns: antique' and 'Models'.
Arms & Militaria Bookshop
34 High St N14. 01-886 0334. Large selection of old model soldiers and books.
Collectors Corner
1 Northcross Rd SE22. 01-693 6285. Militaria of the world, covering all aspects. Parachutist wings and world-wide elite forces. Reference books.
Tradition   2 I 17
10 White Horse St W1. 01-491 7077. Also at 5a Shepherd St W1. Antique weapons and uniforms. Buttons, badges, buckles, helmets and belt plates. Paintings, prints and postcards. Model soldiers.

Military war medals

Services war medals can be bought at Moss Bros military department. Also:
The Armoury of St James   2 I 18
17 Piccadilly Arc SW1. 01-493 5082.

Miniatures

Asprey   2 G 19
165 New Bond St W1. 01-493 6767.
Limner Antiques   2 G 19
The Antique Centre, New Bond St W1. 01-629 5314. Antique portrait/miniature specialists.

Models

Aeronautical Models
39 Parkway NW1. 01-485 1818. Wide range of kits and accessories. Mostly remote-controlled. Expert staff.
Beatties of London   3 I 26
202 High Holborn WC1. 01-405 6285. Model trains, cars, kits, boats, games, radio-controlled toys, diecast aircraft, jigsaws, tools, video and electronic games.
Cherry's
62 Sheen Rd, Richmond, Surrey. 01-940 2454. Second-hand and new model locomotives. Traction and stationary engines. Suppliers of a limited tinplate edition.
Hamleys   2 H 20
188-196 Regent St W1. 01-734 3161.

Good stocks of remote-controlled toys and train sets. Impressive working train system on show.

Henry J. Nicholls & Son
308 Holloway Rd N7. 01-607 4272. A specialist model aircraft shop for the serious enthusiast. All types of aircraft, boat and car models, especially the most sophisticated radio-controlled models.

Hummel   2 I 19
16 Burlington Arc W1. 01-493 7164. Collectors' pieces. Also some collectors' dolls and London souvenirs. Model soldiers.

Julip Model Horses   2 I 12
18 Beauchamp Pl SW3. 01-589 0867. Every breed of horse and pony available, together with tack and other equipment.

Model Aircraft Supplies
207 Camberwell Rd SE5. 01-703 4562. Specialists in working model kits – not only aircraft.

Model Railway   3 C 28
Manufacturing
14 York Way N1. 01-837 5551. Knowledgeable service and stocks for the enthusiast. Top-quality scale equipment. Also railway and transport books.

W. & H. Models   2 D 19
14 New Cavendish St W1. 01-935 5810. Train sets, scale models, plastic kits, and remote-controlled cars. English and Continental stocks. Experienced staff.

Parker Gallery   2 I 19
12a-12b Berkeley St W1. 01-499 5906. Many kinds of ship models. Specialise in military, naval and topographical prints, oils and watercolours.

Steam Age   I E 6
19 Abingdon Rd W8. 01-938 1982. Steam models of all kinds, and railway, ship and traction engines. Books, kits and castings.

Tradition   2 I 19
5a Shepherd St W1. 01-493 7452. The best selection of old and new model soldiers in London. Make their own. Militaria and military books.

Motorbikes & accessories

Gambier Reeks   4 L 4
554 King's Rd SW6. 01-736 3096. The full range of Yamaha motorbikes plus spare parts and accessories can be found here. Also good selection of second-hand bikes and two efficient workshops for repairs.

Lewis Leathers   2 E 21
122 Great Portland St W1. 01-636 4314. Motorbike leather specialists.

Mocheck
24-28 Clapham High St SW4. 01-720 6072. Kawasaki and Honda specialists. Also range of second-hand motorbikes and accessories. Large workshop for repairs and services.

Motorcycle City
535-537 Staines Rd, Bedfont, Middx. 01-890 1849. Huge range of Japanese bikes – new and second-hand. Accessories.

Motoring organisations

Automobile Association   5 J 21
(AA)
5 New Coventry St W1. 01-839 4355. Join the AA at any of the 11 centres in Greater London (check the telephone directory for the nearest). Provides various breakdown and recovery services, as well as legal advice, route details and discounts on various services and publications.

Royal Automobile Club   5 J 19
(RAC)
49 Pall Mall SW1. 01-839 7050. Membership offers a recovery breakdown service and access to insurance schemes and publications at a reduced rate.

Musical automata & boxes

Jack Donovan   I · A 8
93 Portobello Rd W11. 01-727 1485. Musical boxes, barrel organs, street pianos and automata.

Talking Machine
30 Watford Way NW4. 01-202 3473. Deals in early gramophones, phonographs, Victorian sewing machines, primitive typewriters, classic jukeboxes, early radio and TV equipment and old records.

Musical instruments

Andy's Guitar Centre   3 H 23
27 Denmark St WC2. 01-836 0899. New and second-hand electric guitars and basses. Semi-acoustic and classical. Workshop where guitars are made and repaired. Many major pop groups among their customers.

J. & A. Beare   2 H 21
7 Broadwick St W1. 01-437 1449. Fine old violins, violas and cellos. Also restorers.

Bill Lewington   2 I 21
144 Shaftesbury Av WC2. 01-240 0584.

New and second-hand wind and brass instruments.

Bluthner 2 H 19
47 Conduit St W1. 01-439 1166. Pianos.

Boosey & Hawkes 2 G 20
295 Regent St W1. 01-580 2060. Manufacture whole range of brass and woodwind instruments. Sell instrumental accessories, music and books but no instruments from here. Music publishers.

Early Music Shop at Schott & Co 2 G 21
48 Great Marlborough St W1. 01-437 1246. Reproduction instruments mainly from the Renaissance and Baroque periods.

T. W. Howarth 2 D 18
31 Chiltern St W1. 01-935 2407. Manufacturers of oboes d'amore and cor anglais. Woodwind specialists. Music, accessories, woodwind repairs.

Ivor Mairants Musicentre 2 G 22
56 Rathbone Pl W1. 01-636 1481. Specialise in guitars, of which they have a huge range, and other fretted instruments such as mandolins, banjos and ukuleles. 1001 accessories.

The London Music Shop
43-45 Coldharbour La SE5. 01-737 2468. Main branch of this musical education specialist is in Exeter, selling percussion instruments, recorders and clarinets. This is the mail-order division but supplies information on workshops undertaken at local schools.

N. P. Mander
St Peter's Organ Works, St Peter's Clo, Warner Pl E2. 01-739 4747. Antique organs supplied all over the world. Also restorations and new organs built for churches, cathedrals and home use.

Morley Piano & Harpsichord Workshops
34 Engate St SE13. 01-318 5838. Antique, reproduction, second-hand and modern pianos and early keyboard instruments. Domestic long-term piano rental. Also tune, repair, recondition and restore any keyboard instrument.

Paxman 3 J 23
116 Long Acre WC2. 01-240 3642/3647. One of the most famous horn makers in the world, they sell all types, both new and second-hand. All other brass and woodwind instruments supplied. Sheet music and repairs.

Peter Coutts
43 Perryn Rd W3. 01-743 8727. Handmade harpsichords.

Professional Percussion
205 Kentish Town Rd NW5. 01-485 0822. Vast selection of drums, drum kits and other percussion instruments. Accessories and second-hand equipment too.

Raymond Man Chinese Music Shop 3 I 23
64 Neal St WC2. 01-240 1776. Chinese and Indian instruments. Also a selection of Chinese, African, Japanese, Balinese and Indian records. Lessons on Chinese instruments. Hiring service too.

Roka 3 H 23
5 Denmark St WC2. 01-240 2610. Repairs carried out on acoustic and electric guitars, amplifiers and Rhodes pianos. Comprehensive stock of spares and second-hand guitars. Anything new ordered.

Salvi Harps 3 I 23
151-157 City Rd EC1. 01-253 3738. Italian firm which makes and sells harps and everything to go with them.

Schott 2 G 20
48 Great Marlborough St W1. 01-437 1246. Music publishers and sellers of educational and classical sheet music. Sell recorders.

Steinway 2 E 19
Steinway Hall, 44 Marylebone La, Wigmore St W1. 01-487 3391. Wide variety of Steinway pianos.

Musical instrument restorations

F. & H. Percussion Ltd
131 Wapping High St E1. 01-481 3704. Percussion hire, retail and repair.

Fiddles & Sticks
13 All Saints Rd W11. 01-221 4040. Stringed, brass and woodwind instruments restored.

Munson & Harbour
Masterpiece Works, Hampshire St NW5. 01-267 1610. Harp repairers.

Music: printed, antique

Otto Haas
49 Belsize Park Gdns NW3. 01-722 1488. Rare collectors' items – manuscripts and printed music from the Middle Ages to the 20thC. *By appt only.*

Travis & Emery 2 I 22
17 Cecil Ct, Charing Cross Rd WC2. 01-240 2129. Printed music from the 1700s. Also books on music.

Music: printed, modern

Chappell 2 G 19
50 New Bond St W1. 01-491 2777. Established 1811. Publishers with a world-wide

reputation. Also sell a variety of instruments.

Cramer Music   5 **J** 22
23 Garrick St WC2. 01-240 1612. Publishers and stockists of classical, educational and popular music.

Novello   2 **H** 20
8 Lower James St W1. 01-734 8080. Famous publishers of educational, church, vocal, instrumental and orchestral music.

Needlework & embroidery

House of Fraser and John Lewis have excellent needlework departments.

Ellis & Farrier   2 **G** 20
20 Prince's St, Hanover Sq W1. 01-629 9964. Sell all kinds of beads mostly for the embroidery trade; sequins, bugle beads; pearl drops, shaped stones; all colours and sizes. Will dye beads especially to customers' requirements.

Harrods   2 **I** 12
Knightsbridge SW1. 01-730 1234. Needlework department covers Continental merchandise – specialises in tramme tapestries and counted cross-stitch embroidery. Lace-making equipment and thread.

Luxury Needlepoint   2 **I** 12
36 Beauchamp Pl SW3. 01-581 5555. Everything to do with tapestries either to make yourself or ready-made. Furniture to accommodate the tapestries.

Royal School of Needlework 6 **J** 23
5 King St WC2. 01-240 3186. Comprehensive range of embroidery materials and equipment. Also cleaning and repairing of samplers and lace, and the restoring of antique embroideries and textiles. Classes and courses in all aspects of embroidery and related textile crafts and lacemaking.

Pens

Pencraft   6 **J** 25
91 Kingsway WC2. 01-405 3639. Very wide range of ballpoints and fountain pens.
Penfriend   6 **K** 23
Bush House Arc, Bush House, Strand WC2. Large selection.
W. H. Smith   6 **J** 24
11 Kingsway WC2. 01-836 5951. Repairs and sales of Parker pens.

Perfume

Stores and chemists usually stock a large range of all the more popular perfumes. For
something more unusual try the shops listed below. Large shops like Selfridges, Harrods and Dickins & Jones stock 'The Perfumer's Workshop' range which enables you to blend your own.*

Chanel   2 **I** 19
26 Old Bond St W1. 01-493 5040. The whole perfume and cosmetics range.
Floris   5 **J** 20
89 Jermyn St SW1. 01-930 2885. Perfumers to the Court of St James since George IV, specialising in English flower perfumes, matching toiletries and preparations for men.
Mary Chess   2 **I** 17
7 Shepherd Market W1. 01-629 5152. Traditional perfumes and perfumed accessories.
Penhaligon's   2 **G** 19
20a Brook St W1. 01-493 0002. Traditional toilet waters and hand-made fragrances. Also deal in old English silver scent bottles. Other branches.

Pest control

Your local Council offers a free service for the disposal of vermin and insects, or try:
Rentokil   2 **F** 20
37-38 Margaret St W1. 01-493 0061. Gives free surveys for rising damp, woodworm and dry rot. Does the remedial work as well as clearing out pests.

Photographic equipment

Dixons   2 **G** 22
88 Oxford St W1. 01-636 8511. Photographic as well as audio-visual equipment. Over 90 branches in London all with excellent stocks.
Fox Talbot   5 **K** 22
443 Strand WC2. 01-379 6522. Large selection of top names.
Jessops   3 **H** 23
67-69 New Oxford St W1. 01-240 6523. Wide range of photographic and dark-room equipment at competitive prices.
Leeds Camera Centre   3 **F** 23
20-22 Brunswick Centre, Bernard St WC1. Cameras, films and all accessories can be found in the Camera Centre, the Flash Centre or the Film and Hire Centre.
R. G. Lewis   3 **I** 25
217 High Holborn WC1. 01-242 2916. Developing and enlargements. Photographic equipment, telescopes, stereos.
Morgans   3 **E** 23
179 Tottenham Court Rd W1. 01-636 1138.

Extensive selection of good second-hand cameras and photographic equipment.

Pelling & Cross 3 C 24
93-103 Drummond St NW1. 01-380 1144. Large stocks of professional cameras and equipment. Rental and repair service.

Wallace Heaton 2 G 19
127 New Bond St W1. 01-629 7511. High-quality new photographic, cine and projection equipment.

Photography services

Atlas Photography
6 Blundell St N7. 01-607 6767. All aspects of photographic services. Can enlarge, provide exhibition display prints, print T-shirts, supply film.

Studio 10 3 H 28
25-27 Farringdon Rd EC1. 01-404 4044. High-quality, professional and expensive. Re-touching, enlargements, colour prints made into slides.

Picture framing & restoring

Blackman Harvey 3 I 24
36 Great Queen St WC2. 01-836 1904. 48hr framing service. Also do picture and frame restorations.

Bourlet Frames
Unit A, 50-56 Wharf Rd N1. 01-251 9229. Large range of styles and some hand-made frames. Watercolour and oil restoration also undertaken.

F. A. Pollak 5 J 19
20 Blue Ball Yd, St James's St SW1. 01-493 1434. High-quality and expensive bespoke framing service.

J. & L. Tanous 4 L 2
115b Harwood Rd SW6. 01-736 6497. Modern and antique framing of quality. Fine art picture frame makers; gilders, restorers.

Pipes

Astleys 2 I 19
109 Jermyn St SW1. 01-930 1687. Established since 1862. Specialise in briar and meerschaum pipes.

Dunhill 5 J 19
30 Duke St, St James's SW1. 01-499 9566. Exclusive masculine luxury goods including pipes, lighters, cigars, writing instruments and leather goods.

Inderwick 2 H 20
45 Carnaby St W1. 01-734 6574. Esta-

blished in the 18thC. Made pipes for Edward VII. Tobaccos blended for individual tastes.

Plants

See under 'Flowers' and 'Gardening'.

Postcards

John Hall
31 Epple Rd SW6. 01-736 3542. Extensive collection of fine postcards. Also largest private collection in England of lithographs and engraved music covers, plus ephemera of all types 1740-1940. *By appt only.*

London Postcard Centre
21 Kensington Park Rd W11. 01-229 1888. HQ of postcard collecting in Britain. Sell antique picture postcards from all over the world.

Pleasures of Past Times 5 J 22
11 Cecil Ct WC2. 01-836 1142. Extremely large classified collection of early postcards, greetings cards, early children's books and theatre ephemera.

Posters & reproductions

The London art galleries usually sell reproductions of their more popular paintings.

The Arts Council Shop 6 J 23
8 Long Acre WC2. 01-836 1359. Sell a wide range of posters on the performing arts and visual arts.

Athena 2 G 21
119-121 Oxford St W1. 01-734 3383. Main branch. Good selection of cheap posters and reproductions. Other branches.

Imperial War Museum 6 Q 23
Lambeth Rd SE1. 01-735 8922. General selection of World War I and II posters.

The Lords Gallery
26 Wellington Rd NW8. 01-722 4444. Permanent exhibition of European, American and Chinese posters (Lautrec to World War II). Also collages by Schwitters.

Medici Gallery 2 H 19
7 Grafton St W1. 01-837 7099. Reproductions, limited editions, graphics and greetings cards. Exhibitions *Mar-Aug.*

Paperchase 3 F 23
213 Tottenham Court Rd W1. 01-580 8496. Modern posters. Also prints and art books.

The Poster Shop 4 J 10
168 Fulham Rd SW10. 01-373 7294. Other branches. Posters from all over the world covering every subject. Huge selection. Framed posters too.

Press cutting agencies

International Press Cutting Bureau
224-236 Walworth Rd SE17. 01-708 2113.
Monitoring service for world-wide press.

Romeike & Curtice
Hale House, 290-296 Green Lanes N13.
01-882 0155. Extensive cuttings from newspapers, magazines, trade journals as well as advert checking and a foreign department.

Records & cassettes

Don't forget that records can be borrowed like books from local libraries – a particularly good one is Westminster Public Library in Charing Cross Rd WC2.

Caruso & Co   3 H 23
35 New Oxford St WC1. 01-379 5839. English and foreign, vocal and operatic and a large selection of classical records. Also nostalgia and second-hand records.

Cassettes Plus   5 J 22
9 St Martin's Ct WC2. 01-836 8514. Specialist cassette shop offering London's largest selection – 10,000 titles. Also compact discs.

Cheapo Cheapo Records   2 I 21
53 Rupert St W1. 01-437 8272. Jazz, rock, classical and blues – and the name does not lie. All second-hand stock.

Dobell's   2 I 22
21 Tower St WC2. 01-240 1354. Complete stocks of jazz, folk and blues records.

Gramophone Exchange   3 I 23
3 Betterton St WC2. 01-836 0976. Large stock of all types of records, classical specialists. Also Albanian goods.

HMV   2 G 21
150 Oxford St W1. 01-631 3423. Comprehensive stock of all types of music in a very large store.

James Asman   5 J 22
23a New Row WC2. 01-240 1380. Long-established jazz, blues and nostalgia records specialist run by jazz critic James Asman. Lots of imports, deletions and second-hand bargains. Collections bought.

Music Discount Centre   5 K 23
437 Strand WC2. 01-240 2157. Other branches. Huge selection of classical records ranging from the very specialist to the more popular. Inexpensive.

Our Price Records   2 G 23
12 Tottenham Court Rd W1. 01-636 4631. Every taste catered for, though they specialise in pop and rock. Competitively priced.

Ray's Jazz Shop   3 I 23
180 Shaftesbury Av WC2. 01-240 3969. Jazz records, cassettes and compact discs.

Record and Tape Exchange
38 Notting Hill Gate W11. 01-727 2329. Exchange or select from thousands of second-hand records. Rare deletions. Also at 229 Camden High St NW1, 01-267 1898, and 90 Goldhawk Rd W12, 01-749 2930.

Tower Records   2 I 20
1 Piccadilly W1. 01-439 2500. Housed in the old Swan & Edgar building this is said to be the 'greatest record store in the known world'. Full range of sounds and large selection of compact discs, videos and US imports.

Virgin Megastore   2 G 22
14-16 Oxford St W1. 01-631 1234. Progressive and popular music, blues, jazz, classical – almost everything at below the recommended price. Virgin Records has many branches.

Sex supermarkets

Ann Summers   2 I 21
26 Brewer St W1. 01-437 4016. The original sex supermarket, with all types of contraceptives, gadgets, and aids to being a superman or woman. Helpful staff; demonstrations.

Lovecraft   5 J 22
46 Cranbourn St WC2. 01-437 2105. Amusement arcade-like sex supermarket. Wide selection of products.

Shells

Eaton's Shell Shop   2 H 22
16 Manette St WC2. 01-437 9391. Near Foyles. Very varied shop offering as its main line an awe-inspiring selection of shells, minerals, crystals and fossils costing anything from a few pence to hundreds of pounds. Popular with collectors and theatre and cinema prop hunters. Also shell and semi-precious stone jewellery. Natural woven matting, bamboo poles, cane roller blinds made-to-measure and chair cane. Branch at 30 Neal St WC2 (3 I 23). 01-836 5772.

Shoe repairs

Most of the large tube and mainline stations have heel bars for quick repairs.

Jeeves Snob Shop   5 **J** 12
7 Pont St SW1. 01-235 1101. Superlative
repairs and shoe services. Also take on
sports footwear and handbag and luggage
repairs. Collect and deliver within London
postal area and operate nationwide postal
service. Other branches.

Silver

See under 'Jewellery & silver'.

Souvenirs

*It's no problem finding souvenir shops in
London. Oxford St, Carnaby St and Leices-
ter Sq are awash with souvenirs of the
T-shirt emblazoned with British flag calibre.
More sophisticated gifts can be found at a
number of museums and Covent Garden is
an oasis for up-market and quirky gift ideas.
See also 'Gifts'.*

Sponges

Maitlands   2 **I** 18
175 Piccadilly W1. 01-493 1975. Marvellous
selection of natural sponges in all sizes.
Also hairbrushes, shaving brushes and
perfumes.

Sports equipment: general shops

Adidas Connection   3 **G** 23
22 Tottenham Court Rd W1. 01-631 1410.
Complete range of Adidas sports clothing,
footwear and equipment plus other brands.
Astral Sports   2 **F** 19
House of Fraser, 318 Oxford St W1. 01-629
8800. The entire basement of the store is
packed with clothes and equipment for
tennis, squash, badminton, golf, riding, athletics, dance – in fact everything.
Lillywhites   5 **J** 20
Lower Regent St SW1. 01-930 3181. Excellent general stock of top English and Continental equipment. Archery, underwater
equipment, and most other sports.
Olympus Sports   2 **F** 19
301 Oxford St W1. 01-409 2619. Wide range
of tennis, squash and badminton equipment, swimwear, ski-wear; large training
shoe department. Also hand luggage and
sports bags.
Pindisports   6 **J** 27
14-18 Holborn EC1. 01-242 3278. Good

British and Continental skiing, camping and
mountaineering equipment.

Sports equipment: boating & yachting

Arthur Beale   3 **I** 23
194 Shaftesbury Av WC2. 01-836 9034.
Excellent small yacht chandler. Nautical
clothing and books.
Capt O. M. Watts   2 **I** 19
45 Albemarle St W1. 01-493 4633. World-
famous yacht chandler. Inflatable boats,
electronic and optical navigational equipment; charts, books, clothing, gifts and all
boating equipment.
Force 4   5 **L** 16
30 Bressenden Pl SW1. 01-828 3900. Full
range of boating equipment, hardware and
clothing. Smaller dinghies and inflatables in
stock. Nautical gifts, books and charts.
London Yacht Centre   6 **N** 33
13 Artillery La E1. 01-247 0521. Very large
stock of boating equipment with the advantage of being near Liverpool St station –
gateway to the east coast yachting resorts.
Thomas Foulkes
6a Sansom Rd (off Lansdowne Rd) E11.
01-539 5084. Probably the best selection in
London of all types of gear and equipment.

Sports equipment: camping & mountaineering

*Pindisports have good camping stocks;
Simpson and Lillywhites have small camping sections.*
Blacks Camping & Leisure   2 **G** 22
53 Rathbone Pl W1. 01-636 6645. Probably
the most versatile camping shop in London.
Supply the best British and Continental
equipment and clothing: have equipped
many mountaineering expeditions. Specialists in climbing and mountaineering.
Camping Centre
44-48 Birchington Rd NW6. 01-328 2166.
Possibly the largest exhibition of tents in the
country – also trailer tents. Backpacking
and outdoor clothing.
Camping & Outdoor Centre   5 **M** 14
27 Buckingham Palace Rd SW1. Everything you could need to camp, climb or
walk.
Youth Hostels Association   6 **J** 23
14-16 Southampton St WC2. 01-836 8541.
Large stocks of climbing, skiing and camping clothes and equipment. Also an outdoor
holiday travel department.

Sports equipment: fencing

Leon Paul   3 H 25
14 New North St WC1. 01-405 3832. World-famous fencing equipment, designed and tested to Olympic standards.

Sports equipment: fishing

Ashpoles
15 Green Lanes N16. 01-226 6575. Rods, clothing, accessories and bait.

Don's of Edmonton
239 & 246 Fore St N18. 01-807 5396. Knowledgeable proprietor. Good stock. 239 specialises in game fishing, salmon and trout; 246 in salt water and big game tackle.

C. Farlow   5 J 19
5 Pall Mall SW1. 01-839 2423. Modern approach to anglers' needs. Specialists in trout and salmon fishing tackle. Large country clothing section. Staff are all anglers. Established 1840.

Hardy Bros   5 J 19
61 Pall Mall SW1. 01-839 5515. Finest hand-made rods in the world and general fishing tackle.

Sports equipment: football

Soccer Scene West One   2 G 20
24 Carnaby St W1. 01-439 0778. Vast selection of team shirts including all the UK teams, top Continental clubs and national squads. Also footballs and all clothes and accessories.

Sports equipment: golf

Golf City   6 L 27
13 New Bridge St EC4. 01-353 9872. Clubs, trolleys, balls, shoes, clothes and accessories. Half sets of clubs available for the beginner.

Sports equipment: running

Run and Become, Become   5 M 18
and Run
42 Palmer St SW1. 01-222 1314. Specialist running shop. Vast range of running shoes and shoes for many other sports. Plus comprehensive stock of running clothes. Help and advice from running experts. Clinic on Thur eve – by appt only.

Sports equipment: riding & saddlery

Bernard Weatherill   2 H 19
8 Savile Row W1. 01-734 6905. Excellent sporting tailors. Specialists in breeches.

Giddens of London   2 H 19
15d Clifford St W1. 01-734 2788. Top-quality riding clothes. Manufacture their own saddles, harnesses and equestrian accessories.

Moss Bros   2 I 20
88 Regent Street W1. 01-494 0666. Stock saddles, equipment and riding clothes.

Swaine, Adeney, Brigg   2 I 20
185 Piccadilly W1. 01-734 4277. Complete range of equestrian equipment and clothing.

Sports equipment: shooting

See under 'Guns: modern'.

Sports equipment: skiing

Pindisports. Lillywhites. Simpson. Harrods and Moss Bros have good ski clothes and equipment.

Alpine Sports   1 D 4
215 Kensington High St W8. 01-938 1911. All ski equipment and clothing.

Ellis Brigham   6 J 23
30-32 Southampton St WC2. 01-240 9577. Large specialist ski shop with a full range of ski-wear and equipment. Also hire of ski equipment and ski repair workshop. Mountaineering equipment and sportswear.

Snow & Rock   1 D 6
188 Kensington High St W8. 01-937 0872. Clothes and equipment for skiing and mountaineering.

Sports equipment: sub aqua

The basic equipment needed is a wet suit, aqualung and harness, demand valve, weight belt, knife, fins, mask and snorkel. A life-jacket is also considered essential. There are numerous accessones from badges to sophisticated decompression meters. The following shops can fully equip you: they both have compressors (for refilling your aqualung).

Collins & Chambers
197-199 Mare St E8. 01-985 0752. Seibe-Gorman. Farallon. Aquastar and Pirelli concessionaires. Wide range of quality gear. 10% discount to BSAC members.

Firefly Wetsuits

495 Fulham Palace Rd W6. 01-736 3271. Specialise in sub-aqua and water-skiing equipment. Also supply outboard engines and inflatable boats.

Sports equipment: tennis

The Racquet Shop

22 Norland Rd W11. 01-603 0013. Racquets for badminton and squash as well as tennis. Accessories. Regripping and restringing service.

Sports equipment: windsurfing

London Windsurfing & Ski Centre

557-561 Battersea Park Rd SW11. 01-223 2590. Full range of windsurfers and windsurfing gear and clothing. Windsurfer and clothing hire; windsurfing courses. Water skis. Seasonal stock of snow skis and skiwear.

Windsurfer's World

312 King St W6. 01-741 4801. Boards, sails, board accessories, harnesses. Wetsuits and steamers. Windsurfer hire.

Stained glass

Goddard & Gibb Studios

41-49 Kingsland Rd E2. 01-739 6563. Make and repair stained glass for all kinds of windows, door panels and Tiffany lampshades.

Stamps

Cameo Stamp Centre 5 K 22

6 Buckingham St WC2. 01-930 2099. Vast selection of British and world-wide thematics/topicals. Wants lists welcomed. Mail-order catalogue.

Georges Korel 5 J 22

2 Irving St WC2. 01-930 4727. Specialises in collections of all countries, British, foreign and colonial sets and singles, thematics (topicals) and Masonic covers and stamps. Children especially welcome.

New International Stamp 6 J 22
Centre

110 St Martin's La WC2. 01-240 1963. Two dealers under one roof. Leo Baresch deals in all world collections, covers and stamps.

Simon Andrews deals in general and specialist GB stamps and covers.

Royale Stamp Co 6 J 23

42 Maiden La WC2. 01-836 6122. British and Commonwealth Stamps from 1840.

Stanley Gibbons 6 K 23

399 Strand WC2. 01-836 8444. World-famous for stamps and catalogues. New issues to classics.

Vera Trinder 6 J 23

38 Bedford St WC2. 01-836 2365. Everything for stamp collectors, except the stamps themselves. Magazines, albums, catalogues, mounts and magnifying glasses.

Stationery shops

W. H. Smith has branches at the main stations and throughout the suburbs, and most of the big stores have good selections.

Frank Smythson 2 G 19

54 New Bond St W1. 01-629 8558. The absolute tops in posh diaries, stationery and leather goods.

Italian Paper Shop 2 I 12

11 Brompton Arc SW3. 01-589 1668. Beautiful, marbled stationery and desk accessories.

Paperchase 3 F 23

213 Tottenham Court Rd W1. 01-580 8496. Exciting collection of paper products including stationery, cards, gifts and wrapping paper.

Rymans 2 E 21

6-10 Great Portland St W1. 01-636 3468. Stationery, office equipment, business machines, furniture and many other useful things. Nice bright shops. Branches throughout London.

Walton Street Stationery Co 4 G 23

97 Walton St SW3. 01-589 0777. Unique papers, elegant printing and personal design service. Finest hand-made writing ink in the world.

Tea

See under 'Coffee & tea'.

Theatrical supplies

See also 'Fancy dress hire' and 'Antique hire'.

Old Times Furnishing

135 Lower Richmond Rd SW15. 01-788 3551. Stage furniture for hire.

Tobacco & snuff

James J. Fox (Cigar Merchants)   2 I 19
2 Burlington Gdns, Old Bond St W1. 01-493 9009. Specialise in finest cabinet selections of all the choicest Havana cigars. Also wide range of cigars, tobaccos and all smoking accessories.

Robert Lewis   5 J 19
19 St James's St SW1. 01-930 3787. The best Havana cigars, as well as Turkish and Virginia cigarettes. Own mixtures. One of the biggest cigar merchants in Europe.

Smith's Snuff Shop   2 I 22
74 Charing Cross Rd WC2. 01-836 7422. Colourful blue and gold 19thC shopfront. Inside has old Victorian tobacco adverts and rich snuff jars. A great snuff house. Full range of Havana and Continental cigars. Finest selection in UK of Turkish and Egyptian cigarettes.

Tools

See also 'Do-it-yourself'.
Buck & Ryan   3 G 23
101 Tottenham Court Rd W1. 01-636 7475. Very large stock of all essential tools.

Toys

See under 'Children's shopping'.

Umbrellas & walking sticks

Burberrys   5 J 21
18 Haymarket SW1. 01-930 3343. Also at 165 Regent St W1 (2 **H 20**). 01-734 4060. For good selection of umbrellas and raincoats.

James Smith   3 H 23
53 New Oxford St WC1. 01-836 4731. Famous store (established in 1830) for umbrellas, shooting sticks, walking sticks.

Swaine, Adeney, Brigg   2 I 18
185 Piccadilly W1. 01-734 4277. World-famous hand-made Brigg umbrellas and luxury leather goods.

Umbrella repairs

Carter's Umbrellas   6 N 31
30 Royal Exchange Bldgs, Threadneedle St EC3. 01-626 7724. Sale, repair and refurbishment of umbrellas.

T. Fox & Co   6 M 31
118 London Wall EC2. 01-606 4720. Manufacture, sales and repairs. Will undertake repairs of British-framed umbrellas.

Veterinary clinics

Beaumont Animals Hospital   3 A 26
Royal Veterinary College, Royal College St NW1. 01-387 8134. Clinic for domestic animals.

Blue Cross Animals Hospital   5 M 14
1 Hugh St SW1. 01-834 5556. Clinic for domestic animals.

People's Dispensary for Sick Animals
PDSA House, South St, Dorking, Surrey. Dorking 888291. For animal treatment centres in London consult the telephone directory.

Wallpapers

Cole & Son (Wallpapers)   2 F 21
18 Mortimer St W1. 01-580 1066. Exclusive and unusual French and Continental prints. Fine modern and traditional English hand-blocked designs. Complementary fabrics. Telephone orders 01-580 2288.

Colefax & Fowler   2 G 18
39 Brook St W1. 01-493 2231. Exclusive screen-printed wallpapers and co-ordinating chintzes based on 18th and 19thC country house designs.

Elizabeth Eaton   2 I 13
25a Basil St SW3. 01-589 0118. Pretty American and French wallpapers in cottagey prints. Fabrics, upholstery and furniture too.

Osborne & Little   4 L 4
304 King's Rd SW3. 01-352 1456. Wallpapers and fabrics. Exclusive designs.

Quintessence   3 E 29
4-10 Rodney St N1. 01-837 8665. Smart, elegant and chic wall-coverings and fabrics.

Sandersons   2 G 22
52 Berners St W1. 01-636 7800. Very large and well-laid-out showroom displaying 'easy to see' English and Continental papers — hand-printed, textural, flocks, imitation marbles and murals. Also wide range of furnishing fabrics.

G. Thornfield   3 E 27
321 Gray's Inn Rd WC1. 01-837 2996. Large selection of well-known brands at up to half list prices.

Watts & Co   5 O 19
7 Tufton St SW1. 01-222 7169. Unique and

elegant patterns made up in the colour of your choice from original Victorian wallpaper blocks. They have about 32 designs and an unlimited range of colours so you can create your own look.

Wine

Most chain store wine merchants in London belong to big organisations who buy in bulk and offer competitive prices. Also listed are some completely independent shops specialising in individual service and small excellent parcels of wine. Harrods have a good wine department which buys selectively and independently.

Alexander Findlater & Co
77 Abbey Rd N8. 01-724 6311. Large selection of all sorts of wines but specialise in Australian. Good range of French, New Zealand and Californian wines.

Berry Bros & Rudd 5 J 19
3 St James's St SW1. 01-839 9033. Charming old wine merchant's shop. First-class list. Independent merchant.

Bow Wine Vaults 6 M 24
10 Bow Churchyard EC4. 01-248 1121. Old-fashioned wine merchant adjoining a popular City wine bar.

Christie's 5 J 19
8 King St SW1. 01-839 9060. Wine auctions usually held on *Thur.*

Harveys of Bristol 5 J 19
27 Pall Mall SW1. 01-839 4691. Long-established group with excellent list.

Hedges & Butler 2 H 20
153 Regent St W1. 01-734 4444. Long-established reliable wine merchants.

La Vigneronne I I 8
105 Old Brompton Rd SW7. 01-589 6113. Rare vintages of claret, burgundy and Madeira and also specialise in Alsace wines.

Les Amis du Vin 2 C 18
51 Chiltern St W1. 01-487 3419. Large selection of over 500 ports, sherries, wines and champagnes including 20 own-label varieties bottled in the country of origin. Wine club offering good discounts to members.

Oddbins 6 K 28
41a Farringdon St EC4. 01-236 7721. Jumbo bottles of perfectly drinkable plonk as well as bargains in more illustrious wines. Other branches.

Soho Wine Market 2 H 22
3 Greek St W1. 01-437 9311. Cut-price wines and spirits – some excellent bargains.

Wine by the case

You have to buy in bulk from the following – a minimum of 12 bottles – but the wines tend to be correspondingly cheaper and a wide choice is offered.

Bibendum
113 Regent's Park Rd NW1. 01-586 9761. Large selection of fine vintage clarets and ports. Also good general stock at wide range of prices. Antique and modern wine accessories. *OPEN 10.00-20.00 Mon-Sat, 11.00-18.00 Sun.*

Majestic Wine Warehouse 4 N 7
Unit B2, Albion Wharf, Hester Rd SW11. 01-223 2983. Vast selection of wines at varying prices. Good value. Hire of glasses. *OPEN 10.00-22.00 Mon-Sun.* There are now 12 Majestic Wine Warehouses in London and nearly as many in the home counties.

Wine clubs

Berry Bros, Justerini & Brooks, Harveys and some others (see under 'Wine') will lay down wine and help customers invest in good wines.

The Wine Society
Gunnels Wood Rd, Stevenage, Herts. Stevenage 740222. A wine-selling co-operative owned by its members, who receive regularly updated lists. The range offered is wide and reliable.

Wine making

Larger branches of Boots sell wine- and beer-making supplies.

W. A. E. Busby 3 H 28
96 Farringdon Rd EC1. 01-837 2373. Manufacturers of hydrometers and glass airlocks, but will supply all equipment and ingredients for wine-making as well as giving friendly advice.

Markets

There are three main sorts of market: vast wholesale complexes which sell only in bulk where the visitor will be entranced by the bright colours, the noise and the smells; the middle-classy art and craft markets; and those where the stall-holders will mesmerise you into parting with your money under the impression that anything and everything is a bargain – try not to be deceived into believing them. There are literally hundreds of these markets: with their rich variety of goods and people they make shopping an event infinitely preferable to trailing round the chain stores buying canned goods in time to canned music. Some of London's best-known markets are listed below: local Town Halls will supply full details of addresses and times. Remember that on wet days and Mon markets tend to be fairly dead and the opening times given are a guide only. Markets will often close early, depending on the state of business. Also see 'Markets' under 'Antiques'. EC = early closing.

Bermondsey and New   6 R 29
Caledonian Market
Between Tower Bridge Rd and Bermondsey St SE1. A vast number of antique and junk stalls mostly aimed at collectors and dealers, although the large variety and specialist goods make for fascinating browsing. There is a large indoor market and comforting snack bars and cafés for cold early mornings. OPEN 07.00-13.00 Fri only.

Berwick Street W1   2 H 21
Busy and boisterous general market in the heart of Soho: the fruit and vegetables are good, and prices reasonable. Also meat, cheeses, fresh fish and household goods. OPEN 09.00-18.00 Mon-Sat.

Bethnal Green Road E1
General high street market. OPEN 08.30-17.00 Mon-Sat.

Billingsgate (wholesale)
North Quay, West India Dock Rd E14. Europe's principal inland fish market moved from the City to Docklands in 1982. Plenty of activity but can be a very wet and smelly experience! OPEN 05.30-12.00 Tue-Sat, 05.30-10.00 Sun (shellfish only).

Borough Market (wholesale)   6 O 26
8 Southwark St SE1. Wholesale fruit and vegetable market under the railway arches of London Bridge. OPEN 02.00-09.00 Mon-Sat.

Brick Lane E1
An exciting place to go to on a Sun morning when Brick La and the surrounding streets – Cheshire St, Sclater St, Cygnet St and Bacon St – come alive with stalls, stallholders and potential customers jostling for space. Famous for second-hand furniture but come here for almost anything.

Brixton
Radiating from Atlantic Rd SW9. Large general market with a distinct West Indian flavour; exuberant atmosphere heightened by the loud reggae music reverberating

around the railway arches. OPEN 08.00-18.00 Mon-Sat, EC Wed.

Camden Lock
Where Chalk Farm Rd crosses Regent's Canal NW1. Amongst the cobbled courtyards and warehouses of the lock is a huge expanse of market selling everything from designer clothes and pine furniture to antique clothing, junk and bric-à-brac. Also a number of interesting food stalls. Refreshments. OPEN 10.00-18.00 Sat & Sun.

Camden Passage   3 E 32
Islington High St N1. A paved walk lined with a mixture of shops and stalls; the haunt of the trendies, selling mixture of antiques and attractive, but expensive, bric-à-brac. Also second-hand records and books, old clothes, prints and furniture. OPEN 09.00-18.00 Mon-Sat. Market stall days OPEN 08.00-16.00 Wed & Sat.

Camden Town
Inverness St NW1. Fruit, vegetables and a few junk stalls. OPEN 09.00-13.00 Mon-Sat.

Chapel Market   3 E 31
White Conduit St, off Liverpool Rd N1. General market selling cheap fruit and vegetables and tat; also pet stall. OPEN Tue-Sun. EC Thur & Sun.

Chelsea Antiques Market   4 L 8
245-253 King's Rd SW3. 01-352 9695. Large, bustling market spreading back from the King's Rd. Mostly general stock, but some specialists. OPEN 10.00-18.00 Mon-Sat.

Columbia Road E2
Flowers and plants. OPEN 08.00-13.00 Sun only.

Covent Garden WC2   6 J 23
The Piazza is host to a pricey, gimmicky market – a good place for a gift. Clothes, china, jewellery and knick-knacks.

The Cut   6 O 24
Lower Marsh Rd, off Waterloo Rd SE1. Fruit, vegetables and all sorts of household items. Best times 12.00-14.00 Mon-Sat.

East Street SE17
General items sold in the week, but mainly fruit, vegetables, plants and flowers Sun. OPEN 07.00-14.00 Tue-Sun.

Farringdon Road EC1   3 G 28
Old and rare books, manuscripts and newspapers. OPEN Mon-Fri.

Gabriel's Wharf   6 M 24
56 Upper Ground SE1. The South Bank's answer to Covent Garden – a collection of craft workshops including jewellery, fabric and leather designers, plus a restaurant bar and a garden centre. At weekends there is a market which also sells flowers, vege-

tables, designer gimmicks and clothes all to the accompaniment of live street entertainment. Market *OPEN 09.30-18.00 Sat & Sun.* Workshops *OPEN 11.00-17.00 Tue-Sun.*

Greenwich Market
Greenwich High Rd SE10. Almost opposite St Alfege's Church. Second-hand clothes, books and jewellery *Sat & Sun*, fruit and vegetables *Mon-Fri.*

High Street, Walthamstow E17
Over a mile of stalls and shops selling literally everything. Crowded and noisy. *OPEN Thur, Fri & Sat.*

Jubilee Market   6 J 23
Jubilee Hall, Covent Garden WC2. Small-ish market beside the paved shopping and market complex. Antiques *05.00-17.00 Mon*, general *09.00-17.00 Tue-Fri*, crafts *10.00-17.00 Sat & Sun.*

Kensington Market   I E 8
Kensington High St W8. A maze of off-beat clothes mingled with jewellery, antiques and records. Stall-holders prepared to buy, sell and barter. *OPEN 10.00-18.00 Mon-Sat.*

Kingsland Waste E8
For the DIY enthusiast – hardware, tools and timber. *OPEN 07.00-17.00 Sat.*

Kingston Markets
Kingston-on-Thames, Surrey. General market on *Mon* on Cattle Market Car Park, Fairfields Rd. *OPEN 08.00-14.00.* Ancient and Apple Market, Market Pl is mainly fruit, vegetables and fish but has some general stalls. *OPEN 08.00-17.30 Mon-Sat, EC Wed (to 14.00).*

Lambeth Walk SE11   5 Q 21
General market. Vegetables and fruit, clothing, electrical goods, materials. *OPEN 10.00-18.00 Mon-Sat, EC Thur (to 13.30).*

Leadenhall Market   6 O 37
Gracechurch St EC3. General retail market: vegetables, poultry, plants, fish and endless other items. The late Victorian glass and ironwork of the building is superb. *OPEN 07.00-17.00 Mon-Fri.*

Leather Lane EC1   3 I 28
Vast range of goods, very few leather stalls nowadays. Lively patter. Close to London's diamond trade in Hatton Garden. *OPEN 11.00-15.00 Mon-Fri.*

London Silver Vaults   6 J 26
Chancery La WC2. Underground vaults like an Aladdin's cave crammed with antique and modern silverware. *OPEN 09.00-17.30 Mon-Fri, 09.00-12.30 Sat.*

New Covent Garden   5 R 14
(wholesale)
Nine Elms SW8. London's foremost whole-

sale fruit, vegetable and flower market which has been in its present location since the end of 1974. Some of the old charm and vitality have been lost in the move from the age-old site in the centre of London, but it is still extremely lively and well worth a visit if you can get up in time. *OPEN 04.00-11.00 Mon-Fri, 04.00-09.00 Sat.*

North End Road SW6   I F 2
Variety of stalls. Plants and flowers in summer. *OPEN 09.00-18.00 Mon-Sat, EC Thur.*

Northcote Road SW11
Busy market, selling mainly fruit and vegetables, near Clapham Junction. *OPEN 09.00-17.00 Mon-Sat.*

Petticoat Lane   6 N 33
Petticoat La as such does not exist but is the name given to the market which radiates from Middlesex St E1 on *Sun* mornings. Some of the streets – Goulston St (good for fashion), Toynbee St and Wentworth St – are open during the week too. The other streets involved are Bell Lane, Strype St, Cobb St, Leyden St, New Goulston St and Old Castle St. Petticoat La is well-known for selling clothes and the choice extends from designer fashion to tack. The range of other goods on sale is very wide – toys, food and toiletries to luxury goods and shoes. Some streets are better for one item than another, but it is fun to just wander around enjoying the atmosphere.

Portobello Road W11   I A 8
Very well-known and much-frequented market extending into Golborne Rd and Westbourne Gro. Fruit, vegetables and new goods sold *09.00-18.00 Mon-Wed, EC Thur (to 13.00).* Second-hand junk and bric-à-brac sold *08.00-17.00 Fri* and on *Sat* the famous antiques market is held, though it is now too established for many bargains to exist. The arcades off Portobello Rd open on *Sat only.* Antique market *OPEN 08.00-sunset Sat.*

Ridley Road E8
Famous East End market with Jewish and West Indian influences. *OPEN Tue-Sat, EC Thur.*

Roman Road E3
Traditional East End market. Large, busy, with lots of discount fashion stalls. *OPEN 08.30-18.00 Mon-Sat.* Busiest trading days *Tue, Thur & Sat.*

Shepherds Bush W12
Large, general open-air market alongside the railway arcade. Food stalls have a strong West Indian bias. Pets, household goods and the usual market tat. *OPEN 09.30-17.00 Mon-Sat, EC Thur.*

Smithfield (wholesale) 6 J 28
Charterhouse St EC1. World's largest meat market; some interesting architecture and storage techniques but not for the squeamish. *OPEN 05.00-12.00 Mon-Fri.*

Spitalfields (wholesale)
Commercial St E1. Covered fruit, flower and vegetable market – 5 acres (2.1ha). Extensive underground chambers: one of the main centres for ripening bananas. *OPEN 04.00-10.00 Mon-Sat.*

Trafalgar Rd SE10
General street trading in Colom Rd, Tyler St and Earlswood St. *OPEN 09.00-17.00 Mon-Sat, EC Thur.*

Wentworth Street E1
Part of Petticoat La market on *Sun*. Fruit, vegetables and bric-à-brac. *OPEN 08.30-14.00 Sun-Fri.*

Westbourne Grove W11
North end of Portobello Rd market. Clothes, especially leather goods, and some bric-à-brac. *OPEN 10.30-18.00 Mon-Sat.*

Whitechapel Market
Whitechapel Rd E1. Famous East End high street market. Huge array of stalls. *OPEN 08.30-17.00 Mon-Sat.*

Woolwich
Beresford Sq SE18. Variety of goods sold in this well-known south London market and in the adjacent covered market in Plumstead Rd. *OPEN 09.00-17.00 Mon-Sat, EC Thur.*

Social services

Cry for help

Although London boasts an enormous range of helping organisations, it can be very difficult to track down the one you need. If your cry for help is met by a succession of polite or not-so-polite suggestions to try somewhere else, you may end up feeling more desperate than when you started. To help you find your way through the maze of official and voluntary services, this section signposts the main referral agencies who will either be able to offer direct help or can put you in touch with the appropriate organisation. Information or help is given willingly and most of it is free. The publications which follow later contain useful information and addresses and should be available in most public libraries. Post offices display posters and lists giving names and addresses of services available in the area.Some local authorities run their own information centres; particularly useful for finding out about services run by the borough. Contact the local Town Hall for the address.

General

Church Army
Church Army HQ, Independence Rd SE3. 01-318 1226. Offers help to anyone in need: homes, hostels, holidays, youth services, prison welfare and social work.

Citizens Advice Bureaux (CAB)
Look in telephone directory for local branch. General advisory service plus help on any matter.

Chelsea 4 L 9
Old Town Hall, King's Rd SW3. 01-351 2114. *OPEN 10.00-12.30 Mon, Wed & Thur. Also OPEN (by appt only) 17.00-19.00 Tue.*

City 6 L 28
Lower Court Stationer's Hall, Ave Maria La EC4. 01-236 1156. *OPEN personal callers 12.00-15.00 Mon-Thur; telephone callers 10.00-12.00 Mon-Thur. CLOSED Fri.*

King's Cross 3 F 25
74 Marchmont St WC1. 01-837 9341. *OPEN personal callers 10.00-13.00 Mon-Wed & Fri, 17.00-19.00 Thur; telephone callers 10.00-13.00 & 14.00-16.00 Mon, Wed & Fri.*

Marylebone 2 B 18
Westminster Council House, Marylebone Rd NW1. 01-486 6425. *OPEN 10.00-12.00 Mon, 10.00-13.00 Tue, Wed & Fri, 16.00-19.00 Thur.*

Stepney
Toynbee Hall, 28 Commercial St E1. 01-247 4172. *OPEN 10.00-12.30 Mon-Wed & Fri, 15.30-18.00 Thur.*

Citizens Rights Office 3 I 24
1 Macklin St WC2. 01-405 5942. Welfare rights advisory service. Phone *from 14.00-16.00 Mon-Fri.*

Family Welfare Association
501-505 Kingsland Rd E8. 01-254 6251.
Counselling service to individuals, groups and families on all problems from financial to marital. Trained caseworkers. *OPEN 09.00-13.00 & 14.00-17.00 Mon-Fri.*

Help Advisory Centre   I E 6
3 Adam & Eve Mews W8. 01-937 7687/6445. Help on assertiveness and communication skills, workshops on emotional and personal problems, women's and psychotherapy groups. Can also refer to specialists. *OPEN 11.00-19.00 Mon-Thur, 11.00-18.00 Fri.*

Help Line
Capital Radio wavebands: 95.8 VHF, 194 MW. 01-388 7575. Runs many telephone services for listeners: Help Line, *09.30-17.30,* information and advice; flat sharing; job finders; community projects, etc.

International Social Service of Great Britain
Cranmer House, 39 Brixton Rd SW9. 01-735 8941. Helps with personal and family problems extending across national frontiers. Can help with repatriation of immigrants.

Piccadilly Advice Centre   2 I 20
100 Shaftesbury Av W1. 01-434 3773. Free information, advice and referral service on housing and jobs for the young, single, homeless and unemployed. *OPEN 10.00-21.00 Mon-Thur, 14.00-21.00 Fri, 13.00-21.00 Sat & Sun.*

Southwark Day Centre
81 Camberwell Church St SE5. 01-703 5841. Day centre for single homeless people.

Salvation Army   6 M 28
101 Queen Victoria St EC4. 01-236 5222. Help on any problem. *24hr telephone service.*

Samaritans   2 H 21
46 Marshall St W1. 01-439 2224. 14 branches throughout London. Advice and encouragement if you are despairing or suicidal. *Walk-in service 09.00-21.00. 24hr telephone service.*

Women's Royal Voluntary Service
234-244 Stockwell Rd SW9. 01-733 3388. A nationwide service for all kinds of local community welfare work. Trained members help in both local and national emergencies.

Official organisations

Addresses from the local Town Hall, Citizens Advice Bureau or local post office.

Social Services Departments
Have a wide range of duties and responsibilities laid on them by central government concerning the welfare of children, the elderly, and the mentally or physically handicapped. Social workers offer assistance with personal, practical and emotional problems. Some areas are under greater pressure than others, consequently services vary considerably.

Housing Departments
Let and maintain council housing. Deal with problems connected with rents, rates, welfare, maintenance, transfers, homelessness.

Environmental Health Departments
Will investigate 'nuisances' (noise, dampness, smells); food control and hygiene (inspection of premises and consumer complaints); defective housing; responsible for prevention of spread of infection.

Departments of Health and Social Security (DHSS)
The term 'Social Security' covers all the schemes which provide direct financial assistance in time of need. It includes both National Insurance contributory schemes, eg sickness and unemployment benefit, and a range of non-contributory schemes. A great number of free explanatory leaflets on benefits are available from any local office of the DHSS but it is a vast and complicated area which confuses many would-be claimants. To obtain more information, or if in difficulty, it's worth consulting some of the books listed below or contacting the Citizens Rights Office (see 'General') or a local welfare rights group.

Publications

These should be available in most large bookshops like Dillons and Foyles but also from public libraries.

Annual Charities Digest
Family Welfare Association, 501-505 Kingsland Rd E8. Basically for professionals. Lists major charities, what they use their funds for, and those eligible to apply for help.

Consumer's Guide to the British Social Services
Phyllis Willmot. Penguin.

Guide to the Social Services
Family Welfare Association, 501-505 Kingsland Rd E8. 01-254 6251. Published annually.

Women's Rights: A Practical Guide
Anna Coote and Tess Gill. Penguin.

Abortion

Either see your doctor for help through the NHS or contact one of the following non-profit-making organisations. They may be able to help you to get an NHS abortion even if you have been turned down; otherwise they will arrange a private abortion as cheaply as possible. Where indicated contraception is also available. Charge for services unless otherwise stated.

British Pregnancy Advisory 5 N 15
Service
7 Belgrave Rd SW1. 01-222 0985. Pregnancy tests and abortion service. Service for infertility, vasectomy and artificial insemination. *OPEN 09.00-17.00 Mon-Fri. Phone for information/appt.*

Brook Advisory Centre 3 F 23
Central Clinic, 233 Tottenham Court Rd W1. 01-323 1522. Phone 01-580 2991 for an appointment. Services for young people up to 25. Small annual donation covers pregnancy testing and contraception. Counselling and abortion help. Also offer counselling for sexual problems. *OPEN 09.30-18.40 Mon-Thur, 09.30-13.40 Fri.*

Help Advisory Centre 1 E 6
3 Adam & Eve Mews W8. 01-937 7687/6445. Free pregnancy testing and abortion advice. *OPEN 11.00-19.00 Mon-Thur, 11.00-18.00 Fri.*

Life 2 E 20
150 Harley St W1. 01-487 4776. Free pregnancy testing and counselling for women not wishing to abort. *OPEN 10.30-16.00 Mon-Fri (to 20.00 Thur).*

Pregnancy Advisory Service 2 F 22
13 Charlotte St W1. 01-637 8962. London's oldest-established pregnancy advisory service. Pregnancy testing, including test which can confirm pregnancy within 14 days of conception. 'Morning after' contraception effective within 72 hours of unprotected sex. Comprehensive abortion service. Sterilization for women. Pregnancy testing is a walk-in service. Other services by *appt only. OPEN 09.30-17.30 Mon-Wed & Fri, 09.30-20.00 Thur, 09.30-13.00 Sat.*

The Well Woman Centre 2 E 22
Marie Stopes House, 108 Whitfield St W1. 01-388 0662/2585. Pregnancy tests, counselling and abortion services. Contraception and sterilization for men and women. Counselling help for psychosexual problems. Also offers a range of women's health care services including medical check-ups, cancer screening and help with premenstrual and menopausal problems.
For advice on the legal position only:

Abortion Law Reform 3 F 31
Association/A Woman's
Right to Choose campaign
88 Islington High St N1. 01-359 5200. Two pressure groups which have combined to thwart efforts to restrict abortion and work to make abortion more freely available. Advice only; they cannot help you obtain an abortion.

Adoption

Demand is always greater than supply as far fewer babies are now placed for adoption. There are, however, many older, handicapped or black children who need parents. Either apply through the Social Services department of the local authority or direct to an adoption agency. Many organisations cater only for a particular religious denomination so it is as well to get information about all the agencies and their requirements before applying (lists from the British Agencies for Adoption and Fostering).

British Agencies for 6 O 26
Adoption and Fostering
11 Southwark St SE1. 01-407 8800. Not itself an adoption agency but a national federation of adoption agencies through which efforts are made to place children with special needs. Publishes a list of agencies and other literature and information on adoption and fostering including a photo list of children awaiting adoption. Trains social workers and has medical and legal groups.

Independent Adoption Service
121-123 Camberwell Rd SE5. 01-703 1088. Finds families for children of all ages and from all communities.

Parents for Children
222 Camden High St NW1. 01-485 7526. A home-finding agency for older and handicapped children. Offers information and advice to people considering this type of parenthood. Long-term support to family after a child is placed.

Parent to Parent Information on
Adoption Services (PPIAS)
Lower Boddington, nr Daventry, Northants. Daventry 60295. An informal self-help organisation, largely of adoptive parents, who offer advice and support on all aspects of adoption. *Annual subscription.*

AIDS

For information about AIDS (Acquired Immune Deficiency Syndrome) the follow-

ing centres offer advice and counselling, and have facilities for examination and testing.

Body Positive

01-373 9124. An organisation which provides a service for carriers of HIV antibody positive (the AIDS virus) who have not actually contracted AIDS. Telephone 01-373 9124 *19.00-22.00 Mon-Sun.*

The Healthline Telephone Service

01-980 4848. A confidential service which provides information and advice in the form of recorded tapes. Sixteen tapes on AIDS are available and approx. 300 on other medical conditions. Phone and ask the tape operator for the tape you wish to hear. For a free copy of the booklet *AIDS, What Everybody Needs to Know*, write to: Dept A, PO Box 100, Milton Keynes. *OPEN 14.00-22.00 Mon-Sun.*

London Hospital Whitechapel Clinic

Whitechapel Rd E1. 01-377 7307. Free testing for HIV virus and other sexually transmitted diseases. (New patients are asked to come early: it may be necessary to wait, though everyone is seen on the day they attend.) *No appt or doctor's note necessary. OPEN 09.30-17.30 Mon-Thur, 10.30-17.30 Fri.*

Terrence Higgins Trust

52-54 Gray's Inn Rd WC1. 01-242 1010. This is the main organisation dealing with AIDS. *Telephone the AIDS Helpline for information between 15.00-22.00 Mon-Sun, or write enclosing sae.*

Alcoholics

Alcoholism is now widely recognised as an illness. Help and treatment can be claimed under the NHS either through your doctor or through hospitals. Other useful centres are:

Accept 4 **J** 3

200 Seagrave Rd SW6. 01-381 3155. Independent organisation providing a counselling service and treatment centre; for problem and dependent drinkers, their families and friends. Also help for people with tranquilliser problems.

Al-Anon 6 **R** 27

61 Great Dover St SE1. 01-403 0888. Information and help for families and friends of problem drinkers. *24hr telephone service.*

Alateen 6 **R** 27

61 Great Dover St SE1. 01-403 0888. Information and help for teenagers with parents or relatives who have drinking problems. *24hr telephone service.*

Alcoholics Anonymous 4 **K** 5

11 Redcliffe Gdns SW10. 01-352 3001. (Head Office: PO Box 1, Stonebow House, Stonebow, York. York 644026/7/8/9.) Give help to people wishing to recover from alcoholism or in need of the support and companionship of fellow sufferers. Meetings. *Telephone service 10.00-22.00. 24hr answering services.*

Greater London Alcohol 6 **J** 28

Advisory Service

91-93 Charterhouse St EC1. 01-253 6221. For people with drinking problems and their families. Telephone advice and information for Greater London *09.00-17.00 Mon-Fri;* counselling service for the City and Hackney.

Turning Point 6 **K** 29

Cap House, 9-12 Long La EC1. 01-606 3947/9. Runs rehabilitation hostels and advice centres for people with alcohol- and drug-related problems.

Ambulance

*Dial **999** for an emergency, otherwise:*

St John Ambulance Brigade 2 **B** 17

Edwina Mountbatten House, 63 York St W1. 01-258 3456. Will arrange a private ambulance and collection of ambulance cases from airports, docks or rail terminals. Need at least 48 hrs notice. *Charge.*

Animals

Royal Society for the Prevention of Cruelty to Animals (RSPCA)

HQ, The Causeway, Horsham, W. Sussex. Horsham 64181. North London: 01-228 0656; South London: 01-228 1131. Telephone for information on animal clinics and hospitals. All complaints of cruelty to animals investigated in strict confidence. Rescue service for animals in distress. (See also 'Veterinary clinics' under 'Shops & services').

Bereavement

Cruse Bereavement Care

126 Sheen Rd, Richmond, Surrey. 01-940 4818. Counselling service for the bereaved.

Blind people

Social Services departments, either through their own specialist workers or in conjunction with voluntary organisations, provide a wide range of services for blind people. Ask to see a social worker who will be able to tell you how to get any special help you may need and what financial assistance, training and aids are available.

Royal National Institute for the Blind 2 E 21
224 Great Portland St W1. 01-388 1266. Provides active help and advice on practically any problem involving blind people. Also publishes a directory of all agencies for blind people.

Cancer prevention

Cancer can be treated successfully if detected early enough. Women should have a regular cervical smear test; see your GP or local family planning clinic. They will also carry out breast examinations but it is advisable for women over 25 to learn to give themselves a monthly breast examination. The Women's National Cancer Control Campaign publishes an excellent leaflet on this.

The Well Woman Centre 2 E 22
Marie Stopes House, 108 Whitfield St W1. 01-388 0662/2585. Examination and screening for breast cancer and cervical smear test. *Charge.*

Women's National Cancer Control Campaign 2 G 17
1 South Audley St W1. 01-499 7532. Education and information service. Publishes a list of clinics offering check-ups. Send sae for leaflet on breast self-examination and cervical cancer. Mobile screening service for industry.

Cancer relief

Marie Curie Memorial Foundation 5 J 14
28 Belgrave Sq SW1. 01-235 3325. Homes, nursing and welfare service for the seriously ill.

National Society for Cancer Relief 4 L 9
Anchor House, 15-19 Britten St SW3. 01-351 7811. Financial assistance, homes, nursing homes, for needy cancer patients and their families. Any request, however unusual, is always considered.

Children

Social Services departments have a duty to promote the welfare of children in their area. They can do this by offering advice, practical assistance and, in certain circumstances, financial help to prevent family breakdown. They, or the NSPCC, will also investigate allegations of neglect or ill-treatment of children. If you suspect that a child is being seriously ill-treated and you feel prompt action is called for, you can call in the police. If a child shows signs of having psychological or emotional difficulties you can get advice and help from your local child guidance clinic. Your GP or the child's school can put you in touch. MIND (National Association for Mental Health) keeps an up-to-date register of centres and clinics of all kinds throughout the country – see under 'Mental health'. Children who need someone to talk to themselves, can call Childline on 0800 1111. Will offer confidential support and advice. OPEN 24hrs Mon-Sun.

Child Poverty Action Group (CPAG) 6 J 33
4th Flr, 1-5 Bath St EC1. 01-253 3406. Excellent information service on welfare rights. Help with tribunals. Useful publications (available only to advisers and re-presentatives of claimants). Information line 01-253 6569. *OPEN 14.00-16.00 Mon-Fri.*

Invalid Children's Aid Association 5 M 14
126 Buckingham Palace Rd SW1. 01-730 9891. Trained social workers help parents of invalid or handicapped children at home. Also special schools for asthmatic and language disordered children.

National Association for Gifted Children 2 G 17
1 South Audley St W1. 01-499 1188. Advice of all kinds for parents and teachers of gifted children. Activities for the children. Newsletter for members.

National Autistic Society
276 Willesden La NW2. 01-451 3844. Advice or help. Special schools. Playgroup. Publications.

Royal Society for Mentally Handicapped Children and Adults 6 J 31
123 Golden La EC1. 01-253 9433. Help for mentally handicapped people and their families. Care centres, day nurseries, leisure clubs, speech therapy, training schemes.

National Society for the Prevention of Cruelty to Children (NSPCC) 3 I 28
67 Saffron Hill EC1. 01-242 1626. Helps parents with problems concerning their children, marriage and financial difficulties. Investigates reports of neglect or ill-treatment of children. Has set up Child Protec-

tion Line, manned by qualified and experienced personnel, to listen and advise on physical and sexual abuse and neglect. 01-404 4447. OPEN 24hrs.

Shaftesbury Society

Shaftesbury House, 2a Amity Gro SW20. 01-946 6635. For physically handicapped children. Hostels for young mentally and physically disabled people (over 16 years of age). Residential schools. Holiday homes.

Contraception

Contraception is now freely available under the NHS whether you are married or single. You can consult your GP or visit your local family planning clinic. For other organisations offering contraception services see under 'Abortion'.

Brook Advisory Centre   3 F 23

Central Clinic, 233 Tottenham Court Rd W1. 01-323 1522. Eleven clinics in the London area offer sympathetic advice and contraception to young people. *Free to students, unemployed people, and those under 18; otherwise a small annual donation.*

**Family Planning   2 F 21
Association**

27-35 Mortimer St W1. 01-636 7866. Supplies a list of clinics and leaflets on aspects of sex education. Bookshop and mailorder. Phone-in service for information and advice.

**International Planned   2 A 20
Parenthood Federation**

Inner Circle, Regents Park NW1. 01-486 0741. Reading materials on family planning in several languages.

Pregnancy Advisory Service   2 F 22

13 Charlotte St W1. 01-637 8962. Contraception services include post-coital – 'morning after' – contraception, effective within 72 hours of unprotected sex. Services other than pregnancy testing require an *appt*.

Deaf people

Visit your Social Services department for advice on benefits and services available. They, or the CAB, will be able to put you in touch with local and national voluntary organisations.

British Association of the Hard of Hearing

7-11 Armstrong Rd W3. 01-743 1110. A self-help organisation with 220 branches for those with acquired hearing loss, total or partial. Social clubs, lip-reading groups, advice on hearing aids, educational weekends, holidays, etc.

**National Deaf Children's   1 A 10
Society**

45 Hereford Rd W2. 01-229 9272. Information and guidance for parents and those concerned with deaf children. Literature available. Regional branches. Runs a Technology Information Centre in Birmingham, which has a lending scheme for equipment. Birmingham 454 5151.

Royal Association in Aid of Deaf People

27 Old Oak Rd W3. 01-743 6187. Concerned with the spiritual, social and general welfare of deaf and blind/deaf people in London, Essex, Surrey and Kent. Trained staff to act as interpreters and counsellors. Special social clubs.

**Royal National Institute for   3 F 23
the Deaf**

105 Gower St WC1. 01-387 8033. Information, education, training, hostels, homes for the deaf. Hearing aids tested free *(by appt)*. Extensive library. Research laboratories.

Diabetics

**The British Diabetic   2 E 19
Association**

10 Queen Anne St W1. 01-323 1531. Aims to educate the diabetic to come to terms with his or her condition and lead an active and useful life. Literature and advisory services available. Annual holiday camps for children and adult diabetics. Also sponsors diabetic research.

Disabled people

Much more attention has been given to the needs of disabled people in recent years largely due to the efforts of pressure groups working on their behalf. The DHSS publishes a mini-guide to services for disabled people (leaflet HB1), available free from local Social Security offices and Social Services departments. Nicholsons publish a very comprehensive guide to London researched for and by disabled people. Called Access in London it deals with all aspects of getting around and exploring the capital. Available from bookshops.

Artsline   3 A 26

5 Crowndale Rd NW1. 01-388 2227. Telephone or drop-in service offering information and advice to disabled people on all

aspects of the arts and entertainment in London: theatres, cinemas, concert halls, colleges, bookshops, museums and galleries. From access and facilities to opportunities for taking up creative interests. *OPEN 10.00-16.00 Mon-Fri.*

Disabled Drivers Association
Ashwellthorpe Hall, Ashwellthorpe, Norwich, Norfolk. Fundenhall 449. An association 'of the disabled, for the disabled, by the disabled' concentrating on all problems of mobility. Information and advice, help with holidays and travelling arrangements (home and abroad), local groups. *OPEN 10.00-16.00 Mon-Fri.*

Disabled Living Foundation
380-384 Harrow Rd W9. 01-289 6111. Information service. Enquiries by phone or letter (with sae), personal calls by *appt*. Advice on equipment and facilities for independent living. Permanent display of aids and equipment.

Disablement Income Group
Millmead Business Centre, Millmead Rd N17. 01-801 8013. Advice and information service. Issues publications. About 20 branches.

Royal Association for   2   F   21
Disability and Rehabilitation (RADAR)
25 Mortimer St W1. 01-637 5400. Information and advice on education, welfare, mobility, training and employment of the disabled. Help with housing, travel and holiday queries. Publications include *Access for Disabled* guides.

Sexual Problems of the Disabled
286 Camden Rd N7. 01-607 8851. Gives advice and information on sexual matters to disabled people and those working with them. Free advisory leaflets.

Discharged prisoners

These organisations try to welcome the discharged prisoner back into society. You can also go to your local court and ask for the Probation Officer who should give you advice and help.

Apex Charitable Trust
1-4 Brixton Hill Pl SW2. 01-671 7633. Operates a range of centres offering employment services for ex-offenders and youngsters at risk.

National Association for the Care and Resettlement of Offenders
169 Clapham Rd SW9. 01-582 6500. Services voluntary organisations providing facilities for offenders in the community; runs pilot projects to test out new ideas and educates the public about the care of offenders and prevention of crime.

Probation & After Care   6   Q   27
Service
Resettlement Office, 289 Borough High St SE1. 01-407 4611. Helps rootless and homeless ex-prisoners coming to inner London.

Discrimination

If you feel strongly about civil rights, issues of sexual or racial discrimination or inequality, the following organisations may be able to help in individual cases or may welcome your support. They campaign to promote awareness on these issues and to improve or implement legislation.

Commission for Racial   5   L   16
Equality
Elliot House, 10-12 Allington St SW1. 01-828 7022. Investigates complaints of inequalities or discrimination on racial grounds. Brings cases to court if necessary.

National Council for Civil   6   R   27
Liberties (NCCL)
21 Tabard St SE1. 01-403 3888. Campaigning organisation for the protection of civil rights; separate 'Rights for Women' section with special expertise on sex discrimination and equal pay legislation. Campaigns and advises on all civil liberties subjects. All advice by letter only.

Drug dependence

The Misuse of Drugs Act 1971 made it illegal to possess cannabis, LSD, cocaine, amphetamines, opium, morphine or heroin. The police can search suspects and their property with a warrant, not their premises. Your GP, or one of the voluntary organisations below which specialise in counselling people with drug problems, can advise you about treatment. See also 'Drug dependence units' in the 'Hospitals' section.

City Roads (Crisis   6   K   33
Intervention)
354-358 City Rd EC1. 01-278 8671. Provides immediate short-term help (up to three weeks) for young people in a state of crisis through drug abuse. Offers medical and social work support. Links with other agencies to offer long-term rehabilitation. *OPEN 24hrs, 7 days a week.*

Community Drug Project
30 Manor Pl SE17. 01-703 0559. Advice
and counselling for people with drug-
related problems, principally aimed at users
of heroin, cocaine, stimulants or other
injected drugs. Needle exchange service.
*OPEN 10.00-17.00 Mon, Wed & Fri,
14.00-17.00 Tue & Thur. Drop-in service
(no appt necessary) 14.00-17.00 Mon-Fri.
Telephone first, 10.00-17.00 Mon & Wed-
Fri.*

The Hungerford Drug   5 K 22
Project
26 Craven St WC2. 01-930 4688. Counselling information, advice and referral service
for people experiencing problems with their
drug use.

Phoenix House
1 Eliot Bank SE23. 01-699 1515. Long-term
residential rehabilitation for drug addicts
and alcoholics who need extensive support. Therapeutic community staffed by ex-
addicts and social workers. Phone them for
an interview if you think you need such
treatment.

Release
169 Commercial St E1. Emergency: 01-603
8654. Specialise in giving legal advice to
those arrested for drug offences. Drugs
counselling and referrals for illegal and prescribed drugs. General advice and information on drugs, legal and practical help.

Tranx
25a Mason's Av, Wealdstone, Harrow,
Middx. 01-863 9716. Walk-in service and
support group for people wishing to come
off mild tranquillisers or sleeping pills.
OPEN 10.00-16.00 Mon-Fri.

Turning Point   6 K 29
Cap House, 9-12 Long La EC1. 01-606
3947/9. Counselling service and residential
centres for the after-care of addicts who
have undergone treatment.

*Many children and adults are handicapped
by dyslexia (word-blindness).*

The British Dyslexia Association
98 London Rd, Reading, Berks. Reading
668271. Information and advice service.
Branches throughout the country.

The Dyslexia Institute
133 Gresham Rd, Staines, Middx. Staines
59498. Professional assessment and specialist teaching. Advisory service for parents and teachers. Trains teachers and
carries out research. Fifteen regional
centres.

**Anorexia & Bulimia Nervosa
Association**
Tottenham Town Hall, Town Hall Approach
Rd N15. 01-885 3936. Telephone counsel-
ling service.

Overeaters Anonymous
Box 19, Stretford, Manchester. Self-
supporting organisation that follows a 12-
step programme of recovery and offers
advice to anyone suffering from overeating,
anorexia or bulimia. Phone 01-868 4109 for
information on meetings in London and
south east England.

*Most people prefer to stay in their own
homes and retain their independence as far
as possible in old age, and Social Services
departments provide a range of services to
help them do just this, sometimes with the
help of the local voluntary organisations.
Home-helps can be arranged to cope with
housework and shopping for those no
longer able to manage alone, and the
'meals on wheels' service supplies cooked
lunches to the elderly, infirm or house-
bound. Anyone on a pension who needs
extra heating because of illness or
restricted mobility should be eligible for
financial help from the DHSS. Services and
facilities for the elderly vary from district to
district but a call at the Social Services
department, CAB or local 'Age Concern'
branch should help you find out.*

Abbeyfield Society
186-192 Darkes La, Potters Bar, Herts. Potters Bar 44845. Family-sized houses where
seven-nine people live together with resident housekeeper responsible for main
meals. Own bed-sitting room, own furniture. Also 'extra care' houses of 20-25
people requiring more attention.

Age Concern
Bernard Sunley House, 60 Pitcairn Rd,
Mitcham, Surrey. 01-640 5431. The focal
point of all voluntary welfare organisations
for the old. Excellent information service.

British Red Cross   5 J 15
9 Grosvenor Cres SW1. 01-235 5454. Provides regular visitors who act as friends and
helpers. Loans medical equipment for nursing in the home. Organises holidays for
handicapped people.

**Counsel & Care for the Elderly (Elderly
Invalids Fund)**
Turyman House, 16 Bonny St NW1.

01-485 1566. Comprehensive advisory service for the elderly and those concerned with their welfare. Advice about suitable homes and how to apply. Useful fact sheets on care of the elderly. Gives financial help when needed. *OPEN 10.30-16.00 Mon-Fri.*

Country Houses   6   **J**   **25**
Association
41 Kingsway WC2. 01-836 1624. Charitable association for preservation of historic country houses, providing accommodation for retired and semi-retired people.

The Carers National   2   **B**   **13**
Association
29 Chilworth Mews W2. 01-724 7776. Pressure group which aims to improve legislation for those who care for elderly relatives at home. Advice on financial matters and information about short-stay nursing homes.

Pre-retirement Association
19 Undine St SW17. 01-767 3225. Gives advice and information to help people face retirement successfully. Also publications. Details of special courses from 53-66 Chancery La WC2 (6 **J 26**). 01-404 4717.

Pensioners' Links
17 Balfe St N1. 01-278 5501. Local offices throughout London. Volunteers visit the elderly and give practical help. Also organise social activities.

Epilepsy

British Epilepsy Association   6   **Q**   **30**
92-94 Tooley St SE1. 01-403 4111. Head office: 40 Hanover Sq, Leeds, W. Yorks. Leeds 439393. Advisory service covering welfare, training, education, employment and social adjustment.

Gambling

Gambling can be as compulsive as drug addiction and may cause distress to both the addict and his or her family.

Gamblers Anonymous   4   **M**   **8**
17-23 Blantyre St, Cheyne Wlk SW10. 01-352 3060. An organisation with several meeting places in the London area. Constructive help and advice to compulsive gamblers.

Haemophilia

Haemophilia Society   5   **O**   **22**
123 Westminster Bridge Rd SE1. 01-928 2020. A society for sufferers from haemophilia and those interested in their welfare. Advice and assistance given.

Homeless

Local authorities must give housing advice to anyone with a housing problem; enquire at your local housing department. Finding somewhere to live is particularly difficult for young single people coming to London and many of the following organisations offer advice and short-term accommodation. It is important to know your rights if you are a tenant and to get proper advice if you have difficulties.

Alone in London Service   3   **E**   **28**
188 King's Cross Rd N1. 01-278 4224/5. An advice and counselling service for young, homeless people under the age of 21. *OPEN 09.00-16.00 (to 12.30 Wed) Mon-Fri.*

Eddie Brindley Project
166 Benhill Rd SE5. 01-708 1636. For homeless people of any age.

Centrepoint   2   **H**   **22**
Office: St Anne's House, 57 Dean St W1. 01-434 2861. *OPEN 09.00-17.30.* Night Shelter: 65a Shaftesbury Av W1 (2 **I 21**). 01-434 2861. *OPEN 20.00-08.00 every night of the year.* Provides basic accommodation, food and advice for up to 30 young people (male aged 16-19, female aged 16-21) who are new to and at risk in central London. Admission by interview at the gate.

London Hostels Association   5   **N**   **15**
54 Eccleston Sq SW1. 01-834 1545. Hostels for men and women in the London area. Minimum stay one month. Advance reservations for groups. Enquiries to Accommodation Section: 01-828 3263.

SOS Society   4   **L**   **2**
13 Harwood Rd SW6. 01-371 0118. Homes and hostels for elderly men and women, mental rehabilitation patients and ex-offenders.

Southwark Day Centre
81 Camberwell Church St SE5. 01-703 5841. Day shelter for single homeless.

Tent City
Old Oak Common La W3. 01-743 5708. (East Acton tube.) Very inexpensive short-term tourist accommodation. Deposit required from UK residents; passport from foreign visitors. *OPEN May-Oct.*

West End Co-ordinated   5   **M**   **18**
Voluntary Services for Single Homeless
People (WECVS)
16-18 Strutton Ground SW1. 01-799 2404.

Fourteen agencies (including Centrepoint) which have combined to tackle the problem of single homeless people in central London. Advice, help and referral services for accommodation, employment, social security problems. Advice centres at some rail termini. Day centre with washing facilities and social activities. Short-and medium-stay hostels.

YMCA
640 Forest Rd E17. 01-520 5599. Head office which will send lists of hostels catering for both sexes in UK and abroad. Enquiries and bookings should be made direct to the particular hostel.

YWCA of Great Britain
Clarendon House, 52 Cornmarket St, Oxford, Oxon. Oxford 726110. Clubs and hostels for young people and women of all ages, classes and creeds. Temporary accommodation and permanent bed-sitting rooms and flats. For up-to-date information write to YWCA Regional Office, 3rd Floor, 16-22 Great Russell St WC1. 01-580 4827.

Young Women's Housing Project
81 Camberwell Church St SE5. 01-252 7005. For single girls aged 16-25.

Homosexuality

Lesbian & Gay Switchboard
01-837 7324. 24hr telephone service giving information on accommodation, activities and entertainments for lesbians and gay men. Legal and medical referrals. Will put you in touch with local groups.

GLAD (Gay Legal Advice)
01-253 2043. Telephone advice on legal matters relating to lesbian and gay people. OPEN 19.00-22.00 Mon-Fri.

Lesbian Line
01-251 6911. Phone service only. Advice for women only. 14.00-22.00 Mon & Fri, 17.00-22.00 Tue-Thur.

London Friend   3   D   29
86 Caledonian Rd N1. 01-837 3337. Telephone helpline for lesbians and gays every eve 19.30-22.00. Also face-to-face counselling, social support groups, coffee, tea and snacks. Phone for details. Women's number 01-837 2782.

Transvestite & Transexual Support Group
2-4 French Pl, off Bateman's Row E1. 01-729 1466. Support and befriending service. Centre OPEN 10.30-19.30 Wed & from 19.30 Fri-Sun. Telephone helpline OPEN 10.30-16.30 Tue & Wed, 19.30-22.00 Fri-Sun. Women's line (Gat-

wick 545653) OPEN 19.00-21.00 Tue & Thur.

Legal aid & advice

There is a legal aid scheme whereby your legal costs can be subsidised on a means-tested basis. To find out about this and to get legal advice, go to your local Citizens Advice Bureau (see under 'General'); to any solicitor displaying the Legal Aid sign; or to your neighbourhood Law Centre.

Central London Law Centre
13 Ingestre Pl W1. 01-437 5854/5764. OPEN 15.00-19.00 Tue (Employment), 15.00-19.00 Wed (Housing), 15.00-19.00 Thur (Immigration). OPEN at other times by appt.

Legal Action Group
242-244 Pentonville Rd N1. 01-833 3931. Publishes a directory of Legal Advice and Law Centres but cannot help with individual problems. Also publishes a monthly bulletin and runs training courses.

Legal Aid & Advice Centres
Free advice on employment, housing, social security and law. Usually by appt only. Must live in area of the centre.

Mary Ward Legal Centre   3   G   25
42 Queen Sq WC1. 01-831 7009/0. Legal advice. Appt only. OPEN 09.30-17.30 Mon-Fri. Run on a green card legal aid basis. Also has a financial advice service. 01-831 7079.

Release
169 Commercial St E1. Emergency: 01-603 8654. Deals with criminal legal emergencies. General legal advice and information on handling the police, the courts, prisons, lawyers and the legal aid system.

South Islington Law Centre   3   E   32
131/2 Upper St N1. 01-354 0133. OPEN (by appt) 09.30-17.30 Mon-Fri. OPEN for walk-in advice sessions 10.00-14.00 Mon & Fri, 14.00-16.00 Wed.

Southwark Law Centre
29 Lordship La SE22. 01-299 1024. OPEN 16.30-18.30 Tue, 14.00-16.00 Fri. By appt only.

Marriage guidance

Catholic Marriage Advisory Council   1   E   7
23 Kensington Sq W8. 01-937 3781. Help for those, of all denominations, with marital problems. Meetings arranged for parents,

teachers, school pupils and engaged couples. Natural family planning. *Appt only.* Phone for details.

Institute of Marital Studies

Tavistock Centre, 120 Belsize La NW3. 01-435 7111. Professional help with marital problems. *OPEN by appt 09.30-17.30 Mon-Fri.*

London Marriage Guidance   2 **E** 21
Council

76a New Cavendish St W1. 01-580 1087. Confidential counselling and education service for those with difficulties in their personal relationships. *Appt only.* Phone for details.

Marriage partners

There are many commercial organisations in London which offer introductions to suitably matched people who are looking for a marriage partner. Some are less than scrupulous in their attempts to match clients' requirements and/or make exorbitant charges so enquire about terms and conditions before handing over any money.

Dateline International   1 **E** 6

23 Abingdon Rd W8. 01-938 1011. Computer dating service with a complete cross-section of many thousands on file.

Katherine Allen   2 **H** 19

3 Cork St W1. 01-494 3050. Mostly educated, professional and middle-class applicants. A few aristocrats. Personal approach.

The Marriage Bureau   2 **G** 19
(Heather Jenner)

124 New Bond St W1. 01-629 9634. The oldest-established bureau. Famous for creating successful partnerships.

Meeting people

Breakaway

57 Garrick St W5. 01-991 2169. A social club for professional people organising social, sporting and cultural activities in London and the home counties. *Annual or 3-month fee.*

London Village

24 Upper Park Rd NW3. 01-586 7455. Membership organisation created by people aged 20-45 for their own age group. All kinds of social activities arranged. Introductory meetings, Grosvenor Hotel, Victoria Station SW1 *18.30 or 20.00 Tue.* Charing Cross Hotel *18.30 or 20.00 Fri. Charge.*

Mental health

If you have a severe emotional problem, the best person to see is your doctor who may recommend psychiatric help. Social workers are also able to give advice and assistance to the mentally ill and their families and can tell you about local facilities and support groups.

Brent Consultation Centre

Johnston House, 51 Winchester Av NW6. 01-328 0918. Confidential walk-in service for young people from 16-23 years old with personal and emotional problems. Trained psychotherapists. *OPEN 19.15-21.45 Mon, 16.30-19.00 Tue, 12.00-14.30 Thur.*

MIND (National Association   2 **E** 20
for Mental Health)

22 Harley St W1. 01-637 0741. Advisory service on all aspects of mental disorder.

New Grapevine   6 **J** 29

416 St John St EC1. 01-278 9147. Free and confidential help with any personal or sexual problems. *10.30-14.30 Tue, 14.30-18.30 Wed.*

Problems Confidential

1 Clovelly Rd W5. 01-567 0262. Central referral service to a network of over 170 psychotherapists and hypnotherapists. Associated groups include Guilt Confidential, Hypnosmoke Confidential, Neurotics Confidential, Marriage Guidance Confidential and Phobia Confidential. Send SAE for free referral.

Samaritans   2 **H** 21

46 Marshall St W1. 01-439 2224. A voluntary organisation to help people who have thoughts of suicide or despair. *24hr telephone service;* also walk-in service *09.00-21.00.* Totally confidential. Many London branches; see telephone directory.

Westminster Pastoral   1 **E** 7
Foundation

23 Kensington Sq W8. 01-937 6956. A large counselling centre, offering individual, group, or family and marital counselling for those with emotional difficulties. Also has an extensive training programme with both short and full-time courses.

Missing persons

It is advisable to inform the police, although they can do little unless there is suspicion of foul play.

The Salvation Army Social   3 **E** 26
Service Investigation Dept

105-109 Judd St WC1. 01-387 2772.

Enquiries for close relatives are accepted. Also searches abroad. No adoption, business, wills, divorces, friends or under-17s.

Nursing

The NHS can provide a district nurse. Apply to your local health authority. For private nurses look in telephone directory, at the advertisements in a nursing magazine, or contact one of the following:

British Nursing Association   **2 F 18**
443 Oxford St W1. 01-629 9030. Nursing agency supplying all types of nurses.

Langham Nurses   **2 B 12**
Association
85 Maitland Ct, Gloucester Ter W2. 01-723 1444. Private, qualified nurses available (resident or non-resident).

One-parent families & parents

Gingerbread   **6 J 24**
35 Wellington St WC2. 01-240 0953. Network of self-help groups to help one-parent families stay sane. Advice on housing, the law, social security, baby-sitting, etc. Over 300 local groups.

National Council for One-Parent Families
255 Kentish Town Rd NW5. 01-267 1361. Will help and advise single parents and single pregnant women with any problem. Confidential.

Parents Anonymous, London
01-263 8918. *18.00-06.00.* Confidential telephone listening service for parents under stress who fear they may physically or emotionally abuse their children. Can also help with any emotional crisis in the family. One of many OPUS (Organisations for Parents under Stress) groups.

Pregnancy tests

A pregnancy test can always be done by your doctor – or consult your local family planning clinic. Magazines, newspapers and some chemists carry advertisements for private firms carrying out pregnancy tests, at a fee. You can also buy do-it-yourself kits at most chemists. See also 'Abortion'.

Rape

See under 'Emergency and late night help'.

Service & ex-servicemen

Royal British Legion   **5 J 19**
48 Pall Mall SW1. 01-930 8131. Will give assistance and financial aid to service and ex-servicemen and women, and their dependents. Apply to local branch.

Soldiers', Sailors' &   **5 M 19**
Airmen's Families Association
16-18 Old Queen's St SW1. 01-222 9221. Financial advice and other aid for the families of service and ex-servicemen.

Smoking

Action on Smoking & Health   **2 F 21**
(ASH)
5-11 Mortimer St W1. 01-637 9843. Advice on smoking-related problems and addresses of withdrawal clinics in London area.

Smokers' Treatment Unit
Maudsley Hospital, Denmark Hill SE5. 01-703 6333. Help and advice for anyone wishing to give up smoking. Telephone first.

Venereal diseases

See list under 'Hospitals'. All treatment is free, anonymous if desired and completely confidential. You do not need an appointment or letter from your own doctor.

Women's issues

There are many issues which specifically concern women; for example, equal pay, sex discrimination, combining work with child-rearing. Several organisations now exist to monitor legislation, promote research and provide practical help and advice. See also 'Abortion Law Reform Association' in the 'Abortion' section and 'NCCL' under 'Discrimination'. The feminist movement has been growing for years and many groups covering the whole feminist/ political/radical spectrum exist in London. For further information consult the London Women's Handbook *available in libraries and women's centres.* Spare Rib *at 27 Clerkenwell Clo EC1 (3 I 29), 01-253 9792, also publish a monthly feminist magazine and a diary giving useful information on women's issues.*

A Woman's Place   **5 M 22**
Hungerford House, Victoria Embankment

WC2. 01-836 6081. Co-ordinates and gives information on women's groups in London. Drop-in centre. OPENING times vary. Please phone for details. Call or write. Women only.

Equal Opportunities Commission
Overseas House, Quay St, Manchester. Manchester 833 9244. Advice on all queries and complaints regarding the Equal Pay and Sex Discrimination Acts.

Feminist Library &   5 **M** 22
Information Centre
Hungerford House, Victoria Embankment WC2. 01-930 0715. Library and information service on issues affecting women. Collects and collates information on research which has been or is being undertaken. 11.00-17.30 (to 19.30 Thur) Wed-Sat.

London Women's Aid   6 **J** 33
52-54 Featherstone St EC1. 01-251 6537. Help for battered women. Co-ordinates local women's aid centres. 24hr telephone service to put battered women in touch with their nearest women's refuge and to offer advice and support.

Rights of Women   6 **J** 33
52-54 Featherstone St EC1. 01-251 6577. Free legal advice for women by women in the legal profession. Enquiries by letter only or telephone to speak to a qualified solicitor 19.00-21.00 Tue-Thur.

Women's National   5 **M** 20
Commission
Room 50, 4th Flr, Govt Offices, Great George St SW1. 01-270 5902. Publishes a list of established women's organisations in London and the UK.

Voluntary social work

Many organisations rely heavily on volunteers to carry out much needed work in the community. If you can offer skills such as teaching, driving, typing, decorating and maintenance or sewing, so much the better, but many opportunities exist for people who can offer time, patience, good humour and commitment for tasks such as befriending, visiting the elderly or helping in clubs and hospitals.

British Volunteer Programme
22 Coleman Fields N1. 01-226 6616. Send people with professional or technical qualifications or experience for a minimum of two years to help with projects in Third World countries.

Community Service   3 **E** 29
Volunteers
237 Pentonville Rd N1. 01-278 6601. Produce various publications full of unusual suggestions for helping in the community. Minimum of four months full-time work. Board, lodging and pocket money.

London Adventure Playground
Association
28 Underwood Rd E1. 01-377 0314. Helpers and crafts materials often needed, especially in school holidays.

London Voluntary Service   3 **D** 25
Council
68 Chalton St NW1. 01-388 0241. Co-ordinate and support the work of the Volunteer Bureaux in London. Contact them for the address of your local Volunteer Bureau.

Samaritans   2 **H** 21
46 Marshall St W1. 01-439 2224. Volunteers needed to help on 24hr telephone service befriending the suicidal and despairing. Work in one of 14 branches. Information given about selection procedures, training etc.

Voluntary Action Camden   3 **E** 25
Volunteer Bureau, 25-31 Tavistock Pl WC1. 01-388 2071. Guides people into the type of voluntary work that they are most suited to. Work in Camden only. Runs playgroup projects, reclamation of urban wasteland projects, a psychotherapy unit, and provides a salaries administration service for voluntary groups.

Women's Royal Voluntary Service
234-244 Stockwell Rd SW9. 01-733 3388. Men and women volunteers welcome for all kinds of community work.

Police stations

These are the most important police stations within a 3-mile radius of Piccadilly Circus.

City of London

Headquarters & all **departments** 26 Old Jewry EC2. 01-601 2222.	6	**M**	30
Bishopsgate 182 Bishopsgate EC2. 01-601 2222.	6	**N**	33
Snow Hill 5 Snow Hill EC1. 01-601 2222.	6	**K**	28
Wood Street 25 Wood St EC2. 01-601 2222.	6	**L**	30

Metropolitan

Battersea   4 Q 7
112-118 Battersea Bridge Rd SW11. 01-350 1122.
Bow Street   6 J 23
28 Bow St WC2. 01-434 5212.
Cannon Row   5 M 21
Victoria Embankment SW1. 01-839 8888.
Chelsea   4 K 10
2 Lucan Pl SW3. 01-741 6212.
Hyde Park   2 F 14
North of Serpentine W2. 01-434 5212.
Kensington   1 G 5
72-74 Earl's Court Rd W8. 01-741 6212.
King's Cross   3 E 28
76 King's Cross Rd WC1. 01-837 4233.
New Scotland Yard   5 M 18
Broadway SW1. 01-230 1212.
Rochester Row   5 N 17
63 Rochester Row SW1. 01-434 5212.
Southwark   5 Q 27
323 Borough High St SE1. 01-407 8044.
West End Central   2 H 20
27 Savile Row W1. 01-434 5212.

Hospitals

General hospitals: Central London

Guy's Hospital   6 Q 28
St Thomas St SE1. 01-407 7600. *24hr casualty.*
London Hospital (Whitechapel)
Whitechapel Rd E1. 01-377 7000. *24hr casualty.*
New Charing Cross Hospital
Fulham Palace Rd W6. 01-748 2040. *24hr casualty.*
Queen Mary's Hospital
Roehampton La SW15. 01-789 6611. *24hr casualty.*
Royal Free Hospital
Pond St NW3. 01-794 0500. *24hr casualty.*
St Bartholomew's Hospital   6 K 29
West Smithfield EC1. 01-601 8888. *24hr casualty.*
St George's Hospital
Blackshaw Rd SW17. 01-672 1255. *24hr casualty.*
St Stephen's Hospital   4 K 6
369 Fulham Rd SW10. 01-352 8161. *24hr casualty.*
St Thomas' Hospital   5 O 21
Lambeth Palace Rd SE1. 01-928 9292. *24hr casualty.*

University College Hospital   3 E 23
Gower St WC1. 01-387 9300. *24hr casualty.*
Westminster Hospital   5 O 19
Dean Ryle St, Horseferry Rd SW1. 01-828 9811. *24hr casualty.*
Whittington Hospital
Highgate Hill N19. 01-272 3070. *24hr casualty.*

Children's hospitals

Belgrave Unit
King's College Hospital, Denmark Hill SE5. 01-274 6222. *24hr casualty.*
Children's Hospital Sydenham
321 Sydenham Rd SE26. 01-778 7031. *24hr casualty.*
Dept of Paediatrics   6 Q 26
(of Guy's Hospital) Southwark Bridge Rd SE1. 01-407 7600. *24hr casualty.*
The Hospital for Sick   3 G 26
Children
Great Ormond St WC1. 01-405 9200.
Queen Elizabeth Hospital for Sick Children
Hackney Rd E2. 01-739 8422. *24hr casualty.*
St Mary's Children's   2 B 14
Hospital
South Wharf Rd W2. 01-725 6163. *24hr casualty.*
Westminster Children's   5 O 16
Hospital
(Westminster Hospital Teaching Group) Udall St SW1. 01-828 9811. *24hr casualty.*

Dental hospitals

Eastman Dental Hospital   3 F 27
256 Gray's Inn Rd WC1. 01-837 3646.
London Hospital Dental Institute
New Rd E1. 01-377 7000.
University College Dental   3 E 23
Hospital
Mortimer Mkt, Capper St (off Tottenham Court Rd) WC1. 01-387 9300. *OPEN 09.00-14.30 Mon-Fri.* At other times, cases of real emergency may be treated at University College Hospital (see under 'General hospitals').

Drug dependence units

The following hospitals have special clinics to deal with drug abuse and dependency. Each drug unit can accept patients only from its local catchment area. They prefer people to have a letter of referral from a GP but will see them without if necessary. A few units have in-patient facilities but any unit will offer help and guidance for further treatment if required. Emergency cases should go to their nearest casualty department. The Maudsley Hospital operates a 24hr general emergency clinic.

Hackney Hospital
Drug Dependency Unit, 230 Homerton High St E9. 01-986 6816. *OPEN 09.30-12.00 Mon, Wed & Fri* for walk-in service. At other times by *appt only.*

London Hospital (St Clements)
2a Bow Rd E3. 01-377 7000. *OPEN 09.30-17.30 Mon-Fri.*

Maudsley Hospital
Denmark Hill SE5. 01-703 6333.

New Charing Cross Hospital
57 Aspenlea Rd W6. 01-385 8834. *OPEN 09.00-17.00 Mon-Fri.*

Queen Mary's Hospital
Roehampton La SW15. 01-789 6611. *OPEN 14.00-18.00 Mon, 10.00-12.00 Wed.*

St George's Hospital (Tooting)
Blackshaw Rd SW17. 01-672 1255. *OPEN 09.00-17.00 Mon-Fri.* Walk-in service and appt then made.

St Mary's Hospital   2 B 14
Praed St W2. 01-725 6666. Drug Dependency Centre: 01-723 8829.

St Stephen's Hospital   4 K 6
369 Fulham Rd SW10. 01-352 8161. Drug dependence treatment: 01-351 7035. *OPEN 09.30-17.30 Mon-Fri.*

University College Hospital 3 C 23
Drug Dependence Unit, National Temperance Hospital, 122 Hampstead Rd NW1. 01-387 9541. *09.00-17.00 Mon-Fri.*

West Middlesex Hospital
Twickenham Rd, Isleworth, Middx. 01-560 2121. *OPEN 14.15-17.00 Mon, 09.00-17.00 Wed, 09.00-13.00 Thur.*

Eye hospitals

Moorfields Eye Hospital   3 I 33
City Rd EC1. 01-253 3411. *OPEN 24hrs Mon-Sun.*

Foreign hospitals

French Dispensary   2 C 22
6 Osnaburgh St NW1. 01-387 5132.
Italian Hospital   3 G 25
Queen Sq WC1. 01-831 6961.

Homoeopathic hospitals

Royal London   3 G 26
Homoeopathic Hospital
Great Ormond St WC1. 01-837 3091.

Maternity hospitals

Newham General Hospital
Forest La E7. 01-555 3262.
Queen Charlotte's Maternity Hospital
339 Goldhawk Rd W6. 01-748 4666.
Whipps Cross Hospital
Whipps Cross Rd E11. 01-539 5522.

Migraine clinics

New Charing Cross Hospital
Fulham Palace Rd W6. 01-748 2040. *24hr casualty.*
Princess Margaret Migraine Clinic
Fulham Palace Rd W6. 01-741 7833. Walk-in facility *09.30-17.00 Mon-Fri.*

Nursing & convalescent homes

The National Health Service can send you free or at very low cost to one of their many convalescent homes by the sea or in the country – consult your hospital doctor.
King Edward's Hospital   1 B 9
Fund
14 Palace Ct W2. 01-727 0581. A directory for Greater London of places that offer convalescence, rehabilitation and other short-term care.
The London Clinic   2 C 20
20 Devonshire Pl W1. 01-935 4444. Top, private.

Psychiatric hospitals

Castlewood Day Hospital
25 Shooter's Hill SE18. 01-856 4970.
Friern Hospital
52 Friern Barnet Rd, New Southgate N11. 01-368 1288.
London Hospital (St Clements)
2a Bow Rd E3. 01-377 7000.
Maudsley Hospital
Denmark Hill SE5. 01-703 6333. Also drug clinics and drug in-patient facilities. *24hr walk-in emergency.*
Paddington Centre for Psychotherapy
63-65 Lancaster Rd W11. 01-221 4656.

Referral by GP, social worker etc, from anywhere in the London area.

St Thomas' Psychiatric Day Hospital for Children
35 Black Prince Rd SE11. 01-735 1972.

Tooting Bec Hospital
218 Tooting Bec Rd SW17. 01-672 9933. Also drug in-patient facilities, geriatric unit.

Specialist hospitals

Grove Park Hospital
Marvels La SE12. 01-857 1191. Mental handicap.

London Chest Hospital
Bonner Rd E2. 01-980 4433.

London Foot Hospital   2   D   22
33 Fitzroy Sq W1. 01-636 0602.

Maida Vale Hospital for Nervous Diseases
4 Maida Vale W9. 01-286 5172.

Maudsley Hospital
Denmark Hill SE5. 01-703 6333. Special units for anorexia, epilepsy and neurosurgery.

Moorfields Eye Hospital   3   I   33
City Rd EC1. 01-253 3411. *24hr casualty.*

National Heart and Chest   4   J   9
Hospital (Brompton Hospital)
Fulham Rd SW3. 01-352 8121.

National Heart Hospital   2   D   19
Westmoreland St W1. 01-486 4433.

The National Hospital for   3   G   25
Nervous Diseases
Queen Sq WC1. 01-837 3611.

Royal Marsden Hospital   2   E   21
Fulham Rd SW3. 01-352 8171. Malignant diseases.

Royal National Orthopaedic   2   E   21
Hospital
48-51 Bolsover St W1. 01-387 5070.

Royal National Throat, Nose   3   E   27
& Ear Hospital
330 Gray's Inn Rd WC1. 01-837 8855.

St John's Hospital for   2   I   21
Diseases of the Skin
5 Lisle St WC2. 01-437 8383.

St Mark's Hospital for   3   F   31
Diseases of the Rectum & Colon
City Rd EC1. 01-253 1050.

St Mary's Hospital   2   B   14
Praed St W2. 01-725 6666. Special units for allergies, rheumatism and kidney disease.

St Mary Abbots Hospital   1   F   6
Marloes Rd W8. 01-937 8181. Psychiatric and geriatric patients only.

St Paul's Hospital   3   I   23
24 Endell St WC2. 01-836 9611. Genitourinary.

St Peter's Hospital   6   J   23
Henrietta St WC2. 01-836 9347. Genitourinary.

St Philip's Hospital   6   J   25
Sheffield St WC2. 01-242 9831. Genitourinary.

Western Ophthalmic   2   B   18
Hospital
(St Mary's Hospital Teaching Group)
Marylebone Rd NW1. 01-402 4211. *24hr casualty.*

Venereal diseases hospitals

Eastern Hospital
Homerton Gro E9. 01-985 1193.

Guy's Hospital   6   P   29
St Thomas St, London Bridge SE1. 01-407 7600.

London Hospital (Whitechapel)
Whitechapel Rd E1. 01-377 7000.

Middlesex Hospital   2   F   22
James Pringle House, 73 Charlotte St W1. 01-380 9141. *08.00-18.00 Mon-Fri.*

Newham District General
Glen Rd E13. 01-476 1400.

Prince of Wales General Hospital
High Rd N15. 01-808 1081.

Royal Free Hospital Marlborough Clinic
Pond St NW3. 01-794 0500.

Royal Northern Hospital
Holloway Rd N7. 01-272 7777.

St Bartholomew's Hospital   6   K   29
West Smithfield EC1. 01-601 8888.

St Mary's Hospital   2   B   14
Praed St W2. 01-725 6666.

St Thomas' Hospital Special   5   O   21
Clinic, Lydia Dept
Lambeth Palace Rd SE1. 01-928 9292. *09.00-17.30 Mon-Fri.*

University College Hospital   2   E   22
Gower St W1. 01-387 9300.

Westminster Hospital   5   O   19
Dean Ryle St, Horseferry Rd SW1. 01-828 9811.

Donor services

If you wish to donate blood, or to leave your organs or other parts of your body for transplantation or research purposes, these wishes must be recorded in writing on a donor card which should be carried at all times. For further information contact:

Depts of Health and Social Security (DHSS)   6 B 24
Hannibal House, Elephant & Castle SE1.
01-703 6380.

Blood

West End Donor Centre   2 F 20
26 Margaret St W1. 01-580 8772/3.

Eyes

Royal National Institute for the Blind   2 E 21
224 Great Portland St W1. 01-388 1266.

Organs

Depts of Health and Social Security (DHSS)   6 B 24
Anatomy Dept, Hannibal House, Elephant & Castle SE1. 01-703 6380.

Whole body donation

London Anatomy Office
PO Box 915, London W6. 01-741 2198.

Public lavatories

Look out for signs in the streets directing you to the nearest public lavatories, or ask someone likely to be familiar with the area: police, traffic wardens, news-vendors or shopkeepers. All lavatories in this country are divided into separate areas for men and women. Though you may sometimes find them in the same location, there will always be separate entrances. Nearly all large stores, museums and national art galleries have lavatories, as do all mainline stations, and the major ones – Euston, King's Cross, Paddington, Victoria and Waterloo – where train services continue throughout the night are open 24hrs. Some London Transport underground stations have lavatories but owing to staff shortage and vandalism many have been closed down. Refer to the map section at the beginning of this book; find your position and look for the nearest WC sign, station or large public building. All public places must now provide access for the disabled wherever practicable and this includes lavatories; look for the wheelchair symbol. Remember, other terms for lavatories are public conveniences, toilets, loos, or WC. Symbols are frequently used to differentiate between the sexes – otherwise both men and women, ladies and gentlemen are used.

Emergency and late night help

Accident

When in an accident with another vehicle you must stop and exchange names, addresses and insurance details with the other party. There is no need to call the police to the scene of the accident unless a person is seriously injured, in which case dial 999 immediately. In the case of a person being injured but able to walk away, or where the other driver fails to stop, then this must be reported to the nearest police station within 24 hours.

Arrested

Always keep calm and remain polite. You do not have to say anything in answer to

any allegations that are made but it is sensible to give your name and address. Ask to phone your solicitor or phone Release 01-603 8654 (open 24hrs) who will give you advice and get a solicitor if necessary. Appeals for legal representation, legal aid and bail can be made in court. See under 'Legal aid'.

Baby battering & child abuse

If you suspect a child is being ill-treated, phone the local Social Services department (outside office hours the police will give you an emergency number), the NSPCC 01-242 1626, or the police. Alternatively, if you suspect a child is in trouble or danger or if a child would like to seek help himself, phone Childline 0800 1111. OPEN 24hrs.

Bombs

If you see a suspicious looking package:
1 – **DON'T TOUCH IT**
2 – *Get people away from the area*
3 – *Inform personnel in charge of the premises*
4 – *Dial 999 and tell the police where it is*

Broken down

AA Breakdown service
01-954 7373. *24hrs.*
RAC Breakdown service
0923 33555. *24hrs.*

Desperate

New Horizon   3 I 24
1 Macklin St WC2. 01-242 0010. Advice and activities for the young homeless in the West End. *OPEN 08.00-17.00 Mon-Wed & Fri, 13.00-17.00 Thur.*
Piccadilly Advice Centre   2 I 20
100 Shaftesbury Av W1. 01-434 3773. Free information, advice and referral service on housing and jobs for the young, single, homeless and unemployed. *OPEN 10.00-21.00 Mon-Thur, 14.00-21.00 Fri, 13.00-21.00 Sat & Sun.*
Samaritans   2 H 21
46 Marshall St W1. 01-439 2224. To talk about your problem just walk in *09.00-21.00* or phone the *24hr* telephone service.

Emergency birth

Phone the hospital at which the mother is registered – if any – or phone one of the maternity hospitals under the 'Hospitals' section. If all else fails, dial 999 – the ambulance men are trained to cope.

Late-night chemists

Your local police station keeps a list of chemists and doctors available at all hours. Or try:
Bliss Chemist   2 E 16
5 Marble Arch W1. 01-723 6116. *OPEN 09.00-24.00 every day of the year. Also at*

50-56 Willesden La NW6. 01-624 8000. *OPEN 09.00-02.00 Mon-Sun.*
Underwoods   2 I 21
62 Shaftesbury Av W1. 01-434 3647. *OPEN 09.00-23.00 Mon-Sat, 11.00-22.00 Sun.*
Warman-Freed
45 Golders Green Rd NW11. 01-455 4351. *OPEN 08.00-24.00 daily, including Xmas.*

Late post

Post Office   5 J 22
24-28 William IV St, Trafalgar Sq WC2. 01-930 9580. *OPEN 08.00-20.00 Mon-Sat, 10.00-17.00 Sun & B.hols.*

Locked out

The police keep a list of local locksmiths or try the Yellow Pages for a 24hr service or a willing locksmith who will come out after hours.

Lost your car keys

If you know the number of your key (keep a note of it somewhere in your wallet) the AA or RAC can probably help (phone numbers under 'Broken down') if a nearby garage or the police can't.

No cash

Cash dispensing machines outside major branches of most banks operate 24hrs. Ask your bank about obtaining the special card, and a list of branches with dispensers. There are now many places (in small shops, arcades, etc) open till late in the evening, which call themselves Bureaux de Change *and will change travellers cheques. Some are quite unscrupulous and charge a very high commission for the service. It is always best to change money in a proper bank or well-known and established Bureau de Change. The following open longer hours than usual.*
Chequepoint   5 J 21
37 Coventry St W1. 01-839 5072. *OPEN 09.00-23.00 Mon-Sun. Also 236 Earl's Court Rd SW5 (1 G 5), 01-370 3238; Marble Arch W1 (2 E 16), 01-723 1005; 58 Queensway W2 (1 A 11), 01-229 4268. OPEN 24hrs.*

London Gatwick Airport
Lloyds Bank (Crawley 37559) and Midland Bank (Crawley 26934) both operate a 24hr service.

London Heathrow Airport
Thomas Cook (01-897 3361) in Terminals 1 & 2. *OPEN 07.30-23.30 in Arrivals, 06.00-21.00 in Departures.* Travelex (01-759 4800) in Terminal 3. *OPEN 24hrs in Arrivals, 06.30-21.30 in Departures.*

Luton Airport
Barclays Bank (Luton 30700) *OPEN Easter-Oct 06.00-23.00 Mon-Sun. Nov-Easter 07.00-23.00 Fri-Mon, 07.00-19.00 Tue-Thur.*

No petrol

Stuck in the middle of the night? The following have 24hr service unless otherwise stated.

Cavendish Motors
Cavendish Rd NW6. 01-459 0046.

Chelsea Cloisters Garage   4 K 11
Sloane Av SW3. 01-589 1226.

Chiswick Flyover Service Station
1 Great West Rd W4. 01-994 1119.

Fountain Garage   2 G 16
83 Park La W1. 01-629 4151.

Maida Vale Service Station
115-117 Maida Vale W9. 01-286 7321.

Park Lane Underground   2 G 16
Garage
Park La, Hyde Park W1. 01-262 1814. *24hr parking. Petrol OPEN 07.00-22.00 Mon-Fri, 08.00-20.00 Sat & Sun.*

Star Service Station
63 Fortune Green Rd NW6. 01-435 2211.

Nowhere to park

Blue signs direct you to NCP car parks, a lot of which are open 24hrs. Notice boards at the entrance give details of time and charges. Most parking meters and single yellow lines along London streets cease to be applicable as from 18.30 Mon-Fri, 13.30 Sat and all day Sun; but do read the signs on the meters or affixed to nearby lamp posts which give times of operation. Parking on double yellow lines, on the pavement and double-banked parking is forbidden at all times, and you may emerge to find your car has been towed away or that a clamp has rendered it immobile. Collecting your car (or having the clamp removed) is costly and inconvenient (see 'Wheel clamped'). Fines for illegal parking are stiff and worth avoiding.

Nowhere to sleep

See under 'Homeless' in the 'Social services' section.

The police can help you

when you need a doctor or a chemist
Each police station keeps a list of emergency doctors and chemists which are available at all hours.

when you need a garage
Each police station keeps a list of local garages and the times they are open.

when you need a hotel
They keep up-to-date information on hotels and boarding houses in the area, with prices – of course, they don't know if there are vacancies, but at least you'd have somewhere to try.

when you've lost property in the street
It may have been handed in to them, or they will be able to give you a list of lost property offices for things lost in trains and taxis, etc.

when your car has been stolen
Ring them up straight away – it may have been towed away by them for a parking infringement. Otherwise they will circulate its description and let you know if they get it back.

when your dog is lost
It may have been taken to them at the station, in which case they will look after it for one night and then take it to the Battersea Dogs Home, 4 Battersea Park Rd SW8. 01-622 3626.

when you're stranded
If you've come to London from a provincial town and spent your return fare, they can take the name of someone in your home town who will deposit your fare at the local police station and then the London police will give you a travel warrant to get you home. (This applies to British residents only – all other nationalities should apply to their own embassy for repatriation.)

Rape

If you have been raped or sexually assaulted, and need support, information or any other help phone the Rape Crisis Centre, 01-837 1600. OPEN 24hrs.

Robbed

If a theft has occurred from your hotel room contact the assistant manager immedi-

ately, through the reception desk, who will take the appropriate action. The quicker you make the report the faster the hotel security staff can go into action on your behalf. If you are robbed in the street, report the theft immediately to the nearest police station. Here are some useful telephone numbers to call if you lose any of the following:

Access Card
Joint Credit Card Company, Access House, 200 Priory Cres, Southend-on-Sea, Essex. Southend-on-Sea 352211. Phone your own bank during office hours or the above number any time outside office hours (24hr service), then write a confirming letter to the above address within seven days.

American Express Card
01-222 9633. During office hours report the loss to any American Express office or after hours to the above number (24hr service).

Bank cheque cards
Telephone your own bank as soon as possible. Most foreign banks have a branch in London where you can report the loss (see telephone books for numbers).

Barclaycard
Barclaycard Centre, Dept G, Northampton, Northants. Northampton 230230. During office hours report the loss to any branch of Barclays Bank or after office hours to the above number (24hr service), followed by a confirming letter within seven days.

Diners Club Card
Diners Club House, Kingsmead, Farnborough, Hants. Farnborough 513500. Operate a 24hr telephone service for reporting lost cards.

Eurocard
See under 'Access' above.

Mastercard
See under 'Access' above.

Visa
See under 'Barclaycard' above.

Passports
Foreign nationals should apply to their own embassy (see phone numbers under 'Travel' section or in telephone books). If a British passport is lost, inform the Passport Office from which it was issued. Another passport, limited to one year's use, can be obtained by filling in the application form available from any main branch of the Post Office. If you cannot wait for a full passport to be issued, because travel, foreign business trip, etc is imminent, ask for a British Visitors Passport (available from main Post Offices, Mon-Fri only). The Post Office will give you a list of countries for which these

passports are valid, ie those for which visas are not normally required.

Starving at 4am

Late-night supermarkets can now be found in many areas of London, but if you want someone else to cook the food try these:

Canton   2 I 22
11 Newport Pl WC2. 01-437 6220. Chinese food OPEN 24hrs.

Centre Point Snack Bar   2 F 23
279 Tottenham Court Rd W1. 01-636 3563. OPEN 24hrs. Also run an all-night mini-cab service 22.00-04.00.

The Grecian   2 G 22
27a Percy St W1. 01-636 8913. Expensive Greek food and dancing. OPEN to 06.00 Mon-Sat.

Harry's   2 H 20
19 Kingly St W1. 01-734 3140. All-night café serving full cooked breakfasts, toasted sandwiches and snacks. Popular with nightclubbers and night-owls. Fully licensed; excellent value. OPEN 22.00-10.00 Mon-Sat. CLOSED Sun night.

Kentucky Fried Chicken
Take-away service. The following are open late:
132 Uxbridge Rd W12. 01-743 8511. OPEN to 05.00 (06.00 Fri & Sat).
95 Westbourne Gro W2. 01-229 6940. OPEN to 24.00 Mon-Sun.

Terminal Buffets
Terminals 1, 3 & 4 London Heathrow Airport, Middx. 01-759 4321. OPEN 24hrs. Terminal 2 buffet closes 21.00.

Up All Night   4 L 4
325 Fulham Rd SW10. 01-352 1998 Steaks, hamburgers, spaghetti and coffee. Take-away too. OPEN 11.30-06.00 daily.

Taken ill

Whether you are a visitor or a resident, in an emergency dial 999 and ask for the ambulance service, or make your own way to a casualty hospital (see 'Hospitals' under 'Social services' section). If at all practicable, go to your doctor as casualty hospitals are for serious emergencies only. Visitors to London can register as temporary patients.

Transport

The underground system closes down about midnight although the night bus service is good and extends to the suburbs. There are fewer taxis around late at night and prices increase after midnight. Mini-cabs operate 24hr services and the Yellow Pages are full of them.

Avis Rent-a-car　　　　2　E　17
68 North Row, Marble Arch W1. 01-629 7811. 24hr service from Heathrow and Gat-wick airports.

Godfrey Davis Europe Car
London Heathrow Airport. 01-897 0811. Desks in each terminal. 24hr service.

Lady Cabs
150 Green Lanes N16. 01-254 3501. Late-night cabs, for women, driven by women. OPEN 08.00-24.30 Mon-Thur, 08.00-01.00 Fri, 09.00-02.00 Sat, 10.00-24.00 Sun.

Wife battering

If you are being assaulted by the man you live with contact the local Social Services department, the Citizens Advice Bureau or your local Law Centre who will tell you how to go about obtaining an injunction to pre-vent the man assaulting you or to stop him entering your home. A 24hr telephone ser-vice is operated by:

London Women's Aid　　　6　J　33
52-54 Featherstone St EC1. 01-251 6537. Advises battered women and can put them in touch with a women's refuge.

Wheel clamped

Take the label attached to your vehicle, plus the fixed penalty notice, to one of the police car pounds listed below. You will have to pay a fine before the clamp is removed. A.Ax.Dc.V. It can be some hours before the clamp is removed. In an emer-gency telephone 01-252 2222. It is possible if you come back to the place where you left the car only to find it is no longer there, that it has been towed away to one of these pounds:

Hyde Park Car Pound　　　2　E　16
NCP Park La Car Park, Marble Arch W1. OPEN 24hrs.

Camden Town Car Pound
Oval Rd NW1. OPEN 09.00-23.00 Mon-Sat, 09.00-17.00 Sun.

Warwick Road Car Pound　　　1　G　4
245 Warwick Rd W14. OPEN 08.00-24.00 Mon-Sat.

NICHOLSON

THE BEST IN LONDON

NEW £3.50

NICHOLSON
LOOKING *Good* IN LONDON
The HAIR, BEAUTY, FASHION AND FITNESS GUIDE

£2.95

THE GUIDE TO LONDON BY BUS & TUBE

NEW £3.95

NICHOLSON
Out of LONDON
The 60 Best Day Trips

£2.95

NICHOLSON
LONDON
THE GOOD TOUR GUIDE
Visit the 60 most exciting places in town

£3.95

NICHOLSON
LONDON
Arts and CULTURAL GUIDE
THEATRE Dance MUSEUMS Music Festivals HISTORIC HOUSES Galleries

£3.50

NICHOLSON
LONDON RESTAURANT GUIDE
Over 700 places to eat More than 30 national cuisines
NEW EDITION

£3.50

NICHOLSON
LONDON PUB GUIDE

£2.75

NICHOLSON
LONDON DOCKLANDS MAP

NICHOLSON
LONDON DOCKLANDS STREET ATLAS & GUIDE
£5.95

Nicholson publishes a
large range of guide books
covering various aspects of London
life. Whatever your interest you can
rely on Nicholson to give you accurate
up-to-date information in a compact and portable form.

Index